The
Roanoke Valley
in the 1950s

The
Roanoke Valley
in the 1950s

N E L S O N   H A R R I S

To Frank –
Hope you enjoy!
Nelson Harris
5.21.24

H
THE
Hi$tory
PRESS

Published by The History Press
Charleston, SC
www.historypress.com

The Roanoke Valley in the 1950s
Copyright © 2024 by Nelson Harris
All rights reserved

Manufactured in China

ISBN: 9781467155687

Library of Congress Control Number: 2023948252

Notice: The information in this book is true and complete to the best of our knowledge. It is offered without guarantee on the part of the author or The History Press. The author and The History Press disclaim all liability in connection with the use of this book.

Dedication

In memory of mom

Gaynelle Simpson Harris
ALHS, Class of 1958

Contents

Acknowledgements

As an author of books and articles on local and regional history I am indebted to those that also share the same passion, especially to those who dedicate themselves professionally to this subject. This book would not have been possible without the wonderful resources of the libraries, historical societies, and individuals of the Roanoke Valley. I am especially grateful to the Roanoke Public Library Foundation for the funding of my research and this work and to Sheila Umberger, Director of Roanoke Public Libraries, for her friendship and support of many years. Dyron Knick of the Roanoke Main Library's Virginia Room was extremely helpful and my main point of contact for the resources therein. His consistent aid was critical and deeply appreciated. Ashley Webb of the Historical Society of Western Virginia; Fran Ferguson, Alex Burke, and Garrett Channell of the Salem Historical Society; and Judy Cunningham at the Vinton Historical Society were all encouraging and resourceful in providing photographs and other assistance. The Facebook community, known as *Memories of Roanoke*, and its administrator Laurie Platt were the source of many photographs not otherwise available. I also wish to acknowledge the photographic resources made available to me from the Virginia Tech Libraries.

Grammatical editing and wise counsel were provided by Bill Hackworth and the late George Kegley, who read each chapter as it was completed and offered corrections and input.

Kate Jenkins at The History Press, with whom I have had the privilege to work on other books, provided her always steady hand at shepherding this project through the publishing process.

Finally, to my wife Cathy who was often a "microfilm widow" as I scrolled through microfilm many evenings over the past few years to write this book. I appreciate her love, support and patience with all my history pursuits.

Introduction

This volume on the Roanoke Valley in the 1950s was the result of my viewing every edition of *The Roanoke Times* and *The Roanoke Tribune* between January 1, 1950, and January 1, 1960. I began that process in the fall of 2019 and finished four years later. This work is an expression of my passion for local history, as I believe we have much to learn from a community's past.

The 1950s for the Roanoke region was both celebratory and cautionary—celebratory in that so many endearing and enduring aspects of the Roanoke Valley began during the decade. The Children's Zoo on Mill Mountain, the Roanoke Symphony Orchestra, the Roanoke Fine Arts Center, local television, and Showtimers are a few such examples. Roanoke celebrated its Diamond Jubilee and Salem its sesquicentennial, while Vinton launched its Dogwood Festival. There were the stars of the *Grand Ole Opry* that came through Roanoke regularly, usually performing at the Roanoke Theatre, as well as big bands, popular Black entertainers, and even Elvis, who performed for shows and dances at the American Legion and Star City Auditoriums. General Electric opened a plant in Salem and quickly became a leading employer, while at the Norfolk and Western Railway, there was the switch from steam to diesel. This was the age of drive-in theatres and restaurants, cruising on Williamson Road, drag races at Starkey, marble tournaments, the Harvest Bowls, and Miss Virginia pageants. Miller & Rhoads, Sears Town, the Hunter Viaduct, and a new main library changed the landscape of downtown Roanoke, while Roanoke County opened Cave Spring High School and broke ground for Northside.

The Roanoke Valley endured setbacks and faced challenges. American Viscose closed, leaving nearly 3,000 without employment. The US Supreme Court rendered its *Brown v. Board of Education* decision that propelled state and local politicians to respond with massive resistance. Local Black leaders organized and led efforts to integrate schools and other public facilities. The dump in Washington Park remained a constant nuisance and pollutant to surrounding Black neighborhoods. The Roanoke Redevelopment and Housing Authority, using federal funds, embarked on urban renewal—approved by a single-vote margin of Roanoke City Council—that would eventually eliminate most of the Black neighborhoods of northeast Roanoke and, in time, Gainsboro. The American Legion Auditorium burned to the ground in 1957, leaving the valley without a major venue for civic and entertainment events. The Korean War took men from Roanoke to Southeast Asia, with some returning for burial.

At many points, this work uses language that, by contemporary standards, would seem impolite and even offensive. The names of organizations and the words commonly used during the 1950s have not been altered by me, as I believe it is important to understand the evolution of language in advertising, public discourse, titles, and descriptions, as this, too, provides a lens to view another element of our history.

When writing history, no author and sources are perfect. I relied solely upon the newspapers of the time in the spelling of proper names. I am certain there are misspellings and mistakes, hopefully minor. Corrections are welcome.

As with all my local history titles, these are endeavors of my love and appreciation for the Roanoke Valley. I learned much about the region, not just its past but also the individuals and movements that still shape our present. I am better because of what I absorbed through the research for these books, as my perspective has greatly broadened. I hope this work will have the same impact upon those who read it.

Nelson Harris
Roanoke, Virginia
September 2023

1950

The new year was rung in, literally, at Fincastle during an age-old tradition of ringing the bells. The courthouse bell chimed at 11:45 p.m. and was followed in succession at twenty-second intervals by the bells of the Presbyterian, Baptist, Methodist, and Episcopal churches, concluding with the courthouse bell at midnight. A. G. Simmons rang the Botetourt County Courthouse bell, a custom he had performed for forty-six years.

The following banks reported assets and liabilities as of December 31, 1949: First National Exchange Bank, $67,041,577; Mountain Trust, $22,733,900; Colonial-American National, $27,687,228; Southwest Virginia Building and Loan Association, $2,908,137; Bank of Virginia, $66,961,602; and People's Federal Savings and Loan Association, $3,019,362.

Opera soprano Mary Curtis, an alumnus of Hollins College, performed at the school on January 5. She had recently performed with the famed Teatro Lirico in Milan, Italy.

The *Ice-Vogues of 1950* opened for a five-night run at the American Legion Auditorium on January 3. The show featured seventy-five skaters performing dances, tricks, and comedy routines. The main star was ice champion Ilona Vail.

Doormen and bellmen were stationed once again at the Ponce de Leon Hotel to assist patrons. The positions had been abolished in 1941 due to wartime manpower shortages.

The Barter Theatre group performed *Dangerous Corner* at the Jefferson High School auditorium on January 7. Betty Shultz, Virginia Downing, and William Kemp had the lead roles.

Law enforcement officials reported a total of forty-nine violent deaths in Roanoke and Roanoke County in 1949, with most being traffic fatalities.

The bandstand in Elmwood Park was slated to be moved by mid-January to a point northwest of the park's pond. The bandstand had been in the park since 1913 and was originally built to provide a venue for concerts by the Norfolk and Western (N&W) Railway Band. The bandstand had been used for a variety of purposes since then. The move was necessitated by the construction of the new main library.

The *Roanoke Times* introduced two new cartoons on January 2. *Grandma* by Charles Kuhn replaced *Popeye*, and *Uncle Ray's Corner* replaced *The Nebbs*.

The Reverend Spencer Edmunds, former pastor of Second Presbyterian Church, died at midnight on December 31, 1949. Edmunds served the congregation for eighteen years before accepting a call to First Presbyterian Church in Eaton, Pennsylvania. While in Roanoke, Edmunds was active in the city's civic affairs. He was interred at Evergreen Cemetery.

Richard Beck of Martinsville was named as the executive director of the Roanoke Redevelopment and Housing Authority. The authority was tasked with building two 900-unit housing developments, one for whites and one for Blacks.

The "Great Lester," a master magician, performed on the stage of the Roanoke Theatre on January 4. According to ads, he cut a beautiful girl in half with a buzz saw and did the famed Hindu rope trick.

William Wells and Richard Meagher established an architectural firm, Wells and Meagher, which was located at 118 West Campbell Avenue.

N&W Railway made its last Sunday train run to Galax on January 8.

The CBS radio network announced the Reverend William Simmons, pastor of Fifth Avenue Presbyterian Church, would be the speaker for the network's *Church of the Air* broadcast on July 16. The program was to originate from WDBJ in Roanoke.

Charles Begley was indicted by a grand jury for the murder of Ernest Six on December 11, 1949. Begley pled self-defense. The shooting occurred in the City Diner, where Begley was the manager.

The Fulton Motor Company, located at 112 Franklin Road SW, displayed the 1950 models of Chrysler automobiles that included the company's newest car, the Newport, a hardtop convertible.

A biracial committee proposed that a new swimming pool be included in the construction of the new Addison High School master plan. Dr. Harry Penn, a school board member, noted that the pool for Blacks was located eight miles outside the city.

Some ninety former internees and prisoners of war (POW) had filed claims with the Roanoke office of the Division of War Veterans Claims during the first week of January. Applicants from the Roanoke Valley included Mr. and Mrs. Gordon Ells, who were imprisoned by the Japanese when they took control of the Philippines, and Earl Harbour, who spent twenty-two months as a POW in Europe.

Arnold McElyea of Salem was fined by the Roanoke County Court for selling obscene materials at a filling station on Route 11 and for operating at the station two slot machines, four punchboards, and three tip boards.

An architectural rendering of the new Roanoke Main Library was shown to and approved by Roanoke City Council on January 5. The contemporary structure was estimated to cost $575,000 according to its architect, Randolph Frantz.

Fifteen coal cars of a Virginian Railway train derailed near the Wabun station west of Salem on January 5. The accident tore up several hundred feet of track and blocked the single track of the railway's New River Division.

The Wells Furniture Company at Third Street and Elm Avenue SE, was damaged by fire on January 5. L. M. Wells did not provide an estimate of damage but stated the contents were not insured.

The Reverend Daniel Clare, a retired Baptist minister who had served as interim pastor to numerous Roanoke churches, died at his home on January 5 in Roanoke. He was eighty-four.

Horace Mason of Roanoke was killed when he crashed and his auto caught fire at the Tinker Creek Bridge on January 6. Mason sustained serious injuries and died shortly after transport to the hospital. Mason worked for Heironimus.

The Margaret Webster Shakespeare Company presented *Taming of the Shrew* at Hollins College on January 12.

Air traffic at Woodrum Field in 1949 broke all previous records for the airport, according to airport manager Marshall Harris. The three airlines serving the airport—Eastern, American, and Piedmont—brought in 24,333 passengers and took out 22,782. In freight, the airlines brought in 227,516 pounds and took out 135,043 pounds. Airmail amounted to 54,027 pounds.

The Episcopal bishop of Southwestern Virginia announced plans for a new church in the Williamson Road area. A survey had indicated some seventy individuals in the area were interested in establishing a congregation. A meeting was held at Huntington Court Methodist Church on January 9 to determine further plans, and it was decided to proceed with establishing a church. The Reverend Paul Reeves was selected to be the pastor.

The new incinerator for the Town of Salem began operating on January 9. The incinerator for household garbage cost $66,184 and was located at the southern end of Indiana Street.

Reverend Robert Atkins, minister at South Salem Christian Church since 1941, announced his resignation effective April 1. Atkins offered no future plans. He had been involved in religious and civic affairs in Salem for many years.

The bandstand in Elmwood Park, which was moved, met a watery end on January 7 when it slipped from its temporary base and slid into the park's pond. What could be salvaged was used to build a shelter for ten ducks at the pond.

Webb Hamill, CPA, opened his business at 3204 Williamson Road in mid-January.

The Tango Restaurant, at Campbell Avenue and Park Street, opened a ballroom on January 9, where dancing was held each evening. The restaurant specialized in Italian cuisine and was managed by Charles Ramo.

An automobile overturned and caught fire on January 9 at the intersection of Peters Creek Road and Route 11. Those killed were George Akers Jr. and Maggie Patrick. Both were burned to death. Two other passengers were injured, having been thrown from the vehicle.

Roanoke City Council appropriated $1.1 million in bond funds for school construction. Among the projects was the construction of three new schools—Grandin Court Elementary School, Huff Lane Elementary School, and Garden City Elementary School.

Oakey's Funeral Service began advertising its Williamson Road Chapel, located at 2408 Williamson Road. The chapel had formerly been Peters Funeral Home.

Braxton Sumner and his wife were arrested by Roanoke police for neglect of their nine children. Two of the children had been taken by a social worker to the

Memorial and Crippled Children's Hospital with severe malnutrition. Police described the home as "shocking" and "beyond disbelief."

Virginia's Supreme Court of Appeals refused to review the case and sentence of Lee Scott for the murder of Dana Marie Weaver. Both were students at Jefferson High School when the murder occurred. Scott had been found guilty and sentenced to ninety-nine years. Scott's attorney, Warren Messick, had argued for a sentence of twenty years.

A new skating rink, the Sports Arena, opened on Williamson Road on January 13 next to the Plaza Restaurant. The rink was owned by R. A. Ellis. Professional instruction was provided by Earl Mehaffey.

Officials with the Roanoke Red Sox baseball team lobbied Roanoke City Council committee for a five-year lease of Maher Field to justify more than $100,000 in capital improvements. The team president also presented extensive plans for the park's improvement.

William Anderson Jr., a student at Highland Park Elementary School, was discovered deceased in his bedroom by his grandmother on January 13 at their home on Walnut Hill SE. The coroner determined the boy's death was a suicide.

In a Lee Day assembly at Lee Junior High School, Roanoke Vice Mayor Richard Edwards told students, "Robert E. Lee, gentleman of Virginia, was the type of man we should all want to emulate." Edwards cited Lee's efforts to restore Virginia's economy following the Civil War.

The Roanoke Merchants Association agreed to lobby Roanoke City Council to expand its membership from five to seven members. The resolution adopted by the group asked the council to consider asking for a charter change from the General Assembly, such that the change could take effect in two years.

Dr. Hugh Trout Sr., prominent surgeon and founder of Jefferson Hospital, died at his home in Roanoke on January 13 at the age of seventy-two. Trout, a native of Staunton, founded Jefferson Hospital in 1907, with the first patients admitted there in February 1908. At the time of his death, the hospital had been greatly expanded to 150 beds with sixty medical staff. He was president of the Virginia Medical Society in 1940. He was also active in Roanoke's civic and fraternal organizations.

Robert Lunn, known as the "talking Blues singer" of the *Grand Ole Opry*, performed on the stage of the Salem Theatre on January 13.

Herb Lance, along with George Hudson and his orchestra, performed at the American Legion Auditorium on January 16 for a floor show and Blacks-only dance. White spectators were admitted for a discount.

The first set of triplets ever delivered at Lewis-Gale Hospital were born on January 13, when Mrs. Daisy Webb of New Castle gave birth to a boy and two girls.

Marie Beheler Studios opened a charm and modeling school in mid-January. Advertisements stated students would learn "a new hairdo, proper make up, and rhythmic exercises for a slimmer, trimmer you." A forty-hour course was offered for those interested in modeling.

Larry Dow Pontiac, shown here in January 1950, was located at 425 Marshall Avenue SW at that time. *Virginia Room, RPL*

Local No. 11 of the Textile Workers of America erected a new three-story union hall in the 300 block of West Campbell Avenue at a cost of $225,000. The architect was Paul Hayes. The third floor held a 500-seat auditorium.

Members of Central Church of the Brethren burned their mortgage note on January 15. The church at 416 W. Church Avenue also celebrated its twenty-fifth anniversary on the same day. Rev. Merlin Garber was pastor.

Rev. Harry Gamble, pastor of Calvary Baptist Church in Roanoke, received the Junior Chamber of Commerce Distinguished Service Award for 1949. The award was presented by the Jaycees at their annual dinner at the Hotel Roanoke, where US Senator Harry Byrd was the keynote speaker.

Valleydale Packers in Salem announced plans to expand their plant, in effect doubling its size. The company planned to begin the expansion in February. Valleydale employed about 250 persons.

Roanoke College sold a house at 455 High Street to the Kappa Alpha Order to become a fraternity house. The fraternity had been renting a home at 120 N. College Avenue.

The Roanoke Life Saving and First Aid Crew reported it answered 515 calls for service in 1949, up from 296 in 1948. The crew provided aid to 1,582 persons in 1949.

Richard Ferrell, a pianist from New Zealand, gave a concert at the Jefferson High School auditorium on January 18. His appearance was part of the Community Concert Association series. Farrell had performed with numerous symphonies around the world.

Spices of 1950 came to the Roanoke Theatre on January 18. The variety show boasted singing, dancing, novelty acts, and glamorous girls.

Former Roanoker and Hollywood actor John Payne came to Roanoke on January 18 to help promote the local premiere of his new movie *Captain China* at the American Theatre. During his visit he went to view the Roanoke Star on Mill Mountain, having read about the star in *Life* magazine and to see patients at the Veterans Administration Hospital. City officials, the Junior Chamber of Commerce, and the Jefferson High School band greeted Payne when he arrived in the city by train. Mayor A. R. Minton presented Payne with a key of the city. The actor also addressed a student assembly at Addison High School. An estimated crowd of 5,000 jammed a parade route along Jefferson Street as Payne rode from the Hotel Roanoke to the sold-out American Theatre.

Construction began on the Hollins Fire Station in mid-January. The station was located on the north side of Peters Creek Road, just west of the intersection with Route 11. A volunteer crew was to be organized to staff the station.

Roanoke City Council launched an investigation into the prevention of child abuse and neglect as a result of the case of the Sumner family, where two children were discovered half-starved. The council heard from various city officials as to other child neglect cases in the city and the city's response.

A jury found Charles Begley not guilty on the charge of murder in the shooting death of Ernest Six at the City Diner on December 11, 1949. The diner was located at 1013 Orange Avenue NE. Begley had claimed the shooting was in self-defense.

John Willett of Airpoint died on January 19 at the age of seventy-six. Willett was a prominent orchardist in that section of Roanoke County.

Rev. Edward Pruden, pastor of First Baptist Church in Washington, DC, and the pastor to President Harry Truman, spoke to some 350 clergy and laity at the Virginia Baptist Conference on Evangelism held at First Baptist Church, Roanoke, on January 19.

Arthur Taubman, president of Advance Stores Company, joined other businessmen from across the nation on a trip to Israel to determine interest in developing the rubber industry there. The trip lasted about a month.

Broaddus Chewning resigned as head of the Roanoke Community Concert Association, having served in that capacity for eight years. Chewning believed it was time for new leadership. The association brought orchestras and prominent singers to Roanoke for performances.

Roanoke City Manager Arthur Owens estimated it would cost $175,000 to bring the Academy of Music up to fire safety codes. The Academy had been closed since January 1949, but there was significant civic interest in having it reopen. Councilman Benton Dillard suggested diverting bond funds slated for the armory to rehab the academy.

The Women's Division of the Roanoke College Alumni Association met at Longwood in Salem on January 20 and voted to lobby college officials to reinstate football in the near future.

Buddy's Restaurant at 6 South Jefferson Street became the Star City Restaurant. E. C. Sink was the proprietor.

WROV radio announced that the Star City Boys, featuring Hugh Hall and Rufus Hall, would be regulars on the station's *Blue Ridge Jamboree* heard weekdays at 11:30 a.m. The program's emcee was Lee Garrett.

The body of Mrs. Esther Cabaniss of Roanoke was found in the Roanoke River on January 20. Cabaniss had been reported missing by her family on November 19, 1949. The body had been discovered by two young boys walking along the riverbank.

James Lewis, administrator of Burrell Memorial Hospital, reported that the hospital was operating at nearly double its capacity. In mid-January sixty-two patients were being treated in a facility that could care for thirty-four. Even the administrator's office had been turned into a patient room. The news was received as urgent given the Hospital Development Fund campaign to raise monies for both Burell and Memorial and Crippled Children's Hospital. Clem Johnston, chair of the campaign, stated, "We must not continue to put up with conditions existing at present in our hospitals." The campaign goal was $1.5 million.

The first complete shop for students studying agriculture was under construction at Andrew Lewis High School in mid-January. The shop's cost was around $36,000, and it was being added to the south end of the industrial arts shop.

The stage of the open-air chapel at Sherwood Burial Park was completed in late January. Constructed of Catawba stone, the stage was part of a master project for the cemetery that included a reflecting pool, mausoleums, and 1,016 crypts.

An article in the February issue of *Trains* magazine reported that the N&W Railway's *Powhatan Arrow* passenger train, since being launched in 1946, had failed "the kindest yardstick known to passenger accounting." The Cincinnati-Norfolk daytime train "is no gold mine," asserted the article.

Radiant glass heat, a new form of home heating, was introduced to the Roanoke Valley by the Noland Company in January.

Roy Kinsey (fourth from right) and his employees pose in front of the Roy C. Kinsey Sign Company at 22 Wells Avenue NE in 1950. *Bob Kinsey*

Lewis Hodges and Charles Faries, both of Roanoke, were killed in Miami, Florida, on January 22, when their small passenger planeas hit by another, similar plane in midair. The two men were on a routine cross-country training flight. Hodges was a licensed commercial instructor for the Hicks-Kesler Flying School based at Woodrum Field. Faries was logging time toward a commercial pilot's license. The two planes sideswiped near Sunny South Airport and crashed.

Rabbi Samuel Goldenson of Temple Emanu-El in New York City spoke to students at Hollins College and to the congregation of Temple Emanuel in Roanoke on January 25. Goldenson was widely known for his philanthropic work.

Western film star Lash LaRue, along with the Westernettes, gave a stage show at the Roanoke Theatre on January 25.

Roanoke City Council gave preliminary approval for a "Negro residential subdivision" in the Lincoln Court neighborhood adjacent to Addison High School. Prominent Black leaders spoke in favor of the approval, citing the need for city infrastructure to support the development that contained 2,000 home sites.

Two new circles of the King's Daughters were organized, one for Williamson Road and the other for Raleigh Court. Mrs. Everette Jones headed the Williamson Road circle, and Mrs. Claude Brice led the one for Raleigh Court. The King's Daughters' principal project was the operation of the Mary Louise Home for elderly women.

Don Reno, a "hillbilly musician," was arrested by Roanoke Police on a warrant from South Carolina that charged the banjo player with obtaining money under false pretenses. Reno's hearing was set for February 15. Reno played with the Tennessee Buddies.

The Roanoke School Board dismissed the idea of a swimming pool being incorporated into the master plan for the new Addison High School at their meeting on January 24. The idea had been advocated by board member Harry Penn, but the board majority determined the cost was too high.

Roanoke City Manager Arthur Owens reported to the city council that an ordinance banning the dumping of trash in an abandoned quarry near Addison High School would cost the city thousands of dollars. Owens indicated that the city did not have the capacity to absorb the additional trash elsewhere.

The N&W Railway westbound freight train No. 91 derailed near the Vinton station on January 25. The incident involved twenty-two cars, forcing passenger trains to be rerouted. The wreck was caused by a broken wheel on a gravel-carrying hopper.

US Secretary of Defense Louis Johnson, a Roanoke native, addressed the sixtieth annual meeting of the Roanoke Chamber of Commerce at the Hotel Roanoke on January 25. Johnson praised President Truman's foreign and domestic policies, asserting they had brought "unparalleled prosperity both at home and abroad." About 900 chamber members attended the event.

Sixteen trailers in the Veterans Emergency Housing Project located at the Roanoke City Farm were disposed of on a bid basis. The trailers and all other temporary housing units at the projects (one was for whites, one for Blacks) had been conveyed to the city by the federal government in 1949.

The Roanoke Kiwanis Club celebrated its thirtieth anniversary at the Patrick Henry Hotel on January 25. The keynote speaker was Leonard Muse, whose topic was "Keep America American." Special guest was US Secretary of Defense Louis Johnson, brother of the club's president, Gordon Johnson.

The Normandie Inn at Patterson Avenue and Thirteenth Street SW was sold at auction on January 26.

The first public hearing on the proposed $34 million Smith Mountain Dam was held at Moneta High School on January 28. Ben Moomaw, executive of the Roanoke Chamber of Commerce, spoke against the dam on behalf of the group that considered the project an invasion of private property.

Rex Bowen of the Brooklyn Dodgers and Maurice Aderholt of the Washington Senators were instructors for the baseball coaching clinic that was held at Jefferson High School in early February. The clinic was sponsored by the National Association of Professional Baseball Leagues and was for coaches and managers of amateur teams.

Mary Dudley Antiques opened on January 30 in the Patrick Henry Hotel.

The board of the Thursday Morning Music Club sent a resolution to Roanoke City Council advocating the reopening of the Academy of Music.

The Roanoke Valley sent well-wishes to Ed Tuttle, a student at Andrew Lewis High School, who was at a Boston hospital for an experimental artificial kidney. The kidney had been used three times before, twice successfully. Tuttle was suffering from a blood disease that had damaged his kidney. He died three days later, on January 30. Neighbors had raised funds for his hospital care, and his parents were with him when he passed.

The congregation of Trinity Lutheran Church launched a $50,000 capital campaign in early February to build a church at the corner of Williamson Road and Epperley Avenue. The church was founded on February 2, 1947, and dedicated some months later with sixty-two charter members.

Caldwell-Sites broke ground on a new wholesale warehouse in Vinton. The one-story building had an estimated cost of $112,000 and was located at Tinker and Tenth Streets.

Auto Parts, a wholesale auto parts and supply business, was sold to Raymond Brickey, Winfred Smith, and Dallas Scaggs. The business was located at 522 Salem Avenue SW.

The cornerstone for the new Masonic Temple of Williamson Road Lodge No. 163 was laid on January 28 by C. E. Webber of Salem, past Grand Master of Masons in Virginia. Over 200 persons attended the event. The lodge was located on Pioneer Road, behind the post office.

According to figures published in the 1950 city directory, the population of Roanoke was 92,500 as of January 1.

The body of Army Master Sergeant Bernice Martin arrived at Salem on January 30. Martin died in a drowning accident near his base in Kyoto, Japan. He was survived by a wife and three children. He was thirty.

The Roanoke Civic Ballet opened its sixth season with a February 7 performance of *Swan Lake* at Jefferson High School. The ballet had been originally organized by Mrs. Floyd Ward and Mrs. Frank Rogers.

Martha Graham and her dance company performed at Hollins College on February 13. Graham and her twenty-member company were on a national tour.

Some 400 voters in Vinton were sent postcards as a sample ballot on expanding the town council from three to five members. There were 150 in favor and 29 opposed by the ballot deadline. The town council voted to ask the General Assembly for permission to expand.

Roanoke native Captain Harold Wilson was killed on January 31 in a plane crash in Guatemala, where he was stationed at the American consulate. The crash also killed three other men.

Y. Hutsona became the first Black candidate to announce for the Democratic city council primary in Roanoke. A tailor, Hutsona was a member of the City Democratic Executive Committee and was past president of the Roanoke Civic League. Two days later, a second Black candidate entered the race, Eugene Brown. Brown was the president of the Roanoke Civic League and was endorsed by the group's Citizens Committee.

Film comic Al St. John performed on the stage of the Roanoke Theatre on February 1. Known as "Old Fuzzy," he was accompanied by his "Musical Rangers."

Two former pitchers for the Jefferson High School baseball team were given professional contracts by the Elizabethton, Tennessee, team in the Appalachian League. They were Richard Harrison and Duvall Turnbull.

Paul Williams and his Hucklebuckers Orchestra, along with Larry Darnell, performed at the American Legion Auditorium on February 3. White spectators were admitted for a discounted price.

Fire swept through the Hartsook Building on Roanoke's Market Square on February 2. Damage was estimated at $200,000. Two businesses were completely wiped out, Shay Produce Company and Clark Produce Company. Seven other businesses in the building were damaged. Eight engine companies and two ladder trucks responded to the fire.

The annual meeting of the Roanoke Groundhog Club was held at the American Legion Auditorium on February 3. Some 3,000 attended the male-only event that poked fun at local politicians by inviting all council candidates to sing together an impromptu version of *Sweet Adeline.* Music was provided by the Freddie Lee Orchestra and Wayne Fleming and his Hillbilly Band. H. T. Angell was elected as the group's president.

Candidates for the Democratic Roanoke City Council primary for April 4 numbered twelve when the application deadline passed. They were James Bear, Francis Bentley, Eugene Brown, Glenn Culbertson, Benton Dillard, Saunders Guerrant Jr., Paul Johnson, Archer Minton, Walter Nelson, Charles Satchwell, Roy Webber, and Walter Young. Y. Hutsona chose not to file.

Richardson-Wayland Electrical Corporation completed its move from 122 W. Church Avenue to Memorial Bridge between Thirteenth Street and Roanoke Avenue SW in early February.

Pollocks Shoe Store became Butler's Shoe Salon at 13 W. Campbell Avenue. The change was due to the national chain being bought and renamed.

Some 3,000 members Roanoke's all-male Groundhog Club met on Groundhog Day at the American Legion Auditorium. *Historical Society of Western Virginia*

Henderson Pate, a senior at Jefferson High School, was accidentally shot in the chest at a social gathering following a high school basketball game in Salisbury, North Carolina. He recovered following a brief hospitalization.

The Roanoke County Board of Supervisors established a county Board of Health. Among the initial five members were three physicians—H. H. Wescott, John Hurt, and Harold Kolmer. The board was tasked with overseeing the sanitary conditions of the county and directing and preventing contagious diseases.

Dr. Lindsey Martin opened his optometry practice at 313 Campbell Avenue SW. He had formerly been with Martin Optical Company.

The Star City Laundromat opened at 2910 Williamson Road on February 6.

Fast Service Laundry and Cleaning opened on February 6 at 687 Brandon Road. Vincent Wheeler was the owner.

Claude Hopkins and his *Zanzy Barr Revue* of singing, dancing, and novelty acts came to the stage of the Roanoke Theatre on February 8.

Nearly 1,000 Boy Scouts participated in a two-ring circus at the American Legion Auditorium on February 10 and 11. The event closed out a weeklong celebration of the fortieth anniversary of the Boy Scouts of America.

Junius Fishburn donated a thirty-five-acre tract of land adjacent to Mill Mountain to be used for a public purpose. The donation was to allow a connection between Mill Mountain and the Blue Ridge Parkway. The parkway's construction between Bent Mountain and the Peaks of Otter was expected to begin in 1953.

The Roanoke School Board was informed that Thomas Jefferson High School and John Marshall High School dropped Jefferson High School from their football schedules. The two Richmond schools had different reasons for their decisions. Jefferson officials stated that the last game they played against the Roanoke school resulted in players following each other after the game looking to fight. Marshall's coaches said the game with Roanoke simply did not draw enough fans.

Some 500 persons attended a dinner at the Hotel Roanoke honoring Rev. Z. V. Roberson on the occasion of his twenty-fifth anniversary as the pastor of Raleigh Court Presbyterian Church. A gift of silver was presented to Roberson and his wife by the congregation.

Wanda's Beauty Shop opened on February 8 one block east of Lakeside at Laffoon's Store. The owner was Wanda Caudell.

Mickey Harmon of Salem was electrocuted while working on power lines on Long Island, New York, on February 8. He was twenty-seven.

The Salem Chamber of Commerce opened its first full-time office at 308 E. Main Street. John Dennis was the executive secretary.

Due to the coal crisis created by striking miners, Southern Railway diesel engines were used to pull Southern passenger trains operated by N&W Railway between Bristol and Lynchburg in mid-February. N&W Railway was forced to curtail one-third of its passenger service due to a federal mandate in response to the coal situation.

Roanoke native and Hollywood actor John Payne and his wife, actress Gloria DeHaven, were granted a divorce in Los Angeles on February 9. The couple had been married for six years and lived in Beverly Hills. DeHaven had filed for divorce on the grounds of cruelty in that Payne had asked her to give up her movie career.

Roanoke Gas Company received authorization to build a thirty-mile natural gas transmission line between Gala and Roanoke near Eagle Rock. The Federal Power Commission had given the company "what we've been waiting for," reported company president Michael Shea.

Ray Firestone and Ben Firestone opened their new poultry processing plant in Troutville. The brothers' business killed, cleaned, and packed for shipment between 2,000 and 2,400 chickens per hour. The Firestones worked with some 150 farmers throughout Southwestern Virginia. Firestone and Company employed 113 persons.

Rose's *Parisian Midget Follies* came to the stage of the Roanoke Theatre on February 15. It was billed as a showcase of "the most beautiful midgets in the world" that featured sisters Jaqueline and Sonja.

Several hundred persons came to the N&W Railway passenger station in Roanoke on February 11 to see the Southern Railway diesel engines pull the *Tennessean* into the station. It was the first time diesel engines had been used on the N&W Railway's mountainous Radford Division.

An original comic book was produced by four Roanoke men in mid-February. *The Adventures of Flip and Chip, the Chipmunk Twins* was written by Fred Hubbard, illustrated by James Gibson and John Kessler, and printed by Russell Paxton of the Paxton Press.

Calvin Webb of Roanoke was killed in a single-car accident on February 12, when the vehicle he was driving struck a small bridge near the brick plant in Salem. He was twenty-eight.

Band leader and singer Vaughan Monroe, along with his "Moon Maids," performed at a Valentine's Banquet at the Hotel Roanoke for the Hospital Development Fund that that was raising money for Burrell Memorial Hospital and the Memorial and Crippled Children's Hospital. Some 700 persons attended. Clem Johnston was chairman of the $1.5 million campaign. While several prominent businessmen spoke, the press reported that the most moving speech was given by Betty Musselman, who had been stricken with polio in 1949. The *Roanoke Times* reported, "The audience grew more and more quiet until not an eye wandered from the girl on the platform." Musselman described the cramped rooms at the hospital and the need for additional medical equipment and space.

Three members of the Roanoke Kennel Club exhibited dogs in the Westminster Kennel Club Show in New York. Margaret Douglas entered two Welch Corgis; William Hemberger entered three Cairn terriers; and Eric Sachers entered his Labrador retriever.

George Jones died at Burrell Memorial Hospital on February 14, having been struck by a car at the corner of Gilmer Avenue and First Street NW. The driver of the car was Weldon Lawrence Jr.

The new, larger McAvoy Music House opened on February 15 at 122 W. Church Avenue.

Division Five of the Hospital Development Fund campaign had raised over half of their $152,000 goal as reported in their meeting at the Hotel Dumas. The vast majority of the amount came from employees of Burrell Memorial Hospital and the Magic City Medical Society. The society was headed by Dr. L. E. Paxton.

Members of the Salem Penguin Club announced they would move to their new clubhouse on Wildwood Road north of the Andrew Lewis Tavern in early March.

Some twenty employees of the Cold Spring Cooperative Creamery at 532 Loudon Avenue NW went on strike on February 15, claiming several employees had been fired without cause.

Nettie Decker, age fifty, was found beaten to death in the kitchen of her apartment at 915 Salem Avenue SW on February 16. Arrested for the brutal slaying was the victim's son, Clarence Decker. Frank Webb was leading the police investigation.

The First National Exchange Bank formally opened its Williamson Road Branch on February 18 with an open house. The branch was located at Williamson and Pioneer Roads. The building contractor was J. M. Turner. The ribbon cutting was marked by the arrival of Victorian carriages occupied by members of the William Fleming Dramatic Club portraying Col. William Fleming, Gen. Andrew Lewis, and Gen. Edward Watts in costume.

A cornerstone-laying ceremony was held for the First Wesleyan Methodist Church at Melrose Avenue and Sixteenth Street NW on February 19. Rev. Dewey Miller was the pastor. The guest speaker was Rev. E. L. Henderson, a former pastor.

The Simmons Company mattress manufacturers leased the warehouse of the former Central Manufacturing Company and made Roanoke a key distribution center for its products. Paul Piedmont managed the warehouse that was located at corner of Second Street and Center Avenue NW.

George Steffey was profiled in the February 19 edition of the *Roanoke Times*. Steffey had been a barber in Roanoke for fifty-three years and was still working. He began at age seventeen at a shop located in the old Terry Building in Roanoke. He estimated that he had given 513,000 haircuts.

Magic City Launderers and Cleaners reopened at Memorial Bridge the third week in February. The laundry had been gutted by a fire in June 1949. E. C. Tudor was the owner. The new building was located at 902 Thirteenth Street SW, and equipment cost around $200,000.

The Dove-Gillespie Floral Shop opened in the Patrick Henry Hotel. The florists were Devona Gillespie and Harold Dove. Both had been formerly with Fallon Florist.

The activities of the Liberty Trust branch of the Colonial-American National Bank ceased on February 23 as the branch was incorporated into Colonial-American's main branch at Jefferson Street and Campbell Avenue.

Horne's at 410 S. Jefferson Street opened a hair and beauty salon on its second floor.

Rodeo stars Sally and her "Montana Plainsmen," along with Tex Don, performed at the Roanoke Theatre on February 22.

Officials with Burlington Mills Corporation at Vinton announced a planned 60,000 square-foot expansion for the plant. J. C. Cowan Jr., head of the firm, said the expansion would create about one hundred new positions.

Johnny Woods, self-described "human fly," scaled the sixty-foot high Roanoke County Courthouse in Salem on College Avenue. Some 200 persons watched the fifty-three-year-old Los Angeles man climb the structure using only his hands and feet on February 22.

Martha Ann Woodrum of Roanoke was elected president of the Virginia Aviation Trade Association.

A birdhouse was discovered on the grounds of the former German POW camp in Salem with a note inside from the prisoner who built it. The note was from William Schwartz of Kiel, Germany, and asked the finder of the note to write him. The note was dated March 11, 1945.

Addison High School won top honors in the Southwestern District Music Festival held at the school. Some 400 students from Western Virginia participated. Eunice Poindexter was the choir director at Addison.

Bob Porterfield, director of the Barter Theatre, appealed to save the Academy of Music in a speech to the Roanoke Executives Club. Porterfield described the Academy as "one of the finest theatres in America."

Two Jefferson High School wrestlers captured state titles in a tournament held at Charlottesville. Sam Cook won the 138-pound division, and George Preas won the 175-pound division.

Roanoke's second eight-day Preaching Mission opened on February 26. The mission was organized and promoted by the Roanoke Ministers Conference and brought in well-known speakers from various denominations. The services were held at the American Legion Auditorium, and the lineup included US Senator Clyde Hoey, Norman Vincent Peale, Clovis Chappell, and Thomas Carruthers. A mass choir sang nightly.

A show of vaudeville acts and a "scintillating girl show" came to the Roanoke Theatre stage on March 1. Ads claimed patrons could see "Ruthine in her Dance of Desire," and Karston's *Eyefuls of 1950*.

Shirley's Drive-In Restaurant opened on February 28 at 2816 Williamson Road.

The Liberty Trust building at the corner of Salem Avenue and Jefferson Street was sold for $260,000 to Building Management Inc. of Wilmington, North Carolina. The building had been erected in 1909 by the First National Bank.

Roanoke City Council gave final approval to the school board's plans to acquire the Schilling-Liptrap tract in Garden City for a new school. The plan also included the removal of two dwellings on the site. Work on the new school was to begin in May.

Michael's Bakery held a formal opening of their new store at 3336 Williamson Road. This was their third location, with other stores in downtown Roanoke and on Main Street in Salem.

Officials with Appalachian Electric Power Company announced plans for a $1 million high-voltage transmission station on a twenty-acre site halfway between Roanoke and Salem on Route 11.

A fire on March 3 destroyed the two-story sausage plant of Keith Brothers in the Hanging Rock section of Roanoke County. The loss was estimated at $40,000, and the owners indicated the plant would be rebuilt.

A proposed new baseball field and stands for the Roanoke Red Sox was sketched out by the Virginia Bridge Company. A rendering of the $100,000 facility to be built at Maher Field was advocated by Red Sox officials to be constructed of wood, steel, and cinder block. The plan called for 5,000 seats under cover, including 750 box seats. Red Sox President Clarke Wray said construction could begin at any time if a term lease of Maher Field was agreed to.

Detailed plans for the new Addison High School in Roanoke were unveiled to the public in early March. The preliminary architectural sketches were developed by Stone and Thompson architectural firm and approved by the Roanoke School Board. The new $1.1 million school was to be built on a ten-acre tract on Orange Avenue at Fifth Street NW, on the opposite side of Washington Park from what would become the former Addison High School. The original Addison High School was built in 1928 at a cost of $182,000. The school was named for Lucy Addison, a Black educator, who retired from teaching in Roanoke after forty years.

The Vinton Lions Club held their annual minstrel show in the auditorium of William Byrd High School. The fundraiser ran for three nights and included over seventy participants. J. W. Reynolds was the show's director.

The Kazim Shrine-Polack Brothers Circus opened for a six-day run on March 6 at the American Legion Auditorium. Headlining the program was the famous high-wire Berosini Troupe that performed without a safety net. Elephant and chimpanzee acts were part of the other attractions.

The Roanoke Jewish Forum sponsored a series of speakers and music at the Patrick Henry Hotel. The main speaker for the forum was Rabbi James Heller of Cincinnati. Dr. Leo Platt was president of the forum.

The vast majority of workers employed by N&W Railway who were furloughed during the coal miners' strike were called back the second week of March as a result of the strike being over. The railway had furloughed about 1,900 workers in Roanoke. A week later, the railway was able to resume normal passenger train runs.

Doris Milton of Roanoke was held for a grand jury after a hearing in police court on the charge she aided and assisted in an abortion procedure for an eighteen-year-old woman. According to the evidence presented, Milton was paid $175 for assisting in the abortion.

Roanoke City got its first full-time dental health officer in mid-March. Dr. Byron John of West Virginia was employed to carry out dental hygiene work among Roanoke's school pupils, mostly during the summer months. His annual salary was $4,500.

Muddiman Electric Company opened on March 10 at 28 W. Church Avenue. They carried Westinghouse appliances.

The Virginia General Assembly approved a $2.5 million capital improvement plan for the Catawba Sanatorium. The plan was mostly for the construction of a new infirmary.

N&W Railway purchased thirty steam switching engines from the Chesapeake and Ohio (C&O) Railway, as the C&O had changed to diesel engines. N&W officials stated the engines were bought for a bargain price.

Ivory Joe Hunter and his orchestra performed for a Blacks-only show and dance at the American Legion Auditorium on March 15. White spectators were admitted at a discounted price.

The Barter Theatre presented a production of *Thunder Rock* at the Jefferson High School auditorium on March 17.

Ground-breaking services were held for the Williamson Road Church of the Brethren on Pioneer Road on March 12. The Reverend C. M. Key was pastor. The services were part of a $50,000 education building being erected to serve the congregation that was organized in October 1948.

A concert by the National Symphony Orchestra was given at the Jefferson High School auditorium on March 14. Howard Mitchell, whose appearance was sponsored by the Community Concert Association, conducted the orchestra.

The St. Louis Symphony Orchestra performed at the American Legion Auditorium on March 13 under the auspices of the Thursday Morning Music Club. The orchestra was conducted by Vladimir Golschmann.

Kennard-Pace Company held a formal opening of their new showroom at 129 W. Kirk Avenue during the third week of March.

Rudy Lacy of Jefferson High School was the 1949–50 city-county scoring champ in basketball with a regular season point total of 496 in twenty-four games. James Saul of William Fleming High School was second with 267 points.

Roanoke City Council initiated a movement to consider consolidating all Roanoke Valley political subdivisions into one governmental unit during their meeting on March 13. The council invited officials with Vinton, Salem, and Roanoke County to hold a meeting in the near future to discuss the possibility. The motion for the idea was proposed by Councilman Dan Cronin.

The Western film comic Cannonball and his "Country Cousins" performed on the stage of the Roanoke Theatre on March 15.

Students at Conehurst School in Roanoke County continued their studies in the basement of Tabernacle Baptist Church due to the construction of an addition at their school. The county school board authorized a continuation of that arrangement that affected 160 students.

The idea of developing a federal low-income housing project in Roanoke City proved controversial. Some candidates in the Democratic city council primary opposed such a plan, and others demanded there be a voter referendum on the question. The Roanoke Junior Chamber of Commerce was also on record in opposition.

Roanoke Elks Lodge 197 presented its third annual minstrel show at the Jefferson High School auditorium the third week in March. *Holiday Escapades* featured a cast of 125 persons. D. M. Rumisell was general chairman for the three-night show that raised money for the Elks boys' camp near Clifton Forge.

The Salem Lions Club held their annual minstrel show at Andrew Lewis High School for a three-night run. The Salem Lions did their first minstrel show in 1936 to raise funds for their various community projects.

With much fanfare, Roanoke Mayor A. R. Minton threw the ceremonial switch that turned on the new streetlights in downtown Roanoke on March 18. At 8:02 p.m., the lights came on and created what civic and business leaders called "the great white way." Hundreds of Roanokers blocked the streets at the intersection of Jefferson and Campbell to watch the ceremony. This was the third time the streetlights had been vastly improved over as many decades to improve nighttime activity in downtown. The new lighting system cost about $1.2 million, according to officials with Appalachian Electric Power Company, and would be completed in phases through 1951. The new system had all lighting infrastructure below ground, and all light posts, most dating to 1928, would be removed during the project.

The Cosmopolitan Male Choir performed at the American Legion Auditorium on March 19. They were sponsored by Hill Street Baptist Church. The group was well-known nationally on radio.

Revival speaker Rev. Mordecai Ham held a rally at the Market Auditorium in Roanoke on March 19. His topic was "Who sold America's birthright—Christ or communism?" His appearance was sponsored by the Friends of Christ in Roanoke.

Francis Poulene, a composer, and Pierre Bernac, a baritone, presented a concert at Hollins College on March 20. This was part of their second transcontinental tour across the United States.

The Salem Community Players presented *Three Blind Mice* in the Carriage House Theatre at Longwood. It was the first production to be staged in the carriage house that had been converted for theatrical performances. Lead roles were played by Amy Glenn, Dorothy Thompson, and Bill Segall.

This is the intersection of Jefferson Street and Campbell Avenue, looking west on Campbell, in 1950. *Historical Society of Western Virginia*

Roanoke City Council held a public hearing spread across two days on the proposed federal housing project consisting of 900 units with an estimated federal price tag of $6 million. Those opposing the low-income housing were the Roanoke Junior Chamber of Commerce, former councilman Courtney King, and several prominent realtors and bankers. Favoring the project were the Roanoke Building and Trades Council and local attorney Arnold Schlossberg. A majority of the city council was of the opinion the ordinance could not be rescinded as the Roanoke Redevelopment and Housing Authority had been duly empowered and had begun with their work. The council eventually decided to have a representative from the Public Housing Administration come to Roanoke and explain in detail the federal housing project proposal.

The Roanoke County Board of Supervisors agreed to be represented at a meeting to discuss the consolidation of the local governments in the Roanoke Valley, accepting an invitation extended to them by Roanoke City Council.

A six-week evangelistic crusade came to Roanoke the last week of March with services alternating between the American Legion Auditorium and the auditorium of Lee Junior High School. The evangelists were Robert Boothby of Washington, DC, and Leslie Mansell. Both were heard nationally on radio.

The Optimist Club of Roanoke adopted a resolution opposing public housing in Roanoke. Jack Coulter told the club on behalf of the Jaycees that public housing was "another form of socialism" and should be put to an advisory referendum before the public.

The Roanoke Red Sox opened their spring training in late March in Jacksonville, Florida. Thirty-six players participated in the training camp headed by the team's manager, John "Red" Marion.

George Fulton Jr. of Roanoke qualified to play in the Greater Greensboro Open professional golf tournament. Fulton shot two straight rounds of seventy-six each and failed to qualify for the final thirty-six holes of the tournament.

C. A. Kingery of Roanoke fell from a crane while working at the N&W Railway East End Shops on March 23 and was killed. He was forty-five with a wife and two sons.

Garden City Shoe Shop, located in the Garden City Hardware Company at 3331 Garden City Boulevard, opened on March 24.

The body of Alice Taylor of Roanoke was found alongside Route 460 on Brush Mountain, five miles northwest of Blacksburg, on March 24. Taylor, twenty-four, had been missing for three days. The Veterans Administration Hospital clerk lived on Sherwood Avenue SW. The Montgomery County coroner determined that Taylor had died from a cerebral hemorrhage that Dr. R. H. Grubb believed to be the result of an assault. The body was identified by the woman's mother, Mrs. H. P. Taylor, and her brother, Raymond Taylor. Police believed the body was probably dragged from a car and placed along the road. Taylor's body had been discovered midmorning by Bernice Dowdy as he walked along the road. For many in Roanoke and for the police department, the murder reminded them of the Mother's Day slaying of Dana Marie Weaver in 1949. According to her supervisor and family, Taylor had left work at the hospital around 10:00 a.m. on Thursday, March 23, complaining of a headache and that she was going to see a physician. When Taylor failed to arrive at her mother's home for dinner later that day, the family felt something was amiss. Roanoke City Council directed the city manager to offer a reward of $500 to anyone providing information to solve the case, as police had no leads.

Salem Town Council and Vinton Town Council both agreed to send representatives to a meeting requested by Roanoke City Council to discuss the possible merger of all local governments in the Roanoke Valley.

Farr Home Equipment opened at 122 E. Campbell Avenue on March 24.

The Roanoke Ministers Conference launched their "Support the Church" campaign through a variety of advertising that encouraged persons to attend a church of their choice. The conference was joining with other clergy organizations across the country in the nationwide emphasis.

Minnie Spangler of the Williamson Road area was killed in an auto accident at the intersection of Center Avenue and Twenty-Fourth Street NW on March 25.

Over 7,000 people attended the open house of the remodeled Colonial-American National Bank in Roanoke on March 25. Murals around the lobby walls depicted scenes of Mount Vernon, Monticello, Gunston Hall, and Williamsburg. The most popular spot for visitors was the vault that contained 3,200 individual safety deposit boxes. The bank also had a display of old coins for the event.

The Chapman-Rice firm began advertising the new, modern Blair Apartments in Salem as ready for occupancy in late March.

The *Stardust Revue* came to the stage of the Roanoke Theatre on March 29 that featured pro boxer Lou Nova and singers Jimmie O'Brien, Johnny Standley, and the Larry Collins Musical Trio.

Troup Brothers, golf architects and engineers in Miami, Florida, was given the contract to construct the Hidden Valley Country Club golf course. Clearing of the land began on March 28, and club officials hoped the course would be ready for seeding by mid-August.

Dartha Fulton of Bedford County was arrested on March 28 in the death of Alice Taylor. Held as material witnesses were Christine Jones and Woodson Tuck, also of Bedford County. According to law enforcement officials, who obtained a sworn statement from Fulton, Taylor had gone to Bedford by bus on March 23 to get an abortion to be performed by Fulton. Taylor died from the procedure while in the home of Fulton. It was noted that abortions were illegal in Virginia, including even the selling of literature or lecturing on the subject. Officials gave no further details about the case other than the arrest.

Virginia State Police moved into their new headquarters on Route 11 west of Salem in late March. The substation had sleeping quarters, a photography dark room, offices, and a communication room.

The barn of the Baptist Orphanage at Salem burned on March 28. The barn was located on the orphanage's farm off Ashbottom Road northwest of Salem.

Lizzie Price, age 108, died in her log-cabin home in Floyd County on March 28. Price was born a slave in Franklin County near Rocky Mount in 1842.

Rev. Elias Poe, former pastor of Belmont Baptist Church, died in a Roanoke hospital on March 29 at the age of sixty-eight. Poe served as Belmont's pastor for twenty-two years from 1926 to 1948.

Roanoke police filed a charge against Dartha Fulton for performing an abortion in a Roanoke home. According to Detective Frank Webb, Fulton had performed the abortion "several weeks ago." Fulton had been arrested in connection with the death of Alice Taylor, who died during an abortion performed by Fulton in Bedford. Doris Milton of Roanoke had already been charged with aiding in the Roanoke abortion. Bedford County officials gave, on the same day, further details of the Taylor situation, stating that the young woman had died at Fulton's home during the abortion, and that Fulton wanted the body removed from her home. She, aided by Woodson Tuck, drove sixty-five miles with Taylor's body in the trunk of Tuck's auto. Near Brush Mountain, they disposed of the body along Route 460.

Bronze-color parking meters were installed at strategic locations in downtown Roanoke that allowed for twelve-minute parking for one penny. The meters gave a maximum of thirty-six minutes.

A $35,000 warehouse to be occupied by Sunshine Biscuits at 1350 Eighth Street SW was under construction and expected to be completed by late June. The building was adjacent to the Porterfield Distributing Company.

The Burrell Memorial Hospital Association held its annual meeting at High Street Baptist Church on March 30. Dr. E. D. Downing was elected president. James Lewis, administrator, reported that in 1949 there were 2,354 admissions and 459 births.

From left to right are Gabriel Tucker, Alexander Fleming, and Elbyrne Gill in 1950 in Gill's office. Fleming, a Nobel Prize recipient, was a guest lecturer at the Gill Spring Congress. *Historical Society of Western Virginia.*

Moses Esso Service Station opened on March 31 on East Main Street in Salem, near the courthouse. The operator was Johnny Moses Jr.

The Blue Ridge Jamboree was held at the American Legion Auditorium in April. Featured performers included Woody Mashburn and his Wanderers of the Wasteland, Joe Basham, Wayne Fleming and his Country Cavaliers, Clarence Arthur and his Roaming Ramblers, Johnny McDowell, and Florie Belle.

The twenty-third annual spring congress of the Gill Memorial Eye, Ear, Nose and Throat Hospital began April 3. Some 400 specialists in that field attended. Guest faculty members included Sir Alexander Fleming—the discoverer of penicillin—of London and Dr. C. W. Mayo, who was professor of surgery at the Mayo Foundation in Rochester, Minnesota. Fleming had won the 1944 Nobel Prize for medicine.

Officials with the Chesapeake and Potomac Telephone Company reported that since the end of World War II, some 13,000 new residential telephones had been installed in Roanoke. C&P planned to install an additional 1,700 in the Williamson Road section by midsummer.

Glenn L. Martin, pioneer American aviator, addressed a group of Roanoke businessmen on the threat of "push button" warfare. Martin, president of Glenn L. Martin Company in Baltimore, shared his company's development of long-range missiles that could carry atomic materials.

The 147-acre Bush orchard in the Bent Mountain section was auctioned on April 12. The orchard had about 800 fruit trees.

The Roanoke Planning Board gave approval for the Lincoln Court housing development to move forward at their meeting on April 3. John Windel, chairman of the Roanoke Redevelopment and Housing Authority, announced after the meeting that the 300-unit development for low-income Blacks would be built on thirty-three acres east of Washington Park. A similar development for low-income whites was also approved by the planning board. Two days later, the housing authority reported that the W. H. Horton property in northwest Roanoke would be the site for white housing. The thirty-acre tract was bounded by Center Avenue on the south, west to Twenty-Ninth Street, to an area between Lynchburg Road and Melrose Avenue.

Dr. Wayne Shober opened his optometry practice at the corner of Burton Avenue and Williamson Road NW in early April.

The Eden Corporation announced their new housing development, known as Intervale, was underway between Cove Road and Florida Avenue NW. The development consisted of sixty-two homes ranging in price from $6,000 to $9,200. W. A. Ingram was the company president.

The Roanoke Department of Parks and Recreation reported that sixteen rabbits had been donated for Elmwood Park to add to the fourteen ducks there. Park staff had built pens for the rabbits.

A grand jury indicted Dartha Fulton, a former Bedford taxi driver, on a charge of performing an abortion on an eighteen-year-old Roanoke woman in January. Fulton's trial was set for April 21. Fulton had also been charged separately in the death of Alice Taylor. The grand jury also indicted Doris Milton, in whose home the abortion had been performed.

Over 10,000 voters participated in the Roanoke Democratic primary for city council, which was the de facto council election. The record-breaking turnout had the following results: Roy Webber, 7,596; Walter Young, 6,910; A. R. Minton, 5,284; Paul Johnson, 2,835; Benton Dillard, 2,223; James Bear, 2,200; Eugene Brown, 1,118; Saunders Guerrant Jr., 684; Glenn Culbertson, 590; Francis Bentley, 518; Charles Satchwell, 307; and Walter Nelson, 208. Dillard was an incumbent seeking a second term, and Minton also an incumbent. Brown was the only Black in the race. Webber was a florist, and Young was an assistant chief engineer for N&W Railway. The general election would be held in June.

Everything from a bear trap to a demonstration on how to skin a squirrel was part of the Izaak Walton League Sports and Conservation Show held at the Appalachian Building auditorium the first week in April. It was the first such show held in Roanoke. Many considered the most interesting exhibit to be a display of old guns made between 1460 and 1918.

Sir Alexander Fleming addressed students at Jefferson High School during an all-student assembly. Fleming was in the city for the Gill Memorial Hospital symposium.

Ralph Shoaf of Roanoke signed a contract to play professional football with the Washington Redskins. Shoaf played football for Jefferson High School and for the University of Virginia. Shoaf, who was twenty-five, was five feet ten and weighed 195 pounds. At UVA he had played in the half-back position.

The Parfield Golf Driving Range opened in early April on Melrose Avenue.

The Virginia Amateur Baseball League, under president W. C. Wood, announced their league teams for the 1950 season. They were Buchanan, Boone Mill, Clifton Forge, Troutville, Glenvar, Lowmoor, New Castle, Salem, Vinton, and the Veterans Administration Hospital. The season called for thirty-six games to be played between May 6 and August 19 on the weekends.

A jury found Clarence Decker guilty on April 7 of first-degree murder in the death of his mother, Nettie Decker. Mrs. Decker was found dead in her kitchen on February 16. L. E. Hurt Jr. and Rodney Fitzpatrick were Decker's court-appointed defense attorneys. The jurors took slightly more than an hour to deliberate before returning their verdict. Decker brutally stomped his mother to death according to the Assistant Commonwealth's Attorney Beverly Fitzpatrick, who asked for the death penalty. Decker's defense team argued for acquittal on the grounds their client was insane. The next day, Judge Dirk Kuyk sentenced Decker to life imprisonment.

Lucky Millinder and his orchestra performed at the American Legion Auditorium on April 9. The balcony was reserved for white spectators.

The Boston Braves and the Cincinnati Reds played a Major League Baseball exhibition game on April 10 at Maher Field. The starting pitchers were Johnny Antonelli (Braves) and Ken Peterson (Reds). The Braves won, 15 to 12, largely due to a grand-slam home run in the eighth inning by pinch hitter Tommy Holmes. Nearly 5,400 fans turned out for the game that also saw a Reds triple play in the third inning.

Singer Marian Anderson performed at the American Legion Auditorium on April 11. Her appearance was sponsored by the Fifth Avenue Presbyterian Church. Anderson was widely known and celebrated as a singer and most noted for her Easter Sunday concert in 1939 for 75,000 at the Lincoln Memorial. A review of her performance in the *Roanoke Times* noted, "The distinguished artist took breath away from her audience with amazing demonstrations of voice range." The audience demanded and received three encores as Anderson closed with *Ave Maria*.

Carl's Salon of Beauty opened on April 12 on Second Street at Luck Avenue SW. The owners were Carl Blundo and F. M. (Chick) Wilkinson. Both men were formerly employed by Heironimus department store.

A story by Ozzie Osborne in the *Roanoke Times* on April 9 gave a brief history of the Patchwork Players, a homegrown theatre troupe. Barbara Lucas, Sylvia Farnham, Anne Weaver, Betty Coleman, and Lyn Neill started the group for fun in 1945, and five years later the group had performed before over 75,000 people. Home from college for the summer, the group decided to stage plays on Farnham's front lawn. In the first year, the audience barely outnumbered the cast as they performed scenes from various plays. The next year, Francis Ballard stepped in as director, bringing twenty years of professional acting and directing experience. It was that season they took the name Patchwork Players and offered courses in acting, scenery making, and costuming. They also moved from Farnham's yard to doing plays in city parks.

Singer Marian Anderson was welcomed at the N&W Railway passenger station by Roanoke Mayor A. R. Minton. Joining him were Rev. William Simmons (fifth from right) and some members of Fifth Avenue Presbyterian Church. *Fifth Avenue Presbyterian Church*

By 1947, the Players were well-established with Roanoke audiences and became a permanent organization with Clem Johnston as president and Judge Richard Pence as vice president. That same year, college students wanting to act came from several states for the summer. By 1950 Osborne observed they were "Roanoke's most unique and successful cultural venture."

A crowd estimated at 18,000 attended the Easter sunrise service at Natural Bridge on April 9 and heard Rev. Robert Lapsley Jr., pastor of Roanoke's First Presbyterian Church, deliver the message. It was believed to be the largest crowd ever for the event.

Advertisements for the Hospital Development Fund appealed to citizens for donations at the midpoint of the campaign. The goal of $1.5 million was to provide for a new seventy-five-bed Burrell Memorial Hospital for Black patients, a new one-hundred-bed addition to the Memorial and Crippled Children's Hospital (formerly Roanoke Hospital), and a minimum of fifty beds for the care of crippled children due to polio in the twenty-four counties in southwestern Virginia.

Dr. John Everett, thirty-one, was selected to become the new president of Hollins College by the school's trustees, succeeding Dr. Bessie Randolph, who had announced her retirement effective June 30. Everett was chairman of the Department of Philosophy at Columbia University.

Rabbi Morris Lieberman of Baltimore spoke at a dinner at the Hotel Roanoke on the occasion of the sixtieth anniversary of Temple Emanuel. The title of his address was "Affirmations of Liberal Judaism."

The Roanoke Red Sox made their home season debut with an exhibition game against their parent team, the Boston Red Sox, at Maher Field on April 12. Roanoke fans were particularly interested in watching Ted Williams play outfield, as he was at the time the highest-paid player in pro baseball. Also on Boston's roster was former Roanoke player Jim Sucheki. The Roanoke team won, 4–2, before a crowd of 2,243. The game closed when Williams lined out to first base with the tying runs on first and second base. With that, fans rushed the field to congratulate their home team.

The Committee for Home Protection was organized in Roanoke to protest the development of two low-income housing developments in the city by the Roanoke Redevelopment and Housing Authority. Harry East was chairman of the group that declared in ads that the developments were not "slum clearance" but definite steps toward socialism and increased property taxes due to increased public services. A few days later, the Melrose Civic League joined the group in opposing the low-income development for whites in their neighborhood.

The fifteenth annual Roanoke dog show was held in mid-April at the American Legion Auditorium. The show had 375 canines entered from Virginia and neighboring states. The show was sponsored by the Roanoke Kennel Club. The Best in Show award went to a Pekingese owned by John Royce of Brookline, Massachusetts.

Dr. Sherman Oberly was inaugurated as the sixth president of Roanoke College in ceremonies on April 14. The keynote speaker for the installation program was Harold Stassen, former governor of Minnesota and the president of the University of Pennsylvania at the time.

Dr. Sherman Oberly, right, became the sixth president of Roanoke College in 1950.
Virginia Room, RPL

The Hill Top Restaurant opened on April 15 on Veterans Hospital Road. F. T. Wiekel and C. B. Guthrie were the owners.

Firestone and Company poultry processing plant held a public open house on April 19 and 20. The plant was located in Troutville.

The new Marine Corps Reserve Center was dedicated on April 15. The $155,000 training facility located at Maher Field was formally opened in a ceremony preceded by a parade through downtown Roanoke and with a speech delivered at the center by Major General M. H. Silverthorn. An American flag, given in memory of Cpl. Otey Schilling Jr., a marine who was killed at Okinawa, was hoisted over the center to conclude the ceremony.

The new $40,000 plant of the Graham-White Manufacturing Company at 1209 Colorado Street in Salem was completed in mid-April. The firm's former headquarters was at 723 Third Street SW in Roanoke. The new plant was 15,000 square feet and principally manufactured sanders for locomotives.

The Roanoke Civic Chorus and Orchestra presented Mendelssohn's *Elijah* at the American Legion Auditorium on April 19. The soloists were Jean Schneck, John Yard, and Katharine Hansel.

The Roanoke County Board of Supervisors appointed County Engineer Paul Matthews as executive officer and coordinator for the board at their meeting on April 17. His duties would be similar to those of a county manager. It was the first time such a position existed for the county.

Mobile X-ray units paraded through Roanoke in a caravan on April 17 to mark the launch of the community-wide chest X-ray program to check for cases of tuberculosis. Bands from Jefferson High School and Monroe Junior High School participated in the parade. The thirty-four-day campaign had the mobile units stationed at the Municipal Building, Roanoke Theatre, Gainsboro Branch Library, Monroe Junior High School, Booker T. Washington Trade School, and Jefferson High School. The goal was to X-ray 55,000 adults. Mrs. John Grove was campaign chairman.

Martha Anne Woodrum announced she would participate in the annual transcontinental air race for women with her Beechcraft Bonanza. The race from California to South Carolina was to be held in June. It was her first time entering the competition.

Roanoke City Council decided to continue operating the City Farm that produced vegetables and beef for city institutions such as the City Home, Tuberculosis Sanatorium, and the jail. The city had sold its dairy herd and some farm equipment at auction. Farmland owned by the city included tracts at the airport, sanatorium, and the City Home.

Twice-a-day residential postal service was halted by order of the US Postmaster General on April 19. There were fifty-eight postal routes in Roanoke City in which mail was delivered twice daily. The order would take full effect in Roanoke by June 30.

Heironimus department store celebrated its sixtieth anniversary on April 20 with a huge birthday cake that contained fifty pounds of icing and a horse-drawn procession to the store on Campbell Avenue. Some 3,000 persons attended the in-store birthday party. Robert Lynn Jr. was the firm's president.

This 1950 image shows Elmwood Park looking southwest from the corner at Jefferson Street and Elm Avenue. Elmwood Home, which served as the city's library, is in the background. *Virginia Room, RPL*

Doris Milton pled guilty on April 19 to performing an abortion on an eighteen-year-old Roanoke woman. She was sentenced to four years in prison.

Mrs. Everett Repass of Salem was elected as one of the seven vice presidents of the Daughters of the American Revolution during their annual congress in Washington, DC.

Courtney King, representing a group of property owners, filed a petition for a permanent injunction to thwart the development of federal low-income housing units in Roanoke. Defendants were the City of Roanoke and the Roanoke Redevelopment and Housing Authority.

Napier Texaco Station opened on April 22 on Orange Avenue at Seventeenth Street NW.

WROV sponsored a dance to celebrate the opening of the regular season of baseball for the Roanoke Red Sox. The radio station broadcast their games. The dance featured Sonny Dunham and his orchestra at the American Legion Auditorium on April 26.

Clem Johnston of Roanoke was elected to the board of directors of the United States Chamber of Commerce.

The president of Optimist International Franklin Steinko joined the Roanoke Optimist Club in opening and dedicating the addition to their Junior Optimist Club building in Norwich on April 24. Several hundred persons attended the event.

Little Jimmy Dickens of the *Grand Ole Opry* performed on the stage of the Roanoke Theatre on April 26.

Nearly one hundred acres burned on the east slope of Mill Mountain. The fire was brought under control after five hours. More than 150 city employees assisted firemen in battling the blaze that was fueled by high winds.

An overflow crowd jammed the Roanoke City Council chambers on April 24 to hear remarks from A. R. Hanson of the Public Housing Administration in regard to federal low-income housing developments planned for Roanoke. Mayor A. R. Minton had to gavel the crowd to order on several occasions. After three hours, Minton called a halt to the meeting that seemed to alter no one's opinion.

Dartha Fulton was sentenced to four years by Roanoke Judge Dirk Kuyk for performing an abortion on a Roanoke woman. Fulton pled guilty to the charge. Doris Milton had earlier pled guilty and been sentenced in regard to the same case. Fulton was facing a murder charge in Bedford County in the case of the death of Alice Taylor that was the result of a botched abortion in Fulton's home there.

The Boston Grand Opera Company presented *Carmen* at the American Legion Auditorium on April 27. Leonora Corona and John De Merchant had the lead roles.

This is Jefferson Street looking south from a location midway between Norfolk Avenue and Salem Avenue in 1950. *Historical Society of Western Virginia*

For the first time in Virginia history, women were allowed to serve on juries due to a new law effective July 1. Roanoke courts had already drawn their juries, however, such that no woman would be able to serve until 1951. Under the new law, women could opt out of serving, but men had no such choice.

The regular baseball season of the Piedmont League got underway on April 26. League teams were Roanoke, Portsmouth, Norfolk, Newport News, Richmond, and Lynchburg.

Luther Beamer of Roanoke died on April 26 from a shotgun wound in the abdomen that he had received a few days prior. Police arrested John Clay for the slaying.

Kenwood Beauty Shop opened in late April at 1717 Kenwood Boulevard SE. Mrs. R. A. Holland was the owner and operator.

The Lee Shop, a women's apparel store, opened at 118 Lee Avenue in Vinton on April 28. Almeda Foutz was the manager.

The cornerstone for the new St. Paul's Lutheran Church on Peters Creek Road was laid on April 30. Dr. William McCauley of Salem was the acting pastor. The ceremony's guest speaker was Dr. Luther Mauney, president of the Virginia Lutheran Synod.

Buddy Johnson and his orchestra performed at the American Legion Auditorium on May 3. The show also featured Ella Johnson and Arthur Prysack. White spectators were admitted to the balcony for the show and dance.

Progress Laundry and Cleaners opened the first week of May at 1711 Williamson Road. Owners and operators were O. W. Lockett and C. W. Wilcox.

One of the first houses built for paraplegics in the United States for disabled GIs was in Roanoke for William Peters, an infantryman who lost both legs in Europe during World War II. It was located on Golfside Avenue NW, overlooking the eighth tee at the Roanoke Country Club. Peters got $10,000 from the Veterans Administration outright and qualified for a VA loan for the remaining balance under the program.

The *Pin-Up Girls Revue* came to the stage of the Roanoke Theatre on May 3. The show featured Lotus Wing, Dorothy Ates, Denise Lane, and singer George Decker.

An addition to the Auto Spring and Bearing Company at 118 W. Luck Avenue was completed in early May. The addition was to the First Street side of the building, giving it a more modern look with a liberal use of glass.

La Lee Beauty Nook opened at 532 Mountain Avenue SW. The owner was Mrs. Leona Epps.

A section of 1,800 bleacher seats at Maher Field along the first base line were condemned. The decision to close the section of the stands was the result of an underwriter's inspection of the baseball park. Estimates to replace the bleachers were $9,000. Ultimately, the council appropriated $13,000 to replace the bleachers and make improvements to the grandstand.

The Central Church of the Brethren celebrated its twenty-fifth anniversary the first weekend of May. The church's cornerstone was laid on July 20, 1924. On January 3, 1925, the first service was held in the Sunday School auditorium.

The entire stock of farm and hardware supplies of the Roanoke Farm Supply Center, located on Route 221 near Mount Vernon School, was sold at auction on May 4.

W. C. Stouffer, managing editor of the *Roanoke World-News*, was reappointed as a member of the Pulitzer Prize Journalism Jury at Columbia University.

Joie Chitwood's Auto Daredevils came to Victory Stadium on May 9.

Turpin Hardware Company, owned and managed by Ben Turpin, opened on May 6 in Vinton.

A fashion show and dance sponsored by Kann's, John Norman, and WSLS attracted 3,500 teenagers to the American Legion Auditorium. Parents were permitted to watch from the balcony.

The South Salem Home Demonstration Club was organized the first week in May, becoming the twentieth in the county. Mrs. G. M. Shumat was elected president.

Bill Monroe and his *Grand Ole Opry Show* performed on the stage of the Roanoke Theatre on May 10. Other performers included Dave Macon and Dot and Smoky.

The congregation of Virginia Heights Lutheran Church formally dedicated their new building at Grandin Road and Brandon Avenue on May 7. With the relocation, the congregation officially became Christ Lutheran Church. The pastor, Rev. Frank Efird, received the keys to the church and led a procession into the nave.

Thirteen civic organizations—Rotarians, civic leagues, Chambers of Commerce, realtors—went on record in opposition to federal low-income housing in Roanoke. They helped circulate a petition that resulted in some 3,000 signatures opposing the developments. The effort was coordinated by the Committee for Home Protection.

Over 800 women volunteered to conduct the last phase of the Hospital Development Fund campaign by going house to house in their neighborhoods.

Mick-or-Mack grocery chain opened its newest store on May 11 at 2825 Brambleton Avenue SW. Owner-managers were Harry Cannaday and Woody Angle.

Roanoke merchants encouraged all males to participate in the city's "Straw Hat Day" on May 15 in honor of the summer season with the hope that men would wear their hats through Labor Day.

Organizers of the Hospital Development Fund campaign announced on May 12 that the effort had exceeded its $1.5 million goal. Campaign chairman Clem Johnston reported during a press conference at the Hotel Roanoke that slightly over $2 million had been raised or pledged. It was the largest fundraising campaign staged in the Roanoke Valley. The funds raised were for a new Burrell Memorial Hospital and an addition to the Memorial and Crippled Children's Hospital.

The Johnson-Carper Furniture Company won manufacturing first prize in the international low-cost furniture competition sponsored by the Modern Museum of Art in New York City. The winning furniture was by British designers Robin Day and Clive Latimer. The furniture that won was sold locally by Phelps & Armistead.

Pictured are members of the Roanoke Chamber of Commerce's Colored Citizens Committee in 1950. Rev. A. L. James (seated, left) was the chairman that year. *Historical Society of Western Virginia*

Ralph Flanagan and his orchestra performed at the American Legion Auditorium on May 15. The vocalist was Harry Prime. Black spectators were admitted to the balcony.

A new $750,000 dining hall opened at the Veterans Administration Hospital with a formal open house to commemorate National Hospital Day on May 14. Some 6,500 meals were prepared at the hospital daily.

Robert Hurt of Roanoke was elected president of the Virginia Junior Chamber of Commerce at the group's convention in Virginia Beach on May 13. Hurt was a supervisor with Appalachian Electric Power Company.

The Salem Community Players presented *Angel Street* the third weekend in May at the Longwood Carriage House Theatre. Leading roles were played by Herbert Harris, Amy Jo Glenn, and Leroy McFarland.

Jewels that once belonged to the Russian Imperial Family, the Romanovs, were put on display in the First National Exchange Bank the second weekend in May. Among the items were two Faberge eggs.

First Baptist Church, Roanoke, observed its seventy-fifth anniversary on May 14. Guest speaker was former pastor Rev. John Vines. Alma Hunt, executive secretary of the Woman's Missionary Union of the Southern Baptist Convention, spoke at the evening service. Hunt was a Roanoke native.

The senior class of William Fleming High School gave a minstrel show titled *Senior Shenanigans* at the school. The end men were directed by Virginia Mason, and Bill Hale was the interlocutor.

The Alpha Tau Chapter of Phi Delta Kappa, a national professional Black teacher's sorority, was chartered in Roanoke. The organization's charter members were Della Williams, Dorothy Davies, Beatrice Watkins, Thelma Williams, Katherine Jefferson, Zelma Clark, Juanita Clark, Marie Roberts, and Ora Giles.

Western film star Johnny Mach Brown and his Western Entertainers performed on the stage of the Roanoke Theatre on May 17.

The Raleigh Court Lions Club received its charter on May 15. Elected president of the new group was James Hesser. Other officers were William Young, S. F. Hollingsworth, H. S. Leonard, W. R. Harp, and W. A. Brown. It became the third Lions Club in Roanoke and welcomed twenty-three charter members. Roger Hodnett was the tail twister.

The Roanoke County Board of Supervisors voted to hire Eugene Honaker as tenant and driver for the new Hollins Fire Station that was nearing completion at the intersection of Peters Creek Road and Route 11. Honaker was a former captain of the Williamson Road Life Saving Crew. The cinderblock fire station had an upstairs apartment where Honaker and his family would live. The station was activated on May 22.

Twice-daily mail service ended in Salem on May 17 as a result of an executive order from the US Postmaster General that curtailed such service nationwide.

Elected officials from Roanoke, Roanoke County, Salem, and Vinton met to discuss the consolidation of valley governments at a dinner meeting hosted by the city at the Hotel Roanoke on May 17. The consensus was that a single government would be in the distant future, but there were immediate areas in need of valley cooperation. The group decided to hold monthly meetings to discuss valley cooperation. A topic of general concern was providing a civilian defense force in light of the development of the H bomb and the Cold War.

Richardson-Wayland Electrical Corporation held a public open house at its new main office and warehouse below Memorial Bridge on May 19. The company had been located on Church Avenue. J. M. Richardson, president, said his company began in 1913 with four employees and had grown to over 350 employees by 1950.

Rudy Lacy of Jefferson High School was named to the eleven-member all-state basketball team by the Group 1 Virginia Coaches' Association.

A jury acquitted John Clay in the fatal shooting on April 22 of Luther Beamer. Jurors deliberated for less than ten minutes. Clay had claimed self-defense.

The Public Affairs Committee of the Hunton Branch YMCA endorsed the federal low-income housing developments for Roanoke and called for a mass meeting of the Black community to convene at High Street Baptist Church on May 21. Committee chairman C. C. Williams cited numerous Black civic, fraternal, and business groups that had endorsed the endeavor.

Renick Motor Company, shown here in May 1950, was located at 2239 Franklin Road SW.
Virginia Room, RPL

Representatives of all branches of the military participated in the Armed Forces Day parade through downtown Roanoke on May 20. The parade included school bands, Boy Scouts, and civic organizations and was watched by a crowd estimated in the thousands.

"If we expect to follow the fundamental precepts of democracy, we must help our citizens have decent homes," declared Dr. Harry Penn at a mass meeting attended by 300 persons at High Street Baptist Church on May 21. The meeting had been called by the Hunton Branch YMCA to address growing opposition to the federal low-income housing developments planned for Roanoke. Richard Beck, director of the Roanoke Redevelopment and Housing Authority, outlined the program that would provide housing to those who cannot afford to rent from private landlords.

Curtis Turner of Roanoke, driving a 1950 Oldsmobile, won the stock car race feature before 7,000 spectators at the Martinsville Speedway on May 21.

At their meeting on May 22, Roanoke City Council voted 3–2 to give the Roanoke Redevelopment and Housing Authority a vote of confidence in its plans to proceed with federal low-income housing units. Voting against the motion were Mayor A. R. Minton and Benton Dillard. Dillard moved to disband the authority but failed to receive a second. Authority chairman John Windel reminded council of the various actions and resolutions they had adopted that established the authority and acknowledged the need for slum clearance and low-income housing.

The tradition of Sunday afternoon summer concerts at Elmwood Park was discontinued due to the lack of a bandstand and instead moved to Highland Park. The concert series was sponsored by the city's parks and recreation department and involved numerous military and civic bands.

Construction of permanent buildings at the Roanoke Area Boy Scouts Council's Camp Powhatan began on May 24. The new camp was located eleven miles southeast of Pulaski. The 450-acre encampment replaced the old fifty-acre Camp Powhatan near Natural Bridge. The camp was slated to open July 10. The camp was being laid into seven different villages under the supervision of the camp's director Ray Heck.

Frederick Olmstead of Brookline, Massachusetts, visited the Blue Ridge Parkway office in Roanoke on May 23 and conferred with Superintendent Sam Weems. Olmstead was on the advisory board of the National Park Service.

The Roanoke Jaycees held their second annual Talent Scout Show at the American Legion Auditorium that featured twenty mostly local acts. Performers included the Freddie Lee Orchestra, Wanderers of the Wasteland, Remus Belle and the Bellhops, Dick Burton, Leslie Kings, and various high school choirs. The event was attended by 2,000, and the winner of the talent competition was Ottawa Pullen, a baritone. Pullen thereby qualified for an audition competition for the *Arthur Godfrey Show*.

A $25,000 damage suit was filed against Magic City Launderers and Cleaners in connection with a fire at the laundry in 1949. The plaintiff was Price Kingery, proprietor of the Royal Fur Shop on South Jefferson Street. Kingery had furs and other items from customers stored at the laundry and alleged that the laundry had intentionally and fraudulently failed to renew fire and theft insurance and had denied any liability.

Mrs. W. W. Butler of Roanoke was elected president of the Garden Club of Virginia.

Fire swept through the Sunday School building of Calvary Baptist Church in Roanoke on May 25. Damage was estimated at $150,000. Firemen described the scene as a roaring inferno when they arrived. The church used the Kazim Temple and Jefferson High School for classrooms until repairs were made. Rev. Harry Gamble was the church's pastor and indicated insurance was adequate to cover the costs.

A fine arts museum for Roanoke was discussed at a meeting of the Fine Arts Committee of the Chamber of Commerce on May 25. Dr. Sherman Oberly, president of Roanoke College, was chairman of the committee.

Consolidation of the fundraising agencies in the Roanoke Valley into a single solicitation drive was approved by the board of trustees of the Community Fund. The move was proposed by Rev. Richard Beasley. Broaddus Chewning, executive director of the Roanoke City and County Community Fund, stated, "More and more feeling against the multiplicity of appeals for funds is developing in our community."

This early 1950s image is of Firestone, located at the corner of First Street and Tazewell Avenue SE. *Bob Kinsey*

A new marquee went up on the Jefferson Theatre in Roanoke. The new V-shaped sign replaced an old twenty-foot long, twelve-foot wide marquee that had stood for fifteen years. C. A. Posey was the theatre's manager.

Pinky Jackson and his famous chimpanzee, Cheeta, performed on the stage of the Roanoke Theatre on May 31. Cheeta had starred in *Tarzan* movies.

Plans to consolidate the two Catholic high schools in Roanoke were announced by laymen in late May. The merger of the schools operated by Our Lady of Nazareth Catholic Church and St. Andrew's Catholic Church had been discussed for some time. The new school would be known as Roanoke Catholic High School and be located at St. Andrew's on North Jefferson Street. The combined high school would have a potential enrollment of 400 students.

The Hospital Development Fund campaign came to its official end on May 27. Its offices at 25 West Church Avenue were closed. The campaign raised a total of $2.3 million, far exceeding its $1.5 million goal.

Thirty-nine church choirs participated in the Thursday Morning Music Club Church Music and Choir Festival that was held in the American Legion Auditorium on May 28.

Paper milk cartons made their first appearance in Roanoke in late May after Clover Creamery and Roanoke Dairy began using the cartons. The cartons replaced bottles sent to wholesale outlets. Home deliveries continued to be in bottles.

Wyonie Harris, along with Eddie Durham and his orchestra, performed a "battle of the blues" at the American Legion Auditorium on May 30. White spectators were admitted at a discount.

Charlie Ventura and his orchestra performed for a Blacks-only dance at the American Legion Auditorium on June 2. The balcony was reserved for white spectators.

A Memorial Day parade was held in downtown Roanoke that featured a replica of the Liberty Bell, which was rung at the conclusion of the parade in Elmwood Park.

Construction began in late May on the new twelve-room Grandin Court School. The school was located on an eleven-acre site facing Spessard Avenue SW. The contractor was the firm of Lucas and Fralin. Completion was anticipated for January 1951.

The F. W. Woolworth Company reopened on June 1 at 24 W. Campbell Avenue after extensive remodeling. The store had doubled its floor space and expanded its lunch counter to accommodate up to fifty-eight persons. T. J. Seeley was the store manager. Seven thousand people went through the store on that day.

Johnny Olsen brought his nationally broadcast radio program *Ladies Be Seated* to the American Legion Auditorium on June 3. Broadcasting live from Roanoke, the two-hour event was a benefit for the Roanoke Lions Club. The Roanoke show featured the local Dixie Playboys and a forty-member choir of city and county high school students.

St. Paul's Lutheran Church was formally dedicated on June 4. The new church building was located on Peters Creek Road. The church had been organized on April 13, 1913.

The Melrose Postal Station was completed and opened in early June. The station was at 1604 Orange Avenue NW.

The "new" Oak Hall held a reopening gala the first weekend in June to showcase their newly remodeled store on Campbell at Jefferson. The clothier had been operating in Roanoke since 1889.

Coon Electric Company at 3520 Williamson Road announced in early June that they were going out of business.

The Rogers Rodeo and Thrill Circus came to Victory Stadium on June 6. The show featured cowboys, auto stunt drivers, and "Big Syd" the bull. A $1,000 prize was offered to anyone who could stay on Big Syd for more than ten seconds.

Hillbilly comedian Cousin Wilbur from the *Grand Ole Opry* performed at the Roanoke Theatre on June 7. Joining him were Blondie Brooks and the Log Cabin Folks.

Cornerstone-laying services were held at the Williamson Road Church of the Brethren on June 4. The $50,000 structure was being built at the corner of Oakland Boulevard and Pioneer Road NW. Rev. C. M. Key was the pastor.

The Roanoke Chest X-Ray Survey concluded on June 2 with some 61,000 Roanoke area residents having participated. The survey campaign was done to determine cases of tuberculosis.

Dr. Frank Slaughter, a former surgeon with Jefferson Hospital, returned to Roanoke to promote his new novel, *The Stubborn Heart*. He had several speaking engagements and a book signing at the Book Nook. Slaughter had written several books of both nonfiction and fiction such that he was no longer practicing medicine and had moved to Jacksonville, Florida.

Dr. William Elliott of Harvard University delivered the commencement address at Hollins College. Elliott warned the graduates about the rise of Russia in global affairs, calling it "a modern slave state."

Clifford Roberson Jr. won the city-county marbles tournament on June 5. The championship tournament was held at Elmwood Park. He qualified for the National Marbles Tournament to be held in Asbury Park, New Jersey, later in the month. Runners-up were Willard Pacetti and Larry Vinson. Rex Mitchell was the tournament director.

The 1950 census set the population of Roanoke at 91,070 in a preliminary count. Roanoke County had a population of 41,690. The counts showed a gain of slightly more than 18 percent in the overall metropolitan region.

Dr. Charles Grady, administrator of the Veterans Administration Hospital, reported that the average cost for care of a patient at the hospital was $7.08 per day in 1949.

John Blaney wrecked his car into the front of Helms Grocery Store on Water Street in Salem on June 7 and injured five bystanders. Most of the injured were taken to Burrell Memorial Hospital.

The sales and service department of Antrim Motors moved to its new quarters at 510 McClanahan Place in South Roanoke on June 10. The car company had previously been located at 503 Sixth Street SW, where it had been operating since 1935. Blair Antrim was the firm's president; the firm was a local dealership for Dodge and Plymouth.

Harrison Jewelry Company held a formal opening of their newly remodeled store at 307 S. Jefferson Street on June 8. They had been in business in Roanoke for over sixty years.

Louise Thaden, a Roanoke aviatrix who made history back in the 1930s, entered the women's air race from Montreal to West Palm Beach, Florida. Thaden had won the Bendix Trophy in 1936 when she placed first in an air race from New York to Los Angeles with a time of fourteen hours and fifty-five minutes.

US Secretary of Defense Louis Johnson visited his parents in Roanoke on June 8.

Baseball clown Al Schacht entertained the crowd at the Roanoke Red Sox home game on June 13. He was a former professional baseball player who had become more famous for his baseball comedy routines around the country.

Ambassador to Liberia Edward Dudley visited his parents at their home at 405 Gilmer Avenue NW the second weekend in June. He was the first Black person to achieve the rank of ambassador in US history. Dudley was a graduate of Addison High School who left Roanoke in 1928. Prior to being appointed to the embassy in Liberia, Dudley had worked for the attorney general of New York.

The old infirmary at Catawba Sanatorium was razed in mid-June to make way for the new 312-bed hospital. The infirmary had been erected in 1918.

The Roanoke School Board had an ambitious capital program underway by June that included several projects—the new Huff Lane and Grandin Court schools and additions to Woodrow Wilson Junior High School, Crystal Spring Elementary School, and Virginia Heights Elementary School. The new Addison High School was also underway.

The Alumnae association of the Memorial and Crippled Children's Hospital held its first reunion the third week in June. A brief history of the hospital was provided. The hospital began in 1899 with land donated by N&W Railway. The King's Daughters completed the hospital by 1901. The Roanoke Hospital Association was chartered on May 10, 1899. The first graduate of the association's training school was Mary Wills, who was given a diploma in 1901.

Paul Coffey was chosen as Roanoke's Father of the Year by the Junior Chamber of Commerce. Coffey was head of the Roanoke Recreation Association and had been involved with numerous youth organizations and civic groups over the years.

Roanoke firemen battled a blaze on the top of the Carlton Terrace Building on June 12. The structure was nearing completion.

Municipal elections were held on June 13. In Roanoke, the Democratic ticket was unopposed, meaning that A. R. Minton, Roy Webber, and Walter Young were elected. Less than 1,000 persons voted. In Salem, Mayor James Moyer (870 votes) and Councilman Frank Morton (643) were reelected, defeating three challengers—Ernest Obenshain (232), Farland Ferris (14), and E. M. Atkinson (46). In Vinton, three new members were elected to the town council—Gus Nicks (241), Marvin Craig (250), and Augustus Hylton (216). Incumbent Norman Dowdy finished fourth with 171 votes. In Vinton, the town council would grow from three to five members when the new members were seated on September 1.

The cornerstone for the new Huff Lane Elementary School was laid on June 18 in a ceremony presided over by the Williamson Road Lions Club.

Capt. Eddie Rickenbacker, president and general manager of Eastern Airlines, visited Roanoke on June 15 as part of his tour of all Eastern installations. Rickenbacker told city officials that a new terminal was needed even more than longer runways at Woodrum Field.

A never-before-seen baseball uniform style was sported by the Newport News Dodgers in their game against the Roanoke Red Sox at Maher Field on June 14. The team wore shorts. According to the *Roanoke Times*, the team was greeted "with wolf calls and raspberries." The teams split a doubleheader.

The Chicago Colleens played the Springfield Sallies at Maher Field the third weekend in June. Both teams were members of the All-American Girls Baseball League. The games were sponsored by the Roanoke Optimist Club. The league had been organized in 1943 by major league owners due to the shortage of men during the war.

Virginia Bryant, twenty-three, died at Lewis-Gale Hospital on June 16 from a stab wound to the throat. The Roanoke waitress's husband, Roy Bryant, was sought by police based on an eyewitness who saw the stabbing. A taxicab driver took the husband to the restaurant where the wife worked and saw her stabbed. Police caught the husband the following day in downtown Roanoke, and he confessed to the murder. Detective Frank Webb shared that a homemade knife used in the slaying was recovered from the husband. According to Webb, Bryant had gone to a restaurant in the 4500 block of Williamson Road to talk with his wife. When she refused to talk with him, he stabbed her. "I lost my head," Bryant reportedly told police, "I don't care if they give me the electric chair."

Louise Thaden placed third in the women's "powder puff" air derby from Montreal to Florida. She was accompanied by her daughter, Patsy. Thaden won $400 for third place.

The Royal Jubilee Singers, along with Thelma Bumpass and her Royletts, performed at the American Legion Auditorium on June 18. Advance tickets were available at the Dumas Hotel, Hobbie Brothers, and the Gainsboro Grill.

Tommy Collins, Bernice Arnold, and Boots Alexander—all dancers from New York City—performed at the Morocco Club on June 17. They were accompanied by a local band, the Aristocrats. The balcony was reserved for white spectators.

Four fifteen-foot stone pillars removed from the front of the N&W Railway passenger station in Roanoke were resting in a Botetourt County cow pasture owned by A. H. Henderson. Asked by a reporter if he had plans to use them, Henderson reminded the reporter that the contractor on the passenger station renovation in 1948 was looking for somewhere to put the columns. Henderson happened to be looking at the station on that particular February day when the columns were to be removed and volunteered his pasture. The dairy farmer indicated he had no real use for them, but he was inclined to leave them in his cow pasture.

Martha Anne Woodrum and her copilot Mary Ann Weatherby came in second place in the transcontinental women's air race from San Diego to Greenville, South Carolina.

Martha Anne Woodrum (left) and Mary Ann Weatherby stand beside their Beechcraft Bonanza airplane in San Diego after competing in the 1950 Transcontinental Air Race. They were sponsored by the Roanoke furniture company Johnson-Carper. *Historical Society of Western Virginia*

Julian Wise was elected president of the International Rescue and First Aid Association at the group's meeting in Columbus, Ohio, on June 18. Dr. Marcellus Johnson Jr. was named chief medical advisor to the association. Both men were Roanoke residents. Wise was also captain of the Roanoke Life Saving and First Aid Crew and president of the Virginia State Association of Rescue Squads.

George Fulton Jr. won the city-county golf tournament held during the third weekend in June. Ralph English placed second. Fulton carded a three-round total of 217 for the tournament held at the Roanoke Country Club.

The production *Hawaiian Nights* came to the stage of the Roanoke Theatre on June 21 that featured "lovely aloha maids." Other performers included blackface comedians Emmett Miller and Turk McBee.

Black clergy, led by Rev. A. L. James, met with Roanoke City Manager Arthur Owens and Roanoke City Council on June 19 and asked that the city hire Black firemen. They specifically requested that such hires be placed at the new Williamson Road station. The Roanoke Fire Department had never integrated its work force. The city council asked Owens to report back to them on July 10 as to how he would proceed to integrate the department. At the same meeting, Dr. E. D. Downing asked council to make the six tennis courts for Blacks the same quality as those provided for whites. Further, George Lawrence asked the council to name the park and playground designated for Blacks for the first Black casualty from the city in World War II. The council agreed to research the matter.

Acousticon of Roanoke opened in the Rosenberg Building on June 20. The company diagnosed hearing loss and treatment.

The Junior League held a business closing sale at their Opportunity Shop the last week of June. The store was located at 114 W. Salem Avenue.

Roanoke City Council voted 3–2 to allow stock car racing at Victory Stadium on an experimental basis. Two races were slated for July. The request was made by racing promoters Bill France and Curtis Turner. Councilmen questioned the financial viability of stock car racing given that those who had previously promoted midget car racing at the stadium had lost money. Turner assured the council that stock car racing had a very profitable future.

Mrs. Janie Pearson, a fifty-one year-old N&W Railway clerk, was found dead in the basement of her home at 1913 Blenheim Road SW on June 20. Detective Frank Webb reported that he was holding her husband, L. C. Pearson, on a charge of murder. City coroner Dr. Charles Irvin stated Pearson had died of head injuries. Police were called to the Pearson home after the husband's mother noticed bloody footprints in the house and thought something amiss.

Henri Kessler, Roanoke fur dealer, succumbed on June 20 to injuries he had sustained in an auto accident on June 7. He died in a Richmond hospital. Kessler had been a resident of Roanoke for twenty-seven years and was a prominent member of Roanoke's Jewish community.

Alonzo Grate was struck and killed by a truck as he walked along Shenandoah Avenue near the Veterans Administration Hospital on June 20. The driver of the truck was Thomas Vest of Check.

The Roanoke chapter of the National Conference of Christians and Jews welcomed its first female members on June 20 during a luncheon at the Shenandoah Club. Ernest Brown was chapter chairman.

Over 200 horses were entered for the Roanoke Valley Horse Show Association annual competition. The event was held in late June at Lakeview Farm on Route 11 north of Roanoke.

Two residents of Vinton reported seeing flying saucers over their community on June 21. Mrs. A. W. Harvey and her daughter Libby claimed to have seen a round, silvery object moving slowly over William Byrd High School. The object turned a deep red and then rose out of sight.

Five persons were instantly killed on June 22 in the crash of an experimental navy plane, an A-J-1, eight miles from Bedford. The wreckage was scattered in a wheat field on the farm of J. A. Laughlin. A crowd of 500 viewed the wreck site. The plane was from Edwards Air Force Base in California and was en route to Maryland.

General Lucius Clay, former US military commander in Germany, visited the Continental Can Company plant in Roanoke on June 21. Clay was chairman of the board of the company, which had some sixty plants nationwide.

The American Furniture Mart in Chicago named Roanoke's Donald Jordan as its industry's "Man of the Year." When presented the award in Chicago, it was stated that Jordan was "the man who did the most for the furniture industry during the past year." Jordan was president of Johnson-Carper Furniture Company.

The Chili Shop opened at 6 Walnut Avenue SE on June 23. Their opening special of fried chicken, whipped potatoes, vegetable salad, pie, green peas, peaches, and biscuits was offered for seventy-five cents.

Antrim Motors celebrated its twenty-fifth anniversary with an open house at their new showroom at 510 McClanahan Street SW on June 24. The company began operations in Pulaski in 1925 and came to Roanoke in 1931. The contractor for Antrim's new location was B. F. Parrott and Company. Over 5,000 attended the event.

The Patchwork Players opened their summer season on June 26 with a production of *What Every Woman Knows* at the Little Theatre on the campus of Hollins College. The Players were directed by Francis Ballard.

M. J. Schlossberg petitioned for a declaratory judgment in chancery court regarding property located in the Prospect Hills section that had deed conditions and restrictions. Schlossberg, who was Jewish, challenged the decades-old deed restrictions that prohibited the sale of land in the subdivision to "Negroes, Greeks, Assyrians, or by any persons who belongs to any race, creed, or sect which holds, recognizes or observes any day of the week other than the first day of the week to be the Sabbath or his Sabbath." The restrictions, imposed in 1927, were to be in effect for twenty-five years according to deed records. Schlossberg cited a Supreme Court ruling that prohibited private deed restrictions of that nature in his petition, which sought to rule such conditions invalid. According to Schlossberg, the current owner of the Prospect Hills development, C. W. Francis, extended the deed restrictions from the original twenty-five years to fifty years. Schlossberg asserted that he had acquired a lot in the neighborhood but had been denied loans by banks for improvements due to the restrictions.

The Melrose Guild presented the N&W Railway Wheel Rollers and a variety show at the American Legion Auditorium on June 30. The Wheel Rollers were John Canty, Thomas Campbell, Charlie Wiley, Earl Dummings, and Clinton Scott. The emcee for the show was Ernest Canty.

As the Comas Cigarette Machine Company in Salem prepared to celebrate its sixtieth anniversary, some of its history was shared. The company, located at the corner of Fourth Street and College Avenue, was organized on July 12, 1889. The idea for a cigarette machine began earlier with Jacob Bonsack, a Roanoke College student, who developed and patented the first cigarette machine and launched the Bonsack Machine Company that operated at Lynchburg. Eventually the Comas and Bonsack companies became competitors, with D. B. Strouse of Salem serving as Comas's first president. In 1910, the Comas Company outfitted a small building just north of the one on College Avenue. Over the years, the company developed other machines that produced cigarettes and other tobacco-related products. The name Comas came from a Brazilian who lived in a community where many of Comas's first machines were leased. At the time of their sixtieth anniversary, Chester Markley was company president.

Arthur Smith and the Cracker Jacks performed at the Roanoke Theatre on June 28.

Over 800 persons attended the dedication of the Church of Jesus Christ of Latter Day Saints church on June 25. The church was located at the corner of Laburnum Avenue and Grandin Road SW. The keynote speaker was Ezra Taft Benson, a member of the Quorum of Twelve Apostles. The congregation began in 1898 and had been meeting in a house on Patterson Avenue since 1942.

N&W Railway's *Powhatan Arrow* officially opened the new Elkhorn Tunnel on June 26 by snapping a red ribbon emblazoned with the railway's logo stretched across the east portal.

Bower Esso Station was located at 101 Commonwealth Avenue NE, as shown here in 1950. *Virginia Room, RPL*

The Roanoke Booster Club left by train for the Greenbrier Hotel in an effort to "sell Roanoke to Roanokers." The 325-member club had a mission of promoting Roanoke to other communities but used the annual golf trip to build and retain membership. Dr. E. G. Gill was the club's president. The Booster Club was first organized in August 1915.

Johnnie Flint of Roanoke was sentenced to twenty-two years when he was found guilty on two murder charges. Flint was sentenced for the May 19 stabbings of Willie Willis and Lynwood Thompson in northwest Roanoke.

Billy Haupt won the Junior Amateur Golf Tournament at Roanoke Country Club. Three others placed— Johnny Hicks, Moyer Duncan, and Craig Wilton Jr. The four became eligible to play in the state tournament.

Bower Esso Station closed as the lease was acquired by the Hotel Roanoke to be operated by them for the courtesy of their customers. The personnel of the Esso station moved to Willett's Truck Terminal at 324 Orange Avenue NE.

Brenda Rae Fashions went out of business at the end of June. The women's clothier was located at 313 South Jefferson Street.

A contract post office was opened on July 1 at Saunder's Pharmacy, 1232 Jamison Avenue SE. The post office was managed by Earl Buck, operator of the store.

Vance's Esso Station opened at Commonwealth and Wells Avenue NE on June 29.

Eskimo Treat, an ice cream store that specialized in frozen custards, opened on June 29 on Cave Spring Road, one mile south of the Coffee Pot. Giant milkshakes were twenty cents.

Vance's Esso Station, located at 108 Commonwealth Avenue NE, opened in 1950. This image is from 1951. *Virginia Room, RPL*

Addie McCormack, forty-eight, of Catawba died on June 30 at Lewis-Gale Hospital due to injuries she sustained when she was brutally attacked on June 25 at her home. The attacker, who used a hammer, was Floyd Joyner Jr., a trusty at the convict camp near Catawba.

The Roanoke Department of Parks and Recreation held the first of four summer tennis court dances on June 28. Some 1,200 young people attended the event in Elmwood Park.

The Orioles and Cootie Williams and his orchestra played for a show and dance at the American Legion Auditorium on July 2. White spectators were admitted for a discount.

N&W Railway began production of fifteen coal-burning switch locomotives and 1,000 additional seventy-ton hopper coal cars at the Roanoke Shops. The estimated cost was $6.4 million.

The American Viscose Corporation began on July 1 paying the 3,300 employees of its Roanoke plant by check rather than cash.

Roy Acuff and his *Grand Ole Opry* Gang performed at the Roanoke Theatre on July 5. Other entertainers included Pap and his Jug Band, Smoky Mountain Boys, Jimmy Riddle, Jesse Easterday, and Brother Oswald. Ticket prices were fifty-two cents and sixty cents.

Lula Kelley, twenty-one, was drowned in the Roanoke River on July 1. She lived on Twelve O'clock Knob Road in Roanoke County. Her body was recovered by the Roanoke Life Saving and First Aid Crew.

The St. Mark's Lutheran Church congregation approved plans for a new church and parish building to be erected on the southeast corner of Franklin Road and Highland Avenue SW. Norman Mansell of Philadelphia was the architect. The congregation's church at the corner of Third Street and Campbell Avenue SW was to be sold. St. Mark's was organized in 1869 through the merger of two rural churches.

The Patchwork Players presented *The Curtain Rises* at Hollins College and Monroe Junior High School. The lead was played by Barbara Lucas.

The old home of the late Joseph Lancaster was razed in early July to make way for the construction of the Blue Ridge Parkway. The landmark home was located on the Franklin-Roanoke County line in the Bent Mountain section. Nearby was the Baldwin School, a log structure in a dilapidated condition.

Paul's Chicken House, formerly Archie's Tavern, opened on July 2 on Route 11 at Sunnybrook. A dinner special of chicken, french fries, coleslaw, rolls, and a drink was priced at $1.25.

A Fourth of July parade in Salem was watched by over 4,000 persons. The parade began at Langhorne Place, went along Main Street, and eventually ended at Municipal Field, where a patriotic program was held. The theme of the parade was "Homecoming" as former citizens were invited back to their hometown. At night, there were fireworks, a square dance, and exhibits by various organizations.

Rev. Richard Owens, retired pastor of Calvary Baptist Church, died at his home on July 6 at the age of sixty-nine. Owens served as Calvary's pastor from 1921 until 1946. When he retired, membership of the church was around 3,000.

Eight Roanoke merchants were fined $5 each in Roanoke's Police Court for selling groceries on Sunday, and thereby violating Virginia's Sunday Blue Law. All eight immediately filed an appeal to test the validity of the law. The law dated to 1779 in Virginia and dictated that no work occur on Sunday except that "of necessity or charity."

Three members of the Roanoke Red Sox were named to the Piedmont League All-Star Team. They were Bob Mosakoski, outfielder; John Ahern, pitcher; and George Contratto, first base.

Novelist Leonard Kaufman arrived to spend the summer in Salem to write and relax from his touring schedule. Kaufman had friends in the Roanoke Valley. His novels were bestsellers, and some were being considered for screenplays by Hollywood.

The Patchwork Players presented the comedy *Seven Keys to Baldplate* at Hollins College and Monroe Junior High School during the second week in July. William Cain had the lead role.

Roanoke City Manager Arthur Owens reported to the city council that no Black firemen would be hired within the year as there were no vacancies to fill. Owens did state his firm belief that the department should be integrated and that he hoped with the opening of new stations to do that.

Rev. William Simmons, pastor of the Fifth Avenue Presbyterian Church, preached on the nationally broadcast radio program *Church of the Air* over the CBS network on Sunday, July 16.

Everett Custer won the Soap Box Derby held on July 12 on Crystal Spring Avenue in South Roanoke. He was one of sixty-five boys who participated. Custer edged out Billy Whitlow to claim the trophy that was presented by Mayor A. R. Minton. It was the seventh annual derby and attracted a crowd estimated at 6,000. On hand for the occasion, which was preceded by a parade, was the 1949 National Soap Box Derby Champion, Fred Derks.

Some 5,000 spectators watched the inaugural stock car race at Victory Stadium on July 12. Hometown favorite Curtis Turner won the twenty-five-lap event.

Barry's, a men's clothing store, opened on July 14 at 214 Nelson Street. Dress pants were two pairs for $7, and polo shirts were seventy-nine cents.

Jazz artist Illinois Jacquet and his orchestra performed at the American Legion Auditorium on July 17. The balcony was reserved for white spectators.

Studio Scandals came to the Roanoke Theatre on July 19 and was billed as "the nation's most thrilling nite life stars" with the warning, "Girls! Hold on to your boyfriends!" The show also included Slim Williams, a blackface comedian.

Personnel at the Army and Air Force Recruiting Station readied themselves for preinduction examination of hundreds of men for the new draft due to the Korean conflict. The station was located at 609 S. Jefferson Street. The commanding officer was Capt. H. L. Piper Jr.

Foster Sheets was elected president of the National Auctioneers Association. The group's annual convention was held at the Hotel Roanoke in mid-July. During the convention, the association conducted a charity auction at the American Legion Auditorium to benefit the Memorial and Crippled Children's Hospital.

Lyla McDaniel, seventeen, died on July 16 from injuries she sustained in a fall from an automobile. McDaniel lived in southeast Roanoke.

Don Leavens of Washington, DC, defeated Heath Alexander of Charlotte, North Carolina, in straight sets to win the ninth annual Exchange Club Invitational Tennis Tournament at Roanoke Country Club on July 16.

Fred Blanding died at age sixty-two at his home near Salem on July 16. Blanding had been a Major League Baseball player who pitched for Cleveland Indians for five seasons. He had been in the auto business in Roanoke since 1935.

Virginia's governor announced the appointment of J. H. Wyse of Salem as the state coordinator of Civilian Defense, a post he also held during World War II.

Officials with Memorial and Crippled Children's Hospital reported that during the first two weeks of July, thirty-five polio victims were admitted. Twenty-six were from Wytheville. Of those admitted, three had died.

John Parrott was elected head of Roanoke Gas Company. He would assume office effective August 1. Parrott was head of the Roanoke Pipe Line Company and previously had been involved in real estate sales.

Of the nearly 62,000 persons who participated in Roanoke's mass chest X-ray campaign, 212 had some form of tuberculosis that required treatment.

Roanoke's Curtis Turner won the second stock car race held at Victory Stadium on July 19. The twenty-five-lap feature drew a crowd estimated at 5,000. The twenty-lap amateur race was won by George Holt of Winston-Salem.

Roanoke's Sixteenth Engineer Company Marine Corps Reserve was notified they were being called up for active duty for the Korean War. Capt. William Hopkins commanded the unit. The company was composed of 205 men and 13 officers.

Garland's Drug Store opened its new jewelry department in July. The store was located at 1232 Jamison Avenue SE.

Hank Snow, Stringbean, and the duo of Hal and Velma, all from the *Grand Ole Opry*, performed on the Roanoke Theatre stage on July 26.

The Rogers Brothers Circus, billed as the fifth-largest circus in the world, came to Oakey Field in Salem in late July. The event was sponsored by the Salem Kiwanis Club. The four-ring circus featured 250 performers and more than 200 animals all under a big top canopy tent that measured 90 by 270 feet.

Finnell Swimming Pool opened for its first summer season on July 23. The pool was located at foot of Bent Mountain on Route 221. Admission was twenty-five cents for adults and fifteen cents for children.

George Fulton Jr. of Roanoke had the lowest amateur score in the Virginia Open Golf Tournament held in Danville. He had a seventy-two-hole total of 298 and received the silver trophy.

Roanoke's Marine Reservists learned they would depart for active duty on August 10. They were part of the Sixteenth Engineer Company and became the first Roanoke unit called to duty in the Korean Conflict.

Curtis Turner scored his fourth victory of the season in the Grand National Circuit of stock car racing in his win on July 24 at Charlotte. He was first among twenty-five racers at the 200-lap event.

The Crystal Spring Laundry, shown here in the early 1950s, was located at 720 Franklin Road SW. *Virginia Room, RPL*

A huge materials bin fell through the roof of the mixing plant at Pre-Shrunk Masonry Sales Corporation on Cleveland Avenue SW on July 25. The crash of the giant steel hopper killed Edward Hairston, twenty-nine, of Roanoke. If the accident had happened five minutes later, Hairston would have been away at lunch. It took two days before his body was found amid the debris. The crash of the 100-foot tall hopper was witnessed by persons from five blocks away. The plant had recently begun renovations that would make it the largest cinder-block plant in the South.

The worst polio epidemic in Virginia history continued unabated by the end of July with the small community of Wytheville being hardest hit per capita. Many of those suffering from the paralyzing disease in southwestern Virginia were being treated at Memorial and Crippled Children's Hospital in Roanoke.

A new Mick-or-Mack Grocery Store opened on July 27 at 3653 Williamson Road. The store managers were G. M. Sprinkle and Joe Hauer. Norman McVeigh was president of the local chain that was part of a national network of fifty-seven stores.

Joseph Logan died on July 26 at his home in Salem. He was fifty-two. Logan was prominent in Salem's business and civic affairs, serving as president of Old Dominion Candy Company. He later established Frigid Freeze Locker plants in Roanoke and Salem.

An old log barn, a landmark in Fishburn Park, was dismantled in late July so the lumber could be used to construct picnic shelters in Mill Mountain Park and Washington Park.

A landmark sign was removed in downtown Roanoke when the marquee at the Raleigh Hotel in the 100 block of W. Campbell Avenue was ordered removed due to recently adopted sign regulations.

Mrs. Barbara Pandlis, eighteen, won the "Miss Star City" contest that was held at the Grandin Theatre on July 28. She was one of over one hundred women who had initially entered the contest before judges narrowed the field to seventeen finalists for the show. The floor and balcony of the theatre were at overflow capacity. The contest was sponsored by the Star City Furniture Company to help promote its grand opening on August 10. Pandlis received enough new furniture to outfit three rooms.

Miss Star City is flanked by the runners-up on the stage of the Grandin Theatre in July 1950. *Avisco News*

Barbara Alcorn Pandlis was crowned Miss Star City in the Star City Furniture Company–sponsored contest. *Avisco News*

Rev. Robert Richards, a former member of the US Olympic track team and the American pole vault champion, spoke at the Central Church of the Brethren on July 30.

Henebry's of Roanoke, a jewelry store, celebrated its fiftieth anniversary with a large sale in early August. The store had been founded in Roanoke in 1900 by Joseph P. Henebry, an iron molder with the N&W Railway Shops. The first store was on Salem Avenue and then relocated to Jefferson Street in 1920. When Joseph Henebry died in 1922, his son Leo Henebry took over. In 1926, Henebry purchased a jewelry store owned by K. W. Green on W. Campbell Avenue and moved his store to that location. In February 1928, the store moved again to the American Theatre building. In 1950, the store had locations at 209 S. Jefferson Street and 215 E. Main Street in Salem. Henebry's also had stores in North Carolina and Tennessee.

Roanoke Housing Agency, located at 113 E. Church Avenue, offered government surplus "wonder homes" that were preconstructed and delivered on site within a twenty-five-mile radius of the city. Four models were available and ranged in price from $1,095 to $2,775.

Amos Milburn and his band, along with Charles Brown and his orchestra, performed at the American Legion Auditorium on August 2. White spectators were admitted.

Jamup and Honey, blackface comedians, and their *Grand Ole Opry* show performed at the Roanoke Theatre on August 2. Joining them were Stringbean and the Double-R Cowboys.

The Patchwork Players presented *Born Yesterday* at Hollins College and Monroe Junior High School during the first week of August. The lead was played by Julann Wright.

Some seventy men were trained to convert stoves, refrigerators, and water heaters in 16,000 homes throughout the Roanoke Valley to burn natural gas. This was in response to the pending completion of the gas pipeline from Gala to the pipelines serving the Roanoke Gas Company.

At the beginning of August, the polio ward at the Memorial and Crippled Children's Hospital in Roanoke had fifty-five patients. A total of ninety had been treated since the outbreak began, mostly in southwestern Virginia. Thirty-three of the fifty-five patients were either from Wytheville or Wythe County. The polio ward was staffed by thirty-one nurses.

Hill Street Baptist Church was remodeled with a permanent stone covering. Additional work involved new stain glassed windows. The original building had been erected in 1885. The pastor was Rev. D. R. Powell, who had been there thirty-three years.

Neighborhood Barber Shop opened at 3607 Williamson Road on July 31.

The Villa Heights Lions Club received their charter on July 31. The group was headed by Lee Hartman and had originally formed on June 20.

Newman's Pharmacy opened in the Carlton Terrace Building on August 1.

Shown here is the north side of Roanoke's First Church of the Brethren at the corner of Carroll Avenue and Twentieth Street NW in 1950. *Avisco News*

At a meeting of the Roanoke School Board on August 1, a spirited discussion was held by board members about allowing Monroe Junior High School to be used by the Patchwork Players. Two members, Leroy Smith and Mrs. Kirk Ring, strongly objected to what they considered foul language in some of the scripts, given that there were children in the audiences. The principal target was the play *Born Yesterday*. Board members agreed to meet with the Players group and discuss certain policies the result of which was that children under age sixteen must be accompanied by adults.

Owners of the Roanoke Red Sox appealed to Roanoke City Council to support a fundraising campaign to replace the "splinter bowl" wood bleachers at Maher Field with steel ones. A new steel 5,000-seat grandstand was estimated at $150,000.

Curtis Turner won the NASCAR race held at Victory Stadium on August 2. Turner defeated his ace rival Jimmy Lewallen in the twenty-five-lap event. Attendance was estimated at 5,000.

The Pantry Restaurant at Bent Mountain advertised the formal opening of its new Colonial Dining Room for August 4.

Rugby Grocery opened on August 4 at 1210 Eleventh Street NW. It was affiliated with Blue Jay Food Markets.

Mrs. W. K. Langford of northwest Roanoke reported seeing a flying saucer from her yard on August 4. The "round, aluminum-colored saucer" was headed toward Bedford.

The new road from Hanging Rock south along Route 630 was opened to traffic for the first time on August 4. The road was planned to eventually connect with Route 460 at Lakeside. Universal Construction Corporation of Salem did the roadwork.

C. W. Francis, a longtime realtor, died at his home in Roanoke on August 4. He was eighty-one. Francis was a native of Floyd County and established the Francis Farm Agency in Roanoke in 1910. In 1920, the firm changed its name to C. W. Francis & Son.

Roanoke author Nelson Bond had a new novel published, *Lancelot Biggs: Spaceman*. The work was published by Doubleday & Company in New York. The science-fiction work was set in the year 2115.

A brief history of Roanoke's Washington Park was provided in the August 6 edition of the *Roanoke Times*. The park was composed of two tracts. One was given by Nannie Williamson and Charles Lukens in 1922. The other tract, known as Springwood, was about twenty acres. That tract contained the brick caretaker's house that was built in the late eighteenth century as a tavern and was possibly one of the oldest structures in the city. The tavern's original owner was George Spotts. Along the creek in the park was once a grist mill operated by Spotts. The earliest record had the land being owned by Nathaniel Evans in 1773, with Potts acquiring eleven acres from Evans in 1793. The resident caretaker in 1950 was Sam Callaway.

George Fulton Jr. became the first golfer to capture the Roanoke Country Club golf championship for five consecutive years. He defeated Dr. P. T. Goad 5 to 4 in the tournament finals.

This early 1950s image shows Roanoke Country Club as seen from the fairway. The clubhouse was constructed in 1924. *Virginia Room, RPL*

The first case of polio in Roanoke for the year was reported on August 7. Wythe County remained the epidemic center in western Virginia with a reported 128 cases. Wythe County had erected billboards at the county line advising visitors and tourists to not stop in the county.

Western film star Lash LaRue brought his *Great Western Show* to the stage of the Roanoke Theatre on August 8.

Roanoke City Council adopted a resolution requesting a $475,000 allocation from the federal government for the clearance of blighted areas in the city in conjunction with the planned 900-unit low-income housing project. The council took the action amid protests from several groups to the housing development.

Dr. Elizabeth Durham, a professor at Virginia State College, filed suit in Law and Chancery Court against the N&W Railway for $10,000. Durham alleged she was forced to move from a sleeping car to a coach "solely because she was a Negro." Durham's local attorney was Reuben Lawson. Durham was traveling from Columbus, Ohio, to Petersburg, Virginia, when she was forced to change cars as the train approached Roanoke last January. She was made to move to a coach for whites and then to a coach for Black passengers even though she had purchased first-class tickets. Durham described the coach for Blacks as "small, overcrowded, filled with smoke, dusty, dirty and drafty." The train's conductor, L. L. Crowder of Richmond, was also named as a defendant.

Star City Furniture Company held its grand opening on August 10 at 131 E. Campbell Avenue. The location was formerly the Appalachian Electric Power Company building. The store had sponsored the "Miss Star City" contest as a means of promoting its opening and advertised $12,000 worth of gifts for the opening week. A three-piece walnut bedroom suite was $69, and a four-piece mohair living room outfit was $349. An estimated 15,000 persons attended opening day. The store manager was Kenneth Long.

Clyde Moody, formerly of the *Grand Ole Opry*, performed in person at the North 11 Drive-In on August 10. Joining him were Smiley Wilson and the Range Partners.

Rev. Robert Jett, retired bishop of the Southwestern Virginia Diocese of the Protestant Episcopal Church, died at his home in Roanoke on August 9 at the age of eighty-five. He was consecrated as the first bishop for the diocese in 1920. He retired in 1938.

The Roanoke Ministers' Conference observed a citywide "Day of Prayer" in light of the Korean War. A midday prayer gathering was held at First Baptist Church and attended by about 300 persons. A Catholic prayer service was held at Our Lady of Nazareth Catholic Church.

Stubby Pee Wee Martin of Bassett won the fourth stock car race of the summer held at Victory Stadium on August 10. He bested hometown favorite Curtis Turner who came in second. Some 4,500 fans came out to watch the twenty-five-lap event.

This 1950 image shows the interior of Rainbo Bread which was located at 2609 Plantation Road. *Virginia Room, RPL*

The Southern Railway announced their new dining policy that Blacks and whites would be seated at separate ends of their dining cars. The Southern's old policy of separating the races by using curtains had been ruled illegal by the US Supreme Court.

Hazel Garst was named as "Cop of the Month" in August. She became the first woman to get the award. Garst had been a member of the Roanoke Police Department since January 1, 1944.

Con Davis, former basketball coach at Washington and Lee College, was named as the new head basketball coach and assistant football coach for William Fleming High School for the coming school year.

The section of the Blue Ridge Parkway from Bonsack to the Peaks of Otter opened to traffic on August 12. The parkway extended all the way south from the Peaks to Asheville, North Carolina.

The Patchwork Players presented *The Passing of the Third Floor Back* that involved almost every member of the theatrical group—Joseph Scher, William Cain, Harry Harris, Sally Gearheart, John Weir, Stacey Remaine, Julann Wright, Jeanne Beatty, Barbara Lucas, Fran Smith, and Francis Ballard.

The Carlton Terrace Beauty Salon opened on August 15.

Roanoke County resident and former journalist Eduoard Diamond spoke to the Roanoke Writers Guild at their monthly meeting on covering the Alaskan gold rush at the turn of the century. He gave up his job as a reporter with the *Kansas City Star* after he struck gold himself. He later went to China and covered the Boxer Rebellion.

Additional polio patients were admitted to the Memorial and Crippled Children's Hospital almost daily. The total number of cases reported for Western Virginia was 221, with 146 of those being in the town of Wytheville. Total cases for Virginia were 404 as of August 14.

The contract for the new administration building and terminal for Woodrum Field was awarded to B. F. Parrott and Company pending approval from the CAA. Their low bid totaled $317,432.

Roanoke City Council member Dan Cronin failed in his attempt to dismiss the city manager. Cronin did not receive any support from his fellow members in his bid to oust Arthur Owens from his job. Cronin offered no specific reason for his motion.

Three community sings were sponsored by the Roanoke Parks and Recreation Department during mid-August at Oakland Park, Washington Park, and Raleigh Court Park. In addition, the department sponsored a dance for teenagers at the tennis courts in Elmwood Park. The community sings were led by George Shaw.

Salem Town Council instructed its manager, Frank Chapman, to make a study of the cost of making Salem a first- or second-class city. The council was acting on a recommendation for such a study by the town's planning commission.

Another sign landmark was removed in downtown Roanoke on August 15. The large vertical sign on the American Theatre was removed to comply with a recently adopted sign ordinance. The sign was erected in 1928 when the theatre opened and was believed to be the largest of its kind in the city. The sign was six feet wide and forty feet high and read "American."

In the fall of 1950, construction began on a new terminal building at Woodrum Field. The former control tower and Cannaday home, shown here, would be razed. *Virginia Room, RPL*

William Dupree, a Roanoke tenor and student at Howard University, was selected to sing in Paul Green's symphonic drama *Faith of Our Fathers* that opened in Washington, DC, in early August.

The Stork Shop opened on August 17 at 308 First Street SW. It specialized in maternity and infant wear.

Curtis Turner won the fifth stock car race held at Victory Stadium on August 16. Tim Flock of Atlanta placed second in the twenty-five-lap event. Baldy Wilson of Roanoke won the twenty-lap amateur race.

Little Esther, age fourteen, along with Johnny Otis and his orchestra and Redd Lyte and his Blue Notes, performed at the American Legion Auditorium on August 18. The balcony was reserved for white spectators.

A parade of over 200 children was held in Salem on August 18 as the climax for the summer Camp Salem activities. The parade began at Langhorne Place to Municipal Field via Main Street, College Avenue, and the Boulevard. The white children held a day of activities following the morning parade at Municipal Field, and the Black children did the same at Water Street Park.

The thirty-mile natural gas pipeline from Gala to Roanoke was completed on August 18.

A Self-Service Station opened on West Main Street in Salem on August 19.

Hoover Brothers Grocery opened at 1736 Memorial Avenue SW on August 17. It was affiliated with Blue Jay Food Markets.

The Sixteenth Engineer Company, marine reserves, boarded an N&W Railway train on August 20 to head for active duty in the Korean War. The Roanoke outfit was commanded by Capt. William Hopkins. The men gathered at the Marine

Armory in Roanoke before departing and were seen off by Mayor A. R. Minton. They marched from the armory to the train station and boarded a 10:30 a.m., eleven-car troop train.

Curtis Turner had the fastest qualifying speed at the new Darlington International Raceway on August 19. Turner was set to enter the inaugural Southern 500 on September 4.

Some seventy-five military aircraft were sheltered at Woodrum Field the third weekend in August, having been flown in from East Coast bases being pounded by a hurricane. The display of the latest military planes became a sightseeing event for locals. Airport officials estimated that 5,000 came to see the aircraft.

Big Bend, a restaurant and bar along Bent Mountain Road, was purchased by the Jennings family of Natural Bridge and converted into the Blue Ridge Tea Room.

Glenvar won the regular season Virginia Amateur Baseball League championship by defeating Vinton. Glenvar's pitcher was Bill Baxter. The team finished the season with a 24–12 record.

The first local casualty of the Korean War was Cpl. Eugene Payne, who was killed in action on July 28. He was nineteen and the son of Mr. and Mrs. Ralph Payne of Wise Avenue SE. He enlisted in the army in 1949 and went overseas in March of that year.

Judge K. A. Pate, along with several business and civic leaders, created the Juvenile Court Children's Fund as a means to purchase candy, movie tickets, ice cream, and other items for neglected children. Arthur Taubman was elected chairman of the group.

At back, the employees of Fisher's Supply Company pose for this 1950 image. The store was at 411 First Street. *Virginia Room, RPL*

The Johnson Family Singers performed at the Roanoke Theatre on August 23. The group was popular nationally on the CBS radio network. They also performed the next day at the Veterans Administration Hospital carnival.

An addition to Fire Station No. 7 on Memorial Avenue was underway in late August. Much of the construction work was done by the firefighters. The new addition was done to accommodate a sixty-five-foot aerial ladder truck.

Curtis Turner won the sixth stock car race held at Victory Stadium on August 23. Some 5,700 fans watched Turner win the twenty-five-lap event. Jimmy Lewallen came in second. Baldy Wilson of Roanoke won the amateur race, and Pete Stanton of Salem came in second.

Pvt. Vernon Ferris of Roanoke was reported killed in action in Korea on August 14. He was the son of Mr. and Mrs. J. W. Ferris of Shenandoah Avenue NW. He had enlisted in the army on September 3, 1949. He was eighteen.

L .J. Dove of Roanoke won the city-county horseshoe pitching tournament. He defeated defending champion G. B. Darnell.

A field artillery unit from Roanoke, the first army reserve unit called up for active duty in the region, left on August 28 for the Korean War. The unit was commanded by Lt. Col. Minor Kulp.

The Roanoke Fair opened on August 28 for a five-day run. The fair was held at Victory Stadium and featured the Janet Circus, the Aerial Ortons, acrobats, a unicyclist, singer Gloria Tara, organist Jessie Griffith, fireworks, agricultural exhibits, and a midway.

The Patchwork Players presented *Broadway* as their final production of the summer season.

Haskell Deaton of Charlotte staged an air show at the Montvale airport on August 27. The show featured aerial daredevils and parachutist Don Edwards billed as "The Human Batman."

Ballard Gibbs of Bennett Springs was fatally stabbed by his stepdaughter, Theresa Coleman, on August 27. Gibbs was a custodian at Andrew Lewis High School.

Two retiring members of Roanoke City Council were presented silver trays in recognition of their service. Benton Dillard came off council as he was defeated for reelection, and Richard Edwards chose not to seek reelection.

Fire Station No. 10 was formally dedicated on August 30 by Mayor A. R. Minton and a crowd of about 250 persons. The station was located at Noble Avenue and Wilkins Street NE. The station cost $108,000, and the contractor was Neale Construction Company. Wiley Jackson, president of Neale, handed the keys to the station to the mayor and to Fire Chief W. M. Mullins.

A building permit for a $60,000 office and warehouse was issued in early September for the Strietmann Biscuit Company for 28 Mill Lane in Salem.

The Roanoke City Council selected Roy Webber to serve as mayor and A. R. Minton as vice mayor during its September 1 reorganization meeting. At Salem Town Council, the members reelected James Moyer as mayor, and Vinton Town Council elected Nelson Thurman as mayor.

Tiny Bradshaw and his orchestra performed at the American Legion Auditorium on September 3. The dance and floor show began at midnight and went until four o'clock in the morning. White spectators were permitted.

Roanoke city policeman R. M. Shropshire fatally shot Curtis Simmons of Roanoke County on September 1. According to police, Simmons wrestled the policeman's night stick away and began to assault the patrolman. The shooting occurred in the 30 block of First Street SE when Simmons was resisting arrest for public drunkenness.

Home Food Service began operating in Roanoke in early September as a home-delivery grocery business. The fleet of grocery buses delivered a variety of grocery products. The business was owned by Sidney Lichtenstein and Paul Bernstein.

The Charlotte Doyle Shop opened at its new location at 127-A W. Luck Avenue on September 5.

Pearl Counts opened Pearl's Beauty Salon at 3518 Williamson Road, formerly the location for Lura's Beauty Salon.

The Roanoke Bachelors Club held its first event since being organized. Their dinner-dance was held at the Hotel Roanoke. The club consisted mainly of college-age and post-college men. Jimmy Johnson was the club's organizer.

Huff Lane School opened for the first time at the start of the 1950–51 school year on September 5. Enrollment was 365 students.

Former Roanoker and Jefferson High School graduate First Lt. Eugene Kelly was killed in the crash of a C-119 troop carrier plane in Parsons, Tennessee, on September 1. Kelly was the copilot of the plane that exploded in midair, killing all six persons on board during a training exercise.

Health Spot Shoe Store opened on September 5 at 25 Church Avenue. J. S. Rausin was the store manager.

Landon Buchanan beat Lu Merritt to win the city-county tennis tournament that was held at South Roanoke Park. Buchanan won the title in 1947. Merritt and Paul Rice won the men's doubles tournament, defeating Landon Buchanan and Charley Turner.

Juanita Stanley won the women's singles championship in the city-county tennis tournament. She beat Nell Boyd. In doubles, the champions were Stanley and Kitty Coxe.

The Waynick Furniture Company closed. The store had been in business in Roanoke for forty-one years and was located at 109 E. Campbell Avenue. James Waynick was the manager.

Dr. Lewis Ripley of the Memorial and Crippled Children's Hospital began his work doing physical therapy in Wytheville for polio patients. The therapy center was located in the Veterans' Home in Wytheville.

The Bent Mountain Hunting Club hosted a squirrel supper at their clubhouse with over 150 guests in attendance.

Sidney's held a formal opening of its newly enlarged and remodeled store on September 7. The women's clothing store was located at 501 S. Jefferson Street.

Roanoke City Council voted 3–2 to discontinue modified stock car racing for the remainder of the year at Victory Stadium. Curtis Turner and Bill France had asked for races to be extended through October.

Members of the Bent Mountain Hunting Club pose in front of their clubhouse located on Calloway Road in this 1950s image. *Virginia Room, RPL*

Fire damaged the Salem Hardware Company store at 109 E. Main Street in Salem on September 6. Russell Johnston, owner, estimated the damage at $100,000.

Gene Graybill was sentenced to three years in prison after he pled guilty to a charge of bigamy in Roanoke County Circuit Court. In 1949, he had wed a Roanoke County woman while still married to a woman from Roanoke City.

First Church of the Nazarene at Highland Avenue and Eighth Street SE was dedicated on September 10. The new church had a seating capacity of 450. Rev. C. E. Winslow was the pastor. The church was organized in 1928. Five hundred persons attended the ceremony.

The new store and warehouse for Virginia Supply Company was completed in mid-September. It was located at Shenandoah Avenue and Ninth Street NW.

The comedian "The Duke of Paducah," along with Annie Lou and Danny from the *Grand Ole Opry*, performed at the Roanoke Theatre on September 13.

The Roanoke Country Club golf team won the State Golf Team Tournament held at the country club. The team was led by George Fulton with other members being John Rice, P. T. Goad, and E. J. Keffer Jr.

The Roanoke Red Sox finished second in the regular season of the Piedmont League and faced Lynchburg in the first round of the playoffs.

President Harry Truman dismissed Louis Johnson as his secretary of defense on September 12. Johnson was a native of Roanoke. Truman replaced Johnson with General George C. Marshall. Johnson had come under criticism for reducing military spending too much such that his critics charged he had endangered national security.

The Barter Theatre presented *The Show Off* at Jefferson High School on September 13. The play was sponsored by various women's organizations.

Toot's Drive-In restaurant opened on September 13 at 2729 Williamson Road. The proprietors were L. H. Austin and J. L. Austin.

This September 1950 image shows Train No. 25 at the N&W Railway Station at Salem.
N&W Historical Photographs Collection, VPI&SU Libraries

Erskine Hawkins and his orchestra performed at the American Legion Auditorium on September 15. White spectators were admitted.

Judge Stanford Fellers in Law and Chancery Court denied a petition for a permanent injunction to halt Roanoke's planned multiunit low-income housing program. The petition had been filed by several businessmen and organizations. Courtney King was the attorney for the petitioners.

Pfc. Wallace Witt and Pfc. Marvin Short, both of Roanoke, were reported killed in the Korean War. Witt was killed in Haman on September 2. He had enlisted in the military in 1947 and was part of the occupying force in Japan before being transferred to Korea. Short was killed on September 3. He had joined the army in October 1949 and went to Korea in August 1950.

A campaign to stop drinking at high school football games was launched by Roanoke City Manager Arthur Owens with the broad support of PTAs and spectators. Owens observed that heavy drinking at past games was a source of complaints such that he placed police in the stands.

The Carlton Terrace Barber Shop opened on September 15.

The Raleigh Court Methodist Church began an addition to their church that was a two-story Sunday School building with a recreation room on the first floor.

Jefferson High School defeated William Fleming High School in a football game to benefit the sandlot league. Carl Trippeer was Jefferson's quarterback, who led the Magicians to the 27–0 victory. An estimated 9,000 persons attended the game at Victory Stadium. On the same night, Andrew Lewis High School defeated Emory and Henry College's B team 14–0 at Salem Municipal Field before a crowd of 2,000.

The congregation of Emmanuel Evangelical Lutheran Church voted to construct a new $55,000 sanctuary to be erected at Palmetto Street and Olive Avenue NW, just three blocks west from their location at the time on Lafayette Boulevard at Staunton Avenue. That building had been erected in 1923. Rev. John Utt was the pastor, and Frank Hartman was chairman of the building committee. The new church would seat 250 persons.

Some 400 veteran employees of N&W Railway attended the annual meeting of the Colored Division of N&W Railway that was held at the American Legion Auditorium in mid-September.

Blue Ridge Post 484, Veterans of Foreign Wars, held a note-burning ceremony at the post's home at 1912 West Avenue SW on September 21. The building had been expanded by the post since it was acquired in 1942.

Roanoke police found the body of a newly born baby boy in a locker at the Greyhound Bus Terminal on September 18. The baby had been dead for a week, and police had no leads. The police had been called to the station after a maid discovered a strong odor coming from the women's locker room area. A few days later, Florence Robertson of Salem, age twenty-one, was formally charged with the hiding of the body of her newborn. According to a statement she provided police, Robertson had given birth to the stillborn baby in a rooming house in Salem on September 10. She put the body in a towel in a cardboard box, took a taxi to the bus station, and then placed the body in the locker. According to Det. Capt. Frank Webb, they had investigated Robertson using an anonymous tip.

Some 150 citizens attended the meeting of the Roanoke School Board on September 18 demanding to know why the construction of the new Addison High School had been delayed. Board members committed to the project, though they received sharp comments about other projects going forward ahead of Addison.

Tommy Magness, Red Smiley, Don Reno, Verlon Reno, and Cousin Irv Sharp performed on the stage of the Salem Theatre on September 19.

Floyd Joyner Jr. was sentenced to death in the electric chair after a jury convicted him of the hammer slaying of Addie McCormick in Roanoke County on June 26. She died in a hospital four days later. Judge T. L. Keister set Joyner's execution date for December 4. Joyner claimed he was innocent and had only confessed to the crime when threatened by police officers. Ten witnesses, however, testified for the prosecution.

Dr. J. N. Dudley, Roanoke physician, declared the Roanoke River as the city's "worst health menace" due to its polluted condition that contained many types of intestinal germs. Dudley made his assessment during a speech before the Roanoke Kiwanis Club.

Pvt. Lawrence Fitzgerald of Roanoke County was killed in action in the Korean War on September 1. He was the son of Mr. and Mrs. Fred Fitzgerald.

The abandoned Fire Station No. 2 at East Avenue and Fourth Street NE was converted into a recreation center for Blacks. Some space was also reserved for use by the Gilmer School. The station ceased operating in mid-September when No. 10 Fire Station opened.

Club 52, formerly Jeff's Silk Room, opened on September 23 on Route 11 west of Salem. The club was operated by Skinny Stephenson and Dennis Deeds. On opening night, dance music was provided by the Jack Saunders Quintet.

The Carlton Terrace Building held a grand opening on September 25 with a ribbon-cutting ceremony. Tours were provided along with organ music in the lobby. Besides 150 resident apartments, the building also contained a roof garden, barber shop, snack bar, drugstore, florist shop, milk depot, laundry service, and professional offices. The structure was designed by Tucker Carlton, a former Roanoker.

Haverty Furniture Company opened at 111 W. Campbell Avenue on September 28. Yolande Betbeze, who was Miss America in 1950, made an appearance to promote the grand opening. She was joined by BeBe Shopp, Miss America for 1948. The Roanoke store was the company's thirty-second store nationwide. A crowd of 10,000 attended the grand opening.

Virginia Military Institute defeated William and Mary in football 25–19 in a game played before 12,000 fans at Victory Stadium on September 23.

This image of the Carlton Terrace Building, which was located in the 900 block of Jefferson Street SW, was taken in November 1951. *Virginia Room, RPL*

The 1950 *Fall Fashion Futurama* was held in downtown Roanoke during the last week of September. The event included free city bus service, open houses as all the clothing stores, live models in the store windows, and special events. The week-long event was sponsored by the Roanoke Merchants Association.

Florence Robertson was fined $20 in Roanoke Police Court for unlawfully disposing of the body of her newborn baby. Robertson had placed the body in a box and then put it in a locker at the Greyhound bus terminal.

Allen Ingles Palmer, a well-known Roanoke Valley artist, was killed in a plane crash on September 24. The crash of his Piper Clipper happened southwest of Roanoke City in the backyard of Garland Sheets on Poplar Road in the Cave Spring section. Palmer had taken off just minutes before from his small landing strip at his Cave Spring home en route to exhibit some of his works in New York City. According to eyewitnesses, the plane's engine cut off before it plummeted to the ground, where the gas tank exploded on impact. The fire was too hot for neighbors to remove Palmer from the cockpit, who had already died upon impact. The crash was investigated by Marshall Harris, manager of Woodrum Field, and a CAA officer. According to Harris, Palmer had his plane checked a few days before at the airport. Palmer had studied art at leading schools in the US and under Walter Biggs of Salem. His works had been exhibited at the Metropolitan Museum of Art in New York, the Art Institute in Chicago, the Pennsylvania Academy of Art, and the Virginia Museum of Fine Arts. His trip that resulted in the crash was to exhibit some of his works at the Milch Galleries, and he had thirty-five paintings on board the plane. He was thirty-nine. Palmer's funeral was conducted from St. John's Episcopal Church with interment at Evergreen Cemetery.

Dr. Cameron Zorro and his *Terrors of the Unknown* came to the stage of the Roanoke Theatre on September 27. The show featured Lady Godiva, the ghost with "hex" appeal.

Mayor Roy Webber led a 3–2 vote at Roanoke City Council to cancel all commitments regarding federal low-income housing developments in the city. The mayor appointed a committee of five to meet with the Roanoke Redevelopment and Housing Authority board to determine a way to abrogate all agreements with federal authorities regarding the housing projects.

The newly remodeled People's Credit Clothing held at formal reopening of their store in the 100 block of W. Campbell Avenue.

Dr. Harry Penn, Rev. A. L. James, George Lawrence, Eugene Brown, and Rev. R. J. Smith appeared before Roanoke City Council on September 25 and renewed their appeal for the hiring of Black firefighters. The group was not advocating for a segregated fire station, but for Blacks to be hired to fill vacancies and serve at existing stations. The council referred the matter to the city manager for a response at an upcoming meeting.

The Roanoke School Board purchased the former Antrim Motors Company building at 503 Sixth Street SW for $60,000 for use as additional space for vocational classes.

Salem town manager Frank Chapman told a joint meeting of the Salem Town Council and the Town Planning Commission that a study to consider Salem becoming a second-class city would cost up to $3,000. The council decided to forward the matter to the planning commission for follow-up.

Francis Cocke, president of First National Exchange Bank in Roanoke, was elected vice president of the American Bankers Association at a meeting of the group in New York City. By custom, Cocke was set to become president of the association in 1951.

Roy Bryant was sentenced to life imprisonment after being found guilty in the slaying of his wife, Virginia Bryant, on June 16 at a restaurant on Williamson Road. Lester Pearson was sentenced to twenty years for second-degree murder of his wife, Janie Pearson, on June 17 in the basement of their home on Blenheim Road SW. Both men pled guilty, and both sentences were imposed by Judge Dirk Kuyk.

Joie Chitwood and his auto daredevils came to Victory Stadium on September 30. The show featured stunts, a two-wheel obstacle course, and auto jumps.

Julian Wise was reelected head of the Virginia Association of Rescue Squads at a meeting of the organization in Richmond. Wise was also president of the International Association of Rescue Squads.

The Roanoke Red Sox defeated Portsmouth in a decisive game seven to win the championship tournament of the Piedmont League. They were also the regular season champions.

Louis Jordan and his orchestra performed at the American Legion Auditorium on October 2. White spectators were admitted.

WSLS radio station observed their tenth anniversary on October 1.

The Big Show of 1951 came to the stage of the Roanoke Theatre on October 3. The show featured lingerie models, Roberta the "fig leaf" dancer, and vaudeville acts.

The nation's leading contract bridge player and newspaper columnist, Charles Goren, gave a series of lectures on the card game at the Patrick Henry Hotel. His appearance was sponsored by the Nancy Christian Fleming Chapter of the DAR.

The Roanoke Redevelopment and Housing Authority board refused to work out an arrangement with Roanoke City Council to stop federal low-income housing developments from being built in the city. At the joint meeting held on October 4 between the two bodies, the authority indicated they would forward the Public Housing Administration a copy of the council's resolution to stop such developments.

Cpl. Irvin Adkins of Roanoke was killed in action in the Korean War on September 22. Adkins had enlisted in the army in 1946. He had lived in the Hollins Road section.

The King's Daughters of Roanoke purchased property adjacent to the Mary Louise Home that they operated at 1001 Patterson Avenue SW with the intent of building an annex for the home for elderly women. The home was established in 1925 to house older women without families and was originally located at the corner of Fourth and Washington Streets SW. The home moved to Patterson Avenue in 1930.

C. G. Beckman opened Community Barber Shop at 4840 Williamson Road on October 6.

Clifton A. Woodrum, former Sixth District congressman, died on October 6 in Washington, DC. He was sixty-three. Woodrum served in Congress for twenty-two years and was instrumental in garnering federal funds for Roanoke Airport such that after its expansion it was renamed Woodrum Field. Woodrum was born in Roanoke on April 27, 1887, to Robert and Anna Woodrum. He received his law license in 1908. He was elected Roanoke's Commonwealth's Attorney in 1917. His funeral was conducted at Greene Memorial Methodist Church, and he was interred at Fairview Cemetery.

Clifton Farris of Hershberger Road was killed when struck by an N&W Railway passenger train on October 6 near the Moore Mill crossing in Salem. He was fifty. Witnesses saw Farris step in front of the oncoming train intentionally.

The University of Virginia defeated Virginia Tech in football 45–6 in a game played at Victory Stadium on October 7 before a crowd of 12,000 spectators.

A baseball night game was played at Maher Field on October 11 that featured Dan Bankhead of the Brooklyn Dodgers, the first Black pitcher in Major League Baseball. Other players included Sam Bankhead, Buck Leonard, and Sam Jones of the Cleveland Indians, along with players from leagues in Cuba, Mexico, and Puerto Rico. The players were on hand for an exhibition game between the Homestead Grays and the Roanoke All Stars. The All Stars were picked from various local Black teams by the Roanoke recreation department.

Dr. T. Allen Kirk of Roanoke, an internationally recognized rose expert, was presented with France's Legion of Honor at a luncheon in Washington, DC, in early October. The award was given in connection with his work in cultivating roses.

Brenda Lee Heslep, age three, and Larry Dean Heslep, age eight months, were both killed in a house fire at 1615 East Gate Avenue NE on October 7. They were spending the night with neighbors, Mr. and Mrs. Thomas Ash, when fire swept through the home. The couple and their two children escaped. The city coroner believed the Heslep children died from suffocation. Their parents were T. J. and Dorothy Heslep. Their father was away in the US Navy, and their mother was at work.

Sunshine Biscuits moved into their new warehouse at 1346 Eighth Street SW and held a formal open house on October 13.

Blanche Thebom, a mezzo-soprano with the Metropolitan Opera, performed at the American Legion Auditorium on October 10 under the auspices of the Thursday Morning Music Club.

William Owen of New York opened a school of art in Roanoke in mid-October with weekend and day school classes. Owen had won numerous prizes, studied in France under Andre L'Hote, and had works in the permanent collection of the Art Institute of Chicago. The classes were held in the recreation room of the Bank of Virginia.

Sgt. Walter Johnson of Roanoke was killed in the Korean War on September 30. He was the son of Cora Johnson of Elm Avenue SW and a member of Roanoke's marine reserve unit. Pfc. Guy Underwood was killed in action in Korea, having previously been reported as missing. He was the son of Guy Underwood of Roanoke County.

A 1900s steam fire engine was placed in front of the Municipal Building in October 1950 to promote Fire Prevention Week. *Historical Society of Western Virginia*

Ground was broken in late October for the long-awaited new administration building at Woodrum Field with a new terminal slated for completion by October 1951.

The Virginia Medical Society met at the Hotel Roanoke in mid-October for its annual meeting and voted 53–30 to admit Black physicians into its membership. The vote needed a two-thirds majority to pass and thus fell five votes short of that requirement.

The Virginia Tech freshmen football team defeated the freshmen of VMI 19–13 in a game played at Victory Stadium on October 13. An estimated 2,600 persons attended the game.

The Roanoke Gas Company ended the use of coal at its plant in northeast Roanoke with the completion of the gas pipeline from Gala.

Marine Pfc. William Moore died on October 13 at a navy hospital in Japan of wounds he received in Korea. He was twenty-two.

Doe Hicks became a three-time winner of the Monterey Golf Club championship when he defeated Harry Harris in the thirty-six-hole final.

Sammy White, who played for the Roanoke Red Sox in 1949, signed a contract with the Minneapolis Lakers to play professional basketball.

Roanoke police, in a crackdown on illegal gambling, seized over $20,000 worth of pinball machines from restaurants, gas stations, and pool rooms and issued summons to twenty-nine proprietors of the establishments. The thirty-three machines seized in the nighttime raids were lined up in the hallways of the Municipal Building.

The court case involving Dr. Elizabeth Durham's civil suit against N&W Railway was delayed as the plaintiff's attorney moved to dismiss the case as no Blacks had ever or were serving on juries in Roanoke's Law and Chancery Court. Judge Stanford Fellers took the motion under advisement. Blacks had been appointed to juries in Roanoke's Hustings Court, which handled felony cases, since 1948, but juries remained all white with the Law and Chancery Court that heard civil suits.

Pfc. John Hassell of Roanoke was killed in action in Korea on September 21.

The first polio death of the year of a Roanoke Valley resident occurred on October 17 when Ernest Rutrough, age twenty, succumbed to the disease in Memorial and Crippled Children's Hospital.

Eight Roanoke businessmen had cases against them dismissed in Hustings Court by Judge Dirk Kuyk, who ruled that they were not in violation of the Sunday Blue Law. All the men were represented by Warren Messick, who argued that beer was regularly sold on Sunday and that "if beer is a necessity, everything else is a necessity." The Sunday Blue Law forbade the sale of nonessential items on Sundays.

Vaughan Monroe and his orchestra performed at the American Legion Auditorium on October 19. Monroe was the star of the Camel Caravan heard nationally over the CBS network. Black spectators were admitted for a discount.

Charles Altis, age thirty-one, of Poages Mill was fatally injured on October 19 in an accident at the Harris Hardwood Company where he was a foreman. The coroner believed Altis suffered an electric shock that caused him to fall and break his neck.

A couple was instantly killed and twelve persons injured when an automobile crashed with a Greyhound bus nine miles south of Roanoke on Route 220 on October 20. Marcus and Annette Stickley of Rockingham County died at the scene. The driver of the car they were in was their son, Raymond. The couple was en route to Charlotte, North Carolina, to celebrate with family their golden wedding anniversary.

Professional wrestling returned to Roanoke after a two-year hiatus with four main events at the American Legion Auditorium on October 25. Jack Dempsey, former heavyweight boxing champion, was the guest referee. "The large crowd yelled themselves hoarse when O'Brien (a wrestler) faked a punch at Dempsey early in the feature match. But when Big Jack tapped him with a short left jab, his most famous punch, after the match when O'Brien struck Becker, the crowd roared their approval."

Dr. Sherman Oberly of Roanoke College delivered the main address at the cornerstone-laying ceremony for Garden City School on October 22. The event was attended by city officials with music by the Jefferson High School Band. Three hundred attended the event.

Aerial Gunner from Virginia, a compilation of letters of Cpl. Dallas Moody of Vinton to his mother, was published by the Virginia State Library. Moody was killed in action in World War II. Moody was a 1943 graduate of William Byrd High School.

John Kennett was fatally struck by an automobile while standing on the corner at Morehead Avenue and Ninth Street SE on October 22. Charged with reckless driving and manslaughter was Raymond Scruggs of Roanoke. Kennett was seventy-five.

The Ringling Brothers and Barnum & Bailey Circus came to Roanoke on October 23. The four circus trains arrived the day before, and thousands came to Maher Field to watch the circus set up. The circus included some 2,000 animals and performers and used twenty-one tents, including the big top tent. Among the many attractions was famous circus clown Lou Jacobs. Attendance totaled 17,000.

Western film star Tex Ritter and his *New Western Revue* came to the stage of the Roanoke Theatre on October 25.

The Columbus Boys Choir opened the 1950–51 concert season sponsored by the Community Concert Association with their October 24 performance at the Jefferson High School auditorium.

Trompeter's Bakery opened its new store on October 24 at the corner of Church Avenue and First Street SE. The bakery had been founded in 1929 by Mrs. Hannah Trompeter. She was aided in the business by her two sons, Albert and Herbert. Former State Senator Leonard Muse cut the ribbon.

US Senator Willis Robertson spoke on the steps of the Roanoke Municipal Building to advance the cause of the United Nations. As communities across Virginia observed UN Day, Robertson challenged those present to support the UN as the best protection against Russian aggression.

The Roanoke Merchants Association held an open house on October 24 to formally showcase their newly renovated offices on the second floor of the Walters Building at 22 Luck Avenue SW. The association had moved from its previous location in the Rosenberg Building on July 30. E. C. Moomaw was secretary-treasurer.

Twenty-nine merchants and four distributors were fined in Roanoke Police Court for violating the state's slot machine law in connection with a police raid on pinball machine gambling in the city. The fines ranged from $50 to $100.

The family of Private Will Hodges received good news from the Department of Defense—their son was alive. The department had sent a telegram to the family two weeks prior indicating that Hodges had been killed in action in Korea. To correct the error, Major Henry Watson of the Roanoke army reserves made a personal visit to the Hodges' home on Westover Avenue to deliver the news.

The young Men's Shop at 7 W. Campbell Avenue went out of business in late October due to their lease not being renewed.

Professional wrestling continued on Wednesday nights at the American Legion Auditorium. One night featured "The Blimp," who weighed in at 640 pounds.

Residents of the Kenwood-Idlewild section of Roanoke appeared before Roanoke City Council and asked that they be de-annexed from the city, having been annexed into the city in January 1949. The citizens claimed that promises made had not been kept in regard to their neighborhood. The council voted to establish a committee to review the claims.

The *Glamour Girl Revue* that starred Debbie Durkin performed at the Roanoke Theatre on November 1, and ads read, "Enough girls to start a heat wave in Alaska!"

Willis Jackson and his orchestra, along with Ruth Jackson, performed for a Halloween Ball at the American Legion Auditorium on October 31. White spectators were admitted at a discount.

An estimated 15,000 children jammed city parks for various Halloween night activities sponsored by the Roanoke Parks and Recreation Department. The police superintendent reported that it was the most orderly Halloween in the city in years. In Salem, several thousand participated in a celebration at Municipal Field that included games and square dancing.

Voters in Vinton approved a bond issuance for a sewage treatment plant for the town by a 238–28 margin.

Eric Williams, age sixty-six, died in a hospital on October 31 from injuries he sustained when his automobile was struck a week prior by a shifting engine on a siding at the Pre-Shrunk Masonry Sales Corporation where he worked.

Cold Spring Cooperative Creamery was sold out to three Roanoke dairies—Garst Brothers Dairy, Roanoke Dairy and Ice Cream Company, and Clover Creamery Company. Cold Spring was located at 532 Loudon Avenue NW. The creamery had been in business for seventeen years.

A fire on October 31 destroyed the filling station and grocery store of D. L. Handy on Route 221 near Cave Spring.

A Roanoke City Council subcommittee seeking to stop the development of federal low-income housing in the city canceled a planned trip to Washington, DC, to meet with officials of the Public Housing Administration. Federal officials indicated to them that there was nothing they could do to cancel the agreements they had with the Roanoke Redevelopment and Housing Authority.

Dr. Everett Clinchy, president of the National Conference of Christians and Jews, addressed the local chapter at a luncheon at the Hotel Roanoke and in the afternoon a student assembly at Jefferson High School. His theme was a worldwide brotherhood "united as a fist" as a protection against Communism.

William Worley, age twenty-four, was struck and killed at Brandon Road and Lincoln Avenue SW on November 1. The driver of the car that struck him, Robert Akers, was charged with reckless driving and manslaughter.

Fishing at Carvins Cove on Sundays became permissible when the commissioner of the Virginia Department of Game and Inland Fisheries overruled a Botetourt County Board of Supervisors ordinance that prohibited fishing there on Sundays.

The Roanoke chapter of Alcoholics Anonymous held its first annual banquet on November 3. The group invited business, religious, and education leaders to attend to learn about the work of AA.

Lt. Gordon Craig, USAF, was killed on November 2 in a plane crash at Panama City, Florida, where he was stationed. He was thirty-one and a graduate of Andrew Lewis High School. He was engaged in a routine training flight at Tyndall Air Force Base when the crash occurred.

Officials with N&W Railway announced the intended purchase of Cloverdale and Catawba Railroad subject to the approval of the state ICC. Chartered in 1949, Cloverdale and Catawba was built from Cloverdale up Tinker Creek to the

Botetourt County site of Lone Star Cement. The cement plant was slated to begin operations at the site in 1951. The purchase price was in excess of $1 million.

An indoor skating rink at Williamson road and Barkley Street was sold for $87,000 to the Crystal Spring Land Company. The rink had been erected and was owned by Raymond Ellis. The land company intended to use the building for other purposes.

The airport control tower at Woodrum Field was moved about 150 feet in early November to make room for the new administration building. Operators remained on duty in the tower as it was moved.

Forty women in Roanoke were mailed letters asking if they would be willing to serve on juries in the Law and Chancery Court. The action was directed by Judge Stanford Fellers in response to legislation enacted in 1949 by the Virginia General Assembly allowing women jurors It would be the first time females were allowed to serve on juries in Roanoke's Law and Chancery Court. Under Virginia law, they could decline to serve.

Grand Piano and Furniture Company advertised the formal opening of their "sixth floor" that was really the basement of the store at the corner of Commerce Street and Kirk Avenue SW. The floor contained a piano salon and a kitchen and appliance department.

In observance of National Education Week, the *Roanoke Times* gave a brief history of Roanoke's school system in its November 5 edition. In 1870 there were two schools in the area that would become Roanoke in 1882—New Lick School, which later became Commerce Street School—and they were located at the site of the federal post office downtown in 1950. When Roanoke was incorporated in 1884, William Graybill was appointed principal of the New Lick School that was called First Ward School. Commerce Street School graduated three in 1884. Commerce Street School was razed in May 1929.

The Barter Theatre presented *The Comedy of Errors* in the auditorium of Jefferson High School on November 10.

The Palm Restaurant and its furnishings were auctioned off on November 8. The restaurant was located at the intersection of Route 117 and Route 11, near Hollins College.

WDBJ used its new broadcasting booth in the city room of the *Roanoke Times* and *World-News* for the first time on November 7 to broadcast election returns.

Theresa Coleman was found guilty of involuntary manslaughter in the death of her stepfather, Ballard Gibbs, by a jury in Roanoke County Circuit Court on November 6. Gibbs was fatally wounded at his home on August 27. Judge T. L. Keister sentenced Coleman, age twenty, to one year in prison. The jury believed the young woman mainly acted in self-defense.

Claude Hopkins and his *Zanzy-Barr Revue* performed on the stage of the Roanoke Theatre on November 8. According to ads, the show had "Harlem's top nite life stars!"

Howard Sink, twenty, of Roanoke was killed in a traffic accident on November 7 in McIntosh, Georgia, while he was en route to his naval base in Florida. His motorcycle was struck by a train at a grade crossing.

This 1950s image shows a race at the Starkey Speedway. *Virginia Room, RPL*

Roanoke voters approved a $4 million bond issue by a 2,963–1,091 margin. The bonds were for a major expansion of the city's water system.

Nationally recognized pianist Rosalyn Tureck performed a concert of Bach pieces at Hollins College. She had previously performed there in 1939.

Dr. Wade Bryant, pastor of First Baptist Church in Roanoke, was elected president of the Baptist General Association of Virginia.

The Salem Hardware Company on Main Street in Salem reopened for business in mid-November after recovering from a fire earlier in the year.

The Starkey Speedway officially opened on November 12 with stock car races.

Caldwell-Sites Company moved into its new warehouse in Vinton in mid-November. The structure was located at Tenth and Tinker Streets. Headquarters for the company remained at 105 S. Jefferson Street in Roanoke.

Roanoke County school officials closed two schools in the Catawba section due to polio. High school students from that section were asked to not attend Andrew Lewis High School and Carver High School. There had been five reported cases of polio in the Catawba Valley. A white and a Black elementary school with enrollments of 125 and 22 students, respectively, were closed.

Twenty women from Roanoke and surrounding counties were called to serve on juries for the first time in Federal Court in Roanoke on November 14. One of the women, Lelia Stalker, was a shorthand teacher at Jefferson High School who invited her class to attend the trial and take down the proceedings for practice. Stalker served on a jury that convicted a traveling salesman of impersonating an FBI agent.

Mrs. Bonny Walker, age seventy-six, of Vinton demanded that her pre–Civil War bonds totaling $2,000 be honored by Virginia. She received national media attention for her claim.

Mrs. Josephine Willis Robertson, age ninety-two, died on November 15 at Memorial and Crippled Children's Hospital. She was the mother of US Senator

Willis Robertson. A resident of Salem, Robertson had been a leader in Baptist organizations.

Wiley Jackson of Roanoke was elected president of the Virginia Road Builders Association.

Mississippi newspaper editor Hodding Carter spoke at Hollins College on November 15. As part of his speech, he said the South must advance in the field of civil rights, healthcare, and education.

Charles Downey, age nineteen, of Roanoke died from burns he had received several weeks prior from a boiler blast at the Clover Creamery Company. The blast occurred on August 27.

Charges of manslaughter against Raymond Scruggs in the death of John Kennett were dropped. Scruggs had accidentally struck Kennett with his vehicle.

The Vinton Hardware Company opened at 100 Lee Street on November 16.

The Purple Secret lost his professional wrestling match in one of the many bouts at the American Legion Auditorium on November 15. By losing, he was unmasked and identified as Honey Boy Hannegan of Charleston, West Virginia. Pro wrestling was sponsored by Adolph Kirsch, president of Oak's Enterprises.

Television came to the Roanoke Valley at Harvey Howell's Restaurant at Bent Mountain in mid-November. Reception was received from stations in Greensboro and Richmond. The installation had been done by Hippert Radio Service, and television could be viewed every night according to ads.

Overstreet Food Processing Company opened on November 17 in the Mount Vernon Heights Section, one mile south of the Coffee Pot. The company offered processed meats, kitchen appliances, and meat dressing service.

Blanche Witt, age fifty-two, was struck and killed by a truck as she crossed Ninth Street at Highland Avenue SW on November 18. Howard West was the truck's driver.

The *Roanoke Times* All City-County football team included the following: Carl Trippeer, back (Jefferson); Bobby Eanes, guard (Byrd); Bobby Seal, tackle (Jefferson), Jim Peters, end (Lewis); Herbie Snyder, back (Byrd); Dick Firebaugh, end (Byrd); Bill Rakes, tackle (Lewis); George Preas, guard (Jefferson); Guy McClanahan, back (Jefferson); Jerry Cannaday, center (Jefferson); and John Kreider, back (Byrd). Black players were not eligible to be named.

Recording artist Ivory Joe Hunter and his orchestra performed at the American Legion Auditorium on November 22. The dance and show started at 11:00 p.m. and went on until 3:00 a.m.

Talley Beatty starred in a live musical production of *Tropicana* at the American Legion Auditorium on November 20.

A profile of Mrs. Eve Marie Eanes appeared in the November 19 edition of the *Roanoke Times*. Eanes, nee Eybe, had married Robert Eanes of Roanoke after World War II and relocated from her native Poland to Roanoke. Her postwar activities included being an interpreter at the Nuremberg Trials.

Two schools in the Catawba Valley that were closed due to a polio outbreak in that section resumed classes on November 27. There had been six children with polio in that area prior to the closings.

The Roanoke Star, shown here in 1950, was first lit on Thanksgiving Eve in 1949. *Virginia Room, RPL*

A majority of Roanoke City Council continued their fairly unsuccessful fight to stop federal low-income housing developments in the city. The majority voted to put the matter of such housing to the voters in a referendum on January 2.

The *Tiny Town Revue* came to the stage of the Roanoke Theatre on November 20. The show consisted mostly of animal acts and comedy routines billed as family friendly.

The Roanoke Star celebrated its first anniversary and the beginning of the Christmas retail season by having its red neon tube lighting turned on to complement the white tubes on Thanksgiving Eve. When done, the star looked red and white from a distance.

The congregation of First Methodist Church in Salem voted unanimously to sell its property to Roanoke College. The property included its sanctuary, parsonage, and a school building, which were located on College Avenue. The congregation simultaneously voted to purchase three tracts on West Main Street as a site for a new $700,000 church. The sale to the college was slated for 1952, giving the congregation time to erect their new building.

VMI beat Virginia Tech 27–0 in the Thanksgiving Day football game at Victory Stadium before a crowd of 25,000. VMI's quarterback Jim Coley was the star of the game, throwing four touchdown passes. In addition to the game, the crowd enjoyed the tradition of the game that included the entrance of each school's cadet corps into the stadium following a parade through downtown Roanoke. The game was attended by Virginia Governor John Battle. Both school bands played the National Anthem followed by *Dixie*. The game was followed by a cabaret dance for cadets at the American Legion Auditorium. The next day, the Roanoke Valley was carpeted by a nine-inch snow.

Pvt. Dan Dent of Roanoke, age nineteen, was killed in action in Korea on November 6. He was the son of Mr. and Mrs. T. S. Dent of Rugby Boulevard NW. He had served in Korea for two months.

Charles Lovern, age nine, died at Memorial and Crippled Children's Hospital on November 24 from burns received while playing at his home on Mountain Avenue SW that same day. The boy was playing with other children and poured gasoline on an alley can fire. The fire followed the stream of gas onto the boy.

The forty-member Roanoke Civic Orchestra gave its first concert of the year in the auditorium of Jefferson High School on November 26. The orchestra was directed and conducted by Franklin Glynn.

Horace Heidt and his *Youth Opportunity Show* came to the American Legion Auditorium on November 29. The show included stars of radio and television from the CBS network along with three local acts vying for a spot on his national program. The locals were Ginger Crowley, Ottawa Pullen, and Margaret Neas. The show was sponsored by the Roanoke Jaycees. Crowley was later selected to sing on Heidt's show on December 3. She was the vocalist for the Freddy Lee orchestra.

Photos of the Roanoke Valley were shown on national television as part of NBC's *Ted Mack Amateur Hour* on November 28. The show saluted Roanoke with images provided by B. F. Moomaw of the Roanoke Chamber of Commerce.

The Roanoke Children's Theatre under the direction of Clara Black presented its first play of the season, *Ghost of Mr. Penny*, in the auditorium of Jefferson High School.

The S. H. Heironimus Company opened its new home appliance department in a new location at 25 W. Church Avenue on November 28. It was the third major postwar expansion for the store. M. S. Smith was the department manager.

Pugh's Department Store held weekly fashion luncheons in the main dining room at the Hotel Roanoke during the Christmas retail season. Live models provided by the JoAnn Gimbert Agency paraded through the room wearing the latest fashions.

The Roanoke Hunt Club and the Bent Mountain Hunt Club returned from their respective hunting trips with much success. The Roanoke club went to the Dismal Swamp, and the Bent Mountain club went to their clubhouse in Wakefield, where they had exclusive hunting rights on 1,000 acres.

Southwest Motor Parts Corporation opened in late November as a wholesale business serving Chrysler dealerships. The business was located at 716 First Street SE. J. A. Meador was president.

Roanoke County school authorities released plans for the new Cave Spring High School. The plan was dependent upon a $3.5 million bond referendum being approved on December 12 by voters. The site was purchased in 1945 and encompassed fifteen acres on Route 221.

Mick-or-Mack Grocery opened its new S&H Green Stamp Store in its grocery at 131 W. Campbell Avenue in early December.

Wright Furniture Company, sponsor of the Saturday Jamboree on WDBJ, congratulated "Cousin" Irv Sharp on his tenth anniversary as host of the popular local program.

Dedication services for the new Sunday School addition to Bonsack Baptist Church were held on December 3. The church was started when the Bonsack family donated land for the congregation in 1860 when it was organized as Hebron Baptist Church.

Cpl. Paul Martin, age twenty-two, was killed in action in Korea on November 28. He was the son of Mr. and Mrs. M. R. Martin of Day Avenue SW. He was in the Marine Corps.

Officials with the Piedmont League reported that average attendance at the baseball games had dropped 20 percent as compared to figures from 1949.

Lloyd Lee resigned as executive secretary of the Hunton Branch YMCA effective January 1 to accept a similar position in Fort Lauderdale, Florida. Lee came to the Hunton Branch in 1928 from Birmingham, Alabama.

Appalachian Electric Power Company announced plans for a new $1 million high-voltage transmission station near Cloverdale in Botetourt County. The station was planned for a twenty-three-acre site on Route 11 near the intersection with Route 220.

The mother of former US Secretary of Defense Louis Johnson died at her home at 1611 Memorial Avenue SW on December 4. Catherine Johnson was eighty-nine.

Roanoke city policeman R. M. Shropshire was cleared by a Hustings Court grand jury of a murder charge in the shooting of Curtis Simmons on September 2.

An opening-day ceremony was held for the Red Cross Regional Blood Center on December 7. The center had a staff of twenty-one with Dr. Kenneth Graves as its medical director. Dr. Clark Hagenbuch oversaw the blood mobile operations. The center was located at 723 Third Street SW.

Roanoke police and state ABC agents rounded up nineteen bootleggers in a nighttime raid on December 5. Detectives confiscated ledgers, cash, and illicit whiskey. Of those arrested, eight were later fined and given jail sentences, while the others were fined and given suspended sentences.

The Teen-Age Girl Center was opened at 501-A Campbell Avenue SW by the Junior League. The center was a recreation center for girls only, though boys were allowed in on Friday and Saturday nights.

Walt Millies was signed as the manager of the Roanoke Red Sox for 1951. Millies succeeded John Marion, who was promoted to Birmingham, Alabama. Millies had played in the major league as a catcher with Brooklyn, Philadelphia, and Washington. He had also been a prominent minor league manager since World War II.

The Carriage House Theatre at Longwood in Salem was heavily damaged by fire on December 9. It was home of the Salem Community Players.

The Roanoke headquarters of Appalachian Electric Power Company at 606 First Street, SW, is pictured here in 1950. *Virginia Room, RPL*

Margaret Neas appeared in Horace Heidt's television show on December 17 broadcast from New York City. Neas performed *Harmony in Rose* on the piano. Ginger Crowley was scheduled to appear on Heidt's television program on January 15, 1951, having previously performed on his radio broadcast over CBS.

Carl Trippeer and George Preas of Roanoke were named to Virginia's Group One All-Star High School Football Team. The team was named by the state's football coaches.

The Star City Auditorium held its grand opening on December 15 with a concert and dance that featured Illinois Jacquet and his Little Jumping Jacks. The balcony was reserved for white patrons. The auditorium was at the corner of Henry Street and Third Avenue NW.

The Roanoke Civic Chorus, accompanied by the Roanoke Civic Orchestra, presented *The Messiah* at the American Legion Auditorium on December 12.

Henry Ellis, age twenty-two, was killed in action in Korea on November 29. He had been serving with the marines in Korea since March.

Roanoke City Council was provided an assessment of the Academy of Music by a citizens committee that estimated a cost of $187,000 to rehabilitate the structure such that it could reopen. The report was presented by Ben Parrott and Carl Andrews.

The Roanoke Sales Executive Club was organized on December 11. William Swartz was named president. About fifty persons attended the initial meeting.

Roanoke County voters rejected a $3.5 million school bond issue that would have made significant improvements to existing schools and created new ones. The December 12 vote was 2,220 against and 1,422 for the bond issuance. The increase in births following World War II had resulted in an intensive six-month campaign by advocates for an expanded school capital program to ease overcrowding and address the need for additional schools.

An engineering consulting firm retained by Roanoke City Council recommended a $1.4 million, four-lane viaduct be built to eliminate the Jefferson Street grade crossing over the N&W Railway tracks. The proposed viaduct would have a northern terminus at Wells Avenue and Commonwealth Avenue NE and the southern end at Jefferson Street and Salem Avenue.

Pvt. Carl Rogers, age seventeen, was reported killed in action in Korea, having been reported as missing in action on July 26. He was the son of Dillard Rogers of Salem.

W. A. Ingram donated fifty acres of land in Franklin County to the Roanoke Kiwanis Club for youth camp purposes.

The Varsity Grille opened in mid-December at 4513 Williamson Road in what was formerly the Plaza Restaurant.

Christmas decorations in downtown Roanoke had a star theme throughout the 1950s due to the popularity of the Roanoke Star on Mill Mountain that was first lit on Thanksgiving Eve in 1949. *Bob Kinsey*

Santa and his reindeer were part of the lit Christmas decorations in downtown Roanoke in 1950. *Bob Kinsey*

The entire stock of the Donaldson Furniture Company at 121 E. Campbell Avenue was auctioned off on December 16 to settle the estate of William Donaldson.

Father M. J. McDonald of St. Gerard's Catholic Chapel gave a hard-hitting speech that targeted the majority of Roanoke City Council and their opposition to federal low-income housing in the city. McDonald especially chided Mayor Roy Webber for twisting facts and trying to lead a reversal of already-settled contracts for the developments. He was addressing the Building Trades Council meeting.

Buddy Johnson and his orchestra, along with vocalists Arthur Prysock and Ella Johnson, performed a show and dance on December 24 from midnight until 4:00 a.m. at the American Legion Auditorium. White spectators were admitted to the balcony.

The Lad-n-Lassie Shoe Shop celebrated its first anniversary. The store was located at 205 First Street SW and specialized in shoes for toddlers through teens.

The cornerstone for Grandin Court School was laid on December 17. Rev. H. W. Connelly of Grandin Court Baptist Church was the keynote speaker for the ceremony. Music was provided by the Jefferson High School band. The school's principal, Lucy Buford, was introduced.

An unusual event occurred at Lewis-Gale Hospital in mid-December. A mother and daughter gave birth on the same day. Mrs. Ava Campbell of Moneta, age forty-one, gave birth to a daughter, while her oldest daughter, Mrs. Doris George of

Roanoke, age twenty, gave birth to a son. Both women and their babies were kept in the same room.

Two football players of Addison High School were selected to the Virginia Interscholastic Athletic League's All-State Football Team for 1950. E. L. Burrell was named to the first team as a tackle, and Thomas Bennett was named to the second team as a back.

The Civil Defense Advisory Council for Roanoke held its first meeting on December 18. The coordinator was Robert Thomas. The council felt that up to 15,000 persons in the city would need to be trained in a variety of jobs to prepare for the event of an atomic attack.

The Roanoke Area Boy Scout Council agreed to sell the old Camp Powhatan near Natural Bridge to the Lynchburg Girl Scout Council. The funds from the sale would benefit the council's new Camp Powhatan in Pulaski County.

Cpl. James Akers was killed in action in Korea on December 2. He was a member of Roanoke Marine Corps Reserve Unit. He was a recent graduate of Jefferson High School.

Home Service Foods established a grocery store to complement its mobile grocery delivery service. The grocery opened on December 20 at 709 Franklin Road SW in what was formerly the Ace Super Market. E. R. Chick Jr. was the store manager.

Roanoke's Police Superintendent S. A. Bruce convened his officers and alerted them that a gambling syndicate was trying to establish a foothold in the city and was willing to pay up to $2,500 per officer in bribes. He warned the officers against such tactics. Bruce told his department, "As long as I am in office and vice rears its insidious head, I'm going to strike at it."

The General Electric "More Power to America" ten-car exhibition train rolled into Roanoke on December 20 to showcase various home appliance products and other GE creations. One of the more popular displays was a J-47 turbojet engine. Some 1,000 persons went through the exhibits. The train was on a national tour.

Detective Sgt. Joe Jennings was named Cop of the Year for 1950. Jennings had been paralyzed and residing at Lewis-Gale Hospital since September 26, 1945, when he was wounded while in the line of duty. Every year, city police officials appealed to citizens for a special collection for Jennings, who commanded the respect of his peers and the public.

L. A. Wright of Gilmer Avenue NW was struck and killed by an automobile while he crossed Shenandoah Avenue on December 22. The driver of the car was James Wilhelm.

The *Parisian Nights Revue* came to the stage of the Roanoke Theatre on December 27. The show boasted a "stageful of can-can cuties" and the "Parisian Glamazon Ginger Grey."

Two pedestrians were killed on Christmas Day in Roanoke County when struck by automobiles. Waverly Mitchell, twenty-four, was struck and killed by a hit-and-run driver along Route 460 near the Blue Eagle Tourist Court. Mitchell was knocked or carried 150 feet by the impact. Nelson Foutz, who was walking with Mitchell, was also struck and critically injured. Hunter Thacker of Lynchburg was later arrested as the driver of the auto. L. W. Leflore, thirty, of Hollins suffered fatal injuries when he was struck while walking along Oldfield Road near Murray's Store. He was taken to Burrell Memorial Hospital where he died. The driver that struck him was John Coleman, who was charged with drunk driving.

Lee Sink of Roanoke died at his home in mid-December. Sink had made national news when a photo of him sitting on the front porch of his burned-down home appeared in a 1941 edition of *Life* magazine as the "Picture of the Week." Sink had been shucking corn when his small house caught fire, resulting in the death of his ninety-year-old wife on November 18, 1941. The photo had been taken by *Roanoke World-News* photographer Lambert Martin and resulted in an outpouring of donations from around the country.

For New Year's Eve, there were plenty of dances to attend. Freddie Lee's Band played at the Colonial Hills Club, while Earl Craig and his orchestra entertained at the VFW Post on Patterson Avenue SW. At the Star City Auditorium was Hal Cornbread and his orchestra, and performing at Club 52 were the Rhythm Boys. Price Hurst and his orchestra played at the Apartment Camps, and at the Blue Ridge Hall were the Virginia Pioneers. Wanderers of the Wasteland entertained at the City Market Auditorium.

The Harlem Globetrotters played at the American Legion Auditorium on December 31. The team's main attraction was funny-man Reese "Goose" Tatum, who had the longest reach in basketball—eighty-four inches. Babe Pressley was team captain. They played against the Collegians with vaudeville acts between games.

1951

The *Ice Vogues of 1951* came to the American Legion Auditorium on January 3 for a five-night run. The show featured seventy-five skaters and twenty-eight acts.

Conehurst School reopened on January 2 after getting an addition. Students from the school had been sent temporarily to South View School.

Pfc. James Earles was reported as killed in action in Korea on December 6, 1950. He was the husband of Mrs. J. S. of Melcher Street SE. He had also served in World War II.

United Iron & Metal Company opened on January 3 at 1204 Third Street SE, dealing in scrap iron. Milton Blank was the owner.

The International Sweethearts of Rhythm Orchestra, along with Peg Leg Bates, Spizzy Canfield, the Rhythmettes, and the Shoareguard Dancers, performed at the Virginia Theatre on January 4. The balcony was reserved for white spectators.

Sydney Small was named as the chairman of the Regional Civil Defense Council comprising organizations in Roanoke, Roanoke County, and Botetourt County. He held the same position during World War II. Small was a former mayor of Roanoke and a vice president of N&W Railway.

George Bolden, seventeen, of Roanoke was stabbed on Water Street in Salem on January 5 and died the same day of his wounds at Burrell Memorial Hospital. A few days later, Robert Jackson, twenty, of Roanoke County was arrested and charged with murder. Apparently the two men had an altercation over whiskey.

Every household in Roanoke and Roanoke County was provided a copy of the governmental pamphlet "Survival Under Atomic Attack" as part of the civilian defense effort. The area was also provided with two radiological detection devices for assessing residual radiation following an atomic attack.

The Roanoke Redevelopment and Housing Authority completed the purchase of twenty-five acres of the former Horton property in northwest Roanoke on January 6. The purchase made possible the start of construction work on a 300-unit housing development for low-income whites. The purchase price was $45,000.

The third-oldest Methodist Church in Roanoke was reactivated on January 7 at 4404 Williamson Road. Grace Methodist Church was organized in 1887 and deactivated in 1932. The church began as a mission Sunday School in a brick building at Commonwealth Avenue and Third Street NE. With growth, a Queen Anne–style home was purchased at Third Street and Third Avenue with support from the members of Greene Memorial Methodist Church. Eventually a small church was constructed on the house lot, with the house being moved to the back of the lot. The congregation later declined, and the church closed. The former church building and house later became St. John's Methodist Church.

The show *Skating Follies* came to the Skate-A-Drome, opposite Lakeside, on January 10 and featured Bill Bolonyus, Dean Corbin, the Glamourettes, and the Bloomerettes (a boys' comedy chorus).

Roanoke voters declared a strong "no" in a January 9 referendum on public low-income housing developments in the city. The referendum vote on whether city council should cooperate with the Roanoke Redevelopment and Housing Authority on developing federal low-income housing in the city was 5,009 against to 1,892 for. The debate on this issue had been spirited for months with veterans' organizations, Black clergy, trade unions, and women's organizations backing the housing program, while realtors, the Chamber of Commerce and prominent businessmen sought to eliminate it. Following the vote, the housing authority's chairman, John Windel, declared that the authority board would continue its work and honor its contracts with the federal government. A few days later, the majority of city council proposed to the authority that the 300-unit project for whites on the Horton property be scrapped and the authority only proceed with the planned 300-unit housing development for Blacks in the Lincoln Court section. The authority board rejected that compromise suggestion and countered that the two 300-unit housing developments for both Blacks and whites proceed with the understanding that they would not pursue a third 300-unit development in the future. The council majority rejected the counter proposal.

Woodson's Cafeteria, at 117 Church Avenue, reopened under new management and a new name in mid-January and became the Mayfair Cafeteria. Jimmy Trettel was the new manager.

The Roanoke School Board awarded Lucas & Fralin of Roanoke the contract to construct Addison High School. They were a low bidder at $1.3 million. The board chairman, LeRoy Smith, indicated that work on the school would begin before the end of January.

Justice Abram Staples of Roanoke announced his retirement from the Virginia Supreme Court of Appeals. Staples had served in the state senate, been appointed Virginia's attorney general, and been reelected to that office in 1937, 1941, and 1945 before resigning to accept an appointment to the Court of Appeals. A native of Martinsville, Staples had practiced law in Roanoke for many years before becoming attorney general.

The Roanoke Hell Cats kicked off their basketball season by playing the Virginia State team at the Star City Gymnasium on January 13. The Hell Cats consisted of former high school and college players for Black schools. Starting for the Hell Cats were Marshall Curtis, Ed Davis, Woodrow Gaitor, Wimpy Booker, and Beefbone Dungee. In the previous season, the team lost only one game. Another popular local team was the Kane's Rebels, a white basketball team sponsored by Kane Furniture. The Rebels' starters were Scotty Hamilton, Chuck Noe, Ed Harless, Jim Ruscick, Joe Valalik, and Henry Bushkar. The Rebels' home court was the American Legion Auditorium.

The Roanoke Redevelopment and Housing Authority awarded a contract on January 13 for the construction of the 300-unit low-income housing development for whites to the Goode Construction Company of Charlotte, North Carolina, for $2.8 million. Construction was expected to start within a week. This seemed to bring an end to the controversy as the authority's board proceeded with honoring agreements with federal authorities already in place.

Virginia Tech beat the University of South Carolina 68–64 in basketball on January 13. The game was held before a sold-out crowd at the American Legion Auditorium.

Airline business at Woodrum Field in 1950 broke all previous records. Three airlines served the airport and reported a total of 29,575 passengers as compared to 24,333 in 1949. This was complemented by increases in airmail and freight.

The Longwood Carriage House was razed in mid-January, having been heavily damaged by a fire. The carriage house had been built in 1906 and purchased from the Cooper family in 1943 by the Town of Salem. It was most recently used as a theatre by the Salem Community Players.

The Barter Theatre presented *The Glass Menagerie* in the Jefferson High School auditorium on January 16.

Bull Moose Jackson, along with Frank Culley and his orchestra, performed at the Star City Auditorium on January 15. Jackson was known for his hits *I Love You, Yes I Do* and *Big Fat Mama*.

Basil O'Connor, president of the National Foundation for Infantile Paralysis, launched the nation's 1951 March of Dimes campaign from Wytheville, Virginia, in a live national broadcast on January 14. The town was chosen because it was the site of the worst polio outbreak in America in 1950, with most of the patients that required hospitalization being treated at Memorial and Crippled Children's Hospital. Wytheville's population was 5,405, with seventy-six cases of polio—seventy times what is considered an epidemic rate.

Mayor Roy Webber broke ground for the new Addison High School on January 15. The new Black high school was "the culmination and beginning of a dream which Roanoke citizens have held for a number of years," stated school board member Dr. Harry Penn. About 400 persons attended the event. Music was provided by the Addison High School choir.

Moyer Heslep and Jerry Sink Jr. began operating Heslep & Sink in Salem as agents for Republic Oil Refining Company.

Alexander Terrell was reelected captain of the Hunton Life Saving Crew. The crew answered thirty-seven emergencies, eighty-five first-aid cases, sixty-two oxygen tent cases, sixteen inhaler cases and two iron lung cases and spent numerous hours in training and drills during 1950.

The suit against N&W Railway brought by Dr. Elizabeth Durham in Roanoke's Law and Chancery Court moved forward on January 17. Her attorney had asked for a continuance as there were no Blacks in the jury pool to sit for the civil rights case. Since being granted a continuance, the Jury Commission provided a supplemental list of potential Black jurors. This was the first time in the Law and Chancery Court that Blacks became eligible to be selected as jurors. When the trial resumed, the case made history twice, as one of the jurors selected was a Black female who was also the first woman to serve on a jury in the court.

This Roanoke Police Department image shows Kirk Avenue in 1951. *Virginia Room, RPL*

Joe Thomas and his orchestra, along with Eddie "Mr. Cleanhead" Vinson and his orchestra, performed at the American Legion Auditorium on January 18. White spectators were admitted to the balcony.

W. H. Hoobler, administrator of the Roanoke Hospital Association, reported that the Memorial and Crippled Children's Hospital was under tremendous strain in 1950 due to polio cases. The number of beds required forced hospital staff to take over the entire first floor of the main building for polio patients. The hospital had 518 polio cases from twenty-nine counties with thirty-six deaths from the disease.

Thousands of spectators watched as flames shot through the cupola atop the Hotel Roanoke on January 18. The afternoon fire began in the main kitchen ventilating duct and was brought under control quickly with little damage caused. The smoke and fire, however, forced the evacuation of guests from the upper floors. Damage was confined to the duct and cupola.

Hilda's Beauty Shoppe opened at 3310 Williamson Road in mid-January.

The Ballet Russe de Monte Carlo performed at the Jefferson High School auditorium on January 22.

The US Junior Chamber of Commerce named Dr. John Everett, president of Hollins College, as one of its ten Outstanding Young Men of America. Everett was presented his award at a banquet at the Hotel Roanoke on January 20.

Roanoke City Manager Arthur Owens reported to city council that he had received an offer from a real estate firm to purchase the Academy of Music. The structure had been closed for some time with a prohibitive cost estimate to renovate it. The council was to consider the proposal at an upcoming closed meeting. Owens favored disposing of the property via a public auction.

Dr. Elizabeth Durham lost her suit against N&W Railway when a jury ruled in favor of the railroad on January 19. Durham had sued for racial discrimination and sought $10,000 in damages from an incident while riding a train through Roanoke on January 3, 1950. The seven-member jury, which included a Black female, took one hour to deliberate before reaching a decision.

The City of Roanoke began dumping all garbage in an abandoned quarry in the northwest section of the city in mid-January due to its incinerator being inoperable. It was anticipated the dumping would last no more than three months.

Lucian Glenn of Roanoke was fatally burned in an auto accident on Starkey Road on January 20. He died at Burrell Memorial Hospital. He was forty-six. Three companions in the car with him were also injured.

Judge Samuel Graham, retired judge of the US Court of Claims, died at age ninety-three in his residence at the Hotel Roanoke on January 20. Graham served as assistant to the US Attorney General from 1913 to 1919.

A new volunteer air reserve training group was set up with headquarters at 209 W. Church Avenue. Lt. Col. Murray Coulter was appointed commander of the group.

The Roanoke Junior Chamber of Commerce named Robert Hurt as its Outstanding Young Man of the Year. Hurt was president of the Virginia State Junior Chamber of Commerce.

Salem Lodge 106, IOOF, celebrated its centennial on January 28. The fraternal chapter was organized in 1851 at a meeting held at the William C. Williams Hotel in Salem and installed N. G. Slagle as the first noble grand of the Salem Odd Fellows. Other charter officers were Waddy Thompson and John Minnix. Other charter members were Henry Slagle, Benjamin Brown, John Wade, George Anderson, and Philip Reed. Initial orders of business were purchasing writing paper, wafers, and candle snuffers. In their initial year, the Odd Fellows rented a hall in Salem from P. H. Huff. The lodge did not meet regularly during the Civil War but reorganized on October 31, 1865. Their lodge hall, possibly the same one being rented from Huff, burned in 1867, and they eventually began meeting in the Old Town Hall on N. College Avenue.

Clyde Pangborn, the first man to fly nonstop from Japan to the United States, ferried a twin-engine plane to Woodrum Field for Clayton Lemon, a local airplane dealer. He ferried the plane from Prestwick, Scotland.

Bring On the Girls came to the stage of the Roanoke Theatre on January 24 and featured Margaret Gorham, Billie Cutler, and Grandma Perkins and Company, plus the all-girl band the Martinettes.

James Hicks, war correspondent for the *Baltimore Afro-American*, spoke at the Gainsboro Branch Library on January 23 about his experiences in and assessment of Korea.

Roanoke City Council rejected a $15,000 offer from W. L. Becker & Company for the "as is" purchase of the Academy of Music during its meeting on January 22. The city manager shared with council that other groups had expressed an interest in funding its restoration. The manager also informed the council that the building was deteriorating rapidly such that city workers were often called to remove bricks from around the building that had fallen off.

Clayton Lemon stands in front of his Virginia Airmotive hangar at Woodrum Field in this 1951 image. *Virginia Room, RPL*

Roanoke City Council established a planning commission with new duties and authority as compared to its predecessor, the Planning Board. The seven members of the inaugural planning commission were W. C. McCorkindale Jr., B. N. Eubank, B. F. Parrott, C. H. Broyles, J. A. Turner, George Dunglinson Jr., and W. P. Hunter. The commission was tasked by the city manager with developing a city master plan.

Lipes Pharmacy No. 2 opened on January 25 at 2907 Brambleton Avenue SW. Lipes Pharmacy No. 1 was at 2201 Crystal Spring Avenue SW. The owner was Cecil Lipes.

Three groceries pulled out of the Mick-or-Mack chain to become a Shopwell Food Store in late January. The stores were located at 2825 Brambleton Avenue SW, 2332 Melrose Avenue NW, and 1212 Fourth Street SW.

William Payne, principal of Jefferson High School, tendered his resignation in late January effective July 1 to assume the appointment as superintendent of schools for Henderson, North Carolina.

US Senator Everett Dirksen of Illinois addressed the annual Roanoke Chamber of Commerce dinner meeting at the Hotel Roanoke on January 26. His speech to a crowd of 700 was on the potential loss of freedoms at home while defending freedoms abroad due to poor domestic and fiscal policies.

William Brown, dean of men at Talladega College in Talladega, Alabama, was appointed as the new executive secretary for the Hunton Branch YMCA effective February 1. He succeeded Lloyd Lee, who held the position for over two decades.

Little League baseball was presented to interested parties from communities in southwestern Virginia at a dinner meeting sponsored by the Roanoke Junior Chamber of Commerce on January 29. The Jaycees hoped to bring Little League to

Roanoke. Little League had grown in popularity in other states since its beginning in Williamsport, Pennsylvania, in 1939. The speaker for the event was the league's national commissioner, Carl Stotz.

Officials with N&W Railway announced plans to build six more Y6b freight locomotives, 3,000 seventy-ton hoppers, and 500 fifty-ton box cars in their Roanoke shops over the next few years. The cost of the new equipment was placed at $21 million.

Universal Atlas Cement Company purchased 680 acres of land in Botetourt County on the north side of Tinker Mountain for a cement plant that would adjoin a tract and cement operation of Lone Star Cement Corporation.

Roanoke City Police conducted a nighttime raid of nip joints on January 27 and made nineteen arrests for bootlegging.

Amos Milburn and the Ravens performed for a dance at the American Legion Auditorium on February 1 from 11:00 p.m. until 3:00 a.m. The balcony was reserved for white spectators.

Hot From Harlem, a vaudeville revue, came to the stage of the Roanoke Theatre on January 31.

Pvt. Herman Hill of Route 3, Salem, was killed in action in Korea. He had previously been reported as missing in action.

The H. H. Moore family in the Hollins section lost their home and the entirety of its contents in a fire on January 25. Given the family's needs, Chief Eugene Honaker of the Hollins Fire Station spearheaded a donation drive that provided food, clothing, and furniture for the family.

About fifty Roanoke businessmen met on January 29 to lay groundwork for forming a local branch of Junior Achievement. Don Jordan was named temporary chairman. The meeting was coordinated by the Roanoke Junior Chamber of Commerce.

Charlie Schuler, a Roanoke construction worker, discovered through a story in the *Roanoke Times* that his wife was an amnesia patient at a hospital in Winston-Salem, North Carolina. She had been missing for three days since being in a minor traffic accident on Mountain Avenue SW. How she got to Winston-Salem, she could not recall, nor could she tell doctors her identity. A photo and accompanying story appeared in the Roanoke newspaper on January 29. According to Schuler, his wife had suffered from nervous breakdowns in the past.

W. H. Hoobler, administrator of the Memorial and Crippled Children's Hospital, provided a detailed analysis of the hospital's role in caring for southwestern Virginia polio victims through January 27, 1951. According to Hoobler, the epidemic began on June 28, 1950. Since then, 450 patients had been admitted to the hospital's polio ward, with 395 having been discharged, 19 remaining on the ward, and 36 died. Of the 450 patients, 94 were diagnosed as Bulbar or Bulbospinal, 120 total paralytic, and 200 nonparalytic; a total of 44 were iron lung cases, of which 24 died. The largest number of patients, 169, came from Wythe County and Wytheville. The nursing staff was supplemented by student nurses, and all out-of-town nurses were housed at the YWCA. The National Foundation for Infantile Paralysis sent pediatric and orthopedic specialists to serve the hospital. They were Drs. M. K. Johnson, Thomas Porterfield, Harry Cox, Herman Gailey, and Lloyd

Crawford. When patients were allowed to go home, they had to remain in isolation there for seven days. Of the 450 patients treated, they were from the following counties: Wythe (169), Buchanan (61), Pulaski (35), Roanoke and Roanoke County (32), Grayson County (20), Washington (19), Smyth (17), Tazewell (12), Montgomery (12), Carroll (9), Giles (9), Bland (9), Botetourt (7), Wise (6), Franklin (5), and twelve other counties represented the remaining number.

French pianist Nicole Henriot gave a recital at the Jefferson High School auditorium on January 31 under the auspices of the Community Concert Association.

A campaign to obtain a new branch for the Lula Williams Branch YWCA was recommended by the organization's board in late January.

Mademoiselle Beauty Salon opened on February 1 at 28 W. Kirk Avenue. Ann Slone was the owner.

Home Service Foods Self-Serve Supermarket opened at 709 Franklin Road SW on February 2. Garnett Thrasher was the store manager.

Posey Nester, a thirty-three-year-old Roanoke taxicab driver, was killed when his Yellow Cab rolled down an embankment into a field east of Mount Pleasant on February 2. Three passengers were injured.

Marion Smythe, sixty-five, died on February 2 in Jefferson Hospital. Smythe was the president of National Business College, a position he had held since 1917.

Evelyn Brinkley, twenty-six, was killed instantly when the car she was in as a passenger crashed into an N&W Railway locomotive on the belt line at Franklin Road and Brandon Avenue SW on February 3.

Robert Stewart presented a piano recital at the Carver School auditorium on February 9. John Wesley Methodist Church sponsored the Julliard-trained musician's concert.

Roanoke poet Leigh Hanes published a fourth volume of poetry, *The Star That I See.*

Mrs. Gertrude West was appointed as Roanoke's first "supervisor of instruction for Negro schools." She assumed the position on February 19. She had been a teacher in Roanoke for twenty-five years.

Dusty Fletcher performed onstage at the Virginia Theatre on February 8. The balcony was reserved for white patrons.

Capt. Cecil Ware of Roanoke died in Japan on February 7 from injuries he received in an accident while participating in operations related to Korea.

The Roanoke area was used as a test project in the Booker T. Washington Birthplace Memorial program to raise funds for the organization to combat communism "among uninformed Negroes." Some 2,000 half-dollar coins were to be sold for $2 each, with each being mailed randomly to homes in the city with an appeal letter and a return envelope for the purchase. S. J. Phillips, president of the Birthplace Memorial, had the idea and managed the campaign.

Murray Coulter was appointed the new president of National Business College on February 7. He succeeded Marion Smythe who died a few days earlier. Coulter was an instructor at the college and a Roanoke native.

This is the intersection of Eighth Street and Tazewell Avenue SE in 1951. *Virginia Room, RPL*

Application for a new standard television station on channel 5 was filed by Radio Roanoke, operator of WROV, in early February. Frank Koehler, manager of Radio Roanoke, said the application requested a visual signal of 13,000 watts and a sound signal of 6,550 watts. Koehler noted that the federal government had temporarily halted applications for television stations due to the Korean War.

All traffic in downtown Roanoke was stopped for one minute at noon on February 9 when a special World Day of Prayer message was broadcast over loudspeakers that were installed at the corner of Jefferson Street and Campbell Avenue. The message was delivered by Rev. Mervin Martin of the Oak Grove Church of the Brethren. The loudspeakers had been provided by Lee Hartman. Further, all stores were asked to stop the play of canned music and tune their speakers to the three local radio stations that were also broadcasting the message that focused on praying for a world many believed was heading for a third World War.

A religious census undertaken in Salem in mid-February of some 5,000 people yielded the following responses as to church affiliations: Methodists, 1,450; Baptists, 1,350; Church of Christ, 730; Presbyterians, 375; Lutherans, 230; Pentecostal Holiness, 200; Episcopalians, 200; Brethren, 140; and Catholics, 100. The remainder was spread across other Christian denominations or Jewish. Of those surveyed, 150 said they had no religious affiliation. The survey was sponsored by six Salem churches and conducted by some 300 volunteers.

Rev. Bob Richards, US Olympic pole vault champion, conducted a weekend revival at Central Church of the Brethren in Roanoke.

Opera soprano Lotte Lehmann gave a recital at Hollins College on February 8.

The Virginia Supreme Court of Appeals granted a writ of error to Floyd Joyner Jr. in his death sentence conviction for the murder of Addie McCormack in Roanoke County on June 26, 1950. He had been scheduled for electrocution on December 4, 1950, but was granted a stay of execution until the case could be heard by a higher court. The defense claimed to have received new evidence since Joyner's conviction.

The Houston Symphony Orchestra performed at the American Legion Auditorium on February 19 under the auspices of the Thursday Morning Music Club. Efrem Kurtz was the symphony's conductor.

The Salvation Army dedicated its new transient building at 820 Norfolk Avenue SW on February 14. The forty-bed building contained a full kitchen, dining room, and lounge.

The three-member bloc of Roanoke City Council, led by Mayor Roy Webber, tried two tactics at their February 12 meeting to thwart the Roanoke Redevelopment and Housing Authority's 300-unit development for low-income whites by tabling the housing authority's request to realign streets to serve the development and the request of a subcontractor for sewer connections.

A Cardigan Welsh Corgi owned by Mrs. Margaret Douglas of Roanoke won best of breed in the Westminster Kennel Club Show at Madison Square Garden on February 12.

The Polack Brothers Circus opened for a four-day run at the American Legion Auditorium on February 14. The circus was sponsored by the Kazim Shrine Temple.

"Nudine," billed as "Queen of the cover girls," performed on the stage of the Salem Theatre for a midnight show, adults only, on February 16.

The Roanoke Booster Club announced they were planning to promote an auditorium or multipurpose building for Roanoke to replace the Academy of Music. Dr. E. G. Gill, Booster president, stated a five-man committee would coordinate the effort with other civic groups and organizations.

The Jefferson Apartments at 818 S. Jefferson Street were sold to a Richmond resident for $140,000 by Hedgelawn Nurseries.

The Seventh-Day Adventist Church on Memorial Avenue SW was dedicated on February 16 as the congregation had paid off the mortgage. Leslie Mansell was pastor.

Roanoke's first all-Black art show was held at the Gainsboro Branch Library on the second weekend of February. The show was sponsored by the art department of Addison High School and featured works by Black artists from around the country through the efforts of Mrs. Countee Cullen of New York.

Penn Kime Jr. of Roanoke had his first novel published, entitled *The Bright Circle*. The book was published by the Exposition Press of New York. Kime worked as an editorial assistant for the *Norfolk and Western Magazine*.

Three persons were killed in a shooting on February 17 at the Cinderblock Club east of Salem on Lakeside Road. The fatalities were Mrs. John Levley, thirty-eight, of Salem; Mrs. Louise Gates, twenty-five, of Salem; and William Joyner, twenty-five, of Salem. The women died at the scene, while Joyner was shot in the back as he fled the shooting and died a short time later at his home on Water Street. There were nearly thirty persons in the club when the shooting began. Investigators believed the shooting involved Joyner killing the two women, and the club manager, Robert Burks, then shooting Joyner as he fled the scene.

The Glorious Church of God in Christ at 504 Third Street NE was badly damaged by fire on February 16.

The national radio show *Share the Wealth* came to Roanoke on February 22 and taped for broadcast five episodes from the Jefferson High School auditorium. The quiz show's emcee was Peter Donald, and the broadcast selected participants from the audience. The show was aired over the CBS network.

The *Roanoke Times* conducted a mail-in ballot comic strip popularity contest during the month of February. *Gasoline Alley* was voted most popular, followed by *Joe Palooka* and *Grandma*. The same contest for readers of the *Roanoke World-News* had *Blondie* finishing first, followed by *Dick Tracy* and *Smilin' Jack*. For the combined readership of the Sunday *Roanoke Times* comics contest, first place went to *Uncle Remus*, followed by *Barney Google*, *Donald Duck*, and *Steve Canyon*.

The Roanoke Camera Club was organized on February 21 with forty persons in attendance at the club's initial meeting at the Appalachian Auditorium. The group was headed by A. J. Locker.

Hollins College celebrated Founders' Day by hosting three speakers on American foreign policy. The guests were Pulitzer Prize–winning columnist Edgar Mowrer, Dr. Burt Marshall, and Congressman A. A. Ribicoff of Connecticut.

The Body Beautiful Salon opened on February 23 on Grandin Road at Maiden Lane SW.

This February 1951 image shows the yards of the Norfolk & Western Railway. Hotel Roanoke is in the background. *Virginia Room, RPL*

Audrey Jamerson of Roanoke slipped and fell from Memorial Bridge into the Roanoke River in mid-February. Jamerson suffered a fractured ankle and back from the fifty-five-foot fall that was witnessed by two persons who pulled her from the river and sought immediate help.

The New York–based Silvertones sextet gave a concert at High Street Baptist Church on February 23.

The Roanoke Preaching Mission opened for several nights beginning February 25 at the American Legion Auditorium. The mission was sponsored by the Roanoke Ministers' Conference and featured leading speakers from various denominations.

The first of a series of films on the medical effects of the atomic bomb were shown to area doctors and nurses by the Roanoke Civil Defense in late February.

Barter Theatre presented a production of *The Heiress* at the Jefferson High School auditorium on February 26. Lead roles were played by Rex Partington and Mary Perry.

Madame Grayeb, a women's clothing store, announced in late February that it was going out of business. The store was located at 506 S. Jefferson Street and had been in business for thirty years.

The Cincinnati Symphony Orchestra gave a concert at the Jefferson High School auditorium on February 28 through the sponsorship of the Community Concert Association. Thor Johnson was the conductor.

James Hairston was struck and killed by an automobile along Starkey Road on February 27. Hairston, seventy-seven, died from his injuries at Burrell Memorial Hospital.

The Young Men's Shop at 7 W. Campbell Avenue that had previously indicated it was going out of business due to nonrenewal of their lease announced in early March their lease had been renewed.

Little Esther, Johnny Otis and his orchestra, and Redd Lyte and his Four Blue Notes all performed in one show for a dance at the American Legion Auditorium on March 2. White spectators were admitted to the balcony.

Elia Kazan's New York stage production of *A Streetcar Named Desire* came to the Roanoke Theatre for live performances March 5 and 6.

A stage production of *Snow White and the Seven Dwarfs* came to the American Legion Auditorium on March 6. The cast was from New York.

The Vinton Lions Club presented its annual minstrel show for a four-night run at William Byrd High School the first weekend in March. The show featured a cast of fifty.

The majority of Roanoke City Council voted to reject an extension on reserving $475,000 in federal funds for low-income housing. The move was another attempt to thwart the Roanoke Redevelopment and Housing Authority from moving forward on its housing developments.

Western film star Whip Wilson appeared in person at the Roanoke Theatre on March 7. He was joined by actress Monica Lane and rodeo star Homer Brown.

This March 1951 image is of the Auto Spring and Bearing Company that was located at the corner of Luck Avenue and First Street SW. *Virginia Room, RPL*

This is the interior of the Auto Spring and Bearing Company in 1951. *Virginia Room, RPL*

Bent Mountain's oldest resident Phil Thompson died in his two-room house along Route 221 on March 4. Residents believed he was at least one hundred years old, having been born a slave in Nelson County before moving to Floyd County. He helped make bricks for the Price Home, a landmark in the community, which was built in 1871. He was buried in Webbs Cemetery.

The contract for paving twenty miles of the Blue ridge Parkway from Route 460 to the Peaks of Otter was awarded to Adams and Tate Construction Company of Roanoke. The contract was for $336,041.

Avis Canter, thirty-six, died in a fire in her apartment at 1115 Ferdinand Avenue SW on March 7. Fire officials believed her bed caught fire due to a lit cigarette. She died from smoke inhalation.

Grace Methodist Church was formally reactivated on March 8. The congregation met at 4404 Williamson Road. Rev. Raymond Musser was the pastor.

Justice Herbert Gregory of the Virginia Supreme Court of Appeals died on March 8 at his home in Roanoke at the age of sixty-eight. Gregory was the youngest person ever appointed to the Supreme Court, having been selected at age forty-three.

Robert Jackson was found guilty on March 8 of first-degree murder in the death of George Bolden in Salem on January 5. Judge T. L. Keister sentenced Jackson to thirty years in the state penitentiary. The case made civil rights history in that Mrs. Sally Burks of Salem served on the jury and was the first Black woman to serve on a Roanoke County Circuit Court jury.

Building permits for six additional buildings in the 300-unit white low-income housing development on the former Horton property were issued by the city on March 9. The plot plan had been submitted by the Roanoke Redevelopment and Housing Authority.

Evergreen Burial Park advertised the creation of Fern Cliff Abbey, a garden-type mausoleum, which offered burial above ground. Precompletion sales were being offered. The structure contained 424 crypts.

Antrim Motors, shown here in March 1951, was located at 510 McClanahan Street SW. *Virginia Room, RPL*

A floor show and dance were held at the American Legion Auditorium on March 16 featuring Joe Morris and his orchestra, Lowell Fulsom and his orchestra, Little Laurie Tate, Ray Charles "Boogie Woogie Blind Pianist," and Bill Mitchell. White spectators were admitted to the balcony.

The Boy Scouts of Belmont Baptist Church dug what was believed to be Roanoke's first bomb shelter when they began excavating a vacant lot adjacent to the church on March 10. The shelter was designed after seeing plans in the local newspapers. Carl Cox was Scoutmaster.

The Roanoke Branch of the Division of Motor Vehicles opened in their new location on March 15 on Eighth Street SW, between Marshall and Campbell Avenues. Their previous location was at 1211 Fourth Street SW.

A $350,000 addition to Valleydale Packers in Salem was completed in mid-March. J. M. Turner was the contractor.

The Salem Lions Club presented its annual minstrel show the third weekend in March at Andrew Lewis High School. One of the comedy routines was performed by Salem's mayor, James Moyer.

The Roanoke-Salem Automobile Auction opened on March 15 one mile west of Salem on Route 11. The auction site was operated by Main Street Motors in Salem.

Walter Loebl, head of Loebl Dye Works in Roanoke, was elected president of the Garment Dyers Guild of America during the organization's meeting in Atlantic City, New Jersey.

Leaders within the Black community met with members of Roanoke City Council on March 12 and urged them to be cautious in cutting the number of units for the planned low-income housing development for Blacks as pursued by the Roanoke Redevelopment and Housing Authority. The group included George Lawrence, Rev. A. L. James, Rev. Maurice Macdonald, and Mrs. Juan Nabors. They said such a move could be considered discriminatory.

Jim Slaughter of Roanoke was selected for the Eastern All-Star College Basketball Team that would play the Western team in a game at Madison Square Garden on March 31. Slaughter played basketball for the University of South Carolina.

The first remains of a local soldier killed in the Korean War came to Roanoke on March 13. The body of Capt. Cecil Ware, who died in a plane accident in Japan as prep for a battle mission over Korea, was interred at Evergreen Burial Park.

Construction on the new infirmary at the Catawba Sanatorium resumed in mid-March after work was halted due to the discovery of a large underground cavern. The cavern was filled such that construction could begin. The delay had been for several months.

The Bonsack Garden Club was organized in mid-March. Mrs. Jacob Bonsack was elected president.

Goldie Landreth, forty-four, of Gilmer Avenue NW died on March 15 from injuries she had received on February 11 from being struck by an automobile near Stewartsville.

The Martin-O'Brien Flying Service based at Woodrum Field went out of business. Their hangar was taken over by Garner Aviation Service of Richmond.

Martin-O'Brien was the oldest continuous flight school in Roanoke. It originally operated from Trout Field near Fairview Cemetery beginning in 1940 and moved to Woodrum Field in 1941. The service was owned and operated by Bob Martin Jr. and Van O'Brien.

Fleming Service Center opened on Williamson Road near William Fleming High School on March 16. The managers were Bill Slayton and Noah Brammer.

Roanoke City Manager Arthur Owens declined an offer to become the city manager for Niagara Falls, New York. Owens had been offered the position with a starting salary of $16,000. Owens cited that his reasons for staying in Roanoke was the cooperative relationship he had with the city council and the progress being made.

Rev. Robert Laspley Jr., pastor the First Presbyterian Church in Roanoke, delivered the Easter sunrise service sermon at Natural Bridge on March 25. The service was broadcast nationally over the CBS network. The service, revived in 1947, was attended by 18,000.

The two-week-long Southwest Virginia Gold Medal Basketball Tournament kicked off in Roanoke on March 19 with one hundred teams entered. Rex Mitchell was the tournament director.

Showtimers, a summer stock acting company, was formed on March 17 by the Gamma Si cast of Alpha Psi Omega, the national dramatic arts fraternity, at Roanoke College. The group announced they would present six plays at Roanoke College. Mrs. Elizabeth Ross, drama teacher at the college, was elected president.

The first Black children's theatre group in Roanoke, the Beta Players, presented their first production, *Big Navajo Medicine*, at Addison High School on March 23. The Zeta Phi Beta Sorority sponsored the play.

The first one-man show of watercolors of Allen Ingles Palmer opened at the Virginia Museum of Fine Arts in Richmond on March 20. Palmer had died in a plane crash near his Cave Spring home in 1950. Some of the works displayed included a few pieces removed from the crash.

The three-person majority on Roanoke City Council opposed to low-income housing developments continued their endeavors to thwart the effort by voting down abandoning alleys and a street that existed only on paper so construction could proceed. Those in the majority bloc were Mayor Roy Webber, Walter Young, and A. R. Minton. The two steadfastly supportive of the Roanoke Redevelopment and Housing Authority were W. P. Hunter and Dan Cronin.

Red Hot and Beautiful, advertised as a "peep show with dancing darlings," came to the stage of the Roanoke Theatre on March 21.

Roanoke City Council at their meeting on March 19 rejected a proposal from Bill France of NASCAR to hold races at Victory Stadium during the spring, summer, and fall. The council offered no explanation for its decision.

Jim Slaughter of Roanoke signed to tour with the College All-Americans during the summer. They were scheduled to open their national tour with a game against the Harlem Globetrotters on April 1 at Madison Square Garden.

Roanoke's first double-amputee victim of the Korean War returned home in mid-March. Pfc. Frank Whorley Jr. lost both legs below the knee after he was trapped in fighting at the Chosin Reservoir.

Abram Staples, a former state senator, attorney general, and Virginia Supreme Court justice, died at his apartment in Richmond on March 21. Staples practiced law in Roanoke and was a former president of the Roanoke Bar Association. He served as a state senator representing Roanoke and Roanoke County in 1927 and 1932.

Over 700 persons attended the fiftieth anniversary dinner for the Roanoke Merchants Association held at the Hotel Roanoke on March 21. The Roanoke Star on Mill Mountain was deemed to be the association's greatest promotion effort in drawing attention to Roanoke.

Local Civil Defense officials and citizens visited a mobile hospital designed for the wholesale treatment of patients in the event of an atomic bombing. The hospital on wheels was parked in front of the post office in downtown Roanoke by its Washington distributor. The trailer contained ten oxygen tanks and masks, two fold-down operating tables for surgery and amputations, thirty stretchers, and seventy-five blankets. The unit cost $2,500.

On March 22, the Federal Communications Commission (FCC) announced new television channel assignments for Virginia to permit operation of anticipated new stations. The channels assigned to Roanoke were 7, 10, and 27.

This March 1951 image shows a vendor, Crumpacker Orchards, selling produce at the Roanoke City Market. *Virginia Room, RPL*

Calls poured into Roanoke Valley sheriff and police departments and to Woodrum Field with reports of a fiery red object speeding through the dusk sky on March 22. Further investigation revealed the object to be a high-flying B-25.

The twenty-fourth Home Demonstration Club in Roanoke County was organized on March 22 in Oak Grove at the home of Mrs. C. D. Wertz. Mrs. Luther Martin was elected as president.

Percy Mayfield and his recording orchestra and Cootie Williams and his orchestra performed for a midnight dance at the American Legion Auditorium on Easter Sunday.

Spring training for the Roanoke Red Sox baseball team began March 26 in Cocoa, Florida, under manager Walt Millies. Millies had been in Florida for several weeks scouting other teams.

Craig County celebrated is centennial the third week in March. The county was created from parts of Botetourt, Giles, Roanoke, and Monroe Counties on March 21, 1851, and named for Robert Craig, to whom King George II had conveyed a large tract in 1753. The county courthouse was completed in 1853.

The hot rod racing season began at the Starkey Speedway on Easter Sunday afternoon on a new half-mile dirt track. The speedway could accommodate 4,000 spectators. Buddy Hodges and Charles Williamson won the feature races.

The congregations of Trinity Lutheran Church and West Salem Baptist Church moved into their respective new buildings on March 25. The Lutheran church was located on Williamson Road at Epperly Street, and the Baptist church was on Route 11, west of Salem.

Johnnie & Jack, Kitty Wells, and the Tennessee Mountain Boys—all RCA Victor recording artists—performed on the stage of the Roanoke Theatre on March 30.

The state ABC Board opened its fourth liquor store in Roanoke at 12 Wells Avenue NE. The store was intended to relieve the heavy volume of two liquor stores on Salem Avenue.

Officials with American Viscose announced plans for a major expansion of the Roanoke plant costing millions of dollars. The expansion was awaiting formal approval of a sale of the Muse Spring water supply from Roanoke to the plant. The reported purchase price for the spring was $40,000. The plant had 3,300 employees.

The Floyd Ward School of Dancing opened its new studio on March 30 at 17 Elm Avenue SW.

Grand Piano and Furniture Company opened an annex at 114 E. Campbell Avenue on March 30. H. E. Williamson was the store manager.

The new Garden City School opened on April 2. The thirteen-room school cost $300,000. Miss Margaret Burnette was named principal.

The Salem Community Players performed *The Little Foxes* at the Andrew Lewis High School auditorium on March 30 and 31. Mrs. George Lawson and Herbert Harris played the lead roles under the direction of Mrs. Thomas Gresham.

Jimmy King, state wrestling champion in the 138-pound division, was awarded the first Jimmy Akers Memorial Trophy in recognition of outstanding character and leadership at Jefferson High School. The award was named for Akers, a graduate of Jefferson, who was killed in the Korean War.

Officials with WSLS radio station announced in late March that they had signed an affiliation agreement with the National Broadcasting Company (NBC). The station had been broadcasting many NBC programs prior to the agreement. James Moore was the station manager.

The Roanoke Civic Orchestra presented a concert of classical music at Jefferson High School on April 1. The forty-piece orchestra was conducted by Franklin Glynn.

A group of American-Jewish businessmen headed by Arthur Taubman of Roanoke began construction of a $300,000 tire factory in Israel that was the first rubber industry in Israel. The plant was located in Hadera.

Paul Roland, a pioneer in the treatment of catatonic schizophrenics, spent eight weeks at the Veterans Administration Hospital training doctors and nurses in his treatment strategies. Roland's work had been lauded by several national medical journals.

Curtis Turner of Roanoke won the 150-lap Grand National circuit race at the Charlotte Speedway on April 1. He drove his 1951 Nash Ambassador.

Bernard Gross and E. G. Ferguson, employees of Roanoke Scrap Iron and Metal Company, were killed on April 2 when the truck they were driving for the company went down an embankment and burst into flames on Route 220, five miles north of Fincastle.

The David C. Shanks, troop carrier and auxiliary hospital ship, was named for late Major General David C. Shanks of Salem. He was a graduate of Roanoke College in 1879 and the US Military Academy in 1884. Shanks was a former commandant at VPI and, for two years, governor of the Cavite province in the Philippine Islands. Further, Camp Shanks in New York was named for him.

George Morgan and his Candy Kids from the *Grand Ole Opry* performed at the Roanoke Theatre on April 4.

A new species of salamander was discovered at Dixie Caverns in late March. At least 322 had been counted in the caverns. According to the Natural Academy of Sciences in Philadelphia, it represented the largest aggregation of a plethodontid salamander recorded to date.

The entrance to Dixie Caverns is shown in this November 1951 image. *Virginia Room, RPL*

This April 1951 photo shows the Post Graduate Banquet at Hotel Roanoke for the Gill Memorial's twenty-fourth annual Spring Congress. *Historical Society of Western Virginia*

Some 500 physicians and specialists attended the annual spring medical conference sponsored by the Gill Memorial Eye, Ear, Nose and Throat Hospital. Meetings were held at the Patrick Henry Hotel with clinics at Gill Memorial.

The Southwest Virginia Savings and Loan Association opened at 360 Second Street SW on April 7. It had formerly been located at 112 Kirk Avenue SW and known as the Southwest Virginia Building and Loan Association.

The Virginia Amateur Baseball League went from six to twelve teams for the 1951 season. The teams were Buchanan, Boones Mill, Glenvar, New Castle, Elliston-Shawsville, Veterans Administration, Glasgow, Roanoke, Webster, Starkey, Back Creek, Salem, and Bedford. The league had a forty-four-game schedule.

The 343rd Medical Ambulance Company, a Black unit of the army reserve, relocated from Harrisonburg to Roanoke in early April. The unit's new commanding officer was First Lt. Jacob Thomas.

Civil Defense officials put out a call for 600 persons to be trained as nurses' aides. Local hospitals were prepared to train the volunteers, who would first be interviewed by the local Red Cross.

Weddle Plumbing and Heating moved to its new building at 1129 Shenandoah Avenue NW in early April from its previous location at 210 Fourth Street SW. J. O. Weddle Jr. was the owner.

The *Cotton Club Revue* was at the Roanoke Theatre on April 11. Advertised as "greatest all sepia show to date," it featured Jamaica Lark and her Harlem Girls along with Renee "the tornado from Trinidad."

Roanoke City Council voted 3–2 to delay a proposal to convert the city's Almshouse to a hospital for indigent care effective July 1. The council majority asked the city manager to reconsider the matter with a potential start date of January 1, 1952.

The US Census Bureau released final population figures for Virginia's cities and counties as determined in 1950. Roanoke had a population of 91,921, and Roanoke County's population was 41,486.

The Dairy Bar opened at 4608 Williamson Road on April 11 and sold ice cream, sundaes, blizzard shakes, and other ice cream–related desserts.

I'd Climb the Highest Mountain had run for twenty-six days at the Grandin Theatre and Lee Theatre and had sold 47,344 tickets, making it the largest attendance of any movie ever shown in Roanoke. It was also believed to have had the longest consecutive run of any film in the city.

The Roanoke Kennel Club held its sixteenth annual dog show on April 12 at the American Legion Auditorium, and an Afghan hound from Scotch Plains, New Jersey, was named Best in Show.

Lloyd Smith, baritone, gave a concert at High Street Baptist Church on April 13. Smith was a student at the Julliard School in New York and had been awarded a Rosenwald Scholarship.

The Roanoke Advertising Club adopted a program of various recommendations to boost Roanoke. The main recommendations included a national campaign to hype the Roanoke Star, creation of an annual Dogwood Festival, a Star City Bowl Game to be held annually on New Year's Day, landscaping around the Star with the addition of an overlook, and placing "Star City of the South" on license tags and postmarks. Kirk Lunsford Jr. was chairman of the group.

Lionel Hampton and his orchestra performed at the American Legion Auditorium on April 19. The balcony was reserved for white spectators.

Pfc. Frank Hopkins was killed in action in Korea on March 31. He was from the Mount Pleasant section.

Dr. John Everett was formally installed as the president of Hollins College in ceremonies there on April 15 and 16. Rev. James Pike delivered the inaugural sermon on Sunday, and the main speaker for the installation ceremony on Monday was Ordway Tead, chairman of the Board of Higher Education of the City of New York. The service was held in the Little Theatre and representatives from 142 colleges and universities attended.

Roanoke City Council voted to acquire the Williamson Road Water Company for $550,000 effective June 30.

Jeanne Mann Dickinson of Roanoke won the American Legion's national oratorical contest that was held in Richmond on April 16. She was a senior at Jefferson High School.

The *Peek-A-Boo Revue* came to the Roanoke Theatre on April 18 that featured "gorgeous girls in a musicalulu" along with vaudeville acts.

Lipes Pharmacy held a formal grand opening of its new store at 2907 Brambleton Avenue SW on April 17. As gifts, the store offered free Coca-Cola, balloons, and a booklet entitled *Common Diseases of Farm Animals and Poultry*. They also had cherry sundaes for ten cents all week.

The Booker T. Washington Community Service Club was organized in Roanoke as an extension of the Booker T. Washington Birthplace Memorial. Mrs. Sallie Casey was elected as the club's president.

Business in Roanoke came to a standstill at lunchtime on April 19, as workers stayed in their offices and customers left stores to seek out the nearest car radio. All stations were delivering the live broadcast of Gen. Douglas MacArthur's forty-five-minute address to Congress.

A new Bibee's Supermarket opened in mid-April at 420 Luck Avenue SW.

The Roanoke Red Sox opened their baseball season with a home game against Lynchburg on April 19. Virginia Attorney General Lindsay Almond and Roanoke's city manager Arthur Owens threw out the ceremonial first balls to open the season. Attendance was 4,600.

Famed pianist Arthur Rubinstein performed at the American Legion Auditorium on April 24 under the auspices of the Thursday Morning Music Club.

N&W Railway announced on April 21 a revision to its segregation policy as a result of an out-of-court settlement with Dr. Elizabeth Durham. The revised rule of the railroad was such that passengers would not be ejected if they refused to sit in segregated coaches, and this applied to both intrastate and interstate travel. The railroad would continue to provide separate coaches for whites and Blacks, but Blacks would not be forced to abide by the accommodations.

Hundley Painting and Decorating opened on April 22 at 358 W. Salem Avenue. The proprietor was J. W. Hundley.

The Roanoke Council, Knights of Columbus, celebrated its fiftieth anniversary on April 28 with a banquet at the Patrick Henry Hotel. The banquet speaker was Francis Heazel. There were three living charter members—T. F. Sheehan, Joseph Zerbee, and T. H. Crawley.

The daily arrivals at Woodrum Field went to twenty-six on April 29, the most in its history. American Airlines added two flights, and Piedmont Airlines added three.

A B-29 Superfortress fuselage and an F-84 Thunderjet fighter were displayed on Campbell Avenue and Jefferson Street on April 25. The exhibit was from the Air Force Exhibit Unit and sponsored by the Roanoke Chamber of Commerce.

Waverly Place Baptist Church celebrated its twenty-fifth anniversary on the fourth weekend in April. The church was started April 25, 1926, with 123 charter members. The membership in 1951 was 1,889.

Barnhart's Pure Oil Service opened on April 27 at Shenandoah Avenue and Twenty-Fourth Street NW. Roy Barnart was the owner.

The first female, Barbara Black, was elected as Student Government Association president at William Fleming High School. There had not been a female SGA president in the school's history.

The congregation of Jehovah's Witnesses in Salem dedicated their new church, Kingdom Hall, on April 29.

Rogers Jewelers, located at 110 South Jefferson Street, announced in late April that they were going out of business due to bankruptcy.

Ray Anthony and his orchestra, along with Tony Mercer, Buddy Wise, Kenny Trimble, and the Skyliners, performed for a dance at the American Legion Auditorium on May 2. Black spectators were admitted to the balcony.

The New York cast of *Mister Rogers* performed the production at the Roanoke Theatre on May 2. The touring cast included Todd Andrews, Robert Ross, Rusty Lane, and Lawrence Blyden.

Roanoke County poet Carleton Drewry had published another collection of his poems, *A Time of Turning.*

Baer's, a clothing store located at 109 West Campbell Avenue, announced in late April that they were going out of business due to the loss of their lease. They had been at the location since 1941.

Pfc. Jim Barnes of Roanoke was reported as killed in action in Korea on April 23.

The Roanoke School Board announced the appointment of Gordon Brooks as the next principal of Jefferson High School. Brooks, who succeeded William Payne, had been a teacher and coach at West Point High School, served in the navy from 1941 to 1945, and had most recently served as principal of Brookville High School in Campbell County.

Roanoke City Council agreed to remove the remaining obstacles to the Roanoke Redevelopment and Housing Authority plan for low-income housing developments at their April 30 meeting. Two of the three members who had been part of the opposition bloc conceded defeat and joined the two stalwart supporters of the plan by voting to officially vacate alleys and streets in the Horton tract. Only A. R. Minton cast the lone vote against the housing authority's request. This ended a protracted and bitter dispute between the two bodies.

This circa 1950 image shows Davidson's Esso on Williamson Road, which was owned and operated by C. R. Davidson. *Steven Davidson*

Kroger on Grandin Road reopened on May 1 following an extensive remodel. One of the key attractions advertised in the store was "electric conveyer checkout stands."

General Electric Supply Corporation held a formal opening of its new office and warehouse at 515 Norfolk Avenue SW on May 2.

The second body of a Roanoker to be brought back for burial from the Korean War arrived on May 2. Pfc. Vernon Ferris's remains arrived in a flag-draped coffin that was escorted by an honor guard to the home of his parents, Mr. and Mrs. John Ferris, on Loudon Avenue NW to await interment at the Colonial Baptist Church cemetery at Blue Ridge.

WROV announced it would become an affiliate of the American Broadcasting Company on June 15.

Professional wrestling returned to Roanoke for the year when Two-Ton Tony Galento squared off against Big Jim Austeri as the main event at the American Legion Auditorium on May 3.

Pfc. Wilbur Hairston of Roanoke was reported as killed in action in Korea by the army. He had previously been reported as missing.

A nursery for children of patients at the Veterans Administration Hospital was dedicated on May 4. The frame building had been repaired and remodeled by the Blue Ridge Post of the VFW. It was located between buildings four and six on the hospital's campus and had formerly been used by a contractor as an office during construction of buildings there.

Pfc. Elmore Turner Jr. was killed in action in Korea. He was a member of the Roanoke marine reserve unit.

The Children's Theatre presented *Snow White and the Seven Dwarfs* at the Jefferson High School auditorium the second weekend in May. The theatre was sponsored by the Roanoke Junior League, and the play was directed by Clara Black.

Curtis Turner won the 200-lap Grand National Stock Car race at Martinsville on May 6. He drove a 1950 Oldsmobile and averaged sixty-three miles per hour.

Spices of 1951 came to the Roanoke Theatre on May 9. The show advertised Sateena doing her "H-Bomb Dance" and a variety of vaudeville acts.

Midget wrestling came to the American Legion Auditorium on May 11 that featured "television star midgets." Matches were between Ski Low Low and Fuzzy Cupid, Sonny Boy Cassidy and Pee Wee James, and Jack Curtis and Bobby Britton.

Roy Milton and his orchestra and Charles Brown and his Smarties performed at the American Legion Auditorium on May 15. The balcony was reserved for white spectators.

Floor plans for the new $2.7 million remodeling of the Memorial and Crippled Children's Hospital were revealed to the public. The most noticeable feature of the architectural renderings was the nine-story addition to the front of the hospital. Hospital officials indicated the work would take two years to complete. The architectural firm was Eubank and Caldwell of Roanoke.

The cornerstone for the new Lucy Addison High School was laid in a ceremony on May 13. Several hundred attended the event at the corner of Orange Avenue and Fifth Street NW. The main speaker was Rev. A. L. James of First Baptist Church, Gainsboro, who said the new school was "an indication of improvement in better race relations and better racial understanding." Dr. H. T. Penn, a member of the school board, was singled out for his dedication to the project. The 700-seat auditorium was lauded as a future venue for Black civic and entertainment events. School superintendent Dr. D. E. McQuilkin enumerated the items to be placed in a box for the cornerstone, including a letter written by him predicting that in the future the Roanoke Valley would be one municipality and that schools would be open year round. Other speakers included Penn, Mayor Roy Webber, and the school's principal, Sadie Lawson. Mrs. Anna Keeling was the master of ceremonies.

Roanoke police conducted a roundup of panhandlers and the intoxicated during the third weekend in May on the Roanoke City Market. They made 129 arrests.

The Service League of Burrell Memorial Hospital held its County Fair Day on May 15 at the Star City Auditorium. Part of the festivities included a parade. The event was intended to raise funds for the new hospital.

A delegation of Garden City residents appeared before Roanoke City Council declaring their opposition to the city's parks and recreation department's intention to hold dances at the recreation center there. Most of the speakers were women aligned with the Nazarene and Baptist churches in that section.

Miss Loretta Jean Zeigler of Roanoke became the first female to be sworn into the US Navy in Virginia. She reported to the Naval Training Center in Great Lakes, Illinois. Zeigler was a stenographer at the Hotel Roanoke before enlisting and the daughter of Mr.. And Mrs. Lunie Zeigler of the Williamson Road area.

A member of the Jehovah's Witnesses in Roanoke was sentenced on May 14 to three years in the penitentiary for refusing to register for the Selective Service. Lindsey Martin had asserted he was a minister and therefore exempt, but Judge A. D. Barksdale disagreed, noting that Martin was employed full time by N&W Railway.

Robert Bailey III of Roanoke was awarded a Fulbright Scholarship to study in England for one year. Bailey was a graduate of Addison High School and a senior at Talladega College.

Congressman O. K. Armstrong (R-Missouri) addressed the 115 graduates of the Booker T. Washington Trade School in a ceremony at High Street Baptist Church on May 15.

The Strietmann Biscuit Company moved from 128 Albemarle Avenue SE to their new $85,000 building in Salem in mid-May.

Dr. Joseph Rhine, director of the parapsychology lab at Duke University, delivered three lectures to the doctors, nurses, and administrators at the Veterans Administration Hospital on May 17. His lectures focused on personality theory and "parapsychology and psychiatry." He was famous for his study of and belief in ESP and had authored numerous articles on telepathy.

A traveling horse show and zoo entertained for four nights on vacant land along Williamson Road May 16 through 20. The show, *Animal Oddities*, included the world's largest horse, Belgian Bob; llamas from South America; baby elephant; camels; and wild yak from Tibet.

Hank Snow, Hank Williams, the Duke of Paducah, and other stars from the *Grand Ole Opry* performed at the American Legion Auditorium on May 20.

Strietman Biscuit Company had a manufacturing plant at 1600 S. Jefferson Street, as shown in this July 1951 image. *Virginia Room, RPL*

Wes Hillman purchased the Frantz Flying Service that had been operated by T. F. Frantz for fourteen years. Hillman was a well-known flying instructor in the region.

Grand Ole Opry comics Lonzo & Oscar, Cousin Jody Summy, and Tommy Warren performed on the stage of the Salem Theatre on May 17.

On May 21 a telescope was erected on Mill Mountain to provide visitors views of the city and surrounding region. The telescope was placed on a platform near Rockledge Inn that had a roof to protect visitors from the elements. The use of the telescope cost ten cents.

Fire heavily damaged the Davidow Paint and Wallpaper Company at 24 W. Church Avenue on May 18. Seven engine companies were needed to contain the blaze.

Jane Stuart Smith of Roanoke made her professional opera debut in Detroit on May 18 in the title role of Puccini's *Turandot*. The opera was part of that city's Grand Opera Festival.

The Roanoke Cardinals opened their baseball season with a game against the Winston-Salem Stars at Salem Municipal Stadium on May 20. The Cardinals were managed by "Babe" Davis, former catcher with the Newark Eagles of the American Negro League.

Chief Lone Eagle from Oklahoma wrestled Nick Kondelis of Greece in the main event of pro wrestling at the American Legion Auditorium on May 23.

Roanoke held its second annual observance of Armed Forces Day with a parade of military units, veterans, and bands that was followed by open houses at various military establishments in the region.

The Roanoke Redevelopment and Housing Authority decided to call the low-income housing development for whites "Lansdowne Park." The 300-unit project was located on property the authority had purchased from the Horton family. The units ranged from one to four bedrooms.

First Presbyterian Church in Roanoke began a weeklong celebration of its centennial on May 20. Various speakers from Presbyterian seminaries and former pastors led services throughout the week. First Presbyterian was organized May 28, 1851, by Rev. Urias Powers, who was pastor of Salem Presbyterian Church. First Church was originally called Big Lick Presbyterian Church but changed its name to First on April 25, 1882. The original church was located in the northeast section of the city on two lots at the intersection of Union (now Jefferson) Street and Hart Avenue. The site was occupied until 1875 when the congregation moved to Church Avenue at Third Street SW. The congregation occupied its next location on McClanahan Street SW on June 23, 1929.

Roanoke City Council rejected a second plea to allow stock car racing at Victory Stadium for the summer and fall. G. W. Reed Jr., an attorney representing Bill France and Curtis Turner, appeared before council on May 21 and spoke on his clients' behalf. Councilman Dan Cronin moved that racing be allowed, but his motion died for lack of a second.

The Community Fund for Roanoke City and County formally changed its name on May 22 to "The United Community and Defense Fund." M. W. Armistead III and Arthur Taubman were chairmen of the fund's 1951 campaign that benefited various nonprofit organizations.

Wallace's Drive-In opened at 4617 Williamson Road in late May. Albert Wallace of Framingham, Massachusetts, headed the ownership group that had four similar restaurants in New England.

H. L. Roberts of Roanoke captured the Virginia doubles championship of the Virginia Trapshooters Tournament held at the Roanoke Gun Club on May 24. A. M. Dillman of Roanoke won the singles championship.

Roanoke Goodwill Industries opened a branch store at 122 E. Campbell Avenue on May 26.

Lakewood Park was the scene for the Blue Ridge Game and Fish Association's "fishing rodeo" on May 26 for those twelve and younger. The park's pond was stocked with 5,000 bream. Hundreds of children participated, with overall attendance estimated at 3,500.

Hidden Valley Country Club held an open house on May 27 for its membership to view the nearly completed golf course. A buffet dinner was served at the stable club room.

Mrs. Alyce Moore was honored as Mother of the Year by the National Conclave of Girl Friends during their national meeting in Boston on May 19. Moore was the mother of four children and active in Roanoke's public schools.

West Salem Baptist Church dedicated its new building on May 27. The guest speaker was Rev. Landon Mattox of Villa Heights Baptist Church in Roanoke.

Ray Sloan, fifty-one, was fatally injured when he fell off a ladder in the furnace room at the Stauffer Chemical Company plant on Greenbriar Avenue SE on May 28.

The comic strip *Major Amos Hoople* began running in the Sunday editions of the *Roanoke Times* on June 3.

Brown Antique Shop at 101 Commonwealth Avenue NE closed at the end of May due to the retirement of the owners.

One teenager was killed and three other teens were injured in a single-car accident while joyriding on Hershberger Road on May 29. Hugh Jones, fourteen, died being transported to Lewis-Gale Hospital.

Roanoke citizens were asked to observe a moment of silent prayer on May 30 for the nation's war dead. The call to prayer began at 11:00 a.m. with the ringing of the fire bell at Fire Station No. 1.

Eastern Home and Auto Supply opened at 3326 Williamson Road on May 31.

A ten-foot high replica of a milk bottle was displayed on the front steps of Roanoke's Municipal Building during the first week of June. The bottle's label read, "Dairy foods are essential for a strong nation."

Pfc. Charlie Boitnott died in Korea as the result of a cliff fall on April 13.

W. S. McClanahan & Company, one of Roanoke's oldest insurance firms, formally changed its name on June 1 to Gray & Perdue Insurance Corporation. Their offices were in the Shenandoah Building. The new name reflected the names of the firm's president and vice president, Harvey Gray and Emory Perdue.

The newly constructed overlook on Mill Mountain opened to the public on June 3. The covered platform was officially designated as the "Fishburn Overlook" in honor of J. B. Fishburn.

Blackburn's Pure Oil Service opened at 804 Tazewell Avenue SE on June 1. The operator was William Blackburn.

Roy Brown and his Mighty, Mighty Men Orchestra, along with Willis Jackson and his orchestra, performed at the American Legion Auditorium on June 1. The bands were joined by singer Ruth Brown.

The cornerstone for the education building at Vinton Baptist Church was laid on June 1. Rudolph Cooke, worshipful grand master of Masons in Virginia, had charge of the ceremony.

Editors of the *Roanoke Times* and *Roanoke World-News* announced additions to the comic pages of their newspapers beginning in June. *Caesar, Mandrake the Magician,* and *Cisco Kid* were new to the *Times,* and the *World-News* picked up *The Lone Ranger* and *Mutt and Jeff.*

Boy Scouts from fourteen counties in Southwest Virginia participated in the Camporee at Victory Stadium the first weekend in June. More than 1,000 boys attended.

The congregation of Waverly Place Baptist Church at Kenwood Boulevard and Fourteenth Street SE began construction on an 850-seat sanctuary and an addition to their education building at a cost of $200,000. Membership was approximately 1,300.

A joint Roanoke City Council–Lions Club–Booster Club committee issued a recommendation in early May that the Academy of Music be replaced with a multi-purpose auditorium at Maher Field and financed through a bond issue. Aside from Maher Field, the only other site considered possible was Shrine Hill.

The *Carolina Follies*, billed as an "all colored musical revue" with a "stageful of sepia sirens" came to the Roanoke Theatre on June 6.

The Valley Lee Drive-In restaurant opened near the Veterans Administration Hospital on June 5.

A Roanoke County Circuit Court jury found Hunter Thacker of Lynchburg guilty in the hit-and-run death of Waverly Mitchell on Christmas morning in 1950. The incident happened on Route 460, east of Roanoke. Thacker was given a thirty-day suspended jail sentence and fined $500.

Frank Long was chosen as Roanoke's Father of the Year by the Roanoke Junior Chamber of Commerce. Long, sixty-seven, had been active in youth work through the YMCA.

Goode Construction Company of Charlotte, North Carolina, was the low bidder for development of the 300-unit, low-income housing project for Blacks in the Lincoln Court section. Their bid was $2.9 million.

A family of eight was left homeless when their home along the Cloverdale-Bonsack Road burned to the ground during an electrical storm on June 7. All members of Frank Bowman's family escaped the blaze.

Area high schools held their graduation ceremonies during the first weekend in June. Addison High School graduated 111 students, and speakers were Everette Miller, Lois Hill, Barbara Dodd, and Van Cunningham. Jefferson High School had 384 graduates, and the commencement speaker was Dr. Sherman Oberly of Roanoke College.

Thursday nights at the American Legion Auditorium usually featured professional wrestling. On June 14, the main card featured female wrestlers—Betty Hawkins versus Beverly Lehmer.

Deluxe Laundry and Dry Cleaners opened a branch at 1820 Memorial Avenue SW on June 11. One other branch was located at 3308 Williamson Road. Mrs. Eff Wimmer was the manager of the new one.

The Roanoke Bachelors Club held a formal dance on June 14 that featured Elliot Lawrence and his orchestra.

The Goodwin-Andrews Insurance Company held a formal opening at 306 E. Main Street, Salem, on June 9. W. C. Goodwin was president of the firm.

Salem Town Council appointed William McGhee as town clerk on June 11. He succeeded Woodrow Turner.

The Roanoke Boxing Athletic Association was granted a charter by the State Corporation Commission (SCC) to operate boxing clubs, gymnasiums, and athletic fields. James Keister was president.

Red Hot & Beautiful came to the stage of the Salem Theatre on June 14 and featured Sateena, "the girl with the million dollar figure," who did her famous H-Bomb dance.

The Roanoke Booster Club left for their annual trip to the Homestead resort on June 14. The group of 300 left by train at 7:00 a.m. and returned around midnight after enjoying golf, tennis, and two banquets.

Clifford Robertson from Woodrow Wilson Junior High School captured the Roanoke city-county marbles championship held in Elmwood Park on June 12. Runner-up was Larry Vinson. Both qualified for the national championship tournament in Asbury Park, New Jersey.

The first annual B'nai B'rith Athletic Achievement Award was presented in a ceremony held in the auditorium of Jefferson High School on June 12. The winner was Everett Miller of Addison High School. Miller was quarterback of the football team, guard on the basketball team, an honor student, and president of his senior class. The guest speaker for the event was Charlie Justice, a football standout at the University of North Carolina. The other nominees were George Preas, Jerry Cannaday, James King, Jeanette Semones, Jimmy King, Stan Lanford, Bernie Mitchell, Raymond Dixon, Bill Rakes, Don Thompson, Sonny Loud, Louise Dooley, Bill Schuermann, Dick Firebaugh, Edward Whitlock, Robert Hopson, and Charles Bailey. All were from both white and Black high schools in Roanoke County and city.

Schneider Oil Company, a Sunoco service station, opened on June 14 at 4107 Williamson Road. It was their second retail station.

Davidow Paint and Wallpaper Company opened their new store at 410 First Street SW on June 15.

The First National Exchange Bank purchased the well-known home of Dr. Allen Kirk, a noted rose grower, at the northwest corner of Grandin Road and Westover Avenue SW. Bank officials indicated no immediate plans for the property.

Prince Valiant made it first appearance in the weekly color comics section of the Sunday edition of the *Roanoke Times* on June 17.

WROV affiliated with the American Broadcasting Company on June 17 and altered its program lineup to reflect that change.

Count Basie and his orchestra performed for a dance and floor show at the American Legion Auditorium on June 19. The balcony was reserved for white spectators.

Bill Monroe and his *Grand Ole Opry* Gang performed on the stage of the Roanoke Theatre on June 18.

Camp Powhatan, a $75,000 Boy Scout Camp that served troops from fourteen Southwest Virginia counties, was formally dedicated on June 16. It was completed five years after it was started. Some 500 persons attended the event, and the main speaker was Dr. Charles Smith, provost of Roanoke College. The camp was located on a 400-acre tract along Max Creek in Pulaski County.

Ginger Crowley, seventeen, of Roanoke was selected to go on tour with radio personality Horace Heidt. Heidt had heard Crowley sing when he brought his broadcast to Roanoke some months prior.

The Roanoke County chapter of the League of Women Voters was organized at a meeting in the county courthouse on June 18. Mrs. J. T. Engelby Jr. was elected as the group's first president.

Floyd Joyner Jr. won a new trial in the murder of Mrs. Addie McCormack in Roanoke County on June 28, 1950. The Virginia Supreme Court of Appeals reversed Joyner's conviction on the ground that the jury had been prejudiced by the Commonwealth's Attorney's statement in closing arguments that Joyner's guilt was enhanced by the defendant's failure to testify on behalf of himself.

A new Roanoke Country Club golf record was set on June 16 when George Fulton Jr. shot a six-under 65 on the new layout. Professional golfer Sam Snead once had a 63 on the course, but that was prior to the new course layout.

Pfc. Homer Goad of Roanoke County was killed in action in Korea on June 1. Private Raymond Duncan of Roanoke was killed in action in Korea on June 16.

Herman V. Fink was killed in an accident on his brother-in-law's farm at Blue Ridge on June 19 when the tractor he was driving overturned and pinned him.

The Children of the Confederacy held their fourteenth annual state convention at the YWCA in Roanoke in mid-June. The forty delegates elected Adrienne Gentry of Roanoke as president.

Henry Shank, seventy-seven, died on June 22 at his home in Salem. Shank was prominent in Salem and Roanoke business affairs, as he and two brothers founded the Salem Foundry and Machine Works and in about 1910 established the Shank Milling Company in Salem. He and his sons also operated a furniture business in Salem.

Fulton Motor Company opened an additional new and used car lot at 1515 Shenandoah Avenue in late June.

Grace Presbyterian Church held its first worship service on June 24 at the Cornett School of Business. The independent church had been organized by Rev. John Elliott, who resigned as pastor of Salem Presbyterian Church to serve Grace Church.

The Patchwork Players, a summer theatre group, officially disbanded in late June due to a lack of funds. The organization was formed in 1946 by college students and eventually drew young actors from around the country to participate in its summer productions around the Roanoke Valley.

A crowd of over 1,000 attended the Bridle Club Horse Show at Lakeview Farms during the last weekend in June. The twenty-event program had over one hundred entries.

The 175-foot N&W Railway chimney just east of the Roanoke passenger station at East End Shops was razed on June 25. Built in 1906, the chimney was a local landmark. A New York firm was contracted to do the dismantling.

Ernest Tudor, seventy, died at his home in Roanoke on June 24. Tudor was president and manager of the Virginia Brewing Company, president of Magic City Laundry and Dry Cleaners, and vice president of Peoples Ice and Cold Storage Company, all in Roanoke.

James Wright, twenty-seven, drowned at "Green Hole" in Tinker Creek on June 24. His companions told authorities Wright was an inexperienced swimmer. His body was recovered by the Roanoke Life Saving and First Aid Crew in about ten feet of water.

Three cast members of the Patchwork Players are shown in this early 1950s image. The Players were mostly college students. *Historical Society of Western Virginia*

Connie Sellers won the Roanoke city-county golf tournament with a fifty-four-hole total of 219. Landon Buchanan finished second with 221, followed by Doe Hicks with 224.

Rev. A. L. James, pastor of First Baptist Church, Gainsboro, was named to the Roanoke School Board by the Roanoke City Council to succeed Dr. Harry Penn, whose term ended on June 30. The decision was controversial, as the council voted 3–2 to replace Penn with James after Penn had served only one three-year term. Penn was backed by Councilmen Dan Cronin and W. P. Hunter. Cronin charged that Penn was not supported by the other council members due to animosity from a prior council election. At the same June 25 council meeting, Barclay Andrews was unanimously reappointed to the school board. Penn was the first Black person named to a school board in Virginia. The following evening at his last school board meeting, Penn thanked his colleagues on the school board for their support and stated, "The only regret I have at leaving the board is for the vile, scurrilous campaign that has been used in an attempt to defame my character." Penn said he was pleased with his successor, Rev. James. "He's my pastor and I love him."

The first ever hole-in-one fired on the number eight hole at the Salem Golf Course was made by William Bain of Salem on June 25. The hole was 288 yards and, according to local golf experts, was believed to be the longest hole-in-one on record for the Roanoke Valley.

Redd's Self-Service Shoe Store opened on June 28 at 16 W. Kirk Avenue.

Hawkins Esso Service Center opened at 4707 Williamson Road on June 29.

The city of Roanoke officially took possession of the Williamson Road Water Company on July 1. The company started in 1924 when a fire burned down an old flour mill leaving an exposed spring. In 1928 a new pump house was built on what was the Nininger estate, and that same year the first of three reservoirs was constructed.

Hoffler Funeral Home began operations on July 1 in Salem serving Black clients. The firm was located at 110 Water Street and was owned by R. W. Hoffler.

By late June construction was underway for the Bethel Baptist Church in South Salem.

Walter Howard, twelve, of Roanoke received national recognition when he was named on the "Pop" Warner Foundation 1951 Midget All-American Baseball Team. Howard was named as the starting catcher over candidates from forty-eight states. In Roanoke, he played in the South Roanoke Midget League.

Amos Milburn and his Big Little Band, the Griffin Brothers Orchestra, and Margie Day did a show at the American Legion Auditorium on July 4. The balcony was reserved for white spectators.

Connie Sellers of Roanoke won the Virginia State Amateur Golf Championship on July 4. The competition was held at the Cascades course at Hot Springs. He defeated another Roanoker, George Fulton Jr., who placed second.

Cpl. Paul Crowder of Roanoke died in Korea on June 20 as a result of drowning while swimming.

The second annual homecoming and Fourth of July celebration was held in Salem with a parade, speakers and fireworks. The parade moved from Langhorne Place to Municipal Field, and the keynote speaker was Mac Minnick, former governor of Boys State. J. G. Wertz of Lakeland, Florida, received the prize for the oldest person to attend the town's homecoming. He was eighty-nine. The Salem Lions Club served free lemonade along Main Street.

As its opening performance, Showtimers presented *Arsenic and Old Lace* on July 5 at the Roanoke College Laboratory Theatre. It was the first of six plays for their first summer season. The play was directed by Sam Good. Local actors included Loris Oliver, David Thornton, Wilson Price, Dennis McCarter, Gordon Peters, Burnette Caldwell, Dick Burton, Bill Segall, Dick Normoyle, and Charles Carper. A week later, the group did a production of *The Bat* that was directed by Leroy McFarland.

Miss Alice Horsley, a teacher at Highland Park School, was elected as a vice president of the National Education Association during the group's annual meeting in San Francisco on July 6.

Mick-or-Mack purchased, remodeled, and reopened the former Food Market at 1003 S. Jefferson Street in early July. James Kramer was the store manager.

A fire heavily damaged several buildings in the town of New Castle on July 7. Losses were estimated at $40,000. A three-story frame building at the corner of Main and Commerce Streets that housed the Red A Feed Store was a total loss. A second building owned by the Layman Brothers was heavily damaged.

The Roanoke Junior Red Sox baseball team, composed of boys ages fourteen to eighteen, played their inaugural season against various teams. Their home fields were Maher Field and William Byrd High School. The roster included Kersey Harper, Willard Matherley, Wayne Brown, Donald Basham, Ernest Owens, Clyde Martin, Frank Adams, Wayne Barr, Pete Hall, Lewis Brammer, James Brown, and Ryland Kingery. Ed Alley was the manager.

Cuban Nights Revue came to the stage of the Roanoke Theatre on July 11. Acts included Loleta Vadle and her Rhumba Band and Santa Pagan, who did her "daring dance of the tropics."

Roanoke City Council authorized the Auditorium Committee headed by Dr. E. G. Gill to determine the availability of some experts to survey the needs for a new multipurpose auditorium for the city in light of the deteriorating condition of the Academy of Music. The council also voted to officially abandon the veterans housing project located on the City Farm property effective May 1, 1952, as the low-income housing project for whites would have been completed by that time. The council believed the housing on the farm property would no longer be necessary.

In its July 10 edition, the *Roanoke Times* took an editorial position against desegregation of public schools. Noting the various lawsuits pending against Virginia school districts, the editorial opined, "Radical firebrands of both races need to be restrained and dissuaded from tactics that can cause only harm and impair the existing relations between the white and colored peoples."

Willie Correll, thirty-four, of Vinton was struck and killed by an automobile on July 10 on Route 24, east of Vinton. Correll was survived by his wife and seven children.

Ground was broken on July 12 for a $100,000 Howard Johnson's restaurant on Route 11 near Roanoke. The building location was a quarter mile from Hollins College and adjacent to the Hitching Post Motel. Martin Brothers of Roanoke was the contractor.

Mick-or-Mack grocery chain opened a new store on July 13 at Jefferson Street and Highland Avenue SW.

The Melrose Gulf Service Station opened on July 13 at 3406 Melrose Avenue NW. Proprietors were A. E. Gaylor and A. L. Shelton.

Ivory Joe Hunter and his recording orchestra played for a show and dance at the American Legion Auditorium on July 19. The balcony was reserved for white spectators.

Professional boxing returned to the American Legion Auditorium on July 20. The main event featured Eddie Green against Boyd Smith. Other matches were Freddie Krueger versus Eddie Miller and Bill Muse against Frankie Martin.

Dr. Howard Morgan was chosen as chief medical officer for the Veterans Administration Hospital succeeding Dr. Lee Sewall. Morgan had been on the hospital's staff since 1947 and was a veteran of both World Wars.

A ground-breaking ceremony was held on July 15 for the new Emmanuel Evangelical Lutheran Church at Palmetto Street and Olive Avenue in Roanoke. The congregation was organized in 1923.

Showtimers presented their third production of their inaugural summer season with Eugene O'Neill's play *Anna Christie*. In the lead roles were Kathy Bauer and Harry Mortenson.

More than 1,000 persons attended a community sing on July 14 at Fallon Park. The music programs in local parks were sponsored by Roanoke City Parks and Recreation Department. George Shaw was the song leader.

Don Leavens captured the Exchange Club Invitational Tennis Tournament championship at Roanoke Country Club on July 15 by defeating Doyle Royal. It was the third tournament championship for Leavens, a naval intelligence officer. Leavens and Ralph Adair won the doubles championship.

A controversy erupted during the July 16 meeting of the Roanoke School Board when several men spoke on behalf of Addison High School social sciences teacher Lawrence Jones, whose contract had not been renewed. Former school board member Dr. Harry Penn also appeared before the board but opposed the renewal of Jones's contract. The superintendent stated after the meeting that he did not intend to recommend retaining Jones as a teacher. Several times during the meeting, the board chairman had to interrupt the verbal sparring match between Jones and Penn, with each calling the other "mentally sick." The following day eight student organizations at Addison joined in the protest of support for Jones.

Okie Jones, singing star of the *Louisiana Hayride* national radio program, performed at the Roanoke Theatre on July 18. Joining him were Jimmy Lee, Smoky Davis, and Martha Lawson.

Mrs. Maude Elizabeth Kee, widow of Congressman John Kee (D-WV), was elected on July 17 to fill out his unexpired term in the US House of Representatives. Kee won with heavy support from the United Mine Workers in the West Virginia congressional district that included Bluefield. She became the first woman to represent West Virginia in Congress and was a former resident of Roanoke.

The Salem Chapter of the Women's Christian Temperance Union presented twenty-five petitions to state officials in opposition to a proposed ABC store in the town.

This early 1950s image shows Main Street in Salem. The Bank of Salem is at front right, across from the post office. *Virginia Room, RPL*

Ronnie Irby, thirteen, won the Roanoke Soap Box Derby on July 18, beating out fifty-five other competitors. The derby was held on Crystal Spring Avenue SW, where Irby covered 1,100 feet in 33.40 seconds. Billy Whitlow was second. John Kelley was the race director for the drivers, who ranged in age from eleven to fifteen. Thousands turned out to watch the races.

Vinton received a town clock that was erected in front of the town hall in mid-July. The clock had once been in front of a jewelry store on Second Street SW in Roanoke.

Cpl. Herbert Bruner was killed in Korea on July 5. He was a graduate of Addison High School.

The US Court of Appeals of the Fourth Circuit on July 20 upheld a lower court's sentence of three years imprisonment for Lindsey Martin Jr. of Roanoke for his refusal to be inducted into military service. Martin was a Jehovah's Witness who claimed to be a minister in that denomination.

Net proceeds from the third annual Roanoke Valley Horse Show were earmarked for the Society for the Crippled of Southwestern Virginia. The society was organized in 1926 by orthopedic surgeons to serve the region's indigent patients.

More than 8,500 customers visited the enlarged and remodeled Kroger store during its official opening on July 26 at Eleventh Street and Moorman Road NW.

The Star City Band was organized and gave its first concert on July 27 in Eureka Park. The band was led by Mark Burdette. An estimated crowd of 4,000 attended the concert.

Jane Stuart Smith of Roanoke sang the lead in Puccini's opera *Turandot* before an audience of 4,000 in Venice, Italy, on July 27. It was her European debut.

This image shows Roanoke's Jane Stuart Smith performing on the opera stage in Venice, Italy, in her European debut in July 1951. *Historical Society of Western Virginia*

A stainless steel clock was erected on the north wall of Woodrow Wilson Junior High School in late July. The clock face measured seven feet across.

Auto racing was held most Sunday afternoons at the Starkey Speedway. Regular drivers there included Buford Dillon, Jim Gillette, Gordon Snead, Early Bird Williams, Eddie Bennington, Andrew Eanes, J. B. Gillette, Baldy Wilson, John Knowles, Harry Bratton, J. C. Cash, Carl Graham, Gerald Riley, Bobby Cook, and Charlie Williamson.

Lightning struck the chimney of the Stonewall Jackson Apartments in the 1700 block of Grandin Road SW on July 28, providing a scare to the residents there. Splinters of slate from the roof flew over fifty feet, impacting cars parked on the street. Little other damage was done.

A new apparatus was installed at Lewis-Gale Hospital known as the "Air Lock" that placed newborns in an oxygen-air pressure lock to assist with respiration. It was the only one of its kind in use in Virginia. Within the first few weeks of its use at the hospital, doctors had credited the machine with saving the lives of two infants.

Bessie Harris, forty, was stabbed to death in her home on the New Castle Highway just west of the Catawba Sanatorium on July 22. Her husband, Walter Harris, was held by the sheriff in connection with the slaying.

Roanoke City Council at their July 23 meeting weighed in on the dismissal of Addison High School teacher Lawrence Jones by asking the school superintendent and board to reconsider the decision. A delegation of Black citizens led by Jones's attorney, Reuben Lawson, made an appeal to the council to intervene by lobbying for the teacher's reinstatement. According to Lawson, Jones had not been reappointed because he did not work for the reappointment of Dr. Harry Penn to the school board.

Harry Lancaster of Bent Mountain died in Jefferson Hospital on July 25. Lancaster had been a schoolteacher for twenty-four years and a former postmaster at Bent Mountain. He wrote a social column for the Roanoke newspapers on Bent Mountain for over thirty years as well as historic pieces on his community. He was fifty-five.

This 1950s photo shows Bent Mountain Elementary School. *Virginia Room, RPL*

The Roanoke County Community Cannery in Salem opened for the season in late July. Under the supervision of the Andrew Lewis High School home economics and agricultural departments, J. C. Shelton was charged with its operation. In 1950, some 26,000 cans of food were processed there between July and December by members of the community.

Officials with Continental Can Company announced in late July that the Roanoke Branch of the company would close effective November 1. The space would be taken over by the Kenrose Manufacturing Company. The plant at 315 Albemarle Avenue SE employed fifty persons and was being closed due to the increased cost of materials. A. S. Rapp was the local plant manager. Continental established the Roanoke Branch in 1912.

The Wildwood Civic League continued its efforts to have the Idlewild and Kenwood section de-annexed from the city so that the sections could get school, water, and sewage treatment services through Vinton.

A ground-breaking ceremony for a new $200,000 education building was held on July 30 at Salem Baptist Church. The building project was a shared endeavor between the congregation and the Baptist Orphanage of Virginia.

The Rogers Brothers Circus played to a full house in Salem on July 28. The circus's appearance was sponsored by the Salem Kiwanis Club as a means of raising funds for their children's work. The circus had thirty acts that featured over 200 animals.

Showtimers presented the comedy *Blithe Spirit* during the first weekend in August. Lead roles were performed by Gordon Peters, Kathy Bauer, Jeanne Dickinson, and Betty Thornton.

The Academy of Music was formally classified as a public hazard by city officials in late July due to falling bricks from the front façade nearly hitting pedestrians. Officials found that upon inspection many of the bricks could be pulled out by hand.

Joe Thomas and his recording orchestra performed at the American Legion Auditorium on August 3. The balcony was reserved for white spectators.

Carter's Fruit Market moved to its new location at 2404 Williamson Road in early August. It had previously been at 1916 Williamson Road.

The owners of Bowles Bake Shop opened Bowles Pastry Nook in Stall 26 of the City Market Building the first weekend in August. The bake shop was located at 3150 Williamson Road.

Former Roanoker Chuck Arrington returned to his hometown as a pro wrestler when he sparred against Angelo Martinelli at the American Legion Auditorium on August 2. Arrington had been wrestling professionally on the West Coast for almost two years. His match was one of several that night at the auditorium.

An abandoned concrete pool in Washington Park opened as the city's first municipal pool in early August. The city spent about $500 repairing the pool that was built in 1925 and operated as part of an amusement park, known as Dreamland, at the site for a period of years.

The Roanoke Guidance Center relocated from 1912 Memorial Avenue SW to 1412 Franklin Road SW. The center was often referred to as the Mental Hygiene Clinic as it offered treatment of emotional problems for both children and adults.

This 1943 photo shows the Academy of Music that was located in the 400 block of West Salem Avenue. It originally opened in 1892. *Virginia Room, RPL*

The new Slate Hill Baptist Church on Route 119 near Starkey was dedicated the first Sunday in August. The original structure had been destroyed in a fire. The church was founded in 1888. When the original church burned in 1946, the congregation met for several months in a Primitive Baptist Church before purchasing the Newtown School building and lot, where they worshipped for five years. The new church was built on the Newtown School site. The pastor was Rev. William Scott.

W. H. Humphries assumed ownership of the Riverjack, a local dance hall on Route 11, in early August. The establishment hosted dances every Friday and Saturday nights with the Leonard Trio and the Bill Hawthorne Orchestra providing the music.

Mel Linkous began broadcasting his local *Saturday Night Dance Party* on WSLS radio in early August. The two-hour broadcast invited listeners to phone or mail in their musical requests.

Margaret's Tavern at 1901 Orange Avenue NE became Skirter's Tavern in early August. The proprietors were Ernest Fuqua and Fred Tickle.

Showtimers presented their final play of the summer season with a production of *My Heart's in the Highlands*. Lead roles were played by Jim Welsh, Martha Searcy, and Sam Good.

Harold Sander was named as the head librarian for Roanoke's new main branch library in Elmwood Park. He came from Indianapolis, Indiana, where he was the business librarian at that city's public library. He succeeded Pearl Hinesley, who retired after thirty years in the position.

Bobby Blake (later Robert Blake) performed on the stage of the Roanoke Theatre on August 8. Blake starred in *Red Ryder* western films as the character Little Beaver.

State Senator Earl Fitzpatrick won the August 8 Democratic primary as he sought reelection to his seat representing Roanoke City. He defeated challenger Arthur Schlossberg 5,883 to 2,950. Fitzpatrick carried twenty-one of twenty-eight precincts. Fred Hoback of Salem won the Democratic primary for the Twenty-First Senatorial District by defeating John Spiers of Radford 5,986 to 5,395. Hoback was seeking to unseat the incumbent Republican Ted Dalton in the general election.

Roy Minnix poses in front of his new 1951 Chevrolet in Roanoke's Jackson Park. *Roy Minnix*

In Roanoke County, incumbent House of Delegate member Ernest Robertson held off a challenge by Keith Hunt in the Democratic primary by a vote of 2,354 to 2,243. Sheriff H. B. McManaway defeated Emmett Waldron 3,344 to 1,281. Commissioner of the Revenue W. C. Muse held off Joe Hardison by a two-to-one margin. Only one incumbent on the Board of Supervisors was challenged, and that was Mason Cook, who lost to W. E. Cundiff, 736 to 441, in the Big Lick District seat. Howard Starkey and H. A. Tayloe of the board were renominated without opposition.

Charles Albert, prominent contractor of Salem, died on August 7 at age seventy-four. Albert was president of Albert Brothers Contractors and was chairman of the board of directors for the Bank of Salem. Albert had resided in Salem since 1925.

Dairy Queen opened at 1902 Memorial Avenue SW on August 8. As an opening day special, ice cream cones were one nickel and sundaes were fifteen cents.

The National Duck Pin Bowling Congress ranked Steve Lindamood of Roanoke as ninth in the nation for the 1950–51 bowling season.

Skyline Studio, a combination art, photography, and hobby shop, opened on Clay Street in Salem on August 10.

An extensive fish kill occurred in the Roanoke River from Salem to Buzzard Rock Ford in the first week of August. Officials with Virginia Tech were unable to trace the chemical that resulted in "many tons" of fish being killed.

John Baugh of Roanoke County was killed in an auto accident on August 11 in the Catawba Valley. Baugh was a passenger in a car driven by Arthur Persinger that left the road and struck a fence.

Buddy Johnson and his recording orchestra performed at the American Legion Auditorium on August 16. The balcony was reserved for white spectators.

Fairland Lake just off Cove Road NW was opened to the public for the first time in mid-August for fishing. The lake had been offered to the city for purchase for recreational purposes, but the sale price was deemed too high. M. W. King managed the lake that had been stocked with trout and other species.

A cornerstone-laying service was held on August 12 for the new sanctuary of Waverly Place Baptist Church. Dr. Wade Bryant of First Baptist Church was the guest speaker for the afternoon event.

The third annual Roanoke Valley Horse Show was held August 16–18 at Lakeview Farm, one mile north of the city on Route 11. A crowd of 2,500 attended on opening day.

Mrs. Mary Macgurn retired from the faculty of National Business College after fifty years of service. She came to the college as a student in 1899 and soon became an instructor in shorthand. She later taught in the Department of Dictation and Transcription. It was estimated she had taught 45,000 students during her career.

Sgt. George Cauley of Roanoke County was reported killed in action in Korea.

Three acts performed at the Roanoke Theatre on August 15. Tommy Magness and his Tennessee Buddies, the Johnson Brothers, and Ray Myers—an armless musician from *Ripley's Believe It or Not!*—entertained a packed house.

The Starkey Speedway came under new management in mid-August, as auto races became supervised by Eddie Allgood of the Danville-Lynchburg-Henderson Speedways.

Bush-Flora Shoe Company opened a new store at 109 W. Campbell Avenue on August 16. The company was formerly located at 130 W. Campbell Avenue. The shoe company was established in 1900 by E. L. Bush and for the first twenty-five years was located on Salem Avenue.

Martin Brothers Contractors was awarded a $138,670 contract for an addition to Belmont School that would include two classrooms, a multipurpose room, a cafeteria, and a workshop.

Showtimers ended their inaugural summer season in the black with assets of $300. The plays were seen by 2,988 persons, or an average of 116 per performance. The group also had 211 season ticket holders. Elizabeth Ross was elected president of the group for the next year.

Juanita Stanley won the women's singles championship in the city-county tennis tournament held at South Roanoke Park. She defeated Suzanne Glass. Lu Merritt won the men's singles championship by defeating Charley Turner. Kitty Coxe and Juanita Stanley won the women's doubles championship, and Merritt and Frank Snow won the men's doubles championship. The tournament concluded on August 19.

Leo Henebry of Roanoke was elected president of the American Retail Jewelers Association during the group's annual convention in New York City in mid-August.

A Delaware corporation headed by John Rollins purchased all the stock in the Roanoke Lincoln-Mercury Sales Corporation effective August 8.

Lawrence Jones, former teacher at Addison High School, accepted the position of executive secretary at the P. S. Brodnax Branch YMCA at Danville. He was at one time the acting executive secretary of the William A. Hunton Branch YMCA in Roanoke.

The Hollins Motel was located at 1231 Lee Highway, north of Roanoke. This image is dated August 1951. *Virginia Room, RPL*

Grand Ole Opry star Little Jimmy Dickens performed at the Roanoke Theatre on August 22.

Clifton Britt, thirteen, was honored as Roanoke's first "Young Mr. Baseball" by the city's parks and recreation department. The award was presented to the best player in the city's Midget League. Britt was the catcher for the Norwich Park team.

The First National Exchange Bank began advertising a new service for customers that was available at their Williamson Road Branch—the drive-in window. "No parking worries…bank from your car," read the ads.

A time capsule containing a history of the development of aviation in Roanoke was placed in the floor of the new administration building at Woodrum Field on August 24. While there was no formal ceremony, airport manager Marshall Harris said there would be a gathering of "old-timers" for the occasion. The capsule contained photos, maps, and newspaper clippings pertaining to the valley's early aviation.

Old Dominion Candies began moving its manufacturing plant from Roanoke to Salem in mid-August. The company had about seventy-five employees and produced one million pounds of candy per year.

E. M. Funk, forty, of Harrisonburg drowned in Carvins Cove on August 24 when his fishing boat capsized. Rescued from the accident was M. H. Bradford of Roanoke. Members of the Roanoke Life Saving and First Aid Crew and the Hollins Fire Station worked in vain to resuscitate Funk.

Juanita Stanley of Roanoke lost to Margaret Hench in the Virginia women's singles championship title match in Charlottesville on August 25. Hench was the tournament's top seed.

Fowlkes & Kefauver, a realty company, began advertising house lots in Windsor Court in mid-August for $2,500. C. F. Kefauver advertised house lots in the Summerdean development near Hollins for $1,500.

The Junior League of Roanoke celebrated its twenty-fifth anniversary, having been founded in Roanoke in 1926 by a group of twenty women. The first president was Mary T. Goodwin. By 1951, membership was around 250. In 1928, the Roanoke league qualified to affiliate with the national organization by participating in two community projects—Red Cross public health services and a day nursery. The biggest project undertaken by the league came in 1930–31 when the group built a wing on the Roanoke Hospital and staffed it with volunteers. One of the best fundraisers was a 1932 super dance held at Lakeside with Guy Lombardo as the entertainment.

A new Spanish-style hotel was completed at Traveltown Tourist and Hotel Court northeast of Roanoke on Route 11. The new addition to the tourist court's campus could accommodate sixty persons.

The Roanoke Fair opened on August 27 for six days at Maher Field. The fair had agricultural, industrial, and livestock exhibits, Broadway acts, nightly fireworks, and a midway.

A weeklong Tri-City Youth Revival sponsored by the Baptist churches of Roanoke, Salem and Vinton concluded in late August. It was estimated that over 10,000 persons attended one or more of the services that were led by Howard Butt and Frank Boggs of Texas.

Landon Buchanan won the Roanoke Country Club golf championship, defeating Connie Sellers 7 to 6. Jimmy Trinkle won the club's men's singles tennis championship, and Katherine Lawson captured the women's title. Trinkle defeated Barton Morris Jr., and Lawson won against Kitty Coxe.

Awakening Service, a business that called daily to wake persons up, began operating in late August. The charge for the wake-up calls was $1.50 per month.

Roanoke City Council authorized the city manager to determine the best way to raze the Academy of Music, including any salvaging of its contents, at their regular meeting on August 22.

The Roanoke City School Board was issued a permit to make alterations to Morningside School. The work would include a multipurpose room, kitchen, shop, library, and two bathrooms for a cost of $116,000.

The *Hadacol Caravan Show* came to Maher Field on August 31 with an array of performers, fireworks, clowns, circus acts, and beauty queens all preceded by an afternoon parade. Entertainers and celebrities included Dick Haymes, Carmen Miranda, Jack Dempsey, Canady Candido, Minnie Pearl, and Hank Williams. Attendance was 8,000. The biggest draws were Hank Williams and Minnie Pearl. The show also included Ted Evans of England, who claimed to be the tallest man in the world at nine feet, three inches.

Eddie Allen was crowned as the Salem golf champ when he defeated David Edmunds, 1 up, in the finals of the town tournament staged at the Salem Golf Course on August 27.

Lucky Millinder and his orchestra performed for a floor show and dance at the American Legion Auditorium on September 2. The balcony was for white spectators.

Francis Rivinus, general counsel for N&W Railway, died in a Roanoke hospital on August 30 at age sixty-eight. He had been involved in numerous business and civic activities in the city and had chaired the Roanoke Public Library Board since 1942.

JoBelle, a women's accessories store, opened on August 31 at 22 W. Campbell Avenue.

Northwest Variety Store at 2308 Melrose Avenue NW held a grand opening on September 1.

Devon Cawthorne, twenty-six, was killed when the car he was driving struck a tree at Memorial and Cambridge Avenues SW on September 1. Four passengers were injured.

The subscription price for the daily carrier-delivered *Roanoke Times* increased five cents to forty cents per week.

Warner Brothers Studio signed a contract with Ginger Crowley of Roanoke. Crowley, seventeen, got her start as a singer locally with the Freddie Lee Orchestra.

Lloyd Garrett, twenty-three, of Roanoke was killed in a hunting accident in Franklin County on September 2. It was believed that his shotgun discharged when he slipped down an embankment.

Over one hundred volunteers participated in one of the largest single-day community service projects in Roanoke's history when they cleaned up the Roanoke

River on Labor Day at Wasena Park. The project was sponsored by the Roanoke Civitan Club.

Roanoke City Detective Jack Mitchell went to visit friends in Washington, DC, for Labor Day and took in a Senators-Yankees baseball game at Griffith Stadium. While at the game, he noticed among the 20,000 fans a man whose face he recognized—Henri Meincke of Roanoke. Meincke had been reported missing by his wife and employer since mid-August. Mitchell phoned DC police who, in turn, obtained an arrest warrant and apprehended Meincke on a charge of nonsupport.

Roanoke golfer George Fulton Jr. won the Fair-Acre Golf Tournament at Hot Springs on September 3. He had won the title previously in 1949.

Roanoke City Council chose A. R. Minton as the city's next mayor at their meeting on September 4. His selection was unanimous. Roy Webber was elected to serve as the vice mayor.

Talk About Girls came to the stage of the Roanoke Theatre on September 5 and featured Amy Fong, an exotic dancer, along with a dancing chorus.

Lucky Millinder returned to perform at the American Legion Auditorium on September 11, but this time the dance was for white patrons. The balcony was reserved for Black spectators.

Davidow Paint and Wallpaper held a formal grand opening on September 6 at its new location, 410 First Street SW.

A spokesman for WFMY-TV in Greensboro said that the government's permission for the station to increase its power to 5,000 watts would mean much-improved television reception for the Roanoke Valley. The power increase would go into effect September 22.

Club 88 opened on September 8 at Paul's Steak and Chicken House on Route 11, two miles north of Roanoke. The Leonard Trio performed for the club's opening.

The all-local *Kommunity Kwiz* returned to WROV on September 15. The Friday night game show, which first aired in 1950, was quite popular and involved teams from local clubs and civic organizations competing to answer questions. The host was Hayden Huddleston.

The cornerstone for the new Bethel Baptist Church was laid on September 9. The two-story cinder block building was located at Martin Street and Bowman Avenue in Salem and was erected by volunteer labor. The church's membership was eighty-seven. The guest speaker for the afternoon ceremony was Rev. James Bryant of Richmond.

Miss Lillian Craig of Roanoke, a schoolteacher, published her fourth book. *The Singing Hills* was a novel about the Southern Highlanders of Virginia and surrounding states.

Prominent Roanoke clergyman Rev. Robert Lapsley Jr. announced on September 9 to the congregation of First Presbyterian Church that he would retire effective December 31. Lapsley had served the church as pastor for twenty-one years.

New Castle defeated Salem for the Virginia Amateur League pennant. It was their seventeenth straight win for an overall record of 35–9. The other top clubs were Buchanan, 34–10; Glenvar, 31–13; and the Veterans Administration Hospital, 31–13.

Roanoke City Council denied a long-standing request to de-annex the Idlewild-Kenwood subdivision that it had annexed in 1949. The council voted 4–1 to deny the citizens' request.

Legs and Laughs of 1952 came to the stage of the Roanoke Theatre on September 12. The vaudeville-style variety show featured comedian Sully Mason and dance duo Vance Henry and Anita Ellis and was "jammed packed with girls," according to ads.

Roanoke schools superintendent D. E. McQuilkin reported that total enrollment for the 1951–52 academic year was 13,765 students, the most in Roanoke's history.

A meeting to organize the Toastmasters Club in Roanoke was held on September 10 at the Shenandoah Club. Roy Herrenkohl was elected temporary chairman, while G. S. Dunn acted as toastmaster for the meeting.

One of two massive smokestacks at the N&W Railway Shops was razed, brick by brick, during September. The 175-foot structure had been erected in 1906 and contained over 180,000 bricks. New power plant equipment made the stack obsolete.

Test borings for a proposed viaduct of the N&W Railway tracks at Jefferson Street were begun on September 10. Engineers with the state highway department said that rock was struck at nine feet. Thirty-six borings were done in total over a two-week period. The viaduct would eliminate the grade crossing and replace the East Second Street Bridge.

Roanoke Pet Shop opened on September 12 at 29 W. Salem Avenue. Mrs. Irma Bower was the owner and manager.

The Roanoke Star on Mill Mountain was literally "on the map" when it was placed on all new aeronautical charts for military and civilian flyers being published for 1952.

An organization was formally established on September 12 to develop a fine arts museum in Roanoke. Dr. Sherman Oberly, president of Roanoke College, was named as head of the twenty-one-member board of trustees of the Roanoke Fine Arts Center. The group planned to use the new main library as the site of its first exhibit. The stated purpose of the center was "to encourage and develop interest in and the study of the arts; to provide ways and means for the purchase of works in the arts; and to exhibit fine arts and other works of art."

Calvary Baptist Church in Roanoke dedicated its new youth activities building and renovated education building on September 13. The education facility had been damaged by fire.

Sam Weems, superintendent of the Blue Ridge Parkway, stated that Roanoke was not taking full advantage of its position along the parkway as the largest and most centrally located city. Weems made the comments in an address to the Roanoke Rotary Club. Weems suggested a spur from the Parkway to Mill Mountain and that the city invest more in advertising and promotion.

The Social Service Clubs of Roanoke County, working with the Public Health Administration, formed the County Federation of Social Service Clubs in a meeting at the Hotel Roanoke on September 13. Mrs. C. L. Gregson of Back Creek was elected president.

South Salem Christian Church laid a cornerstone for its new education building on September 16.

Roanoke native Robert Claytor joined N&W Railway's legal staff on September 15 as solicitor. Claytor had been with American Telephone and Telegraph in New York City since 1948.

Two Roanoke brothers, Jerry Newton and Wayne Newton of 1719 Rutrough Road SE, were winners in the *Junior Revue* television show talent contest at WNBW in Washington, DC, on September 9 and became eligible to compete in the semifinals on September 16. Jerry played the Spanish electric guitar, and Wayne played the Hawaiian electric guitar. Both had been commended to the contest after appearing at a Roanoke Parks and Recreation Department Community Sings program.

Old Dominion Motor Corporation moved from 2613 Williamson Road to 308 Orange Avenue NE in mid-September.

Johnny Otis and his orchestra, along with Mel Walker, Little Esther, and Redd Lyte, performed for a show and dance at the American Legion Auditorium on September 17. The balcony was reserved for white spectators.

Renowned concert violinist Quincy Meeks performed at St. Paul's Methodist Church on September 16.

The first N&W Railway Employees' Golf Tournament since 1938 was held at Monterey Golf Course, and the winner of the two-round event was Blake Humphreys with a score of 146. Clyde Angle placed second.

A truck plowed into an automobile on Route 11, west of Salem, on September 17, killing three people. Roy Lowry, forty-eight; Bertha Bradford, twenty-nine; and Betty Witt, fourteen, were killed upon impact. The truck, driven by Arland Taylor, was loaded with seven tons of asphalt mix when it struck the car. Four others in the car were seriously injured. Capt. J. L. Goodwin of the Salem Rescue Squad said it was the worst accident he had ever seen.

Tan, Torrid & Terrific came to the stage of the Roanoke Theatre on September 19. The show featured what ads described as "strange and secret dances," "uninhibited tropical maidens," and "sinuous bodies and hypnotic music," along with a Tahitian native orchestra.

The Ross-Bailey School of Dancing opened on September 22 at 506 S. Jefferson Street.

The Roanoke Junior Chamber of Commerce sponsored a free show for kids at Victory Stadium on September 22. Attendance at the event was estimated at 10,000. The main attraction was child actor Bobby Benson of the *B-Bar-B Ranch Riders* radio broadcasts. John Norman hosted the actor at their store in the second-floor Corral Shop earlier the same day.

Piedmont Airlines began advertising new commuter service. Round trips daily were offered to Lynchburg ($2.65), Richmond ($9.05), Charleston, West Virginia ($7.10), and Norfolk ($14.05), among others.

A jury in Roanoke County Circuit Court found Walter Harris guilty of first-degree murder in the slaying of his wife, Betty Harris, on July 22. His punishment was fixed at life imprisonment.

Club Cherokee formally opened on September 22 at its location along Lee Highway, two miles east of Salem. Dancing was held every Saturday night with music provided by Bill Hawthorne and his orchestra, and television viewing was also provided.

Lester Flatt, Earl Scruggs, their Foggy Mountain Boys, and the Foggy Mountain Quartet performed at Fort Lewis School on September 20. They were also joined by three comedians—Chubby Wise, Everett Lily, and Jody Rainwater. The show was sponsored by the Glenvar Pennington Baseball Club.

Officials with American Viscose announced on September 20 that plans were being implemented to partially shut down the Roanoke plant due to trends in the textile market. Specifically, two of the six spinning departments at the plant were to be closed.

Yale and Towne Manufacturing in Salem accepted responsibility for a large fish kill in the Roanoke River on August 10. The September 20 announcement by company officials resolved the mystery of the kill that was the result of the dumping of twenty gallons of plating waste that resulted in the deaths of thousands of fish.

State Senator Earl Fitzpatrick, who was aligned with the Byrd organization, endorsed fellow Roanoker Lindsay Almond Jr. for governor. Almond had yet to announce but was widely rumored at the time of the endorsement to be a candidate, and Fitzpatrick was the first of the Byrd machine stalwarts to endorse Almond. Almond was serving as Virginia's attorney general.

Phyllis Brown, seventeen, died from injuries she sustained in an auto accident on September 22. She died at Burrell Memorial Hospital and was a resident of Roanoke.

Elsie Durham, fifty-nine, leapt from Wasena Bridge to her death on September 21. Members of the Roanoke Life Saving and First Aid Crew retrieved the body from the Roanoke River. The jump was witnessed by two passing motorists who notified authorities.

To celebrate the company's sixty-ninth anniversary, Kroger held a free community square dance in their parking lot at their Williamson Road location on September 24. Music was provided by Wayne Fleming and his Country Cavaliers.

Dalton McMillan, forty-eight, of Roanoke died on September 22 from injuries he had sustained a few days prior when his motorcycle hit a dog and threw McMillan to the pavement.

The world's largest swing-type bridge was being constructed in Virginia, between Yorktown and Gloucester Point across the York River. The George Coleman Bridge's price tag was projected at $9 million, and it was being fabricated by Virginia Bridge Company in Roanoke.

The cornerstone for Roanoke County's new West Salem School was laid on September 22. Music was provided by the Andrew Lewis High School choir, and the main speaker was the county school board chairman Lester Whitmore. The sixteen-room school on North Bruffey Street had a construction budget of $370,000, plus $50,000 for equipment. Lucas & Fralin of Roanoke were the general contractors. It was to be the first new school in the county since 1940.

Roanoke City Council repealed on September 23 a three-year-old ordinance limiting the term of the presiding officer (mayor) to one year and prohibiting re-election. The council opted for a two-year term instead.

Floyd Joyner Jr. went on trial a second time on September 24 in Roanoke County Circuit Court for the brutal slaying of Addie McCormack in June 1950. Joyner had previously been convicted in the case of first-degree murder, but the verdict was later set aside by the Virginia Supreme Court of Appeals, and a new trial was ordered. The trial lasted two days, and Joyner was again convicted and sentenced to death in the electric chair on December 12. The jury deliberated slightly less than four hours before reaching its decision.

Stuart Saunders was named as general counsel for N&W Railway effective October 1. Saunders had been with the company's legal department since 1939 and had served in numerous civic leadership roles in Roanoke. At forty-two, he became the youngest person to hold the position in the history of N&W.

Roanoke's Board of Zoning Appeals denied the request of Dixie Drive-In Corporation for a nonconforming permit to build a drive-in theatre on a five-acre tract across from Fairview Cemetery.

The International Rescue and First Aid Association held its annual meeting at the Hotel Roanoke that was attended by over 400 volunteers from Maine to California. The meeting was chaired by Julian S. Wise of Roanoke, who helped found the organization in 1948.

Charles Janney, thirty-three, died from injuries on September 29 he sustained when the car he was driving hit a tree along Route 221 south of Roanoke.

Cpl. Samuel Wilkerson, twenty-one, of Roanoke was killed in a Jeep accident in Japan. He had just reenlisted in the army for an additional three years. He had been stationed in Japan for thirty-one months.

N&W Railway announced on September 29 that it had placed an order with Virginia Bridge Company of Roanoke for 1,000 seventy-ton all-purpose gondola cars at a cost of $6.5 million.

Roanoke City Council adopted a real estate tax rate for 1952 of $2.75 per $100 of assessed value, up from $2.66. The reason was the city's increased debt due to capital projects.

Blackface comics Jammup and Honey, along with the Deep Elm Quartet and the Double-R Cowboys, performed at the Roanoke Theatre on October 3. All were part of the *Grand Ole Opry*.

C. Francis Cocke of Roanoke was elected president of the American Bankers Association at their annual meeting in Chicago on October 3.

The Shenandoah Drive-In Theatre Inc. was given permission to construct a drive-in theatre at 3320 Shenandoah Avenue NW. The projected cost was $6,000.

The Vinton Chamber of Commerce received a charter from the State Corporation Commission in early October. The chamber had been organized eighteen months prior. W. H. Harris was president.

A twelve-minute movie showcasing the Hotel Roanoke was made in early October as a means of showcasing the hotel's amenities for potential convention clients. The director was Charles Beeland of Atlanta.

The Roanoke Academy of Medicine responded to serious criticism about its members not answering emergency calls at night such that the medical group provided a list of its members who were willing to assume such duties with the aid of the police department. Any resident needing assistance was to call the police, who in turn would contact a physician. Prior to this, residents simply called physicians directly.

Vincent Engdall, twenty-eight, of Salem was arrested on October 2 by the FBI in Litchfield, Connecticut, for allegedly absconding with over $20,000 of his employer's money. Engdall would face trial in Roanoke.

The Shenandoah Life Insurance Company acquired all the stock in WSLS radio. The insurance company had been a majority owner in the station since 1940.

Arthur Younger of Roanoke was killed in a construction accident while working on the new Addison High School on October 3. Younger, twenty-six, fell from scaffolding and died at Lewis-Gale Hospital.

The Shenandoah Life Insurance Company headquarters, as shown in this 1950s image, was located at 2301 Brambleton Avenue SW. *Virginia Room, RPL*

Sibert Weeks, fifty-two, of Troutville walked into Carter and Jones Dry Cleaning at 502 Eleventh Street NW on October 4 and shot his estranged wife who was working there. Wounding her, Weeks then shot Jesse Dogan, also an employee. He walked out of the dry cleaning plant and, a block away on Moorman Avenue, sat on a curb and committed suicide.

The Christian Fellowship C.M.E. Church held its first service on October 7. The congregation had purchased the former Maple Street Baptist Church at 407 Loudon Avenue NW. Bishop W. Y. Bell was the guest speaker.

Jennings-Shepherd Company opened at its new location at 24 W. Church Avenue on October 5.

Pfc. Elzia Edwards, nineteen, of Roanoke was reported killed in action in Korea. The date of his death was given as September 22.

The Barter Theatre presented the *Merchant of Venice* at the Jefferson High School auditorium on October 7.

The University of Virginia defeated Virginia Tech in a football game, 33–0, played at Victory Stadium on October 5. Attendance was estimated at 12,000. The game was attended by Virginia Governor John Battle and US Senator Willis Robertson.

This circa 1951 image shows the Williamson Building on the northwest corner of Church Avenue and Jefferson Street. The building was razed in 1977. *Virginia Room, RPL*

Jose Limon and his dance company performed at Hollins College on October 15. Limon helped to pioneer the popularity of modern dance.

Movie actress Jane Nigh arrived in Roanoke on October 8 to begin a weeklong tour through Western Virginia. Her trip was in connection with the *Movietime, USA* campaign.

Roanoke Police Superintendent Stuart Bruce suspended four policemen on October 9 for "spreading malicious rumors" about him and a former female city employee. Bruce claimed the policemen had told others that he was named in a divorce settlement suit which he had not been. The officers were each suspended for five days.

Richard Hart, fourteen, of Salem had been missing from the home of his parents for a week, and a search by local law enforcement had yielded not results. On October 9, Hart arrived at the home of his aunt in Denver, Colorado, having hitchhiked for three days across the country.

Newton Light, forty-seven, of Garden City died at the Veterans Administration Hospital on October 9. He was a survivor of the Bataan death march during World War II.

American Floor Covering Company opened on October 10 at the corner of Orange Avenue and Eleventh Street NW.

A Major League Baseball exhibition game between professional white and Black players was held at Maher Field on October 12. Players for the white team were Gil Hodges, Eddie Robinson, Bill Goodman, Sid Gordon, Gene Woodling, Chuck Stobbs, Randy Gumpert, Tommy Byrne, and Gene Hermanski. Players for the Black team were Roy Campanella, Don Newcombe, Luke Easter, Willie Mays, Monte Irvin, "Suitcase" Simpson, and Hank Thompson.

The National Park Service sent a letter to Roanoke officials stating they would provide technical but not financial assistance to the city for a parkway spur at Mill Mountain. The concept of a spur road had been first proposed in 1942.

The Republican Woman's Club was organized in mid-October at a meeting in Salem. Mrs. I. M. Wigginton Jr. was elected club president.

Lt. Stewart Boyden of Roanoke, twenty-four, was killed in action in Korea on October 4.

The Dominoes, along with Cootie Williams and his orchestra, performed for a dance at the American Legion Auditorium on October 16. The balcony was reserved for white spectators.

Spike Jones and his *Musical Depreciation Revue of 1952* came to the American Legion Auditorium on October 15.

Seven of eight siblings from Bent Mountain held their first reunion in forty years in Gloucester. The children were all born to Mr. and Mrs. J. W. Palmer of Bent Mountain. Mrs. Palmer died giving birth to the eighth child, and consequently the children were separated to be raised by others. One sibling was unable to be located for the reunion.

Will Wimmer works on his farm in the Bent Mountain section in this 1950s photo.
Virginia Room, RPL

Municipal officials in Roanoke, Salem, and Vinton all expressed concerns about rickety television antennas being erected on houses and buildings due to improved broadcast wattage from a station in Greensboro. All three governments began developing building codes to regulate the antennas.

Dedication services for the new Trinity Lutheran Church, on the corner of Williamson Road and Epperly Avenue NW, were held on October 14.

John Thornton, sixty-three, died on October 14 in a Roanoke hospital of a heart ailment. He acquired the Salem Publishing Company in 1933 and thereby became publisher of the *Salem Times-Register*. He also helped organize the Salem Chamber of Commerce.

Horace Stone, twenty-nine, of Roanoke died in an auto accident on Route 460 near Montvale on October 14. He burned to death due to a collision with another car. A passenger, W. G. Alouf, was dragged from the burning car by a Bedford County deputy and recovered in a hospital.

New Castle defeated Buchanan to win the Virginia Amateur League championship. They had previously won the regular season pennant.

Metropolitan Opera mezzo-soprano Martha Lipton gave a concert on October 16 at the Jefferson High School auditorium. Her appearance was sponsored by the Roanoke Community Concert Association. The crowd of 1,000 asked for six encores.

The Roanoke Ministers' Conference finalized plans to adopt the Greek village of Pontikates, whereby congregations would provide needed materials and support.

Mick-or-Mack grocery stores began offering Double Green Stamps Day every Tuesday. Customers got two stamps for every dime spent.

Some fifty persons attended a meeting at St. Paul's Episcopal Church parish house on October 15 to form a Salem chapter of the Junior Chamber of Commerce. Charlie Smith was elected temporary chairman.

A copper-clad time capsule was placed in the concrete floor of the auditorium in Roanoke's new Health Center on October 17. The capsule was expected to be opened in 2001. The vault contained letters, pictures, official manuscripts, and other documents that depicted life in Roanoke in 1951.

A parade of entertainers performed at the American Legion Auditorium on October 22. The lineup included Duke Ellington, Nat King Cole, Sarah Vaughan, Timmie Rogers, Peg Leg Bates, Stump & Stumpy, Patterson & Jackson, and the Marie Bryant Dancers. The auditorium was "equally divided for White and Colored patrons" according to ads.

Mrs. William Garst of Roanoke County won $4,000 in prizes through a national contest she entered through WROV. She completed in twenty words the sentence, "Radio has made me a better American because…"

Belmont Baptist Church celebrated its fiftieth anniversary on October 21. The occasion was marked by a weeklong revival led by Rev. P. H. Chelf.

A sixty-five member opera company performed Strauss's *Die Fiedermaus* at the American Theatre on October 22. The performance was sponsored by the Thursday Morning Music Club. A crowd of 2,000 attended the event. The lead roles were played by Irra Petina and Michael Bartlett.

Cpl. Willie Perry of Roanoke was reported as killed in action in Korea.

Charlie Slate and his Smoky Mountaineers performed at the Roanoke Theatre on October 23. They were joined by Ray Lee, Van Howerd, and the Burleson Sisters.

Roanoke City Council expressed their frustration at the state for failing to have adequate laws to protect the Roanoke River from pollution. Such laxness worked against the city's efforts to clean up the river and its banks. One councilman specifically pointed to the town of Salem for dumping sewage and other pollutants into the river.

This October 1951 image shows vendors selling produce at the Roanoke City Market. *Virginia Room, RPL*

For the first time, the Roanoke Star burned red on October 23. The reason was to help promote the United Community and Defense Fund campaign that was lagging in contributions. Thus, a new slogan was developed: "Turn the Star White – Put the Community Fund over the Top." The campaign was cochaired by M. W. Armistead III and Arthur Taubman.

Grace Presbyterian Church acquired a fifteen-acre tract just west of Lee-Hy Gardens for its church building. The property fronted Edgewood Street SW.

Dr. John B. Claytor Sr. died on October 23 at the age of seventy-four. Claytor had practiced medicine in Roanoke since 1907 and had just left his office an hour prior to his death. A native of Floyd County, Claytor was emeritus chief of the department of obstetrics and gynecology at Burrell Memorial Hospital. The funeral was conducted from First Baptist Church in Gainsboro.

Dr. John B. Claytor Sr. is shown in his office in this undated photo. Claytor was a founder of Burrell Memorial Hospital in Roanoke. *Virginia Room, RPL*

Hidden Valley Country Club formally opened at 12:30 p.m. on October 24. Only the front nine holes of the golf course were available for play, however. Howard Wood was the club's president.

Officials with American Viscose Corporation announced on October 25 that production at the Roanoke plant would be further curtailed due to changes in the textile market.

Hippert Appliance Store at 1504 Grandin Road invited patrons to an open house for television viewing on October 26 to watch the boxing match between Joe Louis and Rocky Marciano.

Dr. Pepper Bottling Company launched their Silver Dollar Man campaign over WDBJ radio in late October. If a representative of the company knocked on one's door, the homeowner could receive one silver dollar for every bottle of Dr. Pepper in their refrigerator for up to ten bottles.

Calvary Baptist Church honored its former pastor on October 28 when the congregation dedicated the Richard Owens Memorial Chapel. The chapel seated 180 and contained two gifts honoring Owens—a cross and a leaded stained glass window.

N&W Railway's J-Class No. 600 locomotive marked its ten-year anniversary in October. As of October 1, N&W reported the locomotive had rolled up 1,620,058 miles.

Production employees of the Roanoke Weaving Company plant in Vinton rejected unionization by a vote of 328–184.

Bill Davis stands beside a Dr. Pepper truck outside the bottling company's plant on McClanahan Street in this 1951 photo. *Historical Society of Western Virginia*

Paris Shade Shoppe opened on October 29 at 411 First Street SW.

The local United Jewish Appeal campaign kicked off on September 28 with a dinner meeting at the Patrick Henry Hotel. The guest speaker was Max Lerner, a well-known journalist and author. Arthur Taubman was the campaign chairman.

The US Navy Band performed at the American Legion Auditorium on October 28. Their concert was sponsored by the Izaak Walton League.

Salem Presbyterian Church observed the centennial of the building of its sanctuary on November 2. Dr. Ben Lacy Jr., president of Union Theological Seminary, was the guest speaker.

Bethel Church, Assembly of God, was formally dedicated on October 28. The church was located north of Salem on Route 705. Rev. and Mrs. Giles Elliott were the church's ministers. The congregation was founded in April 1944.

A fifty-gallon moonshine still was destroyed by ABC agents on Brushy Mountain northwest of Salem on October 27. The agents confiscated 150 gallons of ripe grain mash.

Joseph Szigeti, a celebrated concert violinist, performed at the Jefferson High School auditorium on November 1. His show was sponsored by the Community Concert Association.

Allstate Insurance Company, a subsidiary of Sears, Roebuck and Company, opened a Roanoke regional office in the Carlton Terrace Building in late October. Paul Briney was the manager of the new office.

Roanoke City Council at its October 29 meeting initiated the process to acquire eight acres of land between William Fleming High School and the proposed new elementary school east of Williamson Road for park purposes. The land was to be purchased from Lena Nininger.

The American Viscose Roanoke plant hosted the company's sewing contest at the Hotel Roanoke in October 1951 that recognized attire designed and made by employees. Minnie Garnand models a jacket on the runway. *Avisco News*

Louis Jordan and his band performed for a show and dance at the American Legion Auditorium on November 2.

Barbara Shulkcum, age eight, of Tazewell Avenue SE, was killed instantly on October 31 when she stepped in front of a school bus she had just alighted. The accident occurred at the intersection of Tazewell Avenue and Sixth Street.

The president of Optimists International Roly Nall came to Roanoke on November 1 and addressed the local Optimist Club at the Patrick Henry Hotel.

Southwest Supply Company, a hardware and sporting goods store, held its grand opening at 1211 Fourth Street SW on November 1.

Roanoke City Manager Arthur Owens threw out the suspensions of four policemen by the police chief on charges they had spread "malicious rumors" about him. Owens determined after a three-hour hearing that city policy had not been followed and vowed to investigate the matter himself.

The Civil Aeronautics Administration announced in early November that it had allocated $75,000 in federal funds for improvements to Woodrum Field for 1952. The amount was to be matched by the City of Roanoke.

Tuke's Shell Service Station opened on November 2 at 4311 Williamson Road. Bill Tuke was the operator. Roses were given to the first one hundred ladies and a grand award drawing for a General Electric vacuum cleaner was held. Customers were also given a free pound of Old Mansion drip or perc coffee.

The Roanoke Ministers' Conference chartered Greyhound buses for persons to hear evangelist Billy Graham speak in Greensboro, North Carolina, on November 9.

Diplomat Civic Committee, a Black civic association for the southwest section of Roanoke, was organized in early November by Othia Davis for the main purpose of registering 1,000 new voters among the city's Black population.

Harris Cleaners opened a new branch at 1008 S. Jefferson Street on November 5.

A new Black political organization was created by Dr. Harry Penn to increase the political influence of Black citizens in Roanoke. The Allied Civic and Political Council was inaugurated during a meeting at High Street Baptist Church on November 4. A crowd of several hundred attended the event that was highlighted by a speech from William Brown, a member of the Charleston, West Virginia, City Council. Penn stated the group's goal was to register 5,000 new Black voters to address social and economic inequalities in the city and Virginia. Others elected officers were Paul Scott, Y. Hutsona, Madge Wheaton, and C. C. Williams.

Republican Ted Dalton was reelected to the Virginia Senate for the Twenty-First District in the November 6 election. He beat Democratic challenger Fred Hoback 8,073 to 5,550 votes. In local races, Edwin Garner unseated incumbent Herbert Tayloe for the Cave Spring seat on the Roanoke County Board of Supervisors, 484 to 470. Tayloe had been a member of the board for thirteen years. Roanoke County Commissioner of the Revenue W. C. Muse defeated his challenger, Burman Bowman, 2,908 to 1,800. Board of Supervisors incumbent Howard Starkey was reelected by a vote of 1,391 to 1,100 over G. A. Laffoon in the Salem District. In the Catawba District, Minor Keffer defeated Wesley Moses 174 to 46. Other office holders ran unopposed.

This March 1951 photo shows the Central YMCA on the left as one looks east on Church Avenue from Second Street SW. Notice the outdoor gym on the roof. *Virginia Room, RPL*

This image from November 1951 is looking north from the 900 block of Jefferson Street SW. The Carlton Terrace Building is on the right. *Virginia Room, RPL*

Officials with US Steel Corporation announced that the Virginia Bridge Company in Roanoke would get a new name effective January 1, 1952. It, along with other US Steel subsidiaries, would be known as the American Bridge Division of US Steel. Interestingly, American Bridge was the original name of the Virginia Bridge Company when it was founded in Roanoke in 1889. It became the Virginia Bridge Company in 1895.

Malcolm-Seay Appliance opened at the corner of Grandin Road and Memorial Avenue SW on November 9.

The outdoor gym atop the Central YMCA building in Roanoke was dismantled. Built in 1930, the gym was home to a men's volleyball league for many years. It was dismantled due to roof repairs.

Lindsey Martin Jr. of Roanoke lost his appeal to the US Supreme Court of his three-year prison sentence for his refusal to be inducted into the military. Martin, a Jehovah's Witness, claimed to be a minister within that denomination as the basis for his refusal.

Roanoke fielded a team in the Piedmont Roller Hockey League. Their home rink was Skate-A-Drome near Lakeside Park in Salem. Other teams in the league included Charlotte, Henderson, and Burlington. Their first home game was on November 10.

The Carter Sisters and Mother Maybelle Carter of the *Grand Ole Opry* performed at the Roanoke Theatre on November 14. Those attending received free bags of Martha White flour.

The Barter Theatre presented a production of Moss Hart's comedy *Light Up the Sky* at the Jefferson High School auditorium on November 16. Lead roles were performed by Woodrow Romoff and Michael Lewis.

Roanoke native William Prince, a well-known artist and illustrator for the *Saturday Evening Post*, killed himself at his home in Chapel Hill, North Carolina, on November 10. He was born in Roanoke in 1893.

Over 300 newspaper carriers delivered 33,000 copies of the booklet *Survival Under Atomic Attack* to homes in the Roanoke Valley in cooperation with the local Office of Civil Defense.

An open house was held at two low-rent housing units at Lansdowne Park on November 11. The first thirty units of the development for whites became available for move-ins on November 15.

American Legion Post 19 sponsored an oratorical contest for high school students. The winners, both from Andrew Lewis High School, were Beverly Taylor and O. C. Simpson Jr. Both presented their winning speeches on WSLS radio during American Education Week.

Mr. and Mrs. William Garman placed fourteenth in a five-state contest held by Kroger for the largest families. The Garmans of Salem had fourteen children and 113 grandchildren, including great-grandchildren, for a total family size of 127. Other local winners and the numbers of their living descendants were Margaret Colley (119), Columbus McBride (118), Chambliss St. Clair (111), T. W. Warlightner (89), and Mrs. A. R. Leslie (88).

The Roanoke City Health Department moved into the new Health Center at Campbell Avenue and Eighth Street SW on November 15. The health department's offices had previously been located in the school administration building.

Gerald Mundy, owner of the Castle Theatre in Fincastle, announced that construction of a new drive-in theatre for Roanoke would begin in mid-November. The Trail Drive-In Theatre would be located along Route 460, 1.7 miles east of Roanoke. It would be the fifth drive-in for the Roanoke Valley, as the Shenandoah Drive-In was also under construction on Shenandoah Avenue. The contractor for the Trail was Fred Davis.

Bozo, the clown, visited Heironimus on November 17. All children were invited to come and visit him in his polka-dot house.

The Roanoke Boxing and Athletic Association held a round of boxing matches in the American Legion Auditorium on November 16. The main bout was between Manny Gomes and Richie Reed. A preliminary match featured Roanoke's Roy Wirt against Petey Bonnelli of New Jersey.

Dinah Washington, along with Earl Bostic and his recording orchestra, performed for a dance at the American Legion Auditorium on November 21. White spectators were admitted to the balcony.

Lester Flatt and Earl Scruggs, along with their Foggy Mountain Boys, performed at the Roanoke Theatre on November 20.

Worth's, a women's apparel store, announced in mid-November it was going out of business. The store was located at 211 S. Jefferson Street.

Metropolitan Opera tenor Jan Peerce gave a performance at the American Legion Auditorium on November 19. His performance was sponsored by the

Thursday Morning Music Club. The crowd of 2,000 applauded for and received six encores.

Construction began on a sixth drive-in theatre in the valley in mid-November with the building of "The 460" along Route 460 just outside Roanoke. E. C. Creasy Jr. and W. A. Bohon were the owners of the theatre, and they also owned and operated the Dixie Drive-In near Vinton and the Skyview Drive-In at Rocky Mount.

The United Community and Defense Fund board of directors voted to decrease each participating agency's budget by 5 percent to make up for the 1951 campaign's deficit. The drive netted $270,145 toward a goal of $285,837.

The Allied Civic and Political Council presented Roanoke City Council with three main requests on behalf of the city's Black citizens at a meeting on November 19. The requests were for the full development of Hurt Park, the employment of Black firemen, and improved streets in the northwest section.

The *Roanoke Times* began a thirty-five-day serial installment on November 25 of Fulton Oursler's *The Greatest Book Ever Written: The Old Testament Story.*

The state purchased over fifty-four acres of land in the Cave Spring area from Virginia Iron, Coal & Coke Company to acquire rights of way for the ongoing construction of the Blue Ridge Parkway.

Santa Claus officially arrived in Roanoke on November 23 as part of a citywide parade sponsored by the Roanoke Merchants Association. He was joined by thirty-five clowns who threw thousands of lollipops to children along the route. Miss Laura Fox of Lee Junior High School was the parade's Snow Queen.

An estimated crowd of 22,000 attended the annual Thanksgiving Day football game between Virginia Tech and VMI at Victory Stadium. The game was preceded by a parade of the schools' cadets through downtown and into the stadium. The special guest in attendance was Korean War hero Lt. General Edward Almond. Other dignitaries included Maj. General Richard Marshall and Virginia Attorney General Lindsay Almond. VMI won 20–7.

The Salem Community Players presented *The Women*, a play by Clare Boothe on November 30. Proceeds benefited Mercy House. The thirty-five-member all-female cast had Charlotte Martin and Mary Preston Lindsey in leading roles.

In early December, sociology students at Roanoke College began a survey in northeast Roanoke for the Roanoke Redevelopment and Housing Authority as the first step in its "slum clearance" and urban renewal project. Data collected by the students was to be used to determine the most desirable section for urban renewal. Information was obtained on family size, household income, and the type and condition of residences and other buildings.

The Roanoke Civic League met the managers of the Safety Motor Transit Corporation about employing Black bus drivers. The league also encouraged grocery stores in northwest Roanoke to employ Black store clerks.

Jerusalem Baptist Church was given a building permit for a new brick church building estimated to cost $19,500. The church was located at 1012 Norfolk Avenue SW.

Slim Williams, a blackface comedian, performed at the Roanoke Theatre on November 28.

A fire did considerable damage to the Imperial Café at 600 Gainsboro Road NW on November 28. The cause was an oil stove.

Pfc. James Edwards of Roanoke was killed in action in Korea on October 22. He had been in Korea for four months.

A special N&W Railway train made a four-mile run to accommodate Santa Claus and the children in Vinton. One coach and locomotive brought Santa to Vinton on December 1 for a parade, and Santa set up his shop in the railway coach that was parked on a siding.

The American Male Chorus, a group of WWII veterans from all branches of service, gave five concerts in the Roanoke Valley in early December as part of their national tour.

The Addison High School Bulldogs defeated Lincoln High School in a final football game of the season, billed as the "Star City Classic." The score was 19–0. Some 1,500 persons attended the game at Victory Stadium that was a benefit for the Addison Band and Juvenile Court Children's Fund. The Bulldogs' coach was Charles Price.

The Clovers, along with Paul Williams and his orchestra, performed for a show and dance at the American Legion Auditorium on December 4. White spectators were admitted to the balcony.

Norman Cousins, editor and writer, spoke at Hollins College on December 6. His topic was "America's Assets in the Present Crisis."

O. F. Worsho was profiled in the December 4 edition of the *Roanoke Times* for having served and lived at the Fort Lewis forest tower for eighteen years. He only left the tower once every two weeks for groceries. During his off hours, he took care of the game preserve on which the tower was located.

The cornerstone was laid for the new Emmanuel Lutheran Church on December 4. The church was located at Olive Avenue and Palmetto Street in the Forest Park section of Roanoke.

Roanoke City Council at its meeting on December 3 concurred in the recommendation of the city manager that Rockledge Inn on Mill Mountain not be leased in 1952, but that Mill Mountain Park be better utilized by the public and various organizations within the region. They believed that would result in greater use of the inn and the mountain top.

Mrs. Hazel Nichols, forty-one, of Roanoke was fatally struck by a city bus on December 4 at the corner of Campbell Avenue and Third Street SW. Taken to Lewis-Gale Hospital, she died a few minutes after arriving there. Hayman Smith was the bus driver.

Professional basketball player Johnny Norlander of the Washington Capitals gave a free exhibition of his skills at the Roanoke College gym on December 6. His appearance was sponsored by Nelson Hardware Company.

A painting by Mrs. Joseph Kronish of Roanoke was selected for the National Art Exhibit of the American Artists Association in New York City during December. The selected painting depicted a Virginia landscape.

Roanoke City Manager Arthur Owens cleared Police Superintendent Stuart Bruce of any immoral conduct and reinstated the four officers that Bruce had suspended, stating that the men had engaged in "idle chatter." Owens' administrative handling of the situation ended a thirty-six-day investigation of the matter within the police department. A few days later, Superintendent Bruce announced that he would retire in 1952. Bruce was a twenty-six-year veteran of the department.

Owen Sheetz was named as the manager of the Roanoke Red Sox for the 1952 season. He had been in the Boston Red Sox organization for fourteen years and was a pitcher when he played professionally.

Nearly 700 Roanoke City public school students participated in the seventh annual Christmas program sponsored by the music department of the city school system. A multi-school concert was given on December 14 at Jefferson High School.

Roanoke's first full-time Black recreation center opened on December 17 at the old Fire Station No. 2 at Gilmer Avenue and Fourth Street NE. Mayor A. R. Minton cut the ribbon. Directors of the center were Mrs. Alice Moore and Melvin Pawley. Over 500 persons attended the ribbon-cutting ceremony, and music was provided by the Addison High School band and chorus for the occasion.

Legs & Laughs of 1952 came to the stage of the Roanoke Theatre on December 12. The show featured vaudeville acts, singing comedian Sully Mason, and women whose "legs are their fortunes."

James Dooley, eighty-five, died on December 10 from injuries he had sustained a few days prior from being struck by a car in front of his home on Shenandoah Avenue NW.

Mayor A. R. Minton, a staunch opponent of public housing, refused to re-appoint John Windel to the Roanoke Redevelopment and Housing Authority of which Windel was chairman. Under the city charter, the mayor and not the city council made appointments to certain boards.

Roanoke City Council at its meeting on December 10 authorized the city manager to call for bids on the razing of the Academy of Music. The council asked that the city retain certain items from the building for reuse elsewhere.

Nearly one-fourth of Roanoke city's 7,219 residential units "had no private bath or were dilapidated," according to the Census Bureau when the census was taken in 1950. About 60 percent of all the houses were not owner-occupied.

The Charter Study Commission concluded its two-year-long review of every section of Roanoke's charter and forwarded its report and recommendations to Roanoke City Council for action and referendum. Chairman Walter Scott outlined five key areas he believed the commission wished to see council to consider, and those were as follows: a new charter, a tax limit retained (or not) within the charter, a seven-member council versus a five-member body, council salaries, and the status of the board of real estate tax assessors.

Floyd Joyner Jr. was executed in the electric chair at the State Penitentiary in Richmond on December 12 for the murder of Mrs. Addie McCormack in Roanoke County in 1950.

Dr. Sherman Oberly, president of Roanoke College, announced in mid-December a $1 million development campaign for 1952. Half would go to campus improvements and the other half to the endowment.

Rollins Broadcasting applied for a license with FCC to operate a standard radio station in Roanoke and become the fourth such station in Roanoke.

A book signing was held on December 14 for Reba Stanley of Roanoke at the Book Nook for her new work, *It's A Great Life!*

Robert Jones, sixty-eight, died instantly when he was struck by an automobile at Salem Turnpike and Twenty-Fourth Street NW on December 15. Jones was the sixth pedestrian to be struck and killed by an auto in Roanoke during the year.

New landing fees were established for airlines at Woodrum Field effective December 16. The fees would provide additional annual revenue of $13,000 for the airport. City and airport officials said they were braced for protests from the major airlines serving the airport—American, Piedmont, and Eastern.

A side wall and half of the front wall of Wilhelm Cleaners at 721 Franklin Road SW collapsed on December 15, injuring a customer. The cause of the damage was an excavation for a basement of a new building adjacent to the cleaners.

Dorothy Byers of Roanoke brought a bigamy charge against her husband, John Barnes, twenty-one, in Roanoke's Police Court. According to the wife, the two were married in 1950 in Washington, DC, and she had recently learned of a second wife in that city. The court sent the case to a grand jury.

Harlem After Dark came to the stage of the Roanoke Theatre on December 19. The vaudeville-style show featured Great Scott and his Impressionist Orchestra and was advertised as "more girls than Ziegfield."

Grace Presbyterian Church was given permission to use Virginia Heights School until the following September while its church building was being erected. This followed a spirited discussion by the Roanoke School Board, with some members objecting to the use of a school for church purposes unless it was for an emergency.

Richie Reed squared off against Bobby Kirk in a ten-round feature attraction of a night of boxing at the American Legion Auditorium on December 19. Two preliminary bouts featured locals Roy Wirt, who fought Tony Masciarelli, and Bernie King, who boxed Walt Jones. The entire event, however, was declared a farce by the city's boxing commissioner Rex Mitchell. Some boxers did not show, while one event was deemed a "powder puff" such that the ref stopped the match in the second round declaring it "no contest." Three nonlocal boxers had their licenses suspended permanently, and the two local boxing promoters—H. B. Gillespie and Johnny Hodges—had their licenses revoked by the state boxing commission on the recommendation of Mitchell. A crowd of 700 booed throughout much of the evening.

Six local men were listed as official POW in Korea. They were Pfc. Robert Gray, Cpl. Daniel Bolden, First Lt. John Caldwell, Pvt. Clyde Hughes, Cpl. James Valentine, and Sgt. William Holmes. A list of POWs had been provided to military officials by the Chinese Communists.

Virgil Frantz of Roanoke was awarded a patent for the development of a sand-trap nozzle for railroad locomotives. Frantz was vice president of Graham-White Manufacturing Company in Salem. According to Frantz, nearly 90 percent of all new diesel locomotives were using his invention.

G. E.'s Delicatessen opened at 1004 S. Jefferson Street on December 20. The deli specialized in kosher foods.

Players and coaches of Roanoke's 1951 National Midget League Football Team pose at Victory Stadium a few days prior to their championship game in Florida. *Historical Society of Western Virginia*

Erskine Hawkins and his recording orchestra played for a show and dance at the American Legion Auditorium on December 26. Hawkins was best known for his composition *Tuxedo Junction*. White spectators were permitted on the balcony.

Roanoke sent its best sandlot football players to Lakeland, Florida, after Christmas to compete in the Santa Claus Bowl tournament there. The national event was sponsored by the Pop Warner Foundation. Those selected to be on Roanoke's team were John Matthews, Don Vaught, Albert Peverall, Lee Fracker, Red Thomas, Elliott Shaver, Howard Beckwith, David Meredith, Lilburn Ward, Nelson Showalter, Dean Young, Ronnie Hylton, Pat Kiser, Bert Tabor, Billy Seddon, Don Moody, Don Rucker, Bob McConnell, Dickie Woolwine, Tommy Lawson, Marion Costello, Ray Fisher, Jay Blackwood, Walter Howard, John Hurt, Dean Price, Paul Dotson, and Harvey Creasy.

Roanoke County delegate Ernest Robertson announced that at least twenty-five petitions were circulating in Salem to expand the town council from three to five members. Robertson stated he would support the change through legislation in the General Assembly. The three town council members were noncommittal.

The first worship service to be held in the new Bethel Baptist Church building in Salem was December 23. Rev. Palmer Belcher was the pastor.

Ella Brown, secretary of the Christmas Basket Bureau, reported that almost 5,000 Roanokers had benefited from the generosity of those who donated to the bureau's work to secure food and clothing for those in need.

Ben Hardy, who worked for four years in Roanoke at the Associated Press Bureau before the bureau was moved to Norfolk, died in an airplane crash in Iran on December 23. He perished along with twenty others. Hardy was an assistant to Dr. Henry Bennett, director of America's Four Point Program. Bennett was also killed in the crash.

A ground-breaking ceremony for St. James Episcopal Church was held on December 27 at the church's site on Delray Avenue. The first shovel was turned by Mrs. Caroline Kornegay, a charter member. Rev. Manly Cobb was the pastor.

Construction began on the new Keller Machine Company building in Salem on December 28. The location was 1022 Tennessee Street. The company was located on Salem Avenue in Roanoke and did welding and brazing.

The Roanoke all-star sandlot football team won the Santa Claus Bowl in Lakeland, Florida, on December 28 by defeating a team from Omaha, Nebraska, in overtime. In the tournament prior to the championship game, the boys from Roanoke defeated the favored team from New Orleans. Upon their return to Roanoke, the team was greeted by city officials and a crowd of 1,500 at the train station, and their trophy was played on exhibit in the Oval Room of the Hotel Roanoke. Player John Hurt Jr. had been named to the National Midget League All-American team. The coaches were Bob McLelland, Sam Elliott, John Howard, Buddy Hackman and Fred Smith. The trip had been underwritten by the Roanoke Chamber of Commerce.

Some members of Roanoke's National Midget League Championship Team celebrate with their trophy at the N&W Passenger Station after returning from Florida in December 1951. *Historical Society of Western Virginia*

Roy Brown and his recording orchestra performed for a show and dance at the Star City Auditorium, located on Henry Street, on December 31.

Herman Trompeter and Albert Trompeter purchased the old Maurice Twine Mills factory building in Norwich for $82,000 in late December. The Trompeters indicated a desire to rent the building to a manufacturer.

Capt. Julian Wise of the Roanoke Life Saving and First Aid Crew helped to pioneer the use of the Nielsen Artificial Respiration Method in America and was recognized as doing so by the American Red Cross upon its approval and formal sanctioning of the resuscitation method. Wise had been corresponding with the developer of the method, a Swedish physician, for over fifteen years, and the Roanoke crew was recognized as being the first rescue squad in the nation to employ the new technique.

Three persons suffocated to death in a Salem house fire on December 30. The victims were Fred Blaney, thirty; his wife Catherine Blaney, twenty-six; and their six-year-old nephew, Edward Dudley. Two others escaped the fire at 212 Chapman Street. Dudley was the son of Mr. and Mrs. Ralph Dudley of Rutherford Avenue NW in Roanoke.

Lewis Aliff, twenty-eight, of Roanoke died when his car sped through a thicket and dropped one hundred feet into a water-filled quarry off Hollins Road on December 30. Investigators believed the action was a suicide. The following day, hundreds of onlookers gathered at the quarry to watch rescue workers bring up Aliff and the car from fifty feet of water. The quarry was identified as Mundy Quarry in the vicinity of Monterey Golf Club.

The Civitan Club of Roanoke presented a plan to Roanoke City Council at its December 31 meeting for a Children's Zoo in Mill Mountain Park, which would be built and stocked at no cost to the city. Representing the Civitan Club were H. C. Broyles, Stanley Bailey, and Virgil Holloman. The three presented drawings showing the proposed layout and suggested the zoo would have a Mother Goose theme. Some of the amenities for the proposed zoo included Noah's ark, a pony track, a small brick schoolhouse, a goat paddock and castle, Bunnyville, a *Puss in the Well* building, a play area, and the houses of the "Three Little Pigs." According to the Civitan Club, the idea for a children's zoo was proposed by a visitor from British Columbia, where a similar zoo operated. The council referred the proposal to the city manager for further review.

Robert Paine, president of Mountain Trust Bank, died on December 31 at Lewis-Gale Hospital. He was fifty-three. He was elected president of the bank in 1947.

1952

The first day of January was unseasonably warm, as the high temperature recorded at Woodrum Field was seventy-eight degrees.

James Higgs, seventeen, was arrested by the FBI at his home in the 1200 block of Tenth Street NW in the early morning hours of January 1 for a murder committed in Alabama on December 24. Higgs, who had been AWOL from the navy since late November, was arrested for the murder of a marine, Clyde Sharpley. Higgs confessed to the agents.

The first birth of 1952 was Kenneth Burgess, son of Mrs. Barbara Burgess of Roanoke County. He was born at Memorial and Crippled Children's Hospital at 3:20 a.m. on January 1.

A large fire broke out at the city dump located in an abandoned quarry in northwest Roanoke on January 1.

Howard Starkey of Salem was elected chairman of the Roanoke County Board of Supervisors at the annual reorganizational meeting on January 2.

Two trained chickens seen on national television gave exhibitions at the Agnew & Connelly Seed Store in Roanoke on January 3. Rupert (a rooster) and Zenobia (a hen) did math tricks, played cards, and successfully competed in a shell game. They were touring the country with their owner, Dr. Keller Breland, a psychologist.

A group of auditorium consultants recommended a multipurpose auditorium for Roanoke be built in either Elmwood Park or adjacent to the American Legion Auditorium. Their report was given to the city manager, which indicated that the impact of television on live shows may be a negative one. The consultants also recommended a music hall and an exhibition hall for the city. The report was in response to a citizens group that was trying to address the loss of the Academy of Music as a venue.

Roanoke City Council at their January 3 meeting decided on three questions for an advisory referendum set for February 3 pertaining to changes in the city charter. The questions before voters would be: Shall the city retain its present tax limit in the charter? Shall the city retain its present five-member council? Are you for or against the council establishing a continuing board of real estate assessors? The council's action was in response to a study and report by the Charter Study Commission.

The new educational building of Waverly Place Baptist Church in southeast Roanoke was put in use for the first time on January 6. It was part of an overall $200,000 building program at the church.

Work on the new First Methodist Church of Salem building began on January 7. The $240,000 project included a sanctuary, chapel, and tower. Eubank and Caldwell, a Roanoke firm, was the general contractor.

The Shenandoah Drive-In Theatre opened on January 6 at 3321 Shenandoah Avenue NW. It boasted the largest screen in the city. Admission was one dollar per carload, and the opening night had a double feature—*Red Pony*, starring Robert Mitchum and Myrna Loy, and *Challenge to Lassie*.

Roanoke City Council gave the Civitan Club permission to proceed with the building of the Children's Zoo in Mill Mountain Park. At its January 7 meeting, council appointed a committee to oversee the project's development, and the committee consisted of Arthur Owens, John Wentworth, H. O. Broyles, Rex Mitchell Jr., and Virgil Holloman.

Tom Kent, eighty-five, was killed in a house fire in the 700 block of Eighth Street NW on January 7. The fire was caused by an overheated coal stove.

The Roanoke Life Saving and First Aid Crew elected Bernard Cook as president for the year. They also reported that for 1951, the crew responded to 566 calls for service that included 238 general calls, 2 fire calls, 10 iron lung calls, and 21 calls from outside the city. Julian Wise was the captain.

The new $550,000 addition to Woodrow Wilson Junior High School was opened for use on January 10. The main element of the addition was a cafeteria. Prior to January 10, students at the school had been dismissed at 1:00 p.m. due to the lack of a cafeteria during construction.

Sue Lucado, twenty-two, of Route 3 in Salem was struck and killed by an automobile on Route 220 on January 8. The driver of the car was Leonard Leffel, who said the woman was lying on the highway when he struck her at 10:45 p.m. Witnesses agreed with Leffel's statement. No charges were filed against him.

The state health department announced it would establish a clinic for alcoholics at the Health Center in Roanoke. It was the first such clinic in the state outside of Richmond. Dr. Roland Pearsall of Roanoke was named the clinic's supervisor.

Ernest Tubb of the *Grand Ole Opry* performed at the American Legion Auditorium on January 13. He was joined by Stringbean, Ken Marvin, Annie Lou & Danny, and the Texas Troubadours.

Members of the Roanoke Police Department organized a local chapter of the Fraternal Order of Police on January 9. It was the first in Virginia and was named Old Dominion Lodge No. 1. Cpl. G. O. Willis was named temporary chairman.

Henry Fowler, a native of Roanoke, was sworn in on January 9 by the US Secretary of Commerce as administrator of the National Production Authority.

Redd Harper, a Western film actor, spoke at a Christian youth rally held in the auditorium of Jefferson High School on January 12. The event was sponsored by the school's Hi-Y Club.

Pvt. John T. Whitt, having been listed as missing in action in Korea since October 27, 1951, was reported as killed. He was survived by his wife, Katherine Whitt of Roanoke.

This early 1950s image shows Fleming Avenue looking south toward Williamson Road. Bethany Christian Church is on left of street. *Virginia Room, RPL*

Lionel Hampton and his orchestra performed for a show and dance at the American Legion Auditorium on January 18. White spectators were admitted to the balcony.

Grand Ole Opry star Bill Monroe performed at the Roanoke Theatre on January 16.

Two local poets, Marcia Anderson of Hollins College and Carleton Drewry of Roanoke, both participated in the *Week of Poetry* program held in mid-January in the New York Public Library.

The Barter Theatre presented the comedy *The Vinegar Tree* in the auditorium of Jefferson High School on January 14. Elinor Wright and Owen Phillips had the lead roles.

George and Irma Wilde of 1506 Main Street SW were profiled in the January 13 edition of the *Roanoke Times* for their prolific illustrations for popular children's books. The two had created illustrations for over twenty books, including many of the Quizzle Books and several of the Wonder Books, including *The Giraffe Who Went to School*.

Roanoke City Council incumbents Dan Cronin and W. P. Hunter both announced they would not seek reelection. Each had served a single term.

The body of Sarah Arnold of Roanoke was found on January 13 in woods eight miles northeast of Hanging Rock along an old CCC trail. Police stated that the body appeared to have been dragged 150 feet from the nearest road to the woods and covered in leaves. The body was spotted by a passing motorist. The death was investigated by Roanoke County authorities who determined that Arnold had come to Roanoke three years prior from her hometown of Bassett to work. She was employed by McLellan's department store at the time of her death.

Leo Kesler of Roanoke captured the Virginia State Open Duckpins Bowling Tournament championship held in Newport News on January 13. He turned in a record 1,010 seven-game set. He finished fourth in the United States Classic Tournament held the following day in Norfolk.

Walter Scott, chairman of the Charter Study Commission that had recommended several changes to the charter of Roanoke city, claimed that Roanoke City Council had taken "scissors, the knife, the machete, and the axe to our proposals section by section." Scott's comments were in an address to the Roanoke Area Manufacturers Association meeting on January 14. Scott blamed three council members for largely negating the two years' work of the commission.

Carter Machinery Company was organized in mid-January with offices at 1919 Tenth Street NW. It was an affiliate of Virginia Tractor Company of Richmond. R. H. Carter was president of the new company.

Gina Bachauer gave a piano concert at Hollins College on January 14. Bachauer was from Greece and one of only four living pupils of Rachmaninoff. Bachauer was on a national tour.

Virginia Markets took over fifteen Bibee grocery stores in the state, three of which were in Roanoke—400 Luck Avenue SW, 313 First Street SE, and 2106 Williamson Road. J. M. Hamrick of Roanoke and G. W. Lindsay of Salem headed Virginia Markets.

Thomas Parsley was elected president of Mountain Trust Bank on January 15. He succeeded R. E. Paine who died on December 31. He had been with Mountain Trust since 1948.

Lourens DeVries, a retired Dutch army officer, died on January 17. A resident of southeast Roanoke, DeVries had been a former Olympian and the one-time European fencing champion.

Ewald-Clark, camera and gift shop, moved from 7 W. Church Avenue to 17 W. Church Avenue, where it leased the first, second, and third floors of the building in order to expand its business. A grand opening was planned for mid-March. The owners were Charles Clark and Francis Ewald.

Roanoke City Manager Arthur Owens reported on January 18 that twenty-five businesses and individuals had pledged to work on or donate materials for the Children's Zoo for Mill Mountain Park. Arthur also stated that city work crews were clearing the land for the zoo's construction.

Steel Service, a Richmond firm, acquired six acres of land at Starkey and announced plans to build a warehouse and offices there. The business manufactured fuel storage tanks.

Ice Vogues of 1952 came to the American Legion Auditorium for five days beginning January 23. The ice show advertised twenty-eight acts with new stars and new comedians.

Music With the Hormel Girls, a show featuring an all-female orchestra and chorus, gave a radio and stage production at the Jefferson High School auditorium on January 26. They were touring coast-to-coast, and their local appearance was sponsored by the Shrine Kazim Temple.

Dr. and Mrs. William Marshall Jr. of Christiansburg were killed instantly in a collision with a truck on January 20 on Route 220, three miles east of Roanoke. Marshall was a chiropractor. Their six-year-old son, John, was asleep in the back seat and received only minor injuries.

This January 1952 shows the Elizabeth Heights Apartments located at the intersection of Idaho Street and Elizabeth Avenue in Salem. *Virginia Room, RPL*

Frank Stone, a prominent Roanoke architect, died on January 20 at his home on Viewmont Avenue NW. He was sixty-five. He was a partner in the Stone and Thompson Architectural firm. His local projects included the Municipal Building, Colonial-American National Bank, Ponce de Leon Hotel, WDBJ Studios, and First Baptist Church, Roanoke, among others.

Mrs. Sarah Dyer of Roanoke died at her home on Crystal Spring Avenue SW on January 20. She was a charter member of the Woman's Club of Roanoke and helped establish the State Federation of Garden Clubs.

A fire swept through the small village of Eagle Rock in Botetourt County on January 20, destroying the Methodist Church and four homes. Thirteen persons were left homeless.

The Roanoke City Council–appointed committee that was studying a new multipurpose auditorium decided the new site should be in downtown. This eliminated two other sites that had been considered—Maher Field and Shrine Hill.

Roanoke City Manager Arthur Owens reported to the city council that not a single bid was received to raze the Academy of Music, meaning city crews would have to do the job.

Grace Presbyterian Church began holding services in the Masonic Building at 1324 Grandin Road SW in late January. The congregation planned to worship there until their sanctuary was erected. They had previously sought to use Virginia Heights Elementary School.

James Wilson, a passerby, rescued a three-year-old boy from a burning apartment on January 21 at the Veterans Housing Project on the City Farm. The boy, Michael Spradlin, was inside the apartment as the mother tried helplessly to rescue him. Wilson pulled his car over, ran toward the smoke, and went in through a window to rescue the boy.

The state medical examiner's office reported on January 23 to local law enforcement that an autopsy they performed on Sarah Arnold, twenty-eight, whose body was found near Hanging Rock at Brushy Mountain, yielded little information as to the cause of death. The examiner's office indicated they would continue to run additional tests since law enforcement had no leads in the case.

Scott's Cash Grocery at 2303 Williamson Road was liquidated on January 26 through an auction of all the store's stock and fixtures.

Ronald Robertson, four, was killed as a passenger in a car that sideswiped a parked truck on Route 220 south of Roanoke on January 24. He was the son of Mr. and Mrs. Berkeley Robertson of Garden City.

Frank Gettings was sentenced to twenty years in prison, having pled guilty to the first-degree murder of Herman Hairston at 522 Moorman Road NW on the night of October 7, 1951.

Roanoke County Commonwealth Attorney E. W. Chelf announced on January 25 that Sarah Arnold had died from exposure and closed the investigation into her death. Arnold had been found several days earlier lying in the woods near Hanging Rock. An autopsy had concluded there was no evidence of foul play. A local salesman had been the last to see the young woman alive, but authorities did not believe he was involved in her death. The two had been drinking, and Arnold asked to be dropped off along the highway. Authorities believed she walked several miles in the cold before collapsing, possibly from exhaustion.

This early 1952 image shows the former terminal building at Woodrum Field in the background prior to it being razed for the new terminal. *Virginia Room, RPL*

Rev. Bob Richards, national pole vault champion and national decathlon champion, preached for a two-week-long revival at Central Church of the Brethren in Roanoke in late January and early February.

Roanoke's Groundhog Club convened at the American Legion Auditorium on February 2. Jubal Angell, head of the club, emceed a trial of Roanoke City Manager Arthur Owens, City Engineer Cletus Broyles, and Rex Mitchell on a charge of "trying to deprive the groundhog of its civil rights and pursuit of happiness by conspiring to capture him and place him in the zoo atop Mill Mountain." Proceeds benefited the local March of Dimes campaign.

Pianist Rudolph Serkin gave a concert at the Jefferson High School auditorium on February 2 as part of a national tour. Serkin's performance was under the auspices of the Roanoke Community Concert Association.

J. B. Grant of Bent Mountain was named Roanoke County's champion corn grower by the 100 Bushel Corn Club. His crop yielded 163 bushels per acre.

A Time of Turning, a book of poetry authored by Carleton Drewry of Roanoke was named as the best book of poetry published in 1951 by the Poetry Awards Foundation. Drewry received a cash award of $1,200 and recognition at the Poetry Society of America's annual dinner in New York City on January 30. The book was published by E. P. Dutton and Company.

Dancing Dolls Revue came to the stage of the Roanoke Theatre on January 30. Ads boasted the show had "beautiful cover girls on parade" and "the pick of New York's pin-ups."

A group of Roanoke businessmen chartered the Eastern Life and Casualty Company, an industrial insurance company, in Roanoke in late January. Those involved included Craig Miller, T. P. Parsley, Thomas Rutherfoord, Richard Pence, and Herbert Mosley.

James Farley, former chairman of the Democratic National Committee, addressed the Roanoke Junior Chamber of Commerce on January 29 at a meeting at the Hotel Roanoke. Farley spoke about the state of American politics. At the meeting James Long was honored as Roanoke's Outstanding Young Man of 1951.

T. W. Fugate of Roanoke died at his home on Greenwood Road SW on January 29 at the age of seventy-seven. Fugate was president of Fugate Motors and a past president of the former Guaranty Trust Company in Roanoke.

Bruce Griggs, seventy-eight, died in a local hospital on January 29. He was president of Fairview Cemetery, having been born just outside the town limits of Big Lick in 1873.

Howard Johnson's restaurant opened on January 30 on Route 11 east of Roanoke. John LaRicos was the manager.

Tony Proietti became the first man in the history of Roanoke College basketball to achieve a 1,000-point total. He exceeded that mark in a game against Washington College on January 28.

The Griffin Brothers and their orchestra, along with Margie Day and Peppermint Harris, performed for a show and dance at the American Legion Auditorium on February 1. The balcony was reserved for white spectators.

The Howard Johnson's Restaurant on Route 11 east of Roanoke opened in January 1952. This image dates from that year. *Bob Kinsey*

Dr. William Stauffer, a Richmond-based economist, reported to the Roanoke City Council–appointed Tax Study Commission that the absence of a methodical and data-driven assessment of its property taxes was the single greatest weakness in the city's tax structure. Stauffer estimated that the city was losing $1 million annually in revenue. Stauffer also advocated for the repeal of certain taxes and the modification of others.

Miss Marcia Anderson, assistant professor of English at Hollins College, was presented the Reynolds Lyric Award given annually for the best unpublished lyric submitted by members of the Poetry Society of America. The award was made at the society's annual dinner in New York City.

Six persons filed as candidates for the Democratic Primary on April 1 to compete for two open seats on Roanoke City Council. The candidates were Lester Hutts, Paul Johnson, Ernest Light, Robert Wagner, Robert Woody, and Edwin Young.

Nationally syndicated columnist Walter Winchell stirred interest in Roanoke when he wrote in his January 30 column, "If Gypsy Rose Lee decides to change grooms – first call goes to a Roanoke high school teacher." Lee, a famous stripper, had been married seven times.

Representatives of the Roanoke Council of Garden Clubs met with city officials in late January to discuss use of the former Elmwood home as a garden center. The home was being used as the city's main library, but with the opening of a new main library approaching, the garden clubs hoped to use the home.

Wood's Crown Service Center opened at a new location on February 1 at 606 Third Street SE. The location had been formerly occupied by Holt Wood Oil Company. John Wood was proprietor.

Mrs. Catherine Ikenberry, believed to be Roanoke's oldest citizen, died at the home of daughter on Round Hill Avenue NW on February 1. She was 106.

Roanoke Country Club officials announced the hiring of Luke Barnes from Atlanta as their new golf pro. Barnes was the assistant pro at the Charlotte Country Club and began his duties at the Roanoke club in mid-February.

Sherrill's Antiques opened at 4515 Williamson Road on February 4. It was the store's second location, with the other being at 22 W. Church Avenue.

Hamlar-Curtis Funeral Home opened on February 4 at 1002 Moorman Road NW. Proprietors were Lawrence Hamlar and Harry Curtis Jr. Hamlar had been in the funeral business for eight years prior to opening his own funeral home.

Woods Brothers Coffee Company in Roanoke celebrated its twenty-fifth anniversary on February 1. The business began in 1927 when Harold Woods Sr. and his oldest daughter, Billie, started roasting their first pound of coffee. Originally, the business served a local grocery in Grandin Court, and then others in the area were added. The business was first located at 315 Campbell Avenue and then relocated across the street to 316–318 Campbell Avenue SE. In its first year, the company roasted 75,000 pounds of coffee, and in 1951 it was roasting more than four million pounds. The company's brand was H&C, named such for two reasons. First, the Woods brothers were Harold and Clarence, and second, the company's primary market was hotels and cafes.

Grand Ole Opry singer George Morgan and his Candy Kids performed at the Roanoke Theatre on February 6.

This January 1952 shows the English Garden Apartments along Memorial Avenue SW in Roanoke that were representative of the post-WWII housing boom in the valley. *Virginia Room, RPL*

The Roanoke School Board decided at its February 4 meeting to retain the name of Lucy Addison High School for the new Black high school under construction in northwest Roanoke. The former Addison High School would become the Booker T. Washington Junior High School when the new high school was completed.

In charter referenda votes held on February 5, Roanoke City voters approved enlarging the five-person city council by a vote of 3,986 to 3,655. Citizens voted 6,693 to 867 against removing the $2.50 tax limit in the city charter and also defeated having a permanent board of assessors, 5,965 to 1,570. The following day, Roanoke City Council authorized the election of two additional council members in 1953 to serve three-year terms.

The Norwich Mission of the Presbyterian Church resumed using its original name in early February, Woodside Presbyterian Church. It remained, however, a mission of First Presbyterian Church. Woodside was established in 1893, one of nine mission churches started by First. Woodside was dissolved in 1903 as a church and reverted to a mission.

The new terminal building at Woodrum Field was completed on February 7. The structure was formally presented to Roanoke City Council by the contractor, B. F. Parrott and Company, at the council's meeting on February 11. Related work was ongoing, including the relocation of Hangar No. 1 and additional improvements to the airport parking lot. While the terminal was completed, it could not become operational until the related work was finished.

Goodwill Industries formally unveiled their new cartoon character "Good Willy" at its annual meeting on February 7. The cartoon character, developed by Milton Caniff, was to be used in advertising and promotion.

Officials with the Piedmont League said a few Black players may be introduced on teams for the 1952 season. Clarke Wray, president of the Roanoke Red Sox, was asked his response to the discussions, and he said, "To my knowledge there are no Negro players in the Boston Red Sox farm team system. However, if a scout of the organization thinks a Negro player has the ability and is capable of playing Class B ball and he is sent here, we would be obligated by our working agreement with Boston to give the fellow a chance of making the team."

Earl Bryant, twenty-six, of Roanoke County was killed on February 8 when his tractor-trailer left Route 220 and overturned ten miles south of Roanoke. He was a driver for Kroger Company.

Representatives of seven downtown Roanoke civic clubs completed organizing the Inter Civic Club on February 8. Dr. E. G. Gill was elected president. The purpose of the group was to help organize the various clubs' efforts to effect the betterment of downtown.

Kenneth Herman of Roanoke, and a graduate of William Fleming High School, was cast in a role in the film *Condor's Nest* that starred Cornel Wilde. The film was produced by Twentieth Century Fox in Hollywood. Since graduating from Fleming in 1940 and service in the military, Herman had moved to California and appeared in various television, radio, and summer stock productions.

This 1952 image shows the interior of Garland's Drug Store located at 15 S. Jefferson Street. Walter Garland, owner, is on the stool. The store was later razed to make way for the viaduct. *Historical Society of Western Virginia*

The first house to be erected for the Children's Zoo on Mill Mountain was the goat house. Covered in stucco, it was one of many in keeping with the Mother Goose theme of the attraction.

Natalie Shoppe held the opening of its new store on February 12 at 311 S. Jefferson Street. The store was owned by Nat Spigel, who moved the store from its former location at 301 S. Jefferson Street. Spigel started the store in 1932 and named it after his daughter. The new store was designed by Spigel's son, Leo.

For the first time in the history of the *Roanoke Times*, the Sunday comics were printed in color in the February 10 edition. The color supplement was due to contract obligations with the comic syndicates.

Carney St. Clair, thirty-two, formerly of Roanoke, was killed in a plane crash in Elizabeth City, New Jersey, on February 11. He was the copilot of a National Airlines plane that crashed, killing all thirty-one persons on board. His body was returned to Roanoke for burial. It was the third crash of a passenger airliner over Elizabeth City, New Jersey, in as many months and forced the temporary closure of Newark Airport.

The 300 Club, a new social club, was organized and headed by Byron Morgan.

Mrs. Harry Semones was honored by the Belmont School PTA in mid-February, and at the event she provided a brief history of the PTA movement in Roanoke.

Semones organized the Belmont School PTA in February 1920. On April 2, 1921, the Virginia Congress of Parents and Teachers was organized and had its main office in Roanoke. Semones served as president of the state organization during its early years. The PTA grew out of the Woman's Division of the Chamber of Commerce. Semones chaired the education committee of the division and suggested that a PTA be organized at each school in the city. A contribution of $300 from the Men's Division helped get them started.

The formal opening of the new Carole's Shop was held on February 15 at 304 First Street. The new owners and operators were Frank Silek and his sons.

Little Sport, a comic strip, became a regular weekday feature on the sports page of the *Roanoke Times* beginning February 18.

The Bailey Brothers, Grandpa Jones, Sunshine Sue, and the Happy Valley Boys gave a performance at the City Market Auditorium on February 15.

Roanoke's Fifth Engineer Marine Corps Reserves unit was formally activated on February 15 in a ceremony at the Marine Armory. Col. John Oldfield made a presentation of the colors to the unit's new commanding officer, Capt. Charles Mawyer.

Roanoke native Robert Bailey III was one of the representatives of the United States at the proclamation of the accession of Queen Elizabeth II to the throne of England. Bailey, a graduate of Lucy Addison High School, was studying at the University of Birmingham, England, on a Fulbright scholarship. In addition to witnessing the proclamation of the new queen at St. James's Palace, Bailey also attended the public funeral of King George VI at Westminster Abbey. He had been received at the home of the American ambassador in London during the events.

A comedy-romance written by Nelson Bond was the dramatic offering in the CBS nationally broadcast program *Stars Over Hollywood* on February 23. Bond's script was titled *Under A Lucky Star* and was about a young lady who mistakes an astronomer for an astrologer. The lead actor was MacDonald Carey.

Recording artist Ruth Brown, along with Paul Williams and his orchestra, performed for a show and dance at the American Legion Auditorium on February 15. The balcony was reserved for white spectators.

Roanoke's Children's Theatre presented the play *The Indian Captive* for three consecutive afternoons during the third week of February. The play was directed by Clara Black.

St. John's Episcopal Church sent a church bell to a remote mission chapel in Alaska. The Roanoke congregation donated the bell that was shipped to the isolated mission on the lower end of the Yukon River in the village of Shageluk. A freight boat only visited the village once a year.

Evangelist Oral Roberts brought his crusade to the American Legion Auditorium February 19–24. The faith healing and evangelistic campaign was sponsored by the area's Pentecostal Holiness and Assembly of God churches.

On February 19, Roanoke police began destroying thirty-two pinball machines taken from gas stations, restaurants, and pool rooms that were seized in raids in October 1951. Critics complained that the machines were robbing schoolchildren of their lunch money and that they were basically slot machines.

The *Bring On the Girls!* stage show was at the Roanoke Theatre on February 20. It featured novelty acts, "lovely girls," and a blackface comedian.

The Roanoke Area Council of the Boy Scouts announced a plan to spend $4,000 in improvements to Camp Powhatan prior to the summer camping season. Improvements were to include a water tank, rifle range, cook shack, and archery range.

Ground-breaking ceremonies were held on February 21 for the new St. Mark's Lutheran Church at Franklin Road and Highland Avenue SW. The architect for the Gothic-designed structure was Norman Mansell of Philadelphia, and Martin Brothers of Roanoke was the contractor. The guest speaker for the ground-breaking was Dr. Sherman Oberly, president of Roanoke College.

The US House of Representatives voted on February 21 to change the name of the Blue Ridge Parkway to the Robert L. Doughton Parkway in honor of one of their House colleagues. The resolution came as a surprise to many in Congress who had little advance notice and to those employed by and associated with the parkway. At Blue Ridge Parkway headquarters in Roanoke, the staff was completely in the dark, and the immediate aftermath of the vote had many lobbying Congress to reverse course.

For the first time since 1946, Jefferson High School fielded a track team. The move was due to an increase in interest. The high school was unable to have a baseball team for the spring, however, due to a lack of interest.

Construction was ongoing at the Children's Zoo in the winter in preparation for opening day in the spring. This February 1952 image shows construction of "Bunnyville." *Historical Society of Western Virginia*

The Hunton Life Saving and First Aid Crew celebrated their tenth anniversary with a dinner meeting at Hunton Branch YMCA on February 22. Alexander Terrell spoke on the history of the crew and was one of many speakers for the occasion.

The Hotpoint Cooking School was held on February 27 and 28 in the auditorium of Appalachian Electric Power Company. Miss Jo Parks of Atlanta was the brand's instructor, and Hayden Huddleston was master of ceremonies. The school was sponsored by area Hotpoint Appliances dealers.

Grand Ole Opry stars Johnnie & Jack, along with the Tennessee Mountain Boys, performed at the Roanoke Theatre on February 27.

The Polack Brothers Circus came to the American Legion Auditorium for a five-night run on February 27. Ads boasted thirty acts with over one hundred performers.

Appalachian Electric Power Company launched the operation of its new million-dollar John Hancock high voltage transmission station on Route 11 between Salem and Roanoke on February 23. The station was named for John Hancock Jr., a retired Roanoke division manager. Hancock station had a capacity of 45,000 KVA.

An article in the February 24 edition of the *Roanoke Times* outlined the history of the Garst Fort House located on the road to Loch Haven. It was also referred to by some as the Green Ridge Fort. Built around 1760, it was the last of the remaining fort structures in the area used to defend the Virginia frontier against Native Americans. Originally three stories, the log fort was in disrepair. According to area historians, the structure was occupied by Frederick Gharst from 1820 until his death in 1842.

Barter Theatre presented *Mrs. Moonlight* in the auditorium of Jefferson High School on February 28. Lead roles were played by Barbara Jeanne Lucas of Roanoke and Owen Phillips.

Roanoke writer and poet Carleton Drewry was profiled in the *Roanoke Times* on February 24. Among the interesting stories he shared about his writing was a time when noted writer Thomas Wolfe came to Roanoke to speak at the Roanoke Country Club. Wolfe, Drewry, and another companion gathered prior to the event for drinks and conversation such that Wolfe never made it to the country club.

Carol Withers, four, was struck and killed by an automobile on the night of February 24. She was on her way with her sister and mother to church when she was hit at Sixteenth Street and Carroll Avenue NW.

WSLS radio applied in late February for a permit to build a television station in Roanoke. The petition was filed with the FCC on February 21, with an estimated construction cost of $300,000. WROV radio filed a permit for a television station in February 1951. Officials with WDBJ radio stated they were planning to file for a permit as well.

At a Roanoke City Council candidate forum hosted by the Roanoke Civic League on February 25, three of the six candidates stated support for having a Black person on the council when it is enlarged to seven members. The candidates who supported such a move were Lester Hutts, Robert Wagner, and Edwin Young. The other three candidates did not attend the forum.

Roanoke City Council initiated the process on February 25 to acquire almost twenty-three acres in the East Williamson Road area for an elementary school and city park. The property was in the Fleming Court section immediately north of William Fleming High School.

At its February 25 meeting, Roanoke City Council authorized R. T. Winecoff of Cambria to raze the Academy of Music for salvage, with the exception of the boiler and stoker that would be repurposed elsewhere.

A Roanoke landmark, the Moomaw home at Moomaw Spring in northwest Roanoke, was heavily damaged by fire on February 25. The two-story log home was believed to have been built around the time of the American Revolution and had been unoccupied for several years.

Kann's at 309 S. Jefferson Street was heavily damaged by smoke caused by a small furnace fire on February 26.

Gilbert Storage and Transfer Corporation at 1612 S. Jefferson Street acquired George's Storage and Transfer Company in Roanoke in late February.

The Roanoke City Charter Bill passed the General Assembly in late February, making permanent the changes approved previously by the city's voters and passed by the city council.

The Army and Air Force Recruiting Station opened at its new location in the Patrick Henry Hotel on February 28. It was formerly located on Norfolk Avenue.

Watts Hardware Company opened a second store at 2912 Williamson Road on March 1. C. E. Richards was the store manager.

The fourth annual Roanoke Preaching Mission opened on March 2 for five days with midday services at Greene Memorial Methodist Church and evening worship at the American Legion Auditorium. The mission was sponsored by the Roanoke Ministers Conference.

Pfc. Hubert Neal, thirty, of Roanoke was killed in an auto accident near Baltimore, Maryland, on March 1. He was stationed at Bolling Field. He was survived by his wife, Laura, and two young children.

Roanoke City Council gave approval at its March 3 meeting for rental of the old library building in Elmwood Park to the Garden Club Council. The Garden Club would rent the building beginning July 1 for one dollar per month.

Attorney Richard Edwards represented Curtis Turner and Bill France before Roanoke City Council on March 3 and proposed renewing modified stock car racing at Victory Stadium. The council referred the matter for further study. The proposal was to rent the stadium every Wednesday night between April 16 and September 10 for racing under the same conditions racing was held at the stadium in 1950.

Nelson Taylor, forty-two, of Roanoke died at Burrell Memorial Hospital on March 5 from burns he received in an accident at his home on Wells Avenue NW on December 28. Taylor fell across a heater.

Oliver Hill, a Richmond attorney, was the Men's Day speaker at Fifth Avenue Presbyterian Church in Roanoke on March 9. Hill was a member of the Fair Employment Practices Commission appointed by President Harry Truman.

Billy Eckstine, along with Count Basie and his orchestra, performed for a concert and dance at the American Legion Auditorium on March 10. White spectators were admitted to the balcony.

The Salem Lions Club held their seventeenth annual three-day minstrel show March 13–15 in the auditorium of Andrew Lewis High School. The show raised funds for their community service projects.

The YWCA launched a campaign to raise $165,000 for the new Lula Williams Memorial Branch YWCA and to liquidate a mortgage on the Central Branch building. The Williams Memorial Branch was estimated to cost $110,000 and contain 2,400 square feet, with a seating capacity of 400 persons. The Williams Memorial Branch's building was a residence located at 304 Second Street NE and was deemed inadequate.

The Broadway hit *Brigadoon* came to the Jefferson High School auditorium on March 22. The Civic Drama Guild of New York's production of the play was sponsored locally by the Sertoma Club.

Country singer Glen Thompson and the Smoky Mountain Hayride performed at the Roanoke Theatre on March 13. Special guest was Ray Myers, the "armless musician."

John Puhl Products Company officials announced the construction of a $225,000 household chemical plant on Route 11, just west of Salem. Building would begin in June.

Dr. Edward Dudley Sr., seventy, died on March 10 in Detroit, where he had gone for medical treatment. Dudley was a dentist and a past president of the Magic City Medical and Dental Society. He was the father of Ambassador Edward Dudley Jr. He had practiced dentistry in Roanoke for over forty years.

Officials with the American Viscose Roanoke plant announced the plant's shutdown had been extended for four additional weeks to go through April 6. The shutdown may continue beyond that period, officials cautioned, due to the synthetic yarn market. The curtailment of work affected three-fourths of the plant's 3,000 employees.

This is Grandin Texaco fronting Grandin Road SW at Memorial Avenue. Virginia Heights Baptist Church is in the background in this 1950s image. *Pete Wheeler*

Excavation of the underpass under the N&W Railway tracks at South Roanoke was completed by mid-March. The underpass was proposed to become part of the proposed Riverside Drive to help with stadium traffic.

The Salem Sesquicentennial Celebration received its charter from the SCC on March 12. The organization was chaired by M. S. McClung to promote Salem's 150th anniversary.

Dust storms that had originated in Oklahoma, Kansas, and Texas blew through the Roanoke Valley on March 13, creating a haze and covering all exposed surfaces in dust. Visibility went from a normal fifteen miles to four.

The life story of Dr. Fred Garland was produced as a film in Los Angeles. Garland, a Roanoke native, became a Broadway producer before becoming addicted to drugs and imprisoned. While in Tombs Prison in New York City, Garland converted to Christianity and became an evangelist upon his release. He eventually moved back to Roanoke. The film's working title was *The Case of Convict 63913*.

Sherwin-Williams Paints held a grand opening of its second store in Roanoke on March 14 at 1304 Grandin Road, next to the Grandin Theatre. George Noell was the store manager.

Betty Baxter shared her testimony of faith healing to a large crowd at the American Legion Auditorium on March 16. According to Baxter, she was crippled with both arms paralyzed before being healed by prayer. Her appearance was sponsored by the Pentecostal Fellowship of Roanoke.

Earl Scruggs, Lester Flatt, and the Foggy Mountain Boys performed at the Roanoke Theatre on March 19.

Commander William Starkey announced the opening of VFW Post No. 9696 headquarters at 28-A W. Church Avenue on March 16.

The Pittsburgh Symphony Orchestra performed at the American Legion Auditorium on March 22. Cellist Aldo Parisot joined them as a guest performer. The concert was part of the Thursday Morning Music Club concert series. The symphony conductor was Paul Paray.

The Vinton Lions Club held their annual minstrel show for three nights March 20–22. The show raised funds for their community service projects. The show was produced and directed by Jim Reynolds and featured a forty-member chorus.

The new Ewald-Clark store held its grand opening on the evening of March 17 at 17 W. Church Avenue.

The Roanoke School Board awarded the construction contract for the annex to Jefferson High School to Lucas and Fralin for $86,400. When completed the annex would house a vocational education department, physical education offices, and a gymnasium. The board also allocated payment of $34,000 for some thirteen acres of land for the new Preston Park School to be built. The land was purchased from Lena Nininger.

Salem Sesquicentennial signed a contract on March 21 with John B. Rogers Producing Company for celebration of the town's birthday from August 10–16. Preliminary plans called for a religious service, pageant, and a parade.

The Trail Drive-In theatre opened on March 21 and showed a double feature of *Buccaneer's Girl* and *Hold That Baby!* The drive-in was located on Route 460, a mile and a half east of Roanoke.

Conrad and Carolyn Cromer suffered first- and second-degree burns on their bodies as they rescued their two small children from the family's burning house in Catawba on March 20. The two-story frame home was a complete loss.

A residence that had once served as the Salvation Army Hospital was razed in the 500 block of Salem Avenue on March 21. The stately home was built around 1902 and was once the home of Arthur Sibert, a prominent Roanoke businessman.

Owen Scheetz, the new manager of the Roanoke Red Sox, was officially welcomed to Roanoke on March 22 with a banquet at Maher Field. Scheetz was manager of the Oneonta Red Sox in the previous season.

Francis Cocke, president of Hollins College, announced on March 22 a campaign to raise $625,000 for the college to construct a new library to replace the old one and for a small dormitory to house about sixty-five students.

H. R. Johnson Hardware Company opened at 16 W. Main Street in Salem on March 23. It specialized in Westinghouse appliances, radios, and televisions.

More than 1,000 persons inspected the new Knights of Columbus home on Wasena Hill on March 23. The Knights planned to occupy the home in early April. The local chapter of the Catholic Daughters of America acted as hostesses.

The Star City Restaurant at 6 S. Jefferson Street was auctioned off on March 25 due to the health of its owner.

Roanoke City Council candidate Lester Hutts charged on March 25 that the city manager, Arthur Owens, had a "political machine" at St. John's Episcopal Church and that the worship bulletins there were being used to promote two other candidates. Candidates Robert Woody and Edwin Young attended St. John's. The remark drew a strong rebuke from Woody in the press. Councilman Walter Young was a also a member of St. John's, leading Hutts, a Baptist, to charge that the church would control three persons on the five-person council plus the city manager, who was on the vestry at the church.

Eastern Airlines announced on March 25 that it was planning to eliminate five daily flights into Roanoke. The airlines stated the reason for the cuts was the rates being charged at the airport.

Peggy Lou Bower, an eighteen-year-old student at William Fleming High School, won the American Legion State Oratorical contest. The state contest finals were held at Jefferson High School on March 26.

Morton Turner, eighty-two, died at his home on Grandin Road on March 25. Turner was president of the Dixie Finance and Loan Corporation and a past president of the American National Bank in Roanoke.

The Roanoke Red Sox began their spring training on March 27 in Ocala, Florida.

The half-million dollar addition to Woodrow Wilson Junior High School was formally dedicated on March 27. The guest speaker was Rev. Frank Efird, pastor of Christ Lutheran Church, who gave an address on "The Spirit of Woodrow Wilson."

The par for the Roanoke Country Club golf course was changed from 71 to 69 for the eighteen holes under a new system established by the golf pro Luke Barnes.

John Stephens, recreation department director for Salem, tendered his resignation in late March to take effect on April 20. He accepted a similar position in Coral Gables, Florida. He had been recreation director since 1947.

Charles Wiseman, forty-two, of Roanoke was killed when a dump truck he was driving was struck by an N&W Railway freight train on a grade crossing three miles east of Salem on March 28. A passenger, James Flinchum, leapt from the truck moments before the crash and escaped injury.

Tiny Bradshaw, B. B. King, and H-Bomb Ferguson performed at the American Legion Auditorium on April 2.

The Virginia Amateur Baseball League announced the teams for the season that would begin April 20. The commissioner was Joe Woods, and the teams were Vinton Athletic Club, New Castle, Veterans Administration Hospital, Glenvar, Boones Mill, Roanoke-Webster, Elliston-Lafayette-Shawsville, Rocky Mount, Buchanan, Salem-Milliken, Masons Cove, and Back Creek (which would be called "Big Lick" as they were sponsored by Big Lick Motors).

A fire swept through the poultry barn of Horace Harvey at Starkey on March 29, killing 6,000 chickens.

Arthur Taubman left Roanoke on a trip to Israel on April 6 to participate in the dedication of the Alliance Tire and Rubber Company building, of which he was president. Taubman was instrumental in raising $1.5 million in American funding for the plant that was located between Tel Aviv and Haifa.

An Eastern Airlines Silverliner airplane was placed on the steps of the Municipal Building in Roanoke on March 31 during negotiations between the airlines and city officials on landing fees at Woodrum Field.

Aviation Machinist Garland Hostetter of Roanoke was one of nine men rescued on March 31 after spending four days on an Arctic ice pack 500 miles from the North Pole. The men had been stranded there when the plane they were aboard had to make an emergency landing.

Dr. Fred Oast, medical director of the Roanoke City Tuberculosis Sanatorium, announced on March 31 that six of fifty patients there were being treated with a new drug, Nydrazid, which was in clinical trials.

Orkin Exterminators moved to their new building at 2315 Williamson Road on April 1. They had previously been located at 123 Franklin Road since 1947.

Roanoke City Council voted 3–2 on March 31 to repeal its former ban on stock car racing at Victory Stadium and authorized the city manager to negotiate a contract. The swing vote was A. R. Minton, who, formerly opposed, agreed to try racing for one season.

Robert Woody and Paul Johnson won the Democratic Primary on April 1 to run in the general election for Roanoke City Council. The two men would face two Republicans, John Waldrop and Jubal Angell. The vote totals in the primary were as follows: Woody, 3,740; Johnson, 2,854; Ernest Light, 2,577; Lester Hutts, 1,913; Robert Wagner, 1,236; and Edwin Young, 1,118.

Warren Dickerson, fifty-four, fell through an open safety door of a moving elevator in the State and City Building on April 2 and was killed. The Roanoke attorney became pinned between the car and the shaft wall.

William Mitchell, forty-four, of Roanoke was killed instantly when the car he was driving crashed into a loaded dump truck on Route 11 west of Roanoke on April 3.

Bart Galbraith is in the shop of his Virginia Armature Company (electric motor repair) at 314 W. Salem Avenue in this 1950s photo. *John DeCarolis*

A permit for a new drive-in theatre was issued on April 3 to Southeast Theatre Company for erection of a theatre in the Riverdale section of Roanoke.

Wasena Hardware opened on April 4 at 1110 Main Street in Roanoke.

Homer Briarhopper, Maude Hale, Don Reno, and Richard Geary performed for a show and dance at the City Market Auditorium on April 4.

A Black family mutually agreed with their potential landlord to sever a lease agreement to rent a home at 1219 Rorer Avenue SW after the landlord received threatening phone calls from persons upset with her renting the home to a Black family. Mary Welles reported she had received calls from individuals who planned to burn the house down if she proceeded with the lease.

Western film star Lash LaRue, along with his Hollywood Entertainers, performed at the Roanoke Theatre on April 9.

Major League Baseball's Washington Senators played the Cincinnati Reds on April 8 at Maher Field. The Senators won the exhibition game 8–7 before a crowd of 2,000.

The South Salem Citizens' Committee distributed 500 copies of a three-page letter urging incorporation to residents living within the section. The letter advocated the incorporation of South Salem, Orchard Heights, Orchard Court, and Manchester Court into a town for the purpose of contracting for cheaper sewage disposal. Dewey Moore was chairman of the committee.

The twenty-fifth annual Spring Congress of Gill Memorial Ear, Eye, and Throat Hospital opened for its weeklong session on April 7 with over 500 registered attendees. One of the main speakers was Dr. E. C. Kendall of Princeton University, who discovered cortisone.

The legitimacy of evangelist Oral Roberts and his faith healing split the congregation of Grace Baptist Temple at a meeting on April 8. The church's pastor, Rev. Gene Arnold, denounced Roberts and led a walkout of many members, leaving the church in the hands of those who liked Roberts. So heated was the meeting that fists were thrown, and the melee had to be broken up by eight policemen called to the scene.

H. A. Gross, a retailer of building supplies, opened on Route 460 one mile east of Roanoke on April 10.

The Roanoke Redevelopment and Housing Authority announced that the name of the low-income Black housing project would be Lincoln Terrace. The authority's original name for the development had been Crispus Attucks Heights after the Revolutionary War hero.

Johnny Otis and his recording orchestra, along with singer Little Esther, performed for a show and dance at the American Legion Auditorium on April 13. The balcony was reserved for white spectators.

VFW Post No. 9996 was organized in Roanoke. Officers were E. R. Craig, William Starkey, Paul Smith, Grady Lyons, and Harlin Perrine.

Orange Avenue Baptist Church held their first worship service on April 13 at its new location at 804 Orange Avenue NE. The church had been previously located on Ninth Street SE and was formerly Ninth Street Baptist Church. Rev. Everette Whisnant was the pastor. The church had been organized in 1950.

Ground-breaking ceremonies were held on April 13 for Grace Methodist Church in the 4400 block of Williamson Road. The first shovel of dirt was turned by Frank Horner, oldest member of the congregation.

Wilhelm Cleaners opened on April 13 at 719 Franklin Road SW.

Three bear cubs were secured from a conservation officer in Alleghany County for the new Children's Zoo when it opened on Mill Mountain on the condition that the bears would be released back into the wild by the state once they had become grown.

Huntington Court Methodist Church dedicated its memorial window in the sanctuary on April 13. The theme of the stained glass window was *Christian Love in Action*.

Over 1,000 children participated in the annual Easter egg hunt in Salem's Longwood Park on April 12.

An estimated crowd of 18,000 gathered at Natural Bridge for the annual Easter service. The speaker was Rev. Robert Lapsley, retired pastor of Roanoke's First Presbyterian Church. The service was broadcast nationwide over the CBS network. Lapsley was assisted by Rev. Harry Gamble of Roanoke's Calvary Baptist Church.

The FCC lifted its three-year freeze on new television station applications on April 14. This allowed applications from Roanoke to be considered, including one announced by the Times-World Corporation the day prior. It owned and operated WDBJ.

Dr. Walter Newman, president of Virginia Tech, stated on April 15 that he was "interested in exploring" an educational television station in Roanoke, as the FCC had established a channel for that purpose. Officials with both Hollins College and Roanoke College indicated a lack of interest due to the cost.

Roanoke attorney Moss Plunkett filed to oppose incumbent Sixth District Congressman Clarence Burton of Lynchburg in the Democratic Primary on July 15.

First Lt. John Dille Jr. of Roanoke was killed Easter Sunday in a crash of his fighter plane in Asia. He had flown twenty-four combat missions in Korea.

The King Brothers and Cristiani Circus arrived in Roanoke on April 19 for two performances at Maher Field. The circus held a late morning parade along Franklin Road to Elm Avenue, east to Jefferson Street, and then to Maher Field. Twenty-two tents filled the field along with the big top that seated 7,000. The highlight was the Cristiani family that performed bareback horse-riding stunts. Another popular attraction was Hugo Zacchini, who was shot from a cannon across the length of the big top.

The Roanoke Red Sox opened their regular season in the Piedmont League on April 18 in an away game at Lynchburg. Roanoke won, 13–4.

Roanoke Garden Week was held the third week in April. The homes and gardens of Mr. and Mrs. Benjamin Parrott, Dr. and Mrs. Homer Bartley, Dr. and Mrs. W. S. Butler, Mr. and Mrs. Sydney Small, Mr. and Mrs. Murray Hammond, Mr. and Mrs. Larry Dow, Mr. and Mrs. Burwell Ilyus, and Dr. William Bartlett were on the tour.

The Roanoke City Republican Committee was tossed out of office on April 19 due to not having been legally elected at a mass meeting on March 21. The action to dissolve the committee was taken by the Sixth District Republican Committee. The decision was a victory for Linwood Holton, a young Roanoke attorney who had unsuccessfully sought the chairmanship of the Roanoke group and challenged the methods used at the mass meeting in question.

The Burrell Memorial Hospital Service League sponsored County Fair Day on April 24 at the Star City Auditorium located at Wells Avenue and Fourth Street NW. The annual event featured a parade, school bands, and competitions to raise funds for the hospital.

William Wray, fifty-one, of Roanoke committed suicide on April 20 after shooting his wife in an apparent murder-suicide attempt at their home on Memorial Avenue SW. Mrs. Wray was taken to the hospital with a bullet wound to the neck.

The Roanoke Ministers Conference voted on April 21 not to open its membership to Black clergy. The all-Protestant group did vote to study enlarging the membership to Catholic and Jewish clergy.

Roanoke City Council authorized at its April 22 meeting a referendum on June 10 on a ten-year bond issue of $350,000 to help defray the cost of a viaduct to eliminate the main Jefferson Street grade crossing over the N&W Railway tracks. The remainder of the $2.5 million costs would be paid by the state and N&W Railway.

Members of the Phi Beta Sigma fraternity stand in front of the Fifth Avenue Presbyterian Church. Rev. William Simmons, the church's pastor, is fifth from right. The image is dated April 20, 1952. *Fifth Avenue Presbyterian Church*

Davidson's Restaurant opened on April 23 on Williamson Road at the former location of the Palm Room. W. R. Coleman was the owner and manager.

The furnishings and equipment of the Post House Tea Room on Main Street in Salem were auctioned off on April 23.

The Town of Vinton $200,000 sewage disposal system was put into operation on April 23. It was the first such system in the Roanoke Valley. Prior to this, untreated sewage from the town went into Tinker Creek and from there into the Roanoke River.

Editor and author John Temple Graves spoke to the Laymen's League at St. John's Episcopal Church Parish House on April 23. Graves asserted that belief in God was critical to the nation's future, and he denounced communism, socialism, "misdirected" psychiatry, and progressive education theories.

A crowd of 1,200 attended an open house at Woodrow Wilson Junior High School on April 24 to tour the $550,000 addition.

Odessa Bailey of Roanoke was installed as the president of the Virginia Federation of Women's Clubs on April 25 in a ceremony at Richmond during the group's annual convention.

Arless Kemp, twenty-eight, of Dugspur died in Jefferson Hospital on April 25 from injuries he sustained from a car-truck crash in front of the Bent Mountain Post Office on the same day.

The Roanoke School Board voted on April 28 to authorize the permanent closing of Gilmer School at the end of the school year in June. Gilmer students would be absorbed by Harrison School.

Steel workers at the American Bridge plant in Roanoke went on strike on April 29 as part of a nationwide strike by their union. Almost 700 employees were involved in the strike in Roanoke.

Buddy Johnson and his orchestra, along with Arthur Prysock and Ella Johnson, performed for a show and dance at the American Legion Auditorium on May 2. The balcony was reserved for white spectators.

Frederick Kiser, a bus driver for Safety Motor Transit, was declared the first-place winner in the National Safety Council's city bus division contest for the United States and Canada for 1951. Kiser had driven 38,976 miles in 1951 without an accident. He had been an employee of SMT since 1922.

Bobby Myers won the opening stock car race of the season at Victory Stadium on April 30. Local favorite Curtis Turner wrecked in the fourth lap, recovered, and finished fifth.

A brief history of the Thursday Morning Music Club was provided by its founding president, Mrs. George Gravatt, during the group's luncheon at the Hotel Roanoke on May 1. According to Gravatt, the organization started in 1908 and met in her home until 1912, when they moved to the former Terry home after purchasing a piano from Hobbie Brothers. Mrs. Lucian Cocke also helped to start the club along with students from Hollins College.

Roanoke's Optimist Club sponsored a two-night baseball series between the Battle Creek Belles and the Fort Wayne Daises, both affiliated with the American Girl's Baseball League. The manager for the Belles was Guy Bush, former star pitcher with the Chicago Cubs, and the Daises were managed by Jimmie Foxx, a former star player for the Philadelphia Athletics. The games were May 4 and 5 at Maher Field.

R. E. Roop, sixty, of Salem was struck and killed by an automobile on Route 11 near Fort Lewis School on May 2.

Some 300 alumni and friends of Roanoke College attended a capital campaign kickoff in the college's auditorium on May 2. The Roanoke area group pledged $300,000 toward an overall goal of $500,000.

US Secretary of the Treasury John Snyder spoke to southwestern Virginia bankers at the Hotel Roanoke on May 2. His theme was "a strong economy makes for a strong defense."

Missionary Alliance Church dedicated its new church building at 349 Mountain Avenue SW on May 4. The new church could seat 200. The congregation was organized in 1940.

Airheart-Kirk Clothing Company celebrated its fiftieth anniversary the first week of May.

Star City Drive-In Theatre on Route 220, one mile south of Roanoke, opened on May 5. The premier film was *Dancing in the Dark*. Advertisements for the theatre read, "Whites only."

Wilma Lee, Stoney Cooper, and the Clinch Mountain Clan gave a concert at the Roanoke Theatre on May 7.

Joseph Monsour was awarded the bid to operate Washington Park pool and concessions for the summer. He stipulated in his bid to Roanoke City Council that he would not charge children to swim at the pool, which was reserved for Blacks.

American Airlines agreed to a five-year extension of their contract to serve Woodrum Field. Piedmont Airlines also had their contract extended for the same terms.

Vinton Baptist Church dedicated its education building on May 7. The structure contained ninety-one separate rooms that could accommodate over 1,000 persons.

A group of South Salem residents posted their petition on May 7 at the Roanoke County Courthouse seeking incorporation. Their petition was scheduled to be heard on June 11. The main reason for wanting incorporation was sewage treatment.

President Harry Truman nominated former Roanoker Henry Fowler as defense production administrator on May 7.

The Clyde Moody Show came to the American Legion Auditorium on May 8 and 9. Joining the show's main star were Cody & Cody, Frances Parker, Edgar Vernon, Maids of the Golden West, Phil Ross, and Lloyd McClenney.

William Wilson of Little Rock, Arkansas, was hired in early May by the Roanoke Redevelopment and Housing Authority to be the planning technician for its "slum clearance" program. The authority indicated its first plan would target the northeast section of the city and intended to submit a detailed program to the city council.

In 1951, Woodrum Field reported a total of 37,492 ticketed passengers with the three airlines serving the airport. The figures broke down as follows: American Airlines, 13,049 passengers; Eastern Airlines, 12,540 passengers; and Piedmont Airlines, 11,903 passengers.

This 1950s image shows the Kinsey dairy farm in north Roanoke. The Kinsey home is in the background, and where the cows are grazing is the present-day route of I-581. *Bob Kinsey*

Hedrick's Shell Service Station opened its Washmobile on May 9, the first car wash on Williamson Road. The service station was located at 2605 Williamson Road.

The Roanoke Children's Theatre presented *The Steadfast Tin Soldier* for three nights at the Jefferson High School auditorium. The theatre was sponsored by the Junior League.

Arts & Crafts Ceramic Studio opened on May 10 at 2818 Williamson Road.

Charley Turner was named director of the Salem Recreation Department, succeeding John Stephens.

N&W Railway ordered construction of fifteen coal-burning switching locomotives and 2,025 freight cars for a total of $13.5 million. The S1a engines and all but 500 of the freight cars were to be built in the Roanoke and Portsmouth, Ohio, shops.

Linwood Holton Jr. was elected as the new chairman of the Roanoke City Republican Committee at its meeting on May 10. He defeated C. M. Ellis, 82 to 65. The election of a chairman was spirited and followed a tumultuous meeting held on March 21 that resulted in the outcome of that meeting being ruled illegal by state Republican officials. Holton and his group were viewed as insurgents that sought to bring a different vision to the local party, in contrast to establishment Republicans.

Salem Pentecostal Holiness Church held a ground-breaking for its new $40,000 building on May 10 at 307 Bruffey Street. The pastor was Rev. A. M. Long.

The Salem Community Players presented the comedy *On Approval* on May 14 and 15 at Roanoke College Lab Theatre. It was believed to be the first theatre-in-the-round production for a community theatre group. The play was directed by Kathleen Thornton, and cast members were Charlotte Martin, Amy Jo Glenn, William Segall, and Herbert Harris.

Television equipment arrived at WROV radio station the first week of May, as station officials anticipated the approval of its television application with the FCC for channel 7.

Roanoke Mayor A. R. Minton got a free ride on May 10 around the city in a rubber car manufactured by the US Rubber Company. Company representatives had the car on a national tour to showcase their product. The plastic frame weighed 184 pounds and could be mounted on a chassis purchased separately.

Blackface comedian Slim Williams performed at the Roanoke Theatre on May 14.

Roanoke Junior Chamber of Commerce placed before Roanoke City Council on May 12 their plans to have miniature railroad operate at the Children's Zoo on Mill Mountain. The cost for the train was estimated at $13,000. The Jaycees agreed to bear the cost of the added attraction. The council gave its approval for the idea.

A fire destroyed the sign-making shop of J. P. Guerrant at the rear of his home at 1368 Buena Vista Avenue SE on May 12.

An abandoned newborn baby was found wrapped in old newspaper in an alley just off First Street NW on May 12. The infant was taken to Burrell Memorial Hospital.

Fire blight struck numerous peach and apple orchards in Roanoke County in mid-May. There was no cure for the blight, other than to let it run its course.

Cletus Richards of Franklin County was jailed on May 13 for robbing the Bank of Salem of $32,772 and kidnapping a cashier, Frank Booze Jr., as a hostage for a brief period. Richards commandeered a taxicab and led local police on a wild chase that ended in Roanoke. During the chase, Richards shot and wounded the cab driver, who was forced to drive his cab, in a failed attempt by Richards to escape capture. The cab driver was William Akers of Roanoke.

The Hagan-Wallace Circus came to the grounds of Victory Stadium on May 17, sponsored by the Williamson Road Lions Club.

Applications for Black tenants in Lincoln Terrace, a low-income housing development of the Roanoke Redevelopment and Housing Authority, would begin in June. The mid-May announcement came from the Authority's director, Richard Beck, who indicated the first fifty tenants would be able to occupy their residences by July 15.

The South Roanoke Methodist Church was sold to the South Roanoke Baptist Church congregation for $65,000 in mid-May. The Methodists planned to begin building a new church in the 2300 block of South Jefferson Street in June. The contract allowed for the Methodists to use their old church for up to two more years while the new sanctuary was being constructed.

Armed Forces Day was celebrated on May 18 with an afternoon parade that began at Elmwood Park and concluded at Victory Stadium. At the stadium, Rear Admiral John Carson reviewed the parade of military and veteran organizations, and some 2,000 free ice cream cones were distributed.

Richard Poff, twenty-nine, of Radford was nominated by Sixth District Republicans to run as their candidate for Congress. Poff accepted the nomination before a packed ballroom at the Patrick Henry Hotel on May 17. James Moyer of Salem gave the keynote address, where he derided the Truman administration.

Roanoke College president Sherman Oberly announced that the college's library would be moved from Bittle Memorial Hall to the recently acquired education building of First Methodist Church. Oberly stated the move would be completed by 1953.

Joe Chitwood's Auto Daredevils came to the Starkey Speedway on May 20, featuring racing, car jumps, and stunt driving.

Waverly Place Baptist Church dedicated its new sanctuary on May 21. Rev. C. C. Thomas, the church's first pastor, was the guest speaker. The church was organized on April 26, 1926, and built a small tabernacle that year for worship. In 1927 a larger building was erected, with the new sanctuary's construction having begun in 1951.

Christ Episcopal Church broke ground on May 17 for its new parish house at the rear of the church. Two houses were razed to make room for the structure that was part of a $182,000 capital improvement plan.

Jerusalem Baptist Church dedicated its new sanctuary at 1014 Norfolk Avenue SW on May 18. Rising Sun Lodge 146 of the Grand Order of Masons laid the cornerstone.

William Engleby of the Civilian Defense unit announced that Explorer Scouts would man Roanoke's air defense post atop Mill Mountain in the event the area was alerted for enemy aircraft.

Radio personalities the Bailey Brothers and their Happy Valley Boys Quartet performed on May 21 at the Roanoke Theatre.

Dr. E. J. Keffer won the seventy-two-hole medal play golf tournament at Roanoke Country Club on May 18. The tournament was played in four rounds.

Mrs. Howard Johnson won first prize in a contest to determine which ten books should be moved first from the old Roanoke Public Library to the new one. Her list was as follows: the Bible, *In His Steps*, Aristotle's *Ethics*, Plato's *Republic*, *Encyclopedia Britannica*, *Twelve Centuries of English Poetry and Prose*, *American Literature* by Metcalf, *The Wealth of Nations*, and *Robert Edward Lee* by Freeman. Harold Sander, the librarian, reported that volumes from the old library would begin being moved on May 24 with the help of the Boy Scouts.

Charter night for the new Bonsack Ruritan Club was held on May 22 at Bonsack Methodist Church.

States-rights Democrats dominated the Democratic Party mass meeting held in Roanoke on May 20. The main order of business was selecting delegates for the party's state convention. State Senator Earl Fitzpatrick denounced the Truman administration's policies, claiming "the South is the one great hope in breaking the centralized power of the federal government."

Ben Parrott won Best in Show at the Roanoke Rose Society annual show on May 20. Parrott's rose, "Sweet Sixteen," had also been awarded a silver medal from the American Rose Society.

Big Oak Service Station opened on May 22 at 2521 Williamson Road. Gordon Watson was the owner. Opening weekend special was an oil change and grease job for $2.29.

A Christian Businessman's Club was formed in Roanoke on May 21. Organizers were George Hitch, William Lotz, Carroll Traylor, and J. R. Sheppard.

Officials with the Children's Zoo postponed the opening from Memorial Day weekend to midsummer.

The Salem Avenue Parking Center opened on May 23 at 124 W. Salem Avenue.

Roanoke library staff and about thirty Boy Scouts began moving 58,000 volumes from the old library into the new library on May 23. In the evening, members of the Junior Chamber of Commerce aided the move. The new library's formal opening was set for June 2.

Carr's Garage, near the rear of Lee Junior High School, caught fire on May 23.

The Virginia Mountain Baseball League opened its season in mid-May. Teams in the league were Roanoke, Lexington, Buena Vista, Clifton Forge, Ronceverte, Glasgow, Covington, and Westvaco.

Roanoke College students staged a panty raid on May 24. Access to Smith Hall, a women's dorm, was gained through several windows. Local police and the college president halted the raid conducted by about fifty young men. A few days later, twenty-three of the participants were placed by the college on "social probation."

Ruth Brown, Charles Brown, and Shirley Haven performed for a show and dance at the American Legion Auditorium on May 29.

Douglas Doyle, ten, of Salem was struck and killed by a train on May 24 as he was walking home from fishing with three friends. The accident occurred about 400 yards west of Wertz Crossing near Lee Highway.

Berkley Mauck, seventeen, of Roanoke and a star athlete at Jefferson High School drowned at Loch Haven on May 25. Friends saw him go under but could not rescue him. A local rescue squad recovered his body.

South Salem residents began legal proceeding by serving papers to the three members of the Salem Town Council on May 26 to have their section annexed into the Town of Salem.

The Civil Aeronautics Administration greatly expanded Roanoke's airline service in late May when it ruled in favor of expansion of routes by Piedmont Airlines and to allow American Airlines to continue stopping at Woodrum Field. Marshall Harris, airport manager, had lobbied the board heavily for such action.

A ball diamond was constructed on the southwest corner of the County farm at Glenvar in late May. Roanoke County officials granted permission to create the ball field when approached by V. O. McDaniel, business manager of the Glenvar baseball team of the Virginia Amateur League. Albert Brothers Contractors did the grading for the field at the intersection of Routes 11 and 645.

Mrs. Nellie Brophy of Roanoke died at her home on May 27. She was one of the founders of the Roanoke Music Teachers Association and started the choir at St. Andrews Catholic Church, where she served as choir director and organist for over thirty years.

Robert Stone, seventeen, of Jefferson High School was awarded the second annual B'nai B'rith Athletic Achievement Award on May 28. He was the son of Mr. and Mrs. Webster Stone. Bill Dudley, a former football star at the University of Virginia, was the keynote speaker at the awards banquet.

Jack Robinson, former All-American basketball player at Baylor University and a member of the US Olympic basketball team in 1948, came to Roanoke in late May to be the main speaker for a youth revival that was held in the American Legion Auditorium.

Roanoke City Council held "Zoo Days" the first week in June to allow children to buy "stock" in the Children's Zoo on Mill Mountain. Those that purchased the twenty-five-cent stock would be admitted to the zoo on opening day.

First Methodist Church in Salem held a cornerstone-laying ceremony on May 31 for their new sanctuary. Bishop Paul Gardner was the guest speaker.

Roanoke Coca-Cola Bottling Works celebrated its fiftieth anniversary the first week in June. The original franchise in Roanoke was awarded to A. F. Cathey, J. W. Clark, and J. F. Arrowood on August 21, 1902. In 1909, John Riley acquired control of the franchise. The energetic Riley would jump aboard trains and get off at each stop to take orders for each delivery. Unfortunately, Riley was killed by a train in 1906 in Giles County. In fifty years the Roanoke plant expanded, and the local franchise also operated bottling plants in Pulaski, Galax, and Rocky Mount.

This mid-50s image shows the Coca-Cola Bottling Works located at 346 Center Avenue. Coca-Cola had operated a bottling plant in Roanoke since 1902. *Nelson Harris*

Mrs. W. B. Richardson defeated Mrs. E. J. Keffer to win the Nininger Trophy Golf Tournament held at Roanoke Country Club in late May. It was the seventeenth year for the tournament named for Peggy Nininger.

Clifford Roberson, thirteen, won the city-county marbles tournament at the finals, which were held in Elmwood Park. It was Roberson's third title. Douglas Conner took second place, and Dickey Orr was third. The tournament, held over several weeks, had 3,500 competitors.

Detective Capt. Frank Webb was selected to become Roanoke's next superintendent of the police department. He succeeded Stuart Bruce, who had announced his retirement. Webb had been with the department for seventeen years.

A three-alarm fire in downtown Roanoke occurred on June 1 that gutted a three-story building at 22 W. Campbell Avenue. A foot patrolman discovered the fire in the early morning hours that severely damaged the Budget Dress Shop and J-Belle Hat Shop.

Hayden Huddleston launched a new show on WROV radio on June 2 called *Off the Cuff* that was broadcast during the lunch hour on weekdays and was advertised as a "potpourri of facts and fancy."

World's Museum of Strange People came to Roanoke for six days in early June and set up in the 2800 block of Williamson Road. The sideshow had Johann Petursson of Iceland, who was eight feet, eight inches tall and weighed 425 pounds. Others included Ralph, the elephant man; Electra, the atomic girl; Jeff Griffen, the human pincushion; Salerno, the fire eater; Marvo, the armless wonder; and a leopard-skin girl.

American Viscose announced on June 1 the plan for a new powerhouse at its Roanoke plant. The move seemed to quiet rumors that the plant was destined to be closed or relocated.

Powell Chapman, veteran editor of the *Roanoke Times*, died on June 1 at age sixty-three. Chapman had been with the newspaper since 1915. He served as president of the Roanoke Chamber of Commerce in 1945.

Lee-Hy Auto Court
U. S. 11 West of Roanoke
Call 2-6530

Lee-Hy Auto Court, located on Route 11 west of the Roanoke city limits, is shown on this postcard postmarked 1952. *Nelson Harris*

Irving Olds, retired chairman of US Steel's board of directors, gave the commencement address at Roanoke College on June 1. The main theme of his address was the importance of property rights. "One of the primary functions of government is to protect us in our human right to possess property." There were seventy-eight graduates.

Roanoke City Council member Dan Cronin tendered his resignation on June 3 to take effect June 30.

Grand Ole Opry comics Lonzo and Oscar performed at the Roanoke Theatre on June 3.

The Roanoke Ministers Conference initiated a process to form an interracial Protestant ministers' conference during a retreat at Natural Bridge on June 2. The ministers voted to form a committee to work with Black clergy to explore the possibility.

Roanoke's new public library at Elmwood Park opened at 10:00 a.m. on June 3 with little fanfare. A dedication ceremony was planned for the end of the month.

The Roanoke Jaycees selected William Hobbie as their 1952 Father of the Year. Hobbie was general secretary of Hobbie Music Company in Roanoke and an active leader in Boy Scouts. The Jaycees selected Hobbie in early June with a formal celebration on June 11 at the American Theatre.

The Cave Spring Lions Club presented its annual minstrel show at Back Creek School on June 6.

A ground-breaking ceremony was held at Hollins College on June 7 for the new dormitory, Turner Hall, which was named as a memorial for Joseph Turner and his sister, Lelia Turner Rath. Turner was the former business manager for the college.

About 500 Boy Scouts from thirty troops in Roanoke pitched their tents at Carvins Cove the first weekend in June for their annual camporee.

Roanoke businessman Ernest Boone died on June 5 at his home on Wycliffe Avenue SW at the age of eighty-eight. Boone came to Roanoke in 1880 and by 1884 was associated with the E. H. Stewart Furniture Company. By 1889, he had established Lowe and Boone, which became Overstreet and Boone in 1903. With an additional partner, the furniture store became Overstreet, Thurman, and Boone but was later changed to Thurman and Boone. Boone was a charter member of the Roanoke Booster Club.

A service station at Salem Avenue and Second Street SW was razed the first week of June to make room for a new off-street parking lot to be operated by J. D. Smith.

The St. Mark's Lutheran Church property at Campbell Avenue and Third Street SW was purchased in early June by Reid and Cutshall as the future site for their furniture store. The sixty-three-year-old structure was purchased for $50,750. The store would not take possession of the property until April or May of 1953. The church was erected in 1889 as Greene Memorial Methodist Church and was dedicated by that congregation in 1890. St. Mark's and Greene Memorial exchanged structures in 1902.

A crowd estimated at 1,000 attended the fifth annual Bridle Club Horse Show at Lakeview Farm on June 7. Main winners were Amy Bassett, hunter championship; Johnny Ferguson, five-gaited championship; Fred Repass, Tennessee Walking Horse championship; and Cynthia Butts, three-gaited championship.

Bethel Baptist Church in Salem was dedicated on June 8. The guest speaker was Rev. Wade Bryant of First Baptist Church, Roanoke.

Stuart Bruce, former Roanoke police superintendent, became the police chief at Hampton Roads Port of Embarkation.

Estes Cocke announced his retirement as vice president of Hollins College on June 9. He had been with the college since 1897, having been born at the college in 1876. He was appointed vice president in 1935.

Campbell Furniture Company opened at 123 E. Campbell Avenue on June 10.

Calvin Sisson won the Roanoke Junior Golf Championship at Roanoke Country Club on June 9. Alvin Rose finished second.

Roanoke voters elected Robert Woody and John Waldrop to Roanoke City Council on June 10. Woody, a Democrat, led the voting at 5,205, followed by Waldrop, a Republican, at 4,386. Democrat Paul Johnson garnered 3,906 votes, and Jubal Angell, a Republican, finished fourth at 3,447. Property owners approved a $350,000 bond issuance for the viaduct by a vote of 3,623 to 2,850. Woody and Waldrop succeeded W. P. Hunter and Dan Cronin, who decided not to seek reelection. In Salem, Leonard Shank defeated Burman Bowen 570 to 269 for the lone seat up for election on the town council. In Vinton, voters reelected Nelson

Thurman and elected newcomer Letcher Adkins over incumbent Ross McGee for the two seats up for election on the town council.

The *Cactus Jim Rodeo and Thrill Show* came to the Starkey Speedway on June 13 for two days. The rodeo featured trick riders, wild bull and bronco riding, calf roping, and Brahma Steers.

Three hundred businessmen participated in the annual Roanoke Booster Club train trip on June 11 to Hot Springs. Dr. E. G. Gill was the club president, and N&W Railway provided a special train for the occasion, the purpose of which was to help local businessmen get to know one another better.

A near-riot broke out at the American Legion Auditorium on June 10 when the pro wrestler "The Great Togo" from Japan bloodied the forehead of Irishman Jack Moore. As the incident occurred after the bell, the referee could not disqualify Togo, who was deemed the winner. The crowd began throwing shoes and other objects at Togo, and several rushed the ring before Togo could be escorted by local police to the dressing room.

City employees lobbied Roanoke City Council to adopt a five-day workweek akin to what other large businesses in the region had done, as well as state and federal governments. At the time, most city departments were open for a half-day on Saturdays.

Lee Petty won the 150-lap model stock car race at Victory Stadium on June 11. Attendance was estimated at 16,000.

Roanoke Esso Service Center opened on June 13 at 2715 Williamson Road.

The Roanoke Tuberculosis Association purchased X-ray equipment for Burrell Memorial Hospital and agreed to pay the costs of x-raying all patients ages twelve and up. The X-ray equipment was projected to cost $9,000.

John Massey, fifty-eight, of Roanoke drowned on June 13 while fishing in the James River near Buchanan.

Dr. E. W. Rushton, superintendent of the Orangeburg, South Carolina, public schools, was announced on June 14 as the next superintendent for Roanoke Public Schools. Rushton was to serve as assistant superintendent to Dr. D. E. McQuilkin, who was retiring, until July 1 when he would assume the head position.

Clifford Roberson, city-county marbles champion, and Russell Gwaltney, Salem champion, left for the national tournament in Asbury Park, New Jersey, in mid-June.

Nearly 1,000 children and parents turned out for the fishing rodeo held at Lakewood Park on June 14. The pond had been stocked with 200 rainbow trout and numerous kinds of other fish.

Ralph English won the annual city-county golf tournament at Hidden Valley Country Club on June 15. English had a seventy-two-hole score of 289. He was followed by George Fulton with a 292. Defending champion Connie Sellers placed third.

James Higgs, seventeen, of Roanoke was convicted in Gadsden, Alabama, of the December 1951 murder of Clyde Shapley, nineteen. Higgs pled guilty to the charge and was sentenced to thirty-five years in prison.

20 ENROlled

Children and workers in Vacation Bible School at Melrose Baptist Church in NW Roanoke posed for this June 1952 photo. Enrollment was 390. *Melrose Baptist Church*

Former Salem Mayor Wilbur Cross died on June 16 at age eighty-three. Cross was first elected to the town council in 1922 and served until 1928. In 1934, he became mayor.

Clyde Moody gave a concert at the Salem Theatre on June 19.

Roanoke City Council approved improvements to Woodrum Field at their meeting on June 18. With both federal and local monies, the improvements included the removal of Hangar No. 2, sealing portions of the runways, construction of an additional concrete apron at the new terminal, and construction of an access road.

City Manager Arthur Owens reviewed potential sites for a television and radio transmitter and tower proposed by WROV for Mill Mountain. WROV had an application to operate a television station pending before the FCC.

Riverside Drive-In Theatre opened on June 20 in the Riverdale section at 1942 Bennington Street SE. Opening night featured a live stage performance by Wayne Fleming and the Hawaiians. The movie that followed was *Ala Baba.*

Russ Gwaltney of Salem won the National Marbles Tournament championship in Asbury Park, New Jersey, on June 20. The twelve-year-old was given a police escort into Salem on his return and was recognized in a ceremony at Municipal Stadium.

Virginia Governor John Battle spoke at the formal dedication of the Garthright Memorial Bridge in Vinton on June 21. The bridge was named in memory of a local physician, Robert Garthright, who had delivered 1,939 babies in the town. Garthright had died in 1944.

Edwin Phillips, associate professor of education and director of public relations at Talladega College in Alabama, was named as the new principal for Addison High School effective July 1. Miss Sadie Lawson was named as the principal for new Booker T. Washington Junior High School (old Addison School). Lawson had been principal at Addison for the past three years.

A seven-mile section of the new Catawba Road opened on June 24 from Hanging Rock to the top of Catawba Mountain. The road was constructed using prison labor, and the labor camp was located at the base of Catawba Mountain. The road's completion date was set for August.

Kenneth Johnson won the annual Roanoke Soap Box Derby that was held on June 25 on Crystal Spring Avenue SW. Roger Furrow placed a close second. A crowd of 5,000 was on hand to watch the various heats among seventy-five competitors. Mayor A. R. Minton presented Johnson a plaque. Johnson qualified for the national derby in Akron, Ohio.

Edgar Thurman, president of Thurman and Boone Company, died at his home on June 25 at the age of eighty-eight. Thurman was a native of Bedford County who came to Roanoke in 1890. In 1893, he established a furniture store on Campbell Avenue under the name of Thurman and Overstreet. Thurman left an estate valued at $2 million, all of which went to support various organizations that served the region's youth and children.

The Roanoke Pet Shop advertised in late June that it was going out of business before mid-July. The store was located at 29 W. Salem Avenue.

About seventy-five Roanoke barbers met on June 26 and decided to standardize the price of a haircut at one dollar. A majority had been charging seventy-five cents.

The CAA moved into the control tower of the new administration building at Woodrum Field in late June. The old control tower was to be razed. In 1951, there were 81,748 takeoffs and landings that were directed from the control tower.

The Times-World Corporation filed an application with FCC on June 27 to operate a television station in Roanoke. The corporation owned and operated WDBJ radio and planned to spend $525,000 in building and operating a new television station with a transmitter on Fort Lewis Mountain.

By the end of June, the Academy of Music had been half razed. The job was expected to take four months.

Parade, the national magazine, became a regular insert in the Sunday editions of the *Roanoke Times* on July 13.

The Ravens, along with Cootie Williams and his orchestra, performed for a show and dance at the American Legion Auditorium on July 3. The balcony was reserved for white spectators.

Roanoke's new public library in Elmwood Park was formally dedicated on June 28. Keynote speaker was John Settlemayer, director of the Atlanta Public Library. Other speakers included Mayor A. R. Minton and Charles Hurt, president of the library board.

The former civil and police court became known as municipal court on June 28 in Roanoke. The name change was due to changes in the city's charter.

Melrose Avenue Christian Church dedicated its new $42,000 education wing on June 29.

Walter Garland purchased the home of Allen Kirk at Grandin Road and Westover Avenue SW, with plans to raze the residence and erect a new drugstore and a branch of the First National Exchange Bank.

The Children's Zoo on Mill Mountain opened and was dedicated on July 4. Conceived and sponsored by the Roanoke Civitan Club, the zoo was not yet fully complete for the opening that featured speeches by Cletus Broyles, president of the Civitan Club; Junius Fishburn; and Mayor A. R. Minton. Those recognized for their work in developing the zoo included Roanoke Fire Chief W. M. Mullins and John Wentworth, Director of Public Works. The dedication ceremony took place on the top deck of the concession stand. Over 8,000 attended the zoo on opening weekend.

Curtis Turner won a National Championship Modified and Sportsmen's Auto Race of 200 miles at Darlington, South Carolina, on July 4. His time was two hours and seventeen minutes.

Showtimers opened its second summer season on July 10 at Roanoke College with a production of *The Lady's Not for Burning*. Lead actors in the comedy were Kathy Thornton, Betty Thornton, Sam Good, Gene Akers, Dick Burton, and Yvonne Stone.

Piedmont Airlines announced on July 7 that it would begin daily flights from Roanoke to Louisville and Lexington, Kentucky, beginning July 25. That made eighteen daily flights out of Roanoke for the airline.

This is a 1950s billboard for Piedmont Airlines, one of the main air carriers serving the Roanoke Valley during the decade. The company was headquartered in Winston-Salem, North Carolina. *Bob Kinsey*

Rev. Ramon Redford resigned as pastor of Belmont Christian Church to assume the pastorate of Memorial Christian Church in Lynchburg. He had been pastor at Belmont for twenty-five years, and during that time membership grew from 300 to slightly over 1,000.

William Bailey was fatally shot in the back on July 6 by William Welcher at a restaurant in northwest Roanoke.

The Salem Sesquicentennial became organized in early July with the following serving as committee chairs: Jack Dame, special events; Mrs. W. J. Jolly Jr., tickets; Fred Hoback, hospitality; and Kirk Mayberry, finance. Marshall McClung was president of the organization.

Roanoke's new $4 million sewage treatment plant went into service on July 9. Fred Finnell, plant superintendent, started the first pump at 6:07 p.m.

The veterans' emergency housing project at the City Farm was razed during the second week of July. Crews salvaged some materials from the remaining seventeen structures. The housing units were erected shortly after World War II.

WROV conducted a bathing beauty contest at the American Legion Auditorium on July 11 with three top prizes. First-place winner was Barbara Barker, while second and third showings went to Barbara Bower and Charlotte Wade, respectively.

Carva Melon House opened on July 13 at 4311 Williamson Road. The fruit market was owned and operated by Charlie Wade, Dick Callison, and Egg Eggleston.

Vest Drive-In Theatre on Route 221 opened for its first summer season.

The Dominoes along with Billy Ward and his recording orchestra performed for a show and dance at the Star City Auditorium on July 15.

Showtimers presented the comedy *See How They Run* at Roanoke College on July 17. Lead roles were performed by Evans Evans, Edward Tucker, Gary Kremins, and Dorothy Thompson.

Salem Mayor James Moyer declared in mid-July that all men in the town must grow whiskers in honor of the town's sesquicentennial. They may go back to being clean-shaven on August 16. Moyer stipulated that "either a beard, goatee, chin whiskers, van dyke, mutton chops, mustache, sideburns, or any other acceptable facial hair growth of such length and full luxuriance as to be seen at a distance of eight paces." Failing to do so would incur a fine of one dollar. The men were to be known as "Brothers of the Brush."

A cornerstone-laying ceremony was held on July 15 for the new St. Mark's Lutheran Church in Roanoke. Special speaker was Virginia Attorney General Lindsay Almond Jr.

Roanoke City Manager Arthur Owens reported to city council on July 14 that the Roanoke Red Sox baseball team was in dire financial straits, owing the city funds it could not pay. The reason for the financial position was poor attendance.

Roanoke city and county Democratic voters stayed with the Byrd machine in congressional and state primary elections held on July 15. Incumbent US Senator Harry Byrd defeated challenger Francis Miller, and Sixth District Congressman Clarence Burton turned back challenger Moss Plunkett of Roanoke County. In Roanoke City, the vote totals were Byrd, 8,189, and Miller, 4,991; Burton, 8,818, and Plunkett, 4,167. In Roanoke County the election results were Byrd, 3,028, and Miller, 1,597; Burton, 3,312, and Plunkett, 1,226.

Sambo, a six-year-old monkey, escaped from his cage at the Children's Zoo on July 16, leaving behind his mate, Peaches. The monkey was captured three days later along Riverland Road.

Alton Semones confessed to killing his mother-in-law and shooting his wife on July 17 in the Garden City section where the family lived. The deceased was Frances Giesey of Charleston, West Virginia, who was visiting the couple.

E. D. Gryder of Roanoke and Dick Angle of Rocky Mount reported seeing flying saucers over their areas on the night of July 19. Both said the saucers were moving in a northerly direction.

Showtimers presented *The Glass Menagerie* on July 24 at Roanoke College. The leads in the cast were Susanne Joerndt, Dave Thornton, Pat Hooker, and Drew Hierholzer.

Deek Watson and his *Marionette Revue* came to the stage of the Roanoke Theatre on July 23.

Rollins Broadcasting filed an application with the FCC on July 21 to operate a television station in Roanoke. This became the fifth such application for the Roanoke market. Rollins operated two radio stations in Virginia and owned and operated Roanoke Lincoln-Mercury Sales Corporation in Roanoke.

During the first three weeks of being open, the Children's Zoo on Mill Mountain averaged over 7,000 visitors per week.

Three teenagers and two adults reported seeing flying saucers over Roanoke on July 22. The object was described as red with small, flashing red lights. The following evening three adults sitting on a porch on Gilmer Avenue NW reported seeing a green, saucer-shaped disc in the evening sky.

Mr. and Mrs. Othneil Lockett of Roanoke were killed in an auto wreck on Route 460 at Thaxton on July 23 as they were starting for a vacation. Jerry Maxey, twenty-five, of Roanoke died from injuries he received in an auto accident on July 22 on Route 11 near Boxley's Hill.

The Lee Hotel on E. Salem Avenue in Roanoke was leased to the Milner hotel chain that announced it would reopen the hotel in early August under the name of the Earle Hotel. The hotel was built in 1910 and was originally known as the Shenandoah Hotel.

Curtis Turner won the 150-lap, midseason stock car championship race at Victory Stadium on July 23. Jimmy Lewallen placed second, followed by Slim Rominger. The race went past 10:00 p.m., prompting calls to police from surrounding neighborhoods about the noise.

Owners of WROV amended their application with the FCC to operate a television station in Roanoke from seeking to use channel 7 to channel 27.

Two women, Virginia Slough and Mrs. G. M. Jewell, reported seeing a football-shaped object flying erratically over Roanoke on July 24 from their homes on Orange Avenue, while a third woman, Mrs. Mary Moorman of Gilmer Avenue NW, reported seeing a similar flying saucer over her home a few hours later.

Tab Smith and his orchestra, along with Lyn Hope and his orchestra, performed for a show and dance at the American Legion Auditorium on August 1. The balcony was reserved for white spectators.

The Roanoke Scrappers captured their fifth consecutive City A-League Softball pennant in late July by beating Salem Hosiery. Pitching for the Scrappers was Seabiscuit Simmons.

Fred Hickham, thirty-two, succumbed on July 26 to injuries he sustained in a fire at his apartment at 806 Third Street SW a few days prior.

Employees at the American Bridge Division plant in Roanoke began returning to work in late July after a fifty-three-day nationwide strike by steelworkers.

Wray Meador and Woody Greer opened a gun and locksmith shop at 128 E. Church Avenue in late July.

Showtimers presented *The Tavern* on July 31 at Roanoke College. Lead roles were played by LeRoy McFarland, Yvonne Stone, Gary Kremmins, Nettie Kitchen, and Sandra Lee Kitchen.

A kangaroo court was held in the town of Salem on July 26 as eighteen men were fined up to one dollar for failing to have facial hair in honor of Salem's sesquicentennial.

Roanoke singer Ginger Crowley made her first film appearance in Roanoke since going to Hollywood. She had a minor role in the movie *She's Working Her Way Through College* that opened at the American Theatre on July 31. The film starred Ronald Reagan.

Roanoke City Council approved at its July 28 meeting a train to run on a 1,000 foot long track at the Children's Zoo. The miniature train was a project of the Roanoke Jaycees.

The first fifty families moved into residential units at Lincoln Terrace on August 5. Lincoln Terrace was a subsidized housing development for low-income Blacks.

Riverdale School was formally closed by the Roanoke School Board. Students who had attended the four-room schoolhouse were transferred to Morningside School for the next school year.

The initial run of the Zoo Choo at the Children's Zoo was July 31. Passengers of the maiden run included Roanoke Mayor A. R. Minton and over 150 orphans. The train's official was name was the *Jaycee Star Liner* and was painted the colors of N&W Railway.

Municipal Utilities and Development Corporation announced in early August a planned subdivision on 3,000 acres at Fort Lewis Mountain west of Salem. Westward Lakes Estates would have between 500 and 600 homes.

Showtimers presented *Winterset* for a three-night run that began on August 7. Principal actors included Gene Akers and Jeanne Dickinson.

The Garden City Recreation Center officially opened on August 7. Ceremonies included a talent show and community sing. The rec center was the old Garden City School.

A marker about the Roanoke Star was installed in early August at the foot of the Roanoke Star on Mill Mountain. The marker was sponsored by the Roanoke Chamber of Commerce and the Roanoke Merchants Association.

Riverdale School, shown here in 1952, was closed at the start of the '52–'53 school year. Students were sent to Morningside Elementary School. *Carol Fidler*

Dell Sylvia of Richmond captured the Roanoke Exchange Club tennis tournament singles title in early August by defeating defending champion Don Leavens of Washington, DC.

Merritt Branch, twenty, of Roanoke died from injuries on August 5 that he sustained from an elevator accident the day before. He was crushed at the base of the elevator shaft while working at Virginia Foods on Campbell Avenue SE.

Bemiss Equipment relocated from Shenandoah Avenue in Roanoke to the 300 block of West Fourth Street in Salem in early August.

Hundreds of customers piled into B. Forman Sons for their shoe sale on August 5. The police were called, and the store closed after two hours. With so much pushing and shoving for women's shoes, one clerk was knocked off her feet and a customer fainted. After police cleared the store, clerks found boxes strewn across the aisles and over 300 mismatched pairs of shoes about the store.

The fourth annual Roanoke Valley Horse Show was held for the three days beginning August 6 at Lakeview Farm, The show had more than 150 entries.

Judy Holloday of High Street in Salem was crowned as queen of Salem's Sesquicentennial. Holloday, twenty-three, was selected as the result of a contest. Attendants in the queen's court were Barbara Green, Iris Peterson, Marie Mabes, Mary Alice Woods, Minnie Cadd, Betty Sinclair, and Peggy Layman.

An August 7 fire at the Nehi Bottling Corporation at 302 Fifth Street SW did considerable damage, according to its president S. B. Huff.

Samuel Lawson, four, of Roanoke was struck and instantly killed by an automobile on August 8 in the 1000 block of Beechwood Drive NW near his home.

Patterson Drug Company at the corner of Church Avenue and Henry Street closed on August 8.

Lloyd Price and his band performed for a show and dance at the American Legion Auditorium on August 15. The balcony was reserved for white spectators.

The formal sesquicentennial celebration for Salem began on August 10 for one week. Each evening, the play *The Salem Story* was presented at Municipal Field with over 500 in the cast. Religious Observance Day was held on August 10 with an address by Dr. Henry Hanson, retired president of Gettysburg College. Homecoming day was on August 11, and other events included a veterans' parade, youth Olympics in local parks, historic displays, and open houses by businesses and industries in Salem.

Salem's Sesquicentennial Parade moves through the town in this image from August 1952. The backside of the Salem Theater is in the right background. *Salem Historical Society*

Judy Holladay was crowned as Salem's Sesquicentennial Queen. *Salem Historical Society*

Showtimers concluded their summer season with *On Borrowed Time* the second week in August. Lead actors were Herbert Harris, Kyle Umberger, Leroy McFarland, Annell Bell, and Cynthia Dunn.

Old Dominion Restaurant opened on August 10 at 314 S. Jefferson Street. The chef was J. J. Murphy.

US Senator Willis Robertson of Virginia addressed local dignitaries at a dinner on August 11, held in Salem as part of the town's sesquicentennial. Robertson spent his youth in Salem, stating that his father moved the family there for a better education. "The one contribution of Salem which ranks it above all others is the teaching by Roanoke College of the fundamental principles of the Bible to the youth of the area," claimed the senator.

Councilman W. P. Hunter urged his colleagues on Roanoke City Council to authorize the preparation of plans for the expansion of city hall. Hunter advocated that an annex be constructed of the same architectural style as the current Municipal Building to accommodate growing city departments. Hunter's plan called for the razing of the school administration building.

Kenneth Neighbors, twenty-two, of Roanoke was found fatally shot on the kitchen floor of Doris Harris's apartment on August 12. Harris was held by police on suspicion of murder.

Reuben Lovell, fifty-five, of Salem was killed in an auto accident on Route 11, three miles west of Salem, on August 12.

Schulte-United Department Store at 16 W. Campbell Avenue reopened after being closed for two months following a devastating fire. J. J. Pathemore was the store manager.

Jamup and Honey, former stars of the *Grand Ole Opry*, performed at the Roanoke Theatre on August 13.

Lt. William Hazelgrove Jr. of Roanoke was killed in a plane crash at Elgin Air Force Base in Florida on August 13. His P-47 Thunderbolt failed to come out of a dive while he was practicing dive-bombing. The engine failed, and Hazelgrove tried to bail out. The plane was too close to the ground by the time he exited the craft. He was set to be discharged in a few months.

Mimi's, a specialty shop, opened on August 14 at 7 W. Church Avenue.

Amo's Restaurant opened in mid-August on Route 11 west of Salem. R. A. Ellis was the owner and manager.

Holdren's, a refrigeration sales and service business, opened a second store on August 16 at 803 Dale Avenue SE.

Lorraine's Restaurant opened on August 16 at 2404 Williamson Road. It specialized in French cuisine.

Salem's sesquicentennial parade on August 16 was marred by the tragic death of one of the participants. Lincoln Missimer Jr., twenty-nine, of Salem fell from a truck in the parade and was run over by the vehicle. The accident occurred on Sixth Street, just east of College Avenue. The truck had pulled out of the parade and was circling back to reenter it when Missimer fell.

Gordon Hale, twenty-eight, of Roanoke shot his mother-in-law, Beatrice Akers, then shot his wife, Hazel Hale, then shot at his brother-in-law before killing himself on August 16. The shooting occurred in the family's home at 2603 Mount Pleasant Boulevard SE. Akers died four days later in a local hospital as a result of her wounds.

Capt. Lawrence Damewood of Roanoke was part of an elite group of aviators for the US Air Force. Known as the "Skyblazers," the group was a precision-flying team that performed maneuvers around the world. They made their US debut in late August at the International Aviation Exposition in Detroit.

Four Roanokers made their television debuts on August 17 over station WFMY at Greensboro. They were part of a special program, *Roanoke Presents*, emceed by Ray Bentley. The four performers were Mrs. Gene King, pianist; Charlene Eanes, contralto; Frank Blankenmeyer, vocalist; and Ottawa Pullen, vocalist.

The Youth Crusade for Christ opened for weeklong revival services at the American Legion Auditorium on August 18. Several thousand attended opening night to hear Olympian and evangelist Jack Robinson.

Vinton Town Council honored W. R. McGee during its meeting on August 19 for his many years of service as a member of the town council. He was defeated in his bid for reelection, having served since 1920.

This 1950s image shows the B. E. Conner Market that was located on Colonial Avenue SW. It was owned and operated by Bob Conner. *Pete Wheeler*

James Bailey, a native of Roanoke, was sworn in as the Assistant US District Attorney for the District of Massachusetts on August 19. He was a graduate of Addison High School and the son of Mr. and Mrs. George Bailey.

The Rainbow Dining Room opened on August 20 at 1226 Patterson Avenue SW. Eva Price was the manager.

Mrs. Clarke Cannon was elected president of the Roanoke "Women for Ike" organization. The new organization was established for the purpose of assisting the presidential campaign of Dwight Eisenhower.

The annual Roanoke Fair opened on August 25 with competitions in 325 different classifications. The agricultural event at Maher Field also included nightly vaudeville acts and a midway. Final attendance was given as 32,000, down from 38,000 the year before.

American Airlines made Roanoke a primary radio station for its coast-to-coast communications system. Personnel and equipment were moved to Woodrum Field in late August.

A high-powered rotating beacon at the Franklin County Fair at Rocky Mount had many in Roanoke thinking they saw flying saucers over Mill Mountain.

Warren Gardner was named "Young Mr. Baseball" for Roanoke in a ceremony at Maher Field on August 21. The thirteen-year-old was recognized during a Roanoke Red Sox game.

Johnnie and Jack, along with the Tennessee Mountain Boys, all-stars of the *Grand Ole Opry*, gave an outdoor concert at Maher Field on August 23.

G. B. Darnell of Roanoke won the State Horseshoe Tournament that was held in Elmwood Park the third weekend in August. I. J. Dove of Roanoke was the defending champion.

George Tucker, thirty-five, of Roanoke was struck and killed by an automobile on Route 11 at the intersection with Route 117 on August 24.

George Fulton Jr. won the Roanoke Country Club golf championship the third weekend in August. He defeated Connie Sellers.

Lu Merritt won the city-county tennis tournament by defeating Frank Snow on August 24. The event was held at South Roanoke Park. Charley Turner and Doug Craig won the doubles title with a win over Jack Miller and Bob Bolling. Suzanne Glass won the women's singles title with a victory over Kitty Coxe. Coxe and Edith Paine won the women's doubles title.

American Television and Radio Company opened on August 26 at the corner of Brandon Avenue and Main Street, Wasena. The store specialized in the RCA brand of electronics. The owners were Lonnie Carr and Theron Douglas.

Clarke Wray resigned as director, president, and business manager of the Roanoke Red Sox on August 26. Others associated with the team stated that minor league baseball's future in Roanoke was in jeopardy due to low attendance and financial concerns.

State highway officials announced on August 26 that paving of highway over Catawba Mountain had been completed. The seven-mile road was built exclusively with convict labor, cost $750,000, and took forty-six months to complete. During construction, about seventy-five convicts were housed at a camp north of Hanging Rock.

Roy Brown and his Mighty Men Orchestra, Roy Milton and his orchestra, pianist Camille Howard, and vocalist Lilly Greenwood performed for a show and dance at the American Legion Auditorium on August 31. The balcony was reserved for white spectators.

Downtown businessmen and an investor from New Jersey agreed to erect a 500-car parking garage on South Jefferson Street near the Patrick Henry Hotel. The estimated cost for the garage was $600,000, of which $150,000 was being pledged by local business interests.

The new S&H Green Stamps Merchandise Store opened on August 29 at 419 W. Campbell Avenue.

The first worship service was conducted in the new Emmanuel Lutheran Church at Palmetto Street and Olive Avenue NW on August 31. The church had a seating capacity of 225 and cost $63,000.

Margaret Harrison, a native of Roanoke, won a contest in New York City sponsored by a local television station for best legs. The contestants submitted photos of their legs to see who came closest to having those of actress Rita Hayworth. Harrison, a professional model, received luggage, dresses, and other prizes, including much publicity.

The Booker T. Drive-In Theatre opened on September 1 for Blacks only. The theatre was located on Airport Road "near Claytor's Park, just across Peters Creek Road." The opening double-feature was *The Suspect* with Ella Raines and Charles Laughton and *Adventures End* with John Wayne.

Roanoke City Council held its reorganization meeting on September 1 and selected Roy Webber as mayor and Robert Woody as vice mayor. In Salem, the town council reelected James Moyer as mayor. Nelson Thurman was reelected as mayor of Vinton.

The steeple of the new First Methodist Church in Salem was erected on September 2. The seventy-foot steel structure was swung into place using a crane and placed upon its fifty-foot brick case. The job was done by Hawkins and Cox, steel erectors in Roanoke.

Alton Semones was ordered committed to the Southwestern State Hospital for mental observation on September 2 after a Roanoke County Circuit Court grand jury indicted him for the murder of his mother-in-law and the malicious wounding of his wife.

Curtis Turner won the final auto race of the season at Victory Stadium on September 3. Slim Rominger was second in the 200-lap event.

Loch Haven presented its first annual Water Show on September 7 with Mr. Izzo and the Greenbrier Aquamaids.

The "Zoo Choo" at the Children's Zoo on Mill Mountain was a big hit during its first full month of operation in August with 22,642 passengers.

The barns on the Roy Kinsey farm were destroyed in a fire on September 4. The barns, located on Route 626 near the airport, housed farm machinery and feed worth about $40,000.

Eastern Airlines began using new forty-passenger Martin 4-0-4s with its flights serving Roanoke on September 10.

William Equi Jr., the city delinquent tax collector, was arrested by police in his municipal office on September 8 on gambling charges. When the police raided his city hall office, they confiscated Irish Sweepstakes tickets and a jar of cash.

This 1950s postcard shows the Zoo Choo in operation at the Children's Zoo on Mill Mountain. The official name was the *Jaycee Star Liner*, as it was sponsored by the Roanoke Jaycees. *Bob Stauffer*

William McGhee, clerk of the town of Salem, submitted his resignation effective September 19 as he planned to study law at Washington and Lee University.

Radio station WSLS was granted a television construction permit on September 10 by the FCC. Station officials announced that they were granted channel 10 and that the studios would be in the Shenandoah Building with the transmitter on Poor Mountain. The goal was to be on the air in early 1953.

The Dairy Fountain at 1929 Carter Road SW was sold in mid-September and closed for remodeling. John Jackson purchased the building from Fred Kune.

N&W Railway tested a diesel-powered freight locomotive between Williamson, West Virginia, and Portsmouth, Ohio, the second week of September. It was the first time the railway tested a diesel locomotive.

Tracey Wright, twenty-three, of Roanoke became the first Korean War veteran in Virginia to enter a Virginia college under the new GI Bill. He enrolled in an economics course at Roanoke College.

Dixon's Hardware opened on September 13 at 2304 Franklin Road SW. George Dixon was the owner.

The Rogers Brothers Circus came to Salem on September 13 and began with an elephant parade down Main Street. The circus was sponsored by the Salem Kiwanis Club. The circus's big top was located at Oakey Field. The circus had 100 animals and 300 employees.

West End Baptist Church held dedication services at its new location at 2512 Staunton Avenue NW on September 14.

Carl Smith of the *Grand Ole Opry* performed at the Roanoke Theatre on September 17.

Leroy Schneider, a Roanoke businessman, was named as president of Roanoke Baseball Inc., succeeding Clarke Wray. The organization operated the Roanoke Red Sox.

James Hughes, vice chairman of the Roanoke County School Board, died on September 12 at the University of Virginia Hospital. He had been a resident of the Catawba Valley section since 1927 and was credited with the electrification of that section.

B. T. Crump Company, distributors of Norge appliances, held an open house at their new headquarters at 204 Fifth Street SW during the third week in September.

Roanoke police conducted a gambling raid on the night of September 14 at the Subway Pool Room in the 100 block of East Campbell Avenue. Police seized a baseball ticker and cash from a group of seventeen men who were there at the time of the raid.

Bill France and Curtis Turner rescinded their request to have stock car racing at Victory Stadium in 1953. Roanoke City Council was set to consider their proposal, but the plan was strongly objected to by officials with the Memorial and Crippled Children's Hospital and members of the Touchdown Club. The general complaints were about noise and what some considered a misuse of the stadium.

William Equi Jr., Roanoke's delinquent tax collector, was fined fifty dollars and given a thirty-day suspended jail sentence by the Municipal Court on September 16 for gambling-related charges.

Amos Milburn and his Whiskey Band, the Griffin Brothers and their band, and Margie Day performed for a show and dance at the American Legion Auditorium on September 18. White spectators were admitted for half price.

Robert Almond, a resident at the City Home, was struck and killed by an automobile on September 17 at Colonial Avenue and Persinger Road SW.

WROV radio station received permission from the FCC on September 18 to use channel 27 for television broadcasting. The owner of the station, Radio Roanoke Inc., indicated plans to be on the air by the end of the year.

The Trumpeteers gave a concert at the Star City Auditorium on September 22, sponsored locally by the Royal Jubilee Singers.

Henry Fowler was the convocation speaker at Roanoke College on September 20. In his speech, Fowler stressed the need to return to a well-rounded liberal arts education for the future security of the nation. US Senator Willis Robertson gave the convocation address at Hollins College.

William and Mary College defeated Virginia Military Institute in football, 34–13, in a game played at Victory Stadium on September 20. The crowd was estimated at 12,000.

The Carter Sisters and Mother Maybelle performed at the Roanoke Theatre on September 24. They were stars of the *Grand Ole Opry*.

Lansdowne Park, the 300-unit public housing development for whites, was formally dedicated on September 21. The guest speaker was Henry Fowler. Lansdowne was located on Salem Turnpike. Music was provided by the Monroe Junior High School Band.

Chris Ganas, a native of Greece, opened Chris' Dog House, a restaurant, at 136 W. Campbell Avenue on September 21. Ganas was also the owner and operator of the Blue Ribbon Restaurant.

A ground-breaking ceremony was held on September 21 for the new Fellowship Baptist Church in the 900 block of Murray Avenue SE. Rev. Gene Arnold was the pastor.

The Five Blind Boys from Alabama, the Sunset Gospel Singers, and the Star City Harmonizers performed at the Star City Auditorium on September 28.

Community 5 & 10 Store opened on September 21 at 3754 Garden City Boulevard.

The Virginia Hospital Advisory Council appropriated $1.6 million in Hill-Burton funds for hospital construction in Roanoke. Roanoke's share of the federal funds fell far short of what was needed to begin an addition to the Memorial and Crippled Children's Hospital and for the new Burrell Memorial Hospital. The local Hospital Development Association, led by Paul Buford, reported that an additional $800,000 was needed to start construction.

Shirley Dillon, a toddler, drowned accidentally in a five-gallon rinse bucket at her home in the Starkey section on September 23. She was the daughter of Mr. and Mrs. Claude Dillon.

Two US Air Force officers escaped serious injury when their twin-engine plane crashed during take-off at Woodrum Field on September 23. The landing gear folded on the C-45 Beechcraft while it was on the north-south runway.

The main attraction at the Roanoke Home Show held at the American Legion Auditorium was television cameras displayed by WROV radio. The six-day show was sponsored by the Exchange Club. Mrs. Gladys Fulcher, nineteen, won the "Mrs. Roanoke" contest held during the event.

The Democrats and Independents for Eisenhower Club organized in Roanoke on September 24. The group consisted mostly of disaffected Democrats upset with President Harry Truman's civil rights policies and the support of that by the Democratic presidential candidate Adlai Stevenson. Officers of the club were Joseph Hebert, Holman Willis Jr., Ann Shubert, and Robert Meybin.

The new electric scoreboard for Municipal Field in Salem was erected on September 25. It was a service project of the Salem Junior Chamber of Commerce and cost $2,200. The project campaign was chaired by Jim Butler.

Republican presidential candidate General Dwight Eisenhower made a whistle-stop speech in Roanoke on September 26. Speaking from the back of an eighteen-car train in South Roanoke Park, Eisenhower told the crowd of 7,000 that his administration would be fair to all Americans and that America's problems had been caused "by an administration too long in power, with men too small for their jobs and too big for their britches." Eisenhower reminded the crowd of his Virginia roots in that his mother had been born at Mount Sidney in the Shenandoah Valley. His speech lasted about fifteen minutes with the crowd shouting, "We want Ike!" The next day, the *Roanoke Times* endorsed Eisenhower for president.

A crowd gathered in South Roanoke Park to greet General Dwight Eisenhower on his presidential campaign stop in September 1952. *Historical Society of Western Virginia*

Roanoke Mayor Roy Webber greets Dwight and Mamie Eisenhower on the railroad car's speaker stand during their campaign stop in Roanoke. Webber, a florist, presented Mrs. Eisenhower a corsage. *Historical Society of Western Virginia*

Roanoke's first Black junior high school was formally opened on September 26. Booker T. Washington Junior High School was located in the former Lucy Addison High School and had an initial enrollment of close to 500 students. Miss S. V. Lawson was the principal.

Fats Domino and his orchestra, along with the Blazers, performed for a show and dance at the American Legion Auditorium on October 2. The balcony was reserved for white spectators.

A crowd of 1,000 attended the first ever Jaycee Junior Olympics event at Maher Field on September 27. The program featured athletic competitions for children and youth, a horse show, a parade, and dog obedience training.

Homer Smith and his Melodaires performed on October 2 at Addison High School. The group had appeared on television and film and sung on numerous national radio programs. The concert was sponsored by the Hunton Branch YMCA.

Several thousand went to Woodrum Field on September 28 to publicly inspect Eastern Airlines' new *Silver Falcons* forty-passenger aircraft. Eastern offered free trips over Roanoke with twelve flights that contained mostly children as passengers.

Roanoke City Council decided to retain its delinquent tax collector, William Equi Jr., even though he had been convicted of gambling charges and to give him a letter to reprimand. The council did decide to abolish the position effective December 31.

The *All American Shindig* show came to the Roanoke Theatre on October 1. Performances were given by Daisy Mae and Charlie, Jack Espinosa, Tony LaRocca, and comedian Ches Davis.

The airport in Rochester, Minnesota, was officially named Lobb Field in late September in honor of Albert Lobb, retired Mayo Clinic associate business manager, who was instrumental in creation of the airfield. Lobb was a resident of Roanoke at the time of the dedication, having moved to the city in 1950.

Clinton Wright, two months old, accidentally suffocated beneath the blanket in his crib on September 29. He was the son of Mr. and Mrs. S. J. Wright of Roanoke County.

A Black political rally that drew over 1,100 persons on September 30 nominated Dr. Harry Penn, a Democrat, for Roanoke City Council. The main reason for the gathering was a debate between the Republican and Democratic candidates for Congress. Penn planned to be a candidate in the Democratic primary in April 1953.

Several hundred Protestants gathered at First Baptist Church, Roanoke, on September 30, representing several congregations throughout the city, to dedicate the *Revised Standard Version* of the Bible that had been released by a publisher the day prior.

Roanoke native Douglas Talbert was selected by Tommy Dorsey to be the pianist in his band. Talbert had previously worked with Frank Sinatra and Sarah Vaughan and had appeared on numerous television shows.

Hundreds of fish were killed in the Roanoke River in early October due to a leak of tanning liquors from the Leas & McVitty Tannery into Lake Spring Creek that emptied into the river.

The Roanoke Merchants Association sponsored "Greater Roanoke Days" in early October. The event kicked off with a street dance that attracted 20,000 persons to the intersection of Campbell Avenue and Jefferson Street SW. Nineteen bands provided the live music for the crowd that stretched several blocks in each direction. Irv Sharp was the emcee, and the *Grand Ole Opry's* Duke of Paducah provided comic sketches throughout the evening.

The first families began moving into Lincoln Terrace, the Black public housing development, in early October.

Edward Richardson was sworn in on October 2 as Roanoke County Commonwealth's Attorney to fill the unexpired term of Eugene Chelf.

The estate of E. A. Thurman totaled $2.6 million and was left in a trust for the care of needy children. Thurman had died a bachelor on June 26.

Big Lick Motor Company opened at its new location on October 3 at 548 Salem Avenue SW. The company sold Hudson and Willys automobiles. It had formerly been located on Second Street SW.

This October 1952 image shows Porterfield Distributing Company trucks in front of the company's building at 1354 Eighth Street SW. *Virginia Room, RPL*

G. C. Brothers Jr. announced the opening of the new location of his Old Dominion Floor Company at 121 Franklin Road SW in early October.

The University of Virginia defeated Virginia Tech 42–0 in football at Victory Stadium on October 4 in front of a crowd estimated at 14,000.

Harris Cleaners opened a new branch at 10 W. Kirk Avenue on October 5.

Plantation Time Down South Revue came to the Roanoke Theatre on October 8 and 9. The show advertised five big acts, including the Sixteen Roxyettes.

Eighteen persons were charged with various offenses during a nighttime liquor raid on October 5 at the Sycamore, a nightclub off Cove Road in Roanoke County.

Barter Theatre presented *The Curious Savage* in the auditorium of Jefferson High School on October 6. The lead roles were played by Dorothy LaVern, Charles Quinlivan, Tom McKeehan, and Cleo Holladay.

Hallis Jamison was sentenced to twelve years in prison for the fatal shooting of June Logan. Jamison pled guilty to the offense.

A huge air raid siren was installed on the roof of Monroe Junior High School and was tested on October 7.

The First Operatic Sinfonietta gave a concert at the American Legion Auditorium on October 8 to a capacity crowd. The concert was sponsored by the Thursday Morning Music Club.

The Roanoke School Board at its meeting on October 8 voted to purchase a grocery store and four acres adjoining the grounds of Grandin Court School. The store, owned by W. W. Wood, was located at the corner of Spring Road and Spessard Avenue SW and was to be razed.

The new Crystal Spring Pumping Station went into use the second week of October. The new station was part of a $4 million upgrade plan to the city's water supply system.

Walter Stephenson, president of the Roanoke Chamber of Commerce, proposed in a speech on October 9 that a Roanoke Valley industrial foundation be established to acquire and hold business sites for potential development. Stephenson's concern was the lack of industrial sites in the city and the need to think beyond the city's boundaries in terms of attracting future industries.

William Starkey of Catawba was appointed to the Roanoke County School Board to fill the unexpired term of James Hughes.

The Junior Varsity football teams of Virginia Tech and the Virginia Military Institute squared off in Victory Stadium on October 10. VMI won 13–7 before a crowd of slightly over 200 persons.

Louis Jordan and his Tympany Five performed for a show and dance at the American Legion Auditorium on October 17. The balcony was reserved for white spectators.

Jane Stuart Smith, Roanoke opera singer, made her local debut on October 15 in a concert at the American Theatre sponsored by the Thursday Morning Music Club. Smith had sung in operas in Italy and France and had made her American debut in Detroit in 1951. The concert was a sellout.

Dr. William McCauley, pastor of Peters Creek Lutheran Church and Kittingers Chapel, was recognized for fifty years of service as a Lutheran minister in mid-October. McCauley had helped to found Christ Lutheran Church in Roanoke and Church of the Redeemer in Baltimore, Maryland.

Virginia Attorney General Lindsay Almond Jr. kicked off the Roanoke Community Fund annual campaign with a speech on October 12 at the American Theatre. The goal was $281,533. Heather Tweed was mistress of ceremonies, and Francis Ballard produced and directed the program that was broadcast live on three local radio stations.

Dr. Linwood Keyser died at his home in Roanoke on October 12. He was president of the Roanoke Academy of Medicine in 1944 and a founder of the Virginia Urological Society.

Mrs. Sally Stallard of Roanoke won the women's state archery championship in Norfolk on October 12.

Neal Flying School filed its charter of incorporation with Roanoke County on October 13. The school was operated at Woodrum Field by Paul Neal.

Jane Stuart Smith performed at the American Theatre in October 1952. The theatre was located at 215 S. Jefferson Street. *Historical Society of Western Virginia*

Salem Town Council appointed Charles Shelor, a graduate of Roanoke College and Boston University School of Law, as the town clerk.

Joe Stern, a clothing store, opened at its new location at 124 W. Campbell Avenue on October 15.

Mick-or-Mack opened a new grocery store on Colorado Street at Second Street in Salem on October 16. It was the largest of the seven groceries operated by the chain. Noah Gunter was the store manager.

Helen Traubel, soprano with the Metropolitan Opera, presented a concert at the Jefferson High School auditorium on October 24. Her appearance was part of the Roanoke Community Concert Association season.

Five hundred members of the Knights of Columbus and guests attended the dedication of the Knights' new Roanoke home on Wasena Hill on October 19. The event was preceded by a high mass at Our Lady of Nazareth Catholic Church. William Shanks, chancellor of the council, was in charge of the dedication program.

Plans for a $90,000 community center in Preston Park were discussed at the Roanoke City Council meeting on October 20. Most of the funds were to be raised privately.

The congregation of Haran Baptist Church in Roanoke County dedicated their new church building in mid-October. Located on Route 221, the new sanctuary could seat 200 persons. Rev. W. H. Carter was pastor.

This 1950s Mick-or-Mack sign produced by the Roy C. Kinsey Sign Company of Roanoke became a familiar sight throughout the Roanoke Valley with the expansion of the grocery chain throughout the region in the 1950s. *Bob Kinsey*

This March 1963 image shows the sanctuary of Haran Baptist Church that was completed and dedicated in October 1952. *Nelson Harris*

A nine-hole municipal golf course was proposed by the Roanoke Recreation Association for the former City Farm property. Roanoke City Council agreed to consider the proposal presented by Paul Coffey, president of the association.

The US Census Bureau released figures for 1950 pertaining to Virginia in late October. The official population of Roanoke city was 91,921, which included 77,329 whites, 14,575 Blacks, and 17 persons of other races. About 7.5 percent of the population was over the age of 65.

Traffic in downtown Roanoke was halted for one minute at noon on Friday, October 24, as buglers at the main intersections played *Call to the Colors* in honor of United Nations Day.

The Roanoke chapter of the Society for the Preservation and Encouragement of Barber Shop Quartet Singing in America was organized on October 25 in a meeting at First Presbyterian Church. The Roanoke chapter was sponsored by the chapter in Winston-Salem, North Carolina.

Paul Williams and his Hucklebuckers Orchestra performed at the American Legion Auditorium on October 31. The balcony was reserved for whites.

Norfolk and Western Week was observed in Roanoke beginning October 26 in honor of the centennial of the first train in the city. The week's events included a full-size replica of the engine *Roanoke*, which pulled some of the first trains into the Roanoke Valley, a celebration at the N&W passenger station, and a banquet at the Hotel Roanoke.

Roanoke City Manager Arthur Owens announced on October 25 that Capt. Frank Webb would become the city's next superintendent of police effective November 1. He had been the acting superintendent since June 1, when Stuart Bruce retired.

Ringling Brothers and Barnum & Bailey Circus came to Roanoke on October 27 for two shows at Maher Field. The circus arrived by three trains from Bristol.

The circus advertised that it had nearly 2,000 humans and animals in the show, including two gorillas that proved to be a main draw. A troop of one hundred clowns was led by Emmett Kelly. The circus's local appearance was sponsored by the Roanoke Junior Chamber of Commerce, and attendance was estimated at 6,000. The circus went to Lynchburg the next day.

Morning Star Baptist Church held a formal opening of its new location at 1513 Rorer Avenue SW on October 26. Rev. William Moore was pastor.

Judge Thurston Keister died at his home in Salem on October 26 at age sixty-four. He had presided since 1926 over the Twentieth Judicial Circuit that included the Roanoke Valley. He began practicing law in Salem in 1913.

Roanoke City formally accepted the new airport terminal building at Woodrum Field on October 27. The building was to be occupied and operational by mid-November. The contractor was B. F. Parrott.

Officials with the Ponce de Leon Hotel announced that an old building at the corner of Salem Avenue and Second Street SW would be razed to enlarge the hotel's parking lot. The building was occupied by the Patsel Drug Store. The structure was believed to be about seventy-five years old.

Students at Andrew Lewis High School held a mock presidential election. The outcome was 482 votes for General Dwight Eisenhower and 158 votes for Governor Adlai Stevenson. At Roanoke College, a mock election also gave a victory to Eisenhower, 235–87. At Jefferson High School, Eisenhower also won by a vote of 525 to 220. At Addison High School, Stevenson prevailed, 332–44.

The FCC issued a license on October 30 to Cy Bahakel for a daytime-only radio station in Roanoke.

Alton Semones was found guilty of involuntary manslaughter for the slaying of his mother-in-law, Frances Glesey. He was also convicted of unlawful wounding in the shooting of his wife. Semones was believed to be suffering from mental illness, so Judge Earl Abbott sentenced Semones to a suspended six-year sentence and placed him on probation.

Booze Self-Service Grocery Store and Filling Station opened on November 1 on Route 460 at Blue Ridge.

All Aboard for Harlem came to the stage of the Roanoke Theatre on November 5. The show was advertised as "sepia Vaudeville acts."

Officials with WROV radio announced in late October that its television station would go on the air in mid-December and be an affiliate of the ABC Network. Frank Koehler was the station's general manager.

A forest fire consumed one hundred acres at Carvins Cove in early November.

The Roanoke Chamber of Commerce recognized Mrs. Fannie Trent, ninety-two, as the person who had lived in Roanoke city the longest. She had been a resident for eighty-seven years. Trent came to Roanoke with her adopted parents in 1865 and lived in a home near the site of the Ponce de Leon Hotel. She recalled carrying water from the spring over which the hotel was later built. She also shared that from the home she often viewed the corn field that later became the site of the Hotel Roanoke. She was baptized in the Roanoke River as a young girl, only after a hole was chopped in the river's ice.

Professor and theologian Paul Tillich of Union Theological Seminary in New York spoke at Hollins College on November 2. His appearance there was sponsored by the YWCA.

Three nationally known gospel groups performed at the American Legion Auditorium on November 5—Bells of Joy, Harmonizing Four, and the Skylarks.

The Footlighters, a winter theatre group in Salem, was formed on October 2. The group intended to produce plays during the nonsummer months. Officers included Leroy MacFarland, Herbert Harris, Frances Ebeling, and Bill Segall.

Powell's Pharmacy opened on November 7 at 219 E. Main Street in Salem and held a formal grand opening a week later. The pharmacy, managed by Ben Powell, had a sixteen-stool soda fountain that was operated by Margie Bess.

Roanoke Valley voters supported Dwight Eisenhower in the presidential election on November 4. In Roanoke County, Eisenhower received 6,017 votes to Governor Adlai Stevenson's 4,880. In Roanoke City, Eisenhower got 15,674 votes to Stevenson's 8,043. Voters also ousted Democratic incumbent Clarence Burton from his Sixth District Congressional seat in favor of Republican Richard Poff. In Roanoke County, Poff won 4,706 to 3,191. In Roanoke city, Poff received 12,103, and Burton got 9,219 votes. The only Democrat to win in the Roanoke Valley was incumbent US Senator Harry Byrd. The national and regional votes were driven by an intraparty division among Democrats over President Truman's civil rights agenda and the Korean War.

James Sutphin, age eight, was killed when the bike he was riding struck the side of a moving city bus on November 4. The accident occurred at Wise Avenue and Seventeenth Street. He was the son of R. L. Sutphin.

Roy Acuff and his *Grand Ole Opry* Gang performed on the stage of the Roanoke Theatre on November 9. Acuff was also joined by Pap and his Jug Band and the Smoky Mountain Boys.

Glenvar Restaurant opened on November 8 on Route 11, three miles west of Salem. It was operated by Mr. and Mrs. C. M. Short.

The Seven-Up Bottling Company was located at 934 3½ Street in Roanoke. The image is dated 1952. *Historical Society of Western Virginia*

This mid-50s photo shows the Hickory, Dickory Clock at the Children's Zoo on Mill Mountain which was part of the Mother Goose nursery rhymes theme. *Historical Society of Western Virginia*

Bemiss Equipment Corporation opened on November 8 in its new location at 224 W. Fourth Street in Salem.

The Children's Zoo on Mill Mountain was featured in the November 9 edition of *Parade*.

The West Virginia Mountaineers defeated Virginia Military Institute 39 to 21 in football on November 8 at Victory Stadium. The crowd of spectators was estimated at 9,000.

Tommy Dorsey and his orchestra performed at the American Legion Auditorium on November 17. Joining in the show were saxophonist Sam Donahue, vocalist Marietta Know, and Roanoke pianist Doug Talbert.

The Town of Vinton hired its first full-time fireman in addition to the fire chief in early November. He was H. E. Cooper. Cooper's father had been one of the volunteer fire department's charter members when it was formed in 1925.

Edward Saunders, twenty-seven, of Salem died on November 9 from injuries he sustained in an auto wreck the day prior near Back Creek School on Route 221. At the time of the accident, Saunders was fleeing police after he had shot and wounded Thelma Munsey at her home in Roanoke.

Officials with N&W Railway announced they planned to open up a large tract of land for commercial development that was the former site of the West End Furnace.

Grandpa Jones, along with others from the *Grand Ole Opry*, performed at the Roanoke Theatre on November 12.

Roanoke's United Jewish Appeal campaign kicked off on November 10 with a goal of $55,000. Monies raised went to support the needs of Israel. Local leaders included Arthur Taubman, Herbert Kurshan, Udell Pratt, and Leo Pratt. The guest speaker at the campaign banquet was Mark McCloskey, former chairman of the New York City School Board.

The Roanoke Children's Theatre presented its first play of the season, *The Pied Piper of Hamelin*, at the Jefferson High School auditorium on November 11 under the direction of Clara Black.

The *Vinton Messenger*, a weekly newspaper, published its first edition in mid-November.

The Community Fund campaign fell $14,302 short of its goal as final tabulations were reported. Total contributions slightly exceeded $267,230. M. E. Costello and Clifton Woodrum Jr. were cochairs of the campaign.

A three-judge panel ruled on November 13 that Salem could annex 1.8 square miles of new territory effective December 31. The annexation was expected to increase the town's population to 9,790 and thereby make it the largest incorporated town in Virginia. Salem agreed to spend $80,000 in public works upgrades in the annexed areas.

Winston's, a sewing machine store, opened on November 15 at 128 W. Campbell Avenue.

Eastern Stores opened a new branch of its home appliance chain at First Street and Church Avenue SW on November 15. It had another branch at 3326 Williamson Road.

Harper and McGeehan Shell Service Station opened on November 14 at 3151 Williamson Road NE. Opening weekend customers registered for prizes, with first prize being a Philco television. Fred Harper and Ed McGeehan were the proprietors.

Dr. William Fears, a dentist in Roanoke for nearly thirty years, died at Burrell Memorial Hospital on November 12. He was a past president of the Old Dominion State Dental Society. Prior to coming to Roanoke, Fears had been a dentist in Martinsville.

Frank Koehler, manager of WROV radio, announced in mid-November that the station's planned television broadcasts would be delayed past the previously announced launch date due to their inability to get equipment.

West End Baptist Church changed its name to Pre-Millennial Baptist Church in mid-November. It was located at 2512 Staunton Avenue NW.

William Fleming High School defeated Blacksburg High School in football on November 14 and concluded its season undefeated, making Fleming the District 6 champions.

For the first time in the history of the *Roanoke Times*, the paid circulation of its Sunday edition topped 80,000 subscribers. The November 9 edition had a paid circulation of 80,322.

The new terminal administration building at Woodrum Field officially went into use on November 16. The first ticket sold in the terminal was by Eastern Airlines to Connie Colaizzo, a student a Southern Seminary Junior College who was flying home to Pittsburgh.

The Barter Theatre presented the comedy *The Late Christopher Bean* at the Jefferson High School auditorium on November 19.

Krispy Kreme opened a doughnut shop at 503 Campbell Avenue SW on November 20.

The comic strip *Judge Parker* made its local debut in the November 24 edition of the *Roanoke Times*. According to the newspaper, "Judge Parker presides over a typical American court of justice where human drama is constantly unfolding."

A group interested in establishing a Roanoke symphony orchestra met on November 21 at the Patrick Henry Hotel. The meeting was presided over by Mrs. Harry Dixon, and participants included Gibson Morrissey, Bluefield symphony conductor, and John Edwards from the National Symphony Orchestra. The group announced a rehearsal for local musicians for November 25.

Ford Electric Company opened a branch at 311 Ninth Street SE on November 21. They sold appliances and televisions.

The Harlem Globetrotters brought their basketball skills and antics to the American Legion Auditorium on November 23.

The Christmas shopping season officially launched on November 25 with the Retail Merchants Association, which sponsored their annual Santa Claus Parade through downtown. Patricia Atkins, a senior at Roanoke Catholic High School, was chosen as the parade's Snow Queen. The parade contained ten floats, six bands, a variety of civic and fraternal organizations, and many decorated vehicles. A crowd of 25,000 watched the mile-long parade. To commemorate the start of the holiday season, the Roanoke Star was changed to red and white.

Belle Furniture Company opened at 130 W. Campbell Avenue on November 24. On opening day, the store gave away cigars to the men, orchids to the ladies, and 1,000 Buck Rogers space outfits to children.

Carver High School football team finished their inaugural season on November 19 with a 2–6 record. The team began practice on August 26 with thirty boys who had never played the game. The creation of the school's first football team was due to the yeoman efforts of Principal Rush Johnson, who mortgaged his house to buy the team uniforms and equipment, and to the basketball coach, Irvin Cannaday. Teachers provided the team transportation home from practices and to the games using their personal vehicles. Cannaday coached the team, and Alvin Smith was the assistant coach. Miss C. A. Petty organized a cheerleading squad for the games, and the cafeteria staff provided team meals for the games. Dick Sutherland, reporter for the *Roanoke Times*, wrote that the primary motivator for the football program was Johnson. "That is an example of the faith of Carver's principal, a faith in his fellow man, built on the desires of his students for a full athletic program to match their growing spirit and pride." Carver's home games were played at Municipal Field, with the last game being against Dunbar High School that drew a crowd of 800 persons.

Lloyd Price and his band played for a show and dance at the American Legion Auditorium on November 26. The balcony was reserved for white spectators. Price was known for his hit record *Lawdy Miss Clawdie*.

This Roanoke Police Department image shows the intersection of Franklin Road and Elm Avenue SW in the 1950s. *Nelson Harris*

Roanoke City's sewage disposal plant at Buzzard Rock on the Roanoke River was completed in late November and became fully operational. Fred Funnell Jr. was manager of the $2 million facility.

Gospel groups the Rosettes and the Harmonizing Four performed at the Star City Auditorium on November 30.

Johnny Pineapple and his orchestra presented their *South Pacific Revue* at the Roanoke Theatre on November 26.

The Fellowship of Baptist Ministers was organized in late November and was comprised of both white and Black clergy. Its membership numbered seventy-five. The cochairmen of the group were Rev. F. E. Alexander, publisher of the *Roanoke Tribune* and pastor of Buchanan First Baptist Church, and Rev. Wade Bryant, pastor of Roanoke's First Baptist Church.

Leonard's TV and Appliances opened on November 28 at 416 W. Campbell Avenue. It advertised the largest display of television sets in Roanoke. Leonard Friedman was the store owner.

Linwood Atkinson, manager of the Freddie Lee Orchestra, advertised in late November that effective January 1, 1953, the band would be known as the Townsmen.

A crowd of 24,000 watched the annual Thanksgiving Day football game at Victory Stadium between Virginia Tech and Virginia Military Institute on November 27. The game was attended by Virginia Governor John Battle and retired General George C. Marshall. Tech won 26–7. Tech had not won the contest since 1946.

Johnny Daniels, seventy, lost his life in a house fire on November 27 at 226 Gregory Avenue NE. Three others in the home escaped.

Addison High School defeated Lincoln High School of Chapel Hill NC in the second annual Star City Bowl football game played at Victory Stadium on November 29. Charles Price was Addison's coach. At halftime the Addison band performed a hot jazz session that had couples jitterbugging on the stadium track.

The Roanoke chapter of the League of Women Voters was organized on December 4 in a meeting at the Roanoke Main Library.

J. V. Grant of Bent Mountain earned top honors in the Roanoke County corn production contest for the second year in a row. He harvested 163.02 bushels per acre. The runner-up was Joe Powell of Bent Mountain.

Pianist Gina Bachauer gave a concert at the American Legion Auditorium on December 1. Bachauer was one of only four living pupils of Rachmaninoff.

Roanoke's fourth naval reserve unit, the Organized Mobilization Team, was activated on December 1 at the navy training center. Lt. Commander L. W. Calvin was the commanding officer.

Mac's Soda Shop opened on December 1 at 3327 Garden City Boulevard. The special guest was Santa Claus.

The new Emmanuel Lutheran Church building was formally dedicated on November 30 by Rev. John Utt, the pastor. Dr. Charles Smith, president of Roanoke College, delivered the dedicatory sermon. The congregation was organized on August 6, 1922, and its first church building was on the corner of Lafayette Boulevard and Staunton Avenue NW. The new church building was at Palmetto Street and Olive Avenue NW.

Lloyd Overfelt of Boones Mill died on December 1 at Lewis-Gale Hospital from injuries he had sustained the day before while on the job at American Bridge in Roanoke. While operating a drill, Overfelt lost control of it and was struck in the head.

Master Sgt. Edward Schnore of Roanoke was killed in a plane crash of a military C-124 Globemaster in Alaska in late November. Surviving him were a wife and two children who resided on Colgate Street NE.

Evelyn Gates, thirty-six, was found shot to death in her home at 214 Loudon Avenue NW on December 2. Police quickly arrested Ezzie Steele, an escaped convict from North Carolina, for the crime.

The Associated Press announced their selections for the Group 1 All-State Football Team. Paul Rotenberry of Jefferson High School was named to both offensive and defensive teams as a back (offense) and safety (defense).

Carl Beckner, thirteen, of Roanoke County was struck and fatally injured by an ambulance near Mount Vernon School while he was delivering newspapers on his bike on December 3. The accident occurred on Route 221, and Beckner died a few hours later at Jefferson Hospital. The ambulance was operated by Woods Funeral Home in Floyd.

Fink's Jewelers displayed the world's largest sapphire in their Roanoke store on December 4. The Russian Crown Jewel was worn by Catherine the Great and was valued at $200,000.

At a meeting on December 3 to discuss plans for a possible Roanoke Symphony Orchestra, a committee was put together to develop a business plan, organize a symphony society, and solicit public support. Members of the committee were J. P. Allen, Mrs. Harry Dixon, and Adolphe Rachel. The meeting was held at McAvoy Music House, and an inaugural spring concert was planned with Gibson Morrissey of Bluefield, West Virginia, conducting.

Capt. Floyd Davis of Roanoke and a former star athlete at Jefferson High School died of a gunshot wound in France on December 1 while stationed at Chaumont with the US Air Force. He was survived by his wife, Anna, and two sons of Carolina Avenue SW.

The Bailey Brothers and the Happy Valley Boys performed at the City Market Auditorium on December 5.

Insurance authority and businessman Thomas Rutherford, seventy-three, died at his home in Roanoke on December 4. In 1916, he established a local insurance firm, Rutherford and Maher, with Horace Maher and had been in that business all his life.

Fred Hoback of Salem was the unanimous pick of the General Assembly for the bench of the Twenty-First Judicial Circuit that encompassed the Roanoke Valley. He had practiced law in Salem since 1931.

Federal Bake Shop opened on December 5 at 22 W. Campbell Avenue.

Doris Harris was sentenced to eight years in prison by Judge Dirk Kuyk, who found her guilty in the fatal shooting of her boyfriend, Kenneth Neighbors. in August.

Organizers and proponents of the Roanoke Symphony Orchestra announced that an inaugural concert would be held on February 23, 1953, at Jefferson High School. Gibson Morrissey, thirty-four, had been chosen as the conductor and was holding regular rehearsals with local musicians on Tuesday nights at the Parrish House of St. John's Episcopal Church. The group had received numerous endorsements of its efforts from leading civic and business organizations.

College Lutheran Church in Salem began a weeklong celebration of its centennial on December 14. The church was organized on December 18, 1852, with seven charter members. The first church was built on the northwest corner of Main Street and College Avenue in 1856. The second church (and the one in use at the time) was erected in 1921 for $90,000.

Yale and Towne Manufacturing in Salem announced in early December that it would be expanding its production facilities at Salem in order to begin manufacturing several more lines of locks.

Cover Girls of 1953 came to the Roanoke Theatre on December 10. The show advertised "a stageful of sunny honeys!" The show featured a number of vaudeville acts that included former Roanoker Ron Blake, a singer and actor. Blake had appeared in two films, *Anchors Aweigh* and *Tars and Spars*, and had his own television show in Miami. He was the son of Mr. and Mrs. L. R. Shuttles of Jamison Avenue SE.

This image shows the Federal Bake Shop at 22 Campbell Avenue SW, possibly on opening day. *Historical Society of Western Virginia*

Andrew Coxe took over as head of the local March of Dimes campaign. The Roanoke attorney was named to the position after Joseph Herbert resigned in a dispute with the National Foundation for Infantile Paralysis over local fundraising methods. Anna Haley was chairman of the local chapter.

The Roanoke branch of Southern Oxygen Company moved to 603 Center Avenue NW on December 10.

WSLS-TV went on the air at 6:06 p.m. on December 11, several days after initial projections due to delays caused by equipment failures and a lightning storm the day before. A televised inaugural ceremony included a statement from Roanoke Mayor Roy Webber, who was followed by two films projected from the local studios. At 6:30 p.m., viewers saw *The Living Book*, a taped program about the Bible, and then at 7:00 p.m. *The Lone Ranger*. At 7:30 p.m., WSLS joined the regular broadcast of NBC with the airing of the *Dinah Shore Show*. The opening ceremony produced locally had been taped prior to broadcast, but station manager James Moore indicated "live" in-studio broadcasting would occur in about ten days.

Schertle Television and Appliances opened on December 12 at First Street and Franklin Road SW. A grand prize drawing for a new Bendix television set was held for customers who came to the store on opening weekend.

Roanokers had their first opportunity to see themselves on television during a telecast from the showroom of Grand Piano Company on Second Street SW on December 13. The program also became the first to originate in Roanoke. The program aired at 3:00 p.m. for one hour as persons in the store were interviewed. The Floyd Ward Dancers and the Townsmen Trio also performed during the broadcast. A Crosley mobile television unit was brought to Roanoke for the event and fed the live event to WSLS.

Consolidated Bus Lines' new terminal was completed in mid-December on Salem Avenue. The one-story structure eased the burden on the downtown Greyhound terminal.

About one hundred persons attended a rally to denounce the new Revised Standard Version of the Bible at New Hope Baptist Church in Salem. The main speaker was Rev. Robert Miller, pastor of Ghent Church of the Brethren, who declared, "There is only one Bible – the King James Version!"

The *Roanoke Times* began listing television station schedules for the first time in their December 14 edition. Along with WSLS, the programs of other stations included WFMY in Greensboro and WTVR in Richmond. The three stations broadcast between noon and midnight.

Durfee Television Company opened on December 15 at 514 S. Jefferson Street. A grand prize for participating customers was a DuMont television set.

The annual Roanoke Sandlot Football Banquet was held at Monroe Junior High School on December 18. Guest speakers were Virginia Tech football coach Frank Moseley and Tech's starting fullback Don Booth, who got his start playing sandlot in Roanoke.

Eldridge Cundiff Inc. moved to its new location at 2203 Patterson Avenue SW in mid-December.

Local sales of television sets sharply increased the week WSLS went on the air. It was estimated that 4,000 sets had been sold locally within the first weeks of December. The average price for a television set was $250.

Bob Williams and his Cumberland Mountaineers, along with Joe Binglehead, performed for a three-hour round and square dance at the City Market Auditorium on December 19.

Don "Red" Barry and his *Hollywood Show* performed at the Roanoke Theatre on December 17.

The Dairy Fountain at 1929 Carter Road SW held its formal opening the third weekend in December. The store and soda fountain had been completely remodeled by its new owner and operator John Jackson.

Marvin Long, twenty-four, of RFD 3 in Salem was fatally wounded on December 19 at the home of his father, A. D. Long, located three miles west of Salem on Route 11. Police arrested Charles McCarty for the shooting, who was Long's brother-in-law. Long was a veteran of the Korean War.

Buddy Johnson and his orchestra, along with vocalist Ella Johnson, performed for a midnight show and dance at the American Legion Auditorium on December 24. The balcony was reserved for white spectators.

N&W Railway's Santa Claus train rolled into Roanoke on December 21. The train traveled through the railway's service region for five days distributing candy and other items to children. N&W was the first and only railway in the nation to sponsor a Santa Train, which it began in 1950.

Ground-breaking ceremonies were held for South Roanoke Methodist Church on December 21 at the church's new location at South Jefferson and Twenty-Fourth Streets SW.

Roanoke's first municipal Christmas pageant was staged on the steps of the Municipal Building on December 22. The pageant featured a sixty-person choir and a play involving school children as well as adults. Traffic was halted in front of the Municipal Building for the late afternoon performance. Staging and directing for the pageant were done by Francis Ballard, Genevieve Dickinson, Clara Black, and Betty Thornton. The pageant was sponsored by the city and the Junior Chamber of Commerce. The national Jaycees had adopted a theme of "Putting Christ Back into Christmas," and their sponsorship of the local pageant was in service to that effort. Several hundred attended the event.

The Roanoke County Community Cannery ceased operations the third week in December. Those using the cannery numbered 492 and canned 16,985 quarts of food. Almost 2,000 pounds of lard were produced. The cannery was located on Water Street in Salem and was operated by J. C. Shelton and Ida Gray.

Girl Scout Troop Number 7 of Belmont Methodist Church celebrated its twenty-first birthday on December 23. It was the oldest Girl Scout Troop in Roanoke, having been started by Bee Bell in 1931.

WROV continued a long-standing tradition as they broadcast live the midnight Christmas Mass from St. Andrew's Catholic Church.

The final performance of twelve of the Emmanuel Pilgrim Church Christmas pageant was December 26. Total attendance for the dozen performances was 8,000. The outdoor production was held at the corner of Melrose Avenue and Nineteenth Street NW and was under the direction of the church's pastor, Rev. Joseph Brown.

Milt Larkin and his orchestra, along with the X-Rays, performed for a show and dance at the Star City Auditorium on December 31. White spectators were admitted for half price.

Two Bibee grocery Stores closed at the end of December due to nonrenewal of leases. The stores, owned by Virginia Markets, were located at 420 Luck Avenue SW and 3324 Williamson Road NW.

Roanoke City Council voted at its December 29 meeting to purchase twenty-two acres known as the Tazewell Morgan property for recreational use and future site of a fire station. The property, acquired for $20,000, was located on Vinton Road just south of Orange Avenue NE.

Hospitality Unlimited, a film about the operations of the Hotel Roanoke, was aired on December 30 over WSLS-TV and became the first local film shown on television in Roanoke. The film had aired at conventions around the country to promote the hotel.

The Mick-or-Mack Grocery Store chain announced on December 31 that it was planning to close some of its smaller stores. The first to close would be their grocery at Highland Avenue and Jefferson Street SW.

A murder charge against Cophas Smith was sent to a grand jury on December 31 for the bayonet slaying of Howard Brown earlier in the month. Both men were from Roanoke. The incident occurred during an argument between the men at First Street and Wells Avenue NW on December 4. Brown succumbed to his injuries two days later at Burrell Memorial Hospital.

1953

Roanoke City Council authorized City Manager Arthur Owens to end farming and dairy operations at the City Farm along Colonial Avenue to help balance the city's budget. The City Farm was one of three farms operated by the city, with the other locations being at the tuberculosis sanatorium at Coyners Spring and near the airport.

Philip Grosso was the first baby born in the Roanoke Valley in 1953. He was delivered at 1:55 a.m. at Lewis-Gale Hospital, the son of Mr. and Mrs. Joe Grosso of Woods Avenue SW.

Alfred Thomas, twenty-three, died from head injuries on January 1 when he fell from a moving truck in the alley of the 600 block of Tazewell Avenue SE. Thomas lived in Salem.

Dr. John Boyd Jr. died at his home on Second Street SW at the age of seventy-one. Boyd had practiced medicine in Roanoke since 1906 and was a past president of the Roanoke Academy of Medicine.

Professional boxing returned to Roanoke on January 5 with five matches at the American Legion Auditorium. The marquee fight was between George Wilson and Eddie Marshall. The event also included two locals, Don Webber and Lou Yonkers.

Colonial Place Radio and TV opened at 3762 Williamson Road on January 3. They carried General Electric television sets.

Skating Varieties of '53 came to the Skate-A-Drome near Lakeside the first week in January. The roller-skating show featured seventeen acts.

WSLS-TV began broadcasting morning shows on January 5. The lineup of network shows included *Today with Garroway, Morning Chapel, TV Coffee Time, Ding Dong School, Prologue to the Future*, and *There's One in Every Family*. Prior to this, WSLS had not begun broadcasts until noon.

Cowboy Copas, Kathy Copas, and Jim Day from the *Grand Ole Opry* performed at the Roanoke Theatre on January 7.

Federal authorities granted permission and funds to the Roanoke Redevelopment and Housing Authority on January 5 to develop a detailed slum clearance plan for the city. The plan would require the approval of Roanoke City Council.

Ezzie Steele, a fugitive from North Carolina, was indicted by a grand jury on January 5 for murder in the death of Evelyn Gates. The trial date was set for January 19.

At least eighty young men from Roanoke were reported as AWOL from military bases by federal authorities in early January. According to Roanoke police, only twenty had been apprehended.

Wards Television Company opened a branch at 1229 Williamson Road the first week of January. The store manager was Sheldon Shapiro.

Fred Waring brought his *Festival of Song* to the American Theatre on January 7. The performance was sponsored by the Thursday Morning Music Club as part of their annual concert series.

Dominion Signs acquired the Harley Webster Company, which had been in the sign business for two decades. Dominion had previously absorbed Stanford, a sign company in Salem, in 1952.

The congregation of St. James Episcopal Church worshipped for the first time in their new building at 4545 Delray Street NW on January 11. The new building cost $54,000.

Ice Vogues of 1953 came to the American Legion Auditorium for a weeklong run that began January 15. The show featured seventy-five ice skaters and dancers.

The Clovers, a quartette, along with Fats Domino, performed for a show and dance at the Star City Auditorium January 15. The balcony was reserved for white spectators.

Grand Ole Opry stars Johnnie and Jack and their Tennessee Mountain Boys performed at the Roanoke Theatre on January 14.

Howard Rice proposed to the Salem Town Council at their January 12 meeting that they swap him Younger Park for "Boxwood," a historic home on Main Street, as the location for the town's library. The council rejected the proposal.

A 200-foot transmission tower was erected on Mill Mountain in mid-January for WROV-TV, which was set to air at the end of the month, according to station manager Frank Koehler. The station's studios were in the Mountain Trust Bank Building.

The Roanoke City Democratic Committee opted to not have a primary for City Council in April at their meeting on January 13. The decision meant that the city would have its first nonpartisan City Council election since June 1918. The proposal to do so was made by State Senator Earl Fitzpatrick.

The Civitan Club announced plans to sponsor a local talent show on Saturday evenings on WSLS-TV called *Variety Revue of Virginia*. The goal was to showcase local talent in the hopes they might be given a chance to perform on national television.

A $650,000 capital campaign for Hollins College was launched with a dinner at the Hotel Roanoke on January 14 for the Roanoke phase of the effort. Around 400 persons attended the event that was hosted by the college's president, Dr. John Everett. R. H. Smith, president of N&W Railway, was general chairman of the campaign.

Paul Rotenberry, a senior at Jefferson High School, was named to the All-America High School football squad of *Scholastic Magazine*. He was the only Virginian named to the squad.

In the January 18 edition of the *Roanoke Times*, Melville Carico wrote about the early history of Roanoke aviation. The first opportunity for Roanokers to ride in an airplane occurred in the fall of 1919 when a barnstormer landed in a field on the Horton farm near Forest Park School and offered rides for fifteen dollars. Among those in the crowd that day was Clayton Lemon, who would become a Roanoke aviation pioneer. One of the earliest airfields was Cook Field, located where the Appalachian Power substation is on Route 11. Frank Reynolds and Lemon operated from there in the later 1920s. There was also Cook Field and later Trout Field adjacent to Fairview Cemetery.

Belmont School, the city's oldest school for whites, held an open house on January 22 to allow the public to view the $185,000 annex that had been completed. The school was built in 1891. Nell Walters was the principal.

Sonny Denton of Roanoke won the *National Amateur Time* contest in Baltimore, Maryland, by singing *Don't Let the Stars Get in Your Eyes*. The show was nationally televised.

"Sugar-foot Sam from Alabam" and his *All-Colored Revue* performed at the Roanoke Theatre on January 21.

The Brambleton Junior Woman's Club sponsored *Dixie Minstrel* at the Jefferson High School auditorium on January 22 as a fundraiser for their club. Ernest Robertson was the master of ceremonies.

The Roanoke Development Corporation received its charter from the SCC on January 22. The corporation was formed by those associated with the Roanoke Chamber of Commerce to assist in industrial and commercial development in the Roanoke Valley.

The Roanoke Chamber of Commerce expressed its thanks to its retiring executive director Ben Moomaw at the group's annual dinner at the Hotel Roanoke on January 23. In what was believed to be the largest attendance at an annual dinner, Moomaw received a sustained standing ovation for his thirty years of service to the chamber.

Officials with Montgomery Ward and Company announced the opening of a new catalog office at 414 First Street SW on February 5 for mail-order business.

Young's Store at Edgewood near Peters Creek was razed the third week of January due to the widening of Route 460 to a four-lane highway. It had been used for years as the polling station for the Peters Creek precinct in Roanoke County.

The Star City Club of the Deaf was a basketball team that competed against other teams of the hearing-impaired. In their inaugural season, they were coached by Edward Howell.

Little Jimmy Dickens brought his *Grand Ole Opry* show to the Roanoke Theatre on January 28.

Kroger held a free cooking school for three nights each at the Lee Theatre and Grandin Theatre during the last week of January. Groceries, kitchen appliances, and cookware were given away as prizes. Grace Reeder was the instructor. The average attendance at each presentation was 500.

The Footlighters presented their first production of a play, *The Philadelphia Story*, at Roanoke College on January 30. Lead roles were played by Sam Good and Betty Thornton.

Comic books proved quite popular in Roanoke. A leading distributor, American News Agency, estimated that over 150,000 comic magazines were sold monthly in the city based on their reports.

John Quarles, forty-five, of Roanoke died on January 25 from burns he sustained in a house fire a day prior at 27 Elm Avenue SW. Quarles had been taken to Lewis-Gale Hospital after he was rescued by firefighters.

Officials with the National Municipal League and *Look* magazine announced on January 26 that Roanoke had been selected as an All-American City for 1952 due to its building program and efforts to rejuvenate the city. Roanoke was one of eleven cities selected for the honor from among eighty entries. The city celebrated its achievement with a sold-out banquet at the Hotel Roanoke on January 28 where pollster George Gallup spoke and formally presented to city officials the award. Gallup was introduced by Carl Andrews, chairman of the Roanoke Awards Committee.

WROV-TV received its power plant on January 29 that was quickly installed at its transmission tower on Mill Mountain in preparation for launching its broadcasts in less than two weeks. The station's UHF transmitter was one of only nine in the nation. Most television sets would need a low-cost adapter for reception station officials indicated.

Paul's Steak and Chicken House reopened on January 30 under the new management of Virginia Stanley. The restaurant was located on Route 11, two miles north of Roanoke.

Carl Tabor, general manager and vice president of N&W Railway, died at his home in Roanoke on January 31. He was fifty-nine. Death was attributed to a heart attack while he slept. H. C. Wyatt was appointed as Tabor's successor a few days later.

Lionel Hampton brought his *Variety Revue of 1953* to the American Legion Auditorium on February 4. White spectators were admitted to the balcony for the floor show and dance event.

Bill Bailey's *All-Star Minstrels* show was at the American Legion Auditorium on February 7. The show featured well-known minstrel acts and comedians. The performance was sponsored by the Rajah Temple Dokies.

Peoples Federal Savings and Loan acquired the Liberty Trust Building for $250,000 with plans to make the building its corporate home effective April 1. The property was located at Jefferson Street and Salem Avenue SW and was owned by Wilmington Bank and Trust of Wilmington, North Carolina, as a trustee.

First National Exchange Bank displayed ancient coins in its lobby during the first week of February. The collection had been assembled by Chase Manhattan Bank.

The Thursday Morning Music Club concluded its 1952–53 season with a concert by the Boston Pops Tour Orchestra on February 6 at the American Legion Auditorium. The orchestra was conducted by Arthur Fiedler.

Guy's, a Roanoke restaurant, was purchased by Fred Kune from John Hunter in early February. The restaurant was located in the Shenandoah Building.

Dr. J. G. Davis, Roanoke's oldest practicing physician, died at his home in Roanoke on February 1 at the age of eighty-nine. Davis was considered the last of the "horse and buggy" doctors. He began his practice in Roanoke in 1905 making house calls on a horse and then switching to a Model-T in 1909. He practiced medicine up until two days before his passing.

Grandpa Jones and his *Grand Ole Opry* show came to the Roanoke Theatre on February 4.

The Roanoke Groundhog Club held its annual dinner on February 2 that included roasts of politicians and humorous acts. H. T. Angell was president of the "Groundhog Club of America No. 1."

During the first several weeks of 1953, several grocery stores closed. They were Mick-or-Mack at Highland Avenue and Jefferson Street SW, Martin Brothers Grocery at 714 Third Street SW, Echols Cash Grocery at 501 Thirteenth Street SW, Virginia Markets (Bibee) at 420 Luck Avenue SW and 3324 Williamson Road, Shopwell Food Store at 1322 Grandin Road SW, Murray's Cash Grocery at 831 Salem Avenue, and Home Service Foods at 709 Franklin Road SW. Local grocers indicated the reasons for the rash of closings were tough competition from chains with larger groceries, poor locations, or the retirement of the owners.

Francis Ballard and John Creasy formed the Roanoke Cinema Group in early February to bring early films to Roanoke for viewing. The movies were from the library of the Museum of Modern Art in New York and were shown at the Bank of Virginia.

Greene Memorial Methodist Church kicked off a debt-retirement campaign with a dinner at the American Legion Auditorium on February 5. The monthlong pledge drive sought to raise $150,000.

Lloyd Lovern, thirty-five, of Roanoke fell to his death while working on a sign for Old Dominion Signs in Fluvanna County on February 4.

This postcard, mailed in 1953, shows Bradford's Seafood Restaurant that was located at 2523 Franklin Road SW. *Bob Stauffer*

Ray Mond brought his *Voodoo Show* to the Roanoke Theatre on February 6. The horror show included "night-mare creatures that come right into the audience," according to ads.

S&W Cafeteria signed a thirty-year lease on the Greyhound Bus Terminal building on Church Avenue that was to be vacated by Greyhound and remodeled for the cafeteria. S&W opened in 1930 at 412 S. Jefferson Street. It would take several months for the remodeling before S&W could occupy the terminal space.

The Children's Shop opened at 4 E. Main Street in Salem on February 7.

Roanoke City Manager Arthur Owens asked City Council to delay any consideration of converting the former site of the veterans' emergency housing project into a municipal golf course as had been advocated. Owens cited budget constraints and that the one-hundred-acre site might be better used as a park.

Carleton Drewry had a volume of poetry, *The Writhen Wood*, published by E. P. Dutton & Company of New York in February. Drewry had numerous poems published in national magazines and was president of the Virginia Poetry Society. He worked for N&W Railway.

The William A. Hunton Branch YMCA celebrated its twenty-fifth anniversary on February 8 with a special program held at First Baptist Church, Gainsboro. The keynote speaker was Thomas Young, a publisher from Norfolk.

Doctors Ambulance Service began operations in early February from headquarters at 1929 Patterson Avenue SW.

Dr. J. D. Riddick, former principal of Jefferson High School, died at a hospital in Pearisburg on February 8 at age fifty-nine. He served as principal at Jefferson High School from 1935 to 1945.

Leaders of the Hunton Branch YMCA pose in front of their 1953 membership campaign visuals. *Virginia Room, RPL*

Mrs. Henrietta Woods celebrated her one-hundredth birthday at her home on Chestnut Avenue NW. She was born of slave parents on a farm near Stewartsville.

The Inter-Club Council of Business Women's Club of Roanoke sent out a letter to recruit a woman to run for Roanoke City Council in 1953 or 1954. "Roanoke needs a woman on City Council. The entire community will benefit from the experience, viewpoint, and rich contribution which a qualified woman can give," stated the letter.

The Negro Veterans Emergency Housing Project was razed in mid-February. The project, located at the west end of Salem Avenue, was provided by the city for housing Negro veterans of WWII and their families.

Grace Presbyterian Church dropped "Presbyterian" from its name effective in mid-February. The congregation would be called Grace Church, Independent, to reflect its nondenominational stance.

The daughter of Booker T. Washington and an associate in Washington, DC, filed suit in US District Court in Roanoke on February 12 with a charge of breach of contract against S. J. Phillips and the Booker T. Washington Memorial in Franklin County. The suit involved the sale of the memorial half-dollars and the distribution of the proceeds.

Managers of the two Roanoke public transit companies sent letters to the Roanoke city manager asking for fare increases to help their balance sheets. Passenger volume had dropped, and they indicated the reason was too many were staying home watching television.

The Salzburg Marionette Theatre performed at Hollins College on February 16. The three-foot size marionettes did a production of Mozart's *The Magic Flute.*

Roy Brown and his Mighty Men, along with the Five Royales, performed for a show and dance at the Star City Auditorium on February 17. White spectators were admitted for a discount.

Sydney Small, vice president of N&W Railway, announced on February 14 plans for a $1 million expansion of the Hotel Roanoke that would include fifty-six guest rooms, a new exhibit hall, and a larger dining room.

Roanoke Electronic Supply, a wholesale dealer in television and radio parts and Emerson brand electronics, opened at 1322 Williamson Road on February 16.

WROV-TV, the first UHF station in Virginia, did a test pattern on the air on February 16 with only dealers and service technicians getting advance notice. Channel 27 was used. Station officials said programming will not start until dealers are satisfied that set owners will get satisfactory reception.

Blue Cross and Blue Shield signed a five-year lease on the former Flikwir house at 903 S. Jefferson Street. The mansion, constructed in 1906, provided more room for the expanding agency that had been located in the Colonial-American Bank Building.

The Polack Brothers Circus came to Roanoke February 25 for four days sponsored by the Kazim Shrine Temple. The circus included a new act, Jack Joyce and his trained camels. Gene Randow headed the clowns.

Roanoke opera singer Jane Stuart Smith performed at Carnegie Hall in New York on February 20 as part of the annual American Music Festival.

Jo Anne (Elmore) Lantz is shown on the set of her WSLS-TV show, *Songs by Jo Ann Lantz*, in this May 1953 image. Lantz won a talent competition and sang on Horace Heidt's national radio broadcast. *Avisco News*

Billy Eckstine, Ruth Brown, and Count Basie and his orchestra performed for a show and dance at the American Legion Auditorium on March 4. White spectators were admitted to the balcony.

The *Horace Heidt Show* came to the American Legion Auditorium on March 1. In addition to Heidt, other well-known entertainers from the show also performed, including Johnny Standley, Ralph Sigwald, Doodles Weaver, Lila Jackson, Conley Graves, Bud Messenie, and Lizabeth Lynch. The show was sponsored by the Roanoke Jaycees. Some seventy-five locals participated in tryouts the week prior at the Appalachian Power Company Auditorium for a chance to perform on the nationally broadcast show, and two singers were selected—Jo Anne Lantz and Evelyn McLaughlin.

Sonny Bridges and his *Basin Street Revue* came to the Roanoke Theatre on February 25.

The Sertoma Club sponsored the Roanoke Golden Gloves boxing tournament the third weekend in February. Robert Humphries of Villamont was named outstanding boxer of the event. Boxers from around the state competed in the tournament. Local winners were Neil Mullen, John Tyree, Ed Crigger, Walter Daniels, Paul McAllister, William Goodman, and Larry Craighead.

Roanoke Commissioner of the Revenue John Hart announced in February that he would not seek reelection. Hart had served as commissioner for twenty years.

Rev. Frank Efird resigned as pastor of Christ Lutheran Church on February 22 to assume the pastorate of the largest Lutheran church in the South, St. John's Lutheran Church in Salisbury, North Carolina. St. John's membership was 1,700.

The Barter Theatre presented a production of *The Virginian* on February 24 at the Jefferson High School auditorium. Robert Porterfield played the lead in the Western play.

Bedford TV Stores opened a Roanoke branch at 2817 Williamson Road on February 24.

Roanoke stepped into the national boxing spotlight when it hosted the American Bantamweight Championship fight at the American Legion Auditorium on February 23 before 2,300 fans. Henry Gault defeated Buddy Baggett in a unanimous fifteen-round decision to retain the title. The match was broadcast nationally over radio.

Goode Construction Corporation of Charlotte, North Carolina, was awarded a $343,000 contract to construct Roanoke's first parking garage. The 500-car garage was to be built on Jefferson Street between Bullitt Avenue and Day Avenue SW. Construction was to start March 9.

In late February, construction began on a $19,000 swimming pool and pavilion at Hidden Valley Country Club. The project was to be completed by May 1.

Ell-an's Beauty Salon opened at 1327 Grandin Road SW in the rear of Garland's Drug Store.

The *Roanoke World-News* began running two new comic strips, *Twin Earths* and *Peanuts*, on March 2.

The Paganini Quartet presented a concert of chamber music at the Jefferson High School auditorium on March 4, sponsored by the Community Concert Association.

The Children's Zoo underwent enhancements during the off-season in preparation for its second's year. Projects included a new lookout that included steps down to the "Zoo Choo," a tunnel for the train to pass through, clearing of wooded areas around the zoo, and an outdoor children's television viewing area coordinated with WROV-TV.

Construction began on March 2 of a new forty-room motel at Lakewood Farm. The Lakewood Motel was expected to be completed by July 1.

This late 1950s postcard shows the Lakeview Motor Lodge on what was formerly Lakeview Farm near Hollins. Construction on the motel began in March 1953. *Bob Stauffer*

WRIS Radio went on the air on February 28 on channel 1410 with a 5,000-watt transmission, making it one of the more widely broadcast stations in Southwest Virginia. Frank Tirico was the station manager, and Rod Stevens and Herm Reavis were the main announcers. The transmitter was located on Luckett Street near Shenandoah Avenue. A dedication ceremony was broadcast at 3:00 p.m. on March 1.

Horace Heidt announced that Jo Anne Lantz, singer-pianist, of Roanoke had been selected by him to perform on his national radio show on March 4.

WROV-TV went on the air on channel 27 on March 2 for two hours from 8:00 to 10:00 p.m. Station officials claimed success as they received hundreds of calls from viewers saying their reception was good. The station continued to broadcast only in the evenings with a plan to have programming throughout the day beginning March 15 when they officially affiliated with the ABC network. The first night's broadcast included a travelogue on St. Petersburg, Florida, and a full-length movie, *Shanghai Gesture*.

The first local television panel program aired on WROV-TV on March 4 when Coleman Austin moderated *Topics for Teens*, a local show of high school students discussing various issues. Prior to being televised, the show had been aired on WROV radio. On March 6, the station aired *Kommunity Quiz*, which allowed members of local clubs and organizations to compete in answering questions about various topics.

The Lee-Hi Drive-In Theatre and the Trail Drive-In Theatre advertised that for the 1953 season, they would run the same films simultaneously.

Hugh Zirkle, sixty-six, of Roanoke Country was struck and killed by an automobile near Salem on March 4.

Power Equipment Center opened on March 6 at 25 Shenandoah Avenue NW.

The Grandin Road Community Center held a formal grand opening of all its tenants on March 6. The adjoining stores were located in the 1300 block of Grandin Road and mainly included Garland's Drug Store (1327) and Frederic's Flowers (1329). Mrs. Brownie Eunice was the general contractor. For Garland's, it was their sixth drugstore in the city. Within the drugstore were Ell-Anne's Beauty Salon, Paul Shelley's Barber Shop, and Peter's Jewelry.

The American Legion Auditorium was standing-room only for professional wrestling on March 5 as the Smith Brothers squared off in a tag team match against the Jungle Boy and the Great Togo. It was believed to be the most-attended wrestling event in Roanoke's history. The *Roanoke Times* reported, "A mass of shouting humanity jammed around the ring...At times all four wrestlers were in the ring mauling and kicking each other."

Kay's Ice Cream opened a new store at 1306 S. Jefferson Street on March 7. They also offered fresh bakery products from Michael's Bakery.

Katz Food Company at 1621 Shenandoah Avenue NW was purchased from Harry Katz, founder, by Pete Apostolou.

This shows Garland's Drugstore at 1327 Grandin Road SW in the mid-1950s. The store opened in March 1953. *Virginia Room, RPL*

This March 1953 image shows the soda fountain inside Garland's Drugstore on Grandin Road SW. *Virginia Room, RPL*

Johnson Service Company of Milwaukee opened at branch office at 2418 Durham Street NW in early March.

The Cole Porter musical *Kiss Me Kate* with its New York touring cast was performed at the Jefferson High School auditorium on March 14.

The local *Hayden Huddleston Show* debuted on WROV-TV on March 8, having been on WROV radio previously. The variety show featured local talent, quizzes, and prizes.

A stage production of *Oklahoma* presented by the Theatre Guild National Company came to the Roanoke Theatre on March 13. Blacks were admitted to the balcony. Lead actors included Florence Henderson as "Laurey" and Ralph Lowe as "Curley."

The Roanoke Civic Ballet presented its annual program on March 9 at the Jefferson High School auditorium. The program included *Aurora's Wedding* and *The Fantastic Toyshop*.

The Vinton Lions Club presented its annual minstrel show for three nights beginning March 12.

The first of five custom-built fire trucks made for Dallas, Texas, left the factory of the Oren Roanoke Corporation on Salem Avenue at Twelfth Street SW on

March 9. The fire trucks were shipped by rail. The trucks were the largest postwar order received by Oren, and Dallas was the largest city to order from Oren.

Over one hundred women from various organizations attended a meeting on March 9 to better organize a campaign to elect a female to Roanoke City Council. A committee of twelve was selected to solicit nominations for potential candidates.

A ground-breaking ceremony was held on March 9 for the 500-car parking garage in downtown Roanoke at Jefferson Street and Day Avenue. One hiccup in the construction process was the contractor initially being unable to get a building permit as there was no provision for a parking garage in the city code. City officials worked quickly to rectify the matter.

WROV-TV began airing national programs of the ABC network on March 8.

A cornerstone-laying ceremony was held on March 14 for the new home of Melrose Lodge No. 139, AF&AM, at Carroll Avenue and Twenty-First Street NW. The lodge was chartered in 1928.

Charm Shop, a women's clothing store, opened at 12 W. Campbell Avenue on March 13.

Willie Mabon and his orchestra performed for a show and dance at the American Legion Auditorium on March 16. White spectators were admitted to the balcony.

Evangelist and faith healer Oral Roberts held a two-day revival at the American Legion Auditorium on March 17 and 18.

First National Exchange Bank opened its Grandin Road Branch on March 20 at 1323 Grandin Road. The first customer was Mrs. D. E. Peery, who opened a new savings account with a three-dollar deposit. Over 4,000 persons attended the opening-day event that was enhanced by twenty-six 1953 model cars displayed by local dealers in adjacent parking lots.

In 1952, Roanoke Merchants Association added sixty-two new firms as members, making it the largest trade association of its kind in the South.

The Salem Lions Club held its annual three-night minstrel show the third weekend in March.

Dr. Cecil Jackson of Jackson, Mississippi, was appointed as the new superintendent of Catawba Sanatorium in mid-March. He would assume his duties April 15.

Col. Chesley Davis and his *Chicago Follies* came to the Roanoke Theatre on March 18. According to ads, the show included international pinup girls.

The Chuck Wagon Gang, along with Wally Fowler, Martha Carson, and the LeFevre Trio, presented a concert at the American Legion Auditorium on March 21.

Elmer Yoter, newly appointed manager for the Roanoke Red Sox, arrived in Roanoke in mid-March to begin promoting the 1953 season. He succeeded Owen Sheetz. Yoter had over thirty years of experience in professional baseball as a player, manager, and scout.

A touring basketball team, the New York Colored Clowns, played an exhibition game against the Sportsmen at Carver School on March 20. Many of the players were associated with teams in the National Basketball Association. The star player for the Clowns was Curtis Johnson.

Dr. Edgar Lawrence, physician, died on March 21 at a Roanoke hospital. He was eighty-four. He first practiced medicine in Floyd County before coming to Roanoke in 1919 as a general practitioner.

WSLS-TV boosted its transmission power from 12,600 watts to 25,600 watts on March 21. This allowed for those beyond the Roanoke region to receive the station's broadcasts.

The Piedmont League released its 1953 baseball season schedule in mid-March. The league consisted of eight teams. In addition to the Roanoke Red Sox, the other teams were the Lynchburg Cardinals, Richmond Colts, Portsmouth Merrimacs, Newport News Dodgers, Norfolk Tars, York (Pennsylvania) White Roses, and Hagerstown (Maryland) Braves.

Microfilming of practically all Roanoke County records from its founding in 1838 through the Civil War period was started in mid-March by representatives of the Church of Jesus Christ of Latter Day Saints.

W. B. Littrell announced he was retiring as the last old-style blacksmith in the Roanoke Valley. Littrell's business had been located on the Boulevard in Salem since 1909. Littrell recalled being in the business with his brothers and making horseshoes, repairing carriages, and forging tools. Littrell was seventy-five.

Mrs. Mary Pickett was formally nominated for election to Roanoke City Council on March 23 by a large gathering of women interested in having a female perspective on the council. The women in attendance pledged to work daily for her election. Pickett was a past president of the Roanoke Central Council PTA. A committee formed by representatives of ninety-three women's organizations selected Pickett from among nineteen nominees who had been submitted to them. The meeting to announce their selection of Pickett was held at the YWCA. In accepting the backing of the women, Pickett said her candidacy did not represent a dissatisfaction with the current members of council, just the need to have a "woman's perspective." Mrs. Edward Moomaw presented Pickett to the group and stated, "She is young enough to grasp the scope of what will be expected of a woman on council and to have the vitality to cope with the problems that will arise with that position." Pickett joined four others who had also been announced for the first nonpartisan council election in thirty years. The announced candidates included Rev. F. E. Alexander, Paul Puckett, James Breakell, and Clarke Wray.

Roanoke City Council authorized the city manager to enter into a contract with the Commonwealth of Virginia and N&W Railway for construction of a grade crossing elimination project at Jefferson Street. The viaduct's construction was to be funded through a combination of local, state, and federal funds.

Blue Ridge Beverage Company opened in its new location on Route 460 opposite of Lakeside on March 23. Hugh Gish was company president. They were distributors of Red Top Ale and Miller High Life Beer.

The 164-foot high radio tower on top of the Shenandoah Building in downtown Roanoke was removed on March 23. The tower once transmitted for WSLS radio but was no longer needed.

A large addition to the Belmont Church of God in southeast Roanoke was dedicated on Sunday, March 22. The addition had been designed by the church's pastor, Rev. Benjamin Jenkins.

The student government of Jefferson High School presented *The Showboat Minstrels* at the school on March 27.

The Submarine Shop on Jefferson Street at Bullitt Avenue was sold in late March in order to be razed for off-street parking.

The *Roanoke Times* began running the daily comic strip *Twin Earths* on March 29. The sci-fi strip was already running in the *World-News*. The futuristic comic included flying disks, space stations, autoplanes, handbag televisions, and wireless telephones.

Cletis Richards was sentenced to twenty-five years in prison on March 27 for his bizarre armed robbery of the Bank of Salem that also included kidnapping. Richards pled guilty to the charges and had been under court-ordered psychiatric care.

Woodlawn Methodist Church in Roanoke was formally dedicated during its note-burning ceremony on March 29. The seven-year-old congregation had 249 members. Methodist church buildings were not dedicated until they were debt free.

The Roanoke Symphony Orchestra held its debut concert on March 31 in the Jefferson High School auditorium before 900 patrons. Weeks prior to the concert a fundraising campaign had raised $1,000 for the orchestra's inaugural performance. Chairing that effort was Mrs. Hoge McIlhany. The symphony was conducted by Gibson Morrissey, who had been guest conductor for orchestras in Europe and the United States to much acclaim. A graduate of the Julliard School of Music and Columbia University, Morrissey conducted the New York Philharmonic Orchestra at Carnegie Hall for a performance in May 1952. The symphony played three pieces for the concert—*Symphony No. 5 in E Minor* (Dvorak), *Young Person's Guide to The Orchestra* (Britten), and *Suite from the Opera Carmen* (Bizet).

Wasena Hardware at 1110 Main Street SW went out of business at the end of March.

Twenty drawings and four gouaches by Alfred Maurer, a pioneer in American modern art, were displayed in an exhibit sponsored by the Roanoke Fine Arts Center in early April at the Roanoke Library.

Blackstone and his *Big Magical Revue* came to the Roanoke Theatre on April 1.

The Roanoke School Board ruled that if families had television sets in their homes, then their children were ineligible for free school lunches. The board at its March 29 meeting heard a report from Mrs. Hester Webb, director of school cafeterias, that 17 percent of those receiving free lunches had televisions in the home.

The Roanoke Red Sox began their spring training in late March at Ocala, Florida. At the same time, the Portsmouth Merrimacs became the first team in the Piedmont League to integrate as eight black players participated in their spring training program. Portsmouth was affiliated with the Cleveland Indians.

Roanoke Symphony Orchestra director Gibson Morrissey gives advice to brothers Edward (left) and Jerry Webb during a March 1953 rehearsal. *Avisco News*

Peoples Federal Savings and Loan Association completed the purchase of the Liberty Trust Building on March 30. People paid $250,000 for the eight-story building on Jefferson Street at Salem Avenue in addition to conveying to the seller its building at 132 W. Campbell Avenue.

Sister Rosetta Tharpe along with Marie Knight, Marion Williams, Jimmy Roots, and the South Wind Quartet gave a concert of gospel and spiritual music at the Star City Auditorium on April 1.

Richard Beck, executive director of the Roanoke Redevelopment and Housing Authority, announced on April 1 plans for the development of 102 acres in northeast Roanoke. The plan called for the acquisition of about 400 pieces of property through purchase or condemnation. According to Beck, displaced persons would have access to residential units in the Lincoln Terrace public housing project. The area involved was bounded by Shenandoah Avenue on the south, Orange Avenue on the north, Second Street on the west, and Fourth Street in the east.

The Dominoes performed for a show and dance at the American Legion Auditorium on April 5. White spectators were admitted to the balcony.

Sidney Lattimore, eighteen, of Roanoke died at Burrell Memorial Hospital on April 3 of injuries he sustained the same day in an auto accident at Gilmer Avenue and Fifth Street NW.

The sanctuary of the Salem Pentecostal Holiness Church, shown here on this 1950s postcard, was dedicated in April 1953. It was located on North Bruffey Street. *Virginia Room, RPL*

Sam Krisch, a Roanoke pawnbroker and optician, died on April 3 at the age of sixty-six. A native of New York, Krisch came to Roanoke in 1918 and established the United Pawn Shop at Salem Avenue and Jefferson Street.

The Boston Red Sox and the Philadelphia Phillies played an exhibition baseball game at Maher Field on April 7. Philadelphia won, 15–2. Attendance was 2,556.

Salem Pentecostal Holiness Church was dedicated on April 5.

A crowd estimated at 20,000 attended the Easter sunrise service at Natural Bridge. The sermon was delivered by Rev. Harry Gamble, pastor of Roanoke's Calvary Baptist Church. It was the seventh such service held there and was broadcast nationally on radio by the CBS network.

Bill and Mary Reid, the Melody Mountaineers, Burk Barbour, Curly Lambert, and Jim Eanes with his Shenandoah Valley Boys brought their *Hillbilly Jamboree* to the Roanoke Theatre on April 8.

The Roanoke Red Sox agreed to an installment plan to pay debt owed to Roanoke City. According to city officials, the baseball team owed $1,496 from 1952 and $142 for 1951. The Red Sox had struggled with attendance and making payments to the city.

Miles Garage, an auto repair shop, opened at 527 Rorer Avenue SW on April 8. Charles Miles was the owner.

The Roanoke City Health Department reported that in 1952 there were around 600 cases of polio diagnosed, with twelve resulting in some form of paralysis. At the end of the year, the department had seventy polio-stricken children under its supervision, along with 325 tubercular patients.

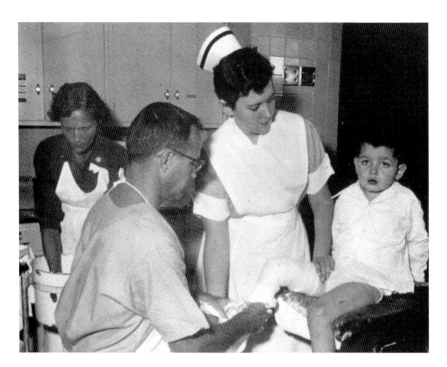

Dr. Louis Ripley works with a patient who had corrective surgery for polio at Roanoke Memorial Hospital. *Carilion Clinic*

Appalachian Electric Power Company received a permit in early April to convert its car barn at 315 Walnut Avenue SW into offices and a warehouse. The car barn had formerly housed streetcars.

Martha Anne Woodrum, well-known Roanoke aviatrix, married Dr. J. C. Zillhardt of Binghamton, New York, on April 11 at Greene Memorial Methodist Church.

The Roanoke Kennel Club held its annual dog show on April 9 at the American Legion Auditorium. There were 375 canine entries from all across the country. Best in Show went to a four-year-old English Setter owned by William Holt of Richmond.

The new Trailways-Consolidated bus terminal opened on April 17 at 215 W. Salem Avenue with thirty-six arrivals and departures daily. J. H. Terry was the terminal manager.

Nat King Cole, Sarah Vaughan, Billy May and his band, and comedian Gil Lamb performed at the American Legion Auditorium on April 15. For buying tickets, advertisements read, "Kindly state White or Colored Section, First or Second Show. House equally divided down center for white and colored." Tickets for whites were available at Hobbie Brothers and for Blacks at Nabor's Grill.

The Roanoke Executives Club was entertained by a mentalist and magician simply named Cleveland at their meeting on April 10. The self-proclaimed mind reader did numerous parlor tricks that amazed his audience.

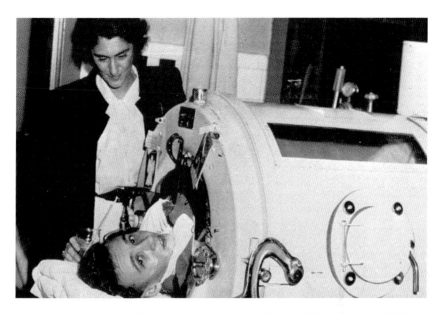

A polio patient is treated with an iron lung at Roanoke Memorial Hospital in this 1950s image. The hospital was the main center of treatment for polio patients in Western Virginia. *Carilion Clinic*

The Golden Gate Quartet performed at the American Legion Auditorium on April 16.

The Dunn Brothers' Miniature Circus went on display at Pugh's Department Store in Roanoke during the last two weeks of April. The toy circus had 750,000 pieces. Proceeds from ticket sales to view the display went to support the Children's Zoo on Mill Mountain. The circus required twenty-three years to build and was insured for $500,000. It occupied 2,000 square feet of floor space.

The Mexican Craft Shop opened at its new location in mid-April in the log cabin on Route 11 across from Hollins College.

The Johnson-Carper Furniture Company unveiled a new *I Love Lucy* bedroom suite in mid-April. The company, known for a sleek, modern design for its signature furnishings, created a bedroom suite that was selected by Desi Arnaz and Lucille Ball for the bedroom furniture that would appear on their popular television show. Johnson-Carper officials considered the partnership an advertising bonanza as the show was seen weekly by an estimated 40 million viewers. The bedroom suite was designed by Edmond Spence.

George Gearheart, seventeen, of Vinton was killed in an auto accident on April 12 on Route 460 east of Roanoke. Gearheart was a student at William Byrd High School and the son of Vinton Town Manager Guy Gearheart.

The congregation of St. Mark's Lutheran Church held its final worship service in the main auditorium of the church on April 12. Worship for the following two Sundays was held in the Sunday School building, and afterward the congregation moved into its new sanctuary on Franklin Road at Highland Avenue SW. The former church was a Roanoke landmark at Campbell Avenue and Third Street SW for over seventy-five years and was first used by Greene Memorial Methodist Church before the congregations swapped buildings.

A delegation of seventy-five Black citizens appeared before Roanoke City Council on April 13 to express opposition to the "slum clearance" plan of the Roanoke Redevelopment and Housing Authority for northeast Roanoke. The group presented petitions bearing almost 400 signatures. Spokespersons included Mrs. Cordelia Williams, Ira Womack Jr., and Rev. M. T. Coker of Mount Zion Baptist Church. Speakers asked the council as to the purpose of razing good homes in order to eliminate substandard ones and noted that traffic issues in the section could be addressed without the razing of residences. Council members responded that the plan had not been formally presented to them by the authority, so comments were received and filed.

The first woman to run for the House of Delegates in the Roanoke Valley was Mrs. Louise Cutts who declared her candidacy on April 13. Cutts stated she would seek one of the two seats allotted to the city. She was principal at Mount Vernon Elementary School and was active in numerous women's organizations.

Blackface comedian Slim Williams and a chorus of dancing girls brought their *Show of Shows* to the Roanoke Theatre on April 15.

Tastee-Freez opened on April 15 on Route 460 just east of the Roanoke city limits.

Matt Cvetic gave a lecture entitled "I was a Communist for the FBI" on April 16 in the Jefferson High School auditorium. His spy stories had been widely broadcast over national radio.

The Roanoke Redevelopment and Housing Authority held a public meeting on April 15 at Lincoln Terrace to explain the proposed redevelopment of northeast Roanoke. The overflow crowd listened as Richard Beck, the authority's executive director, explain that a sufficient number of residential units would be built such that no person or families would have to leave the area. Families whose residences would be razed would be given the opportunity to move into public housing. According to Beck, over half the homes in the area being considered were substandard. A number of pointed questions were directed at Beck about the plan, especially by Dr. Harry Penn. Penn raised concerns about valuations, aged citizens on fixed incomes, and the overall necessity of the plan.

Western film star Gene Autry and a friend halted their private flight from New York to Dallas with a ten-hour layover in Roanoke on April 16 for the weather to clear. While in the city, Autry and his business manager dined at the Hotel Roanoke where they were staying and were presented with a Virginia country ham by local restaurant owner Bradford Lipscomb. Autry's thank-you was to allow Lipscomb to fly with them the next day to Dallas aboard his twin-engine Beechcraft so Lipscomb could visit his ill sister.

Bus Terminal Restaurant formally opened on April 17 in the Trailways-Consolidated Bus Terminal. Plate lunches were fifty-five cents.

The King Brothers and Cristiani Circus came to Maher Field on April 21 sponsored by the Exchange Club. The circus had 150 performers, 250 animals, and a 5,000-seat big top.

Grand Ole Opry stars Red Foley, Rod Brasfield, Moon Mullican, Grady Martin, Jimmy Selph, and Sally Sweet performed at the American Legion Auditorium on April 20.

The first 3D movie to be shown in the Roanoke Valley was on April 19. The North 11 Drive-In and the Shenandoah Drive-In showed the film short *A Day in the Country*. Patrons were required to pay ten cents for the special glasses that were needed.

The Virginia Amateur Baseball League began its season on April 25. The teams in the league were Boones Mill, Back Creek, Buchanan, Elliston-Lafayette-Shawsville, Glenvar, New Castle, Roanoke, Roanoke-Webster, Rocky Mount, Salem, and Vinton.

The Piedmont League opened its baseball season on April 23. For the first time in the league's history, Blacks played in the league. Four teams had Blacks on their rosters—York (PA), Portsmouth, Newport News, and Richmond. The Roanoke Red Sox had not allowed Blacks to try out for their team as their parent organization, the Boston Red Sox, had not yet chosen to integrate. One of York's Black players, Joe Van Durham, had formerly played with the Chicago team in the American Negro League.

The Footlighters presented *Night Must Fall* at Roanoke College on April 24. The play was staged with arena-style seating. Lead roles were played by David Cross, Nettie Kitchen, Elizabeth Ross, and Sam Good. Ross also directed the play.

Construction on a new Mick-or-Mack grocery store began in late April on Windborne Street SW. The store was intended to replace the chain's grocery at 1330 Grandin Road SW.

Construction of the Mick-or-Mack grocery store, located at 1312 Winborne Avenue SW, began in April 1953. *Virginia Room, RPL*

Ken Herman, a 1942 graduate of William Fleming High School, appeared (uncredited) in the film *The Treasure of the Golden Condor* that opened at the Grandin Theatre and Lee Theatre on April 23. The movie starred Cornel Wilde and Ann Bancroft. Herman had been active in Fleming's student productions as a student and had appeared in several television shows since moving to New York, including the *Dinah Shore Show, Hollywood Theatre Time, Studio One*, and *I'm The Law*. He also had numerous roles with stage productions in New York, Chicago, and Los Angeles.

Sunshine Sue and the *Old Dominion Barn Dance* came to the stage of the Roanoke Theatre on April 22.

William Parsons, a seventeen-year-old student at Jefferson High School, of Roanoke won second place in the national finals of the American Legion oratorical contest on April 20 in Jersey City, New Jersey. He was awarded a $2,500 college scholarship. Parsons was also president of the Jefferson SGA.

In late April, the *Roanoke Times* began including Lynchburg television station WLVA, channel 13, in its daily listing of programs as its transmissions reached the Roanoke Valley.

Robert Bennett, twenty-eight, of Roanoke was killed in Smyth County when his car was struck on April 21 by an N&W Railway train. *The Tennessean*, powered by the J-Class 600 locomotive, carried the car 600 yards from the point of impact. Bennett owned and operated Bennett Supply Company in Roanoke.

Judge Stanford Fellers ordered in Law and Chancery Court on April 21 a sixty-day injunction against N&W Railway and seventeen nonoperating Brotherhoods from signing a union shop contract. The contract would have made union membership a condition of employment. Fellers stated he needed more time to study the case that had been brought by three nonunion employees.

James Carden, twenty-five, a native of Roanoke and a graduate of Jefferson High School, was killed in a military aircraft accident in the Gulf of Mexico on April 21. The training crash was the result of his overshooting a landing strip at Tyndall Air Force Base.

Eugene Carbaugh Jr. announced that he was planning to build a second parking garage in Roanoke as soon as the one under construction on Elm Avenue was completed. The second garage was to be constructed on the northeast corner of Salem Avenue and First Street SW and would house between 400 and 500 cars. The Roanoke Chamber of Commerce would act as trustee for the financing of the garage.

Hodges Lumber Company broke ground on April 22 on a new $35,000 warehouse at 908 Shenandoah Avenue NW.

Rev. J. E. Patterson delivered his farewell sermon on April 26 to the Mountain View Brethren Church. Patterson had previously announced his retirement to the congregation that he had served for forty years and helped organize in 1913.

Roanoke city officials offered citizens the opportunity to send their pets to an all-expense paid vacation for the summer as exhibits at the Children's Zoo on Mill Mountain. In a media release on April 22, recreation department staff stated, "An old sheep, two lambs, an old pretty cat and five kittens, three pigs, a gray fox and a red fox" were needed. Other animals needed included a calf, white rats, guinea pigs, hamsters, squirrels, monkeys, a parrot, pheasants, and a chipmunk. If people had animals on the list, they were encouraged to call the recreation department. The zoo's summer season began on May 15.

Roanoke Mayor Roy Webber threw out the first pitch to open the Roanoke Red Sox's 1953 season on April 23. Their opening game was against Lynchburg.

Calvin Wade of Blue Ridge and Henry Alls of Vinton were both killed in a traffic accident on April 24 on Route 460 at Blue Ridge Stone Corporation. Both were in an auto that was struck by a truck.

Amos Milburn and his orchestra performed for a show and dance at the American Legion Auditorium on May 1. White spectators were admitted to the balcony.

Capt. Herbert McClanahan Jr. was killed when the B-29 he was copiloting crashed over Long Island Sound, New York, on April 24. A native of Roanoke and a graduate of Jefferson High School, McClanahan was thirty and veteran of World War II. Five other crewmen aboard the plane also died.

Lady Minstrels from Dixie with an all-girl cast that featured dancers, singers, and musicians was presented at Addison High School on April 27 to benefit the student newspaper.

Over 1,000 persons attended an open house on April 26 of the new Addison High School. Although the school had been open since the fall, some parts of the school had just been completed. The school cost $1.5 million.

This early 1950s postcard shows the Noah's Ark animal exhibit at the Children's Zoo on Mill Mountain. *Bob Stauffer*

This early 1952 image shows Addison High School under construction. Addison was the city's Black high school during the years of segregation. *Virginia Room, RPL*

Cephas Smith was sentenced to five years in prison on April 26 for the slaying of Howard Brown with a bayonet on December 4. Smith pled guilty in Hustings Court to voluntary manslaughter.

Arthur Weakley, sixty-four, died in a fire at his home on Stewart Avenue SE on April 28.

Harvey Robinson Jr. was sentenced to four years in prison, Walter Miller to one year, and Earl Jones was placed on probation all in connection with the fatal stabbing of Robert Rhodes, seventeen, of Roanoke. All pled guilty to various charges surrounding their involvement in the event that involved an argument over a bottle of wine.

Elsie Hartwell of the Colonial-American National Bank was elected president of the Roanoke Chapter of the American Institute of Banking on April 28. She was the first female president in the chapter's thirty year history.

Radio Supply Company, a wholesale distributor, held a formal opening on May 1 at 2009 Williamson Road.

Charles McCarty pled guilty to the December 19 murder of Marvin Long in Roanoke County Circuit Court on April 29 and received a life sentence.

Brothers Samuel Trumpeter, Albert Trumpeter, and Herbert Trumpeter bought the Shenandoah Hotel and the Earle Hotel along with adjacent properties for $175,000 in late April.

The Salem Junior Chamber of Commerce launched a petition drive on May 1 to expand the Salem Town Council from three to five members.

Six persons were certified by the board of elections as candidates for the general election for Roanoke City Council slated for June 9. The candidates in the nonpartisan contest were Clark Wray, James Breakell, Paul Puckett, F. E. Alexander, Mary Pickett, and Leigh Hanes Jr.

In advance of the dedication of the new terminal building at Woodrum Field, four veteran Roanoke aviators were profiled in the May 3 edition of the *Roanoke Times*. They were Roy Richardson, Clayton Lemon, Frank Reynolds, and George Mason. The senior among them was Roy Richardson, who shared about his entrance into the world of flying. He recalled that in 1920, two World War I veterans were flying a Jenny from Langley Field to Pennsylvania. In a takeoff from a cow pasture where the Twenty-Fourth Street NW fire station was located, the motor conked out, forcing the two the crash-land the craft at Seventeenth Street and Third Avenue NW, killing a cow. The two pilots had minor injuries, but the plane was too damaged to fly. Richardson was working for the city police force and at the time was assigned to stand guard at the wreckage to prevent the curious from taking souvenirs. As he stood there overnight, he decided to buy the plane, which he did for $250, and take it to the city garage for rebuilding. He spent $1,150 for two new wings, landing gear, and a propeller. He took the repaired Jenny out to Williamson Road, near where the First National Exchange Bank branch was later located, and soloed after two hours of ground instruction from Dun Steel, a World War I pilot. On that same day, Richardson got his first paying passenger, a man from New York who happened to be driving by, and earned five dollars. Richardson earned the distinction of being the first pilot in Roanoke to have "passenger service" and was the first pilot to land a craft at Cannaday Field, which later became Woodrum Field.

This early 1950s photo shows Roy and June Holcomb (center right) and the employees of State Office Supply. The Holcombs owned the store, which was located at 511 S. Jefferson Street. *Tommy Holcomb*

The Barter Theatre Players presented the comedy *George and Margaret* at the Jefferson High School auditorium on May 6. Lead roles were played by George Phillips and Dorothy LaVerne.

The congregation of St. Mark's Lutheran Church worshipped for the first time in their new sanctuary on Franklin Road SW on May 3. The service was attended by an estimated 750 persons.

Mason-Dixon, a trucking company, opened its new terminal on Rhodes Avenue in late April.

The Booker T. Drive-In Theatre closed at the end of April. Days later, the Loch Haven Drive-In Theatre opened on May 3 at the same location on Airport Road (later Wood Haven). The opening night films were *Carrie* and *Pigmy Island*. It advertised, "White Only." Ironically, the Booker T. advertised as Blacks only.

Bob McGinis won the feature race at Starkey Speedway on May 3, the first race there of the 1953 season.

Jack Hunt and his Rhythm Ranch Hands performed at the Roanoke Theatre on May 6.

Television sets in the Roanoke Valley were able to receive broadcasts from CMQ-TV, a station in Havana, Cuba, when the atmosphere was just right. Viewers claimed the reception was as good as what they received from stations in Greensboro and Richmond.

Some 8,500 spectators attended that Virginia State-wide Safety Conference Circus held at Victory Stadium on May 7. They watched as a bank was robbed, a train crashed into a car, people were rescued from burning buildings, and other assorted acts of public safety. The event was billed as the first of its kind in the nation. The purpose was to inform and educate the general public about safety measures and demonstrate appreciation to those serving in public safety.

James Brooks of Roanoke married radio and singing star Martha Tilton on May 7 in Las Vegas, Nevada.

N&W Railway announced in early May that it expected delivery on its first coal-burning, turbo-electric locomotive sometime in the summer. The experimental motive power unit was being built at the Baldwin-Lima-Hamilton locomotive shops near Philadelphia. N&W officials anticipated a 40 percent savings in fuel costs with the new locomotives.

Paul Smith, twelve, of Botetourt County drowned in Tinker Creek near Hollins on May 8.

Well-known evangelist Mordecai Ham conducted a revival at Orange Avenue Baptist Church, across from the Virginia Bridge Company, on May 9.

Johnny Otis with his vibraharp and recording orchestra performed for a show and dance at the American Legion Auditorium on May 14. He was joined by singer Marie Adams. White spectators were admitted to the balcony.

The first full-length 3D movie to be shown in Roanoke premiered at the Grandin Theatre on May 10. *Bwana Devil* starred Robert Stack, Barbara Britton, and Nigel Bruce. Polaroid viewers were provided to patrons.

The Footlighters presented their final play of the season on May 15. The lead roles in *Years Ago* were played by Cynthia Dunn, Herbert Harris, and Marion White.

Some seventy acres of the Garst estate were sold in early May to Westhampton Homes Inc. for residential development. The tract was located between Grandin Road Extension and Rosalind Hills.

The Goodyear Service Store opened at Second Street and Luck Avenue SW on May 14. The tire store offered a grand prize drawing for a Console Motorola television set during opening weekend.

The Booker T. Drive-In Theatre on Airport Road reopened on May 13 under new management, effectively ending the short stint of the drive-in as the Loch Haven. Ads read, "Colored Only."

Acme Typewriter Company opened a customer drive-in store at 541 W. Campbell Avenue on May 14.

The Roanoke City Republican Committee "recommended" Leigh Hanes Jr. for election to Roanoke City Council. The move was seen by some as violating the nonpartisan character of the race. The chairman of the committee was Linwood Holton Jr., who stated that the committee was fulfilling its obligations to inform voters of competent candidates.

Some 500 Boy Scouts participated in the spring Camporee at Carvins Cove on May 16.

The new terminal building at Woodrum Field was formally dedicated on May 15. Famous aviator and president of Eastern Airlines Eddie Rickenbacker declared in his keynote that the terminal was "a bridge to a greater future." Some 2,000 persons attended the outdoor event in eighty-degree heat. Rickenbacker called for even more improvements to the airport, primarily the extension of runways to accommodate larger planes. In other events of the day, a plaque honoring the late Congressman Clifton Woodrum was unveiled in the lobby by his widow and daughter, Martha Ann Zillhardt. A flight of twenty-four B-26s from Langley Field flew overhead twice for the dedication, and music was provided the William Fleming High School and Jefferson High School bands. *Dixie* was played as the Virginia flag was hoisted over the new terminal. Marshall Harris was manager of the airport and coordinated the various activities of the day, including the honoring of local aviation pioneers George Mason, Roy Richardson, Frank Reynolds, and Clayton Lemon. N. W. Kelley acted as master of ceremonies. The event also celebrated the thirty-fifth anniversary to the day of airmail service to Roanoke.

Fellowship Baptist Church worshipped in its new sanctuary at 929 Murray Avenue SE on May 17.

Officials with American Viscose Corporation announced in mid-May plans to enlarge the powerhouse plant at its Roanoke facility. The company planned to spend $3.5 million on the project.

The Silver Beaver Award, the highest honor in Boy Scouts, was presented to James Taylor at Addison High School on May 15. Taylor was the first Black in the Roanoke Valley to ever receive the award.

An Aldersgate Rally, a mass meeting of Methodists, was held at Victory Stadium on May 24. The speaker was Rev. F. S. Hickman of Duke University. Attendance was estimated at 10,000.

Alfred Hartman, fifty-five, of Roanoke was killed in a single car accident on Route 311 near Hanging Rock on May 17. He ran off the shoulder and the car flipped.

A small tornado did thousands of dollars worth of damage in the Starkey area on May 18. The Crescent Heights residential section was hardest hit, with up-rooted trees, torn roofs, and dismantled garages. A car with a father and daughter was picked up and carried forty yards. No injuries were reported.

Grand Ole Opry stars Cowboy Copas and his Oklahoma Cowboys, along with Jim Day, performed at the Roanoke Theatre on May 20.

Dr. Walter Claytor was released from his Armed Services duty and resumed his medical practice at 413 Gainsboro Road NW in mid-May. He operated the Claytor Memorial Clinic.

The first official "Miss Roanoke" pageant was held at the American Legion Auditorium on May 23 with fifteen contestants. The average height of the contestants was five feet, six inches with an average weight of 124 pounds. Average measurements were 34–23–36 (bust, waist, hips). This was the first pageant affiliated with the Miss Virginia contest, the winner of which competed for Miss America. The Roanoke pageant was sponsored by the Valley Junior Woman's Club. The day before, the contestants were paraded through downtown in a motorcade and "were greeted with wolfish whistles." Frank Morris was master of ceremonies, and the judges were mostly college professors from Western Virginia. The winner was Annette Garst, seventeen, of Roanoke County, whom the *Roanoke Times* described as "a sun-kissed…combination of beauty, bearing and ballet…with perfect pin-up proportions." Second and third place went to Carolyn Jones and Nancy Stockton, respectively. City Manager Arthur Owens presented Garst her crown and her $200 scholarship. The pageant was followed by a Coronation Ball. All contestants received flowers from their sponsors, inscribed scrolls, and the bathing suits they wore from Smartwear-Irving Saks.

The Edgewood Lions Club received their charter on May 21. Charles Coffey was president of the club.

Alvis TV and Appliance Store opened at 2404 Williamson Road on May 22. They carried Westinghouse brand products.

Rev. Robert Lapsley Jr. died at the age of sixty-eight in a Roanoke hospital on May 22. He was the well-known, retired pastor of First Presbyterian Church in Roanoke. He came to the church as pastor in 1930 and retired after twenty-one years there in 1951.

Dr. Dwight McQuilkin, the retiring superintendent of Roanoke City Public Schools, was honored at a testimonial meeting at Jefferson High School on May 22. He was presented with a watch and a check for $1,000. He had served as head of the school system since 1918, having first come to Roanoke as a high school teacher in 1908. His retirement was effective July 1.

Over 500 persons enjoyed the May Day festivities at Back Creek School on May 22. The theme was "Around the World" and featured folk songs, contests, and a May pole.

This 1950s image shows Back Creek Elementary School, which was located along Route 221 in the Poages Mill section of Roanoke County. *Virginia Room, RPL*

Wasena Hardware on Main Street SW reopened under new management on May 23.

The *Roanoke Times* and the *Roanoke World-News* published their first ever direct wire transmission photos from the Associated Press in their May 24 editions. Wire transmission allowed the newspapers to receive a photo within one hour of it being taken.

James Hobbs Jr., thirty-four, accidentally drowned at Loch Haven on May 23. He was a shop inspector for N&W Railway.

Some 900 children participated in the fishing rodeo at Lakewood Park pond on May 23. It was the Blue Ridge Game and Fish Association's third annual Trout Fishing Rodeo. The rodeo trophy for the largest trout went to Shelby Bivens.

Bobby Cruickshank of William Fleming High School won the B'nai B'rith Athletic and Achievement Award for 1953. The presentation and announcement were made over live television by WSLS-TV. The Fleming senior played football, wrestled, and ran track while maintaining a 4.1 GPA.

Roanoke Parks and Recreation Department announced that their summer programs for children in city parks would be "Indian-themed." Each park would have the name of a Native American tribe, contain teepees, and provide Indian games and powwows.

The Roanoke Life Saving and First Aid Crew celebrated its twenty-fifth anniversary the last weekend in May. Capt. Julian Wise and the entire crew attended worship together at Calvary Baptist Church as Rev. Harry Gamble was the crew's chaplain. Later that afternoon, the crew hosted an open house at their headquarters on Kirk Avenue.

A group of northeast Roanoke citizens filed a petition with Roanoke City Council asking the body to delay any action on the redevelopment of their section to give them time to participate in a fair and impartial hearing on the matter. The petition was submitted by the Commonwealth Citizens Association. The petitioners contended that the procedure proposed for the purchase and resale of property for business use was unfair to property owners.

Rush Anderson, principal of Carver High School, was killed on May 25 in an auto accident at the corner of Melrose Avenue and Sixteenth Street NW. The car that struck Anderson's was involved in a hot rod chase, according to police.

A cave-in occurred on May 25 in the 1100 block of Indiana Street in Salem. The twenty-five-foot wide and twenty-foot deep pit threatened undermined the foundations of two homes. A cave-in of smaller proportions had occurred a week earlier at Valleydale Packers requiring several truckloads of dirt to fill the hole. The following day, town officials authorized drilling to be done to determine the cause.

The Roanoke Public Library Foundation applied for a charter from the SCC as a nonstock, nonprofit corporation on May 25. Francis Cocke, president of First National Exchange Bank, headed the foundation board that sought to raise funds for the library.

Western film comedian Fuzzy St. John and his Musical Rangers brought their *Western Revue* show to the Roanoke Theatre on May 27.

Peter Wreden, a Roanoke artist, received a $1,500 grant from the Virginia Museum of Fine Arts to support his painting career. Wreden had two exhibitions slated for later in the year at Hollins College and with the Roanoke Fine Arts Center.

Professional boxing returned to Roanoke on May 28. Five matches were held at the American Legion Auditorium. Feature bouts were Biff Jones versus Tony Gallagher and Eddie Marshall versus Tex Newby. The promoters were D. L. Johnson and Bob Riley.

Officials with the Roanoke Redevelopment and Housing Authority shared with the city's planning commission on May 27 that their proposed redevelopment and slum clearance program for northeast Roanoke would cost an estimated $1 million with the authority providing two-thirds of the funding from federal dollars. The discussion about the plan was held with the planning commission in closed session.

The Children's Zoo on Mill Mountain received a donation of fourteen prairie dogs from Lubbock, Texas, in late May, just in time for the season's opening day.

The Booker T. Washington Trade School in Roanoke closed its doors on May 31. The school was operated as a service by the Booker T. Washington Birthplace Memorial headed by S. J. Phillips. During its five years of operation, the school served 518 black adults.

Clifford Roberson won the city-county marbles tournament on May 29. It was his fourth time winning the tournament. Danny Likens placed second, and Ralph Esco came in third. All three qualified to go to the national tournament.

This January 1955 image shows Prairie Dog Town at the Children's Zoo on Mill Mountain. The exhibit became one of the most popular in the zoo. *Historical Society of Western Virginia*

Beltone Hearing Service opened at its new location at 404 First Street SW on June 1. Mr. H. S. Cato was the manager.

The Orioles, along with Bull Moose Jackson and his Buffalo Bear Cats, performed for a show and dance at the American Legion Auditorium on June 5. The balcony was reserved for white spectators.

The Roanoke Council for Retarded Children, formed in October 1951 and the first of its kind in Virginia, worked with Roanoke public schools to set aside two classrooms at West End School for special instruction for children in their programs. The two classrooms were to be equipped by the Brambleton Junior Woman's Club for the start of school in the fall. Two teachers were trained over the summer at the University of Richmond.

Bailey's Antique and Gift Shop opened on June 1 at 1025 S. Jefferson Street.

Charles Jennings of Abingdon was named as the new principal for William Byrd High School to replace P. E. Ahalt.

An estimated 1,000 persons visited the Children's Zoo on Mill Mountain on opening day on May 30. The main attraction was the prairie dog exhibit. Other new additions to the zoo were bears, a tunnel for the Zoo Choo, and a goldfish pond surrounding a concrete Willie the Whale.

The Roanoke Symphony Orchestra gave its second concert of its inaugural season on June 2. The concert featured former Roanoker and Hollywood actor John Payne, who narrated Prokofieff's *Peter and the Wolf.* The concert opened with Rossini's *Semermiade Overture* and closed with Grieg's *Peer Gynt Suite No. 1.* Other selections included Mactucci's *Nocturne,* Sibelius's *Finlandis,* and *Sleeping Beauty*

Waltz by Tchaikovsky. A matinee concert for families with children was in the afternoon, followed by the main concert that evening. Musicians from Southside and the New River Valley had joined the symphony since the first concert. The evening concert was attended by 500 persons at the Jefferson High School auditorium.

Robert Lipscomb, seventeen, of Hardy died on May 31 from injuries he received the day prior when he wrecked his three-wheel motorcycle on Orange Avenue NE.

Arthur Camper was named acting principal of Carver High School following the death of Principal Rush Anderson. Camper was on the faculty at Carver.

Western film stars Wild Bill Elliott and Jack Sparks came to the Roanoke Theatre on June 3.

Mrs. Estill Ellis, a thirty-eight-year-old mother of three, was shot twice in the back on June 4 when she returned to her Mountain Avenue SW home from work. Police arrested her husband, who was brought to police headquarters by his two brothers.

Daniel Hale was sentenced to twenty-five years in prison on June 4 for the murder of his wife, Ruth Hale, on April 9. Judge Dirk Kuyk found Hale guilty of first-degree murder.

The Blacks-only Booker T. Drive-In Theatre reverted to the whites-only Loch Haven Drive-In Theatre on June 6.

Russell Henry, retired general superintendent of motive power of N&W Railway, died on June 6 in a Roanoke hospital at the age of sixty-nine. Henry worked for the railway for over four decades and was instrumental in the design and construction of roller-bearing locomotives built in the Roanoke Shops.

Between 1948 and 1952, thirty Class Y6b engines were produced in the N&W Railway Shops. Engine No. 2200, the last of the Y6bs, is shown in this 1953 image at Roanoke. *Virginia Room, RPL*

Neighbors in the Garden City section gathered to erect a frame addition to the home of the Orange family on Bandy Road as a bedroom for their stricken son Paul Orange, who was wheelchair bound. The three-week effort was led by Rev. D. F. Herman.

The students of Stonewall Jackson Junior High School in southeast Roanoke celebrated the thirtieth anniversary of their school on June 6, then formed an "I" and sang *Through the Years* as a farewell tribute to their retiring principal, W. C. Ikenberry.

The Park Theatre in Roanoke closed for the summer due to competition from drive-in theatres and television. Elmore Heins, president of the National Theatres Corporation that operated the Park along with three other downtown movie houses, said that Park would reopen in the fall. It was the first time since the Depression that a local movie house had closed.

The Roanoke Fine Arts Center opened a one-man show on June 9. The exhibit at the Roanoke Library displayed eighteen works of Walter Biggs, a native of Salem. Biggs had lived and worked in New York for the past fifty years. Biggs was widely known as an illustrator for *Harper's Magazine, Scribners, Century*, and *Ladies Home Journal*.

Hammersley-Nash, a car dealership, opened their second location at 1929 Franklin Road SW on June 7. They sold the Nash brand of autos as well as used cars.

Before a gallery of 500 persons, Ralph English won the four-round city-county golf tournament that was held over the first and second weekends in June held at Hidden Valley Country Club. English had a final score of 292. He was followed by George Fulton (295), Connie Sellers (298), and John Rice (303).

The Roanoke Area Council of the Boy Scouts officially became the Blue Ridge Council of the Boy Scouts on June 8. The name change was favored due to the council having Scouts across a fourteen-county area.

I. N. Moseley announced he would not seek reappointment to the Roanoke County School Board. Having served twenty-three years, Moseley said, "I have served long enough."

In the June 9 general election for Roanoke City Council, Mary Pickett and Leigh Hanes Jr. won the two open seats. Pickett became the first woman elected to the council in the city's history. Pickett received 4,454 votes and Hanes, an attorney who was endorsed by the local Republican party, received 2,952 votes. The other candidates were Paul Puckett (2,729 votes), James Breakell (1,746 votes), Rev. F. E. Alexander (1,414 votes), and Clarke Wray (863) votes. Alexander was editor and publisher of the *Roanoke Tribune* newspaper and the only Black candidate on the ballot. Pickett's victory was due to the well-organized campaign by several women's organizations to have a female elected. On election night at Pickett's campaign headquarters, all was relatively quiet; however. Ozzie Osborne, in writing for the *Roanoke Times*, penned, "Mrs. Odessa Bailey, Mrs. E. C. Moomaw, and Marie Hazlewood were the only three women at the headquarters when the returns came in. The other workers…were home fixing supper for their families."

This 1953 photo is of Kirk Avenue looking east toward First Street SW. Roanoke Book and Stationary is across Kirk Avenue from the woman with the umbrella. *Historical Society of Western Virginia*

Norman Gravely, fourteen, won the Roanoke Negro marbles tournament on June 9. Ronald Perry came in second. It was the third time Gravely had won the tournament that was sponsored by the *Roanoke Times.*

The body of Lawrence Clement, age ten, of Roanoke was found in the Roanoke River on June 10. The boy drowned on June 8, and his body was found about a quarter of a mile downstream from where a friend saw him go under. He was a student at Belmont School and the son of Mrs. A. P. Clement.

Roanoke's Father of the Year for 1953, as chosen by the Jaycees, was John Howard, manager of the local branch of the Pittsburgh Plate Glass Company. Howard was instrumental in organizing "Howard's Little League," a baseball league for boys that had seventy boys across four teams.

The first worship service to be held in the new sanctuary of First Methodist Church in Salem was on June 14. The sanctuary could seat up to 700 persons and cost $260,000.

The Moon Glow Inn opened in mid-June. It was formerly the Sycamore.

Rev. Richard Beasley, rector of St. John's Episcopal Church, delivered the sermon for the *Church of the Air* program over the CBS radio network on June 14. The program was broadcast nationwide.

A geologist's report on the numerous cave-ins that plagued the town of Salem was released to the public on June 13. The report concluded, "The new well on the property of Valleydale Packers is very probably the source of the trouble." The meat packing company agreed to shut down the well that had been pumping at a rate of 200 gallons per minute. The Ninth Street area of the town was the most impacted. Citizens petitioned the town council to release the report that had been in the town's possession since May 31.

Mrs. Esther Hale retired from teaching in Roanoke Public Schools in mid-June after thirty years. She came to Roanoke in 1926. She taught at Gainsboro School, Harrison School, and Loudon School. In her thirty years as a teacher, Hale had not missed a single day on the job.

The congregation of Hollins Road Baptist Church held a cornerstone-laying ceremony on June 14. Rev. Wade Bryant of First Baptist Church was the guest speaker. The church was organized on July 3, 1949, with seventy-one charter members. W. B. Fralin was the general contractor.

Mrs. Bertie Ellis died on June 15 from gunshot wounds inflicted by her husband on June 4. Murder charges were placed against Estill Ellis later that day, who had previously told police he shot his wife in the back for nagging him about getting a job. They had three young children.

Amana Food Plan of Roanoke, a supplier of prepared meals, opened at its new location at 127-A W. Luck Avenue on June 17.

Salem's two community theatre groups decided to merge. The Footlighters and Showtimers combined and kept the latter's name. Showtimers operated as a summer stock theatre, while Footlighters did plays in the winter. By combining, the new group planned to produce plays year round.

Wilson Adkins was appointed to the Roanoke County School Board on June 16 to represent the Town of Vinton for a four-year term. The seat had previously been held by I. N. Moseley.

Richard Geary, thirteen, of Roanoke signed a one-year recording contract with Decca Records. The student at Stonewall Jackson Junior High School had performed on the *Old Dominion Barn Dance* radio program and had been offered jobs with Sunshine Sue and Red Foley. Foley was the one who alerted Decca to Geary's singing talent.

Self-Service Station opened on Route 220, one mile south of Roanoke city, on June 19.

Wayne Haley of Bassett won the first annual state junior amateur golf tournament that was held at Hidden Valley Country Club the second week in June. Paul Kosko of Roanoke came in second.

The South Salem Lions Club received its charter on June 22. Rev. Virgil Lilly was club president.

Piedmont Airlines, which had twenty-one flights per day at Woodrum Field, boarded 24,442 passengers in the previous month of May. According to Piedmont officials, that set a national record for one month's passenger count for a local service airline.

James R. Jordan Jr., owner and operator of Jordan Funeral Home at 601 Loudon Avenue NW, died in mid-June. McKinley Rice assumed operations of the funeral service.

The new chapel in Raleigh Court Methodist Church was formally dedicated on June 21. The Angelus Bible Class presented the chapel to the church during an afternoon service.

George Kosko won the eighth annual junior golf tournament held at Roanoke Country Club on June 21. The tournament was sponsored by the Roanoke Jaycees.

The Roanoke County Government Study Committee that had been appointed to look at county services considered favorably a surprise proposal at their June 23 meeting which was to explore incorporating the county as a city. A four-person subcommittee was developed to research the matter with Nelson Thurman as chairman.

The Roanoke Valley was well-represented in the July issue of *Reader's Digest* with articles by Roanoke school teacher Lillian Craig and the review of a biography of Mary Lincoln that had been written by Ruth Randall, formerly of Salem.

Christ Episcopal Church dedicated its new parish house on June 26. The new addition included a parish hall and dining room, church library, classrooms, modern kitchen, offices, and a chapel. Rev. Van Garrett was the rector.

Jerry Furrow, twelve, won the Roanoke Soap Box Derby on June 24 among eighty boys who entered. Frankie Fairburn came in a close second. The derby was held on Crystal Spring Avenue in South Roanoke. John Kelley was the derby director. Furrow qualified to compete in the national Soap Box Derby in Akron, Ohio.

Leggett's department store at 112 Campbell Avenue SW installed a Chrysler Airtemp system in late June and became the first department store in the Roanoke Valley to be air-conditioned.

A 200-year-old barn on Hershberger Road was destroyed by fire on June 25. C. W. Hawkins was the owner.

Roanoke County's cannery on Walker Street in Salem opened on June 30 for the summer. Nearly 500 persons used the cannery the previous summer. Jim Peters and R. E. Kinzie were the managers.

Officials with WROV-TV notified the FCC on June 26 that they wanted to bid for VHF Channel 7 as UHF was not profitable. That put WROV-TV in direct competition with the Times-World Corporation, operator of WDBJ radio, for channel 7. WROV officials stated that only 20 percent of local television owners obtained UHF receivers.

In a special session of the Salem Town Council on June 26, the council decided to petition the circuit court to hold a referendum on enlarging the council from three to five members in response to petitions from Salem citizens requesting the change.

Charles and Dianne Edwards opened an Arthur Murray Dance Studio at 314 S. Jefferson Street on June 29. They held a weeklong open house where persons could receive a free dance analysis and learn new steps.

Trumpeter Erskine Hawkins and his orchestra, along with pianist Ace Harris and saxophonist Julian Dash, performed for a show and dance at the American Legion Auditorium on July 3. White spectators were admitted to the balcony.

The official transfer of the First Methodist Church property in Salem to Roanoke College took place at the end of June when the college made its final payment of $30,000 to the church's treasurer. The Methodists had erected a new sanctuary elsewhere in Salem.

The first of the summer's tennis court dances launched in early July at Elmwood Park. The City of Roanoke sponsored the events. The Elmwood Park dance was attended by 500 persons.

Officials with Mohawk Rubber Company of Akron, Ohio, announced on June 29 plans to locate a rubber plant in Salem to manufacture plastic products. They planned to occupy a factory formerly used by the Blue Ridge Chemical Company.

Chauncey Harmon was named as the new principal of Carver High School in Salem by the county school superintendent on June 29. Harmon had for the previous nine years been principal at Scott Memorial High School in Wytheville. Harmon was a native of Pulaski and a graduate of the Tuskegee Institute and Columbia University.

Salem held its annual Huck Finn Day at Lake Spring on July 1 with some 300 youngsters participating in the fishing competition and a costume contest. Betty Branum and Jimmy Bohon won the costume contest, and A. C. Lyon caught the biggest fish.

State and federal agencies gave final approval on July 1 to contracts for two large hospital projects. A contract for the expansion and remodeling of the Memorial and Crippled Children's Hospital was officially awarded to B. F. Parrott and Company for $2.4 million. English Construction of Altavista was formally awarded a $1.3 million contract for the new Burrell Memorial Hospital.

Pentecostal evangelist Oral Roberts held a weeklong tent revival on the grounds of Maher Field beginning July 3. His big top had a seating capacity of 12,500.

Club Cherokee announced its formal reopening on July 4. The nightclub was located at 829 W. Main Street in Salem. Hal Humphries was the manager.

Roanoke police launched a preholiday raid on reputed bootleggers in the city on July 3. They arrested about a dozen individuals and seized more than 150 pints of whiskey. Most of the raids were of residences, but police did raid two businesses—the Anderson Hotel on Second Street SE and the Star City Chicken House on Commonwealth Avenue NE.

Patsy Braden, a senior at Jefferson High School, was killed in auto accident on July 4 on the Blue Ridge Parkway near the Rockingham-Augusta County line. Also killed in the accident was Carl Custer, twenty-five, of Catawba. Three days later, a third companion in the car, Samuel Campbell of Roanoke, died from his injuries in a Lexington hospital. Campbell was nineteen. A fourth occupant of the vehicle, Lois Campbell of Roanoke, was seriously injured.

Virginia Heights Baptist Church used its new pipe organ for the first time in worship on July 5.

Showtimers opened their summer season with the comedy *Engaged* on July 9. The lead roles were played by James Fulghum, John Marstellar, Betty Thornton, Evans Evans, and Jeanne Dickinson.

The Fine Arts Center held an exhibit of large Mexican oils and watercolors at the Roanoke Library in July. The works were on loan from the collection of IBM Corporation.

Trinity Methodist Church in Roanoke celebrated its fiftieth anniversary on July 12. The principal speaker was Rev. Nolan Harmon. The church was planted by Greene Memorial Methodist Church in 1891 and dedicated its sanctuary on July 12, 1903.

Guy Morton, catcher, was the only member of the Roanoke Red Sox baseball team selected for the season's Piedmont League All-Star team.

Roanoke race car driver Curtis Turner was voted by fans as the most popular driver to compete regularly at the races at Bowman Gray Stadium in Winston-Salem, North Carolina. It was the second year in a row Turner received the honor.

Roanoke Church of Christ broke ground on its $45,000 church at 2606 Brandon Avenue SW in the third week in July.

Area banks reported the following total liabilities and capital accounts as of June 30: Colonial-American National Bank, $34.5 million; First National Exchange Bank, $79.0 million; Bank of Virginia, $96.3 million; Mountain Trust Bank, $25.2 million; Roanoke Industrial Loan Corporation, $0.5 million.

Earl Bostic and his orchestra, along with the Bostican Stompers, performed for a show and dance at the American Legion Auditorium on July 15. The balcony was reserved for white spectators.

Showtimers presented the mystery *An Inspector Calls* on July 16 at the Lab Theatre in Salem. Lead roles were performed by David Thornton, Robert Darst, Virginia Holton, Dean Doss, Patricia Clark, John O'Neill, and Nancy Moore. The play was directed by Sam Good.

Police Superintendent Frank Webb publicly warned couples against "spooning" on Mill Mountain after the park closes. Webb reported that three couples had been fined for such activity in July.

Standard Drug Company at 30 W. Campbell Avenue closed at the end of July due to losing its lease. The owners stated they planned to build a larger store in the near future.

Residents of three blocks of Crystal Spring Avenue petitioned Roanoke City Council on July 13 to relocate the annual Soap Box Derby races. Residents complained of damaged lawns, noise, blocked driveways, and a general nuisance being created by the race that turned their residential street into "a college athletic field." The matter was referred to the city manager.

Local Democratic primaries were held on July 14. Roanoke County state delegate Ernest Robertson defeated challenger George Draper, 1,207 to 721. In Roanoke City, James Armstrong defeated Robert Thomas for the nomination of Commissioner of Revenue, 2,647 to 2,577. W. B. Carter came in third with 2,085 votes. Johnny Johnson won over John Martin, 4,285 to 2,841 votes, for the city treasurer nomination. Julian Rutherfoord and Kossen Gregory were nominated for the House of Delegates. They finished ahead of J. W. Lindsey, Mosby Williams, and Louise Cutts. Cutts was the first female in the region to run for a state office.

A major remodeling program of the Hotel Roanoke began in mid-July with renovations to the main dining room, with the lobby scheduled for remodeling later in the summer.

WROV-TV went off the air at the end of programming on July 18. Station officials said the operation had lost money with their UHF Channel 27. It was the region's second television station and had operated since March 2. WROV officials had applied to the FCC for VHF Channel 7 along with WDBJ radio. A couple of days later, WSLS-TV received permission to air programs of the ABC network in addition to the CBS and NBC networks.

Excavation work for the new addition to the Memorial and Crippled Children's Hospital began the third week in July. Construction was anticipated to take three years.

The clinic building at Burrell Memorial Hospital was razed on July 13 to make room for the new eighty-bed hospital.

Officials with Shenandoah Life Insurance Company announced on July 13 plans to purchase a plot of land at Third Street and Church Avenue SW for $10,000 to build new studios for WSLS radio and WSLS-TV. The studios would replace the studios on the seventh floor of the Shenandoah Building.

Raymond Barnes began selling subscriptions to his forthcoming book, *A History of Roanoke*. Barnes hoped to get 500 or more advance subscriptions as he neared completion of the work.

A fire and explosion on July 17 destroyed a large metal building at the metal products plant of John W. Hancock Jr. Inc. at 427 McClanahan Street SW. Firemen attributed the blaze to a hot piece of metal dipped into the paint tank.

Sheriff Harry McManaway of Roanoke County died on July 18 of a heart attack. He was fifty-three. McManaway had first been elected county sheriff in 1947 and reelected in 1951.

Roanoke Scrap Iron softball team (a.k.a. the Scrappers) captured the A League regular-season championship for the sixth year in a row.

James Honaker, twenty-three, of Salem was fatally injured on July 18 when his car went down an embankment on the Route 460 bypass near Lakeside.

Showtimers presented *Skylark* the third weekend in July. Leading roles were played by David Cross, Patricia Hooker, Robert Bradshaw, and Sandra Kitchen. The play was directed by Genevieve Dickinson.

The new method of collecting garbage in Salem changed the way residents handled their waste. Prior to July, citizens had to separate their garbage into burnable and unburnable parts for the incinerator. With the use of a landfill, garbage no longer needed to be separated. The town had started a landfill on a fifteen-acre tract between the N&W Railway tracks and the Roanoke River near the Yale and Towne Manufacturing plant.

The Roanoke Branch of Lawyers Title Insurance Corporation opened on July 20 in the State and City Office Building. W. N. Minter was branch manager.

Officials with the Roanoke Red Sox announced on July 21 that the debt-ridden team was dropping out of the Piedmont League. Poor attendance was a major factor in forcing the Red Sox to end their season. Paid admissions to home games for the 1953 season averaged 906 per game. The debt of the club was estimated at $50,000. The next day, Piedmont League officials voted to allow Petersburg to field a team in the league to replace the Roanoke Red Sox The Boston Red Sox, however, declined to move their team to Petersburg but to disperse the Rosox players to their other farm teams.

Over 300 Roanoke business and civic leaders participated in the Roanoke Booster Club annual day trip to the Greenbrier Hotel on July 22. N&W Railway provided a special train for the occasion.

The fifth annual Roanoke Valley Horse Show opened on July 23 at Maher Field with over 160 entries. Horses from seven states competed for $4,000 in prize money. The show was jointly sponsored by the Roanoke Valley Horse Show Association and the Roanoke Life Saving and First Aid Crew.

Henry Clark was sworn in as Roanoke County's new sheriff on July 27. Clark had been a Virginia State Trooper since 1936. He was forty-one and a native of Prince Edward County.

Two journalists refused to leave the room where the Roanoke City Planning Commission was meeting on July 23 to consider the "slum clearance" program relative to northeast Roanoke. Having been advised by the city attorney that the planning commission could meet in executive session for the discussion, reporters from the *Roanoke Times* and WSLS radio asserted their rights to be present. After an hour of deliberation over the reporters' presence, the planning commission meeting was adjourned without discussion of the redevelopment plans.

The 1953 racing season at the Starkey Speedway opened on July 24. The season offered for the first time night racing under the newly installed lights at the speedway.

B. M. Phelps of Roanoke offered to donate a bell to Botetourt County, which he believed to be the one which hung in the courthouse in Fincastle prior to the 1846 erection of the new courthouse building, at which time the old bell was removed.

Nearly 1,000 persons attended the thirty-fourth annual reunion of the Eightieth Division soldiers that was held at the Hotel Roanoke the last weekend in July.

The Roanoke Pentecostal Fellowship, an organization composed of various Pentecostal, Holiness and Church of God congregations in the Roanoke Valley, reported that the fifteen-day evangelistic crusade held by Oral Roberts at Maher Field in mid-July had an average nightly attendance of 8,000 with 3,500 professions of faith.

The Roanoke Red Sox played their last game at Portsmouth on July 24. They lost 4 to1. The next day, the players received assignments from the Boston Red Sox to other minor league clubs within the organization.

A new branch of Deluxe Laundry and Dry Cleaners opened at 1101 Brandon Road SW on July 27. Ethel Mitchell was the manager.

Lionel Hampton and his orchestra performed for a show and dance at the American Legion Auditorium on July 31. The balcony was reserved for white spectators.

Showtimers presented *Out of the Frying Pan* at Roanoke College this first weekend in August. The cast was led by Cindy Dunn, Judy Bate, Ann Thomason, Jack Kesler, John O'Neill, Wilton Sale, Pat Clark, and John Martsellar.

Charles Rogers, a well-known contractor in Roanoke, died on July 25 at his home on Patton Avenue NE. He was seventy-six.

This is a view of the Oral Roberts tent revival campaign in July 1953. The photo was taken from the top of Victory Stadium. *Virginia Room, RPL*

The actor Jeffrey Hunter and the producer Frank McCarthy appeared in person for the opening of their film *Sailor of the King* at the Grandin Theatre and Jefferson Theatre on July 31. Earlier that day, the two were feted at a luncheon at the Hotel Roanoke, visited patients at the Veterans Administration Hospital, and toured the Children's Zoo on Mill Mountain.

Red Line, a trucking company, occupied its new terminal and garage at 2310 Orange Avenue NE in late July. The business was founded in Roanoke in 1932. E. H. Deacon was president.

A new 500,000-gallon water tank was installed in the Washington Heights section at the end of July. The $50,000 tank on a tower was the fifth such tower in Roanoke City.

Roanoke's newest public swimming pool opened in late July. Fairland Lake, just off Cove Road in the Villa Heights section, also had picnicking and boating facilities.

The Roanoke Ministers Conference conducted a weeklong crusade at the American Legion Auditorium the first week of August. The guest evangelist was well-known athlete Rev. Bob Richards. This effort replaced what been annual preaching missions sponsored by the conference that involved clergymen from various denominations and often nationally known.

Actors Jeffrey Hunter and Frank McCarthy came to Roanoke for the premier of their film *Sailor of the King* at the Jefferson Theatre in July 1953. *Historical Society of Western Virginia*

Thousands of fish in the Roanoke River were found dead at Salem on July 30. There were immediate demands for state investigations into what many believed was industrial waste being dumped in the river.

William McCorkindale Jr. died at a hospital in Charlottesville on July 31 at age fifty-six. He was prominent in Roanoke civic and business affairs, serving as chairman of the city's planning commission and as president of McCorkindale Mortgage Loan Company.

Bradford's Restaurant at 2523 Franklin Road SW was sold to Archie's Inc. for $90,000 on July 31. Bradford Lipscomb stated that Archie Parish would continue to operate the restaurant under the Bradford's name for a few months.

Appalachian Electric Power Company began rebuilding their Niagara Hydro Plant near Vinton in late July. Located on the Roanoke River, it was the oldest power facility in the region. Constructed in the early 1900s, it was the first rebuild of the plant in its operating history.

Shadow and Substance was the fifth play of the season for Showtimers, presented the first weekend in August. Lead roles were played by Betty Jean Carper, Herbert Harris, and Sam Good.

This 1950s postcard shows Bradford's Restaurant, located on Franklin Road SW. *Bob Stauffer*

A campaign to raise $150,000 for a Preston Park Community Center kicked off on August 3. The campaign consisted of the sale of one-dollar share subscriptions and was chaired by Robert Senft. The center would sit on a nine-acre parcel to include a wading and swimming pool, a playground, athletic fields, picnic areas, and tennis courts.

A ground-breaking ceremony was held on August 2 for the new $1.7 million Burrell Memorial Hospital. The first shovel of dirt was turned by Dr. J. H. Roberts, one of the cofounders of the hospital. Rev. A. L. James was master of ceremonies. Dr. L. C. Downing, chief surgeon at Burrell, gave the main address. Dr. Roberts shared a brief history of the hospital. He stated that the earliest effort to establish a hospital for Blacks was Medley Hospital in northeast Roanoke. When Medley did not succeed, a second hospital in northeast was begun, Charity Hospital, but it closed after two months. Finally, Dr. Roberts and four other physicians established Burrell Memorial Hospital in honor of Dr. Isaac Burrell, in a residence on Henry Street in 1915. In 1921, the hospital relocated to a former school building (Alleghany Institute) on McDowell Avenue NW.

Bobby Payne of Richmond won the twelfth annual Exchange Club Invitational Singles Tennis Tournament that was held at the Roanoke Country Club the first week of August. Payne and Dell Sylvia won the doubles championship.

John Strickler was sworn in as US attorney for the Western District of Virginia on August 3.

Participants in the ground-breaking ceremony for the new Burrell Memorial Hospital are seen in this August 1953 image. The old hospital is in the background. *Virginia Room, RPL*

Salem voters approved, by an 8-to-1 ratio, enlarging the Salem Town Council from three to five members in an August 4 referendum. Voters also approved allocating $44,000 for a community center for Blacks on Water Street.

Turpin Hardware at 301 Pollard Street in Vinton became Dixie Hardware Company on August 5. The owners were Tyree Dowdy and Joe Tompkins.

David Thornton resigned as director of development for Roanoke College in early August to assume the position of editor of the *Salem Times-Register*. Thornton's father had been the newspaper's editor from 1933 until his death in 1951.

Cpl. Daniel Bolden of Roanoke was released by North Korea where he had been held as a POW for thirty-two months. Bolden's mother, Betty Bolden, of Gilmer Avenue NE learned of his release over the radio.

Lakeview Motor Lodge at Routes 11 and 220 north of Roanoke held an open house to celebrate their grand opening on August 9. The forty-unit motel advertised "air-conditioned, 24-hour room telephone service…wall to wall carpets, TV and radio, tile bath with shower and tub."

Magic City Collection and Detective Agency opened on August 10 with an office in the Liberty Trust Building.

Showtimers presented their final play of the summer season the second weekend in August. Lead roles in *The Happy Time* were played by Jeanne Dickinson, Addington Wise Jr., Sam Good, David Cross, John Martsellar, and Natalie Spigel. Genevieve Dickinson was the director.

George Sheffey, eighty-eight, died on August 8 in a nursing home. He was a well-known, retired barber in Roanoke, operating a shop in the former Terry Building beginning in 1893.

Roanoke City Council became so frustrated with Salem officials' delay in doing their part to clean up the Roanoke River that the Roanoke council threatened to shut down its own sewage treatment plant if the state water control board did not intervene. City Council authorized the city manager to attend the WCB meeting in Salem in mid-August and complain about Salem treating the river as an "open sewer."

At its August 10 meeting, Roanoke City Council continued the process of acquiring, through purchase or condemnation, properties needed for construction of the Jefferson Street viaduct. The properties involved were the H. B. Barnes building, a house owned by Mary Ford, a garage operated by O. B. Martin, a pawn shop, a walk-up hotel, and a hardware store. All total, the city needed to acquire and raze forty-two pieces of property.

The Boy With A Cart opened for a two-month run at the outdoor amphitheatre at Sherwood Burial Park on August 17. A local cast of fifty persons was involved in the production that Roanoke leaders hoped would rival *The Common Glory*, an outdoor drama performed annually throughout the summer in Williamsburg. The Roanoke play was performed every weeknight, weather permitting, and featured as primary actors Skippy Doss and Maxine Bulbin. H. M. Webber was the business manager.

The Community Polio Committee was organized on August 10 to recruit nurses to care for polio patients at the Memorial and Crippled Children's Hospital. The nurse shortage was so acute that an all-out effort was deemed necessary to obtain and train nurses for the polio wards in Roanoke. Many of the patients needed round-the-clock care. Mrs. Charles Hefner chaired the committee that was largely composed of members of the Red Cross. At the time the committee was formed, the Roanoke hospital had thirty-two polio patients.

The Roanoke City Planning Commission voted on August 13 to recommend approval to Roanoke City Council of the proposed "slum clearance" program developed by the Roanoke Redevelopment and Housing Authority for northeast Roanoke. The commission voted 4–1 for the Commonwealth Redevelopment Project, its formal name, which involved some eighty-four acres and would cost an estimated $3 million.

Kay's Ice Cream opened another store in the Roanoke Valley on August 15. The store was located at the intersection of Williamson Road and Airport Road. Opening-day special was two ice cream cones for ten cents.

This 1954 image shows a Kay's Ice Cream Truck. Kay's was a popular ice cream parlor chain in the Roanoke Valley during the 1950s. *Virginia Room, RPL*

Over 1,500 Legionnaires came to Roanoke for the American Legion convention the second weekend in August. The event was marked by a parade through downtown.

John Puhl Products Company of Salem agreed to pay the Town of Salem $300 for a massive fish kill in the Roanoke River. Company officials admitted to spilling chemicals into a sewer leading to the river. The company manufactured household bleaches and detergents.

Hayden Huddleston launched his *The Hayden Huddleston Show* on August 17 on WROV radio. Huddleston's two-hour weekday program included news, interviews, quizzes, and giveaways.

C. B. Darnell of Roanoke won the AAU state horseshoes tournament in Richmond on August 15. He also won the tournament in 1952.

Luther Wilson, thirty-five, of Loudon Avenue NW in Roanoke was shot to death on August 15. Police arrested his wife, who admitted to firing three shots into her husband.

Mrs. Ida May Martin graduated with a bachelor's degree in education from Roanoke College on August 15. The reason it was newsworthy was that Martin had been a student there "off and on" for twenty-nine years.

The Merchants Parking Center on South Jefferson Street opened its ground floor for parking on August 14, and 200 autos filled the spaces. The upper floors of the garage were slated for completion in late September.

Col. W. M. P. Northcross of Salem was awarded in mid-August the Ulehi Distinguished Military Medal, one of the highest decorations of the Republic of Korea, for his role in the development of Korean Army Ordnance Corps.

Check-R-Board Feed Store opened at its new location at 908 Shenandoah Avenue NW on August 18.

Second Lt. George Brown of Roanoke died in a Japanese hospital of bulbar polio on August 15. Brown had been stationed with the Fifty-Fourth EFM Engineers in Korea when he was stricken with polio in late July. He was twenty-three.

The residence of Curtis Thomas of Route 3 in Salem, was completely destroyed by fire on August 19. The family of four escaped unharmed.

The Salem Jaycees sponsored a talent show, *Tripping Around*, for two nights at Andrew Lewis High School auditorium August 20 and 21. A highlight of the show was the baby contest that was won by Annette Grubb and Barry Zion. Audience members voted for the cutest baby by voting with pennies.

According to the 1950 Agricultural Census, there were eighty-six farms operating within the City of Roanoke with a total of 2,009 acres. The largest was the Huff Farm on Hershberger Road with 225 acres.

This August 1950 shows the pasture at the Lutheran Orphanage in Salem being seeded. It was one of many farms operating in the valley during the 1950s. *VPI&SU Libraries*

Ralph English defeated Charley Turner in the finals of the Hidden Valley Country Club golf tournament to win the championship. The tournament started with 150 players.

WSLS-TV received a new 25,000-watt VHF transmitter that made it the most powerful television station in Virginia. The transmitter was erected on Poor Mountain in late August and was to become operational in mid-October.

Steel framework for the new Roanoke Church of Christ on Brandon Avenue SW was erected the third week in August. The church was located at 1501 Patterson Avenue SW with plans to relocate to their new building upon completion.

Downtown Parking Company received its charter from the SCC for a second parking garage in downtown Roanoke. The garage would accommodate 450 cars and be located at the corner of First Street and Salem Avenue SW. Eugene Carbaugh Jr. was the company president.

Southern Refrigeration Corporation held an open house on August 28 to celebrate their new location at 1627 Shenandoah Avenue NW. The company was a wholesale distributor.

Spur Filling Station opened at 417 E. Campbell Avenue on August 28.

Pfc. Robert Gray of Roanoke and Sgt. William Holmes of Salem were released as POW on August 28 by communists in Korea. Holmes was captured on November 25, 1951, and Gray had been held since November 1950. They were part of a release of some 400 prisoners held by the North Koreans. Lt. Myron Stouffer of Roanoke was freed days later.

Mrs. Sugar Ellett and Mrs. Tommy Hopkins defeated defending champions Kitty Coxe and Edith Paine to win the women's doubles championship in the twenty-fifth annual city-county tennis tournament on August 29. The finals match was held at South Roanoke Park. Bob Bolling won the junior singles title by defeating Jay Walker. The two teamed up to win the junior boys doubles title. The next day Lu Merritt defeated Jack Miller for the men's title, and Charley Turner and Doug Craig won the men's doubles championship. Suzanne Glass defeated Sugar Ellett for the women's single title.

On August 30, Roanoke city police put their brand new paddy wagon to use by hauling a stray cow across the city. The cow had been found wandering in the vicinity of Gainsboro Road and had been tethered at the Gainsboro Branch Library. When no owner was found, police transported the cow to a local stockyard.

Seventy-five speckled trout kept in a large spring in the basement of the Ponce de Leon Hotel as an attraction were accidentally killed in late August. Garland Miller, hotel manager, stated that refrigerator fluid accidentally leaked into the spring.

A 750,000-gallon standpipe water tower was completed in the Grandin Court section in late August and was part of a $4 million capital program of the city's water department.

A cornerstone-laying ceremony was held on August 30 for the new Lula Williams Branch YWCA at Orange Avenue and Peach Road NW. Mrs. Madge Wheaton presided, and the main speaker was Rev. A. L. James. Dr. Harry Penn was the campaign chairman.

Modern Tailors relocated to their new store on August 31 at 512 S. Jefferson Street.

The annual Roanoke Fair opened at Maher Field on August 31 for a weeklong run. The week included grandstand acts and fireworks at Victory Stadium, a beauty contest, agricultural exhibits, and a midway. The fair drew 2,000 persons on opening night with the main attraction being the Flying Valentines, an aerialist act.

The congregation of Oakland Baptist Church broke ground on a new education building on August 31. The $200,000 structure would contain fifty-six classrooms. Membership of the church was 1,479. Rev. James Lippincott was the pastor.

Schneider Oil Company Station opened at the intersection of Routes 460 and 630 at Lakeside on September 3. They sold Sunoco-brand fuel.

Lloyd Price and his band performed for a show and dance at the American Legion Auditorium on September 6. Price was known for his hit song *Lawdy Miss Clawdie*. The balcony was reserved for white spectators.

Sgt. James Valentine of Roanoke was released as a POW by North Korea on September 4. Valentine had been held by the Communists since December 1950. Valentine's mother, a resident of Fairfax Avenue NW, learned of the news when a reporter with the *Roanoke Times*, who learned the news from the Associated Press, contacted city police, who drove to her home to share the news in person. Lt. John Caldwell of Roanoke was released a few days later by the North Koreans.

Mrs. Hank Williams, widow of the country singer, performed at the Roanoke Theatre on September 9. She was joined by Paul Howard and the Arkansas Cotton Pickers.

To celebrate its fortieth anniversary, Glenn-Minnich Clothing Company, a men's store in Roanoke, had employees dress in the fashion of 1913 and parade along downtown Roanoke sidewalks. The store was founded that year in the 100 block of W. Campbell Avenue by C. B. Minnich, Myrl Glenn, and H. A. Glenn. At that time, the store's location was considered outside the city's main business district and many questioned if the company could survive. In 1935, it moved one store over to 108 W. Campbell Avenue.

Washington Heights Church of the Brethren held a ground-breaking ceremony on September 6 for their new building at Westside Boulevard and Michigan Avenue NW.

The Southern Railway *Tennessean* hit a car at the Elm Street crossing in Salem on September 6, killing Louise Dooley, fifty-three, of Salem and injuring three others.

Dawson Ruff, twelve, of Salem was accidentally killed on September 7 when an old .22-caliber target pistol discharged while he and two other friends were playing. He died from a wound to the chest before reaching the hospital. He lost consciousness and died just blocks from the hospital. According to members of the Salem First Aid and Life Saving Crew, seconds before he died, Ruff said, "Take off my shoes. I'm going to die." He was the son of Mrs. Leo Flowers of High Street.

Emil Klein became the first full-time cantor of Beth Israel Synagogue. A native of Czechoslovakia, he was a prisoner in a Nazi concentration camp in Germany for two years. He came to America in 1948. Before coming to Beth Israel, Klein was at a synagogue in Passaic, New Jersey.

Roanoke stock car racer Curtis Turner finished third in the Southern 500 held at Darlington, South Carolina, on September 7. A crowd of 36,000 witnessed thirty-five lead changes.

Mrs. E. J. Keffer won the women's golf tournament at Roanoke Country Club on September 7. She defeated Mrs. W. B. Richardson.

Eddie Crawford and his *Atlantic City Follies* came to the American Legion Auditorium for a cabaret dance and floor show on September 12.

On September 8, Roanoke City Council adopted a five-day, forty-hour workweek for municipal employees with the exception of public safety workers. Prior to this, city offices were open for half-days every Saturday. The meeting was also the first for the seven-member council (previously the council had been five members), and for the first time in the city's history, a woman, Mary Pickett, was a council member.

The Mohawk Rubber Company plant in Salem began "spot runs" the second week in September, which eventually broke off into regular production runs days later. V. M. Mershon was the plant manager.

Operations began on September 8 at the Roanoke County branch of Roanoke Mills. The branch site was the former Thaden-Jordan Furniture Company near Lakeside. The branch had 115 employees.

Roanoke was one of four cities nationwide to be a test site for the Hollywood film *Halfway to Hell*. The movie was shown at the Lee-Hi Drive-In and the Trail Drive-In. Audience members were interviewed at intermission for their reactions to Hollywood's depiction of the evils of Communism.

Trailways began its new President Route bus line in mid-September that operated between Memphis, Tennessee, and Washington, DC, with stops in the area at Galax, Roanoke, and Lynchburg.

As of September 9, polio patients admitted to Memorial and Crippled Children's Hospital for the year totaled 149. One hundred had been discharged, and one had died.

The 24th Street Men's Store at Shaffer's Crossing reopened under new management on September 11. Mr. and Mrs. L. E. Turnage were the owners.

Edmund Chamberlain, thirty-two and a native of Roanoke, died on September 9 when the plane he was piloting crashed in the Potomac River as he was approaching National Airport. Witnesses stated the plane caught fire, forcing the pilot to ditch the aircraft.

Irv Sharp, the "Silver Dollar Man," celebrated his second anniversary in that role on WDBJ radio by holding a contest that offered not one but two silver dollars for every cold Dr. Pepper in one's refrigerator during an unannounced visit by a station representative.

The state water control board, at a meeting on September 11, ordered the Town of Salem and Leas and McVitty Tannery to stop polluting the Roanoke River by October 15, 1955. Both were ordered to have antipollution facilities in operation by that date or face judicial action.

Wayside Furniture Shop opened on September 14 at 4515 Williamson Road, formerly the home of Sherrill's Antiques.

Professional boxing was at the American Legion Auditorium on September 17 with three main events—Joe Green versus Eddie Marshall, Don Webber versus Puggy King, and Biff Jones versus Jackie Alexander. In other matchups, Charles Lucado of Roanoke fought Ronald De Priest, and Johnnie Rooney boxed Joe Gibbons. Event promoters were D. L. Johnston and Bob Riley.

Sandlot football practice began in mid-September in Roanoke with the first games scheduled for September 22. Some 650 boys signed up to play on twenty-six various teams scattered throughout the city.

The Rt. Rev. Msgr. James Gilsenan, pastor of Our Lady of Nazareth Catholic Church, died on September 12 at Memorial Hospital in Chattanooga, Tennessee. Gilsenan had been active in Roanoke's civic life and was forced to diminish his pastoral duties due to ill health several months prior to his death. He was invested with the purple robe of a monsignor in June 1940.

Peerless Hardware Company at 21 E. Salem Avenue in Roanoke was purchased by the Katz brothers, who owned Ace Hardware and Economy Hardware. Sidney Katz stated that Ace Hardware would be combined with Peerless Hardware at the Peerless location.

The Roanoke Area Council of Christian Churches voted on September 13 to form a new congregation in southwest Roanoke by purchasing a lot at the corner of Grandin Road and Carlton Road SW. The council agreed to hire a minister to help start a congregation in the Raleigh Court section and lead them to build a church on the lot. This would become the home of Westhampton Christian Church.

Roanoke City School Superintendent E. W. Rushton announced on September 14 that he would make every effort to abolish school hazing of freshmen with the next school year. His office had received numerous complaints from parents about injuries and humiliations, especially among and between males.

The Roanoke County School Board voted on September 14 to purchase ten acres for an elementary school that would be located on the Catawba Mountain Road near Hanging Rock.

Members of the Washington Heights Civic League met on September 14 and decided to approach Roanoke City Council about "shallow graves" in Lincoln Memorial Park. League members reported that the city health department had been made aware of the matter but claimed no action had been taken. The following day, the cemetery's owner, C. C. Williams, claimed that league members were prejudiced against a Black cemetery being near their neighborhood. He intended to also attend the city council meeting and respond.

The Children's Zoo on Mill Mountain reported that for their summer season (the zoo opened on Memorial Day and closed on Labor Day), they had 86,656 paid admissions though the zoo had an operating loss of close to $2,000.

Erskine Hawkins and his orchestra, along with Jimmy Mitchell and Julian Dash, performed for a show and dance at the American Legion Auditorium on September 18. The balcony was reserved for white spectators. One local group also performed, the Four Sounds.

Mick-or-Mack opened its largest and newest grocery store on September 17 at 1312 Winborne Street SW. Ads read, "Roses, cigars and refreshments for everyone."

Grand prize drawings included a Frigidaire clothes dryer, Crosley table radio, and a Rival broil-o-mat. The grocery chain closed their store on Grandin Road. The Winborne Street store was the forty-ninth store for the chain. W. C. Humphreys was the store manager.

The newly remodeled Shopwell Food Store reopened on September 18 at 1212 Fourth Street SW.

Hal & Luke's Drive-In Dari-Delight restaurant opened on September 18 on Lee Highway, west of the Roanoke city limits. They offered curb service.

A fire destroyed a fruit packing house at Wrights siding on N&W Railway between Starkey and Boones Mill on September 19. The packing house was owned by C. W. Guilliams of Salem.

Davidsons, a men's clothier, reopened its completely remodeled store on September 21. With the purchase of a suit or topcoat came a complimentary ticket to the Virginia Tech versus William and Mary football game scheduled for November 7. Davidsons was located at 303 S. Jefferson Street and had been closed for several weeks for the $35,000 remodeling. Joseph Davidson opened Davidson Tailoring Company at 102 Jefferson Street in 1910. In 1913, Davidson moved to 303 S. Jefferson Street.

Clyde Woody and his Woodchoppers performed at the Roanoke Theatre on September 23.

Former heavyweight boxing champion Jack Dempsey came to the American Legion Auditorium on September 22 to referee a professional wrestling tag team match between the Becker Brothers and Roy Shire and Bobby Wallace. According to the *Roanoke Times*, "At one point of the bout, Dempsey gave Shires a short slug with his elbow that sent Shires flying out of the ring. And the crowd, several of whom were actually hanging from the rafters, practically raised the roof with an approving cheer."

E. L. Flippo sold his controlling interest in the Roanoke Photo Finishing Company to his best sales agent, William Swartz Jr. on September 21. Flippo was believed to be Roanoke's oldest active businessman, having begun by operating Roanoke Cycle Company in 1898, of which he became the sole owner in 1904. Swartz stated that he would continue to use the company's motto, "You snap the picture; we'll do the rest."

The congregation of First Methodist Church in Salem dedicated their new building on September 20.

Roanoke City Public Schools Superintendent D. E. McQuilkin recommended a $7 million capital program to the Roanoke School Board on September 21. His plan included a new senior high school at Shrine Hill Park, four new elementary schools, and additions to four existing elementary schools. The proposal was in response to increased enrollment.

Work began the third week in September on a $30,000 addition to Kroger Grocery at 1319 Grandin Road SW. Paxton Judge was the branch manager.

This mid-'50s image shows the Kroger grocery store that was located at 1319 Grandin Road SW. *Virginia Room, RPL.*

A group of Black citizens gathered on September 22 to express concerns about the City of Roanoke continuing to operate a city dump in the northwest section near Addison High School, the Lincoln Terrace development, and residences. The dump regularly caught fire, was rat infested, smelled, and was a general health hazard. The citizens met at the offices of the *Roanoke Tribune* and elected a committee to formally appear before Roanoke City Council with their complaints in an ongoing effort to have the matter addressed. The committee consisted of Dr. F. W. Claytor (chairman), Rev. F. E. Alexander, Dr. Harry Penn, L. A. Sydnor, Edwin L. Phillips, Dr. L. E. Paxton, James Lewis, George Lawrence and Eugene Brown. The group included school administrators who asserted that flies, rats, smoke, and odor from the city dump had infiltrated their schools.

James Lazenby of Roanoke was killed in September when he was struck by an automobile in the 700 block of Third Street as he walking on the side of the road. He was fifty-eight.

The Young Democrats Club was started on September 24 in Roanoke with a meeting at the Patrick Henry Hotel. Andrew Coxe, an attorney, was elected head of the group that consisted of about sixty persons.

Roanoke City Council reduced the city's real estate tax rate from $2.74 to $2.73 per $100 of assessed valuation.

The Check-R-Board Feed Store, located at 908 Shenandoah Avenue NW, held its grand opening on September 26. Glenn Howell and his *Straw Hat Hoedown* show performed, which included the Four Little Hillbillies and the Wood Sisters.

Det. Sgt. Joe Jennings began his ninth year as a paralytic because of a bullet wound in the back that he received on September 26, 1945, by a youth whom he was arresting in northwest Roanoke. Jennings had been confined to Lewis-Gale Hospital ever since.

The Clovers, T-Bone Walker, Little Esther, and Rhythm Blues performed at the American Legion Auditorium on October 2. The balcony was reserved for white spectators.

The Clyde Beatty Railroad Circus came to Maher Field on September 30 for two performances.

The *Four Star Revue* came to the Roanoke Theatre stage on September 30 and featured vaudeville acts by Sully & Thomas, the Graysons, Al Avalon, and the De Haven Sisters.

A permanent Roanoke Symphony Orchestra became a reality the third week in September when the governing board made the decision to apply for a charter from the SCC. The group was founded in 1952 and had provided two concerts. Mrs. Harry Dixon was president of the board.

Rev. John Utt tendered his resignation on Sunday, September 27, as pastor to the Emmanuel Lutheran Church, bringing to an end thirty-one years of pastoral ministry in the Roanoke Valley as he retired at age seventy-five. Utt had served Lutheran parishes for a total of forty-six years, beginning with his first church in Floyd County. According to Utt, he had received over 1,200 persons into the Lutheran Church and had performed 641 marriage ceremonies.

Town & Campus Men's Shop opened on October 1 at 213 E. Main Street in Salem.

Black leaders spoke at the Roanoke City Council meeting on September 28 and demanded an end to the city dump in northwest Roanoke. Dr. F. W. Claytor served as spokesperson for the group and also lived within one hundred feet of the dump. City Manager Arthur Owens agreed to study alterative refuse disposal sites and methods. The dump was located in an abandoned quarry north of Orange Avenue.

Plasti Industries of Winona, Minnesota, began leasing a warehouse at 2420 Shenandoah Avenue NW in late September to serve as a distribution point for their plastic footwear products. Their brand names were Puddler, Rainstormer, and Pud-Lucks.

Hollywood actor and Roanoke native John Payne married Alexandria Curtis on September 27 in Hollywood. It was Payne's third marriage.

Some fifty residents of South Roanoke formed the South Roanoke Civic League in a meeting on September 29. Clifton Woodrum Jr. was elected president. One of the league's first goals was to establish a city recreation center in the neighborhood.

Philip Levy's Underselling Store advertised a going out of business sale in late September. The store was located at 3 E. Salem Avenue in Roanoke.

Former US Vice President Alben Barkley visited Roanoke on October 2 to address the annual meeting of the Virginia Real Estate Association at the Hotel Roanoke. He did not discuss politics during his address but spoke to economic trends impacting American business.

Nat Spigel, Roanoke businessman, died at age sixty-five in a Roanoke hospital on October 2. Spigel owned Natalie Shoppe and was active in many business and civic organizations.

Former Olympian Rev. Bob Richards conducted a weeklong revival at the American Legion Auditorium that began on October 4. The evangelistic campaign was sponsored by the Roanoke Ministers Conference.

A father and son were shot dead at a tourist court that they operated by the owner of the property. Elvin See and his father, Earl See, were killed at a gas station and restaurant that they ran at the Roanoke Tourist Court located on Route 460, a mile east of Roanoke City. Both were residents of Roanoke. Police arrested Abe Huddleston, who drove himself to police headquarters in Roanoke and surrendered. He was taken into custody later by the Roanoke County sheriff. The October 3 incident had apparently started with an argument over the sale of the property. Prior to killing the Sees, Huddleston killed five of his pets at a junkyard business he ran, leaving a note for employees to bury the animals. Claude Wright, a soft drink truck driver, was an eyewitness to the slayings as he was inside the gas station at the time the younger See was shot.

Henry Stuhldreher, one of the "Four Horsemen" of the 1920s Notre Dame football team and a 1924 All-American, spoke to the Touchdown Club at the Hotel Roanoke on October 5. He had also written numerous books on the sport.

Western film actor Lash LaRue and his *Great Western Show* performed on the stage of the Roanoke Theatre on October 7.

Robert Bailey III of Roanoke and a graduate of Addison High School addressed the Gainsboro Branch Library Reading Club on October 5. Bailey had received a Fulbright Scholarship in 1951 that allowed him to do postgraduate study in England and Germany. He was a graduate of Talladega College and had also studied at Cornell University.

One Hour Valet, a dry-clean service for men's laundry, opened on October 5 at 26 W. Church Avenue.

Belle Furniture Company closed on October 3. The store sold mostly television sets and was located at 130 W. Campbell Avenue.

The Orioles, Buddy Lucas, Spo-Dee-O-Dee, McHarris and Delores performed at the Virginia Theatre on October 6. The balcony was reserved for whites for the midnight show only.

The Floyd Ward School of Dancing opened a branch at 3609 Williamson Road on October 8. Mrs. Marion Windley was the manager.

Nora Epperley, seven, was fatally injured on October 7 when she fell from a moving vehicle. The Roanoke County girl's accident occurred on Route 117, and she was deceased when she arrived at Lewis-Gale Hospital. She was the daughter of Mr. and Mrs. Leon Epperley.

A three-alarm fire at Harris Hardwood Company on October 8 destroyed a huge warehouse. The company, located in the Norwich section of Roanoke, suffered losses estimated at $100,000.

Attorneys for the Times-World Corporation (WDBJ radio) and Radio Roanoke (WROV radio) argued their respective cases before the FCC on October 7 in the fight for a new television station in Roanoke. The new station had been assigned channel 7 by the FCC. The hearing was the second of three before the FCC.

George Trout, founder and owner of G. E. Trout and Sons general contractors, died at seventy-one at his home in northwest Roanoke on October 7.

The new pipe organ at Virginia Heights Baptist Church was dedicated on October 11 with an afternoon recital by Dr. Clifford Loomis of Sullins College at Bristol.

The parking garage at Jefferson Street and Bullit Avenue SW, known as Merchants Parking Center, was formally dedicated on October 10. Roses were given to ladies and windshield wipers were given to men who parked there that day.

The "pay mistress" on the national television show *Beat the Clock* came to Roanoke on October 12 to help launch the local United Red Feather Campaign. Known only as Roxanne, she headlined a locally broadcast talent show that evening on WSLS-TV from the Appalachian Auditorium.

Irmgard Seefried opened the 1953–54 season of the Community Concert Association with a performance on October 7. The soprano sang a variety of classical compositions.

Hennis Freight Lines, headquartered in Winston-Salem, opened a branch terminal at 711 Norfolk Avenue on October 8.

When asked what they considered their biggest problems, some 160 Roanoke city teachers responded in a survey that those were low pay, no free time to eat lunch, poorly disciplined children, and unequal pay between men and women.

Roanoke City Manager Arthur Owens stated on October 9 that the city had no authority over the manner of burials in response to alleged shallow graves some residents were reporting in regard to Lincoln Memorial Park. He said he could find no law dealing with the depths of graves. Owens did report to Roanoke City Council a few days later that a review of the cemetery did find that some graves were only thirteen to sixteen inches deep.

Washington, DC, journalist David Brinkley took part in the local United Red Feather Campaign kickoff that was held in Appalachian Auditorium on October 12. Brinkley spoke briefly about the United Defense Fund during the hour-long talent show that marked the event. Brinkley was part of the NBC national news staff. He was joined by television celebrity Roxanne for the show. Nearly 250 persons attended the show in person that was televised by WSLS-TV. Miss Martha Parrish of Roanoke was selected as "Miss Red Feather of 1954."

Merchants Parking Service Center, an Esso station, opened on October 10 at Jefferson Street and Bullitt Avenue SW. Operators were Ira Hundley, Harry Withers, Harold Dannel, and John Blankinship. Customers got two hours of free parking in the adjacent parking garage with the purchase of eight gallons of gas.

Biller's Physical Culture Studio opened at 114 W. Salem Avenue. The gym had separate hours for women and men.

St. Mark's Lutheran Church dedicated its new $400,000 sanctuary at 1008 Franklin Road SW on October 11.

Dr. Byron Cooper, a geologist at VPI, delivered his report to Salem Town Council on October 12 regarding the various cave-ins that had occurred in Salem. He concluded the cave-ins were the direct result of heavy underground pumping related to the Valleydale Packers well.

Salem Town Council accepted a contract offered by Roanoke for joint use of Roanoke's sewage treatment plant. This brought to an end a protracted and spirited discussion from both sides on the issue.

A two-alarm fire on October 13 gutted Rakestraw's Dry Cleaners and Dyers at 508 Center Avenue NW.

Carl Storey and his Rambling Mountaineers, along with hillbilly comics Homeless Homer and Ray Atkins, performed at the Roanoke Theatre on October 14.

The Roanoker Motor Lodge opened on Route 11, two miles north of Roanoke, on October 15. Harry and Helen Deal were the owners.

Peoples Federal Savings and Loan Association began operating in their new corporate headquarters at 101 S. Jefferson Street on October 19. The structure was the former Liberty Trust Building.

Roanoke Merchants Association sponsored *Greater Roanoke Days* on October 22–24 as a means to highlight downtown retail. The event included music and dancing at the Merchants Parking Center with performances by Doug Wilson and his Trail Dusters, Andy Anderson and his string band, Jo Ann Lantz, and the Leonard Trio. There were two fashion shows at the American Theatre involving seventy-five models. The "None of Your Business" window shopping contest encouraged shoppers to spy in a merchant's window an item they did not have for sale. The Saturday morning youth talent show at the American Theatre included several cash prizes, and top prizes were won by Phyllis Barnard, the Melody Boys, and the ukulele-playing duo of Harry Phipps and Bill Baker.

Sugar Ray Robinson, Joe Scott, Billy Ward, the Dominoes, T-Bone Walker and Count Basie and his orchestra performed for a show and dance at the American Legion Auditorium on October 30. The balcony was reserved for white spectators.

The Thursday Morning Music Club presented the Agnes De Mille Dance Theatre performance at the American Legion Auditorium on October 24 as part of their annual concert series.

Atlantic Greyhound Lines moved to its new terminal building at First Street and Bullitt Avenue SE on October 20. Their previous terminal was at 16 Church Avenue SW.

The Floyd Ward School of Dancing opened its Salem branch in mid-October. Mrs. T. J. McCown was the branch manager.

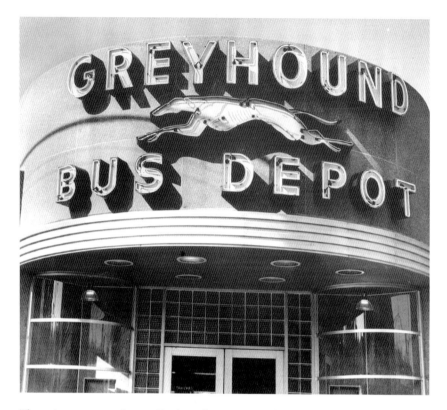

The main entrance to the new Greyhound Bus Depot is shown in this 1953 image. *Virginia Room, RPL*

The Roanoke Symphony Orchestra presented its first concert of its second season on October 19 at the Jefferson High School auditorium. The concert showcased piano compositions as well as Hanson's *Serenade for Flute, Harp and Strings,* Frank's *Symphony in D Minor,* Alfven's *Swedish Rhapsody.*

The Roanoke County Sheriff's Department, along with state police, conducted the largest gambling raid in the county's history on October 18. Twenty-two men were arrested at an isolated cabin near Hanging Rock. Among them was Charles Assaid, who was charged with operating a gambling house.

Western film star Tim Holt performed at the Roanoke Theatre as part of his *Western Wrangler Revue* show on October 21.

Rev. W. N. Hunter headed a delegation of Black citizens who appeared before the Roanoke School Board on October 19 and asked that a new elementary school for Blacks be built in the southwest quadrant of the city. The school board responded there was no money available for any new schools.

Dr. E. G. Gill, chairman of a study committee for a new auditorium for Roanoke, recommended to Roanoke City Council that a new municipal auditorium be erected on the southwest corner of Elmwood Park. The proposed structure was intended to replace the Academy of Music on Salem Avenue that had been razed. Gill estimated the cost of the building would be between $1 million and $1.5 million with a seating capacity for 3,500 persons.

Ewald-Clark took over operations of the Hotel Roanoke gift shop in mid-October. The gift shop had formerly been operated by Caldwell-Sites.

Officials with the Virginian Railway announced on October 23 that they would begin testing diesel locomotives within the next ten days. The Virginian used electric locomotives from Roanoke west to Mullens, West Virginia, and steam locomotives on the nonelectrified sections between Roanoke and Norfolk.

Uncle Tom's Barbecue opened in mid-October at 2926 Franklin Road SW.

Several hundred volunteer firefighters battled a large forest fire that swept across Fort Lewis Mountain north of Salem on October 24 and up the south slope of Catawba Mountain. The Roanoke Valley had experienced severe drought making the forest dry.

The Roanoke Fine Arts Center held an exhibition of abstract paintings by Peter Wreden and William Owen in October.

The Barter Theatre presented *Ah, Wilderness* at the Jefferson High School auditorium on October 27. Lead actors were Owen Phillips, Dorothy Lavern, Sam Greene, and Frank Lowe.

Over one hundred families petitioned Roanoke County to stop dumping garbage on the County Farm property. Residents along Dowdy Hollow and Church Hollow Roads said the situation had become a health hazard and threatened legal action.

First Federal Savings and Loan Association purchased the Perry Building on the southeast corner of Church Avenue and First Street SW in late October for $150,000. The bank planned to raze the building and build a new one.

The second Highway Post Office delivery bus for Roanoke was launched on October 31 between the city and Martinsburg, West Virginia. A postal bus had linked Roanoke and Greensboro three years earlier.

Binswanger and Company assumed the assets of the Virginia Glass Company on October 22. The Roanoke branch was located at 206 Fifth Street NW.

The Roanoke Real Estate Board declared its opposition to the proposed slum clearance program and urban redevelopment slated for northeast Roanoke. The board called for a public referendum on the matter that involved eighty-three acres in northeast. The board made their opposition known at a public hearing before Roanoke City Council on October 28. At that hearing, many residents of Northeast voiced opposition as well. The plan proposed the razing of 251 homes and the relocation of 176 other residences. The council deferred a decision until a later date.

The Baptist Bookstore opened at 36 W. Kirk Avenue on November 2. Kittie Sullivan was the manager.

Virginia Tech defeated the Citadel 22–0 in a football game on October 30 at Victory Stadium. The Southern Conference game drew an attendance of 4,000.

Emory and Henry College played Lenoir Rhyne College in the Pythian Bowl football game at Victory Stadium on October 31. Lenoir Rhyne won 20–7 in the benefit game with 1,800 spectators.

Halloween dances were held at several nightclubs and other venues that included the following: Club Cherokee with music by the Diplomats, Blue Ridge Hall with the Drifting Playboys, City Market Auditorium with the Virginia Pioneers, American Legion Auditorium with Wayne Fleming and his Country Cousins, and Apartment Camps with Cecil Kincer and his orchestra.

The first motion picture in Cinemascope to be shown in the Roanoke Valley was *The Robe*, which began a run at the Grandin Theatre on November 11. A premiere event was held the evening before for city officials, clergy, exhibitors, and other guests. Cinemascope was the screen process that provided the illusion of depth with the use of 3D glasses.

Roanoke Times reporter Ozzie Osborne profiled a popular new Christmas toy being stocked in stores—Mr. Potato Head: "Ideal for rainy days when you might otherwise have to sit inside and watch television. Perfect for travel, too. $1."

In elections held on November 3, Roanoke City voters chose Democrat James Armstrong over C. B. Thornton Jr. for commissioner of revenue and Democrat Johnny Johnson over Republican Price Hylton for city treasurer. In state races, however, Roanokers voted overwhelmingly for Republicans Ted Dalton for governor and Stephen Timberlake for lieutenant governor, though both lost their statewide contests to Democrats. Former Roanoke attorney Lindsay Almond Jr. won reelection in Virginia as attorney general. Voter turnout in Roanoke city was 16,269 votes and was the largest nonpresidential ballot count in the city's history. In Roanoke County, Delegate Ernest Robertson, a Democrat, was reelected over Republican opponent Byron Gochenour. Roanoke City's two Democratic members of the Virginia House of Delegates, Julian Rutherfoord Jr. and Kossen Gregory, were returned to Richmond without opposition.

This 1953 image is a view of Campbell Avenue looking west from Williamson Road. Star City Furniture is in the left foreground, and the Earle Hotel is in the right foreground.
Blair Sherertz

Belmont Christian Church, at the corner of Eleventh Street and Jamison Avenue SE, installed a lighted revolving cross on the church roof in early November.

Roanoke race car driver and lumber operator Curtis Turner filed a petition for bankruptcy in US District Court in early November, listing liabilities of $135,393 and assets of $76,245. Turner owned two farms, one each in Roanoke and Franklin Counties.

The first week of November, the Roanoke chapter of Council of Church Women marked its tenth anniversary, having been organized on November 4, 1943, at St. Mark's Lutheran Church. The interdenominational Christian organization had as its goal to proclaim the gospel and to improve the city. Women from the following congregations comprised the inaugural group: St. Mark's Lutheran Church, Virginia Heights Lutheran Church, Williamson Road Presbyterian Church, South Roanoke Methodist Church, Central Church of the Brethren, and Virginia Heights Baptist Church. The group's first president was Mrs. E. E. Leiphart.

Excavation was begun the first week in November on a three-story, $80,000 activities building at Virginia Heights Baptist Church, on the corner of Memorial Avenue and Grandin Road SW. W. R. Harp was the building committee chairman. Membership of the church was around 1,500.

The third annual Shrine Bowl football game was held on November 7 at Victory Stadium. The day began with a midmorning Shrine Parade through downtown. The event was a fundraiser for Shrine hospitals. The afternoon football game was between VMI and William & Mary, which VMI won 20–19 with a touchdown in the last minute of the game. Attendance was estimated at 5,000.

Mrs. John Jones, forty-four, and Nancy Olive, eight, were killed in an auto accident on November 7 on US 460 near Prospect. Both were from Roanoke. The two-car collision also injured five others.

Dudley's Nurseries opened a branch in Roanoke on November 9 at 1403 Williamson Road NE.

Noted American poet and literary critic Mark Van Doren spoke at Hollins College on November 15. He won the Pulitzer Prize for poetry in 1940 and was on the faculty of Columbia University.

Roanoke City Council approved fluoridation of the city's water supply on November 9 but off an appropriation for the necessary equipment and installation until a later date. The move had been endorsed by the Roanoke Academy of Medicine, the Roanoke Dental Society, the Junior Chamber of Commerce, and the Central Council PTA.

Hugh Moulse opened a new hardware store on Grandin Road in the former location of Mick-or-Mack grocery. The store, Grandin Road Hardware, was located at 1330 Grandin Road SW.

The Roanoke United Red Feather Campaign for the Community Fund ended with a total pledged of $281,414 which was about $16,000 short of its goal. The Community Fund supported nineteen local charities and other agencies.

General Motors exhibits, known as the *Parade of Progress* caravan, came to South Roanoke Park the second weekend in November. The display of science and engineering auto achievements was held under an aero-dome tent that could seat over 1,200 people.

The Hotel Roanoke's Fountain Room, pictured here in May 1950, would be replaced by a coffee shop with the hotel's remodel in 1954. *Norfolk Southern Collection, VPI&SU Libraries*

Officials with N&W Railway announced in mid-November a $1.2 million expansion of the Hotel Roanoke that would include fifty-six additional guest rooms, a large coffee shop, and a convention exhibit hall. Work was slated to begin in early December. The coffee shop would replace the Fountain Room with seating for 225 diners.

Officials of the Virginian Railway announced on November 13 that the railroad planned to purchase twenty-five diesel-electric locomotives for use in the coal fields. It was a move away from the use of steam locomotives.

The congregation of the Ninth Street Church of the Brethren in southeast Roanoke dedicated their new $30,000 education building on November 15. Rev. Ray Showalter of Bridgewater College was the guest speaker.

Tidewater Supply Company opened in their new location at Shenandoah Avenue and Fourteenth Street NW on November 16.

The nation's first Artmobile, a project of the Virginia Museum of Fine Arts, came to Roanoke for a five-day exhibition that began November 19. The museum on wheels displayed sixteen paintings from the VMFA's collection.

The new Hollins Road Baptist Church was dedicated on November 15. The congregation was organized on July 3, 1949. The congregation purchased property for the church and began its construction earlier in the year.

Lloyd Electric Company moved to its new location at 521 W. Salem Avenue in mid-November. It had formerly been located at 334 W. Salem Avenue.

Shirley Parker of Roanoke was charged by Roanoke police with murdering her newborn infant on November 15. Parker had delivered her baby unassisted on a sidewalk along Wells Avenue NW and then put the child in a shopping bag. Taking it to the N&W Railway passenger station, Parker was seen trying to flush the infant down a toilet when a maid called the police.

Kroger formally reopened its remodeled grocery store at 1319 Grandin Road SW on November 19. The building was enlarged by an additional 8,000 square feet, equipped with a "magic carpet" that opened doors for customers as they entered the store, and given a new front entrance at the corner of the store to provide direct access to the parking lot. The store manager was Joe Keeler.

Rev. William Marmion, rector of St. Andrew's Church in Wilmington, Delaware, was elected bishop of the Episcopal Diocese of Southwestern Virginia in a meeting held at St. John's Episcopal Church in Roanoke on November 18. Marmion gained a majority vote of both clergy and laity on the fifth ballot.

The Roanoke Junior Chamber of Commerce decided not to participate in the Santa Parade scheduled by the Roanoke Merchants Association prior to Thanksgiving. The Jaycees wrote a letter to the association asserting they remained engaged in a campaign "to put Christ back into Christmas" and their disappointment that Christmas decorations and a parade in downtown were preceding Thanksgiving.

Two professional basketball teams, the Philadelphia Sphas and the Toledo Mercurys, of the American League played a game at the American Legion Auditorium on November 20.

The freshman squads of Virginia Tech and VMI played each other in football at Victory Stadium on November 21. Tech won 34–0 before a crowd of 850 spectators.

Ruth Brown, Paul Williams and his orchestra, and Margie Day performed for a show and dance at the American Legion Auditorium on November 25. The balcony was reserved for white spectators.

The Santa Parade was held in downtown Roanoke on November 24. Shelby Agee, a student at Jefferson High School, was selected as the Snow Queen for the event. The parade included numerous school bands, city officials, business and civic organization floats, and a "Candy Express" that preceded the parade giving candy to children. Attendance along the route was estimated at 25,000.

Queen Frederika of Greece received a corsage from Roanokers as she and King Paul passed through the city on their way to Williamsburg on November 21. The royal couple had a half-hour layover as their rail coach was switched from *The Pelican* to *The Cavalier*. A. U. Noble, a local florist, delivered the flowers he had arranged, a two-orchid lavender corsage.

The Roanoke Woman's Club purchased a lot at the corner of Grandin Road and Brandon Avenue SW with plans to erect a new clubhouse. The club had been without a clubhouse since it sold the one on Patterson Avenue SW in 1944.

Rev. J. E. Patterson, pastor of Mountain View Brethren Church at Hollins for forty years, died at his home on November 22 at the age of seventy. Patterson was believed to have held the longest continuous pastorate of any minister in the Brethren denomination at the time of his retirement.

Joseph King, thirty, was fatally shot in the lobby of the Dumas Hotel, 110 First Street NW, on November 25. Police arrested Matthew Williamson Jr., twenty, who confessed to the shooting.

Two additional groups joined the Roanoke Jaycees in protesting the Santa Parade that was held the evening before Thanksgiving in Roanoke. The Salem Junior Woman's Club and the Roanoke Retail Furniture Dealers Association both issued statements concurring in the Jaycees' effort "to put Christ back into Christmas" and protesting the lack of a Thanksgiving celebration.

VMI defeated Virginia Tech 28–13 in the annual Thanksgiving Day football game at Victory Stadium. A crowd of 26,000 watched the game. The Fifth Engineer Company, marine reserves, erected a pontoon bridge across the Roanoke River connecting South Roanoke Park with Victory Stadium to better handle parking and pedestrian access for the game.

This 1953 photo shows the Rockledge Inn on the top of Mill Mountain. The lodge would eventually be turned into a theater space in the 1960s. *Historical Society of Western Virginia*

Charm Shop, located at 12 W. Campbell Avenue, announced in late November it was going out of business due to a loss of lease.

Jobe Florist opened a new shop at 215 S. College Avenue in Salem on November 30.

Metropolitan Opera singer Cesare Siepi gave a concert at the Jefferson High School auditorium on November 30 that was sponsored by the Community Concert Association.

The Roanoke Valley Kiwanis Club received its charter on December 1 in a meeting at the Patrick Henry Hotel. Frank Angell was president of the new club that had 150 members. The club's sponsor was the Kiwanis Club of Roanoke.

Four stone columns that stood at the intersection of Grandin Road and Windsor Avenue SW were removed on December 1. The columns had once marked the entrance to Raleigh Court at Grandin Road. Roanoke City Council had authorized their demolition as they obstructed the views of motorists.

Lancaster, Pennsylvania, became the eighth baseball club in the Piedmont League. League officials announced the team for the next season as the replacement for the Roanoke Red Sox that had dropped from the minor league circuit due to financial hardship.

Petitions were presented to Roanoke City Council in early December opposing the city's fluoridation plan for its water supply. A citizens committee had organized to oppose the plan headed by Malcolm Worrell, a retired navy captain. The main arguments were that fluoride was not a proven benefit for teeth and that the chemicals used damaged the water system.

Roanoke city began hauling in tons of dirt to fill an abandoned quarry at Washington Park that had become a city dump. The dirt was a response to nearby citizens' complaints about the health hazards and fires associated with the open-air dump.

Santa Claus arrived in Vinton on December 5 aboard *The Tennessean*. Santa participated in the town's annual pre-Christmas program and was greeted by the William Byrd High School band, town officials, and hundreds of children.

Malcolm-Seay announced in early December it was going out of business. The appliance and television store was located at the corner of Memorial Avenue and Grandin Road SW.

A large residence built in 1891 and considered a landmark in Roanoke was razed in early December to make room for the new Central YMCA. The home, formerly owned by Dr. Albert Cannaday, was located on the northeast corner of Church Avenue and Fifth Street SW.

Salem merchants sponsored the Electric Cooking School on December 8 at the Salem Theatre. Demonstrations were conducted by home economists of Appalachian Electric Power.

Metropolitan Opera singers Irra Petina, Lillian Shelby, Hugh Thompson, and Lanny Ross presented a concert *Immortal Musicals* at the American Legion Auditorium on December 7. The concert was under the auspices of the Thursday Morning Music Club.

Officials with Shenandoah Life Insurance Company announced the opening of three new branches in Philadelphia, Baltimore, and Springfield, Ohio.

The new Vinton Post Office opened on December 7 at 115 W. Lee Avenue. It had formerly been located at 210 S. Pollard Street. Lewis Meador was postmaster.

Forty wives of Roanoke city policemen appeared before Roanoke City Council on December 7 and demanded that their husbands be given adequate pay and better hours. At the time, top pay for a third-year patrolman was $275 per month with an average of 215 working hours per month. That came out to $1.38 per hour. The council referred the matter to budget study.

Andrew Ensley, twenty-two, of Roanoke was shot and killed in a shoeshine parlor on Fifth Street NW, on December 7. He had been home only a few days from serving in the US Marine Corps. Otho Taylor was charged by police with the killing.

Dr. Joseph Webber died on December 8 at the age of eighty. He was Roanoke's oldest practicing druggist. He was president and treasurer of Humphries & Webber, which had been in business at 108 E. Campbell Avenue since 1910. He died an hour after closing his store for the day.

Barber Brothers Gulf Station opened at 3406 Melrose Avenue NW on December 9. Mark Barber and James Barber were the owners and operators.

Steve Lindamood of Roanoke died on December 9 at age thirty-nine. Lindamood was ranked in the top ten nationally for several years in a row in duck-pin bowling.

This December 1953 image shows the N&W Railway S1a No. 244 locomotive at the Roanoke Shops. It was the last locomotive built in the Roanoke Shops. *Virginia Room, RPL*

A standing-room-only crowd attended the Roanoke City Council meeting on December 10 for a public hearing on the council's action to adopt a fluoridation plan for the city's water supply. Those opposed to the plan were met with arguments in favor from local physicians, dentists, and civic organizations.

Well-known missionary Dr. E. Stanley Jones spoke on December 13 at Greene Memorial Methodist Church and later that day at the American Legion Auditorium.

Rev. William Simmons announced his resignation as pastor of the Fifth Avenue Presbyterian Church in mid-December to take effect February 1, 1954. Simmons had accepted a position with Tennessee State University in Nashville. Simmons had come to Roanoke twelve years prior and had taken a leading role in local civil rights activities.

The Roanoke city manager and police superintendent developed a program in mid-December by which physicians at Lewis-Gale Hospital would be used for medical emergencies at the city jail. The need arose when earlier in the month Dr. William Bartlett, chairman of the English department at Roanoke College, collapsed while in a detention cell at the jail. Bartlett had been arrested on a drunken driving charge. Four hours elapsed before Bartlett was transferred to a local hospital, where he died the next day due to a brain hemorrhage. An investigation followed the incident that determined the police department followed the protocol in existence, which was to notify the city physician. However, Bartlett was determined to not have been intoxicated but had slurred speech and impaired driving due to the early stages of his brain hemorrhaging.

Twenty-five air raid sirens were installed throughout Roanoke City in mid-December as part of the Civil Defense program.

An eight-room addition was completed for Blue Ridge Baptist Church, one of the oldest church structures in Roanoke County. Blue Ridge Baptist Church was built in 1854 as a one-room union church for Methodists and Baptists and sat one hundred yards from the Roanoke-Bedford county line.

Glassheat of Roanoke Inc. opened on December 12 at 301 McClanahan Street SW. The business engineered and distributed a system of electric radiant heat developed by the French. Davis Elliot was the firm's president.

Roanoke County Circuit Court Judge Fred Hoback ordered Abe Huddleston to undergo psychiatric examinations at Marion in connection with his confession to the double slaying of Earl See and Elvin See in October.

Water consumption in Roanoke was so high that Charles Moore, project engineer in the water department, reported that filtration equipment at Carvins Cove would have to be enlarged in the near future at an estimated cost of $4 million. According to Moore, water consumption in the summer was at a level not anticipated to happen until the late 1960s.

Long's Restaurant at 1914 Memorial Avenue SW was raided by Roanoke police on December 15 for being a gambling house. Punch cards and other gambling items were confiscated, and J. D. Long Jr. was charged for operating the enterprise and was later fined $100 and given a thirty-day suspended jail sentence.

Basil O'Connor, president of the National Foundation for Infantile Paralysis, addressed 500 March of Dimes volunteers in a banquet at the Hotel Roanoke on

December 16. He predicted a mass testing of a new polio vaccine in the coming months that he believed would eradicate polio. The vaccine, developed by Dr. Jonas Salk, would be given to second graders in those areas with the highest per capita infection rates in the United States.

To honor the fiftieth anniversary of the Wright Brothers flight at Kitty Hawk, North Carolina, Clayton Lemon and Robert Garst, two early Roanoke aviators, gave an on-air interview over WDBJ radio to reporter Don Murray as they circled the valley in an aircraft.

The Roanoke Chapter of the United Cerebral Palsy Association was organized on December 16 at a meeting at the Hotel Roanoke. Judge K. A. Pate was elected president.

The cornerstone for the new Preston Park Elementary School was laid on December 20. The dedication speaker was Rev. A. L. James, pastor of First Baptist Church, Gainsboro, and a member of the Roanoke School Board. The school was located on Preston Avenue NW.

Some 600 sandlot football players attended the annual sandlot banquet at Monroe Junior High School on December 17. The guest speaker was George Preas, All-Big Six tackle from VPI and a Roanoke sandlot football player in the mid-1940s.

Howard Nichols, a sixty-five-year-old freight conductor for N&W Railway, of Roanoke was killed at the West End Yards by a railway car on December 18. He was struck by a car, uncoupled from an engine, and dragged a distance of about 1,000 feet. He had been employed by the railroad since 1911.

The Sweethearts of Rhythm, the Griffin Brothers, and Chuck Willis performed for a show and dance at the American Legion Auditorium on December 24. The balcony was reserved for white spectators.

Roanoke's second annual *Man of the Street* Christmas pageant was performed on the steps of the Municipal Building on December 22. The pageant was given by the city to recognize the sacred significance of Christmas, according to city leaders. The bands of Addison High School and Monroe Junior High School provided the music with sets designed by the parks and recreation department.

W. D. Nunley, lay pastor of Piney Grove Christian Church, resigned his position to help form a new congregation, New Hope Christian Church, which was meeting temporarily at Craighead's Store on Route 220.

Lloyd Electric Company opened its new plant at 521 W. Salem Avenue on December 21.

The congregation of Mt. Zion Baptist Church began work in late December on their new church building by razing a previous structure at Fourth Street and Madison Avenue NW. The new brick sanctuary was estimated to cost $100,000. Church membership was around 700, with Rev. M. T. Coke as pastor.

One of the few very high-frequency, omnidirectional range stations in the eastern United States was under construction at Woodrum Field and slated to begin operations in January 1954. The station would allow airplanes in the vicinity to receive directional signals from any azimuth of the TVOR station. Prior to the station, aircraft received course information from only four points on the compass.

This 1950s postcard shows Woodrum Field's terminal building. An American Airlines plane is in the foreground. *Nelson Harris*

Virginia Governor John Battle granted a conditional pardon on December 21 to Lester Pearson, who was sentenced to twenty years in the penitentiary for the June 1950 slaying of his wife in Roanoke. Pearson pled guilty to murdering his wife, who was found dead in the couple's home on Blenheim Road SW, having been severely beaten. Prison authorities had described Pearson as a model prisoner and noted that he "had reached the peak of rehabilitation."

Frank Sherrill, president of the S&W Cafeteria chain, announced on December 21 that a new S&W Cafeteria would open in the old Atlantic Greyhound Bus Terminal on W. Church Avenue. Work was to begin in January.

William Jenks announced his retirement as chairman of the N&W Railway board of directors effective December 31. Jenks had been with the railroad for sixty-six years. He had served in a variety of capacities with N&W, including as general manager, vice president, and president. He began his career with the railroad as an agent-operator.

Bull Moose Jackson and his orchestra, along with singer Larry Darnell, performed for a show and dance at the Star City Auditorium, located on North Henry Street, on December 31. White spectators were admitted at a discount.

Dave Cather of Roanoke was one of twenty-one boys named to the fifth annual midget football All-America team. The team was under the auspices of the Pop Warner Football Conference. Cather was a student at Woodrow Wilson Junior High School and played for the Raleigh Court Lions 115-pound team.

A forest fire consumed a few hundred acres at Brushy Mountain, northwest of Roanoke, on December 27. Hundreds of volunteers fought the blaze to bring it under control late in the night.

Richard Hale, thirty-eight, of Bradshaw Road was killed in a house fire on Poff Lane in Salem on Christmas night. Hale was visiting the home of Mr. and Mrs. Mark Carroll, owners of the residence. Hale's charred remains were found in the debris that destroyed the home completely. On December 28, Sally Carroll died at Lewis-Gale Hospital from burns she received in the fire. She was seventy-eight. Investigators determined the fire started in the flue.

Several local banks published their balance sheets effective December 31 showing assets and liabilities. The figures were reported as follows: First National Exchange Bank, $86.8 million; Mountain Trust Bank, $28.6 million; Colonial-American National Bank, $35.3 million; Bank of Virginia, $100 million; and Roanoke Industrial and Loan Corporation, $0.6 million.

1954

Rusco Window Company occupied its new $150,000 building on Lee Highway between Roanoke and Salem on January 1.

The Roanoke Chamber of Commerce board voted to oppose the redevelopment plan for northeast Roanoke as planned by the Roanoke Redevelopment and Housing Authority. The opposition stemmed from the use of federal funds and potential strings attached for local governance.

Detective Sgt. J. B. Jennings expressed appreciation to his fellow policemen and friends for their $390 Christmas gift. Jennings resided at Lewis-Gale Hospital and had for several years after being paralyzed in the line of duty with a bullet to his spine.

Robert Johnson, thirty-nine, of Roanoke led police on a wild high-speed car chase on January 2 before he was halted at Big Hill several miles west of Salem. Police confiscated six gallons of bootleg whiskey from his trunk. The chase was initiated at the intersection of Grandin Road and Brandon Avenue SW in Roanoke.

The Roanoke Fine Arts Center opened an exhibit of paintings by two Roanokers, Lewis Thompson and Benjamin Knapp. The exhibit was held at the Roanoke Public Library.

Jane Stuart Smith performed on the NBC radio national broadcast of the Rudolph Frimi's opera *The Vagabond King* on January 4. Other performers included Gordon MacRae and Lucille Norman.

The Blue Ridge Council of Boy Scouts reported that 1953 saw the biggest one-year gain in membership in its thirty-nine year history. Membership increased by 942, bringing the total number of men and boys participating in Scouting to 7,255.

Mrs. Ella Agee, forty-five, died on January 5 from severe burns she received Christmas Day at her home at 609 Stewart Avenue SE.

A fire destroyed a combination store and residence of P. L. Harvey at Midway on January 6.

The Lula Williams Memorial Branch YWCA moved into its new building at 108 Orange Avenue NW on January 6. The new $70,000 building replaced the former location at 304 Second Street NE.

Graham Haynie Jr., an insurance executive, was named Roanoke's Outstanding Young Man for 1953 by the Roanoke Jaycees. Haynie had been involved in numerous civic and business organizations.

Arthur Scholz, seventy-four, of Roanoke died on January 9. A native of Germany who came to Roanoke in 1904, Scholz opened the Dutch Kitchen restaurant in 1910. He closed the restaurant to work for N&W Railway and then reopened Dutch Kitchen in 1936 with co-owner Richard Telchler.

On January 10 WSLS-TV increased its broadcast ability by going to 296,000 watts. *More Power to You*, an hour-long mid-afternoon broadcast, marked the occasion. Tom Wright was master of ceremonies for the show that featured local musical talent, clergy, and station officials.

Ground-breaking ceremonies were held for the new Mt. Zion Baptist Church on January 10 at Fourth Street and Madison Avenue NE. The congregation was meeting at the Lula Williams Branch YWCA. The congregation had 500 members with Rev. M. T. Coker as pastor. C. R. Meadows was chairman of the building committee.

Cellist Leonard Rose gave a concert at the Jefferson High School auditorium on January 14 under the auspices of the Community Concert Association. Rose had played with numerous symphonies around the nation.

The ambulance of the Hunton Life Saving and First Aid Crew was equipped with a radio in mid-January that allowed it to be part of the Civil Defense program. The Hunton Crew had won first prize at a life saving crew convention in Greensboro, North Carolina, for having one of the best life saving vehicles. A. A. Terrell was the crew's captain.

Members of the Hunton Life Saving and First Aid Crew pose for this photograph taken in the 1950s. The crew was organized in December 1941 by Alexander Terrell. *Harrison Museum*

Several Protestant clergy gathered on January 11 at St. Mark's Lutheran Church to explore starting a Roanoke chapter of the Protestants and Other Americans United for Separation of Church and State (POAU). The Roanoke Ministers Conference agreed to form a committee to explore the possibility after hearing a presentation by Dr. Glenn Archer of Washington, DC.

A gas furnace explosion wrecked the home of Mrs. Mamie Sink at 914 Rockland Avenue NW on January 12. Sink's sister was blown through a bedroom window and taken to Lewis-Gale Hospital for treatment. Roanoke Gas Company investigated the explosion that was the first such incident since the company inaugurated the use of natural gas in 1950. Sink, who operated American Lunch, was not at home at the time.

The Roanoke Junior Woman's Club celebrated its twenty-fifth anniversary on January 12 with a dinner at the Elks Club. Clara Black was the club's first president.

Several stars of the *Grand Ole Opry* performed at the Market Building Auditorium on January 17. Performers included Kitty Wells, Jimmy Dickens, Johnnie and Jack, Del Wood, and the Tennessee Mountain Boys.

Dewey Anderson of Roanoke was given a thirty-day jail sentence on January 13 for refusing to get his son vaccinated in accordance with state law. The case was brought by the city school superintendent.

Roanoke City Manager Arthur Owens demonstrated a "drunkometer" device before physicians and attorneys. The device was used by the Richmond police as a means of determining if someone had been drinking. Owens was seeking to address the situation involving William Bartlett the month prior where medical attention should have been given immediately, but officers erroneously assumed intoxication to be the cause of Bartlett's behavior. The device, an early form of the Breathalyzer, was deemed to be valuable by those in attendance.

Roanoke Life Saving and First Aid Crew purchased a lot at the southeast corner of Day Avenue and Fourth Street SW on January 14 for the future site of their crew hall. The crew was using the garage at John M. Oakey Funeral Home on Luck Avenue SW as their garage and meeting place.

Peoples Federal Savings and Loan Association held an open house on January 14 to officially welcome the public to their new building the former Liberty Trust Building at Salem Avenue and Jefferson Street. An element of the open house was the display of the private coin and currency collection of George Walton.

Ken Davidson, a professional badminton player, gave clinics in Roanoke during the third week of January. Davidson was coach of the US International Campbell Cup team and had held clinics around the world attended by over 13 million people.

Kenrose Manufacturing Company was acknowledged for its tenth anniversary of operations in Roanoke City. It was the city's second-largest manufacturer and third-largest employer. The local Kenrose plant at Center Avenue had 500 machine operators that produced 2,100 dresses daily. Another plant and headquarters were located on Albermale Avenue. Kenrose had an office and show room in New York City and a small plant at Buchanan. Total employment by the company was around 1,400, according to Kenrose founder and president Ben Rosenstein.

Marshall Harris, manager of Woodrum Field, reported in mid-January that 1953 was the airport's best year of operations in its history. Total passenger count was 149,634, a 33 percent increase over 1952. Increases were also reported in the sale of gasoline and in cargo transports.

M. W. Armistead III was named publisher of the *Roanoke Times* and the *Roanoke World-News* on January 18. The announcement was made at the annual meeting of stockholders. Armistead had been on the staff of the newspapers since 1936 and took over from William Smith, who was retiring.

Roanoke Commissioner of the Revenue James Armstrong gave his approval to a suggestion that segregation be abolished in the preparation of real estate assessment books. The practice of separately listing properties owned by whites and Blacks was mandated by state law, but Armstrong said he would explore the possibility of being able to simply list all property owners alphabetically without regard to race. A similar request had been made to Roanoke County by real estate attorneys.

Local aviator and airplane broker Clayton Lemon flew to India to shop for planes. India was nationalizing its airlines so many private airplanes were for sale there.

Former Roanoker Carter Lawrence was named by Virginia Governor-elect Thomas Stanley as his executive secretary. Lawrence had served in the same position for Governors John Battle and William Tuck.

The Regina Hotel opened on January 23 on Route 11, one mile west of Salem. L. T. and Elizabeth Clark were the owners.

Starkey Pawnshop opened in mid-January and was owned and operated by Pat Doran. It was located in the Starkey Grocery and Hardware Building.

Joe Morris and his recording orchestra, Al Savage, Faye Adams, and the Orioles performed for a show and dance at the American Legion Auditorium on February 1. The balcony was reserved for white spectators.

Zinka Milanov, a soprano with the Metropolitan Opera and native of Yugoslavia, performed at the American Legion Auditorium on January 25 under the auspices of the Thursday Morning Music Club.

Oscar Giles Lewis, former mayor of Salem and longtime member of the town council, died on January 25 at his home in Salem. He was eighty-six. He was a member of council for twenty years, being first elected in 1928. In 1938 he was chosen as acting town manager. He was elected as mayor in 1946. He had Roanoke County's first Ford Motor Company franchise, which he operated until 1932.

Mabel Logan of Roanoke succumbed on January 25 to burns she had received a week prior when her clothing caught fire at an oil stove. Logan died at Burrell Memorial Hospital. She had severe burns over almost the entirety of her body. She was thirty-three. Logan's clothing caught fire when she was visiting a friend's home on Gregory Avenue NE.

LeRoy Smith, manager of the Roanoke plant of American Viscose, announced on January 26 that the plant would cease production of tire cord fabric for Firestone Tire and Rubber Company. The plant had been making the cord since 1943 and employed some 300 persons in its production.

Showtimers presented *The Madwoman of Chaillot* for a four-night run at Roanoke College in late January. Evans Evans had the lead role. The play was directed by Betty Thornton.

A group of Salem businessmen launched an effort to revive professional minor league baseball team. In a meeting with George Trautman, president of the National Association of Professional Baseball Leagues, they were rebuffed due to unpaid debts from the Roanoke Red Sox. According to baseball rules, no team could be established in a community where creditors were still owed funds by a prior team.

The first woman jury foreman in Roanoke's history served on a Hustings Court panel on January 27. She was Mrs. Frank Claytor, who was also Black. She headed a jury of eight white men, one white woman, one Black woman, and one Black man.

Gibson Morrissey, conductor of the Roanoke Symphony, told the Roanoke Kiwanis Club on January 27 that half of the orchestra was composed of high school and college students. Consequently, he saw as a core mission of the symphony the encouragement of young musicians.

A missing person mystery that had plagued Roanoke police for several months was finally solved on January 29 when the skeletal remains of Mrs. Helena Pietkiswicz were found on an embankment along the Virginia Railway tracks in the 900 block of Ferdinand Avenue SW. Pietkiswicz was a "displaced person" from World War II who had come to the US from Ukraine. The seventy-year-old had been reported missing on June 14, 1953, by relatives. The remains were discovered by three boys who had been fishing in the Roanoke River and had taken a shortcut home. Carson Horseley, Jerry Horseley, and Clarence Henegar found a skull along the embankment while looking for soft drink bottles. On their way home, they took the skull to Saul Reed, who operated a filling station at Eleventh Street and Loudon Avenue NW. Reed notified the police. For several weeks after Pietkiswicz went missing from her Day Avenue home, Roanoke police followed a variety of leads interviewing friends, neighbors, and relatives. According to the husband, Pietkiswicz had left a suicide note. City police dragged the Roanoke River and the pond at Elmwood Park in their attempts to resolve the case.

The congregation of South Roanoke Baptist Church moved to their new home at 2411 Rosalind Avenue on February 3. The site was formerly the home of South Roanoke Methodist Church. The Baptists paid the Methodists $65,000 for the church. South Roanoke Baptist Church had been located in a small frame church at Carolina Avenue and Twenty-Sixth Street SW.

South Roanoke Methodist Church held their first worship service in their new building at South Jefferson Street and Twenty-Fourth Street on January 31. Bishop Paul Garber consecrated the $350,000 sanctuary that had been designed by Smithey and Boynton Architects.

This 1954 image shows the original South Roanoke Baptist Church on Carolina Avenue. It later became the home of the Roanoke Fine Arts Center. *Historical Society of Western Virginia*

Dr. J. D. Willis, a physician in Roanoke for over forty years, collapsed and died of a heart attack on January 29 in his office in the Medical Arts Building. He was sixty-seven. Willis was a past president of the Roanoke Academy of Medicine and began his practice in Roanoke in 1911.

The Lawson Law Building was formally dedicated on January 31. The two-story brick building was constructed for $45,000 and located at First Street and Gilmer Avenue NW. Rev. A. L. James provided the dedicatory address.

Deputy Clerk of the Roanoke School Board A. F. Fisher released a report on February 2 that stated Black elementary schools were overcrowded, more so than white schools. Gilmer School had 136 more students than it could accommodate, and Loudon School had 80 over its capacity. As for white schools, Forest Park had 119 students over capacity, and Oakland had 88. These were but four examples. According to Fisher, the school system needed twenty-two additional classrooms.

The Groundhog Club of America held its annual meeting at the American Legion Auditorium on February 2. The group dispensed heavy doses of humor largely at the expense of local politicians. Frank Angell was master of ceremonies.

The Magic City Medical Society endorsed Roanoke City's fluoridation plan for its water system during the society's February 3 meeting at Burrell Memorial Hospital.

Harris Cleaners opened their Grandin Road branch on February 4 at 1302 Grandin Road.

The price of coffee had soared due to various embargoes placed against the countries from which it was imported. The Texas Tavern responded to the situation by posting a sign inside the restaurant that read, "Valuable gift offer – 1 Cup of Coffee Absolutely Free with Each Purchase of $100 or More."

The *Ice Vogues of 1954* came for a five-night run at the American Legion Auditorium the first week of February. The show was a production of Morris Chalfen and Sonja Henie that featured eight production scenes for a two-and-a-half-hour show.

Shirley's Restaurant reopened at 2816 Williamson Road on February 17 after being remodeled.

Hollins Lion Club, sponsored by the Vinton Lions Club, received its charter in ceremonies at the Hotel Roanoke on February 5. Miller Petty was president of the Hollins Lions Club.

The Ponce de Leon Coffee Shop opened on February 7. John Hunter was the owner and manager, and Babe Haga was the chef. The shop featured the Panel Room, a private room for groups.

This 1951 image shows the Ponce de Leon Hotel at the corner of Campbell Avenue and Second Street SW. It was the third-largest hotel in the city with 200 rooms. *Historical Society of Western Virginia*

Bishop Paul Garber, head of the Richmond area Methodist Conference, conducted consecration ceremonies at the new South Roanoke Methodist Church on February 7.

A sensational trial ended on February 6 when a jury decided that the will of Roanoke businessman Edgar Thurman was valid. Thurman, partner in the Thurman and Boone furniture store, died and willed an estate valued at $2.6 million to a variety of charities for the benefit of children. The bachelor's nieces and nephews sought to overturn the will by claiming that Thurman had been threatened, coerced, and unduly influenced by his live-in housekeeper, Mrs. Mary Barker. Thurman had left Barker his home on Laburnum Avenue SW. The trial was covered daily on the front page of the local newspapers for the two-week duration. As part of the witness testimony, it was revealed that Thurman had fathered a son early in life, but the son was not a litigant. Further, a nephew, who had assumed management of his uncle's furniture store, testified that Thurman had indicated to him verbally that the store would become the nephew's. The will made no such provision. The jury deliberated a little more than an hour before ruling in favor of upholding the will.

The Barter Theatre presented the comedy *Two on an Island* at the Jefferson High School auditorium on February 11.

Ground-breaking services were held on February 7 for the new Grace Church on Edgewood Street SW. The building's projected cost was $51,000, and the contractor was H. A. Lucas & Sons.

A large neon sign was erected at Archie's Lobster House on Franklin Road SW. The sign was one of the first of its kind in Roanoke and was done by Stanford & Inge. Archie Parrish was the restaurant owner.

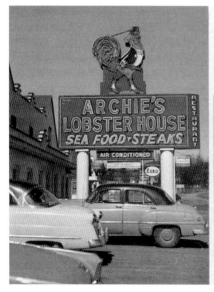

This postcard, which was postmarked 1958, shows Archie's Lobster House and Town House. *Nelson Harris*

Mrs. Vivian Mason, national president of the National Council of Negro Women, addressed the Roanoke chapter of the organization on February 7 at Addison High School.

Raymond Moore and Clyde Bell opened the Villa Heights Barber Shop at 2524 Hanover Avenue NW on February 8.

Roanoke City acquired a strip of business property on February 8 along North Jefferson Street needed for the proposed Jefferson Street viaduct. The property acquired included Barnes Drug Store and the Milner Hotel. The sale delayed the start of condemnation proceedings for other properties.

Roanoke police raided the Anderson Hotel on the evening of February 7 and arrested nine persons on morals charges.

Professional wrestler Gorgeous George came to Roanoke to face George Becker in a night of pro wrestling at the American Legion Auditorium on February 13. The crowd was standing-room only.

More than 1,000 Boy Scouts, Cubs, and Explorers participated in the annual Scout-O-Rama held on February 13 at the marine armory. Paul Reynolds was director of the event.

Renowned duo-pianists Pierre Luboshutz and Genia Nemenoff performed at the American Legion Auditorium on February 17. They were sponsored by the Thursday Morning Music Club. The husband-and-wife team had performed with every major American symphony and with Toscanini.

Andrew Evans purchased the Air-Lee Soda Shop at the intersection of Airport Road and Williamson Road in mid-February. He renamed the business Evans Drugstore.

Moore Business Forms opened its Roanoke sales office at 11 Franklin Road SW on February 15.

Raymond Maxey, captain of the No. 8 Fire Company in Roanoke, collapsed while battling a fire at Roanoke Scrap Iron and Metal Company on February 14. He was taken to Lewis-Gale Hospital, where he died minutes after arrival. Maxey was forty-eight and a resident of Eighth Street SE. Survived by a wife and two children, Maxey's funeral was conducted two days later at Belmont Baptist Church. The scrap iron company was located 2580 Broadway SW.

Mrs. Ida Engleby, a well-known educator and civic leader in Roanoke County, died on February 14. She established the school at the Juvenile Detention Home, where she taught for many years. She ran unsuccessfully for Roanoke County's seat in the Virginia House of Delegates in 1949.

The Wasena Barber Shop at 1118 Main Street SW was heavily damaged by fire on February 13.

A proposal by the Chesapeake and Potomac Telephone Company that several metal telephone booths be placed at strategic locations in downtown Roanoke was rejected by the Roanoke City Council at their meeting on February 15. This was a new idea for the city, and council members and city staff had concerns about blocking off sidewalks and the general appearance of the booths.

This 1950s image by George Davis shows the Wasena Gulf Station located at 1119 Main Street SW. *Virginia Room, RPL*

The YMCA sold its building at the corner of Church Avenue and Second Street SW to the Textile Workers Union Local 11 on February 16 for $255,000. The Y planned to move to its new building at Fifth Street and Church Avenue SW within a few years.

Richard Geary, fourteen, of Roanoke sang on the *Grand Ole Opry* and Ernest Tubb's *Midnight Jamboree* on February 20. The young country music artist was a guest of Jimmy Dickens and Red Foley.

Former speed driver Ab Jenkins spoke to several civic and business groups during a three-day stay in Roanoke in late February. He was touring the country on behalf of Firestone Tire and Rubber Company to talk about highway safety. Jenkins broke many speed records during his professional driving career.

Dr. Benjamin Mays, president of Morehouse College, spoke at First Baptist Church, Gainsboro, on February 21. His appearance was sponsored by the Roanoke Inter-Racial Commission.

Western film star and singer Gene Autry and his horse, Little Champ, performed at the American Legion Auditorium on February 23. Autry was joined by other performers including the Melody Ranch Orchestra, Pat Buttram, Cass County Boys, Rufe Davis, Jemez Indians, Barbara Bardo, and Carl Cotner. Earlier in the day, Autry and his costars performed at the Veterans Administration Hospital.

Pianist Eugene List performed at the Jefferson High School auditorium on February 25. He was part of the Community Concert Association series. List had played with all the major American symphonies.

The Civil Defense Control Center went into service on the first floor of Roanoke's Municipal Building in mid-February. It was constructed in a former vault beneath the main entrance.

A Floyd County man was shot to death by Roanoke police in the early morning hours on February 20 after police discovered him breaking into the Sunoco Service Station at Commonwealth and Gilmer Avenues NE. Arthur Worley of Copper Hill ignored police orders to stop when he broke from the building to run and Patrolman H. A. Thomas and Sgt. J. E. Lemon both discharged their weapons. Worley died at the scene.

Turner Hall, the new dormitory at Hollins College, was dedicated on February 21. The building was named in memory of Joseph Turner, longtime business manager of the college, and his sister, Lelia Turner Rath, a former faculty member. The dorm cost $310,000 and accommodated sixty-eight students.

Virginia's governor signed into law the Shenandoah Life Insurance Company mutualization bill on February 20. The bill allowed the company to complete the conversion from a stock company to a mutual company, a process it had been engaged in for two decades.

Hayes, Seay, Mattern & and Mattern architectural firm broke ground the third week of February on its new building on Franklin Road SW, between King George and Janette Avenues. Martin Brothers was the general contractor. The firm was organized shortly after World War II with the idea to provide full engineering and architectural services within a single company.

This November 1954 image shows the Hayes, Seay, Mattern & Mattern architectural firm building at 1615 Franklin Road SW. *Virginia Room, RPL*

Smokey the Bear received a warm reception in Roanoke when he arrived to help promote the prevention of forest fires. The mascot, a forest service man in bear garb, was welcomed by the mayor, the Jefferson High School Band, the Boy and Girl Scouts, and employees of N&W Railway. He spent a few days visiting local schools.

Dr. Harry Penn proposed to Roanoke City Council at its meeting on February 23 that an interracial commission be established for the purpose of seeking more harmonious working and living conditions between whites and Blacks. One purpose of the commission would be to bring matters of racial discrimination to the attention of the council. The council took the matter under advisement.

Various PTA groups began to align against the suggestion that Roanoke have one consolidated high school. Roanoke School Board members had been discussing building one large high school on the Shrine Hill property in Raleigh Court but had made no definitive moves toward a decision.

Roanoke City Council approved an appropriation of $250 for the purchase of a "Drunk-o-meter" as a scientific means of allowing police to test suspects in regard to intoxication. Six officers were to be trained for its use.

The second annual Golden Gloves Boxing Tournament was held at the American Legion Auditorium the last weekend in February. The local event was sponsored by the Sertoma Club. Over fifty boys and young men participated. James Young, sixteen, of White Sulphur Springs, West Virginia, captured the Most Outstanding Young Boxer award. An estimated 1,000 spectators attended the final night.

Lionel Hampton brought his variety show to the American Legion Auditorium on March 1. Joining Hampton was his son, a four-year-old drummer.

General Electric Company announced on February 26 plans to build a plant in Roanoke County that would eventually employ 2,000 persons. The industry control equipment plant site was a ninety-six-acre tract between Mason's Creek and the Catawba Branch of N&W Railway. It would front on the Veterans Administration Road between Roanoke and Salem. Initial operations were set to begin in 1955 with full operations occurring in late 1957. The plant's anticipated payroll was placed at $8 million annually. It was to be the valley's third-largest employer, behind N&W Railway and American Viscose.

Ruth Ann Gee, a student at Hollins College, became the one millionth passenger of Piedmont Airlines on February 26 when she boarded a Piedmont plane in Roanoke to fly to Richmond. The airlines became the first "feeder" airline in the United States to carry one million passengers. Gee was presented a bouquet of flowers by Roanoke Vice Mayor Robert Woody.

Pat Murphy, fifty-six, was stabbed to death on February 27 in an alley behind 632 Norfolk Avenue SW. Police arrested Sally Biglow for the killing, which she claimed was in self-defense following an argument.

Residential lots in the Lindenwood Park subdivision went up for sale in late February. Lot sales were being handled by J. P. Branecky and H. L. Wright.

Players Incorporated, an international repertory company based in Washington, DC, presented *Othello* at Hollins College on March 1.

Clover Creamery, shown here in the 1950s, was located on Tazewell Avenue SE. *Nelson Harris*

The Kazim Shrine Circus came to the American Legion Auditorium for a three-day run that began March 4. One of the main attractions was the Wallenda Family, tight rope artists.

Officials with General Electric announced on March 1 that its decision to locate a plant in Roanoke County would result in the company moving its headquarters for the industry control business to the new plant. Company officials visited Roanoke and were honored at a dinner at the Hotel Roanoke by the Roanoke Chamber of Commerce.

The Garden Store, owned and operated by William James and Jimmy James, opened at 1322 Grandin Road on March 2.

The W. T. Grant Company store reopened at 21 W. Campbell Avenue after being closed for a substantial remodeling. The store had operated in Roanoke for twenty-six years.

O. P. O. Clothes, a men's store, opened the first week of March at 106 S. Jefferson Street.

McCarty Bedding Company opened on March 5 at 2906 Williamson Road.

Allen's Pharmacy opened on March 5 at 2523 Melrose Avenue NW. It was affiliated with the Rexall Drug Store chain.

Rusty Nichols and Doug Talbert formed a new orchestra that played at local clubs. The group debuted at the Plantation Club, 826 W. Main Street, in Salem on March 6.

William Fleming High School captured the District 6 basketball championship with a 59–51 victory over Martinsville on March 6. Three thousand people watched the game that was played in War Memorial Gymnasium at Virginia Tech.

Harris Hardwood Company erected a new metal-flooring warehouse at its plant in Norwich in early March. The structure cost $100,000 and replaced a warehouse that had been destroyed by fire a few months prior.

Jane Stuart Smith presented an opera recital at Hollins College on March 8. Smith had toured the United States and Europe singing with various opera companies.

General Lawnmower Shop opened on March 8 at 2904 Williamson Road in the former Williamson Road firehouse.

Paint and Wallpaper Service Center opened on March 8 at 120 W. Church Avenue.

Dick Kepley, junior center for the Jefferson High School basketball team, was the Group 1 scholastic basketball scoring champion with an average of 26.2 points per game. He defeated Edgar Baird of Richmond's Thomas Jefferson High School, who often was in the lead during the season.

The scoreboard at Maher Field used for the Roanoke Red Sox games toppled over due to strong winds on March 9. Many likened the fate of the scoreboard as a symbol of the lack of minor league baseball in the Roanoke Valley.

The Salem Lions Club presented its annual minstrel during the second week of March for three nights. Leading the cast of fifty was Salem Mayor James Moyer.

A "Wholesale Row" plan was announced on March 12 for the western end of Patterson Avenue, the site of the old West End Furnace. American Brokerage was the first to commit to that location for its merchandise warehouse.

The Roanoke Symphony Orchestra performed *The Ordering of Moses* along with a 400-voice choir at the American Legion Auditorium on March 15. Gibson Morrissey was the orchestra conductor, and the lead singers were Florence Vickland, Hartwell Phillips, Thilde Beuing, and Jack Wimmer.

Parisian Nights Revue came to the Roanoke Theatre on March 17, featuring showgirls and the Jimmy Jackson Quartette.

Billy Eckstine, Ruth Brown, the Clovers, and Johnny Hodges performed for a show and dance at the American Legion Auditorium on March 18. White spectators were admitted.

Officials with the Virginia Amateur League announced in mid-March that seven teams would compete during the 1954 season, and those were Glenvar, Elliston, New Castle, Buchanan, Blacksburg, Veterans Administration, and Roanoke. W. C. Woods was the league president. Salem opted to switch to the Virginia Mountain League. Efforts by Salem to field a semipro Class D league team fell through.

William Fleming High School won the state Group II basketball championship on March 13 at Blacksburg. They defeated Bristol, 71–58. Corbin Bailey, Fleming guard, was named as the outstanding player of the tournament. Phil Crabtree was the Colonels' coach. Other members of the team included Bill Bryant, Denny Weddle, John Willhide, P. T. Johnson, Wesley Ayers, Leon Turner, Russell Moon, Carlton Assaid, Bob Stevens, Bill Stevens, and Johnny Martin.

The Mexican Craft Shop reopened on March 16 on Route 11 directly across from Hollins College. Ads read, "We have just returned from a six week shopping tour in Old Mexico." The store was owned by R. B. Preston.

Ireland's Dublin Players presented *The Playboy of the Western World* at Hollins College on March 17. The lead roles were played by Phyllis Ryan and James Kenny.

William Flowers, president of the National Bar Association, spoke at the memorial service of Gamma Alpha Chapter of Omega Psi Phi Fraternity held at High Street Baptist Church on March 14.

The Roanoke Merchants Association agreed to not hold the 1954 Christmas Parade before Thanksgiving in response to concerns of the Roanoke Ministers Conference and other groups that doing so added to the commercialization of the holiday.

Mrs. James Riggle of Roanoke and Mrs. Hugh Lee of Salem were named as the winners of the "Mrs. Roanoke" and "Mrs. Salem" contest on March 16. The winners received a one-hundred-dollar wardrobe from Heironimus and one hundred dollars worth of groceries from Mick-or-Mack. The contestants were judged on table decorations, their planning balanced meals, and their preparation of a dinner menu for Roanoke Gas Company. Local winners were eligible to compete in the state contest.

South Salem Christian Church voted in mid-March to change its name to First Christian Church of Salem. The church was organized in 1891 and was the first Disciples of Christ congregation in the Salem area. Rev. Virgil Lilly was the pastor.

The Lee-Hi Drive-in Theatre advertised that it had installed new projection equipment such that it was the first drive-in with wide-screen viewing in Virginia when it opened for the season on March 19.

H. C. Barnes Drug Store moved to 130 W. Campbell Avenue in late March. It had been in its original location at 2 S. Jefferson Street for sixty-three years. The reason for the move was to make way for the viaduct.

An automobile collision at Dale Avenue and Eleventh Street SE on March 20 killed Richard Peggins, thirty-one, of Roanoke. Peggins was an employee of the Roanoke Bridge & Iron Works.

Caldwell-Sites opened their newest warehouse at Tenth and Tinker Streets in Vinton in mid-March.

Organization of a new Baptist church in the Rosalind Hills section was announced in late March for April 4 on a lot purchased in 1950 for that purpose. A three-and-a-half acre tract had been acquired by the Roanoke Missionary and Social Union that fronted Route 11 and extended back to Laburnum Avenue SW. A group of Baptists had been meeting in the home of Leslie Ellis at 2642 Laburnum Avenue since that time. Rev. H. W. Connelly was the pastor of what would become Rosalind Hills Baptist Church.

Carl Smith, the Carlisles, Betty Amos, Richard Geary, and the Wood Sisters presented a *Grand Ole Opry* Show at the American Legion Auditorium on March 28.

Salem officials selected Carver School to be the site of the new playground for Blacks, replacing the one on Water Street.

Gene Sweeney opened Crescent Flying School at Woodrum Field in mid-March. He had logged more than 10,000 hours of flying time and held twenty different ratings with the CAA. Among Sweeney's accomplishments were fifty-one round trips over the Pacific and a dozen over the Atlantic. He also piloted the fifth

American plane to ever land in Shanghai. He was also a founder of the Acorn Flying Club in Roanoke.

The Roanoke County School Board purchased a ten-acre plot on Catawba Mountain Road near Pratt's Store for the purpose of erecting a future school. The land was purchased from C. P. Horne.

Junius P. Fishburn, fifty-eight, died of a cerebral hemorrhage at a hospital in Washington, DC, on March 24. Fishburn was in the city participating in hearings before the FCC about the application of the Times-World Corporation for a television license. Fishburn was president of the Times-World Corporation, a position he had held since 1923. Fishburn was a leader in many civic and business organizations in Roanoke.

Betty Jean Rivers, twenty, was sentenced to fifteen years in prison after pleading guilty to the slaying of James Hamilton in December 1953. Judge Dirk Kuyk imposed the sentence.

Dick Kepley of Jefferson High School was named to the 1954 All-Group 1 scholastic basketball team of the Associated Press sportswriters in Virginia. Kepley set a new per-game average record in Virginia of 26.2 points per contest on 471 points in eighteen games.

Crobuck's Drug & Variety Store opened on March 26 at 2310 Melrose Avenue NW. They offered a quart of free ice cream with each prescription and free bottles of aspirin.

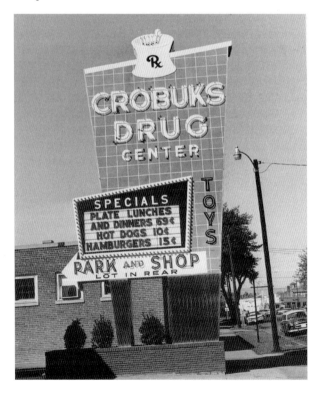

This mid-'50s photo shows the sign for Crobuck's, which was located at 2310 Melrose Avenue NW. The drugstore opened in 1954. *Virginia Room, RPL*

United Pawn Shop opened at its new location on Salem Avenue in late March. Joel Krisch was the owner. The pawn shop was forced to relocate due to the plans for the viaduct.

Three N&W Railway brakemen in Roanoke brought a suit against the railroad and the Brotherhood of Railroad Trainmen in US District Court on March 26 for discrimination. Sam Clark, Robert Coles, and Robert Hamlar charged that they did not get promotions because they were Black. Each had worked for the railroad for over thirty years. The three sued for damages of $115,000 and asked the court to stop the railroad and union from practicing discrimination. According to the suit, a union contract classified Negro brakemen as "non-promotable." Further, the union prohibited Blacks from its membership, yet the union was responsible for negotiating the work contracts for brakemen. The suit was filed by George Lawrence, a Roanoke attorney, associated with a Washington, DC, law firm.

Grace Church held a cornerstone-laying ceremony on March 28 at its site on Edgewood Street SW.

Buddy Johnson and his orchestra, along with singers Norma Lewis and Ella Johnson, performed for a show and dance at the American Legion Auditorium on March 31. White spectators were admitted to the balcony.

Hypnotist and magician Polgar performed at the American Legion Auditorium on April 3.

Mayfair Cafeteria, DuPont Nyloners, and Grayson All-Stars captured championships in the A, B, and C divisions of the Southwest Virginia Gold Medal Basketball Tournament held at Monroe Junior High School on March 27.

After being closed for over three years, Pre-Shrunk Masonry Sales Corporation resumed production of its masonry products in late March. Prior to closing, it was one of the largest producers of cinder block in the South. M. W. Ferguson was the company's president.

Over 2,250 employees of N&W Railway returned to work on March 29 after being furloughed for a week due to a drop in business. Most of those furloughed worked in Roanoke.

Parents of Dewey Anderson withdrew their son from Virginia Heights Elementary School in late March after they refused to comply with having him vaccinated for smallpox according to state law. The child was enrolled in a private school.

A forest fire burned over fifteen acres on Fort Lewis Mountain in late March.

The Vinton Lions Club held their annual minstrel show at William Byrd High School the first weekend in April. The show raised funds for the club's community projects.

A bond referendum passed with voters in Salem on March 30. The main bond issue totaled $1 million and was for connecting Salem sewer lines with those of Roanoke City. By a margin of 3 to 1, voters approved the measure that paved the way to eliminate Salem dumping raw sewage into the Roanoke River.

Williamson Road Dairy Bar Restaurant opened on March 31 at 4608 Williamson Road NW.

Roanoke's civil defense truck arrived on March 30. The truck carried hundreds of pieces of equipment including gas masks, torches, crow bars, and hammers for use in the aftermath of bombing raids. The truck was housed at Fire Station No. 1 on E. Church Avenue.

The Roanoke County Board of Supervisors rezoned a ninety-six-acre parcel on March 30 for heavy industry to make way for the planned General Electric plant.

Postal officials announced on March 31 that the fourth-class post offices at Starkey and Airpoint would close on April 30. The Airpoint post office served about sixty families and had been in operation for almost a century. Miss Inez Conner was the postmaster at Airpoint, which was located in her father's grocery store filling station. The Starkey post office opened in 1892 as Farland with Miss Mantle Short as the postmaster. At the time of the announcement, Estes Terry was the postmaster, and the post office was located in Terry's television and radio repair shop near the N&W Railway depot.

Paul Hahn, a trick shot artist with golf balls, gave an exhibition on April 3 at Hidden Valley Country Club. Hahn had traveled the world conducting his clinic-style play.

Elder D. C. Naff, a minister in the Church of the Brethren for more than fifty years, died at his home on Cove Road on March 31. He was seventy-eight. Among the congregations served was Peters Creek Church of the Brethren, his home church.

Johnny Green was struck and killed by the Southern Railway passenger train, the *Tennessean*, on April 1. Green, age eight, was on his way home from school and was crossing the double N&W Railway tracks at Glenvar when the accident occurred. Two other students from Fort Lewis Elementary School witnessed the tragedy, and both stated the train blew its whistle twice. Green was apparently watching another train and did not see or hear the Southern locomotive. The victim was the son of Mr. and Mrs. T. L. Green of the Waldron community.

Otha Taylor drew a twenty-seven year prison sentence in the death of Andrew Ensley and the wounding of William Dungee. He pled guilty to both charges.

The Trail Drive-In Theatre opened for the summer season on April 2 by advertising a new "curved wide screen."

Mrs. James Riggle of Roanoke won the "Mrs. Virginia" crown in Richmond on April 2. She had been crowned "Mrs. Roanoke" and with the state title was qualified to compete in the "Mrs. America" contest in Florida.

Kay's Ice Cream opened a new store at Eleventh Street and Center Avenue NW on April 3.

The twenty-seventh annual spring congress of the Gill Memorial Eye, Ear, Nose and Throat Hospital opened on April 5 with 400 doctors from across the United States in attendance. Faculty for the congress was headed by Dr. Paul Hawley, director of the American College of Surgeons.

A three-day Roanoke Auto Show was held at Merchants Parking Center the first week in April. All area car dealerships participated to showcase their 1954 models. It was the first auto show in Roanoke in almost two decades.

The Wildwood Civic League at a meeting on April 5 suggested proposed that a new park located between Route 460 and Vinton be named "Thrasher Memorial Park" after a pioneer family in that area. Paul and Sally Thrasher settled in the area, and their home was a popular with visiting clergy. The civic league had planted numerous trees and shrubs in the park.

In the Democratic primary for Roanoke City Council held on April 6, Paul Puckett, Roy Webber, and Walter Young prevailed. Webber and Young were incumbents, though Puckett led in votes received. Lester Hutts finished fourth. The number of voters participating was 3,389.

The Virginian Railway Company petitioned the SCC on April 6 to abandon passenger service in the state on the basis that it was a deficit operation. According to the railway's president, the company carried an average of 1.6 passengers per railway mile in Virginia during 1953. The Virginian inaugurated passenger service in 1909 and in the 1920s was carrying over one million passengers per year.

M. W. Armistead III was named as the head of the Times-World Corporation on April 7. He succeeded the late Junius P. Fishburn, who had died on March 24.

Hake Manufacturing Company of Depew, New York, announced on April 7 it would relocate to Roanoke within sixty days. The plastics manufacturer employed about one hundred persons.

Allen Fry, forty-three, of Roanoke died in a fire at a tourist cabin on Route 11 just north of Roanoke on April 7. Fire officials believed he had been smoking in bed and fell asleep as the mattress caught on fire.

First services for the Westhampton Christian Church were held on April 11 in the Grandin Court Recreation Center.

This 1950s image shows Elbe Reed (right) in his store on Route 221 at Bent Mountain. His store also served as the post office. *Virginia Room, RPL*

Roanoke's Easter Seals campaign kicked off on April 10 with an appearance by Betty Ann Grove, singing star of *The Big Pay Off*, a daytime television show. Grove appeared on a WSLS telecast from Appalachian Auditorium that also included the Freddie Lee Orchestra and the Jefferson High School choir. Easter lilies were sold in downtown Roanoke as a means of assisting the campaign.

The Cosmopolitan Enterprise Agency, a partnership of Clarence Davis and James Chambers, opened on April 8.

The New York Symphony Orchestra performed at the American Legion Auditorium on April 10. The 104-member orchestra was conducted by Dimitri Mitropoulos. The concert was sponsored by the Thursday Morning Music Club. Local restaurant owner Nick Thanos was provided a personal meeting with Mitropoulos as twenty-four years prior he had sung as a tenor in Athens, Greece, during a performance with Mitropoulos.

The Seated Woman, a painting by Pablo Picasso, was displayed at the Roanoke Public Library as part of an exhibition by the Roanoke Fine Arts Center. The Picasso was on loan from the Museum of Modern Art in New York City.

Roanoke City Council formally terminated the lease of Maher Field by the defunct Roanoke Red Sox on April 12. The action allowed the city to open the field for other uses and agreements.

Three racing promoters presented Roanoke City Council with requests to allow stock car auto racing at Victory Stadium. Council delayed taking any action until officials with Memorial and Crippled Children's Hospital could be heard on the matter. The council's Stadium Advisory Committee was on record as opposing the request.

A movement to draft Roanoke's Assistant Commonwealth's Attorney Beverly Fitzpatrick fell short in mid-April when Fitzpatrick announced he would not be a candidate in the June Democratic primary to field a candidate against Rep. Richard Poff in November. Roanoke Democrats had hoped to field a local candidate in the Sixth District primary contest.

Count Basie and his orchestra performed for a show and dance at the American Legion Auditorium on April 18. The balcony was reserved for white spectators.

Dominion Company, a real estate and insurance firm, opened on April 15 at 1320-A Grandin Road SW. The firm was owned by Charlie McNulty and Bill Towles.

Garland's Amana Food Plan, an appliance store, opened at 1328 Grandin Road SW on April 16. Frank Mundy was the manager.

An English cocker spaniel was judged Best in Show at the nineteenth annual Roanoke Kennel Club dog show held at Victory Stadium on April 15. The dog was owned by Giralda Farms in New Jersey. There were 432 dogs entered in the show.

The board of directors of the Memorial and Crippled Children's Hospital was of the unanimous opinion in opposition to auto racing at Victory Stadium due to noise. The board expressed the opinion in a letter to the Roanoke City Council.

The *Country-Western Caravan* show came to the American Legion Auditorium on April 26. Performers included Hank Snow, Minnie Pearl, Charlie Arthur, Chet

Atkins, Betty Cody, Davis Sisters, Hawkshaw Hawkins, Eddie Hill, and Hal "Lome Pine."

Garden Week was observed in Roanoke April 28–29. Homes on the tour included *Lindisfarne* of Dr. and Mrs. Edwin Palmer, *Annsfad* of Ernest Fishburn, *Woods End* of George Ellis, *Merimont* of Grattan Lindsey Jr., the home of John Windel, and the home of Harley Vaughan.

Francis Cocke, president of First National Exchange Bank of Roanoke, announced in mid-April plans to expand the bank. The $500,000 building plan would extend the bank's building along Campbell Avenue.

Barter Theatre presented the comedy *Mr. Pim Passes By* at the Jefferson High School auditorium on April 20. The lead actors were Owen Phillips and Dorothy Lavern.

Vivian Craighead, forty-six, of Roanoke County was found dead in a cabin at the Welcome Valley Tourist Court on Route 220 on April 18. The cause of death was a severe head injury. A few days later, Linwood Burroughs confessed to staying with Craighead at the cabin where they had registered as husband and wife. Burroughs told authorities that she had slipped and hit her head on the baseboard. Burroughs was not charged in relation to her death but was charged with unlawful cohabitation. Craighead was married. Burroughs was from Bedford. Based upon the coroner's report and the sheriff's department investigation, Commonwealth's Attorney Edward Richardson concluded Craighead's death was accidental.

The Easter sunrise service at Natural Bridge drew an estimated 20,000. Rev. A. H. Hollingsworth, pastor of Roanoke's Second Presbyterian Church, delivered the sermon, which was broadcast nationally over the CBS radio network.

The City of Roanoke purchased an old pontoon bridge from the Fifth Engineer Corps, USMCR, to move pedestrians across the Roanoke River between Victory Stadium and South Roanoke Park. The purchase price was fifty dollars. The bridge was to be stored at the marine armory when not in use.

Shenandoah Life Stations broke ground on its new radio and television center in late April at Church Avenue and Third Street SW. The building would house WSLS radio and WSLS-TV, along with a branch office of the insurance company.

Two miniature golf courses, the Minnie Tour and Wee-Tee, opened for the season in late April. They were located across from Lakeside and on Lee Highway between Roanoke and Salem, respectively.

Roanoke City Clerk Maston Moorman resigned in late April to assume the position of administrator of Shenandoah Hospital. Moorman had been clerk since 1947.

Equipment for a 200-bed emergency hospital was acquired for Roanoke in connection with its Civil Defense program. The equipment was stored at Hollins College. The college agreed to serve as a hospital should Roanoke suffer an enemy attack.

The newly formed Blue Ridge Negro Amateur Baseball League began its season on May 1. The eight teams were as follows: Roanoke Royals, managed by J. C. Simms; Roanoke Cardinals, managed by James Jones; Radford Athletics, managed by Walter Hickman; Wake Forest Eagles, managed by R. S. Milton; Altavista Senators, managed by J. C. King; Rocky Mount Hawks, managed by

Theodore Muse; Rocky Mount Clippers, managed by Alfred Hicks; and the Hooker (Martinsville) Red Socks, managed by Grant Wilson. League president was Woodrow Gaitor.

The Orange Avenue YWCA was dedicated on April 25. Guest speaker was Dr. John Everett, president of Hollins College. The Y was located at Orange Avenue and Peach Road NW. An estimated 250 persons attended the event that was presided over by Mrs. Madge Wheaton.

Roanoke City Council at its April 26 meeting banned auto racing at Victory Stadium indefinitely. Only Mayor Roy Webber dissented in the vote. The council majority deemed auto racing to be a nuisance to the patients at Memorial and Crippled Children's Hospital. The council had received letters and a 1,000-name petition in support of racing.

Elizabeth Hambrick, a senior at William Fleming High School, won the girls' state high school public speaking championship that was held at the University of Virginia.

Clem Johnston of Roanoke was elected president of the US Chamber of Commerce at the chamber's forty-second annual meeting in Washington, DC, on April 28. Johnston, fifty-seven, was a wholesale grocer and had served in various leadership positions within the chamber and with other organizations. He also had a 450-acre cattle farm outside of Roanoke.

Stuart Saunders was appointed vice president and general counsel of N&W Railway on April 28. Saunders had been with the railroad's legal department since 1951. He was the youngest person to hold the position of general counsel in the company's history.

Louis Armstrong performed for a floor show and dance at the American Legion Auditorium on May 3. The balcony was reserved for white spectators.

Koppers Company announced on April 29 that it would build and operate a wood preserving plant two miles west of Salem, which would employ sixty persons. The announcement was made by Walter Arnold, vice president of the company that was headquartered in Pittsburgh.

The Texas Tavern announced the opening of its newest Texas Tavern...in Kobe, Japan. Ads that ran on April 30 stated that the new restaurant would operate under the personal supervision of Harold Woods Jr., formerly of Woods Brothers Coffee. "We cordially invite all our old friends and customers to visit the newest Texas Tavern on your next trip to Kobe."

Meyer Hotels withdrew its management of the Patrick Henry Hotel effective June 30, though it retained a financial interest in the hotel. Meyer Hotels had managed the hotel since 1925. The Patrick Henry was to be managed locally with John Shires being appointed as the general manager. The hotel was owned by the New Hotel Corporation of Roanoke. John Parrott was secretary-treasurer of the NHC.

Lawrence Memorial Methodist Church at Bent Mountain dedicated its sanctuary on May 2 during a note-burning ceremony. The structure was built in 1947. The original church, known as Mt. Zion Methodist Church, was built in 1896 and sold to the Primitive Baptists when the new church was constructed.

This mid-1950s image shows the Patrick Henry Hotel on Jefferson Street SW, as viewed from the roof the Roanoke Public Library. *Virginia Room, RPL*

Officials with the Miss Virginia Pageant announced in early May that the 1954 pageant would be held in Roanoke at the Hotel Roanoke. The Valley Junior Woman's Club was given the state franchise. It would be the first time Roanoke hosted the event. The event in prior years had been held at Cape Charles and Norfolk.

Camporees were quite popular for Boy Scouts during the 1950s. This image shows the camporee held at Victory Stadium in May 1954. *WSLS-TV News Film Collection, UVA Libraries*

The American Bridge Division Plant in Roanoke was working on 7,000 tons of steel in early May for the Hudson River Crossing, a large segment of the New York State Thruway.

The Boy Scout Camporee was held the first weekend in May at Victory Stadium. An estimated 4,000 boys participated in the annual event. A main attraction during the camporee was the appearance of the Cisco Kid on Saturday. Various bands also performed during the evening events.

Members of the Roanoke Chapter, UDC, attempted in May to contact descendants of Confederate soldiers buried in Mountain View Cemetery at Vinton. The chapter intended to erect a memorial stone at the cemetery later in the month. At least forty known Confederate veterans were interred at Mountain View, and many unknown were also buried there according to the chapter. The first burial in the land, which later became the cemetery, was in 1889. The dead were two small girls who had been killed by a train.

Jesse Sink of Roanoke was shot and killed on May 2 by Bruce Lail. The two had an argument, and Lail admitted he shot Sink to police. Sink was shot at Lail's home on Route 11.

Dr. Robert Newman of Vinton, a physician for forty-three years, died on May 3 at the age of sixty-eight. Newman had practiced medicine in Vinton since he moved to the town in 1929. He was also a member of the N&W Railway surgical staff.

An intensive search was conducted by the Roanoke County sheriff's department for three young boys who went missing on May 3 after they left home to attend Clearbrook School. Nolan Johnson, Lomax Johnson, and Roger Johnson had been missing for forty hours when the sheriff launched an aggressive publicity campaign to bring attention to the search. All were brothers and the sons of Mr. and Mrs. Joe Johnson, who lived near Wright's Siding at Starkey. On May 5, neighbors found the boys when they crossed a road in search of food. Apparently the brothers skipped school and were afraid to return home and face their parents.

Frank Angell started his new business, Angell Mortgage and Realty Company, in early May. He had previously worked for Shenandoah Life Insurance, which his father helped to start.

The Jewell Gospel Singers and Orchestra performed at the Star City Auditorium on May 9. The group was from Jewell Academy and Seminary in Nashville, Tennessee.

The local teams in the Virginia Mountain Baseball League opened their season on May 7. Salem played Roanoke at Salem Municipal Field. The Virginia Amateur Baseball League opened its season on May 8. Teams were Buchanan, Glenvar, New Castle, Salem, Elliston-Lafayette-Shawsville, and Back Creek. W. C. Woods was league president.

Mrs. Dorothy Deyerle of Roanoke, who was an employee of Rusco Window Company, was featured in an article in the May 9 edition of *Parade Magazine* on working mothers.

Wigington Jeweler opened at 1302-A Grandin Road on May 10. H. C. Wigington was the owner.

Glamour Girl Revue came to the stage of the Roanoke Theatre on May 12.

A citywide campaign to raise $150,000 for the Preston Park Memorial Center was launched on May 10. Judge K. A. Pate was honorary chairman of the campaign. The proposed center was to include a recreation center, swimming pool, athletic fields, and picnic areas on a nine-acre tract opposite Preston Park Elementary School.

Plans for a new barn at Mercy House were unveiled in early May. Materials and labor were donated by the Roanoke and Salem building trades firms. The barn would contain a milking parlor, pasteurizing room, and feed room.

North Cross School celebrated its tenth anniversary with the spring dance recital on May 15 in the Andrew Lewis High School auditorium.

The Children's Zoo on Mill Mountain prepared for the season with the addition of a new entrance that included blocks as pillars with letters that spelled out "Baby Pets," which supported an arch sign that read, "Children's Zoo."

The Clearbrook Lions Club received its charter on May 7 in a ceremony at Clearbrook School. Paul Hartman was president of the new club.

Charles Quinn, a former employee of N&W Railway, was profiled in the May 11 edition of the *Roanoke Times* about the early days of the city. He recalled coming to Roanoke in 1901 as an electrical engineer for the railroad. "If anyone built a house on Jefferson Street south of Mountain Avenue, they were ridiculed. 'What did that fool out that house way out in the country for?' people asked. And on Campbell Avenue there was only one building, a small store, in the block between First and Second Streets SW. You could live at the Hotel Roanoke, meals included, for $35 per month."

This 1950s postcard shows the main entrance to the Children's Zoo. The blocks spelling out the zoo's name were added in 1954. *Nelson Harris*

Roanoke City Council voted at their May 10 meeting to demolish the remaining wooden stands at Maher Field rather than repair them. Box seats that belonged to the defunct Roanoke Red Sox would remain with a seating capacity of 650.

Roanoke City Council elected Robert Thomas as the new city clerk to succeed the retiring Maston Moorman. Thomas was an assistant city auditor and one of nine candidates to apply. Thomas began his duties on May 17.

Some 700 Episcopal clergy filled the nave of St. John's Episcopal Church on May 13 as nineteen bishops consecrated Rev. William Marmion bishop of the Episcopal Diocese of Southwestern Virginia.

Lloyd Engleby Sr., fifty-nine, died at a Roanoke hospital on May 13. He was head of Engleby Electric Company, a position he assumed in 1918 upon the death of his father.

The stained glass windows at Huntington Court Methodist Church were dedicated on May 16. The guest speaker was Dr. Manning Paris, editor of the *Upper Room*. The windows were given by Minnie Webb in memory of Dr. Frank Richardson, former pastor.

The Jefferson High School golf team won the annual Virginia High School League golf tournament held in Portsmouth with an aggregate team total of 670 for thirty-six holes. Jefferson's foursome was composed of Jimmy Darby, David Edmunds, George Kosko, and Paul Kosko.

The cornerstone for the new Burrell Memorial Hospital was laid in a ceremony on May 16. Speakers at the occasion included Dr. L. C. Downing and Dr. J. H. Roberts, two of the hospital's cofounders. James Lewis was the hospital administrator. Several hundred attended the event.

This clip shows Maher Field's wooden baseball stands prior to its partial demolition in May 1954. *WSLS-TV News Film Collection, UVA Libraries*

Douglas Brown, five, of Roanoke County died on May 16 after being struck by a car on Route 220 just south of Roanoke. The boy and his sister were playing along the highway when he was hit.

The US Supreme Court rendered a decision on May 17 that segregation in public schools was unconstitutional. The decision was met with silence by local school board members and superintendents. The only school leader who offered an opinion was Rev. A. L. James, member of the Roanoke School Board. "The Supreme Court…handed down a decision which meets the approval of all who believe in the practice of true democracy and the teachings of brotherhood. God has made of one blood all the nations of men to dwell on the face of the earth."

Kroger opened its newly remodeled store on May 18 at 3215 Williamson Road. The store's remodel cost $149,000 and brought the length of the store to 210 feet, nearly five times the length of an average grocery store in Roanoke. Paxton Judge was the branch manager.

The Theron Williams Negro Community Center was formally opened in Salem on May 23. Dr. W. R. Brown served as master of ceremonies.

Allen's Hair Styling and Reducing Salon opened on May 20 at 137 W. Campbell Avenue.

Wes Livengood and Pat Colgan, scouts with the Philadelphia Phillies, conducted a baseball school in Wasena Park the third weekend in May for boys between the ages of eight and twelve.

Brown's Beauty Salon opened on May 21 at 420 Hershberger Road NW.

A ground-breaking ceremony was held on May 22 for the new building for Second Methodist Church of Salem. The structure was to be located on South

College Avenue and cost $100,000. Mrs. Sarah Trent moved the first shovel of dirt, being the last living charter member of the congregation.

Twenty-three sirens that composed Roanoke's air raid warning system were mass tested at noon on Saturday, May 22. The event was coordinated through the Civil Defense Communications in city hall. Robert Thomas was the city's Civil Defense coordinator. Roanokers were asked to mail in coupons printed in newspapers as to the level of sound they heard.

N&W Railway brought its longest locomotive to Roanoke on May 22. Labeled as the world's longest, the engine was en route to the Bluefield Coal Show. Built by the Baldwin-Lima-Hamilton Locomotive Works near Philadelphia, it was 161 feet in length and weighed 586 tons. Locomotive No. 2300 was a coal-burning steam turbine electric. It could achieve a maximum speed of sixty miles per hour.

The Roanoke Symphony Orchestra performed at the Jefferson High School auditorium on May 24. The program included Dvorak's *New World Symphony No. 5*, Mozart's *Concerto for Horn No. 2*, and Borodine's *Polovetsian Dances* from *Prince Igor*. Attendance was estimated at 500.

Rusco Window Company held a ribbon-cutting ceremony on May 21 at its new building on Route 11 between Roanoke and Salem. The company was organized in 1947 and was owned and operated by R. J. Grammer and Alton Robertson.

Luke's Hamburger Haven Dari-Delite opened on May 23 on Lee Highway just west of Roanoke and next to the Lee-Hi Pool.

George Fulton Sr., Roanoke auto dealer, died at age fifty-six at his home on May 23. He moved to Roanoke in 1932 and had opened his dealership.

Rev. F. E. Alexander of Roanoke joined Oliver Hill and three other Black leaders for a press event in Richmond on May 24 to call on Virginia's governor to lead the way in removing barriers to integration of public schools in the South.

Grady Cates, owner of C. Grady Cates Inc., a metal buildings product firm, died on May 25 at age sixty-two. Cates came to Roanoke in 1912 and opened his business in the city in 1921.

Shank Furniture Company in Salem went out of business in late May. They auctioned off their stock by conducting two auctions daily for several days.

City work crews began dismantling the wooden stands at Maher Field on May 26. The stands were nicknamed the "splinter bowl" and were constructed from salvaged lumber when wooden bleachers were cleared to make way for Victory Stadium. The stands were mostly used for baseball games, particularly by the Roanoke Red Sox.

Many employees at the American Viscose plant in Roanoke believed the company's closure of the plant in Marcus Hook, Pennsylvania, would be a boon to the Roanoke plant, as the same products manufactured at Marcus Hook could be produced at Roanoke.

Campbell Furniture Company at 123 E. Campbell Avenue went out of business at the end of May.

Charles Brown, Johnny Ace and his orchestra, and Willie Mae "Big Mama" Thornton played for a show and dance at the American Legion Auditorium on May 30. The balcony was reserved for white spectators.

This 1951 photo shows the Sportsman, located at the northwest corner of Church Avenue and Jefferson Street. The second floor was a billiards room, and the third floor was a duck pin bowling alley. *Historical Society of Western Virginia*

Roanoke City Council met for the first time in its newly remodeled chambers on June 1. The room doubled as a courtroom with a seven-chair jury box and witness box that could be rolled away for council meetings.

The Roanoke Chapter of the United Daughters of the Confederacy dedicated a memorial stone on May 29 in honor of Confederate veterans buried at Mountain View Cemetery in Vinton. Nearly one hundred descendants of the veterans attended the event. Mrs. Leonard Key was in charge of the program.

The Floyd Speedway, located on Route 8 a mile outside of Floyd, opened on May 30 under the management of Curtis Turner of Roanoke. A crowd estimated at 3,200 attended the inaugural races.

The Williamson Road Lions Club presented *Broadway Toppers* at the American Legion Auditorium on June 12. The show and dance featured the Charm Sisters, Rex Kramer, Mike Monroe, the Great Ray-Mond and his Musical Maidens, and Jimmy Jackson with his Pit Band.

Ralph Escoe won the annual city-county marbles championship on May 29. The final round of the tournament was held in Elmwood Park. Escoe, thirteen, was a student at Lee Junior High School. Dickie Orr placed second.

The N&W Railway Band gave its final performance at the Bluefield Coal Show in late May. The band had been in existence for seventy-one years and was originally founded in 1883 as the Roanoke Machine Works Band. G. F. Fraser of

London, England, started the group. Declining rail revenues and subsequent economic measures were the reasons given for the band's dissolution.

Gorgeous George teamed up with Hans Schnabel in a tag team wrestling against the Beckers Brothers for the feature match at the American Legion Auditorium on June 1.

Grading for the new General Electric plant near Salem began on June 3. Robertson-Henry Company of Huntington, West Virginia, was the contractor for the work on the ninety-six-acre site.

Clara Ward and the Ward Singers, a gospel group, performed at the Star City Auditorium on June 6.

Roanoke City Council voted at its June 1 meeting to impose a 1:00 a.m. curfew on drive-in theatres due to noise complaints. Councilman Walter Young, sponsor of the measure, also voiced concerns about young people staying out too late due to midnight showings.

Ground-breaking services were held on June 13 at Central Church of the Brethren at 416 Church Avenue SW for their new $100,000 education building.

Sunshine and Meeker-Durant, dry cleaners, merged and relocated to 20 E. Campbell Avenue in early June.

Augustus Hylton, a member of the Vinton Town Council, died on June 3 at his home. He was serving out his second term. He was eighty-one.

The Henry Hill Bell Tower at Roanoke College was dedicated on June 5 as part of the college's annual Alumni Day program.

Ground-breaking services for the construction of the $125,000 Church of Christ of Salem were held on June 6. The first shovels of dirt were turned by two living charter members, Mr. and Mrs. B. V. Duke. The church was organized in 1904 and had 400 members. It was located on W. Main Street.

The Brambleton Junior Woman's Club held its third annual carnival to benefit the Retarded Children's School in mid-June. The carnival was held in Raleigh Court Park. The school was two rooms at West End School dedicated to fifteen students.

W. B. Clements Inc. opened at its new location at 534 W. Campbell Avenue on June 5. The auto parts firm had operated in Roanoke for seventeen years.

Swartz and Company began advertising in early June a new invention for commercial kitchens—the rotisserie barbeque machine.

George Fulton Jr. won the city-county golf tournament that was held the first weekend in June. Connie Sellers placed second. Fulton carded a three-round score of 288. The tournament was held at Hidden Valley Country Club.

Marvin Martin, an escaped patient from the Veterans Administration Hospital, was captured on June 8 after an intensive manhunt by the Roanoke County Sheriff's Department. Martin had been hiding in woods in the South Salem section for about two weeks, robbing homes of groceries and other items. Finally, a young boy saw the man hiding in his playhouse and the mother contacted authorities. He had been missing from the hospital since April 25.

Mayor James Moyer, James Peters, Howard Roberts, and Emmett Hart won seats on Salem's new five-person town council in an election held on June 8. They were selected from among ten candidates on the ballot. In Vinton, S. M. Craig, O. L. Horn, and S. D. Crowder were elected to the town council from among seven candidates. In Roanoke, three candidates, all Democrats and unopposed, were elected to the city council—Paul Puckett, Walter Young, and Mayor Roy Webber.

Flames ignited by a lightning strike destroyed the home of Mr. and Mrs. Price Lawrence in Clearbrook on June 9. The only things saved from the home were the clothes the couple was wearing when they fled the house.

Barney Haley, a Boy Scout leader, was named as Roanoke's Father of the Year by the Roanoke Junior Chamber of Commerce. He received a trophy in ceremonies held at the American Theatre on June 16.

Billy Ward and his 60-Minute Men, the Dominoes, and Paul Williams and his Huckelbuckers performed for a show and dance at the American Legion Auditorium on June 14. The balcony was reserved for white spectators.

The Brook Club, formerly Apartment Camp, opened on June 11 after the building was completely remodeled to accommodate a larger dance floor. Opening-night music was provided by the Rhythmaires.

Dewey Marshall and Tom Deyerle opened a real estate firm, Marshall & Deyerle, in mid-June at 21 W. Church Avenue.

Piedmont Stores of Salem, formerly J. M. Logan Company, opened on June 15 at 21 E. Main Street in Salem. The store sold clothing.

Roanoke City Council at its meeting on June 14 set in motion the process to lengthen one of the runways at Woodrum Field and to provide for radar approach. Land had been offered to the city for purchase relative to the runway extension.

The Cloth Stores announced in mid-June it was closing. The shop was located at the rear of Woolworth's at 26 W. Kirk Avenue.

Paul Kosko won the Jaycee Junior Golf Tournament held on June 14 at Hidden Valley Country Club. He shot an 80, edging out by one stroke Gayle Naff.

Officials with the Veterans Administration in Washington, DC, announced that if the nation's capital were attacked, they would move the national office to Roanoke. Such would involve the transfer of nearly 1,000 personnel.

Bent Mountain Swimming Club, formerly Bent Mountain Lakes, opened for the season in mid-June. The club was operated by Paul Coffey.

Roanoke police revealed they had broken up a petty theft ring at the city garage. Twenty municipal employees were discovered to be stealing gas, oil, tires, and car parts. As a result of the investigation, the city manager terminated nineteen employees, and among the group were three police officers, a fire captain, and fifteen garage workers.

Family Jewelers at 509 S. Jefferson Street announced in mid-June it was going out of business.

G. W. Nicks Furniture and Appliance Company opened in Vinton at 107 Pollard Street on June 18.

Kermit Hunter, creator of *Unto These Hills* and *Horn in the West* outdoor dramas, conferred with Salem officials about creating and staging an outdoor drama at the amphitheatre in Sherwood Burial Park.

This Roanoke Police Department image shows the intersection of Franklin Road and Marshall Avenue SW in the 1950s. *Virginia Room, RPL*

Hunter expressed optimism that such a large production could succeed in the Roanoke Valley.

Bonnie Dell, a restaurant, opened on Route 311, a quarter mile north of Hanging Rock, on June 18.

Clarabelle, star of television's *Howdy Doody Show*, gave four free shows at the Memorial and Crippled Children's Hospital and in South Roanoke Park and Washington Park on June 26. The shows were sponsored by Kay's Ice Cream Company.

Hollins College trustees authorized on June 19 $850,000 worth of construction and maintenance at the college, including a new dorm and a new library. The new library was to be named in memory of Junius P. Fishburn, a college trustee since 1931 before his death.

Layman Garst opened Garst's Shoe Hospital at 5 E. Walnut Avenue on June 21.

Two twelve-year-old boys were killed and a dozen others injured when the back of a truck they were riding in swerved into a rock near the Starkey Speedway on June 20. Tyrone Brown died on impact, and Luke Keeling died en route to Burrell Memorial Hospital. All involved were traveling home from a family picnic and swimming party at Back Creek. The rear wheel and fender of the truck struck a rock, and all the passengers were thrown from the truck bed. Mrs. Sadie Muse was the driver.

The congregation of Rosalind Hills Baptist Church worshipped in their new sanctuary building at 2711 Laburnum Avenue SW, on June 27. Rev. W. H. Connelly was the pastor.

Grand Ole Opry star Webb Pierce along with the Wilburn Brothers and the Wondering Boys performed at the American Legion Auditorium on June 27.

Thousands lined Crystal Spring Avenue SW in June 1954 to view the annual Soap Box Derby. *WSLS Television News Film Collection, UVA Libraries*

Paul Palmer, eleven, drowned in the Roanoke River on June 22 at Kumis in Roanoke County. The incident occurred at what was commonly called the "Deep Hole" where youngsters swung out into the river from a rope tried to a tree.

Sixty-three boys competed in Roanoke's annual Soap Box Derby on Crystal Spring Avenue. The starting line was at Twenty-Sixth Street and the finish line near Twenty-Third Street. The race was sponsored by the Optimist Club, Johnson-McReynolds Chevrolet, and the *Roanoke Times*. The winner was Linwood Johnson, thirteen. He nosed out Earl Cook by six inches. A crowd estimated at 3,000 watched the various heats and the championship run.

The first health department for Roanoke County was launched on July 1. Dr. W. P. Jackson was appointed as the director, and the department was located at 231 College Avenue in Salem.

Orchardists in Roanoke and Botetourt Counties were given demonstrations in the chemical thinning of apple trees versus pruning them with saws.

The Virginian Railway began using single-unit diesel-electric switch engines at its Roanoke Yard in late June. The 1,600-horsepower units arrived from Mullins, West Virginia, and were purchased from Fairbanks-Morse & Company of Beloit, Wisconsin.

Grace Church held its first service in its new building at 2731 Edgewood Street SW on June 27. The cost of the building was $51,000.

LeRoy Smith, manager of the American Viscose Roanoke plant and chairman of the Roanoke School Board, died at Duke Hospital on June 26 at the age of fifty-six. His death was attributed to a heart attack.

Joe Morris and his orchestra, Faye Adams, and Al Savage performed for a show and dance at the American Legion Auditorium on July 4. White spectators were permitted to the balcony.

Appalachian Power Company completed the renovation of its Niagara hydro plant in late June. The plant was located on the Roanoke River east of Vinton and was constructed and placed in operation in 1906. The renovation was done by Cofer Construction Company of Roanoke. Paul Johnson was the plant's supervising engineer.

Dixie Caverns was listed for sale at the end of June. The asking price was $72,000 for the eighty-acre property. Clayton Lemon was the owner who placed the attraction up for sale.

Roanoke City and County state legislators unanimously agreed to oppose any effort to abolish the public school system in Virginia as a response to the US Supreme Court's decision declaring segregation to be unconstitutional. Virginia's governor had stated that he would consider proposing to amend the state constitution requiring a public school system as a means to not comply with the ruling.

Roanoke City Council initiated the purchase of thirty-four and one-half acres of land to expand Woodrum Field at its June 28 meeting.

The state highway department advertised for bids in late June for the construction of the largest single urban project ever undertaken by the department for a cost of $3 million. The project was the overpass to eliminate the grade separation of US 11 on Jefferson Street. The project would consist of a four-lane overpass and approaches extending from the intersection of Commonwealth Avenue and Second Street to the junction of Salem Avenue and Jefferson Street. There would also be a four-lane connection to Second Street SE as an overpass of the railroad.

William Barton was named manager of the Roanoke plant of American Viscose on June 29, succeeding the late LeRoy Smith. Barton was a native of Preston, England. He came to Roanoke in 1917 to help start the Roanoke plant.

The Garden City Rural Station post office opened on July 1 at 3329 Garden City Boulevard. The station was operated by Sterling McGregor at Mac's Soda Shop.

With a new management agreement, the Hotel Patrick Henry officially became the Patrick Henry Hotel on July 1. Management was transferred from Meyer Hotels to Patrick Henry Hotel Inc., which was composed of local businessmen.

The Roanoke Public Library announced in early July the beginning of a new service—microfilm. The first microfilm undertaken was the first *Roanoke Times* edition published in 1886.

Henry Hill, custodian and official bell-ringer at Roanoke College, died on July 2 at his home in Salem. He was seventy-eight. Hill had rung the college's bell for forty years, and the college had dedicated its bell tower to him on June 6. The Henry Hill Memorial Bell Tower was dedicated as such during the annual alumni weekend.

Showtimers opened their 1954 season on July 8 with a production of *Pygmalion*. Lead roles were performed by Dean Goodsell, Mrs. David Thornton, Joyce Wood, Gayle Rubenstein, and Addington Wise.

George Fulton Jr. of Roanoke won the Virginia State Amateur Golf Tournament in Hot Springs on July 6. Fulton became the third Roanoker to win the title in the tournament's history. Paul Jamison won it in 1924, and Connie Sellers defeated Fulton in the finals for the win in 1951.

Willett's Esso opened on July 8 at 324 Orange Avenue NE.

A group of prominent Salem businessmen applied for a charter for a new national bank in Salem in early July. Officials with Farmers National Bank and the Bank of Salem engaged legal counsel to oppose the plan.

A twenty-acre forest fire burned throughout the day on July 7 in the Cave Spring section.

The Dairy Fountain on Carter Road SW was purchased by the Garland Drug Store chain from John Jackson in early July.

Bradford's Restaurant opened on July 8 at 14 E. Salem Avenue. Proprietors were Bradford Lipscomb and Fannie Lipscomb.

William Hoobler resigned as administrator of the Memorial and Crippled Children's Hospital in early July. William Flannagan, administrator of the Franklin Memorial Hospital in Rocky Mount, was named as his successor.

Grand Ole Opry stars Little Jimmie Dickens and Del Woods performed at the American Legion Auditorium on July 14.

Roanoke City Manager Arthur Owens agreed to rehire eleven men involved in the mass firing on June 17 following an investigation into thievery at the city garage. Nineteen men were terminated, but Owens offered other positions to the eleven whose terminations he rescinded. The situation was exacerbated by Councilman-elect Paul Puckett who asserted via affidavits that more persons were involved in the affair than the nineteen alleged by Owens. Puckett made his charge at a city council meeting but offered no evidence.

Texas Ranger Championship Rodeo came to Victory Stadium for a four-day run on July 15. The event was sponsored by American Legion Post No. 3 Drum and Bugle Corps.

Gospel singers the Skylarks performed at the Star City Auditorium on July 16, sponsored by Hill Street Baptist Church.

J. H. Wyse, Virginia's Civil Defense Coordinator, told a citizens committee on July 10, "Roanoke County is prepared for an A-Bomb attack but in H-Bomb danger." His presentation was meant to motivate the county to overhaul its preparedness program.

Showtimers presented *Bell, Book and Candle* at the Lab Theatre in Salem on July 15. The five-member cast included Evans Evans, William Blackard, Cindy Dunn, John Marsteller, and Wilton Sale. Betty Thornton was the director.

Roanoke City Council named John Thornton, Dr. L. G. Downing, and incumbent Barclay Andrews to the Roanoke School Board at their meeting on July 12.

Ernest Robertson, a Salem restaurant operator, was nominated by Democrats to stand for election for Congress in the Sixth District. He defeated Powell Glass Jr. of Lynchburg and Carl Poindexter of Salem. Robertson would face incumbent Republican Congressman Richard Poff. Over 11,000 votes were cast in the primary.

This mid-1950s image is of the Perry Building, located at the corner of First Street and Church Avenue. First Federal Savings and Loan is to the left. Note the phone booth on the corner. *Historical Society of Western Virginia*

Theodrice Bonds, seventeen, died on July 13 in Burrell Memorial Hospital from a gunshot wound he received a few days prior from his brother. Police ruled the shooting an accident. The incident occurred at the boys' home on Wells Avenue NE.

The temperature reached 106 degrees on July 14, breaking the previous record high of 105 recorded in August 1930 and again in July 1936. The 106-degree mark was recorded at the South Roanoke weather station by O. P. Estes who, along with his father, had been voluntarily recording Roanoke's weather since 1910.

Due to legislation adopted by the Virginia General Assembly, local banks were able to be closed on all Saturdays beginning July 17. Prior to the legislation, banks were required to have Saturday hours.

The local Lincoln-Mercury auto dealership came under new ownership and management in mid-July. The dealership at 402 W. Luck Avenue became Sylvan Lincoln-Mercury owned by William Sylvan.

Magic City Insulating Company opened in its new location on W. Main Street in Salem in mid-July.

Ralph Gunn, former president of Mountain Trust Bank, died on July 15. He joined the bank when it opened for business on December 15, 1919, and became president in 1932. He retired from that position in 1949.

Felton, a carpet retailer, opened on July 16 at 914 Fourth Street SE.

Monsignor Louis Flaherty, superintendent of schools for the Richmond Diocese of the Catholic Church, announced on July 15 that parochial schools would begin admitting Black pupils to white schools in the coming school year. This meant that Roanoke Catholic Schools would be among those to abide by the new policy. At the time of the announcement, Roanoke Catholic had registered thirteen Black students, twelve in lower grades and one in the high school.

McAvoy Music House at 122 W. Church Avenue advertised in mid-July that they were closing out their record album department to make room for their band instrument and high fidelity phonograph departments.

General Motors Corporation announced that Jim Elliot had been appointed as its new Salem Buick dealer. The new corporation would be known as Elliot Buick with Elliot as president. The firm would purchase the assets of Kasey Buick in Salem. Elliot was the used car sales manager for Johnson-McReynolds Chevrolet in Roanoke prior to his appointment.

A mobile unit displaying costumes, jewels, weapons, and furnishings from the film *The Egyptian* parked at Pollard's Oil Company, opposite the Bank of Virginia, in downtown Roanoke on July 20 and then that evening at the Grandin Theatre. The mobile exhibit, a cross-country promotion for the film by Twentieth Century Fox Studios, featured New York model Theona Bryant and a cheetah.

Showtimers staged *The Showoff* as their third production of the season in late July. Lead roles were played by Barry Boardman, Linda Neill, Nettie Kitchen, Conny Brown, and Bernard Bradshaw.

Roanoke officials received a report that recommended constructing a tunnel through Tinker Mountain to access the flow of Tinker Creek to increase the capacity of Carvins Cove and to build an intercept at Catawba Creek. The report stated that such actions would meet the city's water demands until the year 2000.

Mrs. Ross Fagan won first place in the *Roanoke Times* and *World News* Cake-Baking Contest with her coconut cake. Some 300 women attended the judging event held in the auditorium of the Appalachian Power Company on July 17.

The Roanoke County Board of Supervisors adopted an ordinance that ordered the closing of all outdoor and drive-in theatres by 1:00 a.m. The supervisors were responding to complaints about noise and young people staying out too late.

Wright Furniture Company opened an annex at 123 E. Campbell Avenue on July 21 to sell used furniture.

Some 350 members of the Roanoke Booster Club attended the club's annual retreat at White Sulphur Springs in late July. The club endorsed a bond issue for a new civic auditorium for Roanoke and expansion of the school system's facilities. Club members also voted in favor of a municipal golf course being constructed on the city-owned Poor House tract.

A county welfare worker found that four adults and five children had been living in a parked car west of Salem for three months. Residents near Lawrence's Store reported the family to Salem officials. Welfare staff secured an apartment in Salem for the family.

Marshall Quinn, president and treasurer of Virginia Metal Manufacturing Company, was found dead in his garage on Maple Avenue SW on July 22. The cause of death was accidental asphyxiation as he had left his car running in the garage while he ate breakfast in his home. When he returned to the garage, he was overcome. He was eighty-four.

This mid-1950s photo shows Café Astor, located at 19 E. Salem Avenue. The restaurant was operated by George Ziompolas. Ace Hardware is to the left. *Historical Society of Western Virginia*

Valley Cadillac-Oldsmobile moved to its new location at 2743 Franklin Road SW on July 23. It had been formerly located at 620 Second Street SW.

The new Vinton Post Office on Lee Street was dedicated on July 24 with remarks by Congressman Richard Poff. A community picnic on the street preceded the event. The first post office in Vinton opened in 1868 or 1869 in the home of John Fox whose daughter, Jennie, was the first postmaster. When she married Dr. George Walker, the post office was moved to the Walker home at 118 N. Maple Street. The third location was on the corner of Washington Avenue and Maple Street, but that building burned in 1887. The fourth location was 119 E. Lee Avenue. In 1929, the post office was moved to 210 S. Pollard Street, and in 1953 to 115 W. Lee Avenue.

Arnett Cobb and his orchestra, Ruth Brown, and the Orioles performed for a show and dance at the American Legion Auditorium on July 30. White spectators were admitted to the balcony.

The congregation of Salem Pilgrimage Holiness Church at Eighth Street and Caroline Avenue worshiped for the first time at that location on July 25. Rev. Paul Bauer was the pastor.

Showtimers presented an all-female cast in their production of *Ladies in Retirement* on July 29. The suspense drama was performed by Dorothy Turner, Ethel Neal, Elizabeth Pettrey, Ciddy Young, Amy Jo Glenn, and Anna Canary. Genevieve Dickinson was the director.

Medical authorities at the Southwestern State Hospital in Marion found Estill Ellis of Roanoke, who killed his wife in 1953, "insane and incompetent." The finding meant that Ellis would live the remainder of his life at the facility in Marion. He had been at the hospital since September 30, 1953.

Officials with N&W Railway announced on July 28 the purchase of the Chesapeake Western Railway in the Shenandoah Valley for $825,000, pending approval by the ICC. The Chesapeake Western operated on fifty-four miles of track from Elkton to Harrisonburg, then south to Staunton. It also had an eight-mile branch from Harrisonburg to Bridgewater.

The Greyhound Lines "Scenicruiser" made its inaugural appearance in Roanoke at the end of July. The bus had an elevated rear passenger deck with a curved windshield around the forward section providing an unobstructed view. The bus carried forty-three passengers instead of the usual thirty-seven

The sixth annual Roanoke Valley Horse Show was held at Maher Field at the end of July. The four-day event had entries from six states.

Abe Huddleston pled guilty in Roanoke County Circuit Court on July 29 to the double-murder of Earl See and Elvin See at a filling station restaurant. Huddleston, a wealthy garage owner and well-known in the county, was sentenced to forty years in prison for the slayings by Judge Fred Hoback.

Lewis Meador, Vinton's postmaster, was arrested on July 30 on a charge of embezzlement in connection with the post office there. Margie Gray was appointed interim postmaster.

Three top favorite NASCAR drivers competed in a one-hundred-lap race at Starkey Speedway on July 31. Among them were Jim Reed of Ossining, New York, and Lee Petty of Randleman, North Carolina. The winner was Dick Rathman of Daytona Beach, Florida. An estimated 4,000 spectators attended the race.

The Noel Coward comedy *Private Lives* was presented by Showtimers as their fifth production of the season at the Lab Theatre in Salem. The cast included Evans Evans, Sam Good, and David Thornton. Dean Goodsell was the director.

Budd Sterns opened Furniture Fair on Route 11 at Hollins in late July.

The Miss Virginia Pageant came to the Hotel Roanoke on August 4. Evelyn Ay, Miss America of 1954, was a featured personality at the event which began with a parade through downtown Roanoke. Julie Ann Bruening, nineteen, of Augusta County won the pageant. As *Carry Me Back to Ole Virginny* was played on an organ, Bruening was crowned and also received a key to the City of Roanoke.

The Reverend Lewis Bates was called as pastor of Vinton Baptist Church in early August. He began his duties there on September 1, coming from Colonial Heights, Virginia.

Roanoke County's first public health nurse Sarah Earhart died in early August in Bradenton, Florida, at the age of seventy-nine. Earhart served as the county's nurse from 1919 until 1922.

Jim and Betty Gentry assumed the ownership of Woodward Studio at 33 Main Street, Salem, in early August.

Rea Construction Company of Charlotte was the low bidder for the construction of the Jefferson Street viaduct with a bid of slightly more than $1.6 million. The viaduct plan was to do construction in four phases—on the east side of the N&W Railway tracks, the Second Street span of the Y, the Jefferson Street leg, and an underpass of the tracks for pedestrians at Jefferson Street.

George Hill of Salem was killed in an auto accident on Goodwin Avenue near Salem on August 7. Three passengers were injured.

Sprinkle Brothers Auction House opened on August 11 opposite Lakeside.

L. D. Filson of the Mount Pleasant section took his first flight on August 7 at Woodrum Field. Filson flew the small craft at Woodrum Field under the supervision of his flight instructor, Lawrence Bohon. Filson's flight made news because of his age—ninety-six.

Holman Willis Sr., a prominent Roanoke attorney, died at Lewis-Gale Hospital on August 9 at the age of seventy-five. He had practiced law in Roanoke since 1909 and was a former member of the Virginia state senate.

Roanoke City Council appropriated money for the purchase of land to extend one of the runways at Woodrum Field. The council agreed to purchase thirty-two acres on the northeast side of Route 118 for $32,000.

Showtimers concluded their season with *You Can't Take It With You* on the second weekend in August. Lead roles were played by Herbert Harris, Rosalie Turner, Patti Jones, Gayle Rubinstein, and Michael Mansiter. The play was directed by Leroy McFarland.

Kay Lee, advertising director for Smartwear-Irving Saks in Roanoke, accepted a position as a senior writer for *Glamour* magazine in New York City. She moved to Roanoke in 1941 and had worked for WSLS radio and Houck & Company advertising before going with Smartwear-Irving Saks.

The Valley Cadillac-Oldsmobile showroom, seen here in 1954, was located at 2743 Franklin Road SW. It opened in 1954. *Virginia Room, RPL*

Valley Cadillac-Oldsmobile formally opened their new location at 2743 Franklin Road SW on August 12. Joe Hill was the company president.

A young boy, Jimmy Goad, wading in the Roanoke River near Wasena Park discovered the decomposed body of Clarence Redford, fifty, of southeast Roanoke on August 11. Redford had been reported missing on July 14. The medical examiner concluded there was no foul play in his death and that it was probably due to drowning.

ABC officials, along with the Roanoke County Sheriff's Department, raided a 200-gallon moonshine still in the west end of Roanoke County near Dixie Caverns on August 11. Law enforcement completely destroyed the still along with one hundred gallons of whiskey and 1,000 gallons of mash.

Judge Stanford Fellers ruled in Law and Chancery Court on August 12 that the will of the late Edgar Thurman, a prominent Roanoke businessman, creating a charitable trust of $2.6 million was valid. Thurman's nieces and nephews had made various attempts to challenge the will.

The board of visitors of Roanoke College voted for a slight increase in room and board costs for students. Board during the 1954–55 Session was to be $380, and room rent would be between $108 and $144.

Heironimus presented a campus-career fashion show at the Hotel Roanoke on August 13. The guest commentator on outfits worn by the local runway models was Edith Raymond, associate fashion editor of *Mademoiselle* magazine.

Shank Furniture Company of Salem held at grand opening at 2 W. Main Street on August 13.

John Rowland opened his Pure Oil Service Station at N. Jefferson Street and Wells Avenue NW on August 13.

WDBJ radio began programming at 5:30 a.m., an earlier time, on August 16 with *The Daybreaker*. The local show played country music and popular favorites and was hosted alternately by Dexter Mills, Dick Morgan, and Hal Grant.

Roanoke Record Shop opened at its new location at 116 W. Church Avenue on August 16. Their relocation was due to the construction of the viaduct.

A new parking garage for downtown Roanoke opened on August 17 at Salem Avenue and First Street SW. The garage accommodated 500 cars and the ribbon-cutting ceremony included Mayor Roy Webber; Ben Parrott of the Chamber of Commerce; and Miss Roanoke, Norma Jean Thompson. The multistory garage operated as Downtown Parking Inc. Parking rates were twenty-five cents for the first hour and ten cents for every hour thereafter.

Ray Lewis, forty-three, died of an accidental self-inflicted gunshot wound on August 16. The man was joking with his wife as he held a pistol against his head. The shooting occurred at the Lewis home on Route 117.

Estes Cocke, retired vice president and treasurer of Hollins College, died on August 16 at the age of seventy-eight. Cocke served the college for over a half century. Cocke had been born and raised on the Hollins campus. His body laid in state in the drawing room of the college prior to the funeral at Enon Baptist Church.

Miller Manufacturing Company of Richmond announced on August 17 that it had purchased five acres of land in Roanoke to construct a new plant to make corrugated containers. Company officials stated that the plant would employ about 250 persons. The plant would be located in northeast Roanoke between Old Hollins Road and the N&W Railway tracks.

The Mad Doctor and his *Voodoo Show* came to the stage of the Roanoke Theatre on August 20. Ads read, "Monsters run loose in the audience!"

The first unified pageant sponsored by the Roanoke City Parks and Recreation Department was held in Highland Park on August 18. Children from across the city joined parks department staff in presenting the play *Hiawatha*. Some 500 persons attended the event.

Murtchen's opened at its new location at 11 S. Jefferson Street on August 19. The department store had to relocate due to construction of the viaduct.

Nine of Roanoke's elementary schools adopted split sessions for the fall due to rising enrollments. Morning sessions went from 8:00 a.m. until noon, and afternoon sessions were from noon until 4:00 p.m.

The *Salem Times-Register* celebrated its centennial with a forty-page extra edition on August 20. The paper was founded in 1854 by Jordan Woodrum.

Officials with WSLS radio announced plans to open a broadcast studio in Salem near its 1,000-watt transmitter.

George Fulton Jr. set a new course record at Roanoke Country Club on August 21 when he shot a round of 64. Professional golfer Sam Snead once shot a 63 there, but he did not use the same tee locations as Fulton.

This mid-1950s photo shows National Business College located on the SW corner of S. Jefferson Street and Franklin Road. *Historical Society of Western Virginia*

Hundreds of residents in Schenectady, New York, spent several weeks learning about Roanoke due to the plan by General Electric to transfer some 200 employees from there to its new plant in Salem. The presentations were conducted by Paul Thomson, who helped the company produce a thirty-four-page booklet on Roanoke for those employees being transferred. The cover of the booklet contained a picture of the Roanoke Star on Mill Mountain.

A cow milking contest was held on the lawn of Roanoke's Municipal Building on August 21 for the benefit of Mercy House. The contest was sponsored by the Roanoke and Salem Chambers of Commerce to raise funds for pasteurization equipment for Mercy House. Winners were Thomas Gwaltney in the senior division and Linda Jarrett in the junior division.

Roanoke City Council approved at its August 23 meeting doubling the filtering facilities for Carvins Cove. The plan called for the construction of six additional filter beds in a filter house.

The Veterans Administration Hospital held its seventh annual carnival on the hospital grounds on August 24. Some 1,500 attended the event that included various booths and musical entertainment.

WRIS Radio opened a new studio in Salem on August 24 at the Shank Furniture Company building, 6 W. Main Street.

Paul Woodward was named as temporary manager for the American Viscose plant in Roanoke, succeeding W. A. Barton, who retired effective September 1. Woodward came from the company's Parkersburg, West Virginia, plant.

Camp Powhatan, the Boy Scout camp in Pulaski County, completed its summer season and reported a record 948 attendees.

Actor Bill Holland, star of the movie *Violated*, appeared in person at the North-11 Drive-In prior to the showing of the adults-only film on August 26.

George Jack, a veteran newspaper reporter for Roanoke papers, died at his home on August 25 at the age of eighty-five. Jack also coauthored a history of the Roanoke Valley with E. B. Jacobs that was published in 1912.

Roanoke County's new health department opened on College Street in Salem in late August under the direction of Dr. W. P. Jackson.

Fire gutted Woodward Studio in Salem on August 27, causing $5,000 worth of damage.

Francis Holdren was named as the postmaster for Vinton on August 27 succeeding Marjorie Gray.

Colonial-American National Bank opened a branch at 3403 Williamson Road on August 30.

This photo of the Colonial-American National Bank branch office at 3403 Williamson Road NE was taken soon after it opened in 1954. *Historical Society of Western Virginia*

Judge Samuel Price of Municipal Court died on August 28 while spending the weekend with his wife at their summer home in the Alleghany Mountains. Price had served as Roanoke's commonwealth's attorney and was appointed to the bench in 1948 to fill the unexpired term of Richard Pence. In 1950, he was elected to a full four-year term by Roanoke City Council.

The Roanoke Fair opened on August 30 at Maher Field. The multiday event consisted of livestock, poultry, agricultural and industrial exhibits. Grandstand entertainers were Jessie Griffiths; LaFlotte Duo cyclists Clem Bellings & Company with trained dogs, dancing, and juggling; Blackie Troupe, a comedy novelty act; and the Sparklettes, a revue show.

Lionel Hampton and his orchestra performed for a show and dance at the American Legion Auditorium on September 5. The balcony was reserved for white spectators. Admission was $1.75.

Ray Price and the Western Cherokees brought their *Grand Ole Opry* show to the City Market Auditorium on September 5. They were joined by Tommy Hill.

Officials with N&W Railway announced on August 28 that the Roanoke ticket office at 507 S. Jefferson Street would close effective September 30. Only 10 percent of tickets sold in Roanoke were purchased through the downtown office. All future tickets would be purchased at the passenger station.

Fitch Dustdown Company of Baltimore opened a district store at Twelfth Street and Patterson Avenue on August 30. David Fann was district manager.

Ralph English won the Hidden Valley Country Club golf tournament on August 29, and George Fulton Jr. captured the same title at the Roanoke Country Club. English defeated Glenn Thomas, and Fulton bested Connie Sellers.

Rev. Zebulon Roberson, pastor of Raleigh Court Presbyterian Church, was elected moderator of the Presbyterian Synod of Virginia in late August during the synod meeting Staunton.

Roanoke City Council held its reorganization meeting on September 1 and elected Robert Woody as mayor and Leigh Hanes as vice mayor. In Salem, the town council reelected James Moyer as mayor. In Vinton, the town council gave Nelson Thurman a third term as mayor.

Roanoke City Council named Beverly Fitzpatrick to serve the unexpired term of the late Municipal Court Judge Samuel Price. Fitzpatrick, thirty-four, was serving as assistant commonwealth's attorney.

Roanoke Record Shop held a grand reopening at its new location at 116 W. Church Avenue on September 3.

N&W Railway announced in early September that it would discontinue mining coal for its own locomotives effective October 1. The decision impacted some 600 employees, as the railroad planned to curtail operations at its Pond Creek colliery and mines at New Camp and Goody, Kentucky. The railroad would buy coal from commercial producers along its lines.

Air-Lee Superette, a grocery store, opened at 5002 Williamson Road on September 3.

Frank Anderson of Roanoke County was arrested on September 3 and charged with kidnapping and felonious assault for seizing Hubert Moore of Roanoke at gunpoint and striking him over the head with a shotgun.

Parker Pen Service, a subsidiary of the Parker Pen Company, announced in early September plans to open a regional office at 931 S. Jefferson Street on October 1. Thomas Allman was named as the regional manager.

Robert Hubard retired on September 4 as trial justice and judge of the Juvenile and Domestic Relations Court in Roanoke County. Salem attorney Norman Moore was appointed as his successor.

The Kelly Morris Circus came to the Starkey Speedway on September 6. The circus advertised "Big Blanche" as the world's largest pachyderm, Capt. Ernest Engerer and his ferocious firefighting lions, and bareback riders the Christiani Family. The circus was sponsored by VFW Post No. 1264.

Steve Lindamood Jr. of Roanoke was one of four Virginians named to the sixth annual Pop Warner All-America Boy Baseball Team. The fifteen-player team was announced by officials with the Pop Warner Conference in Philadelphia.

Elaine Bailey, twenty-four, of Gandy Drive NW was found slain on September 5. Wilbert Rosby of Roanoke was charged with her murder. Rosby was discovered by police with self-inflicted knife wounds to his neck and throat and taken to Burrell Memorial Hospital, where he confessed to police.

Lewis Hunt, head waiter in the dining hall at Hollins College, died at his home on September 5. He had worked at the college for fifty-two years before retiring in 1950. His first job, at thirteen, was tending the sheep that grazed on the campus and running to the top of the main building every hour to ring the bell for the start of classes. He was sixty-nine.

Charley Turner won the annual city-county tennis tournament the first weekend in September, defeating Frank Snow. It was Turner's fourteenth championship title. The event was held in South Roanoke Park. Suzanne Glass and Jeane Bentley won the women's doubles championship, while Jay Walker won the boys' division singles title.

Clarence King of Roanoke won the Thirtieth Fairacre Invitational Golf Tournament at Hot Springs on September 6.

Roanoke's parochial schools held desegregated classes for the first time on September 7. According to school officials, twelve Black students were enrolled at St. Andrew's Elementary School, seven at Nazareth Elementary, and two at Roanoke Catholic High School. Public schools remained segregated.

Stogner's Shoes opened at 1324 Grandin Road SW on September 9. The owner and manager was Ned Stogner, formerly a merchant in Waynesboro.

Preliminary work for the viaduct in downtown Roanoke began on September 10 with grading and construction. Demolition work was done by the Cleveland Wrecking Company. Some thirty-four buildings were slated for demolition.

Mill Mountain Zoo reported a record 95,055 visitors to the zoo during its summer season, from May 30 through Labor Day. The zoo remained open on weekends during the fall.

This 1950s postcard shows the "Three Little Pigs" exhibit at the Children's Zoo on Mill Mountain. *Nelson Harris*

Roanoke City Public Schools reported an enrollment of 16,302 students for the school year. High school enrollments were as follows: Fleming, 859; Jefferson, 1,430; and Addison, 621. The racial breakdown was 13,189 whites and 3,113 Blacks. Enrollment in Roanoke County was 9,214.

WSLS-TV transmitted a program in color on September 12 as an experiment. The program was a movie, *Satin and Spurs*. Most viewed the telecast in black and white as the station manager acknowledged there were few color televisions in homes within the viewing area.

Detectives with N&W Railway broke up what they described as a "nip joint" operating in a remote basement room within the railway's General Office building. The investigation and raid was prompted by a custodian's report to his supervisor of the number of whiskey bottles he was disposing of each morning.

South Roanoke Methodist Church dedicated its new pipe organ on September 12 with a concert by Helen Williams of Lynchburg.

Cave Spring Methodist Church observed its centennial on September 12 with worship in its original building. The church was founded in 1853, and the building was erected the following year with bricks made by Ben Deyerle, who lived in the Cave Spring area. The brick was laid by one of Deyerle's slaves, and the carpentry was done by George Hartman, a cabinetmaker. Founders of the church were Hartman, Henry Shaver, and Billy Martin. Early church records indicated that there were both Black and white members, including immediately after the Civil War.

Slim Whitman and the Stardusters, Mac Wiseman and the Country Boys, and Rusty Gabbard performed at the City Market Auditorium on September 14.

Oakland Baptist Church dedicated its new education building on September 19. The four-story structure cost $230,000.

Nat King Cole, the Buddy Johnson Orchestra, and Ella Johnson performed for a show and dance at the American Legion Auditorium on September 22. The balcony was reserved for white spectators.

Roanoke County's last one-room schoolhouse, where seven grades were taught by one teacher, was closed for the start of the school year. The Catawba Colored School was built in 1922 and was officially closed on September 10 when students were transferred to Hollins School. The Hollins School, with four rooms, had an enrollment of 125.

Dr. F. G. Anderson, ninety-one and a retired physician, of Roanoke was killed in a four-car collision on Route 11 near Christiansburg on September 12. Prior to his retirement, he had served on the medical staff of the Catawba Sanatorium.

The *Roanoke Times* published its circulation numbers in mid-September for the six month period that ended on March 31. Average paid daily circulation was 84,733 and on Sundays was 80,216.

Catalina Drive-In Restaurant opened on September 17 at 2905 Shenandoah Avenue NW. Billy Souma was the manager.

Hollins College inaugurated the "Hollins Abroad" program for its students during the 1954–55 academic year. College leaders stated that the program offered two semesters at the Sorbonne in Paris, spread across two academic years, with three months of travel throughout Europe during the summer break.

This early 1950s image shows the Continental Can Company on Albemarle Avenue and along the N&W Railway tracks. *Historical Society of Western Virginia*

James Akers, forty-five, of Roanoke County died on September 19 from injuries sustained when his car left the road and plunged into Peters Creek at Shenandoah Avenue.

Blake Humphries captured the championship title in the annual N&W Railway golf tournament held at Monterey Golf Club. His two-round score of 149 edged out J. D. Sisson by two strokes.

Bennie Carroll, sixty, of Salem died on September 20 from injuries he sustained in auto accident on September 19. The accident occurred at Fourth Street and McClelland Street, only a block from his home.

Salem physician Dr. Eugene Senter died on September 20 at his home on High Street. He was forty-eight. Senter was prominent in community affairs also had served for many years as the physician for Roanoke College.

At its meeting on September 20, Roanoke City Council voted against selling three parcels of land to the Seventh Day Adventist Church for the purposes of erecting a parochial school near Wasena Park. The parcels would have involved the entire north side of the 900 block of Winchester Avenue SW. Council kept with its practice of not selling park land.

A Roanoke County Circuit Court jury found Bruce Lail guilty of voluntary manslaughter in the shooting death of Jesse Sink on May 2. Lail was fined $1,000.

Walsh Construction Company of New York City and William Muirhead Construction Company of Durham, North Carolina, were awarded contracts by General Electric for erection of the company's multimillion dollar industrial controls plant near Salem. The new plant was estimated to cost $10 million, and some 750 construction workers would be employed for work on the project.

Booth's Self-Service Grocery opened at 537 Pollard Street in Vinton on September 24.

The City of Greensboro, North Carolina, placed an order with Oren Roanoke Corporation to manufacture a fire engine that was believed to be the most powerful in the South. The apparatus would have a 300-pound horsepower engine capable of pumping 1,500 gallons of water per minute at 150 pounds of pressure.

Carter Burgess, thirty-seven and a native of Roanoke, became the assistant secretary of defense in charge of manpower and personnel on September 24. He was appointed to the post by Defense Secretary Charles Wilson.

Hayes, Seay, Mattern & Mattern moved into their new offices at 1615 Franklin Road SW the third week in September. The firm employed around one hundred architects, engineers, and clerical personnel.

Loudon Avenue Christian Church held a note-burning ceremony on September 26. The guest speaker was Rev. Emmett Dickson.

James Lewis, fifty-nine, died on September 28 while fighting a grass fire near his barn. According to the county coroner, Lewis's death was brought on by natural causes due to exhaustion. His farm was located on Peters Creek Road near South View School.

This November 1954 image shows employees of Hayes, Seay, Mattern & Mattern at work in the drafting room. *Virginia Room, RPL*

Jefferson Beauty Shop opened in late September at 820 S. Jefferson Street. Dorothy Setliff was the owner.

Roanoke Fine Arts Center opened its new headquarters at 215 Franklin Road SW on September 29. While exhibitions would continue to be held at the Roanoke Public Library, art classes for various age levels were to be offered at the center.

The Speech and Hearing Center opened at 1529 Williamson Road on October 1. The center was jointly sponsored by the Roanoke County Junior Woman's Club and the Virginia Society for Crippled Children and Adults.

The Orchard Club opened on Kessler Mill Road on October 1. The nightclub offered dining and dancing each evening. Opening night featured music by the Leonard Trio with vocalist Thornton Marshall.

Martha Carson, Marty Robbins, Ferlin Husky, and Mac Wiseman brought their *Grand Ole Opry* show to the American Legion Auditorium on October 3. Admission was $1.25.

Col. Sinclair Brown stepped down as president of the Farmers National Bank of Salem on September 30 after serving over thirty-two years in the position. He was succeeded was C. E. Webber, a director of the bank for over twenty years.

Samuel Turner, thirty, of Catawba was found stabbed to death on the back porch of his home on September 30. A. D. Foster of Catawba was charged with the murder after he confessed to the crime. Foster and Turner lived in the same home.

A Clover Creamery delivery truck is shown in this 1954 image. Clover was one of the main dairies operating in Roanoke during the 1950s. *Virginia Room, RPL*

A. A. Woodson, a Pontiac dealer in Salem, took over the Larry Dow Pontiac dealership in Roanoke on October 1. Dow had retired. The new name of the entity would become Woodson Pontiac Company. A formal opening of the new dealership occurred on October 8 at 425 Marshall Avenue SW.

Williamson Road Baptist Church was formally dedicated on October 3. The guest speaker was Dr. R. J. Barber of Danville.

Fort Lewis Baptist Church observed its centennial on October 3 with a day-long homecoming. The guest speaker was Rev. Jesse Davis of Virginia Heights Baptist Church in Roanoke. The church was formed in 1824 and was one of the oldest Baptist churches in the Roanoke Valley. Membership was 300.

The Larks, Pork Chops, the Savoy Hepcats, and a variety of showgirls performed for a show and dance titled *Midnite at the Savoy* at the American Legion Auditorium on October 9.

The investigation into a "nip joint" being operated in a basement room of the N&W Railway general office building came to an end on October 2 when two employees were fired and eight others were given thirty-day "record suspensions," meaning a notation was placed in their personnel records. All ten employees were charged with drinking on the job.

Hollins College broke ground in early October on a new dormitory planned to house eighty-three students. The expected completion date was August 1955. The contractor was J. M. Turner and Company of Roanoke.

Garland's Drug Store at the corner of Salem Avenue and Jefferson Street SW closed on October 1 to make way for the construction of the viaduct.

The Cleveland Wrecking Company offered a variety of construction salvage prior to demolishing over thirty buildings for the viaduct. Their early October ads offered doors, lumber, toilets, flooring, sheathing, window sash, and bricks. Their sales office was at 120 E. Salem Avenue.

Roanoke City Council named a six-man steering committee on October 4 to begin planning for the city's seventy-fifth anniversary in 1959. Chairing the group was Shields Johnson of the Times-World Corporation. Other members were A. M. Krebs, Carl Andrews, A. S. Rachal Jr., E. C. Moomaw, and Arthur Owens.

Jessie Brown, fifty-three, was shot to death in the kitchen of her home at 518 Rutherfoord Avenue NW on October 5. Police arrested William Strange, thirty-three, who confessed to firing the shot that killed Brown but claimed it was accidental.

Second Methodist Church in Salem became Central Methodist Church by a vote of the congregation on October 6. The church was formed in 1908. The church planned to adopt its new name beginning October 30 following the cornerstone-laying ceremony for its new building at 425 College Avenue.

Owen's Market opened at the intersection of Hershberger and Cove Roads on October 8. The owner and manager was Harold Owen.

Ringling Brothers and Barnum & Bailey Circus came to Maher Field on October 11. Emmett Kelley led the clowns, and the show included aerialists, the Nerveless Nocks. Tickets were $0.75 for children and $1.50 for adults. The circus arrived in a three-section train and unloaded at the N&W Railway siding on Third Street SE. Several thousand turned out to watch the circus unload and set up at Maher Field. Combined attendance for the two performances was 12,000.

The Roanoke Department of Parks and Recreation held their inaugural dance for teenagers with music supplied by a disc jockey on October 9 at the marine armory on Reserve Avenue. Plans were to offer all teenagers in Roanoke a dance every Saturday night through May 1 at the armory with the program to also be aired over WSLS radio. The dress code was informal, but blue jeans were not permitted. A separate monthly dance program was being planned for Black teenagers.

Leon Miller, a Roanoke native, was named US attorney for the Virgin Islands on October 8. Miller, fifty-five, earned a law degree from the University of Pennsylvania and was the first Black to be named as an assistant prosecuting attorney in a West Virginia county. He had also served as a member of the city council for Welch, West Virginia.

Fred Astaire Dance Studios opened at 506 S. Jefferson Street on October 10.

A production of the opera *The Barber of Seville* was held at the American Theatre on October 13, given by Boris Goldovsky's Opera Theater. The opera was sponsored by the Thursday Morning Music Club.

Adult art classes were held for the first time at Roanoke Fine Arts Center headquarters. Instructors were Nicholas Wreden, Peter Wreden, and James Yeatts.

The first outdoor mass in Roanoke's history was held on October 10 at St. Andrew's Catholic Church as a special Marian Year event. Over 1,000 persons attended the mass.

Walter Scott, a prominent Roanoke attorney, was fatally injured from a fall from the third floor of the building where his office was located. Scott fell thirty feet from a window to the alley, and investigators believed he leaned against the window and the sash was loose. Scott represented the city in the Virginia House of Delegates from 1932 through 1942.

Roanoke's 1955 Community Fund campaign kicked off on October 11 with a one-hour television program broadcast on WSLS-TV. The show featured speakers, local talent, and special guests highlighting the eighteen agencies to benefit from the drive. Dick Burton was the emcee. The campaign's theme was "Let's make the town of tomorrow today." It was also the thirtieth anniversary of the Community Fund.

Walter Giles, eighty-six, died at his home on October 12. Giles operated Giles Brothers Furniture Company in Roanoke for many years. The store was founded by Giles and his brothers in 1902.

Pre-Millennial Baptist Church was renamed Trinity Baptist Church in mid-October by a vote of the congregation. The church was located at 2312 Staunton Avenue NW and had been in existence about three years.

This 1953 image shows the Veterans Administration Building located at 211 Campbell Avenue SW. *Historical Society of Western Virginia*

Dixie Caverns was sold on October 14 to Sam Garrison, manager of Shenandoah Club, for $72,000. Garrison indicated plans to make the caverns a major tourist attraction. The caverns, along with eighty acres, were purchased from Clayton Lemon. Garrison planned to leave the Shenandoah Club to focus full time on the caverns.

Sixth District Democrats held a campaign rally at the American Legion Auditorium on October 16. The speaker was Congressman Sam Rayburn.

The outer perimeter of Hurricane Hazel hit the Roanoke Valley on October 14 and produced rain for thirteen hours. While there were no injuries, streets were flooded in downtown Roanoke and swollen streams plagued Roanoke County. The weather station at Woodrum Field reported 4.95 inches of rain fell. High winds also blew down the big screen at the North-11 Drive-In.

Washington Heights Church of the Brethren dedicated its new $40,000 education building on October 17. The church was located at 3833 Michigan Avenue NW.

The Salem Moose Lodge established their first headquarters on the second floor of a building at 210 E. Main Street.

A fire on October 15 destroyed a restaurant owned and operated by J. L. Hurley in the Pinkard Court section along Route 220.

The drivers and their trucks are positioned in front of the Porterfield Distributing Company at 1354 Eighth Street SW in this 1954 image. *Virginia Room, RPL*

Colonial Store held its grand opening on October 20 at 2613 Williamson Road near Liberty Road NE. It was part of a national chain of grocery stores.

An outdoor religious drama was being planned for the summer of 1956 by a group that had contracted with Kermit Hunter, author of *Unto These Hills* and *Horn in the West*. Landscaping of the amphitheatre in Sherwood Burial Park had begun for the intended drama. The organizing group was Shenandoah Drama Inc. The plan called for a 2,000-seat amphitheater and a 1,000-car parking lot. The outdoor drama would run from July 4 through Labor Day.

The Brambleton Junior Woman's Club announced a campaign in mid-October to rid Roanoke of undesirable comic books. A community meeting was held on October 19 at the Grandin Court Recreation Center with various religious, civic, and PTA groups represented. The group decided to launch a "good book" campaign by approaching merchants who sold objectionable horror and sexual thriller comic books and asking them to curtail sales. In addition, the group planned to place "good book" boxes in schools where young people could trade in their comic books for books deemed more appropriate.

The Roanoke Symphony Orchestra presented a concert on October 18 at the Jefferson High School auditorium. Selections included *Triple Concerto* by Beethoven, *Elegy* by Deems Taylor, and *Overture to Tannhauser* by Wagner.

Seventeen persons were fined by Roanoke County Trial Justice Norman Moore for participating in an illegal poker game in the back of a store on Water Street in Salem. The cases were the result of a raid conducted by the sheriff's department on the night of October 16.

Louis Jordan and his Tympany Five performed for a show and dance at the American Legion Auditorium on October 22. The balcony was reserved for white spectators.

Western Auto opened a store at 13 E. Main Street in Salem on October 22. It was owned and operated by W. H. Christie.

Roanoke Tourist Motel and Restaurant opened on October 22 on Route 460 east of Roanoke. Tommy Edwards was the manager. The restaurant's quarter-pound hamburger was twenty-four cents.

Kitty Wells, Johnnie and Jack, and the Tennessee Mountain Boys brought their *Grand Ole Opry* show to the American Legion Auditorium on October 25. Tickets were one dollar.

Dr. William Powell died on October 21 at Memorial and Crippled Children's Hospital. He had practiced medicine in Roanoke for forty-eight years, having come to Roanoke in 1906 to serve as superintendent of the then Roanoke Hospital. He was a past president of the Medical Society of Virginia.

The Sunday edition of the *Roanoke Times* hit an all-time-high paid circulation of 83,192 on October 17.

The Columbus Boychoir opened the Community Concert Association season with a performance on October 25 at the Jefferson High School auditorium.

Virginia Tech defeated the University of Virginia 6–0 in a football game held at Victory Stadium on October 24. Attendance was 16,000.

Paintings by John Thompson, a local artist, went on display at the Gainsboro Branch Library in late October. Thompson gained local notoriety when his paintings were part of an exhibit at Heironimus Department Store in Roanoke.

Soprano Muriel Rahn, a star of Broadway musicals, performed at the Star City Auditorium on October 27.

A ground-breaking ceremony was held on October 24 for the new Goodwill Industries building at 3121 Salem Turnpike NW. Mrs. R. B. Jennings turned the first shovel of dirt, having been a member of the original board of directors. The concrete block structure was expected to cost $91,000.

The ICC gave formal approval on October 25 to the N&W Railway purchase of the fifty-five-mile Chesapeake Western Railway.

The sale of Woodson Pontiac in Salem to Fred Gates and James Gates was announced on October 25. The Salem dealership had been owned for many years by A. A. Woodson, who had purchased the Larry Dow Pontiac dealership in Roanoke a few weeks prior.

A panty raid at Hollins College on the night of October 25 was thwarted by law enforcement. Some one hundred young men from area colleges made the attempt by making wolf calls and howling at the moon.

William Rosby was sentenced to life in prison by a Hustings Court judge on October 26 for the murder of his girlfriend, Elain Bailey, on September 4. He stabbed her through the throat after learning she had dated another man.

The drying house of Roanoke Apple Products was gutted by fire on October 28. The fire at 1521 Seventh Street NE also destroyed thirty tons of apples.

The Roanoke Chapter of the Muscular Dystrophy Association received its charter in late October. Leaders of the local chapter included Mrs. Hugh Anderson, Bentley Reed, Louise Stanley, Mrs. T. C. Ferguson, and Mrs. M. R. McCorkle.

Wildwood Chapel, a Presbyterian mission north of Salem, was granted independent status in late October to take effect November 21. The congregation was a mission of Salem Presbyterian Church and was organized on November 19, 1944, when a group of eight persons met at the home of Mr. and Mrs. S. E. Cundiff.

The cornerstone for the new Cave Spring Baptist Church on Route 221 was laid on October 31. The bell from the old church was removed for the new church when completed. The church bell was first rung in 1879.

Mareta's opened in its new location at 6 W. Main Street in Salem on November 4. The store had previously been at 206 E. Main Street.

Virginia Hardware Company held a grand opening at 2319 Melrose Avenue NW on October 29.

Blues musicians Joe Turner, Chuck Willis and his orchestra, and Herm Jackson performed at the Star City Auditorium on October 30. The balcony was reserved for whites.

Schertle Television and Appliances announced in late October it was going out of business effective November 15. The owner, Charles Schertle, had purchased the Roanoke Tourist Court property from Abe Huddleston and was planning to devote his energies to that business. The appliance store was located at 105 Franklin Road SW and had been operating for two years.

The Roanoke Public Library recognized the birthday of George Forsea on October 30. Forsea was born in Hungary in 1874 and immigrated to the United States in 1905. He came to Roanoke in 1920 and became the owner of the Blue Ridge Grill at 1300 S. Jefferson Street. When he died on November 12, 1943, he had no heirs and left his estate, valued at $12,140, to the public library. The bequest became the Forsea Endowment and helped to create the Roanoke Public Library Foundation.

Television clowns Clarabell and Buffalo Vic of the *Howdy Doody Show* came to the Colonial Store on Williamson Road on October 30 for a special program for children and families.

Commonwealth Discount Corporation announced in late October the purchase of the stock of the Roanoke Industrial Loan Corporation effecting a reorganization of the latter.

A cornerstone-laying ceremony was held on October 30 for Central Methodist Church in Salem on October 30. The $150,000 building was expected to be completed in the summer of 1955. Membership was 662. The church was established in 1908 as Second Methodist Church at 501 Colorado Street. The new structure was on College Avenue.

Alfred Hurt, basketball coach at Jefferson High School, announced in early November his plans to retire after twenty-eight seasons. Hurt was succeeded by Preston Brown Jr. Hurt coached his Jefferson squads to five state titles (1929, 1930, 1934, 1935, and 1941) and coached Jefferson's state championship football team in 1928.

Republican Congressman Richard Poff won reelection on November 2, defeating Democratic challenger Ernest Robertson in the Sixth District 32,850 to 19,725. Poff won both Roanoke city and county. In the city, Poff received 10,825 votes to Robertson's 5,258. In the county, the vote was 4,543 to 2,320. Poff's victory was due, in part, to the popularity of President Eisenhower.

United Pawn Shop opened in its new location at 3 E. Salem Avenue on November 3. It had vacated its previous location directly across the street due to the construction of the viaduct. It also opened a branch at 101 N. Henry Street a few days later.

Appalachian Electric Power Company acquired the lands and rights at the Smith Mountain dam site on the Roanoke River on November 3. The company had purchased the site and all other real estate owned by the Roanoke-Staunton River Power Company, which had promoted the idea of a dam for a quarter century.

The congregation of Central Baptist Church at Starkey approved a new $60,000 sanctuary building on November 3. The sanctuary would have seating for 350.

Tommy Dorsey and his orchestra, along with saxophonist Jimmy Dorsey, performed at the American Legion Auditorium for a show and dance on November 8. The balcony was reserved for Black spectators.

VMI defeated William and Mary 21–0 in football on November 6 at Victory Stadium. A crowd of 12,000 watched the annual Shrine Bowl game that benefited the Shrine Crippled Children Fund. A parade through downtown Roanoke was held before the game that involved over twenty high school and junior high school bands from around the state.

Valley Antique Shop opened on November 7 at 4803 Williamson Road. It was owned and operated by Mrs. E. L. Purvis and Miss Annie Purvis.

Jan Lee Laundry opened at its new location at 114 E. Campbell Avenue on November 7.

The national convention of the United Daughters of the Confederacy was held in Roanoke the first week in November at the Hotel Roanoke.

The Roanoke Ministers Conference voted on November 8 to send a letter to Virginia's governor and the chairman of his Commission of Education stating the group's opposition to any effort to evade the Supreme Court's ruling outlawing segregation in public schools. The conference declared the ruling "morally right."

A group of forty businessmen who were touring the Gainsboro Elementary School on November 9 for Education-Business-Industry Day were appalled by what they saw. The group declared the conditions of the school to be "a disgrace to the city." The school was erected in 1898 and had space heaters in the classrooms and outdoor toilets. It was located on four-tenths of an acre, which left little room for recreation.

Roanoke Civil Defense officials conducted surprise drills during the first of November. One daytime drill evacuated Wasena Elementary School, Addison High School, and Roanoke Catholic High School. Students at Wasena were bused to Back Creek Elementary as part of the exercise.

Judge Beverly Fitzpatrick announced on November 9 that smoking would no longer be allowed in Municipal Court and that all in attendance must rise when court was called to order. These initiatives were part of implementing a plan endorsed by the Roanoke Bar Association to bring dignity and decorum to the court.

This 1950s postcard shows a view of Jefferson Street looking north from Mountain Avenue SW. Jefferson Apartments are in the right foreground. *Nelson Harris*

The Barter Theatre presented *Macbeth* at the Jefferson High School auditorium on November 9. Lead roles were performed by Paul Lukather and Jenny Davis.

The Midnighters, Tod Rhodes and his orchestra, and Bill Davis performed for a show and dance at the American Legion Auditorium on November 15. The balcony was reserved for white spectators.

Julien's Shoes celebrated its fifth anniversary in early November. The store was located at 205 First Street SW.

William Fleming High School football team won the District 6 championship in a title game against Blacksburg High School on November 12. Fleming won 51–13. The coach was Fred Smith.

Wheel Room Steak House opened at 217 Twenty-Fourth Street NW in mid-November.

Fulton Motor Company advertised its new remodeled and expanded facilities via advertisements in mid-November. The Chrysler and Pontiac dealership was located at 114 Franklin Road with a service department annex at 620 Second Street SW.

Belmont Christian Church held a ground-breaking ceremony on November 14 for its new three-story education building. Dr. Orville Wake, president of Lynchburg College, was the speaker. The ceremony was part of the congregation's fiftieth anniversary celebration. The building was estimated to cost $150,000. Membership of the church was 1,000.

Roanoke City Council exonerated three of its appointed municipal officials of alleged wrongdoings as had been charged by Councilman Paul Puckett. Puckett had claimed that the city manager, city auditor, and city clerk were involved in the irregularities of some months ago pertaining to the city garage. No evidence was produced by Puckett in that regard, though he had made many public comments insinuating he had proof. The council conducted its own inquiry as a committee of the whole and voted to end the matter with no further actions. Puckett was the only one to dissent.

IBM formally opened its new sales and service office at 933 S. Jefferson Street on November 17.

The Stevens Gospel Singers of New York City performed at Butler Temple, 15 Fourth Street NE, and at Loudon Avenue Christian Church in mid-November. The singing group had regularly performed on national radio and television programs.

The Harlem Globetrotters came to the American Legion Auditorium on November 28.

Ground was broken in Vinton in mid-November for the construction of a professional building at Pollard Street and Jackson Avenue. The two-story structure, when completed, would be occupied by three physicians and an insurance agency. A corporation headed by Dr. John Hurt was constructing the building.

Family Jewelers at 509 S. Jefferson Street announced in mid-November that it was closing.

The Angus House, a restaurant, opened at Jefferson Street and Elm Avenue on November 19. The establishment was in the old Storiesifer house and was decorated in an 1890s motif. The restaurant was owned by Anson Jamison and managed by Thomas Lee.

Julius Prufer, debate coach for Roanoke College, stated on November 19 that no students on the Roanoke College debate team would argue in the affirmative to the question, "Should the US recognize Red China?" Prufer had been interviewed by national journalist Edward R. Murrow for Murrow's CBS newscast. According to Pufer, when the Roanoke College debate team competed against Wake Forest University in North Carolina and was told to argue the affirmative to the China question, a congressman later asked for the names of the students who had done so. "It's a shame that in this country it is getting so you cannot say what you think," Pufer remarked. The professor said he did not want to get any of his debate students in trouble. The interview with Pufer and other college debate coaches on the same matter aired on CBS on November 23.

The Gift Box opened on November 20 next to Howard Johnson's on Route 11 North.

The Orioles, Joe Morris and his orchestra, Al Savage, and Amos Milburn performed for a show and dance at the American Legion Auditorium on November 24. The balcony was reserved for white spectators.

Seven thousand telephone customers of the Chesapeake and Potomac Telephone Company received new numbers on November 21 due to the opening of the company's new telephone exchange on Barkley Avenue. The new exchange also meant telephone service for an additional 1,400 homes. Those switched over to the new exchange had been previously served through the exchange on Luck Avenue.

Dr. Hugh Trout Jr., president of the YMCA, announced plans for a $750,000 campaign to construct a new Y building at the corner of Church Avenue and Fifth Street SW. The YMCA's building at Church Avenue and Second Street SW was deemed inadequate and had already been sold.

Renick Motor Company at 2239 Franklin Road SW was named as the Roanoke area dealer for Nash automobiles. Roanoke had not had a Nash brand dealer since Fugate Motors closed in 1952. Renick also sold Kaiser automobiles and Willys cars and trucks. The company had been in Roanoke since 1919.

A cornerstone-laying ceremony was held for the new National Guard armory on November 20. The $413,000 building was being erected adjacent to Maher Field.

Roanoke Trunk Company held a grand opening on November 22 at 19 W. Church Avenue. The store sold luggage and related items.

Dr. George Kolmer of Salem died at his home on November 21 at the age of seventy. Kolmer was vice president of Farmers National Bank and a former Roanoke County medical examiner. He had practiced medicine in Salem for forty years.

Roanoke City Council ordered on November 22 a proposed contract with the Roanoke Redevelopment and Housing Authority for a "slum clearance" and redevelopment project encompassing 83.5 acres of northeast Roanoke. This was the result of a two-hour hearing where many citizens voiced opposition to the program and council members had objections to some elements of the project. A six-person committee was tasked with developing a contract that would contain more specifics as to the financing and goals of the RRHA's plan.

English Village

This early 1950s postcard shows the English Village, a cabin motor lodge, which was located on Route 11 at Route 117. *Nelson Harris*

John Largin, seventy-eight, of Roanoke was killed by a hit and run near Salem on November 22. Largin's body was discovered lying in a ditch beside Veterans Facility Road.

The SCC authorized the Virginian Railway to abandon passenger service between Roanoke and the West Virginia line effective December 31.

Oren Roanoke Corporation announced on November 23 an order for six of their fire trucks had been received from Turkey for use in that country's oil fields. The trucks would be shipped overseas from New York City.

The Roanoke Symphony Orchestra performed in Bluefield, West Virginia, on November 23, the hometown of its conductor, Gibson Morrissey.

Fink's Jewelers opened a new store in Salem on November 26. Max Spigle was the manager of the store located at 206 E. Main Street. For the grand opening, a $250,000 diamond belonging to Harry Winston of New York was put on display.

Virginia Tech defeated VMI 46–9 in the annual Thanksgiving Day football game at Victory Stadium. Attendance was estimated at 26,000.

The S&W Cafeteria on South Jefferson Street closed on November 26 in preparation for the opening of the new S&W Cafeteria in the 100 block of W. Church Avenue on December 1. The cafeteria had been on Jefferson Street for almost twenty-five years. The new cafeteria could seat 625 and had three serving lines. It also had two private dining rooms, the Train Room and the Hideaway. Frank Sherrill was president of the company, and M. D. Booth was the cafeteria manager. An estimated 10,000 attended the open house, at which ladies were given souvenir spoons. The S&W was part of a nine-cafeteria chain.

This undated photo shows the S&W Cafeteria in the 100 block of Church Avenue SW. *Bob Kinsey*

WLVA-TV near Lynchburg relocated its transmission tower to Johnson Mountain south of Evington in late November. This allowed some in Roanoke to receive their broadcasts on channel 13 as long as the "rabbit ears" were pointed toward Evington.

Pat Poindexter, a ninth grader at Woodrow Wilson Junior High School, was selected by the Roanoke Merchants Association as the Snow Queen for Roanoke's annual Santa Claus Parade that was held on November 30. The parade began at Elm Avenue SE and included decorated autos, eight bands, floats, clowns, ponies, and horses. Police estimated the evening parade crowd was between 30,000 and 35,000.

Two singers with the Metropolitan Opera performed on November 29 at the American Theatre. Brian Sullivan and Hilde Gueden were part of the Thursday Morning Music Club concert series.

Piedmont Stores held a grand opening of its department store in Salem on December 3.

Roanoke's oldest practicing attorney, James Hart, died at his home at the age of eighty-four on December 3. He came to Roanoke around 1900 and started a law practice with his brother, John Hart.

Vinton held its annual Christmas Parade on December 3, and some 2,000 persons lined the streets to see the town's first nighttime Christmas parade.

Virginia Tech tackle George Preas was named the best collegiate football player in the state by the Roanoke Touchdown Club. Preas was presented a trophy at the club's dinner on December 6 at the Hotel Roanoke.

Forty newspaper boys in the Roanoke Valley were presented the new *Webster's Unified Dictionary and Encyclopedia* in early December as part of 900 newspaper carriers selected throughout the state for demonstrating outstanding customer service and scholastic achievement.

Forty-three original old masters from the collection of Dr. Armand Hammer were put on display by the Roanoke Fine Arts Center and Hollins College. The monthlong exhibit included works by Rembrandt, Rubens, Titian, Filippo, Lippi, and Brugel. The exhibit was displayed at both Hollins College and in the auditorium of the Roanoke Public Library.

The Men's Garden Club, the first all-male garden club in the Roanoke Valley, was formed on December 6. A. O. English was named as temporary chairman.

Johnson-Vest Electric began advertising Motorola color televisions in early December. The price for the Mahogany finish consolette with two matched speakers was $895.

The local Fraternal Order of Police moved to their new lodge hall at 3031 Preston Avenue NE, the second week in December. The hall was adjacent to Preston Park.

The search for two young girls, missing from their home in Beckley, West Virginia, since November 1, centered upon Roanoke by the end of the first week in December. West Virginia authorities believed they may have been brought to Roanoke shortly after their disappearance. Local law enforcement began checking motels, transient centers, and rooming houses, but the girls were not found.

Twenty British brides gathered at the home of Mrs. Dorothy Hamilton on December 8 to form a social club. All had married American men who served with US troops in their country during World War II. According to Hamilton, there were fifty British brides living in the Roanoke Valley.

Carl Smith and his Tunesmiths, June Carter, Dale Potter, Rusty Gabberd, and the Wood Sisters, all from the *Grand Ole Opry*, performed at the American Legion Auditorium on December 12.

Bush-Flora Shoe Company, located at 109 W. Campbell Avenue, opened a children's shoe department in mid-December on the second floor of its building.

The Roanoke Merchants Association sent a letter to Roanoke City Council asking that the city pay for the lighting and maintaining of the Roanoke Star on Mill Mountain, a cost borne by the association since the star was lighted in 1949.

Pete Moore's Appliance Center opened on December 13 at 2912 Williamson Road.

George Lawrence, spokesman for the trustees of Burrell Memorial Hospital, asked Roanoke City Council on December 13 that it pay Burrell the same per diem rate for indigent Black patients that the city was paying to other hospitals for indigent white patients. The rate Burrell was being paid was $11.55 per day as compared to $16 per day given to white hospitals. Lawrence reported such funding should be retroactive to the first of the year. The council agreed to the request.

Roanoke City Council member Mary Pickett christened the *City of Roanoke* Trailways bus on December 14. The new forty-passenger bus inaugurated Trailways's new through service from Bluefield, West Virginia, to Washington, DC, via Roanoke. The occasion also marked the acquisition of Consolidated Bus Lines into the Trailways system.

The University Club, a new downtown Roanoke social club for business and professional men, was chartered in mid-December. The group, headed by George Betsold III announced the club would be housed in a former residence at 9 Elm Avenue SW, which would open on February 15.

Salem merchants held Stag Night on December 16 for men-only Christmas shopping. Participating stores were Mareta's, Shank Furniture Company, Zand's, Piedmont Stores, the Children's Shop, Kay's Sportswear, Carper's Gifts, Modern Dress Shop, and Fink's Jewelers. Women were invited to dine and drink at Webber's Pharmacy while the men shopped. In Roanoke, Heironimus and Pugh's Department Store held Stag Night as well. Both stores provided live music using local bands, and runway models showcased dresses, coats, and jewelry.

Larry Hughes, fourteen and a student at Broad Street School, won first place in the statewide one-hundred-bushel corn contest. A resident of the Catawba Valley, Hughes produced 192.72 bushels of corn per acre.

Mayor Robert Woody lit Roanoke's Christmas tree positioned on the lawn of the Municipal Building. Music was provided by the William Fleming High School Band and the choir of Booker T. Washington Junior High School.

More than 500 boys gathered for dinner at the Monroe Junior High School cafeteria on December 15 for the annual city sandlot football banquet. Don Divers, a Virginia Tech fullback, delivered the main address after the awards presentation.

Roanoke City Council member Paul Puckett submitted his resignation on December 16 to take effect on December 31. Puckett had accepted a managerial position in another city with Westinghouse Electric Corporation.

Five coal cars of the Virginian Railway derailed near Wasena Bridge on December 16. No one was injured.

John Mullins, a forty-eight-year-old Roanoke city fireman, died on December 16 from brain injuries he received from a fall from the roof of a residence the previous day. He was cleaning a gutter when he fell.

The Lucado family, which included five children, lost all their belongings in a house fire in the Glenvar section on December 17. They rented the residence from Mrs. Norma Baker.

The Associated Press named their 1954 All-Group I state football team. Included on the eleven-player first team roster was Jack Reynolds of Jefferson High School who played end. On the second team were Carol Jamison, guard for Jefferson High School, and Ken Norton, back for Andrew Lewis High School.

Mr. and Mrs. Meade Harris presented the Roanoke Fine Arts Center with the former South Roanoke Baptist Church building on December 18 for use as the center's headquarters. The building was located at the corner of Carolina Avenue and Twenty-Fifth Street SW. Mrs. Arthur Ellett accepted the deed to the building on behalf of the center. The fine arts group planned to take several months to remodel and prepare the building for its use.

The Roanoke Photo Finishing Company was located on Second Street, SW, as seen in this image from the 1950s. *Bob Kinsey*

A record 41,915 cans of fruits, vegetables and meats were produced at the Roanoke County Cannery in 1954. More than 700 persons used the cannery between July 1 and December 16.

Three persons were killed in a two-vehicle accident on Route 11 at Big Hill near Dixie Caverns on December 19. Emery Smyth, fifty-seven, and his wife, Edna, forty of Kingsport, Tennessee, were killed as was Nancy Nolen, fourteen, of Pearisburg. Nolen was returning home from practicing for a Christmas pageant.

On December 20, Gustavus Whitlock of Floyd County died in a wreck on Route 221. three miles west of Roanoke. His truck collided with a car and went over a forty-foot embankment into Back Creek. Whitlock was seventy-two.

William Strange was sentenced to fifteen years in prison for the murder of Jessie Brown at a home they shared on Rutherfoord Avenue NW. Strange pled guilty to second-degree murder.

Roanoke City Council agreed to assume payments for the electric bill and maintenance of the Roanoke Star at their meeting on December 20. The payments would begin January 1 and was in response to a request by the Roanoke Merchants Association.

The Drifters, La Vern Baker, and saxophonist Red Prysock performed for a show and dance at the American Legion Auditorium on December 25. It was a midnight Christmas dance that began at midnight and went until 4:00 a.m. The balcony was reserved for white spectators.

Leggett's department store, located at 112 Campbell Avenue, was decorated for Christmas in this 1950s image. *Virginia Room, RPL*

Cory Caldwell, twenty-two, of Roanoke County died on December 24 as a result of an auto accident on Kessler Mill Road, about a mile north of Lakeside.

The Roanoke Altruist Club held its annual debutante ball on December 30 in a setting depicting ancient Rome. Twenty-three young women were presented in the event held at the American Legion Auditorium. A few days prior to the ball, the women attended a charm school at the Orange Avenue YWCA.

William Ware, thirty-eight, died on Christmas Day in Burrell Memorial Hospital from a knife wound to the stomach. Nola Taylor, twenty-seven, was charged by police for the slaying.

Frank LaBrie, sixty-five, of Roanoke County, who had been brutally beaten in early December, died on December 27 in a Roanoke hospital. Police had already arrested Theodore Allen of Bluefield, West Virginia, for the beating and then upgraded the charge to murder. Allen had been jailed in Princeton, West Virginia.

Roanoke City Council decided to begin the process of closing the city's tuberculosis sanatorium at Coyner Springs effective June 30, 1955. The decision was prompted by the state's decision to no longer reimburse the city for any of the state's patients at the facility. The city built the sanatorium in 1939 when the state lacked adequate beds. The state, at the time of the council decision, had sufficient beds for white patients and was building a new 250-bed sanatorium at Burkeville for Black patients.

The Colonial Hills Club was purchased for $65,000 from Lucy Rorrer by a new corporation, Colonial Hills Inc., headed by Alonza Larch. The entertainment and dance club was located at 2728 Colonial Avenue SW.

The deed for two lots in the 800 block of McDowell Avenue NW was presented to the congregation of St. Luke's Episcopal Church on December 25 for the construction of a future church. The church was served by Rev. Turner Morris on a part-time basis and was a mission of the Episcopal diocese.

Directors of the Class D Appalachian Baseball League invited Salem to join the circuit on December 29. A ruling by George Trautman, head of the minor leagues, prevented Salem from accepting the invitation until the affairs of the Roanoke Red Sox were cleared up from when that team folded in 1953.

Virginian Railway passenger service west of Roanoke officially ended on December 31 after forty-five years of operation with the arrival of the eastbound train in Roanoke at 4:55 p.m. The westbound train finished its run at Page, West Virginia, earlier in the afternoon. Dozens of people took the train for a farewell ride. The last passenger train to Roanoke was manned by Fireman E. S. White, Engineer A. A. Akers, Conductor H. R. Harvey, and Brakeman I. C. Reese. The Virginian Railway continued to operate passenger service between Roanoke and its eastern terminal at Norfolk.

Detective Sgt. Joe Jennings was given a cash Christmas gift by members of the community and Roanoke police. Jennings had been a resident at Lewis-Gale Hospital since being paralyzed while making an arrest in 1945.

At their meeting on December 31, Roanoke City Council chose Herbert Davies to fill the unexpired term of Paul Puckett. Davies was the retired vice president of American Bridge in Roanoke, a division of US Steel, which was formerly Virginia Bridge and Iron Company.

Paul Williams and his orchestra, along with Margie Day, performed for a show and dance at the Star City Auditorium on December 31. The balcony was reserved for white spectators.

1955

Douglas Ayers, the town clerk of Salem, and his fiancée Joyce Djuvik appeared as contestants on the nationally broadcast quiz show *The Big Pay-Off* over the CBS network on January 3. The show devoted its Monday time to interviewing engaged couples with a chance to win appliances, trips, and clothing.

Roanoke banks reported their year-end 1954 financial positions on January 2. The reports for assets and liabilities were as follows: First National Exchange Bank, $86,007, 378; Mountain Trust Bank, $30,083,551; Colonial-American National Bank, $37,606,220; Peoples Federal Savings and Loan Association, $7,058, 235; Bank of Virginia, $110.874,487; First Federal Savings and Loan Association, $12,722,926; and Southwest Virginia Savings and Loan Association, $5,839,258.

The Roanoke Fine Arts Center opened a three-woman exhibition of paintings by local artists on January 4 at the Roanoke Public Library. The artists were Laura Meagher, Evelyn Thompson, and Priscilla Young.

State Farm Insurance Companies opened its new eight-room office building at 5005 Williamson Road NW on January 3. Fred Gates was the district manager.

Some local television sets began receiving WFMY-TV out of Greensboro on channel 2 in early January. The station began using a new 100,000-watt transformer and was a CBS affiliate.

Roanoke City Council advertised for bids in early January for the razing of the Cannaday home at Woodrum Field. The landmark home had served a variety of purposes for the airport.

Sam Pollock purchased the Natalie Shoppe at 311 S. Jefferson Street from the estate Nat Spigel.

The Roanoke Academy of Medicine voted on January 3 to open its membership to Black doctors. The academy's vote was unanimous. Dr. Allen Barker was the academy's president. The action by the Roanoke Academy allowed Black physicians to be eligible for membership in the Virginia Academy of Medicine and the American Medical Association.

A campaign to qualify 150,000 Blacks as new voters in Virginia was outlined in Roanoke on January 3 by Dr. Harry Penn as part of a nationwide voter registration drive sponsored by the Omega Psi Phi fraternity. Penn, a former national head of the fraternity, was the campaign chairman for Virginia, West Virginia and North Carolina. Penn made his announcement during a meeting at the Hunton YMCA.

This mid-'50s photo shows Vance's Esso, located at 108 Commonwealth Avenue NE. Hotel Roanoke is in the background. *Virginia Room, RPL*

Sixth District Congressman Richard Poff was elected secretary of the Republican conference of the US House of Representatives on January 4.

Donald Bernard, twenty-six, died at Lewis-Gale Hospital on January 5 from what police stated was a self-inflicted gunshot wound. According to witnesses, Bernard was sitting with several friends at the Normandie Inn at Patterson Avenue and Thirteenth Street SW when he shot himself. According to the friends, Bernard told them he was AWOL from the army and did not want to return to the military.

Royal Loan Corporation opened at 124 W. Church Avenue on January 6.

Paul Matthews, Roanoke County administrator, announced that the county would discontinue using a lakebed in Westward Lakes Estate, west of Salem, as a garbage dump. Nearby residents petitioned for the decision, asserting that the garbage contaminated a creek that flowed through the area.

Members of the Magic City Medical Society, the organization for Black doctors, expressed pleasure and approval of the Roanoke Academy of Medicine decision to open membership to Black physicians during their meeting on January 5. Most indicated they planned to join the academy. The Magic City Medical Society was headed by Dr. F. W. Claytor.

The Flamingo Restaurant opened on Route 460 east of Salem on January 7.

Kay's Ice Cream of Roanoke was purchased on January 6 by a new corporation, High's Ice Cream of Roanoke, headed by J. R. Gregory. Gregory, of Richmond, purchased the Kay's stores throughout Virginia including the five in Roanoke and Salem.

A head-on auto collision near Fincastle on January 7 killed eight persons, including three from one family. The fatalities were Mr. and Mrs. Julian Wills, Wilmer Wills, William Clay Jr., Gilbert Wiley, Robert Pettus, Joe Willis, and George Brown. All were from Botetourt County. It was the worst two-car accident in Virginia's history.

WSLS radio formally opened its new studios in Salem on January 7. More than 1,000 persons visited during the open house conducted at the studios on West Main Street. Pat Murphy was the studio director.

The Charms, Chuck Willis and his orchestra, and Lowell Wilson performed for a show and dance at American Legion Auditorium on January 14. The balcony was reserved for white spectators.

WSLS-TV began a new locally produced program for preschool children, *Romper Room*, which premiered on January 10. The host was Mrs. Elsie Tanner. The series aired Mondays through Fridays from 9:00 a.m. until 9:45 a.m.

Vogue Beauty Shop opened at its new location at 19-A W. Church Avenue on January 10.

Eastern Airlines began advertising in local newspapers in mid-January for stewardesses. Applicants had to have the following qualifications: ages twenty-one to twenty-six; single (never married); height between five foot three and five foot six; weight between 110 and 130 pounds (in proportion to height); two years of college; and normal vision, not requiring glasses. Training was conducted in Miami, Florida.

Russian pianist Alexander Brailowsky gave a concert at the American Theatre on January 10. The concert was sponsored by the Thursday Morning Music Club. The audience of 2,000 demanded three encores.

Roanoke City Council gave its authorization on January 10 for the razing of the Cannaday farmhouse at Woodrum Field. The landmark structure was located on a knoll that needed to be leveled for airport improvements.

The City Rescue Mission opened its doors for women transients for the first time in January. Superintendent G. A. Johnson said ten beds had been placed in quarters at 108 E. Salem Avenue. In 1954, the mission provided lodging to 2,472 persons and provided 12,390 free meals.

Roanoke City Council questioned members of the Roanoke Redevelopment and Housing Authority before a packed chamber on January 11. Most of those in attendance were Black citizens who would be forced to move under the housing authority's "slum clearance" program. Most of the questions dealt with the financial aspects of the proposal. It was the first in a number of public hearings slated on the matter. Council members were the only ones allowed to ask questions.

Roanoker Rora Penn, sixty-one, was murdered in the state penitentiary in Richmond on January 11. Penn had been sentenced to life in 1943 for murder. According to the coroner, Penn was strangled to death.

Emmett Shelor, fifty-one, of Salem died on January 12 at his home two hours after being in an altercation following a traffic accident. The coroner attributed Shelor's death to a heart condition that was aggravated by the altercation. The identity of the other person involved was unknown.

The Barter Theatre presented James Thurber's *The 13 Clocks* at the Jefferson High School auditorium on January 12. Lead roles were played by Owen Phillips, Peggy Collins, Dorothy LaVern, and Paul Lukather.

Charles Johnson, president of Fisk University, spoke at High Street Baptist Church on January 16. The title of his address was "The Maturing of Democracy."

Roanoke City Council held another public hearing on January 13 regarding the housing authority's "slum clearance" plan for northeast Roanoke. Two spokesmen were heard representing Blacks whose homes would be impacted. Both urged the council to allow the residents of northeast to develop their own plan for addressing the issues of housing and blight. Mrs. C. S. Williams asked the council to look at ways other cities had addressed similar challenges by involving the residents. Ira Womack was the second to speak and asserted that plans were lacking for the proper relocation of those that would be displaced, including financial remuneration.

Officials with Shenandoah Christian College announced on January 13 plans to organize a college in Roanoke in the fall. Rev. James Comstock was head of the organization.

Robert Jackson, Roanoke's oldest attorney, died on January 15 at the age of ninety-four. He came to Roanoke in 1907 and was Roanoke's first city attorney under the city manager form of government. He served as city attorney from 1918 until 1936.

Harwood Brothers, a paint and hardware store, opened on January 17 at 404 Campbell Avenue SW.

Officials with Hotel Roanoke announced that for 1955, 103 conventions had been booked with anticipated convention visitors expected to number over 25,000.

Metropolitan Opera baritone Theodore Uppman gave a concert at the Jefferson High School auditorium on January 17 under the auspices of the Roanoke Community Concert Association.

The first Black clergyman was admitted to membership in the Roanoke Ministers Conference on January 17. Chaplain Robert Johnson of the Veterans Administration Hospital, formerly the pastor of High Street Baptist Church, was received unanimously by the conference.

The Booker T. Washington Birthplace Memorial, started in 1946, announced on January 18 that it was bankrupt and was selling the Washington home place land, about 400 acres in Franklin County, to pay its creditors. The memorial owed about $140,000. The founder, Sidney Phillips, stated that the birthplace memorial failed to receive support from blacks. Phillips had minted 15 million commemorative half-dollars, but only 2.2 million were purchased. Of those purchased, Phillips said only 3 percent were purchased by Blacks. Phillips stated, "Every program we have attempted has been supported almost entirely by white persons, with little patronage by Negroes generally and almost without any exercise of interest and influence on the part of Negro leaders." Phillips, who was Black, and the birthplace memorial had been the subject of several lawsuits that had dampened interest in the effort. He operated a training school for five years that served some 2,000 students during the period it was open. Phillips had been a salesman with the NeHi

Corporation prior to taking a leave of absence to lead the birthplace memorial campaign. He planned to return to his former position.

The Hotel Roanoke Coffee Shop opened on January 19. It seated 200 people and was located off the main lobby.

Enon Baptist Church on Route 11 at Hollins celebrated its centennial on January 23. The first clerk of the church was Dr. Charles Cocke, who was also the founder of Hollins College. The church's first building was erected in 1855 and then rebuilt and enlarged in 1917.

Virginia's School Segregation Study Commission, a thirty-two-man body, sent its report to the governor on January 19. The six-page report expressed the view that integration "would virtually destroy or seriously impair the public school system" in many sections of the state such that the commission's goal would be to preserve segregation "within the framework of the law." State Senator Earl Fitzpatrick of Roanoke, a member of the commission, commented on the report. "We are working on the basis that the Supreme Court has declared that segregation in the public schools in unconstitutional. With that thought in mind we are working towards means whereby we will not have enforced integration of the race in the public schools of Virginia."

A group of Black leaders in Roanoke pushed back against comments made by Sidney Phillips, founder of the Booker T. Washington Birthplace Memorial, that the effort to establish a memorial had failed due to a lack of support from Black leaders. Some thirty-five Black clergy and businessmen signed a letter that asserted that Phillips's lack of ability to properly develop the plan was a major factor in its failure.

Famous radio singer Martha Tilton visited Roanoke the third week in January. She had wed Jim Brooks of Roanoke and wanted to see his hometown. Tilton was the costar of the weekday program *Curt Massey Time* heard over the CBS network. The couple lived in California, where Brooks was a test pilot.

Showtimers announced on January 22 that they would begin offering a comprehensive survey course on play production beginning in February. The class was sponsored by the University of Virginia Extension Division. Nelson Bond was the business manager for Showtimers and helped organize the course.

Charles McInturff of Starkey was profiled in the January 23 edition of the *Roanoke Times* for his unusual hobby. He collected neck ties, mostly purchased at secondhand shops. His collection consisted of 1,827 ties.

The *Ice Vogues of 1955* came to the American Legion Auditorium for a five-day run in late January. The show featured well-known skaters Chet Nelson and Sheila Hamilton.

The longest single unit shipment ever moved by N&W Railway arrived in Roanoke from Winston-Salem on January 25. It was a treating cylinder for use at the Koppers Company plant west of Salem. The cylinder was 145 feet long and required the use of three flat cars.

Roanoke Coca-Cola Bottling Works purchased an eleven-acre site in late January for a future expansion on Route 11 north of Roanoke. The tract was purchased from the estate of the late W. W. Boxley.

The B. F. Goodrich Home and Auto store was located at 3520 Williamson Road NW, as seen in this mid-1950s photo. *Virginia Room, RPL*

George Preas, a tackle for Virginia Tech, was drafted in the fifth round on January 27 by the Baltimore Colts. Preas, of Roanoke, had played for Jefferson High School.

Showtimers presented the comedy *Goodbye, Mr. Fancy* on January 27 at the Lab Theatre. The cast included Jane St. Clair, Betsy Maxwell, Bettie Jones, Betty Shaner, and Nell Hollingsworth.

Officials with the Times-World Corporation and Radio Roanoke agreed to end their contest for channel 7 television station. The end of the yearlong battle between the two before the FCC was announced on January 28. The Times-World Corporation agreed to purchase television equipment, rights, and privileges owned by Radio Roanoke with the latter agreeing to drop its application for channel 7. The two companies had waged a spirited battle for the channel for nearly eighteen months. There was no timetable given with the announcement as to when Roanoke's second television station might go on the air. The announcement was made jointly by M. W. Armistead III president of Times-World, and Leo Henebry, president of Radio Roanoke. Radio Roanoke owned and operated WROV radio, and the Times-World Corporation published the two Roanoke newspapers, as well as owned and operated WDBJ radio.

S. H. Heironimus Company announced on January 28 it had leased the Thurman estate property at Jefferson Street and Church Avenue, known as the Thurman and Boone Building. Heironimus officials planned to do $1.2 million worth of remodeling to create "an ultra-modern department store." Thurman & Boone planned to go out of business. Heironimus signed a twenty-five-year lease on the property. Heironimus was started in Roanoke in 1890 in a small store at 206 Second Street SW by S. H. Heironimus. Originally known as Heironimus & Brugh, the store moved in 1900 to the northeast corner of Campbell Avenue and First Street, and in 1915 to the corner of Jefferson and Church. In 1936, it relocated again. The founder of the store and its namesake severed ties with the business in 1913. At the time of the announcement, Heirnomius had 400 employees.

The Barter Theatre presented *My Three Angels* in the auditorium of Jefferson High School on February 2. Lead roles were performed by Owen Phillips, Severn Darden, and Frederick Combs.

Kuda Bux and his Pakistani mystics performed at the American Legion Auditorium on January 31. According to ads for the show, Bux walked through fire barefooted, read books through solid walls of steel, and did miracles of magic.

The Community Concert Association, Roanoke's oldest organization supporting public concerts, announced on January 31 the suspension of operations. Richard Pence, the association's president, said the membership made the decision after twenty-three years of operation due to other organizations providing public music programs.

At its January 31 meeting, Roanoke City Council agreed to appoint a five-person study committee to explore the various aspects of a proposed theatre-type civic auditorium which had been recommended for construction in Elmwood Park. Dr. E. G. Gill had led an informal group of businessmen and civic organizations in advocating for such a move.

Robert DeVault, sixty-five, a veteran railroad conductor from Bluefield, West Virginia, was fatally injured at the N&W Railway passenger station in Roanoke on February 1. He was struck by the tender of a locomotive.

Salem's first church-sponsored kindergarten was announced on February 1. The kindergarten would open on March 1 in the Wiley House of First Methodist Church.

Dr. Leo Platt relocated his optometry practice from the Mountain Trust Building to 507 S. Jefferson Street in early February.

Saxophonist Earl Bostic and his orchestra performed for a show and dance at the American Legion Auditorium on February 4. The balcony was reserved for white spectators.

A crowd of 3,000 men turned out for the traditional annual meeting of the Roanoke Groundhog Club on February 2 held at the American Legion Auditorium. Reporter Melville Carico wrote, "The main floor...looked like an acre of bald heads shining in a mist of tobacco smoke under the strong arena-type lights." The group was entertained by hillbilly entertainer Doug Wilson, and several local politicians were roasted in good fun.

The first service for a new church in Salem, Evangelical Methodist Church, was held on February 6 by Rev. E. W. Dean at Third and Colorado Streets.

The St. Louis Symphony performed in Roanoke on February 5 at the American Legion Auditorium and was sponsored by the Thursday Morning Music Club. The eighty-five-person symphony was conducted by Vladimir Golschmann, who led the program while in a fourteen-pound cast due to a broken ankle.

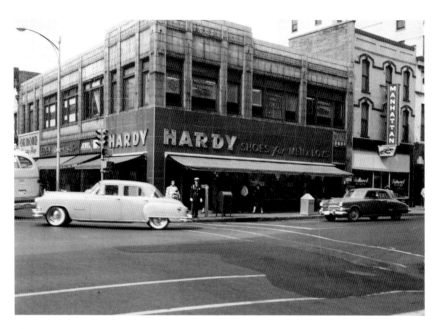

This circa 1955 photo shows Hardy Shoes for Men and Boys, which was located at corner of Campbell Avenue and Jefferson Street. *Virginia Room, RPL*

James Lewis announced on February 4 that he was resigning as administrator of Burrell Memorial Hospital effective March 1. He had served in the position since 1947.

Lou Thesz, reportedly the world's number one ranked professional wrestler, was the mat feature at the American Legion Auditorium on February 8. He squared off against Kinji Shibuya, billed as the Japanese villain. Attendance was 2,250.

A crowd of 1,000 persons attended a voter registration drive rally for Blacks at the American Legion Auditorium on February 6. The principal speaker was Judge William Hastie of Philadelphia. The event was organized by Dr. Harry Penn.

Thirty-four students from Hollins College boarded the French liner *S.S. Liberte* in New York for their transatlantic crossing to study for a year at the Sorbonne in Paris. They were the first participants in Hollins's new study abroad program.

Kay's Restaurant and Gift Shop on Route 11 west of Salem closed the first week of February due to the loss of their lease.

Roanoke City Council approved a $775,000 improvement plan for Woodrum Field at their meeting on February 7. The plan included an extended runway, land acquisition, and improvements to facilities.

The Hitching Post Motel on Route 11, north of Roanoke, announced plans for a $150,000 addition that would bring the motel to having fifty-five units. Mr. and Mrs. Carl Windel were the owners.

Albert Farnham, well-known Roanoke landscape architect, died at his home on February 9 at age sixty-two. He had a leading role in the postwar development of the Virginia Tech campus and was employed by urban planner John Nolan earlier in his career.

James Maxey of Roanoke shot and killed his wife in their home on Eleventh Street NE and then turned the gun on himself. Gladys Maxey was killed instantly, while the husband died a few days later at Lewis-Gale Hospital. The couple, in their forties, had five children.

Prominent Roanoke businessman Littleberry Boxley died on February 13 at age sixty-seven. He entered the contracting business in 1909 and became a member of the W. W. Boxley & Company in 1914. He was president of Blue Ridge Stone Corporation and the Pounding Mill Quarry Corporation. He also served on the board of several businesses and as a trustee of Hollins College.

A new puzzle feature, *Jumble*, began appearing regularly in the two Roanoke newspapers in mid-February.

Lonnie Miller, fifty, lost his life in a house fire on Riley Road NE on February 12. Fire officials believed the blaze was caused by an overheated coal stove.

Pianist Leon Fleisher performed at the Jefferson High School auditorium on February 15. His concert was sponsored by the Roanoke Community Concert Association. He had won numerous piano competitions in Europe.

Douglas Nininger, superintendent of Roanoke County public schools, announced his resignation on February 14 effective June 30. Nininger was appointed as superintendent on July 1, 1945.

The Roanoke County School Board adopted at its February 14 meeting a $4.4 million capital plan that included Cave Spring High School, four new elementary schools, a new high school, and additions to several schools. The plan was designed to meet the system's needs through 1960.

Rev. LeRoy Gresham, the retired longtime pastor of Salem Presbyterian Church, died on February 16 at eighty-three. Gresham served the Salem congregation for thirty-seven years before retiring in 1946.

Brother Joe May performed at the Star City Auditorium on February 21.

The 220 Diner opened on February 18 on Route 220 south of Roanoke.

Theodore Allen was sentenced to life imprisonment on February 18 after he pled guilty to the savage beating of Frank LaBrie on December 5. LaBrie died a few weeks later from his injuries.

Garden City residents petitioned Roanoke City Council for a fire station in that section to be staffed by paid firemen. The section was served by a volunteer squad even after being annexed.

Roanoke's commissioner of the revenue released real estate valuations for the city. The assessed value for white properties was $119.4 million, and the assessed value for Black properties was $3.7 million.

High's Ice Cream opened at Liberty and Williamson Road on February 19.

Three young adults lost their lives on February 19 when the car they were in went off Hollins Road and into Tinker Creek where they remained trapped. David Palmer of Roanoke, Edward Gillespie of Salem, and Christine Johnson of Salem died from drowning according to the medical examiner. The accident happened near the Palmer Park community.

This 1955 image is of Michael's Bakery on Williamson Road at Huntington Boulevard.
N&W Historical Photographs Collection, VPI&SU Libraries

J. G. Sheets, a veteran real estate broker and auctioneer, died at his home on February 19 at age seventy. Sheets came to the Roanoke area from Walla Walla, Washington, and founded the firm of J. G. Sheets and Sons. He also helped develop sections of the Williamson Road area.

The Kazim Shrine Circus came to the American Legion Auditorium the last weekend in February.

The Roanoke Civic Ballet performed the *Nutcracker* at the Jefferson High School auditorium on February 25.

The Roanoke Symphony Orchestra and a chorus of some 500 voices presented *The Ordering of Moses* on February 28 at the American Legion Auditorium. Vocal soloists included Florence Vickland, Mrs. Thilde Beuing-Edele, Hartwell Phillips, Jack Wimer, and James Reynolds.

Well-known radio gospel group Sons of the South performed at High Street Baptist Church on February 20.

Roanoke City Council at its February 21 meeting voted to cease operating the city's Coyner Springs Sanitarium for white patients and turn over the forty beds for Black tubercular patients on a statewide basis. All white patients would be transferred to state tuberculosis sanitariums, and Coyner Springs would be dedicated to the treatment and care of Black patients from across Virginia.

The *Roanoke Tribune* resumed publication in late February after suspending operations due to a roof collapse that occurred on February 13. Rev. F. E. Alexander, publisher of the weekly, was having the newspaper printed at the *Salem Times-Register* plant temporarily.

Edwards Dungan was named as manager of the American Viscose Roanoke plant on February 22. He was promoted from being chief plant engineer.

A. D. Foster pled guilty to voluntary manslaughter on February 22 in the slaying of Samuel Turner of Roanoke County on September 29, 1954.

Nola Taylor pled guilty to voluntary manslaughter on February 24 in the stabbing of Willie Ware. She was sentenced to five years.

A delegation from Roanoke went to Norfolk and toured that city's "slum clearance" program and returned to Roanoke impressed. Mayor Robert Woody, the city manager, city attorney, Councilwoman Mary Pickett, and Councilman Herbert Davies toured Norfolk's redevelopment area with peers on February 25. Norfolk had redeveloped 193 acres that was occupied exclusively by Black residents and businesses. Woody stated that Norfolk "was sold" on the program.

Miller & Rhoads of Richmond announced on February 26 their plan to establish a store in downtown Roanoke on the site of the McBain Building, corner of Campbell Avenue and First Street SW. Construction would start as soon as S. H. Heironimus Company vacated the McBain Building in April 1956. Miller & Rhoads hoped to occupy the new building in the fall of 1957. The McBain Building was built in 1904 opposite a livery stable and was one of the few remaining landmarks of Roanoke's early days. The structure was originally known as the Watt & Clay Building, which was first occupied by the Watt, Rettew, and Clay Mercantile. The business was bought out by George McBain, a native of Scotland, who moved to Roanoke around 1890. The building was eventually occupied by Heironimus and remodeled in 1935.

Westhampton Christian Church announced plans for a new building to be located on the corner of Grandin Road and Carlton Road SW. The congregation was organized in May 1954 and had been meeting at the Grandin Court Recreation Center. Rev. Walter Calhoun was the pastor.

Demolition of the Cannaday house at Woodrum Field began on February 29. The knoll upon which it sat was to be leveled.

The Second Street Bridge over the N&W Railway tracks was razed at the end of February. The bridge was over sixty years old and in a poor state of repair.

The Smoke Shop Barber Shop at 28 W. Church Avenue relocated 127 Luck Avenue SW on February 29. The barbershop was operated by E. C. Allman and W. W. Reid.

Salem Town Council gave permission for a new cab company to operate within its corporate limits at its February 28 meeting. Hickson Cab Company was allowed one cab. Two other cab companies were already in Salem: Barnett Cab Company and Lawson Cab Company.

Follies of the Night came to the stage of the Roanoke Theatre on March 2. Ads stated it was a "show of 1001 delights" that featured pinup models, comedians, and variety acts.

This mid-1950s photograph shows the new terminal at Woodrum Field with the Cannaday home in the background. The home was razed soon after this image was taken. *N&W Historical Photographs Collection, VPI&SU Libraries*

The Clovers, Faye Adams, Joe Turner, Bill Doggett, the Charms, Lowell Fulson, the Moonglows, Paul Williams and his band, Al Jackson, the Spence Twins, and the Moonlighters performed for a coronation ball at the American Legion Auditorium on March 4. The balcony was reserved for white spectators.

Stein's, a men's clothing store, held a grand opening of their remodeled store on March 3 at 216 S. Jefferson Street. Tropical suits were $34.95.

Central Church of the Brethren began using its new educational building on March 6. The twenty-seven-room building cost $100,000. Rev. Merlin Garber was the pastor.

Congressman Richard Poff announced on March 4 that Roanoke would get a new $422,000 army reserve training center. The center would be built opposite the Veterans Administration Hospital entrance. The center, at the time of the announcement, was located in rented space on Norfolk Avenue SW.

A. D. Foster was sentenced on March 4 to five years for the slaying of Samuel Turner. Foster pled guilty to the charge.

The Class D Appalachian League announced on March 5 that Salem would have a baseball team in the eight-club league for the coming season. Salem's home games would be played in Municipal Stadium.

Dick Kepley of Jefferson High School set four records for Group 1 scholastic high school basketball players in Virginia during the 54–55 Season. First, he set a record for most points scored in a regular season: 564. Second, he averaged 29.7 points per game. Third, he made 213 field goals, and fourth he netted 148 free throws. Kepley, a senior, played center and was six feet, eight inches tall.

The *American Alumni Council News*, a national periodical, named America's oldest-living alumnae in its March edition. It was Miss Ella Miller of Lynchburg, a graduate of Hollins College. She attended the school in 1867, when Roanoke was known as Big Lick. She recalled being driven to the school in a "coach and four."

Construction on a new store by Mitchell's Clothing began the second week in March at 28 W. Church Avenue. The store, a men's clothier, had operated in the Shenandoah Building at 307 First Street SW for twenty-five years. At the site of the new store was Muddiman Electric Company, which would be razed. Muddiman planned to relocate to 1925 West Avenue SW. Ernest Mitchell was president of the clothing company.

The Dublin Players from Ireland presented a production of *Juno and the Paycock* at Hollins College on March 8. The Irish thespians were on a national tour.

New Hope Christian Church met for the first time in the first unit of their new building on Route 672 in Roanoke County on March 7.

The Goodyear Service Store at Second Street and Luck Avenue SW advertised it would be showing the telecast of Mary Martin in *Peter Pan* on their Motorola color television for the community to enjoy in their showroom on March 7.

Grand Ole Opry star Little Jimmy Dickens performed at the Roanoke Theatre on March 9.

The Carlton Terrace Coffee Shop opened on March 8 and offered breakfast, lunch, and dinner.

Six Black doctors were voted into the membership of the Roanoke Academy of Medicine on March 7. They were first to become members of the previously all-white organization. Those voted in were Drs. W. R. Brown, John Claytor Jr., Frank Claytor, Richard Fisher, Harry Lockard Jr., and L. C. Downing.

Officials with General Electric informed government officials that 300 families were being transferred to the Roanoke plant with 575 children. Most were coming from Schenectady, New York.

Three local basketball players were named by the Associated Press to its All-Western District Team. They were Dick Kepley (Jefferson), Glenn Parr (Andrew Lewis), and Louie Mills (Jefferson).

The public health directors of Roanoke city and county jointly announced on March 8 that they were working on plans to administer polio vaccines to 6,900 children in their jurisdictions. The plan would go forward provided the Salk serum was licensed. The plan had been unanimously endorsed by the Roanoke Academy of Medicine.

Dr. Andrew Shapiro was granted a building permit to construct a fifteen-room, one-story clinic to be operated at 1201 Third Street SW. Shapiro was a pediatrician.

The Flower Shop, a women's and children's clothing and accessories store, opened on March 11 at 1502 Grandin Road SW.

A. M. Bowman Jr. announced his retirement as president of the Bank of Salem effective April 11. Robley Wood was selected as his successor.

Patty Jo Divers was one of twelve Senior Girl Scouts selected nationwide to participate in an international summer exchange program. She would go to Canada.

J. R. Kirby purchased and began managing the North 11 Drive-In in mid-March.

Lt. Melvin Thomas Harvey of Roanoke was killed on March 10 when his F8F Bearcat Fighter plane caught fire and crashed just south of the Chincoteague Naval Air Station. He was survived by his wife, Marie, and their five children.

Dick Kepley set another high school basketball individual scoring record on March 10 when he netted thirty-seven points in a Group I tournament game. The previous high was thirty-four points set in 1948. It also propelled Jefferson High School to set a new scoring record for a team, seventy-six points. The game was played in Richmond against Maury High School of Norfolk.

Jack Crosswhite was named as the manager for Salem's team in the Class D Appalachian League. Crosswhite was a native of Salem, a graduate of Andrew Lewis High School, and had been in organized baseball for over two decades. Jack Dame was the team's president.

The Manhattan Restaurant at 109 S. Jefferson Street opened its Colonial Room in mid-March for banquets and private parties. On Saturdays, the Colonial Room had dining and dancing.

Harlem Holidays came to the stage of the Roanoke Theatre on March 16.

Nearly 120 teams entered the eighteenth annual Southwest Virginia Gold Medal Basketball Tournament in Roanoke. Games were played across five gyms and six classes.

William Fleming High School repeated as the Group II state basketball champions. They won the championship game at Blacksburg on March 12, defeating George Mason High School 53–32. Members of the team were Carleton Assaid, Bill Stevens, Bob Stevens, Ronnie Griffin, Leon Turner, Denny Weddle, Chester Rogers, John Willhide, P. T. Johnson, Jack Morey, Bill Miller, and Leroy Ferris. The coach was Phil Crabtree, and the team manager was Wayne Parks.

Coach Phil Crabtree (seated, far right) and members of the state championship William Fleming High School basketball team pose with their trophy. *Karen Weddle Baker*

The 1955 Jefferson High School state basketball championship team pose for a team photo with their coach Preston Brown (seated, far left). *JHS Annual, 1955*

Jefferson High School won the Group I state basketball championship on March 12 in Richmond, defeating Washington-Lee High School of Arlington, 42–41. Walter Howard shot a game-winning field goal with eight seconds left to secure the win. It was Jefferson's first state championship since 1941. Team members were J. Arnold, P. Fetzer, Louis Mills, D. Moody, J. Dean, K. Catron, W. Howard, Don Campbell, Dick Kepley, C. Saul, C. Stephens, and D. Lennon. The coach was Preston Brown. Mills was voted Outstanding Player of the Virginia High School State Basketball Tournament.

Myrl Glenn Sr. and his son announced on March 12 they had sold their interest in Glenn-Minnich Clothing to C. B. Minnich and Herman Glenn. The men's clothing store was located at 108 W. Campbell Avenue.

Mrs. Edith Croxford, fifty-five, of Roanoke was killed in a two-car accident on Route 24 east of Vinton on March 12. She died at Lewis-Gale Hospital from her injuries following emergency surgery.

Another suit was brought against the estate of the late Edgar Thurman on March 14. Everette Thurman, a longtime employee of Thurman and Boone Company, claimed that Edgar Thurman had promised the business to him.

The Children's Theatre presented a production of *The Clown That Ran Away* the second week of March. The play was directed by Clara Black and given at Monroe Junior High School.

Ginger Crowley, a former Roanoke singer, was surprised by her family as she appeared as a guest on the NBC television network show *Truth or Consequences* on March 15. Her parents and two brothers were flown from Roanoke to Hollywood for the surprise reunion by the show's sponsors. Crowley was working for Universal Studios.

A Roanoke Chamber of Commerce Committee announced on March 15 exploratory efforts on establishing a technical institute in Roanoke to train for industries. The committee was chaired by Roy Herenkohl which had been working closely with officials at Virginia Tech.

Piedmont Airlines expanded its service to Roanoke on March 18 by offering passenger service between Charleston, West Virginia, and Columbus, Ohio. This increased the airline's flights into Roanoke to twenty-two per day.

Phil Crabtree, the basketball coach at William Fleming High School who led the Colonels to two Group II state championships, announced his resignation on March 15 to accept a position with a local sporting goods firm effective April 1.

A new weekly newspaper debuted in Vinton on March 18. The eight-page *Vinton Booster* was published Fridays by A. R. Powers and was located at 208 Walnut Avenue.

Zand's Department Store, at 3 E. Main Street in Salem, was sold to the DeLong family, owners of the DeLong Department Store in Vinton. The store was purchased from Ralph Snapp.

Melvin Franklin, nineteen and a graduate of Addison High School, left on March 18 for Brunswick, Georgia, to try out as a pitcher for the Pittsburgh Pirates. Franklin had pitched for three seasons with the Roanoke Cardinals in the Negro Blue Ridge League, where he won thirty-four games and lost three. Joining Franklin was Mack Craighead of Vinton and a graduate of Carver High School. Craighead played as an outfielder for the Roanoke Royals in the Negro Amateur League. Both were scouted for Pittsburgh by R. W. Holland of Salem.

The Cincinnati Symphony Orchestra performed at the Jefferson High School auditorium on March 19. The program was sponsored by the Roanoke Community Concert Association and was their swan song production as they had voted to disband.

The congregation of Holy Trinity Greek Orthodox Church announced plans in mid-March for a new church in the Williamson Road section. The congregation had purchased a home and lots on Huntington Boulevard. The congregation had a membership of sixty Greek families.

A twenty-three-acre tract fronting Edgewood Street SW was purchased to serve as the future home of Shenandoah Christian College. The college planned to begin offering classes in September in rented quarters.

The Salem Theatre celebrated its twenty-fifth anniversary on March 24 with a benefit gala and show by the Salem Kiwanis Club. The Kiwanis had sponsored the theatre's grand opening in 1930.

This mid-1950s postcard shows the Old Dominion Motel that was located on Route 11 near Hollins. *Nelson Harris*

This June 1959 photo shows the Catawba School, located in the Catawba Valley section of Roanoke County. *Library of Virginia*

Six evacuation centers, an emergency hospital, and emergency first aid stations had been located throughout Roanoke County for use in the county's Civil Defense program. In a mid-March report to the county Board of Supervisors, Charles Via stated the stations were at Catawba School, Back Creek School, Burlington School, Fort Lewis School, Clearbrook School, and Stewartsville High School in Bedford County. Each station would be served by a team of doctors and nurses. Further, all county schools had been furnished with an air raid drill plan.

The Men's Garden Club of Roanoke, an affiliate of the Men's Garden Club of America, received its charter on March 21. A. O. English was the club's president.

Horace Heidt brought his stage show to the American Legion Auditorium on March 24. Performers included The Ink Spots, Ralph Sigwald, Johnny Standley, Doodles Weaver, and the Horace Heidt Steppers. Heidt had a popular nationally televised variety show. Local young people auditioned for the stage show with the chance that Heidt might select them to appear on his television show. Bob Law of Salem won the local talent competition.

Ruth Townsend, fifteen and a student at William Fleming High School, placed first in a statewide oratorical contest held at Lexington on March 21. The contest was sponsored by the American Legion.

The trustees of Memorial and Crippled Children's Hospital voted on March 22 to drop "Crippled Children's" from the hospital's name effective April 1. The new name would be Roanoke Memorial Hospital. This was in keeping with a national trend of dropping names of ailments or afflictions from hospital names.

William Flannagan was the hospital administrator, and he stated that the new name would clarify that the facility was a general hospital.

William Davis of Roanoke and a Dr. Pepper bottler for nearly twenty years was elected to the company's board of directors at Dallas, Texas.

Dick Kepley, a Jefferson High School senior, was the first ever chosen unanimously to an Associated Press All-Group I basketball team. Kepley was named honorary captain of the 1955 Virginia All-Group I scholastic basketball team. Kepley's Jefferson teammate, Lewis Mills, was also selected to the All-Group I team of five.

Construction of a three-acre lake at Camp Powhatan in Pulaski County was approved by the Blue Ridge Boy Scout Council on March 23. The lake was part of an expansion plan to increase the capacity of the camp to serve up to 200 boys per week. Four new campsites were to be opened there for the summer—Ranger site with Baker tents, Crow's Nest, Adirondack, and Cherokee. White scouts would camp there the first eight weeks and Black scouts the ninth week.

James Archer, twenty-seven, of Roanoke County died on March 24 when his car struck a tree at the intersection of Grandin Road and Brandon Avenue SW following a police chase.

The Gross Furnace Manufacturing Company, located at 510 Rorer Avenue SW, announced on March 24 plans to move to the former Blue Ridge Chemical Building in Salem. Sol Gross was the general manager.

Officials with the Times-World Corporation announced plans for a $200,000 addition to the newspaper building with construction set to begin in mid-April. The new, three-story addition would give the company an extra 18,648 square feet. B. F. Parrott was the general contractor for the project.

This late 1950s postcard shows the Times-World Building on Campbell Avenue SW after its mid-'50s expansion. *Bob Stauffer*

The *Roanoke Times* began running a new daily feature on March 28, Walt Disney's *True Life Adventures.*

The Lee-Hy Supper Club opened in late March next to the Lee-Hy Swimming Pool on Route 11. It offered "home-cooked food served smorgasbord style."

Dillard Paper Company began construction on a $100,000 warehouse in the 2400 block of Patterson Avenue SW in late March. Roanoke Wholesalers planned to move into the vacated paper company's warehouse at 819 Seventh Street SE once the new warehouse was completed.

Isaac Mintz Jr. was found dead in a garage in the 400 block of Third Street SE on March 28. His body was wrapped in newspapers, and the coroner determined he had frozen to death and suffered from acute alcoholism. He was fifty.

Powell's Pharmacy at 219 E. Main Street in Salem enlarged its store by taking over the former Kay's Ice Cream next door. The pharmacy also contained the offices for Western Union.

Two-thirds of the apple crop and almost all peach yields were wiped out in Roanoke County by a cold snap in late March.

Alvis-Barber Appliance Center opened on March 31 at 2404 Williamson Road. The owners were Jim Alvis and Lew Barber.

The official opening of the Roanoke Fine Arts Center Studio at Carolina Avenue and Twenty-Fifth Street SW was March 31. The studio was formerly the South Roanoke Baptist Church and was purchased by and given to the arts organization by Mr. and Mrs. Meade Harris.

Roanoke's second television station was given final approval by the FCC in Washington, DC, on March 31. Channel 7 was awarded to the Times-World Corporation and that set in motion plans by the company to begin construction on a transmitter building and the installation of equipment.

William Parsons, retired educator in Roanoke, died on March 31 at the age of seventy-nine. Parsons was best known as being the principal of Roanoke High School and later Jefferson High School from 1918 until 1936. He then served as assistant superintendent, retiring in 1947.

A community meeting was held at Pilgrim Baptist Church on March 31 to discuss the "slum clearance" plan for northeast Roanoke being advocated by the Roanoke Redevelopment and Housing Authority. Nearly one hundred residents, most homeowners in the area, heard about a do-it-yourself plan that neighbors could engage in as an alternative to the RRHA proposal. A ten-person committee was selected to lobby Roanoke City Council to hold plans in abeyance until the neighborhood's alternative plan could be organized and presented. The neighborhood-based plan was advocated for by the Roanoke Real Estate Board, the Roanoke Chamber of Commerce, and the Neighborhood Improvement Council.

Junius B. Fishburn, a longtime business and civic leader in Roanoke, died on April 1 at the age of eighty-nine. He was chairman of the board of First National Exchange Bank and of the Times-World Corporation.

Krispy Kreme Doughnut Company opened at its new drive-in location at 1923 Williamson Road NE on April 2.

Officials with Roanoke Electric Steel Corporation announced on April 1 plans for a million-dollar steel mill in Roanoke County to be located on a nineteen-acre tract bordering Peters Creek and near the N&W Railway West End Yards. John Hancock Jr. was president of the firm.

James Amos, forty-one, of Roanoke was killed instantly in an auto accident on April 2 on Route 221 a few miles south of Roanoke. On the same day, Katherine Rogers, thirty-three, of Salem died from injuries she had sustained in an auto accident on Melrose Avenue NW. Both were single-vehicle accidents.

The new wing of the Hotel Roanoke was completed in mid-March and fully open by the end of March. The $1.2 million addition included the Shenandoah Room, a new 225-seat coffee shop with murals depicting Mount Vernon, and fifty-six guest rooms. The coffee shop replaced the Fountain Room.

Paul Coffey, general manager of Evergreen Burial Park and active in civic and recreation affairs, died at age fifty-three on April 2.

A Salem landmark known as the Old Salem Tourist Home (also the Biggs home place) was razed at the intersection of College Avenue and the Boulevard in early April to make room for a new gas station. The house had an interesting history. It was originally located in Elliston and then dismantled, piece by piece, and brought to Salem by horse-drawn wagons in 1900 and reconstructed. The home belonged (in both locations) to Walter and Annie Biggs, parents of well-known artist Walter Biggs Jr. The Tyree family later purchased the home and used it to board Roanoke College students.

Jeanne-Mann Dickinson, a graduate of Jefferson High School and the Carnegie Institute of Technology, was signed to a contract with the Northport County Playhouse of Long Island, New York, to be their leading lady for the summer season. In Roanoke, she had been a charter member of Showtimers and acted with the Patchwork Players when in junior high school.

Ruby Shelton, nineteen, of Salem died in a cabin fire at Twelve O'Clock Knob on April 3. Five others in the cabin managed to escape but could not reach Shelton. The cabin was owned by Oren Wade.

The congregation of Tabernacle Baptist Church voted on April 3 to construct a $165,000 education building adjacent to the church. The four-story building would contain fifty-five classrooms. Membership was over 1,100.

The board of the Roanoke Symphony Orchestra voted on April 4 to change the name of the group to the Roanoke Symphony Society and enlarge the board of directors to forty members.

Management of the Jefferson Theatre announced on April 4 that the movie house would undergo a $50,000 remodel to include a wider screen for Cinemascope, new seats and drapes, and upgrades to the interior.

A Night in Miami stage show came to the Roanoke Theatre on April 6 that featured singers, dancers and vaudeville acts.

The Boston Red Sox and the Philadelphia Phillies played a major league exhibition baseball game at Maher Field on April 6. The Sox won 9–3 before a crowd of 3,200. Ivan Delock was the starting and winning pitcher for Boston.

Ruth Brown, along with Willis Jackson and his orchestra, performed for a show and dance at the American Legion Auditorium on April 10. The show began at midnight and ran until 4:00 a.m. The balcony was reserved for white spectators.

Brambleton Amoco Service Station opened at Brambleton Avenue and Harris Street SW on April 8. The operator was Carl Peters.

Physicians in Roanoke and Western Virginia viewed a firsthand report on the Salk polio vaccine via closed circuit television on April 12 in the auditorium of Appalachian Power Company. The broadcast was from the University of Michigan and arranged locally by WSLS-TV and the Roanoke Academy of Medicine.

The City of Roanoke was bequeathed the residence of the late Junius Fishburn at 714 Thirteenth Street SW. The surrounding grounds of 4.3 acres were also part of the gift. Under the terms of the estate, the family could continue to occupy the residence for fifteen more months.

Pro wrestler Gorgeous George took on Wild Red Berry in a match at the American Legion Auditorium on April 12.

Over 20,000 persons attended the Easter sunrise service at Natural Bridge on April 10. Rev. Earl Mitchell, pastor of Roanoke's First Church of the Brethren, delivered the sermon that was nationally broadcast over the CBS radio network. In the Roanoke Valley, a crowd of 1,000 attended the sunrise service held at Sherwood Burial Park. The sermon was delivered by Rev. George Holmes, associate rector of St. John's Episcopal Church. A sunrise service was also held on the top of Mill Mountain.

Emily Bowen, a nineteen-year-old student at Sweet Briar College, of Roanoke died due to injuries suffered in an auto accident on April 11 on Route 60. She was returning with friends to the college.

The controversial "slum clearance" plan of the Roanoke Redevelopment and Housing Authority was approved by Roanoke City Council on April 11 by a vote of 4 to 3. The plan involved the redevelopment of about eighty-three acres of land in northeast Roanoke, mostly involving Black property owners. Mayor Robert Woody and council members Roy Webber, Walter Young, and Mary Pickett voted in the affirmative. Opposing the action were Leigh Hanes, John Waldrop, and Herbert Davies. The three in the minority argued that the matter should be to a referendum and let the voters decide on the $3 million plan. Hanes argued that the redevelopment would only financially benefit contractors and real estate developers and not the property owners impacted. Waldrop opposed the motion due to the share of the cost to be borne by the city, $1 million. Many attending the meeting spoke in opposition to the measure. Former mayor A. R. Minton stated, "This plan is not worth the evacuation of people." There were moments of heated exchanges between those in attendance and members of the council.

The well-known Anthony van Dyk painting *Holy Family* went on display in the Roanoke Fine Arts Center in mid-April. The painting was on loan from the New York House Galleries.

WSLS radio launched a new local program on weekday afternoons, *An Afternoon Affair*. The host was Andy Petersen, who also hosted *Club 88* on WSLS-TV.

The banner headline "Salk Conquers Paralytic Polio" greeted readers of the *Roanoke Times* on April 13. In anticipation of the approval and licensing of the Salk vaccine, Roanoke city and county school officials and public health directors began initiating their well-prepared plans to inoculate the area's children.

William Morris, a twenty-nine-year-old student at Virginia Tech, of Roanoke was killed in an auto accident on April 9 in Montgomery County.

Harwood Brothers, a paint store, opened at 404 W. Campbell Avenue on April 14. Ben Eubank was the branch manager.

WROV radio was sold in mid-April to a group of businessmen in Arlington, Virginia, by Radio Roanoke.

Duke Ellington and his orchestra performed for a show and dance at the American Legion Auditorium on April 18. The balcony was reserved for white spectators.

Miss Georgia Crawford of Salem was crowned "Miss Roanoke" in a pageant held at the American Theatre on April 15. She became eligible to compete in the Miss Virginia contest affiliated with the Miss America pageant. The Roanoke beauty contest was sponsored by WROV. Martha Meredith was runner-up.

The Salk polio vaccine arrived in Roanoke on April 16 via an Eastern Airlines plane from Indianapolis. There were enough doses of the vaccine to inoculate 20,000 children in the Roanoke Valley and surrounding counties.

The Times-World Corporation signed a contract with the CBS Television Network on April 16 under which WDBJ-TV would receive programming once the station began operating. Ray Jordan was the station manager.

Russian violinist Tossy Spivagovsky performed at the Jefferson High School auditorium on April 16. He performed using a 1721 Stradivarius.

A new local television program debuted on WSLS-TV on April 18, *The Betty Bond Show*. The midafternoon show, hosted by Betty Bond, featured "information of interest to the feminine eye."

The Roanoke City Parks and Recreation Department announced on April 17 that it would sponsor sandlot baseball in the same manner it had offered sandlot football. The department planned to have an eight-team league, and it was the first time sandlot baseball had been offered. The league was for boys under the age of thirteen.

Walker Nelms & Company, an interior decorating firm, opened at 21 W. Church Avenue on April 18.

A four-acre tract at Woodrum Field was selected by the US Air Force as the site for an air reserve training center. The Roanoke City Council was asked to lease the land for that purpose by the commander of the 9108th US Air Force Reserve Group.

Belmont Baptist Church held a ground-breaking service on April 17 for a new $150,000 education wing. Rev. Gordon Keller was the pastor.

Houck & Company, an advertising firm, held an open house on April 18 at its new headquarters at 2013 S. Jefferson Street. The firm had been previously located at 625 First Street SW. It was Virginia's largest advertising agency. The agency was founded in 1938 by C. B. Houck.

The Roanoke Auto Show was held at the Merchants Parking Center Jefferson Street and Bullitt Avenue SW the third week in April. A dozen auto dealers participated by showcasing their 1955 models. An estimated 30,000 persons came to the auto show over the three-day period.

This mid-1950s photo is looking east on Campbell Avenue from First Street. *Virginia Room, RPL*

Dynamic Service Corporation, a television and appliance store, opened at 715 Franklin Road on April 18. A seventeen-inch Philco television set sold for $49.80.

Roanoke's first children received the Salk polio vaccine on April 18. According to health officials, 1,151 first and second graders received the vaccine, representing 90 percent of those enrolled in the two grades. Roanoke and Alexandria were the first two communities in Virginia to administer the vaccine. Carolyn Sue Starkey, a second grader at Belmont School, was the first child to be inoculated. Mrs. Helen Killinger, nursing director of the Roanoke Health Department, oversaw the vaccine program and reported that the first day went "like clockwork." Vaccines continued to be administered throughout the week at the health department. Roanoke County's vaccine program began on April 25.

Everette Reynolds, forty, of Roanoke was killed on April 17 when the delivery truck he was driving struck a pole in the Catawba section.

Some of the last remnants of Roanoke's streetcar system were removed on April 19 when city crews ripped out ties along Fifth Street SW between Marshall and Elm Avenues. Crews removed ties from Twenty-Second Street SW, as well. The work was done in connection with street paving.

The Roanoke Redevelopment and Housing Authority ratified the contract with Roanoke City Council for the authority's "slum clearance" plan for northeast

Roanoke on April 20. The authority's board approved the $3 million project on a unanimous vote.

County Appliance Company held a grand opening for its garden center on April 21. The business was located on Route 24, one mile east of Vinton.

Jefferson Street Baptist Church at the corner of Albemarle Avenue and Jefferson Street SW held a note-burning service on April 24.

J. G. Sheets & Sons auctioneers held a complete liquidation auction of Thurman and Boone furniture store on April 27.

A new plant for the Pepsi-Cola Bottling Company was announced on April 21. The plant would be located on Route 11 near Hollins and would replace the company's plant at 6 Laconia Avenue NE. The bottling company served eleven counties.

Dr. Herman Horn, associate professor of political science at Virginia Tech, was named superintendent of Roanoke County schools on April 22. Horn would begin his duties July 1. Horn had been a teacher and principal in public schools in Virginia for nineteen years before becoming a faculty member at Tech. Horn had served as principal of William Byrd High School in Vinton from 1930 to 1940.

Sixteen percent of pledges to the Roanoke Hospital Development Fund were outstanding by mid-April. The pledges were used in the financing of Roanoke Memorial Hospital and Burrell Memorial Hospital expansions. The fund's board of directors voted to pursue legal action against those who had not paid their pledge by May 1. The unpaid pledges amounted to $376,000.

Mrs. Jane Kirk, believed to be Roanoke's oldest resident, died on April 22 at the age of 105 at the home of her daughter in Norwich.

Cpl. Frank Blankenmeyer of Roanoke appeared on the nationally televised broadcast of *Horace Heidt's Talent Show* on April 24.

The Mayflower Hill Club, a nightclub, opened in late April at the intersection of Routes 618 and 658 beyond Riverdale.

Jane Stuart Smith, an opera singer from Roanoke, completed a six-week singing engagement in Egypt in late April to rave reviews by the Egyptian press. Smith was part of an Italian opera company at the time.

Mitchell's Clothing Company announced on April 23 that its new store at 28 W. Church Avenue would cost about $100,000. Martin Brothers was the local contractor. An August 1 completion date was anticipated.

Roy Clark, owner of Citizens Undertaking Establishment, died on April 22 at Burrell Memorial Hospital. Clark came to Roanoke from Pulaski County in 1925 and established his funeral business. He was also a leader in many civic and business organizations.

Dominion Company Realtors advertised over sixty house lots for its development known as Summit Hills in late April. The subdivision was located off Melrose Avenue NW. Lot prices ranged from $1,500 to $2,000.

Mrs. Golda Quesenberry, sixty-seven, of Salem died at Lewis-Gale Hospital on April 24 from severe burns due to a furnace fire in her home.

Stephen Finney, fifty-four, of Roanoke died in an auto accident on April 24 on Route 220, two miles south of Roanoke.

John Eure, a reporter for the *Roanoke Times*, along with C. E. Cuddy and Bob Donahoe of Roanoke, were among hundreds of local Civil Defense officials who witnessed an atomic test blast at Yucca Flats, Nevada, in early May as part of what defense officials called Operation Cue.

Mrs. Daisy Schley was honored at a banquet held at the Orange Avenue YWCA on May 1 for having been a nurse for fifty-nine years. Schley graduated from St. Paul's Institute in 1896 and had been nursing since then, including as a head nurse at Burrell Memorial Hospital and a school nurse in Roanoke.

The Square Dance Club, sponsored by the Roanoke Parks and Recreation Department, began their weekly dances at Rockledge Inn on Mill Mountain in late April. Andy Anderson's band played, and Luther Turner called the figures.

Nearly 1,000 Roanoke County first and second graders received the Salk polio vaccine on April 25 at West Salem School in the first series of shots to be administered in the county.

John Browning, winner of the Steinway Centennial Award, presented a piano concert at Hollins College on April 25.

Eagle Stores Company opened at 120 E. Main Street in Salem on April 28. It was part of a fifty-two-store chain headquartered in Charlotte, North Carolina. W. A. Doniel was the store manager.

Clara Black was named as executive director of Showtimers for their summer season.

The Life Insurance Company of Virginia opened its new district office at 3021 Fleming Avenue NW on April 28.

The first local polio case of the year was diagnosed on April 27. Harry Smiley, nine, began showing symptoms and was admitted to Roanoke Memorial Hospital with no signs of paralysis.

Roanoke schoolchildren are being given the Salk polio vaccine by public health nurses in this image from April 1955. *WSLS-TV News Film Collection, UVA Libraries*

Sterling Studio opened at 411 S. Jefferson Street in late April.

Lemon & Painter Insurance Agency opened in late April at 30 W. Kirk Avenue. Those with the agency were Curtis Lemon, E. B. Lemon, and Harry Painter Jr.

Local shows hosted on WSLS-TV by Hayden Huddleston moved to new times in late April. *Klub Kwiz* began airing at 10:15 p.m. on Thursdays, and *Musical Showcase* aired on Mondays at 6:30 p.m. Both shows were sponsored by Fink's Jewelers.

Posey Lawrence, seventy-seven, of Roanoke County died from injuries sustained in an auto accident on April 28 on Route 11 near Fort Lewis.

The Roanoke chapter of Americans United for Separation of Church and State received its charter on April 29 in a meeting at the Roanoke Public Library. Rev. Luther Vann headed the Roanoke chapter, which had forty members.

Westhampton Christian Church held a ground-breaking ceremony on May 1. Rev. Walter Calhoun was the pastor. Dr. Orville Wake, president of Lynchburg College, was the main speaker.

The Roanoke Life Saving and First Aid Crew received a building permit in late April for a crew hall to be located at 374 Day Avenue SW. It would be the first permanent home for the organization.

The Roanoke Merchants Association announced its six Mother of the Year honorees on May 1. They were Mrs. Max Murray, education; Mrs. William Kavanaugh, community affairs; Mrs. Devona Gillespie, business and professions; Mrs. Arthur Ellett, arts and sciences; Mrs. Viola Scott, family life; and Mrs. Boyd Tyrrell, religious activities.

On May 2, the biggest girder for the Jefferson Street viaduct was swung into place. Fabricated locally, it weighed seventy-four tons and was eighty feet long. Three derricks were used to raise the girder into position.

Posie Powell won the Roanoke Checker Championship in late April. It was his thirteenth title.

Stephen Laurie of Virginia, a home supply business, opened on May 2 at 227 Franklin Road SW.

Salem played its first game of the regular season in the Class D Appalachian Baseball League with an away game against Pulaski on May 1. They won 6–5. The following night, Salem played its first home game at Municipal Field before 1,155 fans, also against Pulaski. Prior to the season openers, a contest was held to name the team. Marion Long of Salem won the contest with her entry of the Salem Rebels. She received a savings bond and a season ticket.

Roanoke City Council at its meeting on May 2 formally approved the contract with the Roanoke Redevelopment and Housing Authority for the redevelopment plan for northeast Roanoke on a vote of 5–2. The formality of the contract approval was required after the housing authority approved it. Councilman Herbert Davies, who had initially voted against the plan at a prior meeting, voted in favor, stating he did not want to be "an obstructionist" as the plan was going forward anyway.

Plans for a new $100,000 home for elderly women to replace the Mary Louise Home in Roanoke were announced during a convention at the Hotel Roanoke on May 2 by the Order of King's Daughters and Sons. The Mary Louise Home was located at 1001 Patterson Avenue SW, with eighteen residents and five staff.

The Virginia Mountain League opened its baseball season on May 5. The league consisted of six teams—Hot Springs, New Castle, Buchanan, Vinton, Glasgow, and Lexington.

The Virginia Amateur League opened its baseball season on May 5 with five teams—Back Creek, Elliston, Glenvar, Salem, and Moneta. Salem's home field was at the Veterans Administration Hospital.

Waverly Place Baptist Church opened a mission chapel in the 100 block of Seventeenth Street SE in April with evening services.

R. V. Fowlkes, a Roanoke realtor, announced plans in early May for a new subdivision for Blacks with a potential of 300 homes. The residential area was to be located northeast of Tinker Creek and south of Orange Avenue.

Roanoke City Manager Arthur Owens announced in early May that he was opening Lakewood Park pond to children and youth (under age sixteen) for year-round fishing, and no license was needed. The city planned to stock bream and blue gills year round there.

The Roanoke Symphony Orchestra presented a concert of the music of Jean Sibelius on May 9 at the Roanoke Theatre. The selections included *Finlandia* and *En Saga*.

Magic City Motor Corporation opened its new truck service and repair facilities at 406 Rorer Avenue on May 9.

The Clovers, Paul Williams and his orchestra, and the Five Keys performed for a show and dance at the American Legion Auditorium on May 13. The balcony was reserved for white spectators.

The Community Council on Education was formed on May 10. The group's mission was to work for the improvement of Roanoke's schools. The council consisted of 140 persons representing civic groups, PTAs, and business organizations. Mrs. Nelson Bond was named temporary chairman.

Rev. D. R. Powell, pastor of Hill Street Baptist Church, died on May 11 at Burrell Memorial Hospital. The interment was at Lincoln Burial Park.

The Meadow Swimming Club opened for the summer along Route 221 at the base of Bent Mountain. The members-only club leased a pool and grounds from B. G. Finnell. Kirk Johnston was club president.

Hank Snow, Faron Young, Martha Carson, the Wilburn Brothers, Slim Whitman, Elvis Presley, the Davis Sisters, Jimmy Snow, and Onie Wheeler performed at the American Legion Auditorium on May 18.

The New York Black Yankees played the Indianapolis Clowns in baseball at Maher Field on May 26. Both teams were in the Negro American League. Joining them was famed baseball clown Ed Harman.

The golf team of Jefferson High School captured their second consecutive Virginia scholastic golf championship played at Hidden Valley Country Club the third weekend in May. The team members were George Kosko, Paul Kosko, Danny Keffer, Al Peverall, D. Edmonds, G. Naff, and Jim Darby.

This is the 1954–55 Jefferson High School state golf championship team. Sitting are J. Darby (left) and A. Peverall. Standing (left to right) are G. Kosko, D. Edmonds, P. Kosko, D. Keffer, and G. Naff. *JHS Annual, 1955*

Doctors at the Veterans Administration Hospital reported some success with a new drug they were trying on patients suffering from psychosis. Reserpine had been used at the hospital for about a year and was considered a better alternative to another common form of treatment that had been used at the hospital—the lobotomy.

The Lee-Hi Drive-in Theatre was purchased by the Craver Theater Company of Charlotte, North Carolina, in mid-May. The company closed the theatre for two weeks and made extensive repairs, including a larger screen. John Garst was the new manager.

The Hillcrest Chapter of the Eastern Star, No. 159, received its charter in mid-May. The chapter met in the Melrose Masonic Temple. The chapter was instituted in June 1954 by Veva Spain, worthy grand matron, with forty charter members.

Elizabeth Leonard, thirty-two, died in Lewis-Gale Hospital on May from four gunshot wounds inflicted on her by her husband, Francis Leonard, at their home on Marshall Avenue SW.

Sixth District Congressman Richard Poff voted against statehood for Alaska and Hawaii in mid-May stating he believed states should only be admitted to the union via a constitutional amendment. The US House voted against statehood for both, 218 to 170.

On May 16, Roanoke City Council approved two areas along Melrose Avenue for shopping centers.

William Goodwin, eighty-two, died on May 17 in a Staunton hospital. Goodwin was a well-known merchant in the Glenvar area, having operated the W. O. Goodwin & Company store there from 1913 until 1946. He also served as a member of the Roanoke County School Board.

American Finance Corporation opened at 128 Campbell Avenue SW on May 18.

The Queen Drive-In Theatre opened on May 18 on Route 11 west of Salem. Opening-night movies were *Elephant Walk* and *Pleasure Island*. The owners were J. D. Poff and Waller Bohon.

The board of directors of the Thomas Jefferson Memorial Foundation named James Bear Jr., a native of Roanoke, as the first full-time curator for Monticello. His duties began June 1.

Campouts involved over 1,000 Boy Scouts during the Roanoke Valley the third weekend in May, all sponsored by the Blue Ridge Boy Scouts Council. A camporee for the Roanoke District was held at Carvins Cove near the Bennett Springs entrance; for Salem-Craig at the foot of Catawba Mountain; and for the Northern Division at Washington Park.

Moser Furniture Company opened at 3326 Williamson Road on May 23.

Maury Strauss, Stanley Weinburg, John McCoy, and L.L. Rush petitioned the Roanoke Planning Commission for a rezoning of their adjoining properties along Brandon Avenue and Mudlick Creek from residential to commercial for the purposes of creating a community shopping area in mid-May.

High's Ice Cream opened two new stores on May 21. The locations were 1941 Franklin Road SW and West Main Street in Salem at its intersection with Route 11.

"Roxann" performed a midnight burlesque show on the stage of the Salem Theatre on May 21.

Shirley Henn, the executive secretary of the Hollins College Alumnae Association, had her first book published by Exposition Press in May. *Adventures of Hooty Owl and His Friends*, a children's book, was also illustrated by Henn.

A rhythm and blues show and dance was held at the American Legion Auditorium on June 2. Performers included Roy Hamilton, LaVern Baker, the Drifters, the Spaniels, Jimmy Reed, Willie Mabon, the Hearts, Willie Walker and his orchestra, and Erskine Hawkins. The balcony was reserved for white spectators.

The oldest continuously sponsored local radio program celebrated its twentieth anniversary on May 23. *The Musical Clock* made its debut on May 23, 1935, on

WDBJ at 7:00 a.m. Dudley Townsend was the announcer. The longtime sponsor was Rainbo Bread.

Joseph Spigel, president of Joseph Spigel Inc. died in a Roanoke hospital on May 21 at age seventy-two. He came to Roanoke in 1907 and established his women's clothing store. He was also active in several business and civic organizations.

Armed Forces Day was observed in Roanoke with a 1,200-pariticpant parade through downtown on May 21. Consisting of mostly military reserve units, school bands, and veteran organizations, the parade's reviewing stand was at Elmwood Park.

The Roanoke Kennel Club held its twentieth annual all-breed dog show on May 29 in the Merchants Parking Center. Fifty-three breeds were represented with 345 entrants.

Two businessmen from Elkins, West Virginia, were killed in a plane crash on May 22, fifteen miles east of Roanoke near Stewartsville. James Ketterman, thirty-three, and Harold Herring, forty, were in a single-engine Navion aircraft when they encountered bad weather.

Roanoke County Civil Defense officials successfully tested an air raid warning system on May 22 that consisted of a Civil Air Patrol plane blaring sirens. It was the first time in the nation that Civil Defense warnings were given from a plane. The pilot was Lt. James Poole.

About 3,000 spectators attended the fourth annual model airplane show at Woodrum Field on May 22. The event was sponsored by the Roanoke Exchange Club and the Roanoke Gas Model Planes Club.

An auto daredevil show, *Tournament of Thrills*, came to Victory Stadium on May 27. It was sponsored by American Legion Post 202.

Dr. P. T. Goad of Roanoke won the Southern Seniors Golf Tournament held at Roanoke Country Club the last weekend in May. His two-round score was 143. Eight players from the East Coast participated.

US Secretary of State John Foster Dulles landed at Woodrum Field on May 23 as he headed to a conference at White Sulphur Springs.

Clem Johnston of Roanoke went on an extended tour of Australia, New Zealand, India, and Pakistan for the US Department of State in early June under the department's international exchange program. Johnson was the immediate past president of the US Chamber of Commerce.

Ernest Thurman, thirty-nine, of Roanoke and a N&W Railway brakeman was killed in a fall from a hopper on May 25 near Shaffer's Crossing. He was riding a hopper being pulled westward for a coal wharf when he fell.

Davy Crokett became highly popular with young boys in May as the *Roanoke Times* ran a sixteen-part serial on the frontiersman's life and department stores sold Crokett coonskin hats, comic books, and other related items. The serial ran in many newspapers around the nation. The *Times* offered a pen-and-ink print of Crokett and received over 5,000 orders.

A group advocating a technical institute in Roanoke met at the Hotel Roanoke on May 26 and decided to form a committee of industry and civic leaders to better organize their efforts. The lead advocate was the Roanoke Chamber of Commerce.

The Children's Zoo opened for the season on May 28 with added attractions that included pony rides and a Dream Castle with Mother Goose and Walt Disney characters painted on the walls.

Roanoke Cab Company was acquired by Checker Cab Company in late May. Cleatis Sisson was the operator of Roanoke Cab and stated that the company would continue to operate under the Roanoke name.

The director of the William Byrd High School band was arrested on a morals charge and convicted on May 27 of four charges of indecent exposure. He was immediately terminated by the county school system.

N&W Railway announced on May 28 that it planned to purchase eight general-purpose diesel locomotives at a cost of $1.4 million with delivery expected in September. Railway President R. H. Smith said, "This does not mean that we have changed our view that our modern roller bearing coal burning steam locomotives can handle the major part of our traffic economically. Nor does it mean that our interest in new and better types of coal burning locomotives has diminished in any way." The same announcement contained news that the railway would be ordering 500 steel boxcars from the Pullman Standard Car Manufacturing Company at a cost of $3.6 million.

Reid and Cutshall announced on May 29 that a new store would be built on Lee Highway between Roanoke and Salem with the plan to open in mid-August.

The inaugural flight of local first-class and registered mail left Roanoke at 8:05 p.m. on June 1 for Cincinnati on a Piedmont Airlines plane. It was deemed to be experimental by postal officials.

Dedication services for the new Salem Church of Christ on West Main Street were held on May 29. Rev. R. M. Miller was the pastor.

Piedmont Airlines inaugurated direct flight service from Roanoke to Myrtle Beach, South Carolina, on June 1. One flight each way daily was scheduled.

The congregation of Fairview Methodist Church voted on May 29 to construct a $90,000 sanctuary. Rev. Charles Bright was the pastor. The new sanctuary would be located at Van Buren Street and Virginia Avenue in the Washington Heights section. The congregation held a ground-breaking ceremony the following Sunday.

A thunderstorm accompanied by lightning played havoc with the Children's Zoo on May 29. Lightning struck the merry-go-round at the pony riding rink, killing one pony. Five other ponies were rendered unconscious, as all were tied to the metal fencing.

Bill and Mary Reid, known as "the Shenandoah Valley Sweethearts," performed at the Roanoke Theatre on June 1. They were joined by the Melody Mountaineers.

Jimmy Moore was named as the new basketball coach at William Fleming High School. Moore was the coach at Troutville High School.

The US Supreme Court ruled on May 31 that state and local officials should seek to end segregation in public schools "as soon as practicable." The court set no deadline. Most Virginia officials believed that school segregation would continue for one more year, giving local education boards and superintendents time to develop and implement desegregation plans. Virginia's Attorney General Lindsay Almond, a Roanoker, continued to remain an ardent segregationist and called on the governor and others to take executive actions to obstruct desegregation, including the closing of public schools or having an indefinite deadline for compliance. Roanoke Mayor Robert Woody stated, "I am glad it was a moderate decision and not an immediate attempt to solve the problem." Dr. Harry Penn, a former member of the Roanoke School Board and leader in the Black community, said, "I don't say it is the most satisfactory way to handle it, but I trust it will work out."

Former Roanoke Mayor Richard Edwards was elected president of the Community Council on Education in Roanoke on May 31.

Producers for the Hollywood movie *Giant* that starred Rock Hudson and Elizabeth Taylor needed a locomotive from the early 1920s for a train scene being filmed between Keswick and Charlottesville. The C&O Railway, which operated on that track, borrowed a mountain-type K-1 locomotive from N&W Railway, painted it in C&O colors, and put its own engineer, W. N. Gibson, behind the throttle for the scenes.

An infant a few days old was abandoned on June 1 on the front porch of G. W. Holland on McDowell Avenue NW. The infant was taken to Burrell Memorial Hospital in a healthy condition. The baby was left in a paper box, fully clothed, with additional garments and a baby bottle.

Sunday night worship services were held in Highland Park beginning the first Sunday in June and continued through August. The services were ecumenical and involved various neighborhood Protestant clergy.

Nathan Hale of Bent Mountain School won the 1955 city-county marbles tournament. Ray Stanley from Back Creek School finished second. Hundreds of boys entered the multiround tournament that took a few weeks to complete.

Western Auto held a grand opening for its housewares department on June 3. The store was located at 325 W. Campbell Avenue.

This 1955 image shows the Salem Creamery that was located at 736 W. Fourth Street in Salem. *ALHS Annual, 1956*

Mrs. Billy Sunday, widow of the famous evangelist, spoke at an afternoon worship service at First Baptist Church on June 5. Her appearance was sponsored by the City Rescue Mission, where she spoke later that evening. Eight hundred attended the afternoon service at First Baptist.

Kiyoshi Tanimoto, a survivor of the atomic bomb drop on Hiroshima, spoke at First Methodist Church in Salem on June 8. His speech, *Surviving the Atom Bomb*, was sponsored by the Salem Chamber of Commerce, the Salem Ministers Conference, and First Methodist. Tanimoto was on a tour of the United States on behalf of the Hiroshima Peace Center Foundation and was the pastor of a Christian church in Hiroshima.

A new radio aid for pilots was completed at Woodrum Field in late May and flight checked by the CAA on June 7. Known as the TVOR-terminal, the unit permitted instrument approaches from any direction and was located in the island between the runway intersections.

James Barringer of Roanoke was selected by the US Department of State for a 1955 Fulbright Scholarship. Barringer planned to study comparative philosophy and linguistics at a university in Bonn, West Germany. Barringer was a graduate of Addison High School.

Jimmy Robertson, a senior at William Fleming High School, was presented the 1955 B'nai B'rith Athletic and Achievement Award.

Linwood Holton, in a speech to the local League of Women Voters on June 4, stated about the matter of desegregation, "There is likely no painless method of readjustment to such a revolutionary change in a basic social concept. Thoughtful, active, and cooperative consideration on the part of cool-headed leaders will, if devoted to the effort, find a way which will create the smallest amount of friction."

George Fulton Jr. won the city-county golf championship held the first weekend in June. The tournament was sponsored by the Times-World Corporation. Fulton posted a seventy-two-hole score of 284 to achieve his second consecutive title. The tournament was held at Roanoke Country Club. Ralph English finished second.

A high-speed chase through the western half of Roanoke City on June 6 involved seven police cruisers in pursuit of a car loaded with illegal whiskey. Shots were fired between police and two persons in the car. Mrs. Gracie Warfe, who was standing on Patterson Avenue when the car went past her, was struck in the hip by a bullet. Robert Johnson, forty, of Roanoke was arrested on various counts, while his passenger leaped from the car during the chase. There were two bullet holes in Johnson's car.

Norwood Corporation purchased almost fourteen acres of land to complete its Rosemont subdivision near Monroe Junior High School in northwest Roanoke. The land was purchased from the W. K. Andrews estate. W. E. Cundiff was president of the Norwood Corporation and indicated the twenty-six-acre subdivision would have about one hundred house lots.

On June 8, the Roanoke Jaycees named their Fathers of the Year. They were Judge Beverly Fitzpatrick (religious affairs), John Cruickshank (education), and Fred Smith (recreation). The men were handed their awards the following evening during televised ceremonies on WSLS-TV.

George Fulton Jr. receives the championship trophy after winning the annual city-county golf tournament in June 1955. *WSLS-TV News Film Collection, UVA Libraries*

William Carr was appointed Clerk of Courts for Roanoke on June 10, succeeding Russell Watson, who had died a week earlier. The appointment was made by Judge Dirk Kuyk.

William Howland of Roanoke was appointed by President Dwight Eisenhower to the US Board of Parole on June 10. Howland was the chief federal probation officer for the Western District of Virginia.

A windstorm blew through the Blue Ridge section of Botetourt County on June 11, ten miles east of Roanoke. The storm ripped off the top story of a three-story pre–Civil War home, unroofed a barn, blew down trees, and splintered a large turkey house belonging to William Lavender, killing an estimated 1,000 turkeys.

Blues musicians Joe Turner, Joe Morris, and Gene & Eunice performed for a show and dance at the American Legion Auditorium on June 17. The balcony was reserved for white spectators.

Ray Stanley from Back Creek School won the Southern Marbles Championship during the first weekend in June that was held in Greensboro, North Carolina.

With the newfound interest in frontier hero Davy Crockett, Roanoke's own Davey Crockett was profiled in the June 12 edition of the Roanoke Times. Roanoke's Crockett was eighty at the time of the article and was well-known in the valley. He was born in Roanoke County in 1875 and became a professional baseball player at the age of twenty-four when he was signed by a team in Raleigh, North Carolina. He played in Detroit for one season and then was traded to a team in Indianapolis. His Detroit contract was for $175 per month in 1901. He later played in the Three-I League for several years. Crockett retired from baseball when he was forty-five. He also recalled at the age of six watching the N&W Railway Shops being built. His family lived at Eleventh Street and Tazewell Avenue SE. He told the reporter about the day the whistle, Old Gabriel, first blew. "When she cut loose with that whistle, nothing like it had ever been heard in Roanoke. I was six years old and I thought the world was coming to an end. I hot-footed it for the bed and slid to base against the wall in one sweep. Horses at the stores broke loose from the hitching posts and wrecked a buggy or two." According to Crockett, the whole town was scared, so N&W toned down the whistle.

Arthur Fralin, twenty-three, died in an automobile crash in Salem on June 11. His collision with a truck occurred at the intersection of Fourth and Union Streets.

Lowell Roberson, twenty-five, of Roanoke won the state archery championship sponsored by the Virginia Bow Hunters Association on June 12 at Fishersville.

The Times-World Corporation asked the FCC in mid-June for authority to broadcast WDBJ-TV from a temporary transmitter on Mill Mountain pending approval of a permanent transmitter on Poor Mountain. The FCC granted the request a few days later.

N&W Railway Locomotive No. 1219 arrives in Roanoke in this June 1955 photo. The Class A was considered one of the "Magnificent Three" designs developed by N&W. *Virginia Room, RPL*

Plans for Cave Spring High School, first started in 1947, received final approval from the State Department of Education on June 13. The school had been delayed due to annexation, a failed bond referendum in 1950, and requirements by the state to alter the plans.

Roanoke Paint and Glass Company opened at its new location at 110 W. Church Avenue on June 20.

Ruth Thompson, six, of Roanoke was beaten and slashed with a butcher knife on June 14. Her assailant was John Goff, a furloughed patient of a Maryland Veterans Administration Hospital. He was arrested the same day in Lynchburg.

Valleydale Packers in Salem erected a water spear in mid-June to serve as a reservoir for 100,000 gallons of water. Erected by the Chicago Bridge Company, the water tower had a one-hundred-foot spear base capped by a thirty-foot ball.

Sears, Roebuck and Company announced on June 14 plans to build a store on Williamson Road just north of Orange Avenue. The store would be built on a ten-acre site leased for fifty years from the Luckens estate.

Mrs. Frank Thomas and Herbert Tayloe were reappointed to the Roanoke County School Board on June 14 by members of the School Trustee Electoral Board.

Leaders of Roanoke city government were moved out of the city in a mock air raid alert conducted by Civil Defense officials on June 15. They were transported to a high school near Webster. Similar mock drills were conducted in fifty major cities on that same day.

The inaugural issue of a monthly magazine, *Focus on Roanoke*, was distributed to motor courts and hotels in the city in mid-June. The magazine, targeted to those visiting Roanoke, was published by Walters Printing.

The congregation of Franklin Road Chapel, in existence since 1935, voted to build a new church in the 2600 block of Colonial Avenue SW. The church was located at 2001 Lynn Avenue. Rev. Kathryn Gorman was the pastor.

A cornerstone-laying service was held at Belmont Christian Church on June 19 for their new education building.

Roanoke's twenty-one playgrounds opened for the summer season on June 20 with thirty-six recreation leaders. The theme for the summer was "Davy Crockett." Leon Briggs was in charge of the summer programs.

Dr. Theodore Banks opened his private dental practice in the Lawson Building at 401 First Street NW on June 20. He was a member of the Magic City Dental Society and had been a public health dentist in Roanoke since 1949.

Flora Reality advertised new three-bedroom brick homes in the recently developed subdivision known as Green Valleys off Colonial Avenue. Prices ranged from $10,950 to $12,750.

Chick-Inn, a barbeque drive-in restaurant, opened on June 19 at 3719 Williamson Road.

The A&B Cash Grocery at 523 Vinton Road NE caught fire on June 20. The co-owners were W. N. Aylor and J. I. Brown. The grocery had opened in September 1954.

This image shows the students and faculty for Vacation Bible School in front of Belmont Baptist Church in Southeast Roanoke in the summer of 1955. *Linda Ferguson Armetta*

Five Black citizens filed for a permanent injunction on June 20 to stop the Roanoke Redevelopment and Housing Authority from proceeding on its "slum clearance" project in northeast Roanoke. Those that filed, naming the RRHA and the City of Roanoke as defendants, were H. J. Walker, Grace Walker, Cordelia Williams, Blanche Markhame, and Henry Markhame. All claimed to be of advanced age and unable to purchase new homes. The RRHA plan called for the redevelopment of eighty-three acres, impacting 436 houses, twenty-seven businesses, and eight public buildings such as schools.

Francis Leonard pled guilty on June 21 to the May 15 slaying of his wife. Judge Dirk Kuyk delayed sentencing until a probation report was provided.

William Jackson, twenty-two, of Roanoke was killed in an auto accident on June 20 at the intersection of Routes 117 and 118. He died in an ambulance en route to a local hospital.

Roanoke's twelfth annual Soap Box Derby was held on June 22 on the Salem Turnpike near Twenty-Fourth Street. The location had been on Crystal Spring Avenue in South Roanoke, but residents had complained about congestion and pedestrian traffic in yards so the popular event was moved to Salem Turnpike. The derby was sponsored by the Times-World Corporation, the Optimist Club, and Johnson-McReynolds Chevrolet. Seventy-two boys entered the competition. Roger Simpson, a student at Jackson Junior High School, won the derby before a record crowd estimated at 7,000.

The Virginia Methodist Conference approved the organization two new Methodist churches, one on Cove Road and the other in the Windsor Hills section. Rev. David Smith began work to organize the congregations in late June. The Cove

Road church would be located near the Cove-Hershberger Roads intersection, and the Windsor Hills Methodist Church near Mudlick and Deyerle Roads SW.

Richardson's Super Market opened at 18 E. Main Street in Salem on June 23. The owner was Frank Richardson. The grocery was affiliated with the Blue Jay Markets.

Officials with the Times-World Corporation announced personnel for WDBJ-TV in preparation for the station to begin broadcasting. Ray Jordan was named managing director. Jordan had been with WDBJ radio since it went on the air June 20, 1924. John Harkrader was named the assistant managing director.

Inez Brown had a book of poetry published by Pageant Press in early July. The author of *Will O' the Wisp* had at one time been a schoolteacher in Roanoke before moving to Georgia.

John Howard defeated Shack Moorman for the Roanoke Jaycee junior tennis championship on June 25 at Roanoke Country Club.

Martha Huffstetler, age nine, became the first person in the Roanoke region to receive a new form of heart surgery known as Brock's Procedure. Having been born with a heart defect, the girl underwent the medical treatment at Hahnemann Hospital in Philadelphia. The congregation of Virginia Heights Baptist Church had assisted with medical and travel expenses.

Lone Star Cement Corporation announced on June 27 plans for a fourth kiln at their plant in Botetourt County. The fourth kiln would expand the plant's capacity to 3.2 million barrels per year.

Showtimers presented its first play of the season, *The Moon Is Blue*, the last weekend in June at Roanoke College. The risqué comedy's lead roles were performed by Kathy Thornton, David Thornton, Willard Hart, and John Lyle. Clara Black was the director.

Johnson and Reid Realtors, located at 404 Gainsboro Road NW, began advertising fifty-four houses for sale in the Rugby section. The ads stated the homes were for Blacks.

Roanoke attorney Linwood Holton stated that Roanoke should establish a committee of white and Black citizens to work together to accomplish desegregation of the schools. Holton shared his thoughts during an address to the Roanoke Republican Women's Club on June 28.

Col. Joseph Thomas, a native of Vinton, was killed in a plane crash near Utica, Kentucky, on June 28. He was piloting a military plane from Little Rock, Arkansas, to Columbus, Ohio. One other officer died in the crash. Thomas was the commanding officer of the air force base at Little Rock. He was a graduate of William Byrd High School.

Fats Domino and his orchestra, along with Bill Doggett and his combo, played for a show and dance at the American Legion Auditorium on July 3. The show went on from midnight until 4:00 a.m. The balcony was reserved for white spectators.

Advance Stores opened a new store at 31 E. Main Street in Salem on June 30. The store gave free orchids to ladies, a key case to men, and balloons to children during its opening weekend.

The Ninth Street Church of the Brethren conducted a "Drive-In Church" on Sundays in the summer at the Dixie Drive-In Theatre in addition to their regular services.

Traveltown Amusement Park on Route 11 at Cloverdale opened to the public with a miniature golf course and swimming pool on July 2. The park was adjacent to the Traveltown Motel.

Norwood Middleton was named the news editor of the *Roanoke Times* on July 1. He had been a reporter for the *Times* since 1949.

Adam's Men Shop at 104 S. Jefferson Street announced in early July it was going out of business.

Roanoke City Council at its July 5 meeting authorized a $1.5 million bond referendum in November's general election for a multipurpose auditorium in Elmwood Park. By a vote of 4–3, the council forwarded the matter to the voters, as the issue had been discussed and advocated for by a citizens committee headed by Dr. E. G. Gill.

William Mullins, chief of the Roanoke Fire Department, announced on July 6 his retirement effective July 16. He had served as chief for twenty-seven years during a career with the department that spanned forty-three years.

Rowena Grisso returned to Salem on July 6 after spending four years as a patient at the Medical College of Virginia in Richmond. The twenty-year-old polio victim was paralyzed from her neck down and was taken to the Green Lawn Rest Home at Salem. She was required to spend seven hours per day in an iron lung.

Negro League baseball came to Maher Field on July 9 when the New York Black Yankees played against the Indianapolis Clowns.

Public Loan Corporation opened at 132-A W. Campbell Avenue on July 7. The manager was Tom Delaney.

Virginia's Attorney General Lindsay Almond Jr. of Roanoke adamantly opposed the desegregation of the state's public parks to comply with a court ruling. Almond told reporters on July 8, "It seems like a century to me that I have been carrying the burden of this desperate fight. I am willing to continue the fight to the last ditch, and then dig another ditch…If they want my advice: Get out of the public park business as quickly and as completely as possible."

Officials with N&W Railway announced on July 9 construction of a new $1 million freight car shop in Roanoke to replace the old one. The ten-acre installation would extend some 1,600 feet east from the Roanoke Shops entrance near Eighth Street and Campbell Avenue.

Clyde Johnson was named the new golf pro at Hidden Valley Country Club. He succeeded Johnny Galdun. He had previously been the golf pro at Blue Hills Golf Club in 1940 and later at the Cascades in Hot Springs.

Catawba Sanatorium treated 634 patients during their fiscal year that ended June 30. The tuberculosis hospital had an average daily occupancy of 293 patients during the period.

Showtimers presented *Come Back Little Sheba* the second weekend in July. Lead roles were played by Elizabeth Pettrey, Leroy McFarland, Sandy Richards, and Sol Katz. The play was directed by Genevieve Dickinson.

This mid-1950s image shows the Rosenberg Building at the corner of Campbell Avenue and Jefferson Street, possibly decorated for the Fourth of July. The building housed the Joy Shop, Barr Brothers Jewelers, and Oak Hall Clothing. *Virginia Room, RPL*

Roanoke Republicans unanimously nominated two candidates for Roanoke's seats in the House of Delegates on July 11—Linwood Holton and Hazel Barger. They would face the Democratic incumbents.

John Walker of Roanoke was elected grand exalted ruler of the Benevolent and Protective Order of Elks of the USA at the organization's convention in Philadelphia on July 11. Walker, forty-nine, was an attorney.

The *Roanoke Times* began running a new comic strip on Sundays beginning July 19, *Legends of Davy Crokett*.

In the Roanoke County Democratic primaries on July 12, Vinton's Mayor Nelson Thurman unseated incumbent State Delegate Ernest Robertson, 2,619 to 1,248. W. C. Muse held off a challenge for the Commissioner of Revenue post by Wesley Chapman, and Roland Clark defeated Katherine Groseclose for the nomination for the Salem District on the Board of Supervisors. Sheriff H. W. Clark defeated a challenge from J. D. Altizer.

General Electric opened a temporary employment office at 501 W. Campbell Avenue in mid-July. E. B. Petersen was supervisor of personnel.

John Hayslett opened his Sunoco Service Station at 901 Orange Avenue NE on July 14 with free pony rides for children and double S&H Green Stamps with every purchase.

First National Exchange Bank held an open house on July 16 to showcase their remodeled and expanded lobby at the main office in downtown Roanoke. A crowd of 4,000 attended.

This July 1955 photo shows the lobby of the First National Exchange Bank, which was located at the corner of Jefferson Street and Campbell Avenue SW. *Historical Society of Western Virginia*

Bo Diddley, Etta James, Charlie and Ray, and Jimmy Witherspoon and his orchestra performed for a show and dance at the American Legion Auditorium on July 22. The balcony was reserved for whites.

Myrl Glenn and Sam Glenn leased space in the Shenandoah Building and announced plans to open a men's store later in the year. They would be occupying the former space of Mitchell's Clothing at 307 First Street SW. The two men had sold their interest in Glenn-Minnich Clothing earlier in the year.

B. F. Parrott and Company was awarded a $1.5 million contract for the new S. H. Heironimus Department Store to be built at Jefferson Street and Church Avenue.

Time Out for Ginger was presented by Showtimers the third weekend in July. Lead roles in the comedy were performed by Raymond Doss, Wilson Price, Holman Willis Jr., Maxine Rulbin, Jean Turner, Patricia Laurie, and Jane Stockman.

The Roanoke plant of American Viscose Corporation began operation of its new powerhouse in mid-July. Approximately 400 tons of coal daily was required for the boilers, and there were also eight turbo-generator units operating with electricity. The new powerhouse meant the abandonment of the old powerhouse built in 1919.

The Roanoke Booster Club took some 350 businessmen from Roanoke by a special N&W Railway train for a day outing at White Sulphur Springs on July 20.

Mr. and Mrs. W. L. Martin began advertising house lots in mid-July for their subdivision Broadview that was along Route 11 west of Salem.

The Roanoke County Board of Supervisors approved funds for two large school construction projects on July 18. A new fourteen-room Cave Spring High School was appropriated almost $800,000, and a six-room addition to Southview School was given $179,000. The contract for the high school was awarded a few days later to H. A. Lucas and Sons by the school board.

Roanoke City Council decided at its meeting on July 18 to celebrate the city's seventy-fifth anniversary in 1957 and not in 1959, per the recommendation of a citizens committee. Thus, an ordinance that had designated 1959 as the year was repealed.

Don Bartol was named as the basketball coach at Jefferson High School. He came from Virginia Episcopal School where he had coached.

Roanoke City Council appointed Col. L. D. Booth, Clarence Hawkins, and John Thornton to four-year terms on the Roanoke School Board.

A second Colonial Store opened on July 20 at 3200 Brandon Avenue SW. Well-known television home economist Nancy Carter appeared in person for the grand opening of the grocery. Children got free pony rides, and women received orchids. A crowd of 8,000 attended the opening.

Edward Jones, thirty-three, of Roanoke County died in a cabin fire in the Glenvar section on July 20.

Seven hundred National Guardsmen from Roanoke and surrounding counties left Roanoke on July 22 for two weeks of training at Indiantown Gap, Pennsylvania. They traveled in a ninety-vehicle convoy.

Famous baseball clown Jackie Price entertained fans during a baseball game at Municipal Field in Salem on July 31.

Crystal Spring Laundry and Dry Cleaners opened a branch at 3008 Williamson Road on July 25. Their main facility was located at 720 Franklin Road.

A WSLS-TV truck is parked in front of the Municipal Building. The station was televising the Diamond Jubilee in 1957 in this image, indicative of local television to air live local events. *Historical Society of Western Virginia*

Showtimers presented *Sabrina Fair* the last weekend in July with a cast that included Sally Babb, Jinx Holton, Rosalie Turner, Robert Gardner, John O'Neil, and English Showalter Jr.

Virginia Anderson, thirty, of Bluefield, West Virginia, drowned at Lee-Hy Pool on July 26. Lifeguard Don Alouf administered aid but with no success.

Francis Leonard was sentenced on July 29 to twenty-five years in prison for the May 15 killing of his wife. Leonard admitted guilt at the time of his arrest.

Oscar Martin, sixty-two, died on July 28 when a ten-foot sewage ditch caved in between Market and High Streets in Salem. Martin was part of a work crew digging the ditch and was a town employee.

Ben Moomaw was selected to serve as executive director for Roanoke's Diamond Jubilee set for 1957. Moomaw was a retired Chamber of Commerce official who was active in a variety of civic and business organizations.

Seven hundred white citizens signed a petition requesting the Roanoke Planning Commission and Roanoke City Council "discourage" the use of the section east of Tinker Creek and south of Orange Avenue for Black housing they felt would be created with the Roanoke Redevelopment and Housing Authority plan to redevelop northeast Roanoke.

Burrell Memorial Hospital staff began transferring patients into its new hospital the first week in August. A public open house was held on August 1. Once the patients were transferred, the old hospital was to be razed. The new $1.6 million hospital, on the same campus as the old one, had Theodore Frazier as its administrator with a staff of ten doctors, eighteen registered nurses, six practical nurses, and ten nursing aids. The new hospital had eighty-one beds, two main operating rooms, an outpatient department, a tumor clinic, a dental clinic, and a prenatal clinic, among other necessities for a fully equipped hospital. The new hospital was paid for by a combination of private donations through the Hospital Development Fund and state and federal aid under the Hill-Burton Act.

Showtimers presented the mystery *Rebecca* the first weekend in August. The cast included Mel Ryman, Genevieve Dickinson, and Dean Goodsell.

An N&W Railway ad that had run in the *Roanoke Times* on July 4 was read into the Congressional Record, broadcast nationally over radio, and had been requested by several thousand in letters to the railway's public relations office. The ad was a patriotic piece titled *I Am the Nation* that apparently had been authored by someone on the staff of the railway.

Mary Coon unplugged her last telephone on July 31 as she retired from a job she had held for over thirty-five years—the switchboard operator at the Ponce de Leon Hotel. Coon had worked in that capacity at the hotel since 1920 and recalled when Eleanor Wilson stayed as a guest, as well as numerous stage actors who lodged there when touring through Roanoke.

Bobby Bortner of Richmond won the first annual Roanoke Valley Invitational Tennis Tournament the last weekend in July, which was held at the Roanoke Country Club. Bortner teamed with Bobby Figg to also win the men's doubles championship.

A delegation of citizens from the Colonial Heights and Beechwood Gardens sections came before Roanoke City Council on August 1 to complain about a dump near their neighborhoods which adjoined a junkyard on Colonial Avenue SW.

Gibson Morrissey, conductor of the Roanoke Symphony, left on August 1 for four weeks to study conducting in Lucerne, Switzerland. Morrissey was one of seven conductors selected to study under Herbert von Karajan, conductor of the Berlin and Vienna Philharmonic Orchestras.

Roanoke's oldest retail pharmacy, H. C. Barnes Drug Store, went into bankruptcy in early August. The pharmacy had been in the same family's hands since its beginning. The business was established at Norfolk Avenue and Jefferson Street in May 1891 by H. C. Barnes and Chris Haller. In 1892, Barnes bought out his partner and incorporated the business in 1907. The pharmacy was forced to move from its original location in 1953 to its second location at 103 W. Campbell Avenue to make way for the downtown viaduct.

James Snyder, eighteen, of Roanoke was killed when his car went out of control on Route 687 in Roanoke County on August 3. The accident occurred not far from Route 221.

Harry Wisemen was appointed production manager for WDBJ-TV in early August. The former Roanoker came from a television station in Indianapolis.

Capt. Ruth Edna Dickson, a US Army nurse, of Vinton was awarded the Associate Royal Red Cross for her services to British forces in Korea. The decoration was presented to her on August 5 in Rome by Ambassador Sir Ashley Clark on behalf of Queen Elizabeth. Dickson was the matron in charge of the 6055 Mobile Army Surgical Hospital in Korea.

This 1955 photo is looking west along the 100 block of Lee Avenue in Vinton. *Historical Society of Western Virginia*

Wilfred Spangler, sixty-seven, of Roanoke died in a local hospital on August 5 from injuries he sustained as a pedestrian when struck by an automobile on July 16. The accident occurred on Jefferson Street at Kirk Avenue SW.

Betty Sue Matthews of Norfolk was crowned Miss Virginia during the pageant held at the Hotel Roanoke on August 6. She was among seventeen contestants who competed for the crown before 1,000 in attendance. The pageant was sponsored by the Valley Junior Woman's Club and was preceded with a parade through downtown. Andy Petersen of WSLS-TV was the master of ceremonies.

Richard Teichler, seventy, of Roanoke died at a local hospital on August 6 from head injuries he sustained when he was struck by an automobile on August 1 at Franklin Road and Allison Avenue SW. At the time of his death, he was the operator the Dutch Kitchen restaurant on West Salem Avenue. Prior to that, he had operated the Jefferson Restaurant.

Roanoke's building inspector ordered that the former Academy Hotel be torn down due to its deteriorated condition. The hotel was located in the 400 block of Salem Avenue SW. At the time of the inspection, the hotel was being used as a warehouse.

A chemical spill from the American Viscose plant into the Roanoke River on August 9 resulted in a significant fish kill. Plant managers admitted to the spill, calling it an accident.

Sgt. William Dupree of Roanoke and a tenor with the US Air Force Symphony Orchestra was offered a two-year contract to sing with the Mainz Opera Company in Mainz, Germany. He was a 1947 graduate of Lucy Addison High School and earned a music degree from Howard University. In early August, Dupree had appeared on national television as part of Ed Sullivan's program *Toast of the Town*. He had also sung on the Gordon MacRae television show and toured for six weeks with the Broadway cast of *Carmen Jones*. He was the son of Mr. and Mrs. C. C. Dupree of Loudon Avenue NW. When in high school, Dupree had studied voice and music with Adelaide Campbell, Arthur Talmadge, and Mrs. Whitwell Coxe.

Piedmont Airlines began offering three round-trip flights daily to Washington, DC, in mid-August. The cost for a ticket was $13.40.

Showtimers offered its final play of the season the third weekend in August, *The Curious Savage*. The cast included Betty Shaner, Wilton Sale, Jean Michie, and Dick Burton. The play was directed by Kathy Thornton.

A *Farm Talent Round-Up* was held at Fort Lewis School on August 12 as part of the Southern States Cooperative's annual membership meeting. The talent show was sponsored by Salem Farm Supply and W. T. Rierson. The same type of event was also held at Vinton War Memorial on the same night for Cooperatives Nos. 1 and 2.

Cook's Apparel Shop, a women's clothing store, held a grand opening for their second store at 304 First Street SW on August 12. Their other store was on Grandin Road.

Toot's Drive-In Restaurant held a grand opening at their new location at 2729 Williamson Road on August 12. WROV radio broadcasted live from the restaurant on opening night.

Officials with the Times-World Corporation announced that WDBJ radio and WDBJ-TV would occupy part of the new addition to the newspaper plant at the corner of Campbell Avenue and Second Street SW. This would place all media under one roof. WDBJ-TV planned to broadcast temporarily from the Mountain Trust Bank Building until the new wing was completed. Further, the television station was acquiring equipment to allow it to broadcast in color.

North Cross School received a charter of incorporation to operate a private school in Salem. The school had operated for eleven years under the direction of Mrs. Howard Butts with children only through the third grade. The new charter allowed the school to operate for children kindergarten through high school. One of the reasons for seeking a new charter was the desegregation of public schools, though school officials stated that was not the primary reason.

William Lotz, president of Lotz Funeral Home, announced plans for the funeral home to move to Franklin Road SW, between Highland and Washington Avenues. The funeral home was located at 430 Church Avenue SW. Lotz planned to renovate a former residence.

Baseball fans got a treat at the Salem Rebels game on August 20. Frank Jessee, Rebels catcher, wed Carol South at home plate just prior to the start of the game. Rev. Clyde Smith performed the ceremony. The Rebels' pitcher and his wife served as best man and maid of honor.

Mick-or-Mack opened its newest store on August 18 at 2602 Franklin Road. They offered free cigars, balloons, and snacks on opening day to the crowd of 10,000 that came.

The Villa Heights Cubs won Roanoke's first Sandlot Little League Championship. The Cubs were awarded the Paul Coffey Memorial Trophy. They defeated a team from South Roanoke. The cubs were coached by Jerry Nagel.

The Salem Rebels won the Appalachian League pennant on August 14.

Dr. Mordecai Ham, the evangelist who converted Billy Graham, spoke at a tent revival at Eighteenth Street and Orange Avenue NE on August 16. Ham had done revivals in Roanoke on prior occasions beginning with one at the American Legion Auditorium in 1933.

Homes in the new subdivision known as Norwood began being advertised in mid-August. At an open house there, just off Peters Creek Road, some 3,500 persons showed up.

Malcolm Minnick Jr., twenty-three, of Salem was elected president of the Luther League of America on August 16 during its convention at Ann Arbor, Michigan. The 50,000-member organization was affiliated with the United Lutheran Church in America.

The Dixie Caverns Restaurant opened in mid-August. Sam Garrison was the owner and manager of Dixie Caverns.

Fulton Motor Company opened its new used car lot at the corner of Franklin Road and Second Street SW on August 19. A 1948 Packard was on sale for $133.33, as Fulton had been in business for thirty-three years.

Miller & Rhoads gained twenty-five more feet of street frontage for its new store in mid-August when the McBain Building Corporation acquired the adjacent three-story Goodfriend store. Consequently, plans for the new Miller & Rhoads store were reduced from six to five stories.

This mid-1950s photo shows the Joy Shop and other businesses that were located at the corner of Jefferson Street and Campbell Avenue. *Virginia Room, RPL*

Frame buildings were razed at Second Street and Church Avenue SW to make way for the viaduct. The buildings were believed to be eighty years old and once housed a blacksmith shop operated by William Raines and a wheelwright shop next door when Roanoke was Big Lick.

Aubrey Vaughan, basketball coach at William Byrd Junior High School, was named as the varsity coach for the high school on August 18. He succeeded Sam Webb, who had accepted the position of athletic director at Ferrum College.

Antonio Rocca, considered one of the most popular professional wrestlers on the US circuit, headlined the weekly wrestling program at the American Legion Auditorium on August 23.

WDBJ-TV began advertising for talent auditions the third week of August. Print ads read, "If you are an entertainer – amateur or professional – and would like to receive a TV talent audition in the near future, here's your opportunity!"

The body of Francis McCluskey of Beckley, West Virginia, was found in Mason Creek on August 20. McCluskey, twenty-three, was a patient at the Veterans Administration Hospital, and his death was ruled a drowning by the medical examiner.

Eighth-grade students from Ogden School, Clearbrook School, and Mount Vernon School were shifted to William Byrd High School for the 1955–56 school year to alleviate overcrowding at Andrew Lewis High School. Eighth graders at Back Creek School remained at that school for the year.

Mason-Hagan, an investment firm based in Richmond, opened a Roanoke branch in the Colonial-American National Building on August 22. Thomas Martin, formerly of Roanoke, was the branch manager.

The film *Souls in Conflict* was shown at Victory Stadium on August 26. The movie was produced by the Billy Graham organization. Bus service was provided to the big screen event that was promoted by several business and fraternal organizations. An estimated 6,000 attended the event that was sponsored by the Roanoke Christian Businessmen's Committee.

Virginia Wright announced her retirement as the postmaster for Roanoke on August 22 effective August 30 due to her health. When she had succeeded her husband as postmaster in 1941, she became the first female postmaster of a Class 1 post office in Virginia.

Frank Spence, the teenager who shot and subsequently paralyzed Roanoke police Sgt. Joe Jennings in 1945, was charged with murder in Richmond on August 22. Spence was charged in the August 20 killing of James Donivan of Richmond. Spence had a criminal record dating back to 1941, beginning in Roanoke with burglaries.

Jennings Electric Company, a two-year-old firm in Roanoke, filed for bankruptcy on August 23. The contracting firm was located at 3021 Christian Avenue NE and was owned by James Jennings.

The Roanoke Fair opened on August 29 for five days at Maher Field. The agricultural fair featured livestock shows, competitions, John Mark's "mile long pleasure trail," daily grandstand acts, and displays of farm machinery.

The H. C. Barnes Drug Store was sold to David Newman, owner of Newman's Pharmacy, on August 26 for $8,000. Newman stated that the Barnes store would continue to operate for several weeks before being liquidated.

Plans for Roanoke's first regional shopping center were announced on August 27 by Bartin and Stover Realtors. The center was to be located between Roanoke and Salem on Route 11. Leigh Bartin said the shopping center would be sited on twenty-three acres, would have over 200,000 square feet of retail space, and would be called the Roanoke Valley Shopping Center. Stores that had already leased space were W. T. Grant Company, F. W. Woolworth Company, Peoples Service Drugs, Schiff Shoes, and Advance Stores. The center would also have a 2,000-space paved parking lot. The land had been purchased from Bernard Cook with plans to open in the summer of 1957.

Deb Fashions held a grand opening of their newly remodeled boutique on August 29 at 313 S. Jefferson Street.

Burrell Memorial Hospital announced in late August its new rates for hospital stays. The new daily rates were as follows: ward bed, $9; semi-private room, $11; private room with bath, $15; and pediatric room, $9.

This August 1955 image is of what was then the new Burrell Memorial Hospital, located on McDowell Avenue NW. This was the hospital for Blacks during segregation. *Historical Society of Western Virginia*

Piedmont Finance Corporation opened a branch office in Salem at 13 E. Main Street. David Harris was the branch manager.

Charley Turner won the men's Roanoke city-county tennis championship on August 28 when he defeated Lu Merritt. Merritt and Fred Bromm defeated Turner and Doug Craig to win the men's doubles title. Mrs. Watt Ellett and Juanita Stanley won the women's doubles title, and Suzanne Glass defeated Ellett for the women's singles championship.

South Roanoke Barber Shop at 2902 Franklin Road SW opened in late August.

The Royal Fur Shop at 406 S. Jefferson Street went into bankruptcy and was liquidated at an auction held on August 30.

Felton's, a carpet cleaning and retail firm, opened a new office and showroom at 339 W. Luck Avenue on August 30. The cleaning plant remained at 914 Fourth Street SE. Stuart Felton was the firm's president.

The Washington Tea Room opened on August 30 at 310 Washington Avenue SW. It served breakfast, lunch, and dinner.

Ruth Brown, along with Billy Brown and his orchestra, performed for a midnight show and dance at the American Legion Auditorium on September 4. The balcony was reserved for white spectators.

Thelma Housier, forty-nine, of Roanoke was shot and killed on September 1 by her estranged husband, Jack Housier, while she stood outside on the street at Commonwealth and Patton Avenues NE.

Frank Ferguson, a twenty-eight-year-old rookie fireman in Roanoke, died fighting a blaze at the Virginia Scrap Iron and Metal Company on September 2. The scrap metal company was located at 1620 S. Jefferson Street. A brick wall collapsed and killed Ferguson. Ferguson had joined the fire department on August 16. Capt. E. W. Meador was seriously injured.

The Dr. Pepper *Silver Dollar* radio program on WDBJ was ruled a lottery by Municipal Court Judge Beverly Fitzpatrick on September 2. The judge imposed a one-hundred-dollar fine and a thirty-day suspended jail sentence for J. W. Davis, president of the local Dr. Pepper Bottling Company. Davis appealed his case.

A volunteer fire department was organized in the Mount Pleasant section with twenty men. G. C. Foley was appointed chief of the crew at the organizational meeting held in Cooper's Grocery Store on September 2.

A large H21 Piasecki helicopter landed in a parking lot at Wasena Park on September 2 after it failed to make radio contact with Woodrum Field during a thunderstorm. When the weather cleared, the helicopter flew to the airport, but not before being swarmed by hundreds of children and parents.

The Salem Rebels and Johnson City were declared cochampions of the Appalachian Baseball League on September 3. Rain canceled their games such that they could not meet the league's Labor Day deadline for tournament play. Average paid attendance for home games for the Rebels during the regular season was 513.

Patients were moved into the new nine-story wing of Roanoke Memorial Hospital in early September.

"The Blimp," billed as the world's fattest man, was on display at the corner of First Street and Church Avenue SW during the second week in September. His waist measured 104 inches, and he weighed 804 pounds. The show, sponsored by National Exhibits, asked for donations.

Francis Brigham of Roanoke was elected national commander of the Twenty-Ninth Infantry Division Association on September 5 at their annual meeting in Washington, DC.

George Fulton Jr. won the Fairacre Golf Tournament in Hot Springs the first weekend in September. It was his third time winning the tournament.

N&W Railway donated its pedestrian footbridge across its tracks on Jefferson Street to the City of Roanoke for a bridge over the Roanoke River connecting Maher Field with Victory Stadium.

WSLS moved to its new radio and television studios at Third Street and Church Avenue SW on September 6.

A decree was entered on September 8 in Law and Chancery Court that officially ended the mutualization of the Shenandoah Life Insurance Company. The company was awarded possession of all holdout stock by Judge Stanford Fellers.

A dinner meeting was held on September 8 at the Hotel Roanoke to launch a $100,000 building fund campaign for a new synagogue for Temple Emanuel. The site for the new synagogue was at Brambleton Avenue and Persinger Road SW. The congregation was located at 112 McClanahan Street SW. General chairman of the campaign was Arthur Taubman and associate chairman was Samuel Spigel. Temple Emanuel was organized in 1890 and met for its first several years in a building on Franklin Road before moving to McClanahan Street in 1937.

The newly organized Windsor Hills Methodist Church held its first Sunday School on September 11 at Mount Vernon School. Land had been purchased at the corner of Windsor Road and Mudlick Road SW for the church.

Belmont Presbyterian Church dedicated its new education building on September 11. The church was organized on January 2, 1915.

Floyd Ward School of Dancing opened a branch in Salem at the Academy Street School on September 16. Mrs. J. L. McCown was the director.

A ground-breaking ceremony was held for the Clearbrook Fire Station on Route 220 on September 10. The building was a project of the Clearbrook Lions Club.

National Business College marked its seventieth year when classes began for the academic year on September 12. The college opened in 1886 at the northwest corner of Campbell Avenue and First Street SW. In 1896, the college moved to the southeast corner of Jefferson Street and Salem Avenue and again in 1909 to Church Avenue between Jefferson and First Streets. In 1919, the college relocated to Franklin Road.

The Salem chapter of the Order of DeMolay was initiated in ceremonies at the Central Methodist Church on September 10. Master counselor was Ernie Clayton, and the sponsoring lodge was Taylor Lodge No. 23 of Salem.

This 1950s aerial shows Burlington Mills, located on West Virginia Avenue in Vinton. *Virginia Room, RPL*

Stars of the *Grand Ole Opry* presented a show at the American Legion Auditorium on September 15. The headliner was Hank Snow, and the show was sponsored by the Chamber of Commerce to raise funds for sandlot baseball. Other performers included the Rainbow Ranch Boys, the Louvin Brothers, the Alabama Sand Dusters, and Elvis Presley from the *Louisiana Hayride* radio program.

Anderson Renick, a Roanoke automobile dealer, was elected commander of the Virginia American Legion on September 11 at the organization's meeting in Virginia Beach.

Wipeldale farm in Roanoke County became the first operating farm in Virginia to artificially inseminate a cow with frozen semen. H. W. Craun, co-owner of the farm on Route 2, believed the procedure would greatly benefit breeders in the future. Prior to Wipledale, the process had been used experimentally at Virginia Tech.

The Pagoda Restaurant began advertising in mid-September as "Roanoke's only Chinese restaurant." It was located at the corner of Jefferson Street and Salem Avenue. Full-course Chinese dinners were $1.10.

R. L. Rush & Sons realtors announced the opening of a new subdivision, Hidden Valley Estates, in mid-September. Homes were priced between $16,000 and $20,000. Other subdivisions being advertised were Greenbrier Park off Brandon Avenue by the Wilbur Development Company; Spring Valley in Grandin Court; Lindsey-Andrews in Salem; Westward Lake Estates; and Lindenwood near Dixie Caverns.

Linwood Holton Jr. and Hazel Barger kicked off their Republican campaigns for the Virginia House of Delegates on September 12. The main issues they sought to address were a state sales tax, the State Milk Commission, open government, and a strong two-party political system.

Reid and Cutshall opened its second furniture store on Route 11 just west of Roanoke on September 15. The building was done in a Colonial Williamsburg style and was to be called Wayside. The furniture retailer had been in business since 1924.

A Roanoke chapter of the Naturalized Citizens of America was formed on September 13 for those born outside the United States. Alex Apostolou was elected temporary chairman.

Jimmy Board, ten, of Roanoke died on September 12 from what doctors believed was polio. Board became ill that morning and died three hours after being admitted to Roanoke Memorial Hospital. He was the first death in Roanoke from polio for the year.

W. T. Norris Company, a clothing store, announced it was going out of business. The store was located at 216 E. Main Street in Salem.

King Brothers and Cole Brothers Combined Circus came to Maher Field on September 17.

N&W Railway was authorized by the SCC on September 16 to discontinue agency service at Lithia in Botetourt County. The railroad planned to remove the station building there and to maintain a flag stop.

The cornerstone for Fairview Methodist Church was laid on September 17. The church was relocating from 3424 Melrose Avenue to Van Buren Street and Virginia Avenue NW.

Tank Hill in Salem was officially selected as the site for the Salem Civil Defense Ground Observer Corps post. The post was to be manned primarily by Explorer Scouts.

The National Guard armory at Maher Field was officially opened on September 17 following a promise made fifteen years prior when the 116th Infantry was mobilized for World War II. Major General Edgar Erickson provided the keynote speech as army, navy, air force, and National Guard units in Roanoke stood in formation before him. The previous night, Assistant Secretary of Defense Carter Burgess spoke at an armory program at the Hotel Roanoke. Councilwoman Mary Pickett cut the ribbon.

Franklin Road Beauty Salon opened at 2904 Franklin Road SW in mid-September.

The Bandbox, a clothing and accessories store, opened at the Patrick Henry Hotel on September 20.

Arthur Jones, a fifteen-year resident of Roanoke, was identified by the FBI as an escaped murderer from Alabama. Local police had charged Jones with assault on September 10 and took his fingerprints, which were compared to FBI records. Jones had been sentenced to fifty years in prison for murder in 1921 and had escaped from prison after serving several years.

Postal officials announced on September 17 that rail postal service between Roanoke and Norfolk via the Virginian Railway was to be discontinued effective November 1. A new star route would be originated to replace the service.

This mid-1950s photo shows the Melrose Lodge #139 of the Freemasons at Twenty-First Street and Carroll Avenue NW. The building would later become part of Williams Memorial Baptist Church. *Virginia Room, RPL*

Dillard Paper Company formally opened its new office and warehouse at 2490 Patterson Avenue SW on September 20. The company, which came to Roanoke in 1940, had previously been located in the 200 block of Bullitt Avenue SE.

Ken Platt, a shoe store and men's clothing retailer, opened at 37 E. Main Street in Salem on September 23.

Roanoke Gas Company held an open house at its headquarters to showcase "modern kitchen planning in four colors – white, blue, yellow and copper."

N&W Railway presented the City of Roanoke with an 1897 steam locomotive on September 23. The engine, identified as No. 6, was placed in Wasena Park near the east end of Wasena Bridge off Wiley Drive. The donation of the locomotive was the first step toward the creation of a transportation museum the city was planning for the park. The idea for the museum was attributed to Robert Hunter, the city's director of parks and recreation.

In September, many businesses including Kroger began offering Top Value Stamps as an inducement to buy from them. The stamps were a competitor with S&H Green Stamps.

John Wood, twenty-nine, of Salem died on September 23 from injuries he sustained in an auto wreck the day prior on Hershberger Road.

Rev. Edward Zeigler, pastor of the Williamson Road Church of the Brethren, was named as the editor for a new national publication of the Brethren Church headquartered in Elgin, Illinois. The quarterly was *Brethren Life and Thought*.

Clover Creamery advertised its newest flavor of the month in mid-September, Virginia apple. Virginia apple ice cream was "flavored with tantalizing spices."

This circa 1955 photo is of Tom's Potato Chips and the Farm Credit Association, which were located at the intersection of Sycamore Avenue and Williamson Road NE. *Virginia Room, RPL*

N&W Railway announced on September 24 it would begin "piggy-back" rail-truck service out of Roanoke and Bristol to Philadelphia and New York on November 1. Several motor lines had signed contracts for the service with the railroad. N&W was working in tandem with the Pennsylvania Railroad for the new service. The trucks would be loaded on special flatbed rail cars.

Beltone Hearing Service held a grand opening at its newest location at 17 E. Main Street in Salem on September 26.

The *Top Ten Review* came to the American Legion Auditorium on September 30. The show and dance featured the Clovers, Faye Adams, Joe Turner, Bill Doggett, the Charms, Bo Diddley, the Five Keys, Paul Williams and his orchestra, Gene & Eunice, Al Jackson, Etta James, and Charlie & Ray. The balcony was reserved for whites.

The Shrine Bowl football game was held at Victory Stadium on September 24. About 8,000 attended the event where George Washington University defeated VMI 25–6. Pregame activities were called off due to rain.

Second and third graders in Roanoke County received their second Salk vaccine shots for polio the last week in September. The same was scheduled for Roanoke City beginning October 10.

James T. Davis Inc., a paint and hardware store, opened the last week in September at 10 Church Avenue SE, the site formerly occupied by Roanoke Paint and Glass Company.

The through-truss-pin highway bridge erected in 1917 by the Virginia Bridge and Iron Company that connected the company property to the city via Ninth Street SE was removed in late September. A new through-plate-girder type bridge was being built to replace it with completion expected by early December to better serve the Viscose plant.

Jane Price, twenty-three, died on September 26 from injuries she sustained in an auto accident a week prior at Cave Spring on Route 221. She was a waitress at the Chick-Inn on Williamson Road.

Dr. Margaret Glendy was chosen as Woman of the Year for Roanoke by the Business and Professional Woman's Club. She was commended for her many civic and medical activities.

Charlie Spivak and his orchestra played for a Cabaret Dance at the Dixie Caverns Ballroom on September 30.

The newly organized North Roanoke Church of the Brethren held its first worship service on August 2 at Burlington School. Rev. Randolph Abshire was the pastor.

Nelson Hardware Company announced on September 30 that it planned to become a strictly wholesale operation and to erect a warehouse and office building at Gregory and Rhodes Avenues NE. The hardware company opened in Roanoke in 1888 as Nelson and Myers on Second Street SW. The founder of the business was A. M. Nelson, who came from Culpeper. In 1897 the business moved to 17 E. Campbell Avenue. Upon the death of his partner in 1901, Nelson formed a stock company that operated under Nelson Hardware Company.

The first Group 1 intercity football game in Roanoke was held on September 30 between Jefferson High School and William Fleming High School. It was

Fleming's first year in the Group 1 division. Jefferson won 25 to 0 before a crowd of 11,000 at Victory Stadium, which raised funds for the city's sandlot football program.

WDBJ-TV officially went on the air on October 3 at 7:00 p.m. from temporary studios on the sixth floor of the Mountain Trust Bank Building and using a temporary 25,000-watt transmitter on Mill Mountain. The winner of the WDBJ slogan contest was Doug Branham, who received an all-expense-paid trip to New York City. The inaugural broadcast opened with a dedicatory program that included Irv Sharp, Roanoke Mayor Robert Woody, Chamber of Commerce executive A. S. Rachal, and Hal Grant. Rev. J. E. Stockman, president of the Roanoke Ministers Conference, provided the invocation that was followed by the singing of *The Lord's Prayer* by John Newsom. M. W. Armistead III, president of the Times-World Corporation, along with the station's manager Ray Jordan, addressed viewers with a statement of commitment by the station to public service.

The local Fraternal Order of Police, Dominion Lodge No. 1, announced in early October plans to bring amateur boxing to Roanoke. Headquarters for the boxing program would be at 114 W. Salem Avenue and would be strictly supervised by the Police Athletic League. Paul Vest was instrumental in organizing the program.

Polgar, billed as "the world's greatest hypnotist," performed at the American Legion Auditorium on October 7.

Chi Omega installed its 118th chapter at Roanoke College on October 1 in ceremonies at the Hotel Roanoke.

A white Russian man and his Finnish wife were profiled in the October 2 edition of the *Roanoke Times*. George Solonewitsch escaped mass executions in Russia in 1917 by moving with his parents to Europe and then to Argentina. He came to America in 1953, where he dug ditches in New York City while his wife, Inga, helped on a poultry farm. Wanting their own farm, the couple researched various locations and chose Roanoke County. Both being artists, Solonewitsch contacted Houck and Company advertising firm, and he was hired. The couple soon thereafter purchased a 127-acre farm in the Back Creek section. The couple would later change the spelling of their last name to Solonevich.

Koppers Company formally opened its new wood preserving plant west of Salem on October 5. The event was preceded by a luncheon at the Hotel Roanoke. A special train carried the 250 lunch guests from the hotel to the site of the new plant for the ribbon-cutting.

Eddie Fisher and Debbie Reynolds spent the last moments of their honeymoon at Woodrum Field on October 4. They had flown in from White Sulphur Springs on a private plane to catch an American Airlines flight out of Roanoke to New York. During the interim, the couple posed for photographs and autographs and fielded questions from reporters.

Owen-Weaver Sporting Goods held its grand opening at 4221 Melrose Avenue NW on October 7. A. C. Owen and Curtis Weaver were the owners.

Fink's Jewelers of Roanoke purchased Jenkin's Jewelers of Charlottesville in early October. Fink's had stores in Roanoke, Salem, Bedford, Covington, and Harrisonburg.

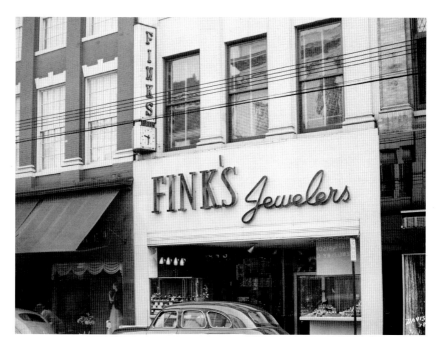

This 1950s photo shows Fink's Jewelers, located at 310 S. Jefferson Street. *Virginia Room, RPL*

Roanokers Luke Barnes and Jack Keffer won the State Pro Am Golf Tournament in Richmond on October 6.

The Police Athletic League formally opened their new gym at 114 W. Salem Avenue on October 6. Emmett Jacobs was the boxing coach.

Bob's Service Station that sold Phillips 66 gasoline opened on October 8 at 3234 Mt. Vernon Drive (Cave Spring Road) SW.

William Wheeling, ten months, drowned while playing in a bathtub at his family's home on October 7. He was the son of Mr. and Mrs. Clarence Wheeling of southeast Roanoke.

Nancy Smith, ten, of Salem was struck and killed by a car near her home on October 7 in the Hanging Rock area. She died en route to the hospital. She was the daughter of Mr. and Mrs. Jesse Smith.

A meeting of Roanoke's Black citizens was held on October 7 at St. Paul's Methodist Church by the United Citizens Appeal, headed by Dr. Harry Penn. It was agreed that a committee would be formed to meet with Roanoke's public school officials to discuss desegregation plans. The group also adopted a resolution to seek changes in state laws affecting illegitimate births. According to Penn, one-third of all Black children born in Roanoke were either in the foster care system or getting government aid due to being born out of wedlock. Penn declared the situation "shocking."

Mitchell's Clothing Company opened at its new location at 28 W. Church Avenue on October 12.

Blue Ridge Gardens opened on October 13 on Route 11 between Salem and Roanoke.

Nationally syndicated columnist Sigmund Blomberg came to Roanoke during the second week of October to give lectures on enhancing one's memory. His column, Improving Your Memory, began appearing daily in the *Roanoke Times* that same week.

Salem Town Council passed a resolution on October 10 to ask the Virginia Division of Military Affairs to construct a National Guard armory in the town. The council agreed to offer $20,000 toward the effort and convey five acres of land. Oakey Field was mentioned as a possible site.

Raymond Wilkerson, thirty-six, of Roanoke was killed on October 10 when he hit a fire hydrant with his car and was thrown from the vehicle. The accident occurred on Dale Avenue SE.

A new Baptist church was organized in mid-October to be located at Hershberger Road and Wayside Boulevard. Rev. H. W. Connelly was leading the effort.

Stars of the *Grand Ole Opry* performed at the American Legion Auditorium on October 16. Headliners were Roy Acuff, Kitty Wells, and Johnnie & Jack.

LaVern Baker, the Drifters, and Sil Austin and his orchestra performed for a show and dance at the American Legion Auditorium on October 19. The balcony was reserved for white spectators.

Shirley's Restaurant at 2816 Williamson Road became Shirley's Barbeque House in mid-October.

The Roanoke Symphony Orchestra performed at the Roanoke Theatre on October 17. The program consisted of two pieces by John Powell, *Overture in Old Virginia* and *Rhapsody Negre*, along with Tchaikovsky's *Symphony No. IV in F Minor*. Kathleen Coxe was the piano soloist.

L&N Stores, a department store with a soda fountain, opened at the corner of Jefferson Street and Salem Avenue on October 19. They held a formal grand opening on November 11. A hamburger, piece of pie, and milk lunch cost thirty-nine cents.

This 1955 image shows the Dixie Caverns Restaurant ballroom, a popular space for dances and civic gatherings. *ALHS Annual, 1956*

Students at Andrew Lewis High School in Salem gathered for a pep rally at Salem's Municipal Field in this 1955 photo. *ALHS Annual, 1956*

Frederic Morrow, administrative officer for President Dwight Eisenhower, spoke at the William A. Hunton YMCA annual Founders' Day event on October 16. The program was held at the Greater Mt. Zion Baptist Church.

The cornerstone was laid on October 15 for the new home of the Roanoke Life Saving and First Aid Crew at Day Avenue and Fourth Street SW. Pleasants Lodge No. 63 conducted the ceremony.

Robert Via, a career postal employee, was sworn in on October 15 as the acting postmaster for Roanoke.

Evelyn Boaz, fifteen, of Salem became the first homebound student in the Roanoke Valley to learn by telephone. A special phone was placed with her teacher and classroom at Andrew Lewis High School, so she could hear instruction and interact. Boaz had been homebound for several months.

Belmont Christian Church dedicated its new $150,000 education building on October 16. The church was located at 1101 Jamison Avenue SE. The congregation had a Sunday School enrollment of 750.

Poff & Arrington Realty Company began advertising house lots in Chatham Hills, a new subdivision that adjoined Roanoke Country Club.

Mrs. W. W. Kavanaugh of Roanoke was elected president of the Virginia Congress of Parents and Teachers on October 18 at the organization's annual convention held at the Hotel Roanoke.

Management of the Park Theatre began showing "art cinema," meaning finer cinema and foreign language films somewhat beyond mainstream tastes. They began advertising as Park Art Theatre in mid-October. The first of such films was *Doctor in the House*. The theatre had been closed for three years before reopening. Louise France was the manager.

The spoon bread recipe of Hotel Roanoke was included among 120 selected recipes in Duncan Hines's new book *Duncan Hines Food Odyssey*.

Top Value Stamps opened a gift store at 318 Second Street SW on October 20. Sylvia Dent was the manager. Over 350 retailers in the Roanoke Valley were giving the stamps to customers. On opening day, the first 500 customers received a free relish dish.

Bowen Motor Sales, a used car dealership, opened at 825 College Avenue in Salem on October 21. Operators were Burman Bowen, Stanley Stutts, and Morgan King.

A framed picture of Daisy Schley was presented to Burrell Memorial Hospital on October 21 by the Roanoke Bugs Pinochle Club in honor of her many years of nursing in Roanoke.

Virginia Tech defeated UVA in football 17–13 at Victory Stadium on October 22. Attendance was 16,000.

Harris Cleaners and Shirt Laundry opened a branch at 122 Twenty-Fourth Street NW on October 24.

Ernest Fishburn, an early Roanoke businessman and part of the well-known Fishburn family, died at his home on October 22. He came to Big Lick in 1882 and was employed by the Roanoke Street Railway Company and from 1900 to 1904 he owned a bookstore, the Fishburn Company. He later went into real estate.

Ewald-Clark, a camera and gift store, expanded in late October by taking over an adjacent property previously occupied by Seay's, an appliance store.

The New York Concert Choir performed at the American Theatre on October 24, sponsored by the Thursday Morning Music Club.

Colonial-American National Bank erected a neon sign and clock atop its bank building in late October. The clockface was fourteen feet in diameter. The overall length of the sign was eighty-six feet, and the height was forty-six feet. The letters were in gold and red, and it was the largest neon sign in downtown Roanoke. It was built and erected by Dominion Signs.

Rish Equipment Company, which started in Roanoke in 1932, announced on October 22 plans to open five new plants in Ohio, bringing the number of plants to twelve across three states.

Henry Wright, forty-one, of Starkey was killed instantly on October 23 when a coal bucket dropped from a tall building at Shaffers Crossing. The N&W Railway employee fell more than one hundred feet from the coal wharf where he was working.

Leed's, a clothing store, announced in late October it was going out of business. The store was located at 203 First Street SW.

The Hitching Post Motel on Route 11 at Hollins was leased by Mr. and Mrs. Carl Windel to three men who had formed a corporation for that purpose. They were Thomas McCarthy, owner of the Maple Shade Inn in Pulaski; Kenneth Hyde, associate manager of the Hotel Roanoke; and James Hunter, general manager of the Natural Bridge Hotel.

Pfc. Paul McAllister of Roanoke was fatally stabbed on October 24 at Fort Knox, Kentucky, while on duty. McAllister had been a star athlete at Jefferson High School who later went on to play football at Georgia Tech. Another soldier at the base was arrested for killing McAllister, who was twenty-one.

Allen Hodges, eighteen, was sentenced to twenty years on October 25 for the fatal shooting of Lewis Austin, thirty-four. Hodges pled guilty to second-degree murder.

This early 1950s image shows Barr Brothers Jewelers, located at 4 Campbell Avenue SE.
Virginia Room, RPL

Kay's Sportswear opened at 114 E. Main Street in Salem on October 26. It held a formal grand opening on November 11.

Auto Spring and Bearing Company opened a new branch on W. Main Street in Salem on November 1. Floyd Anderton was the branch manager.

A ground-breaking ceremony for Glad Tidings Church was held on October 30 at Thirteenth Street and Fairfax Avenue NW. The new church was being erected on a lot adjoining the original church. Rev. Gerald Meadows was pastor and founder of the congregation.

After attacking his wife, son, and daughter with a hatchet, James Thomas, forty-five, of Vinton took his own life at their home on South Maple Street on October 28. The family members' injuries were not life threatening.

Jack Housier was convicted of first-degree murder on October 28 in the killing of his wife on September 1 and sentenced to life imprisonment.

Blue Ridge Barbell Club, a bodybuilding gym, opened at 926 Colorado Street in Salem on October 31. Douglas Biller was the manager.

Leggett's Department Store announced in late October it had signed a lease for 40,000 square feet in the planned Roanoke Valley Shopping Center to be located on Route 11 between Roanoke and Salem.

Nannie Burks, ninety-seven, died at Mercy House on October 29. Burks came to Roanoke with her husband in 1892 and organized the first Woman's Suffrage Club in the city.

The Barter Theatre presented *Dial M for Murder* at the Jefferson High School auditorium on November 1. The production's lead roles were played by Owen Phillips, Jeanette Randall, and George Baron.

Walter Hurt, eighty-six, of Roanoke died on October 30. He rose from a messenger boy to treasurer of N&W Railway, retiring in 1938. He was involved in numerous civic and business organizations in Roanoke.

Ruth Brown and Buddy Griffin, along with his orchestra, performed for a show and dance at the American Legion Auditorium on November 4. The balcony was reserved for white spectators.

N&W Railway authorized the construction or purchase of more than 2,000 freight cars and twenty-five general-purpose diesel locomotives on October 31. The total cost was $20 million.

The City Rescue Mission purchased property on First Street SE, behind Elmwood Park, for the construction of new quarters for the ministry. The mission was located at 111 Salem Avenue SE. The mission had been started by Mr. and Mrs. Gustaf Johnson several years prior.

J. J. Newberry Company, a department store, opened its new store on November 3 on Main Street in Salem adjacent to its old store. M. M. Moore was the manager. The Salem store was one of 490 in the Newberry chain across forty-five states. Newberry first opened a store in Salem in 1929. The new store had two floors with a twenty-eight-stool lunch counter.

Caldwell-Sites, a stationery store, held a grand reopening of its store at 105 S. Jefferson Street on November 3 following a major remodeling and conversion to self-service. The store was established in 1897.

Lendy's Big Boy Drive-In Restaurant opened on Lee Highway (Route 11) between Salem and Roanoke on November 2. Advertisements declared it "the home of the double-decker hamburger."

Nearly 2,500 fans watched professional wrestlers Argentina Rocco and Mr. Motto battle in the main mat event at the American Legion Auditorium on October 2. Rocca pinned the Japanese wrestler in two of three falls. Cowboy Carlson defeated Harry Lewis in the opener.

The Man's Shop opened at 216 E. Main Street in Salem on November 3. It occupied the former location of W. T. Norris.

Henebry's, a jewelry store, opened on Main Street in Salem on November 4.

Shoppers Mart, a department store, opened on November 3 at the corner of First Street and Church Avenue SW, across from the Bank of Virginia.

Airport Esso Service Center opened on November 4 at 4704 Williamson Road.

Captain Kermit Allman and Lt. R. M. Harris of Roanoke flew to Houston, Texas, to personally present bicycles to Jerry Wayne, nine, and his siblings. Wayne had written a heartfelt letter to the Roanoke Police Department requesting one of the hundred bicycles held in storage in the city in a freight warehouse. The Wayne children's parents were both disabled and unable to work.

Hannah Swisher, thirty-six, of Roanoke was shot to death on November 5 on Eleventh Street NW. Police arrested Lucian St. Clair of Roanoke for the slaying.

Windsor Hills Methodist Church received its charter during services on November 6. The congregation was meeting at Mount Vernon School until the church was built.

Clemson College defeated Virginia Tech in football, 21–16, at Victory Stadium on November 5. Attendance was 8,000.

In the general election for state offices on November 8, Nelson Thurman, Democrat, defeated Byron Gochenour, Republican, by 2,000 votes to represent Roanoke County in the House of Delegates. Thurman was the mayor of Vinton. Republican Ted Dalton won reelection to the state senate by defeating former Roanoke County School Superintendent Douglas Nininger, a Democrat, by a vote of 7,541 to 4,240 in the Twenty-First Senatorial District. In the race for the two House of Delegates seat for Roanoke City, the two Democratic incumbents defeated the two Republican challengers. The vote totals were as follows: Kossen Gregory, 7,337; Julian Rutherfoord Jr., 7,086; Linwood Holton Jr., 6,744; and Hazel Barger, 6,180. Holton and Barger both had the backing of organized labor and did well in the Black precincts. The locally contested elections were the Cave Spring District seat on the Roanoke County Board of Supervisors, where incumbent E. H. Garner was defeated by Edwin Terrell, 820–C582; incumbent W. C. Muse won as Commissioner of Revenue over John Rettinger, 3,702 to 2,744; and Sherriff H. W. Clark won reelection Cecil Reynolds. For the Salem District Board of Supervisors seat, Roland Clark defeated Howard Houck, 2,070 to 1,215. Roanoke City's State Senator Earl Fitzpatrick was unopposed.

In Roanoke City, a hotly disputed bond issue was on the ballot for a new civic auditorium in Elmwood Park. Business leaders were divided over the issue, with those in support citing the basic need for a new venue, while those opposed did so on the basis of not wanting to increase the city's debt. The bond issue was defeated, 8,847 to 2,400. It failed to carry to a single precinct.

Fink's Jewelers celebrated its twenty-fifth anniversary in November.

Woodlawn Methodist Church broke ground on November 13 for a new $44,000 education building. The church was located at 3301 Ashby Street SW.

The Harlem Globetrotters came to the American Legion Auditorium on November 16. Bob Hall had replaced Goose Tatum in the lead clowning role for the team. The team was accompanied by variety acts that performed during halftime and before and after the game.

Crouch's Drug Store opened on November 12 on Route 11 near Howard Johnson's Restaurant.

Marcellus Ramsey, one of the founders of First Federal Savings and Loan, died on November 11 at his home in Roanoke. He came to Roanoke in 1892 and opened a shoe store.

Arthur Densmore, fifty-five, of Roanoke died on November 12. Densmore was the owner and operator of the thirty-acre Densmore Poultry Farm in northwest Roanoke.

S. S. Biskind, a builder and developer from Cleveland, released designs for his planned $3 million shopping center at Hershberger Road and Grandview Avenue.

Construction and development of the twenty-six acres was dependent upon rezoning. The land was part of the former Gish farm.

Nell Rankin, a mezzo-soprano with the Metropolitan Opera, gave a performance at Hollins College on November 17.

"Piggy-back" operations on N&W Railway began on November 14, when the first trailers owned by commercial motor lines were placed on flat cars. A special ramp and terminal for the operation in Roanoke was in the 1100 block of Shenandoah Avenue NW.

Star Beauty Shop opened at 1217 Patterson Avenue SW on November 14. Mrs. L. D. Setliff was the owner.

The American Piano Trio performed at the American Theatre on November 16 as part of the Thursday Morning Music Club concert series. The members of the trio were Stephen Kovacs, Naomi Weiss, and Esther Fernandez.

Ida Payne, mother of movie actor John Payne, died on November 14. Payne, a resident of Roanoke, had been involved in church and civic activities. She came to Roanoke in 1906. Upon marrying George Payne, a Roanoke builder, Ida Payne and her husband resided for some time at the historic Fort Lewis home in Salem on Route 11.

Glenn's, a clothing store for men and boys, opened at 307 S. First Street on November 17. The owners were Myrl Glenn and Sam Glenn, formerly associated with Glenn-Minnich's.

Howard Seitz, executive director of the fourteen-county Blue Ridge Boy Scouts Council, submitted his resignation on November 15 effective January 31, 1956. He had accepted the job of executive director of the Far East Boy Scouts Council with headquarters in Tokyo, Japan.

Holdren's, an appliance store, opened a new branch store at Cloverdale on Route 11 on November 16.

Luckett Watkins, Roanoke's city engineer from 1920 to 1940, died on November 15 at the age of sixty-six in a Washington, DC, hospital.

Rankin Jewelers announced in mid-November it was going out of business. It was believed to be the oldest jewelry retailer in Roanoke, having been in operation for over fifty years. The company, located at 301 First Street SW, was closing due to the owner's health. The owner was G. A. Jensen. The retailer began as Ryland and Rankin in 1900, when it was first opened by A. J. Rankin on Jefferson Street. It moved to the corner of the Shenandoah Life Building in 1938.

Automotive Services Depot opened at 335 Shenandoah Avenue NW as a wholesaler. R. L. Brickey was the company's president, who claimed the warehouse was the only one of its kind between Baltimore and Atlanta.

The US Marine Band performed at the American Legion Auditorium on November 18.

Smiley Lewis, Jack Dupree, Willie John, George Smith, Earl King, Marie Knight, Otis Williams and his Charms, and Hal Singer and his orchestra performed for show and dance at the American Legion Auditorium on November 23. The balcony was reserved for white spectators.

John Hollyfield, twenty-seven, of Norfolk died in a car accident on November 18 on Route 221, halfway up Bent Mountain.

This 1955 image shows the interior of Staley's Restaurant, located at Colorado and Fourth Streets, in Salem. *ALHS Annual, 1956*

A November 18 fire gutted the three-story O. P. O. Clothes at 106 S. Jefferson Street. The building was a total loss and was razed a few days later.

Elmore Heins, president of the National Theatre Corporation, announced on November 19 that the Rialto Theatre would close on December 3 and be razed to make room for a parking lot. The Rialto was located at 11 E. Campbell Avenue and had been in continuous operation since being built in 1919. Heins stated the movie theatre was no longer profitable. The Palace Confectionary and Presto Café on the theatre property would remain open through June 1956 due to their respective leases, so the building would not be razed until July.

Movie star Aldo Ray came to Roanoke on November 21 to sign autographs at the Grandin Theatre and Lee Theatre in connection with the premier of his film *Three Stripes in the Sun*. While in the city, Ray made an appearance on WSLS-TV, visited St. Vincent's Orphanage, and gave press interviews.

Cornerstone-laying ceremonies were held for the new educational building of Belmont Baptist Church on November 20.

St. Elias Catholic Church caught fire on November 20, but Roanoke fireman arrived in time to stop the blaze that was about to engulf the whole church.

Another new shopping center was proposed on November 21, when plans were submitted before the Roanoke Planning Commission to rezone property on the south side of Melrose Avenue NW at the city line. The request involved nearly seven acres.

The Roanoke Ministers Conference voted unanimously to oppose the proposed constitutional convention recommended by the Gray Commission. The convention was largely viewed as an attempt to modify the Virginia constitution such that the state would not have to fully comply with the Supreme Court's ruling regarding the desegregation of public schools. The ministers believed the proposal was made in haste and that the segregation issue could be worked out without resorting to changing the state constitution. Further, they held that the Gray Commission was a threat to public education. At their November 21 meeting, they also elected Rev. Van Garrett of Christ Episcopal Church as president.

John Kesler, fifty-two, of Roanoke died on November 22 at the C&O Hospital in Clifton Forge from gunshot wounds he received while hunting near Hot Springs.

The eastern half of the Second Street leg of the new viaduct in downtown Roanoke was opened to auto traffic on November 24, marking the first such use of any section of the viaduct. Trucks and buses were not permitted.

Italian Kitchen restaurant opened in mid-November at the end of Williamson Road near Hollins.

Virginia Tech defeated VMI in their annual Thanksgiving Day football game at Victory Stadium. The score was 39 to 13. It was the fifty-first contest between the two schools. Roanoker Don Divers scored three of Tech's touchdowns and was consequently voted the game's outstanding player. Attendance was estimated at 24,000. As usual, Virginia's governor was in attendance. A new tradition was started as a silver Spanish ceremonial sword, imported from Madrid and purchased by both schools, was held by the winner until next year's game.

The Miller Brothers Circus came to the American Legion Auditorium on November 25. The event was sponsored by the Roanoke Exchange Club.

David Carroll, seventeen, of Roanoke County died in a hunting accident in the Fort Lewis area on November 26. His shotgun accidentally discharged when he sat down to rest.

Seward Mott Associates, a consulting firm in Washington, DC, announced on November 26 plans for a $10 million shopping center development at the intersection of Hershberger Road, Williamson Road, and Airport Road. A group of businessmen from Dallas, Texas, were the investors. It was the largest proposed shopping center for the valley, involving some sixty acres. The tract had recently been rezoned by Roanoke County and was formerly the Greendale Farms estate of the late J. B. Andrews.

Roanoke's Boys Club sandlot football team won the Pumpkin Bowl in Gastonia, North Carolina, on November 26. The team received a large trophy, and each player got a gold football. Morris Rorer was voted most outstanding player.

Harvest House, a gifts and antiques store, opened in late November at 1414 Grandin Road SW.

Greene Memorial Methodist Church began a new ministry in late November, dialing A-S-O-U-L for prayer. By calling that number, listeners would hear a prayer for the day.

Janet Bowman, a senior at Jefferson High School, was selected as the Snow Queen for Roanoke's annual Santa Claus Parade that was held on November 29. Fifty-six entrants participated in the parade that snaked through downtown and was sponsored by the Roanoke Merchants Association. The nighttime parade was broadcast by WSLS-TV and was attended by an estimated 20,000 people.

Concert and Broadway singer Nina Dova performed at the Roanoke Executives Club dinner at the Hotel Roanoke on December 2.

Westhampton Christian Church held its first worship service in its new church at the corner of Carlton Road and Grandin Road SW on December 4. The congregation had been meeting in the Grandin Court Recreation Center.

Ted Krystank, forty-three, was found beaten to death in Roanoke County on November 27. He lived in the Mount Pleasant section. Police arrested his estranged wife and father-in-law for the crime.

Eugene Campbell, forty-five, of Clearbrook died on November 27 from burns he had received the day prior when an oil heater in his cabin exploded. Campbell was living at the rear of the Clearbook Service Station and Grocery.

The Roanoke Chapter of the American Association of University Women went on record on November 28 in opposition to calling a constitutional convention in Virginia as proposed by the Gray Commission. The convention was viewed as an effort to thwart desegregation of public schools.

The Roanoke Redevelopment and Housing Authority, using $700,000 in federal money, began purchasing pieces of property in northeast Roanoke as part of its redevelopment plan for that area. The authority had options on 250 of the 465 pieces of property in the eighty-four-acre redevelopment area.

The Blind Boys of Mississippi and the Blind Boys of Alabama gave a joint concert at Mt. Zion Baptist Church on November 29.

N&W Railway announced on November 29 that it was planning to build 4,000 new freight cars totaling $30 million. All would be built in the railway's shops.

Rev. Clinton McCoy and Rev. J. W. Reynolds Jr., representing the Roanoke Ministers Conference, spoke before a joint committee of the Virginia Assembly in Richmond on November 30 in opposition to a proposed amendment to the state constitution as a means of avoiding desegregation of schools. Both asserted that the assembly was acting in haste and that citizens had insufficient information as to the plans for privatizing education with public dollars. The 150-member Roanoke Ministers Conference had gone on record opposing such efforts.

Kay's Hat Box opened at 9 S. College Avenue in Salem on December 2.

A building permit for a nursing home to be built on Broad Street in Salem, between Main and Clay, was issued in late November to Mrs. Minnie Snyder. The twelve-bedroom home was to cost $40,000.

Charles Moore retired on December 1 as head of the Roanoke Water Department, bringing an end to a thirty-nine-year career with the city. Moore became the head of the water department in 1923 and oversaw the expansion of water utilities into annexed areas and the development of Carvins Cove.

Southern States Roanoke Cooperative held a grand opening at Fourth Street and Mountain Avenue SE on December 3. Roses were given to ladies and cigars to men. N. T. Richardson was the store manager.

Vinton held its annual Christmas Parade on December 2 with 10,000 on hand to welcome Santa Claus as part of the thirty-two-unit parade. Gus Nicks was chairman of the Parade Committee.

Judge Stanford Fellers ruled in Law and Chancery Court on December 2 that five Black homeowners in northeast Roanoke who did not want to sell their properties to the Roanoke Redevelopment and Housing Authority could not block the

development project. Fellers stated in his decision that the city and the housing
authority were acting in accord with powers granted to them by state law.

The Rialto Theatre showed its last movies the night of December 3, Gary
Cooper in *Springfield Rifle* and Roy Rogers in *Song of Arizona*. The movie house
was known for showing mainly westerns. The *Roanoke Times* described the down-
fall of the theatre: "Now young Roanokers lie in front of the television set and see
the same stuff free. Or if they don't like Wild West there are space men."

Both chambers of the Virginia General Assembly voted overwhelmingly to
put the question of holding a constitutional convention to the voters in a January
6 referendum. The only dissenting vote in the entire state senate was Ted Dalton of
Radford. The measure was widely viewed as an opportunity to create an amended
constitution for the purpose of subverting the US Supreme Court's ruling to desegregate public education by creating tax-supported private schools. The *Roanoke
Times* opined in their lead editorial on December 4 that it was "the heedless determination of some to evade what has been declared the law of the land."

The Salem Quarterback Club was organized and held the first of a proposed
annual affair—a testimonial dinner honoring the Andrew Lewis High School football team—on December 4.

The Roanoke Touchdown Club presented its annual collegiate Player of the
Year trophy to Jim Bakhtiar of UVA in a dinner at the Hotel Roanoke on December
5. Special guest at the dinner was baseball legend Ty Cobb. Cobb was in Roanoke
visiting his friend J. J. McIntyre. The keynote speaker was former Notre Dame
football coach Frank Leahy.

Greene Memorial Methodist Church ended its dial-a-prayer ministry in early December because it was too successful. Telephone officials indicated that the
prayer line was receiving 15,000 calls per day, meaning most callers got a busy
signal. Church staff hoped they could find a remedy.

Thomas Boyle Jr. of Roanoke died on December 5 at the age of sixty. Boyle
was a founder and the first president of the Roanoke Optimist Club and later
became a vice president of Optimist International. He was also a partner in Boyle-
Swecker, a tire business.

Mrs. Grace Spaulding John, formerly Mrs. John Hancock, visited Roanoke
in early December to sign copies of a new children's book for which she was the
illustrator. The book, *Azalea*, was authored by Eugene Pilot. John lived in Houston
but maintained an art studio in New York City.

Some local high school football players were named to the Associated Press's
All-Western District Team. They were as follows: Don Edmunds, Jefferson; Milan
Christley, Andrew Lewis; Eugene Ferguson, Jefferson; Jim Worley, Jefferson; Paul
Henson, Andrew Lewis; Walter Howard, Jefferson; and Don Whitley, Jefferson.

The Roanoke Symphony Orchestra, along with local church choirs, presented
Handel's *The Messiah* at the American Legion Auditorium on December 11. Solo
vocalists were Florence Vickland, Elise Hartwell, Oscar McCullough, and Patrick
Byrne.

The Roanoke Police Athletic League amateur boxing team kicked off its inaugural season on December 8 in a match against the team from Charlotte, North
Carolina. The competition was held at the American Legion Auditorium. Boxing

for Roanoke were Wesley McCune, Kenneth Wilson, Bob O'Neill, Bert Hasley, James Muse, Glenn Paxton, Louis Johnson, Luster Brown, James Barnett, Robert Carter, Don Hughetti, Charles Williamson, Robert Thompson, and Lowell Foutz. It was the first racially integrated sports team in Roanoke's history. Paul Vest was the team's manager. Roanoke won, 6–3, before a crowd of 1,800.

The Wee Bee Shop, which sold men's neckties, opened in early December at 609 S. Jefferson Street.

Gloria Balander of Roanoke competed on the nationally televised game show *The Big Surprise* on NBC in early December. Her winnings on successive shows totaled $10,000.

The Roanoke PTA Alliance, an organization of PTAs from Roanoke's six Black schools, voted to be in opposition to the "Gray Plan," the name given to the effort to convene, by public referendum, a constitutional convention in Virginia to make amendments such as to thwart desegregation of public schools. George Lawrence was president of the alliance.

Viaud School, a private school, moved to a twelve-room home at 1101 First Street SW in early December. The school had formerly been located at 105 Mountain Avenue SW. The school had 125 pupils and had been founded by Ms. Gustave Viaud in 1926 at 363 Allison Avenue SW.

Judge John Hart, former Hustings Court jurist and a past commissioner of the revenue in Roanoke, died on December 12. He retired in 1953 due to ill health. Hart had many years of public service as a judge, Roanoke alderman, and state senator. He was also instrumental in bringing the Virginia state bar exam to Roanoke. He was eighty-eight.

Salem officials announced they would tie in their sewage system to that of Roanoke City on January 2. With the announcement came the hope that the Roanoke River would become sewage free by mid-1956.

Virginia Governor Thomas Stanley made a press appearance in Roanoke on December 12 to express confidence that the state's voters would vote in the affirmative on the constitutional convention referendum on January 6. On the same day, former state delegate Ernest Robertson of Roanoke County announced the formation of a pro-segregation group in the county called Defenders of State Sovereignty and Individual Liberty. Further, the Roanoke County PTA voted to take no position on the Gray Plan.

The Virginia Sport Writers and Sportscasters Association announced on December 12 their All-Virginia High School football team that was open to all high school players being eligible. Named to the first team were Ken Norton of Andrew Lewis and Gene Ferguson and James Worley of Jefferson High School.

M. B. Shorter, twenty-nine, of Salem was one of two men killed in Wytheville on December 13 when an N&W Railway locomotive exploded. Shorter was a student brakeman. The explosion also killed the fireman. A third man died the following day. The lone survivor was P. H. Sledd, thirty-one, of Roanoke, who was transferred from Wytheville to Lewis-Gale Hospital for treatment.

An overflow crowd of 300 citizens packed the Appalachian Power Company Auditorium on December 13 to hear State Senator Earl Fitzpatrick and other elected officials in the Virginia General Assembly lobby for the proposed constitutional convention and Gray Plan. Most in the crowd were adamantly opposed. The racially mixed crowd asked pointed questions and heckled Fitzpatrick when he replied to one question with, "If schools are integrated, standards are going to be lowered."

The forty-two-room mansion of the late Junius B. Fishburn was deeded over the City of Roanoke for recreational and cultural purposes on December 15. Known as Mountain View, the home was situated on five acres at 714 Thirteenth Street SW. A brief ceremony marked the transition of ownership, where Mrs. Louise Fowlkes handed the key to the house to Mayor Robert Woody.

Sam Garrison, operator of Dixie Caverns, filed corporation reorganizing proceedings in US District Court on December 15 to head off foreclosures by creditors. Most of the debts were incurred with the construction of a restaurant on the property.

Anderson & Weeks Service Station opened at 1828 Memorial Avenue on December 16.

Two additional community forums were held on the Gray Commission plan and the pending referendum on a constitutional convention for Virginia. State Senator Earl Fitzpatrick in Vinton and then a day later on December 16 at Andrew Lewis High School in Salem. The Salem event was attended by about 250 persons who asked pointed questions of Fitzpatrick and others mostly dealing with tax and financial issues of granting state dollars to private school systems.

The Roanoke School Board initiated the purchase of ten acres in northwest Roanoke for a new elementary school on December 16. The tract was located slightly west of Fairview Cemetery. The land was owned by Maggie Wertz.

Civilian pilots paraded about twenty-five aircraft over Roanoke on December 17 in honor of the fifty-second anniversary of flight of the Wright brothers at Kitty Hawk, North Carolina. Wes Hillman promoted the air parade, the first of its kind for Roanoke.

Two lots at Eleventh Street and Grayson Avenue NW were purchased on December 16 for the construction of an Episcopal church for a mission congregation that was worshiping at the Northeast Recreation Center. This mission congregation was St. Luke's Episcopal Church, with Rev. Turner Morris as part-time pastor.

The Roanoke School Board voted 5 to 2 to support the Gray Plan, the proposed change in Virginia's constitution, at their meeting on December 19. After a vigorous debate, a resolution was presented by Vice Chairman John Thornton. The two dissenting votes were from Barclay Andrews and Dr. L. C. Downing. Thornton asserted that the Gray Plan was a "compromise of widely divergent and deep-seated convictions." Barclay opposed the resolution for fiscal reasons, believing tax dollars would be diverted to private schools created to avoid integration. Downing held that the resolution before the board was not given adequate time for discussion and was concerned about the potential damage to public education by adoption of the Gray Plan.

William Smith, senior editor of the *Roanoke Times* and the *Roanoke World-News* was honored at a retirement dinner on December 19. His retirement took effect December 31. He had been employed by the Roanoke newspapers since 1926 in various positions.

Fats Domino and his orchestra performed for a midnight Christmas show and dance at the American Legion Auditorium on December 25. The balcony was reserved for white spectators.

Patricia Moorman, seven, of Roanoke died on December 21 of burns she had received two weeks prior when her clothing caught fire at her home on Kimball Avenue NE due to a kerosene heater.

The Gamma Alpha chapter of Omega Psi Phi fraternity, a group of about fifty Black businessmen in Roanoke, voted on December 22 to oppose the Gray Plan and a constitutional convention.

The Salem Theatre hosted its first annual Christmas Party on December 24 for children under twelve. The movie house provided an hour of cartoons along with Santa.

A profile of a retired mailman appeared in the December 25 edition of the *Roanoke Times*. Charles Richardson, eighty-eight, recalled the early days of mail in Roanoke. He had served as the first president of the Roanoke branch of the National Association of Letter Carriers in 1906 and retired in 1932 after forty-three years with the postal service. He recalled the thirty-six-inch snow of December 1890 when roofs collapsed and of coming home wet waist-high due to walking through weeds and brush to deliver mail. The first post office he worked at in Roanoke was on Salem Avenue. And one early post office burned to the ground on the night of Grover Cleveland's second inauguration. Richardson stated that all mail was hauled in by trains and placed on two-wheel carts and then handled in a boxcar. From there, he carried the mail using a horse and buggy for $27 per month.

The Altruist Club held its fourth annual debutante ball on December 29 at the American Legion Auditorium. The ball was preceded by weeklong activities including a "charm school" at the Orange Avenue YWCA with Mary Williams as the consultant. There were twenty-three young women who were honored.

Goose Tatum, the "Clown Prince of Basketball," and his Harlem Magicians, which included Marques Haynes, came to the American Legion Auditorium on December 25. They played against Bill Spivey and his New York Olympians. The Magicians won, 81–68.

The City of Roanoke contracted with Consolidated Chimney Company of Chicago to raze the 125-foot, reinforced concrete stack at the city's old incinerator on East Campbell Avenue. The stack had been unused for about fifteen years.

Dr. Charles Smith, retired president of Roanoke College, announced on December 29 his support for the Gray Plan and a constitutional convention. "When the citizens of Virginia enter the polls in this election they will have the duty of deciding whether the entire life of the Commonwealth will be advantaged or disadvantaged by mixing black children and white children in the same schools. Those who vote 'yes' will vote for segregation; those who vote 'no' will vote for integration. It's that simple." Smith, also a Lutheran minister, also addressed those clergy who had spoken against the Gray Plan, believing segregation un-Christian. Smith stated, "There were wide racial and national cleavages in the time of Jesus but I nowhere find Him commanding his disciples to crusade for racial or national amalgamations...I am convinced that both they and the NAACP are rendering a disservice to both races in sponsoring a law which will prove unenforceable, which will create disorder, and which ultimately will prove itself hurtful rather than helpful to all Virginia's children...The recent order of the Supreme Court requires an obedience to a law which millions of people in all good conscience cannot bring themselves to obey." Smith went on to opine that the Supreme Court had overstepped its bounds in their ruling in *Brown v. Board of Education*. Smith, in his lengthy statement, concluded: "I believe sincerely that the intellectual, moral, social and spiritual welfare of both races can be best attained in separate schools...I desire that both Negroes and whites shall retain their racial purity and integrity."

The Roanoke County School Board authorized Superintendent Herman Horn to proceed with plans for two new elementary schools, one of Route 119 between Salem and Cave Spring and the other in the Burlington section.

Vinton Town Council accepted the resignation of Mayor Nelson Thurman at its meeting on December 29. Thurman had been elected to the House of Delegates. The council appointed J. E. Clifton to complete Thurman's term on the council.

The F. W. Woolworth Store at 409 S. Jefferson Street closed on December 24, and customers were directed to the Woolworth store at 26 W. Campbell Avenue.

A group of Black clergy in the Roanoke Valley issued a statement on December 30 opposing the Gray Plan and a constitutional convention. The statement read, in part, as follows: "There cannot be found a single Negro so naïve, or devoid of the experiences of indescribable humiliations, and the unnecessary disadvantages and hardships to which Negroes are subjected resulting from segregation."

The Griffin Brothers and Little Richard performed at the Star City Auditorium on December 31. The balcony was reserved for white spectators.

Banks reported their assets and liabilities as of the close of business on December 31, and they were as follows: Southwest Virginia Savings and Loan, $6.8 million; Mountain Trust Bank, $29.8 million; Colonial-American National Bank, $38.3 million; and First National Exchange Bank, $90.1 million.

Greenvale Nursery purchased in late December over three acres off Veterans Facility Road as a site for a new nursery school. The school planned to conduct a $100,000 capital campaign for the new building. Organized in 1934, the school had been at various locations but had been at 1210 Patterson Avenue SW since the late 1940s.

1956

Roanoke City's first baby of 1956 was Ann Marie Dickerson, born at 9:28 a.m. on January 1 to Mr. and Mrs. H. B. Dickerson.

Roanoke's Curtis Turner won the second annual Tobacco Bowl stock car race at Winston-Salem on January 2 before a crowd of 9,000 at Bowman-Gray Stadium. Turner had won the same race the previous year. Turner's first place award was $300.

The Blue Ridge Boy Scout Council announced the appointment of Joseph Davis as its new executive. Davis would begin his duties in mid-February, coming from the Scout Council in Washington, DC.

Roanoke City Council at its meeting on January 3 refused to rezone a twenty-six-acre tract, formerly known as the Gish property, near Hershberger Road for a proposed $3 million shopping center. The plan was vigorously opposed by nearby residents. The rezoning had been recommended by the planning commission.

W. E. Cundiff of Vinton was selected by the Roanoke County Board of Supervisors to serve as chairman for 1956 during their meeting on January 3.

Clarence Thornton, thirty-nine, shot and killed his wife, Margaret, at their home on Williamson Road on January 4. He then threatened his sister-in-law and children, who were also present in the residence, with the same gun. Police were called and surrounded the house before Thornton surrendered. Police credited a young surgeon, Dr. Houston Bell, whom Thornton knew, with skillfully coaxing Thornton to surrender and therefore possibly saving the lives of the others inside the home.

The *Roanoke Times* endorsed, in part, the Gray Plan and the proposed constitutional convention in their January 5 edition. The editorial asserted that using public dollars for private education may be the better way to avoid racial confrontations and ensure the mass education of Virginia's children. "The best solution…is to provide a means whereby non-integrated private schools can function in those areas which will not accept the Supreme Court edict."

State Senator Earl Fitzpatrick and state education board member Leonard Muse addressed a meeting of the Roanoke chapter of Americans United for Separation of Church and State at First Baptist Church on January 6. The two men specifically addressed concerns by the group that if the Gray Plan was adopted and a constitutional convention was held, it would result in the state-sponsored expansion of Catholic schools in Virginia. Both men reported that no public dollars would be directed to church-operated private schools.

William Parker Sr. of Roanoke died on January 7 at the age of seventy-two. Parker came to Roanoke in 1918 and established his photography business, which he operated until the time of his death.

Martha Anne Woodrum Zillhardt, formerly of Roanoke, became one of the first women in the United States to obtain a helicopter license. She trained for the license at an airport in Boston. She had once operated a flying school at Woodrum Field and was one of the first women in Virginia to earn a pilot's license.

Howard Hammersly of the *Roanoke Times* was named Photographer of the Year by the Virginia Press Association on January 7.

Bishop Karl Block, who served as the rector of St. John's Episcopal Church from 1920 to 1926, was honored as a Commander of the Most Excellent Order of the British Empire by Queen Elizabeth in early January for his service to the British fleet while they were stationed in San Francisco.

Eastern Finance Corporation opened an office at 3 W. Salem Avenue on January 9. Kenneth Wright was the manager.

The Interdenominational Negro Ministers Alliance took out an ad in the January 8 edition of the *Roanoke Times* declaring its strong opposition to the Gray Plan and the proposed constitutional convention on the eve of a statewide referendum. Rev. F. E. Alexander was the chairman of the group.

The statewide referendum on holding a constitutional convention, known as the Gray Plan, passed 2 to 1 throughout Virginia. The Gray Plan passed in both Roanoke City and County. In Roanoke City, the vote was 6,206 "for" and 6,156 "against," with Black precincts voting overwhelmingly against. In Roanoke County, the vote was 3,080 "for" and 2,654 "against."

Petitions were filed on January 9 for rezoning about thirty acres of land between Colonial Avenue and Brandon Avenue SW, for a shopping center. The property was owned by the Times-World Corporation as it was also the site of the WDBJ radio transmitter and towers.

The Salem Junior Chamber of Commerce named Talmadge Jones as its Young Man of the Year on January 9. He was the plant engineer at Yale & Towne.

Ice Vogues of 1956 came to the American Legion Auditorium for a five-night run beginning January 14.

Dr. Charles Grady retired on January 13 as the director of the Veterans Administration Hospital. Grady had served on the staff of the hospital for twenty-six years. He was succeeded by Dr. J. B. Bounds, who was manager of the VA Hospital in Jefferson Barracks, Missouri.

National Timber Sales Corporation opened on January 13 in the Carlton Terrace Building. Curtis Turner was the president.

The Westminster Choir gave a concert at the American Theatre on January 17, sponsored by the Roanoke Civitan Club. The nationally known choir included one Roanoker, Charlotte Nixon.

Westhampton Christian Church dedicated its new building on January 15. The guest speaker was Rev. William Pearcy, executive secretary of the Board of Church Extension in Indianapolis, Indiana.

The Roanoke chapter of Alcoholics Anonymous celebrated its tenth anniversary on January 21 with a banquet at the Hotel Roanoke. The Roanoke group was started by two individuals and had grown to serve 200. The first open meeting of the local AA was in August of 1946 at Lee Junior High School.

Members of the Roanoke Exchange Club held an auction on WDBJ-TV on January 17 of various items which raised funds for the March of Dimes. Various businesses donated goods to be sold.

The newly organized Connelly Memorial Baptist Church broke ground on a building on Hershberger Road NW in early January. Rev. H. W. Connelly was the pastor.

A ground-breaking ceremony was held on January 19 for the army reserve training center, located opposite the Veterans Administration Hospital.

Local Republicans held a "Salute to Ike" fundraising dinner at the Hotel Roanoke on January 20. The keynote speaker was Congressman Dewey Short.

Robert Smith, former Roanoke commonwealth's attorney, died on January 18 at the age of sixty-one. He served as the commonwealth's attorney from 1930 until 1942. He chose Lindsay Almond Jr. as his assistant in 1930.

Wally Fowler, Jimmy Davis, the Sunshine Boys Quartet, the Revelaires Quartet, and the Foggy River Boys gave a gospel concert at the American Legion Auditorium on January 22.

Donald Richberg, a Washington attorney who was a key aide to President Franklin Roosevelt, addressed the annual meeting of the Roanoke Chamber of Commerce on January 20. Some 500 persons attended the dinner at the Hotel Roanoke.

This 1955 image shows the S&H Green Stamp Store at 419 Campbell Avenue. In January 1956, it relocated to Franklin Road. *Virginia Room, RPL*

Excavation was begun the second week of January for the new Sears store, just off Williamson Road. The contractor, Wiley N. Jackson, had to clear a large hill along the western side of the site. Dirt from the construction location was being used to fill private land in the vicinity of Lukens Street and Sycamore Street.

C. R. Davidson announced on January 21 plans for a $1 million shopping center to be located on US Route 11 near Hollins College, to be known as "The Burlington."

The Caine Mutiny Court-Martial was presented by Showtimers the last weekend in January at Roanoke College. Lead roles were performed by Herbert Harris, Ed Johnson, and Arden Kiser. The director was David Thornton.

Roy Milton and his orchestra, Amos Milburn, Little Richard, Mickey Champion, and Lady Dee performed for a show and dance at the American Legion Auditorium on January 27. The balcony was reserved for white spectators.

Fred Waring and the Pennsylvanians brought their musical show, *Hear! Hear!,* to the American Legion Auditorium on January 29.

Directors of First Federal Savings and Loan Association voted on January 23 to build a $1 million seven-story office building at Church Avenue and First Street SW. Daniel Construction Company of Greenville, South Carolina, was the contractor.

The Salem Optimist Club received its charter during a dinner-dance at Dixie Caverns on January 28. William Simmons was the club's president. Optimist Clubs were dedicated to eliminating juvenile delinquency.

The S&H Green Stamp Store opened at its new location, 2514 Franklin Road SW, on January 27. It had previously been located on Campbell Avenue.

This late 1950s photograph shows the S&H Green Stamps Store at 2514 Franklin Road SW. *Virginia Room, RPL*

The Roanoke Junior Chamber of Commerce named William Hopkins, a marine hero and attorney, for is Distinguished Service Award during its annual Bosses Night Dinner at the Hotel Roanoke on January 27.

Mildred Stewart, twenty-eight, was shot and killed on January 27 as she started to get in her car in front of a restaurant on Alabama Street in Salem. Police arrested her estranged husband, Lewis Stewart, for the crime.

The southbound lanes of the Salem Avenue leg of the new viaduct in Roanoke were opened to traffic on January 30, as work on the final stages of the viaduct's construction was underway.

The Blue Ribbon Restaurant, a landmark on W. Campbell Avenue for forty years, announced its new location on January 30, which was next door the old one. The restaurant operators, Mike Ganas and Tommy Spain, planned to open the Blue Ribbon at 138 W. Campbell Avenue on February 13 in what was formerly the Java Restaurant. The Blue Ribbon had been in the Ganas family since 1916.

John Reid in an interview with the *Roanoke Times* on January 29 recalled the early days of golf in Roanoke. A charter member of the Roanoke Country Club, Reid was the only charter member still living. The club was formed in the late 1890s on property owned by the Crystal Spring Land Company in South Roanoke. "It was a crude layout with short, rough fairways, sand greens, and tomato cans for holes." A local tennis club merged with the local golfers to form the country club. Representing the tennis club were Reid, Charley Freeman, and Harry Coleman. The golfers on the organizational committee were Lucian Cocke, William Glasgow, G. H. Dugdale, and R. P. Sanderson. Reid was the youngest man on the committee and was tasked to see how many new members he could get. "We bought an old residence near the present site of the South Roanoke fire station and remodeled it, adding a porch and wooden lockers. We built a couple of sand tennis courts, too." At that time, golf balls were made of juice extracted from an evergreen tree in Malay Archipelago. "We had about three clubs then – a driver, mid-iron, and putter. More came along as the game grew. Also, as the game grew, women became interested. I don't remember my reaction when I first saw a woman golfing, but it might have been, 'They're cluttering up the course.'"

Betty Padget, twenty-five, of Roanoke was killed in an auto accident on Old River Road in Roanoke County on January 28.

Tabernacle Baptist Church dedicated its new education building on January 29. The guest speaker was Rev. Lucius Polhill of the Virginia Baptist Board of Missions. The new building cost $168,000.

The last passenger train of the Virginian Railway came into Roanoke on January 29 at 4:10 p.m., forty minutes late. Virginian officials had received permission to discontinue the service due to few passengers. Making the final trip were three persons who had ridden the Virginian's first train out of Roanoke on July 1, 1909—Essie Martin, Mrs. Fred Meador, and Mrs. Charles Hannabas. S. H. Kirby of Victoria was the engineer on the final run.

Black yard brakemen on N&W Railway won an injunction in US District Court on January 30 barring the railroad and the Brotherhood of Railroad Trainmen from discriminating against them when they sought promotions to car retarder operators. The suit was brought against N&W by three Black brakemen in N&W's Roanoke yard—Robert Coles, Sam Clark, and Robert Hamler.

The gates of the N&W Railway Jefferson Street grade crossing operated for the last time on January 30. The gates had guided traffic for more than fifty years. As soon as the gates came down, workers began excavating under the tracks for a planned pedestrian underpass and a storm sewer line. The project was in connection with the new viaduct, which had begun opening to traffic in phases.

Stars from the *Grand Ole Opry* performed at the American Legion Auditorium on February 4. The show included the Carter Sisters, Audrey Inman, Benny Martin, Charlene Arthur, Jack and Daniel, Porter Wagoner, Tommy Collins, and Sonny James.

N&W Railway ordered fifty general-purpose diesel locomotives in early February for its Shenandoah Division at a cost of $9.3 million. The locomotives would pull passenger and freight trains operating between Roanoke and Hagerstown, Maryland. The order brought the number of diesels on order or in operation by N&W to eighty-three.

Densmore Poultry Farm in Roanoke County was purchased by a new corporation, Densmore Inc., in early February. The new corporation was headed by Frank Oliver and James Hall. The Densmore farm had been in operation since 1903 and was the largest poultry producer in the county.

For the first time in its history, the *Roanoke Times* began publishing all the stock listings on the New York and American Stock Exchanges beginning with the February 2 edition.

The annual meeting of Groundhog Club of America No. 1 was held on February 2 at the American Legion Auditorium. The main topic was whether the athletic field at Fries, Virginia, had groundhog holes in it. Fries High School's principal, N. E. Davis, addressed the matter. Other fun was poked at local and state politics, and music was provided throughout the evening. An estimated 1,000 men attended. The club's president was H. T. Angell.

WSLS-TV advertised in early February its new 6:30 p.m. weeknight show, *Looney Tunes*, hosted by Uncle Looney. The featured cartoons included Porky Pig, Daffy Duck, Buddy Beans, and Bosco.

Hubert Moore, fifty, of Smithfield, North Carolina, and a patient at the Veterans Administration Hospital, was struck and killed on February 4 by an N&W Railway freight locomotive. Moore was struck on the tracks at the rear of the hospital property, and witnesses said he ran toward the westbound train.

Roy Hamilton, Shirley and Lee, pianist Joe Jones, and Erskine Hawkins performed for a show and dance at the American Legion Auditorium on February 10. The balcony was reserved for white spectators.

Roanoke's Police Athletic League boxing team took on amateur boxers from two teams on February 9 at the American Legion Auditorium. Roanoke's boxers participated in over a dozen matches with the boxing teams from Beaumont School in Richmond and the PAL team from Winston-Salem. Attendance was estimated at 2,500.

Heights Club, a new civic organization, was founded on February 4. Membership included residents from southwest Roanoke and adjacent neighborhoods in

Roanoke County. C. G. Haupt was elected president. Membership was by invitation only and limited to businessmen.

Hobbie Brothers, a music store, celebrated its seventy-fifth anniversary on February 7. J. D. Hobbie founded the firm in Lynchburg in 1881. A branch was opened in Roanoke at Salem Avenue and Henry Street (First Street) in 1888. The branch occupied other storefronts along Salem Avenue in the several years that followed before erecting a building of its own in 1906 at 14 W. Campbell Avenue. In 1910, the store moved again to 9 W. Church Avenue.

Residents of the East Gate section spoke out against a proposed refuse dump along Tinker Creek at the Roanoke City Council meeting on February 6. City officials were considering use of an abandoned quarry in the area and the acquisition of twenty surrounding acres for a possible city dump site.

Sample Hash Jr., four, was struck and killed by a gravel truck in front of his home on Route 221 in Roanoke County on February 8. The accident occurred in front of the W. T. Rierson grocery store.

Mrs. Elizabeth Harvey was selected as the new treasurer for the Town of Vinton on February 9. She succeeded Mrs. Florence Hayden, who had served in the position for nine years.

Gene Autry, along with his horse Champion, came to the American Legion Auditorium on February 13. Joining him was Gail Davis, Pat Buttram, the Cass County Boys, the Villemaves, the Promenaders, and Carl Cotner and the Melody Ranch Orchestra.

For the first time in the sixty-six year history of S. H. Heironimus Company, stock in the company was offered for sale to the general public. The company was seeking to raise $900,000 for its expansion program.

Forty-two acres of land in Roanoke County, west of Salem, was purchased in early February by the Roanoke Development Corporation to serve as a future industrial site. RVDC purchased the land from Robah Kerner and Cora Kerner at $1,000 per acre. This was the second piece of large land purchase by the company.

Mrs. Herbert Gregory of Roanoke became the chairman of the all-female Virginia division of motion picture censorship. Every film shown in the state, with the exception of news reels, had to be approved by the censorship division.

Paul Gantt, one of the chief prosecutors of the Nuremberg War Crimes trials, addressed the monthly meeting of the Roanoke Bar Association on February 14. He spoke on the topic of government contracting.

The Barter Theatre presented *Julius Caesar* at Jefferson High School on February 14.

The American Chamber Orchestra gave a concert at Hollins College on February 16. The conductor was Robert Scholz, a native of Austria.

Francis Lane, operator of the Brook Club on Veterans Facility Road near Salem, was fined fifty dollars on February 13 in Roanoke County Trial Justice Court for running a dance on a Sunday. Law enforcement testified that patrons were dancing instead of just listening to a band in violation of the county's local Sunday dance ordinance.

The Roanoke Symphony Orchestra and Chorus pose for a photograph prior to their performance at the American Legion Auditorium in February 1956. At the time, it was the largest musical performance in Roanoke's history. *Virginia Room, RPL*The first glimpse of CinemaScope 55 was previewed at the Grandin Theatre on February 14. The new technique was a process of filming movies on fifty-five-millimeter film and then reducing the picture to thirty-five-millimeter film. This produced a sharper focus and eliminated distortion. *Carousel* was the first major motion picture to use the technique.

The South Central Golf Association was formed on February 15 during a meeting of female golfers in Roanoke, who represented various area country clubs. Mrs. Karl Kregloe of Roanoke was elected general chairman of the association, the mission of which was to promote women's golf.

Dr. Jekyll and His Weird Show came to the stage of the Roanoke Theatre on February 22.

The Roanoke Symphony Orchestra performed Mozart's *Requiem* on February 20 at the American Legion Auditorium. The production also included a 500-voice chorus from surrounding colleges and universities, and over 600 musicians were involved. It was believed to be the largest musical production in Roanoke's history.

An official planting of a dogwood tree on the grounds of the Vinton War Memorial on February 18 marked the first step in the town's effort to become the "dogwood capital of Virginia." The effort was launched by the band boosters of William Byrd High School, who sold more than one hundred dogwood trees to raise money for instruments and uniforms. A Dogwood Band Festival had also been planned for May 5. J. H. Sims, director of Byrd's band, had sent out invitations to over one hundred bands in the state to participate.

Hollins College dedicated its new Fishburn Library on February 21 as part of its annual Founders' Day celebration. The $440,000 library was named in honor of the late Junius P. Fishburn, who was for many years a trustee of the college.

Mrs. Callie Whitenack, seventy-eight, of Roanoke died on February 19 from injuries she received when struck by a car on Orange Avenue NW earlier that day.

The Fishburn Library at Hollins College, photographed here in 1956, was named in memory of Junius P. Fishburn a longtime trustee of the college. *Virginia Room, RPL*

Elections were held across Virginia on February 21 to select delegates to the state's upcoming constitutional convention. The race for Roanoke City's delegate seat was won by Sydney Small, an executive with N&W Railway. He defeated Black civic leader Dr. Harry Penn by a vote of 3,481 to 1,068. In the Twenty-First Senatorial District, which included Roanoke County, Virgil Goode was elected without opposition.

The Polack Brothers Shrine Circus came to Roanoke for a three-day run beginning February 23 at the American Legion Auditorium. George Henneford was the ringmaster.

Roanoke Junior Chamber of Commerce leaders reported on February 22 that the organization was losing money sponsoring performances by the Barter Theatre in Roanoke due to low attendance. Robert Porterfield, director of the Barter, blamed the issue on having to do productions in the auditorium of Jefferson High School. "I don't blame anyone for not going to that auditorium," he said.

Earle Offinger, sixty-six, of Roanoke was found dead in his wrecked car on US Route 11 at a Roanoke River bridge on February 23. Police believed his car hit the bridge railing.

The Appalachian Baseball League announced on February 24 that it was folding. The league was the oldest Class D circuit in organized baseball. Bristol, Johnson City, and Kingsport had announced earlier in the year they would not be fielding teams. The president of the Salem Rebels responded that his club would then not field a team in 1956 or 1957 as there were only four teams left.

O. P. O. Clothes, a men's store, held a grand opening at its new store at 314 S. Jefferson Street on February 27. The chain first opened a Roanoke branch in 1925 at 116 S. Jefferson Street, until it was destroyed by fire. The new location had been formerly occupied by the Old Dominion Candy Company.

The contents of United Pawn Shop, located at 3 E. Salem Avenue, were auctioned off in late February to settle the estate of Miriam Krisch. Rosalie Shaftman was the executrix.

Curtis Turner of Roanoke won the 160-mile NASCAR-sanctioned race at Daytona Beach on February 25 for late-model convertibles. He beat the second-place winner by five miles. Curtis's average speed was 96.1 miles per hour.

Oliver Hill, a prominent civil rights attorney who grew up in Roanoke, spoke on WDBJ-TV on February 25 as part of the station's series titled *Virginia's Dilemma* dealing with school segregation. Hill predicted, "There will unquestionably be further legal action this year" in the Prince Edward County school case. Hill headed a committee of lawyers representing the NAACP in Virginia.

The Roanoke Civic Ballet performed two ballets at Jefferson High School on March 5, *Strauss Suite* and *Serenade for Strings*. The latter was done with modern choreography. Joining the civic ballet was Robert Lindgren, who had danced professionally for six years with the Ballet Russe de Monte Carlo.

Mezzo-soprano Nan Merriman gave a concert at the American Theatre on March 1, sponsored by the Thursday Morning Music Club.

Stars from the *Grand Ole Opry* performed at the American Legion Auditorium on March 4. The show included Carl Smith, Duke of Paducah, Kathy Copas, Danny Dill, Annie Lou, Johnny Sibert, Curly Rhoades, and the Tunesmiths. Tickets were available from the Roanoke Record Shop at 116 W. Church Avenue.

This 1956 image shows the reading room of the Fishburn Library at Hollins College. The library was formally dedicated in February 1956. *Virginia Room, RPL*

The Cadillacs, Ray Charles, and Mary Ann Fisher performed for a show and dance at the American Legion Auditorium on March 2. The balcony was reserved for white spectators. Tickets were $1.50.

The congregation of Pilgrim Baptist Church voted in late February to purchase the Rugby Church of God for $37,500. The Rugby congregation was located at Rugby Boulevard and Thirteenth Street NW and was planning to build a new church. Rev. C. H. Gill was the pastor of Pilgrim Baptist Church.

In a meeting at the Hunton YMCA on February 28, the United Citizens Council nominated Dr. Lawrence Paxton, a dentist, to run for Roanoke City Council. He won over two other candidates considered by the council, Rev. Robert Smith and Rev. F. E. Alexander. The council election was slated for June 12. In accepting the nomination from the Black civic organization, Paxton stated, "I feel that Negroes should have representation on Council."

A Salem unit of the National Guard was activated on March 1. The 418th AAA Battalion had fifteen men and two officers.

The congregation of Enon Baptist Church voted to construct a $70,000 education building. Rev. William Corder was pastor of the 300-mmember congregation.

The contract for the new Miller & Rhoads department store in Roanoke was awarded to B. F. Parrott and Company of Roanoke. The Roanoke store was estimated to cost $2.5 million.

This is a father-son banquet of the Hunton YMCA held at the Star City Auditorium in 1956. *Virginia Room, RPL*

Ground was broken in early March for a new $100,000 gymnasium and a $50,000 boys' cottage at the Virginia Baptist Children's Home in Salem. Both were being built by English Construction Company of Altavista.

A new Presbyterian congregation was formed in the Starmount section of Roanoke County, just off Peters Creek Road, in early March. Rev. Bernard Bain was leading the mission.

Jasper Walters, forty-one, of Roanoke died on March 2 from injuries he sustained eight months prior in an industrial accident. He had remained unconscious the entire period. He was employed at Auto Springs Works and was struck in the head by a disintegrating grinding wheel.

A group of seven doctors announced in early March plans to erect a $125,000 office and clinic on the northeast corner of Franklin Road and Walnut Avenue SW. The building would be located on property that was used by Jefferson Hospital as a parking lot. The group of doctors was Hugh Trout Jr., W. W. Butler, W. W. Butler III, A. P. Jones, Horace Albertson, and Robert Keeley.

The Virginia constitutional convention was held in Richmond on March 7. The convention delegates voted unanimously to enact an amendment that made lawful the expenditure of state funds for education in nonsectarian private schools as a means of avoiding desegregation of the public schools.

Clarence Thornton pled guilty in Hustings Court on March 7 to the fatal shooting of his wife on January 4 and was sentenced to life in prison.

James Ayers, nineteen, at Roanoke College was given a 1956 Ford Thunderbird on March 8 as a contest prize by the Brown & Williamson Tobacco Company of Louisville, Kentucky, for choosing a name for the filter tip of Viceroy cigarettes.

Count Basie and his orchestra, along with Joe Williams, performed for a show and dance at the American Legion Auditorium on March 15. The balcony was reserved for white spectators.

Roanoke police launched an intensive manhunt the second week of March for a man that had been molesting women in the northwest section of the city. Three couples had been attacked separately by a masked man who tied up the males and then sexually assaulted the females. The couples had also been robbed.

The Eagles Nest restaurant opened in the terminal at Woodrum Field on March 10. The restaurant was operated by Ward Cleaves and Fred Stout and consisted of fourteen counter seats and eighteen tables.

Leroy Ferris of William Fleming High School was named by the Virginia Sports Writers and Sportscasters Association to its All-State basketball team.

Campbell Memorial Presbyterian Church in Vinton dedicated its new education building on March 11.

The Inland Lakes Yacht and Boat Club was organized in Roanoke with a planned base of operations at Claytor Lake. About thirty men formed the club and elected Dewey Robertson as first commodore.

Roanoke's PAL boxing team won its fourth straight victory on March 10 when they defeated the Washington Athletic Club by winning six of ten matches. An estimated 1,700 fans watched the event that was held in the American Legion Auditorium.

The campaign to raise $35,000 to underwrite the cost of staging Roanoke's Diamond Jubilee celebration was formally launched in mid-March. Edward Ould headed the effort.

The Dublin Players from Ireland presented the comedy play *An Ideal Husband* at Hollins College on March 12.

The Carib Singers, a group from the Caribbean Islands, performed at Addison High School on March 16.

Roy Summitt, sixteen, of Roanoke pled guilty on March 12 to the murder of John Bray, a movie theatre supervisor, last September in Smyth County. The trial was held at Marion, where Summitt was sentenced to fifteen years.

Roanoke Mayor Robert Woody announced on March 12 that he would not seek reelection to Roanoke City Council. Woody cited time constraints as his reason.

Williams P. Hunter, Roanoke's former city manager who was later elected to the city council, died on March 13 at Roanoke Memorial Hospital. He was seventy-one. He was Roanoke's first city manager, having previously been the resident engineer at the Greenbrier Hotel. His council colleagues selected him as mayor after being elected to that body following his retirement.

Fred Yates of Roanoke County bowled a 204 duck pin game at Luckland Bowling Alleys on March 13. It was the highest single line rolled at the alleys since it opened in 1939.

The Board of Trustees of Hollins College adopted a new annual salary scale for instructors at their meeting on March 14. The scale was as follows: instructor, $4,500; assistant professor, $5,500; associate professor, $6,500; and professor, $7,500.

The Salem Lions Club held its twenty-first annual minstrel show at Andrew Lewis High School on March 15. The show was the club's primary fundraiser. James Moyer was the interlocutor. The Vinton Lions Club held their annual minstrel show the following week at William Byrd Junior High School, where George Austin served as interlocutor.

A new local country music band was formed in mid-March, Jayhue Hall and the Blue Ridge Entertainers. They debuted on WROV radio, performing every weekday at 5:45 a.m. The group consisted of Carl Moody, Bob Bryant, Jayhue Hall, W. J. Wood, Lane Wimmer, George Kennedy, and Pete Goad.

The Roanoke Ministers Conference adopted a resolution at its March 19 meeting calling on Roanoke City Council and the Roanoke County Board of Supervisors to each appoint a biracial commission for their respective localities. The commissions would serve to "make recommendations for the solution and clarification of racial problems." The proposal was endorsed by the *Roanoke Times*.

Ruth Townsend, a William Fleming High School student, won the nineteenth annual American Legion Virginia oratorical contest.

Students of Washington and Lee University performed their minstrel show, *The Deevine Comedy*, at Hollins College on March 21. The show featured over seventy students and raised funds for college scholarships.

Mrs. Margaret Starkey won the "Mrs. Salem" contest on March 21 that was sponsored by Roanoke Gas Company. The competition was based on cooking skills and earned Starkey an opportunity to compete in the "Mrs. Virginia" contest.

Carey Powell, the Vinton fire chief, died on March 21 at his home at the age of forty-four. He had been the town's fire chief for fourteen years and also operated the Pollard Restaurant in Vinton.

Ground was broken for the new Mary Louise Home on March 22 by the King's Daughters. Mrs. Katie Green and Mrs. Pattie Poole did the honors. The new home's location was at the intersection of Cambridge Avenue and Mountain View Terrace Avenue SW.

The State Water Control Board announced on March 23 the no future permits would be issued by them for discharges into the Roanoke River that would contain pollutants. This was in response to the City of Roanoke and others who had complied with pollution control measures.

The number of candidates for the general election for Roanoke City Council grew to four on March 23 with the announcement by Rev. F. E. Alexander, publisher of the *Roanoke Tribune*, of his candidacy. The other announced candidates were Dr. L. E. Paxton, incumbent Mary Pickett, and Selby McMillion. Three incumbent council members had previously announced they were not seeking reelection. Alexander's main reason for running was to close the city dump at Washington Park.

Officials with the Boston Red Sox floated the idea of an experimental-type Class D minor league for the Roanoke Valley with two teams each from Roanoke and Salem. The teams would be composed of rookies from high school or college. The Red Sox stated they would sponsor one of the teams and indicated there was interest by other major league teams in sponsoring the remaining three.

Mrs. Leona Trippeer, who raised ten children and worked later as a "mother" in Roanoke's Juvenile Detention Home, was named Virginia Mother of the Year by a select committee of judges involved in youth work.

The local children's television program *Romper Room* was profiled in the March 25 edition of the *Roanoke Times*. The program was hosted by "Miss Elsie," who was Mrs. Frederick Tanner, and the classroom was Studio 1 of WSLS. The program aired weekday mornings at 9:30. The inaugural broadcast was on January 10, 1955, with five students and became known as "Roanoke's kindergarten."

Fairview Methodist Church held its first worship service in its new church building on March 25. The building was located at Virginia Avenue and Van Buren Street NW and cost about $100,000. Rev. Charles Bright was the pastor.

Virginia Attorney General Lindsay Almond opined on March 26 that high school athletics should remain segregated as the General Assembly had adopted a resolution declaring such. That meant the Roanoke Valley high schools would continue to not have interracial competitions.

This 1950s Roanoke Police Department photo shows a view of Grandin Road SW, looking north from the 1400 block. *Nelson Harris*

The Roanoke Valley Regional Planning and Economic Development Council held its inaugural meeting on March 27 and chose G. L. Mattern, a civil engineer, as its chairman. The council was created by the governing bodies of Roanoke, Roanoke County, Salem, and Vinton for conducting overall planning for the Roanoke Valley and to advise local planning commissions.

Illinois Jacquet and his orchestra, along with the Cardinals, performed for a show and dance at the American Legion Auditorium on April 1. The balcony was reserved for white spectators.

Wally Fowler, the Oak Ridge Quartet, Kat Freeman, the Chuck Wagon Quartet, and the Dixieaires presented a gospel concert at the American Legion Auditorium on April 2.

The medical case of Anne Kahle of Roanoke was profiled in the March 31 issue of *The Saturday Evening Post*. Kahle had suffered from epilepsy since the age of ten but underwent successful operations to treat her seizures at the National Institutes of Health in Bethesda, Maryland.

W. B. Carter and Dr. C. M. Cornell both announced they would be candidates for Roanoke City Council in the general election on June 12. Carter had previously served on the council in the 1940s.

Blacks in Roanoke raised about $700 to aid Blacks in Montgomery, Alabama, with boycotting the bus system there. The effort was spearheaded by Rev. F. E. Alexander and the Roanoke Baptist Pastors Conference. The money was sent directly to Rev. Martin Luther King Jr. from the Roanoke Branch NAACP.

This is another 1950s police department image showing the view looking south from the 1400 block of Grandin Road SW. *Nelson Harris*

Roanoke Woodworking Corporation announced in late March that it occupy a new warehouse on Kessler Mill Road around May 1. The warehouse and other operations to be relocated there would occupy over twenty acres.

The story of formation of life saving crews around the world after the first one was established in Roanoke in 1928 was the subject of an article that appeared in the April edition of *Reader's Digest*. The magazine had previously profiled the Roanoke Life Saving and First Aid Crew in its February 1945 issue.

Three more candidates entered the race for Roanoke City Council on March 31. Vincent Wheeler, Fred Reynolds, and Bowman Harris expanded the field to nine candidates.

The twenty-ninth annual spring congress of Gill Memorial Eye, Ear, Nose and Throat Hospital was held the first week in April with over 400 specialists in attendance. Lectures were held at the Patrick Henry Hotel.

The Barter Theatre presented *Sabrina's Fair* at Jefferson High School on April 3. Leading roles were played by Jeanette Randall, Owen Phillipps, Dorothy LaVern, and Del Close.

Rev. Kern Eutsler, pastor of South Roanoke Methodist Church, spoke to 17,000 worshippers at the annual Easter sunrise service at Natural Bridge on April 1. Local sunrise services occurred at Washington Park, Shenandoah Drive-In Theatre, Mountain View Cemetery, Sherwood Burial Park, and on top of Mill Mountain.

A ground-breaking ceremony was held on April 2 for the new Sears Town shopping on Williamson Road. The store plans included 60,000 square feet of retail space in addition to a new Kroger grocery store. Several officials with Sears's national office were on hand for the event.

WDBJ-TV began full-scale broadcast operations on April 8 with a host of new CBS programs. Prior to the date, WDBJ had had limited airtime. The new schedule allowed the television station to begin broadcasting at 10:00 a.m. on Sundays, 7:00 a.m. Mondays through Fridays, and 9:30 a.m. on Saturdays. On April 4, the FCC gave the station permission to move its transmitter to Poor Mountain to provide better area coverage.

Two landmark smokestacks on Walnut Avenue were razed in early April. The smokestacks had been in place for over fifty years and were part of the Appalachian Electric Power Company generating plant along the Roanoke River. The Chicago Chimney Company did the demolition.

Thomas Williams of Roanoke was arrested and charged on April 6 with trying to rob the First National Bank of Ferrum. Williams's attempt at armed robbery was thwarted when bank officials subdued him and called the sheriff's department.

W. L. Duggins and John Dillon opened D&D Auto Upholstery Shop at 624 Second Street SW on April 9.

Charles Wosaba, a sophomore at William Fleming High School, won top honors in the Western Virginia Science Fair held on April 7. He was awarded a trip to the National Science Fair in Oklahoma City, Oklahoma, by the Times-World Corporation. His science fair exhibit was a walking robot.

The Roanoke Sales Executive Club sponsored a program, *120 Minutes That Can Change Your Life*, at the American Theatre on April 11. The event was a presentation by two nationally known speakers, Dr. Norman Vincent Peale and Millard Bennett. Earlier in the day, Peale signed copies of his books at Pugh's Department Store.

United State Plywood Corporation opened a distribution warehouse at 2502 Patterson Avenue SW during the first week in April.

Roanoke City Council authorized the acquisition of land for extension of the northeast-southeast runways at Woodrum Field during its meeting on April 9. The extension would cause the relocation of Route 118 (Airport Road).

Con Davis, a teacher and coach at William Fleming High School, was named principal of the new Cave Spring High School by the Roanoke County School Board on April 10.

Bluefield Hardware Company established a distribution warehouse at 302 Campbell Avenue SE in mid-April.

Roanoke's Commonwealth's Attorney C. E. Cuddy stated on April 12 that Virginia's segregation law applied to seating at church services. Cuddy's opinion came as a response to a reporter's question about the matter. Cuddy said his statement was not a formal legal opinion or order, per se. Roanoke Police Superintendent Frank Webb responded by saying that local police "will enforce the segregation law where we know there is a violation." Cuddy said churches services are public gatherings and therefore there must be segregated seating.

Roanoke's PAL boxing team defeated the Petersburg team 6–3 in bouts held at the American Legion Auditorium on April 12. A crowd of 1,300 viewed the matches.

State officials announced on April 13 that patients being cared for at the city-owned tuberculosis sanatorium at Coyner Springs would be taken over by the state after July 1. The forty-nine-bed sanatorium was a Blacks-only facility that had been taken over by the state pending completion of a 250-bed hospital in Richmond. All patients at Coyner Springs would be moved to the new hospital by September 1.

Starkey Racing Grounds Inc. purchased the former Starkey Speedway and announced plans to spend $70,000 on the tracks and grounds with work set to begin in mid-April. The new owners intended to bring NASCAR races to the track and horse racing.

Eugene Ormandy conducted the Philadelphia Orchestra in a performance at the American Legion Auditorium on April 17. The concert was sponsored by the Thursday Morning Music Club. Attendance was 2,500.

E. B. Broadwater, principal of Andrew Lewis High School for thirteen years, was named director of instruction for Roanoke County Schools on April 14. DeWitt Miller was named as the new principal for Andrew Lewis.

Showtimers presented a four-night run of *Gigi* that began April 19. The play was directed by Kathleen Thornton, and the title role was played by Martha Ann Miller.

Pat Martin, president of Martin Brothers Contracting, died at the age of sixty-nine on April 16.

Theodore Frazier, administrator of Burrell Memorial Hospital, resigned his position to become the administrator of Florida A&M University.

The Times-World Corporation sponsored and conducted a "Church News Clinic" on April 19 for churches to send their secretaries, education directors and publicity committees to learn best practices for church newsletters and promotion.

Charles Minnich died on April 17. Minnich was president of Glenn-Minnich Clothing Company, a firm he helped found in 1913.

The Woman's Auxiliary of the Hunton Life Saving and First Aid Crew was organized on April 18 at a meeting at the Gainsboro Branch Library. The group's purpose was to help raise funds for the life saving crew. Mary Williams was elected president. Other officers were Bessye Terrell, Genevieve Ford, Lessie Polk, Mary Younger, and Katherine Swain.

Reservations for coach seats on the *Powhatan Arrow*, the N&W Railway passenger train between Norfolk and Cincinnati, were discontinued on March 5. This was the only N&W passenger train that required reservations.

Congressman Richard Poff spoke at the dedication of the Clearbrook Community Center and Roanoke County Fire Station No. 7 on April 21. Harry Wade was master of ceremonies. The Clearbook Lions Club had sponsored the building.

Advance Stores announced on April 20 that it would move its downtown Roanoke store into the building occupied Sears, Roebuck and Company farm store on East Church Avenue. The move was scheduled to occur in January 1957 following an extensive remodeling of the space.

A forest fire burned over twenty-five acres on Reed Mountain on April 21.

Hollywood actor and former Roanoker John Payne celebrated twenty years in film in April. *Slightly Scarlet*, starring Payne, opened at the Grandin Theatre and Lee Theatre on April 22.

Connelly Memorial Baptist Church held its first worship service in its new sanctuary at Hershberger Road and Westside Boulevard NW on April 22. Rev. W. B. Denson was the guest speaker. The congregation had been meeting at Southview School.

Gordon Snead of Roanoke won the one-hundred-lap sportsman stock car feature race at Martinsville Speedway on April 22, edging out Glen Wood of Stuart.

Ground was broken on April 23 for the new Nelson Hardware Company warehouse at Gregory Avenue and Eleventh Street NE. Martin Brothers was the contractor. The warehouse was to be for wholesale goods, as Nelson Hardware planned to close its retail hardware store at 131 E. Campbell Avenue when the warehouse was completed.

When the US Supreme Court ruled on April 23 that segregation on intrastate public transportation was illegal, Roanoke transportation officials indicated little impact would be felt locally as they had not been enforcing segregated seating on city buses for some time. Greyhound Bus Lines officials reported they planned to remove immediately signs designating segregated waiting rooms within their terminal. Trailways had removed such signage some months prior.

Judge Thomas Hutton struck down prosecution evidence on April 24 and freed Frank Johnson, fifteen, of Roanoke on a charge of murder in the slaying of John Bray of Abingdon. Roy Summitt, also of Roanoke, had been found guilty of the killing and had been given a fifteen-year sentence in a trial a month prior to Johnson's.

William Paxton Jr. was named as the Salem town clerk on April 24. He succeeded Douglas Ayers, who resigned to accept a job in Washington state.

Television personality Ted Mack conducted Roanoke's own amateur show, *You've Got A Chance*, on WSLS-TV in person on April 25. The winner earned an appearance on his national show in New York, *Ted Mack Amateur Hour*. Earlier in the day, Mack signed autographs at Heironimus.

White Rock Baptist Church near Hardy was organized on April 22 and held its first worship service in the old Sandy Level Church. A building site had been acquired on Route 634 in Roanoke County. The organizing pastor was Rev. T. R. Brown of Waverly Place Baptist Church.

The "new" Heironimus Department Store held a grand opening on April 26 at South Jefferson Street and W. Church Avenue. The mayors of Roanoke, Salem, and Vinton participated in the ribbon-cutting ceremony with music provided by the Monroe Junior High School Band. Eve Nininger played the Hammond Organ on the mezzanine level throughout the day. Some 3,000 customers were waiting outside the doors prior to the 10:00 a.m. opening, and it was estimated that over 20,000 customers came through the doors by the end of the day. The new store cost approximately $1.75 million and was the store's fourth location in Roanoke since its founding in Roanoke in 1890 with two employees. The store was decorated throughout in pink and turquoise. The store included the "Laurel Room," which offered high-end women's fashion. Other amenities within the store were a beauty salon, access via the "Silver Corner" to the S&W Cafeteria, six escalators, a women's lounge equipped with telephones, a gourmet foods shop, and Roanoke's largest men's shop. Robert Lynn was Heironimus's president.

Jennings-Shepherd Company opened a new wholesale warehouse and show-room at 357 W. Salem Avenue in late April. The company was founded in 1946 by George Jennings and Jackson Shepherd and had a retail store at 24 W. Church Avenue.

Scott, Horner & Mason, an investment firm, opened their new office at 301 First Street SW on May 1.

Two warehouses at the east end of the 100 block of Norfolk Avenue SW caught fire on April 29 causing dense smoke to blanket downtown Roanoke. The wholesale warehouses of Allied Sales Company and Arthur G. Meier were a total loss, and the fire was responded to by all Roanoke fire stations. The flames also attracted thousands of spectators. Shannon Hollingsworth, owner of Allied Sales, stated there were ninety railroad carloads of merchandise in his warehouse.

Senator Alben Barkley from Kentucky and former US vice president collapsed with a sudden heart attack and died while delivering the keynote address at the mock Democratic convention at Washington and Lee University on April 30. Dr. Robert Munger, a Lexington physician, administered oxygen to Barkley for fif-teen minutes on the platform before a stunned and silent audience. Barkley was seventy-eight.

This April 1956 photo shows the corner of First Street and Church Avenue. In the foreground is the Perry Building, which was being prepared for demolition. *Historical Society of Western Virginia*

Herman Keaton was stabbed to death at a house in the Starkey section on April 29. Keaton of Roanoke died at a local hospital an hour after the incident. Police arrested Randolph Maxwell of Starkey for the killing, which occurred at Maxwell's home.

A dinner attended by 600 congregants of St. John's Episcopal Church was held on April 30 at the Hotel Roanoke to launch the church's $250,000 building fund campaign. Francis Cocke was chairman of the campaign to remodel the parish house.

W. B. Carter of Roanoke was reelected president of the Virginia Tuberculosis Association during the group's annual meeting at the Hotel Roanoke on April 30.

Lewis Stuart was sentenced by Judge Fred Hoback on April 30 to life imprisonment for the shooting death of his former wife, Mildred Stewart, in Salem on January 27. Stewart pled guilty to the charge.

Garland's Drug Stores affiliated with the Rexall chain of drugstores on May 1. Garland's Drug Stores were located at 1327 Grandin Road SW; 1102 Loudon Avenue NW; 1232 Jamison Avenue SE; and 1216 S. Jefferson Street.

Fats Domino, Ruth Brown, the Clovers, the Cadillacs, Little Richard, Little Willie-John, Ann Cole, Al Jackson, Joe Medlin, and Choker Campbell performed for a show and dance at the American Legion Auditorium on May 4. The balcony was reserved for white spectators. Following the dance, fights broke out among whites and Blacks such that all on-duty Roanoke police officers were called to the scene to restore order. No one was seriously injured in what the local newspapers called "a racial disturbance that attained riot proportions." According to witnesses, the melee started when a white spectator threw a bottle from the balcony that led to bottles being thrown from all directions. Five persons were arrested.

Josef Loebl, eighty-two, died on May 2 in a Roanoke hospital. Loebl was the founder and president of Loebl Dye Works. In 1922, he served as president of the National Society of Dyers and Cleaners.

The $480,000 addition to the Carvins Cove Filter Plant went into service in early May, tripling the capacity of the facility. The addition was designed by the engineering firm of Alvord, Burdick, and Howson of Chicago.

The Motoramic Fair came to Roanoke the first weekend in May in set up along Route 11 between Roanoke and Salem. The fair advertised as having the world's only two-headed cow, other "freak animals and fowl," and Tony the dancing ape.

A cross was burned on the lawn of a Black family in northwest Roanoke on May 3. The incident occurred at 1016 Watts Avenue, a home owned by Mr. and Mrs. Melvin Meadows. There were no suspects for the incident.

William O'Neal, fifty-two, of Salem died on May 3 from injuries he sustained in an auto accident in late April on Route 11. O'Neal died at Burrell Memorial Hospital.

WDBJ debuted a local teen dance program in late April, broadcast live from their studio. *Saturday Session with Dudley Townsend* could be seen every Saturday at noon.

The Monroe Junior High School band won first place in the junior high school division of the National Safety Patrol Parade held in Washington, DC, on May 5. They competed against over one hundred bands from twenty-one states.

This 1956 image shows Loebl Dye Works and Loebl Cleaners, which occupied a series of buildings along Salem Avenue. *Virginia Room, RPL*

More than 800 children participated in the annual Spring Lake angling rodeo in Salem on May 5. The event was sponsored by the Optimist Club. Kenny Norris, seven, won Best in Show.

Vinton held its first annual Dogwood Festival on May 5 as a step to becoming "the dogwood capital of the world." A parade down Vinton's Main Street began the festival with numerous floats and numerous high school bands. Janet Bowman of Jefferson High School was crowned queen at the band festival. The event was sponsored by the Vinton Band Boosters, of which Mrs. Curtis Kirby was president.

The Roanoke Merchants Association named their Mothers of the Year in early May. Those honored were Mrs. Harry Carper Jr. (education), Mrs. William Urick (community affairs), Mrs. Reba Burnett (business and professions), Mrs. Phillip Trout (arts and sciences), Mrs. Lottie Hoback (family life), and Mrs. Robert Little (religious activities).

Calvin Williams, twenty-nine, of Roanoke was struck and killed by an automobile on May 6 while crossing Route 220 in the Pinkard Court section, a mile south of Roanoke.

A Scottish Terrier won Best in Show at the Roanoke Kennel Club dog show on May 6. Over 300 canines were entered. The terrier was owned by Mrs. Leon Godchaux of Chicago.

Dances with white spectators admitted to the balcony were banned in the American Legion Auditorium by Legion Post No. 3 effective May 7. The unanimous decision by the post came as a response to the melee that followed a show and dance headlined by Fats Domino that resulted in several arrests. The Legion post decided to take such action as a means of preventing future disturbances and of having Roanoke City Council decide the matter. The council did appoint a four-person committee to study the matter and develop policies that might prevent future racial confrontations at entertainment events. The *Roanoke Times* editorial board observed, "But behind the trouble lies something else which should cause concern for all the citizens of Roanoke…there has developed a worsening of race relations, a situation that has accompanied the controversy over segregation."

Elwood Richardson was indicted for armed robbery on May 7 in a case that involved one of several couples who had been the target of robbery and sexual assaults in northwest Roanoke. Roanoke police continued to develop evidence against Richardson for the sexual assaults.

Flora Realty Company advertised three-bedroom brick ranch homes in the new subdivision of Green Valley, off Colonial Avenue, with prices ranging between $13,000 and $17,000.

The Church of God of Virginia purchased a forty-five-acre tract or orchard land along Route 117 to build a state headquarters and camp. Plans called for a 5,000-seat tabernacle, cafeteria, dormitories, and recreation areas.

A Presbyterian mission congregation purchased a three-acre tract and a house near Burlington School in early May. The organizing pastor was Rev. Bernard Bain.

Four members of the Roanoke PAL boxing team won titles at the state Golden Gloves Boxing Tournament finals held in Richmond on May 8. The team members were Bert Halsey, Billy Young, Bill O'Neill, and James Muse.

Attorneys for Sam Garrison filed bankruptcy papers for Dixie Caverns on May 9. Garrison, the owner and operator of the caverns and a restaurant on the site, hoped to keep the business open.

R. H. Smith, president of N&W Railway, told select stockholders on May 10 that the railroad still had confidence in steam locomotives. N&W Railway was manufacturing all parts of its steam locomotives as components were almost impossible to acquire elsewhere.

Shirley Hurt, eighteen, of William Fleming High School won the "Miss Roanoke" contest and became an entrant in the Miss Virginia pageant slated for the following month. June Ferris was runner-up in the contest that was held at Andrew Lewis High School on May 10.

The new $1.5 million Burrell Memorial Hospital was dedicated on May 13. The dedication speech was delivered by John Wheeler, attorney and president of the Mechanics and Farmers Bank of Durham, North Carolina. Other program participants included Dr. E. D. Downing, Clem Johnston, Arthur Owens, Mayor Robert Woody, and Theodore Frazier. George Lawrence was master of ceremonies, and music was provided by Mrs. E. P. Nabors and the Carver High School Band. An estimated one hundred persons attended the event.

The Arrow Hardware, Paint, and Feed Company at 1105 Curtis Avenue NW was damaged by fire on May 10.

Clayton Lemon was appointed factory direct dealer for Cessna Aircraft Company. Lemon's firm was located at Woodrum Field. A formal grand opening was held on May 11.

The Virginia Amateur Baseball League opened its regular season with games on May 12. The seven-team league consisted of Price's Fork, Blacksburg, Salem, Moneta, Elliston-Glenvar, Back Creek, and Catawba.

The annual children's fishing rodeo was held at Lakewood Park in southwest Roanoke on May 12. The pond had been stocked with over 1,000 trout. The event was sponsored by the Blue Ridge Game and Fish Association. Over 3,000 children participated, and the largest trout was caught by Pittman Johnson.

WDBJ-TV began advertising the lineup of CBS daytime soap operas. The list consisted of *Love of Life*, *Search for Tomorrow*, *Guiding Light*, *As the World Turns*, *The Brighter Day*, *The Secret Storm*, and *The Edge of Night*. Each episode aired for fifteen minutes.

The Rugby Church of God announced that its new house of worship would be built on Curtis Avenue NE. The congregation had sold its former sanctuary to Pilgrim Baptist Church.

Sheena, Queen of the Jungle, appeared on the local *Betty Bond Show* and *Uncle Looney Tunes* on May 17. Both were on WSLS-TV. The television star also signed autographs as the Grandin Theatre, Lee Theatre, and Heironimus on May 19, visited the pediatric wards of local hospitals, and appeared at the Boy Scout Camporee being held at Victory Stadium.

During her visit to Roanoke, Sheena visited local businesses. Here the Queen of the Jungle (center) is at the Harris & Huddleston Super Market on Pollard Street in Vinton. William Harris (left) and Warren Huddleston (right) pose with her. *Judy Cunningham*

The Roanoke Symphony Orchestra gave a concert on May 14 at the Roanoke Theatre. A late-afternoon children's matinee was held at the American Legion Auditorium due to the volume of tickets sold. The program consisted of *Overture No. 3* to *Leonore* by Beethoven, the Bruch *Concerto*, Britten's *Guide*, Martucci's *Nocturne*, and Wagner's overture to *Tannhauser*.

A ten-year-old Roanoke girl was abducted and raped on May 13. The girl was taken near her home on Patterson Avenue SW and then dropped off near her residence by her abductor. Taken to a hospital, the girl was treated for lacerations and kept for observation. Police pursued one suspect on a high-speed chase through the western half of the city, but the driver of the car eluded them and escaped. On the same night, a thirty-year-old Roanoke County woman reported she had been raped while she walked along Route 220. A man pulled up in a car beside her, held her at knifepoint, and dragged her down an embankment. Early on the morning of May 14, police found the car they had been pursuing abandoned along Route 11 near Hollins College. It was determined the auto belonged to Frank Snider, thirty, of Michigan. Later in the same day, FBI agents were involved in the case, conducting a manhunt for Snider.

George Lawrence, an attorney and leader in the Black community, proposed to Roanoke City Council at their May 14 meeting that a biracial "Commission for Community Harmony" be named to seek a solution to the racial stress in the Roanoke community. The council chose to refer the matter for future consideration.

F. W. Woolworth Company reopened their newly remodeled store at 26 W. Campbell Avenue on May 16. The department store included a lunch counter. T. J. Seeley was the store manager.

Ideal Laundry and Dry Cleaners purchased the locations of the Deluxe Kwik-Way Laundry and Cleaners and turned them into Ideal branches. The four new branch stores were located at 2602 Franklin Road SW; 1125 W. Salem Avenue; 1820 Memorial Avenue SW; and 1104 Brandon Road SW.

John Edmunds, a senior at Duke University, was named as the head football coach at the new Cave Spring High School when it opened in the late summer. Edmunds was a graduate of Jefferson High School and was an all-state football player in 1949.

J. P. Cruickshank, chairman of the Roanoke School Board, stated before PTA leaders on May 15 that unless there was a fifty-cent real estate tax hike in Roanoke providing for additional schools, then seven schools would be forced to integrate. If the tax increase were to pass, the chairman said, "Roanoke will be fortunate in having an almost segregated school system by natural causes." The tax hike was to be voted on June 12. Cruickshank's comments were the first of any city official on the matter of segregation. The chairman outlined in his comments to the Crystal Spring School PTA that new schools would be constructed in white and Black neighborhoods of the city should the tax hike become implemented, thereby allowing all children to attend one in their neighborhood.

A proposed all-rookie, semipro Class D baseball circuit for Salem and Roanoke was scrapped by major league teams in lieu of doing the same setup in Nebraska.

Frank Snider Jr., wanted for two rapes in Roanoke City and County, was apprehended in Gadsden, Alabama, on May 16 at his father's home by FBI agents.

Snider had been the object of an intensive manhunt following the sexual assaults of two females on May 13. At the time of his arrest, Snider was facing a similar charge in Alabama. A few days after his arrest, police in Baltimore indicated an interest in Snider relative to several rapes in that city.

S. H. Heironimus Company opened its men's store on Jefferson Street on May 17. Described as the largest in Roanoke, the company's men's department occupied the building that was formerly F. W. Woolworth Company and Nell Good Studio. Claude Robertson was the store manager.

Herbert Tayloe, a longtime member of the Roanoke County Board of Supervisors, died on May 17 at the age of fifty-nine. He had also served as a member of the county's school board. Tayloe was chairman of the Board of Supervisors from 1949 to 1952 and worked for N&W Railway.

A National Armed Forces Day Parade was held in Roanoke on May 19 and featured several high school bands, reserve units, and floats. The two-mile-long parade was viewed by more than 3,000 along Jefferson Street.

The Judy Memorial Baptist Church held its first service on May 20. It was located in the 700 block of Jamison Avenue SE. C. B. Blevins was the pastor.

Paul Brugh opened Brugh's Auto Paint and Body Shop at 926 Moorman Avenue NW on May 19.

Over 4,000 Boy Scouts participated in the Boy Scout Camporee at Victory Stadium on May 18 and 19.

Woodlawn Methodist Church held an open house on May 20 for its newly completed education building. The 4,000-square foot building cost $44,000.

Elwood Richardson, twenty-seven, of Roanoke received life imprisonment for a robbery at the Elmwood Diner in which two waitresses were attacked. Police indicated Richardson was their primary suspect in a series of robberies and sexual attacks on couples in the Roanoke Valley. The next day, Richardson was sentenced to a second life term for convictions of robbery and sexual assault on a couple. The commonwealth's attorney had asked that Richardson be executed. During the police investigation of Richardson, he was taken to Marion and given "truth serum" and later to Arlington for lie detector tests.

Roanoke Vice Mayor Leigh Hanes Jr. concluded his service on Roanoke City Council on May 21, leaving three months left on his term, in order to become an assistant US attorney for the Western District of Virginia.

Jimmy's Golf Driving Range opened in late May along Route 11, just east of the Lee-Hi Drive-In Theatre.

A Roanoke County chapter of the Virginia League of Planned Parenthood was organized on May 21. Mrs. George Downing was elected chairman.

Sullivan Supply Company, a hardware and appliance store, opened at South Colorado Street in Salem on May 24.

The Salem courthouse clock received a facelift the last week of May. The wooden hands, believed to have been in service since 1909, were replaced due to cracking and splintering. The work on the clock was done by Hill Clock Shop of Harrisburg, Pennsylvania.

Roanoke's PAL boxing team defeated the Charleston, West Virginia, PAL team, 4–1, in matches held on May 24 at Pearisburg. Over 1,000 were in attendance.

Auto racing returned to the Starkey Racing Grounds on May 25. The race was limited to late-model convertibles for the 200-lap race over the half-mile dirt track. The race was won by local favorite Curtis Turner, who drove a 1956 Ford. Attendance was estimated at 6,000.

Elmore Heins and his wife, Reba Heins, applied to the FCC for a license to operate a radio station in Roanoke. It would be the fifth commercial station in the area.

The Roanoke Youth Symphony gave its first performance on May 25 when it played at William Fleming High School and two junior high schools. The next morning, the symphony gave a live performance on WDBJ-TV. Gibson Morrissey was the conductor of the orchestra that was sponsored by the Junior League.

The Virginia Mountain League began its baseball season on May 25. Teams included Salem, Hot Springs, Buchanan, Glasgow, Clifton Forge, New Castle, and Buena Vista. The Salem Rebels had previously been in the Appalachian League. Salem's home field was at Salem Municipal Stadium.

The National Smart Set held its annual convention in Roanoke at the Pine Oak Inn. Delegates from several states attended the three-day event. The Roanoke chapter was the only southern chapter in the organization.

Don Pullen, a freshman at Addison High School, won the state title in the Negro Division of the James A. Bland Memorial Music Scholarship competition on May 26. Pullen was a pianist and was sponsored by the Raleigh Court Lions Club.

Frank Snider was brought back to Roanoke from Alabama on May 27 to face two rape charges. Det. Capt. Kermit Allman went to Alabama to get Snider.

Roanoke City Council at its May 28 meeting agreed to lease four acres in the Garden City section for a playground and baseball field. The land was located between Garden City Boulevard and Bandy Road.

McLellan's held a grand opening for its remodeled store on May 31. The department store, located at 17 W. Campbell Avenue, advertised a new, modern luncheonette.

Dr. Franklin Fry, the top official with the United Lutheran Church in America, spoke at a rally closing Lutheran Mission Week in the Roanoke Valley on June 1. The rally was attended by nearly 1,000 persons and held at First Baptist Church.

The new asphalt track at Starkey Racing Grounds was used for the first time on June 1. The asphalt track was a quarter-mile layout. Some of the races were NASCAR sanctioned.

Roanoke's PAL Boxing Team defeated a team from Richmond, 5–0, on May 31 in Richmond. It was the seventh straight victory for the Roanoke team. Those that fought for the Roanoke team in the event were Bert Halsey, Jimmy Muse, Nick Nichols, Robert White, and Ed Keeling.

Roanoke native and professional tenor William Dupree starred in the Broadway revival of *Carmen Jones* that began its run on May 31 at the New York City Center Theatre. He played the character Joe.

The Dixie-Aires, a gospel quartet, performed at the American Legion Auditorium on June 3.

Grand Ole Opry star Little Jimmy Dickens performed at the Roanoke Theatre on June 5.

Leonard Electronics held a grand opening on June 6 at its new location, 405 Shenandoah Avenue NW. The radio and television parts store first opened on June 6, 1946, at 106 Second Street SW. The business was owned and operated by James Leonard and his wife, Estelle.

Bascom Blair of Roanoke drowned at Claytor Lake on June 4 while boating with friends. He was the former manager of Shenandoah Auto Parts.

William McGee, a longtime member of the Vinton Town Council, died on June 4 at the age of seventy-one. He had twice served as the town's mayor and was instrumental in the campaign to build the Vinton War Memorial.

The trustees of Temple Emanuel purchased a lot at the intersection of Persinger Road and Brambleton Avenue SW on June 4 to be used for the construction of a new temple. The land was purchased from Mrs. Margaret Slusser.

William Muse, Roanoke County's commissioner of the revenue since 1937, died at his home on June 5 at the age of seventy-six. He had worked in the commissioner's office since 1923.

The razing of the McBain Building at Campbell Avenue and First Street SW was completed the first week in June to make way for the new Miller & Rhoades department store. The final cleanup of the remains of the building came just a little more than a month after demolition began.

Beverly McClure was named Roanoke's Father of the Year, primarily for his longtime work with the Boy Scouts. McClure was bestowed the honor by the Roanoke Junior Chamber of Commerce. For 1956, the Jaycees had decided to return to the practice of having just one Father of the Year.

Ray Stanley of Back Creek School won the twenty-sixth annual city-county marbles tournament in the championship playoff on June 6. The tournament was sponsored by the Times-World Corporation. The tournament began with a field of over 2,500 from twenty-two schools.

William Lotz was appointed to the Roanoke County School Board on June 8 to represent the Cave Spring District. The School Trustee Electoral Board also reappointed Arthur Trout (Big Lick District) and W. H. Starkey (Catawba District) to four-year terms.

The Roanoke Chapter of the SPCA purchased on June 8 a half-acre site for a new animal shelter in the Glenn Falls Addition on US 460. The Roanoke Chapter was formed in 1953.

Mountain Motor Company, located at 201 S. College Avenue in Salem, became a Nash-affiliated dealership in early June. The company sold Nash brand Ambassador and Statesman Ramblers. D. W. Davidson was the dealership's manager.

Bobby Myers of Winston-Salem won the thirty-lap feature race at the Starkey Racing Grounds on June 8 before a crowd of 1,800.

Shirley Vaughan, twenty-one, of Roanoke sang *Ivory Tower* during a coast-to-coast radio broadcast of the *Old Dominion Barn Dance* of the CBS Network on June 16. She was introduced to listeners by "Sunshine Sue."

This 1950s image is looking north on Jefferson Street from the intersection with Elm Avenue SW. Elmwood Park, prior to the construction of the new main library, is in the right foreground. *Nelson Harris*

Boy Scout Troop No. 2 of Raleigh Court Presbyterian Church presented fourteen Eagle Badge awards at a single honor court on June 10. It was a record number for a single honor court in the Roanoke area and believed to be a national record as well. The scoutmaster was Barney Haley.

Luck Richardson Jr. was appointed as Roanoke County commissioner of the revenue by Judge Fred Hoback on June 9, replacing the late W. C. Muse.

A new Lutheran church in the Cave Spring section of Roanoke County held its first service on June 10. The congregation, later to be known as St. John Lutheran Church, was to worship temporarily at the former Cave Spring Baptist Church through the courtesy of the Cave Spring Lions Club. Dr. William McCauley was the organizing pastor.

The Roanoke Branch of the NAACP held its first Father's Day mass meeting on June 17 at High Street Baptist Church. Guest speaker was Elwood Chisholm, assistant special counsel for the NAACP from New York. Reuben Lawson was the Roanoke Chapter president.

George Fulton Jr. won his third straight city-county golf championship the first weekend in June. The tournament was played at Hidden Valley Country Club. The tournament began with a field of 187 golfers. Finishing second was K. R. English. Fulton had a four-round total of 275, sixteen strokes ahead of English, for a tournament record.

The Virginia Amateur Roller Hockey Association was formed in early June by representatives of Skate-A-Drome and Roanoke Rams, the local roller hockey team.

They met with groups representing Buena Vista and Lynchburg. The association's season would begin in early August. It was the first of its kind in the state.

Norman White, forty-three, of Roanoke died on June 11 in Burrell Memorial Hospital from burns he received in a house fire on June 3.

On June 12, voters in Roanoke city participated in one of the most important and competitive city council elections while soundly defeating a proposed fifty-cent increase in the real estate tax rate to support school capital projects. Those winning seats on Roanoke City Council were Benton Dillard, Mary Pickett, W. B. Carter, and Vincent Wheeler. Vote totals were as follows: Dillard, 6,256; Pickett, 6,107; Carter, 5,574; Wheeler, 5,411; Charles Cornell, 4,016; Bowman Harris, 3,593; Kirby Poindexter, 3,532; Fred Reynolds, 3,467; S. J. McMillion, 1,762; John Crowgey, 1,629; B. B. Albert, 1,468; L. E. Paxton, 1,446; and F. E. Alexander, 1,144. Pickett was the only incumbent and female candidate, and Paxton and Alexander were the only Black candidates. City voters defeated a proposed tax ceiling increase by a margin of 3 to 1.

In Vinton, incumbent town council members Letcher Adkins and J. E. Clifton were reelected, defeating Norman Dowdy and G. W. Nicks. In Salem, Mayor James Moyer and Councilman Leonard Shank were reelected without opposition.

The Christian Business Men's Committee recommended to the Roanoke Ministers Conference via a resolution that the conference extend an invitation to the evangelist Billy Graham to conduct a crusade in Roanoke in 1958 or soon thereafter.

Dr. Charles Irvin, Roanoke health commissioner, proposed in a meeting with city officials on June 13 that the tuberculosis sanatorium at Coyner Springs be converted into a home for the aged and chronically ill. The sanatorium was erected in 1938 at a time when the state lacked facilities for TB patients. During the past year, the sanatorium had been used by the state for Black TB patients, but the state was planning to end that service in August.

Green Ridge Presbyterian Church was organized in the Burlington section of Roanoke County in early June by Rev. Bernard Bain. The congregation planned to petition the Montgomery Presbytery for formal organization of the church in late July.

Roanoke City Council tapped Benton Dillard, who had recently been elected to the council, to fill the unexpired term of Leigh Hanes Jr., who had earlier resigned to become assistant US district attorney for Western Virginia.

Two tracts of land were purchased by Roanoke City for expansion of Woodrum Field, which would necessitate the rerouting of Route 118. The city planned to expand runways as part of the improvement plan.

Shoney's Big Boy Drive-In Restaurant opened in mid-June along Lee Highway between Roanoke and Salem.

Gary Smallwood, thirteen, of Roanoke was struck in the face on June 16 by a cherry bomb firecracker that left a two-inch hole near his jaw. The boy was sitting in a car watching a movie at the Lee-Hi Drive-In Theatre when someone threw the firecracker over the fence as a prank and sped away, according to witnesses. Four youths were later arrested in South Roanoke for the incident.

A new type of home construction was used by Watts and Breakell, local builders, for a house on Grandview Avenue NW. The house was constructed from precut framing lumber and wall panels moved en masse to the site and assembled. Described as "The House of Vision," it was the first of its type in the Roanoke Valley. It was engineered by American Houses Inc.

Dickie Layne defeated Herman Moorman to win the Roanoke Jaycees junior tennis tournament held at Roanoke Country Club in mid-June.

The Roanoke Parks and Recreation Department launched their summer tennis court dances on June 17 at South Roanoke Park with music provided by Doug Talbert and his orchestra.

Reuben Lawson, president of the Roanoke Branch NAACP, stated on June 17 that the organization was preparing to ask the Roanoke School Board if it "really means to treat our children like its own." Lawson delivered his comments at the branch's Father's Day mass meeting. Lawson noted that school officials had promised little progress in desegregation. "Jim Crow is dead," he said, "but you'll have to be the undertakers to bury it." The following day, the *Roanoke Times* opined in its editorial page the following as a response: "What was told the group of Roanoke Negroes is typical of NAACP rashness. The organization wants to mingle the races. It is not concerned about the disastrous effects which attempts to force integration upon the white people of Virginia will have upon Negro education."

Roanoke City Council appointed John Cruickshank, Mrs. Grover Ligon, and J. W. Rhodes to the school board at their June 18 meeting. Rhodes was named to fulfill the unexpired term of Lucian Booth.

The New York Black Yankees played the Indianapolis Clowns in baseball at Salem Municipal Field on June 19. The game also included a comedy show. The same week, the New York Giants scouting staff held a tryout camp and baseball school.

Natalie Shoppe, located at 311 S. Jefferson Street, began advertising in mid-June that it was going out of business after twenty-one years. The store carried women's clothing and accessories.

Appalachian Electric Power announced on June 20 that it was proceeding with its long-debated Smith Mountain Dam project at an anticipated cost of $20 million. The power company secured the dam site in 1954 on the Roanoke River. The company planned to submit permit applications with the Federal Power Commission for the dam and hydroelectric power plant immediately.

The spire of the old St. Mark's Lutheran Church was removed on June 21 to prepare for the demolition of the structure, located at Campbell Avenue and Third Street SW. The church was being razed to make way for a store. Crowds gathered to watch the event, as the spire was swung from its perch by a crane. One workman was injured, receiving a broken leg, when the wall he was working on collapsed.

The price to play a record on a jukebox in Roanoke went from three cents to ten cents in mid-June. For three records, the price was twenty-five cents.

Roanoke Steam Laundry and Dry Cleaners opened at their new location at 3308 Shenandoah Avenue NW on June 21 opposite the Shenandoah Drive-In Theatre. The dry cleaning business first opened in Roanoke in 1887.

This June 1956 image shows St. Mark's Lutheran Church being razed. The congregation sold the structure and relocated to Franklin Road SW. *Historical Society of Western Virginia*

A Hustings Court jury sentenced Frank Snider Jr. to the electric chair after deliberating on June 26 in the case that involved the Mother's Day rape of a ten-year-old Roanoke girl. The jury met for less than forty-five minutes before returning their guilty verdict and punishment by death. Snider was a steel worker from Gadsden, Alabama. Snider showed no emotion while the verdict was read and casually read a newspaper as the jury was deliberating. Commonwealth's Attorney C. E. Cuddy asked the jury for the death penalty as he described the crime as one of the worst in the city's history. Judge Dirk Kuyk upheld the jury's sentence the next day, setting Snider's execution for August 3. Snider was also wanted in Baltimore, Maryland, for sex attacks on children in that city. It was the first death-sentence verdict in Roanoke City since 1935.

The Chesapeake and Potomac Telephone Company achieved 50,000 telephone lines in Roanoke on June 26 when it installed a line in the home of Robert Taylor on Circle Drive SW. Roanoke acquired its first thirty-four telephones under Southern Bell Telephone on May 1, 1884. C&P took over on June 30, 1912, when there were about 2,000 phones in Roanoke.

Jimmy Rinehart beat seventy-two other young racers to win the thirteenth annual Roanoke Soap Box Derby on June 27. A crowd of 7,500 lined the Salem Turnpike racecourse. Rinehart, a student a Lee Junior High School, qualified to compete in the national Soap Box Derby in Akron, Ohio, on August 12. Bobby Giles finished second.

The Curtain Shop opened at its new location at 408 S. Jefferson Street on June 29. The store had been in business for fifteen years.

Allen Chappell, twenty-nine and a Korean War veteran, jumped to his death on June 28 from the water tower at the Veterans Administration Hospital. Chappell was a native of Carroll County, Virginia.

Becky Richardson, twenty-four, of Martinsville was crowned Miss Virginia on June 29 at the American Legion Auditorium. The pageant was sponsored by the Valley Junior Woman's Club. The crown was presented by Sharon Kay Ritchie, Miss America of 1956.

High's Ice Cream opened its newest store on June 30 at Ninth Street and Highland Avenue SE.

The Kansas City Monarchs and the Detroit Stars, both of the Negro American League, played baseball at Salem Municipal Field on July 2. Both teams were on a tour of southeastern states.

Sears began advertising in early July its next-day service on catalog orders. "Now orders wired by Western Union direct to Greensboro for next day delivery."

Little Richard, Faye Adams, Paul Williams, and Bobby Parker performed at the American Legion Auditorium on July 3. The whites-only show and dance was from 8:30 p.m. until 11:30 p.m., while the Blacks-only show and dance began at 12:30 a.m. The separate events were probably due to the racial unrest that followed the Fats Domino show a few weeks prior.

Professional women wrestlers grappled at the American Legion Auditorium on July 4. The main feature was between blonde-haired Judy Grable and "Slave Girl Moolah" from South Africa. According to the *Roanoke Times*, "The female wrestlers have proved more popular with local fans than the males." Professional wrestling was often held Wednesday or Thursday nights at the auditorium.

Charles Lunsford Sons and Izard announced the admission of Bolling Izard and Irving Slaydon as partners in the firm on July 1.

The twenty-bed Gresham Cottage at Mercy House was dedicated on July 1. It was the eighth cottage at the county home and was named in honor of the late Rev. LeRoy Gresham, pastor of Salem Presbyterian Church. At the time Mercy House was caring for 117 elderly patients.

Catawba Stone Company became Stone Service of Roanoke on July 1 due to new management. George Maxey was the company's president. The business was located at 1929 Franklin Road SW.

Garry Jones, six, of southeast Roanoke drowned at Sun Valley Pool on July 1, which was located in the Mount Pleasant section.

A strong thunderstorm sent the forty-by-eighty-foot screen at the Shenandoah Drive-In Theatre to the ground on July 2. Winds surpassed fifty miles per hour.

Fes Saunders of northwest Roanoke was fined $6,000 in Roanoke Municipal Court on July 2 for making indecent telephone calls. He had been arraigned on sixty charges and given a one-hundred-dollar fine for each. Defense Attorney Wilbur Austin Jr. protested the hefty fine to Judge Robert Quarles, stating that two of the four complainants testified that Saunders did not use profane language. Quarles responded, "I consider any telephone call of this nature from a Negro man to a white woman...indecent. They were all in the nature of propositions."

More than 600 Roanoke employees of the American Bridge Division of US Steel went on strike beginning July 2 as part of a nationwide walkout of steelworkers due to a contract dispute.

Bank of Salem officials announced on July 3 a $150,000 modernization and expansion of the bank that would triple its floor space. The bank would be expanded into the adjacent building formerly occupied by J. J. Newberry Company. The Bank of Salem was organized in 1891.

Oscar Creech Jr., a native of Kentucky, died at Lewis-Gale Hospital on July 6 from injuries he sustained in a fall at the Lone Star Cement Company plant in Botetourt County a few days prior. He was working on an addition to the plant when the accident occurred.

Seats from the old Rialto Theatre found a new home in the Lab Theatre at Roanoke College, home of Showtimers. It was estimated that twenty pounds of chewing gum had to be scraped off of them before being installed. Showtimers presented *The Desperate Hours* under the direction of David Thornton the first weekend in July at the Lab Theatre.

The congregation of Melrose Presbyterian Church voted on July 8 to accept a three-acre tract on Peters Creek Road as a future church site. The church was organized in 1916 and had been located at Fifteenth Street and Moorman Road since 1928.

This undated image shows the Big Lick Post Office, which was located on the corner of Orange Avenue and Williamson Road in the 1950s. *Virginia Room, RPL*

The Big Lick Post Office was to be spared from demolition, according to Roanoke officials, from the "slum clearance" effort of the Roanoke Redevelopment and Housing Authority for northeast Roanoke. Original plans called for the raising of the white clapboard cottage located on Fourth Street. Ben Moomaw, executive director of Diamond Jubilee, argued to city officials that the historic structure should be spared giving its place in the city's history. The RRHA's director, Richard Beck, agreed to move the structure to another site. Most believed the former post office building was not located on its original site, but all were agreed that the small cottage was the original post office building for Big Lick. There seemed to be consensus that the original site was probably in the vicinity of Second Street and Shenandoah Avenue NW. The structure had been saved from deterioration by the Big Lick Garden Club with renovations some years earlier.

Kroger opened its newest store at Ninth Street and Bullitt Avenue SE on July 10. The opening of the new store necessitated the closing of two smaller Kroger stores on July 7, the one in Vinton and the other at Ninth Street and Jamison Avenue SE. Frank Davis was manager of the new Kroger.

Three names for the new Roanoke County high school to be located in the Cave Spring area were submitted to the county school board on July 10. The names were Clifton A. Woodrum, James Madison, and John Tyler, and all were offered by the PTA groups in that section of the county. The preference was for Woodrum, according to a spokesperson for the PTA.

Charles Evans, fifty-one, of Roanoke died on July 12 when the truck he was driving wrecked near the foot of Bent Mountain on Route 221. Evans was making a delivery to Floyd County.

This photo shows the Kroger grocery store on Ninth Street SE shortly after it opened. *John Boothe*

Stephen Morgan, seven, of Roanoke drowned at Lakeside Pool during a family outing on July 12. It was the first drowning at Lakeside in sixteen years.

Roanoke's newest naval reserve unit was commissioned on July 12. Rear Admiral I. N. Kiland was the main speaker at the ceremony that commissioned Naval Reserve Composite Company 5-60 at Roanoke's naval reserve training center. The company, which had sixteen members, was headed by Lt. Commander Richard Pence.

Don Reno, Red Smiley, and the Tennessee Cut Ups performed at the City Market Auditorium on July 20.

A significant step toward the production of *Thy Kingdom Come*, an outdoor drama planned for the Sherwood Burial Park Amphitheater, was taken in mid-July when ten area Lions Clubs agreed to launch the sale of $100,000 worth of bonds for the Roanoke Valley Drama Association. The author of the drama was Kermit Hunter, who wrote *Horn in the West*, an outdoor drama at Boone, North Carolina. The Roanoke drama's opening was planned for the summer of 1957 and would be one of the first such outdoor dramas in the United States with a religious theme.

Showtimers presented a production of *Holiday* at the Lab Theatre the third weekend in July. Sam Good was the director with lead roles performed by Libba Francis, Ann Fox, and Paul Crawford.

Three auto daredevil shows were held at the Starkey Speedway on July 17. The daredevils were Dick Rogers' Motor Maniacs, the Canadian Aces, and Ward Beams' Auto Daredevils.

The Roanoke School Board deferred answering the question posed to them by the Roanoke Branch of the NACCP as to school integration occurring in the fall. The question had been submitted in writing by the branch's president Reuben Lawson for the board's July 16 meeting. The board decided to table the matter until its August meeting.

The Roanoke branch of Bluefield Hardware Company opened on July 19 at 302 E. Campbell Avenue. Charles Southern Jr. was the store manager.

A cave-in occurred on Ninth Street in Salem on July 16, which was the same vicinity as a series of cave-ins that plagued the Florida-Indiana Avenue area in 1953.

Saks and Company was purchased by Sidney's, which was owned and operated by J. H. Weinstein and his son, Sidney Weinstein. The Saks store was located in the American Theatre Building. Both stores sold women's clothing.

Gold Seal Aluminum Window Company opened at 2923 Brambleton Avenue on July 17.

Robert Janney, twenty-seven, of Roanoke County died in an auto accident in Salem on July 17.

Villa Heights Church of the Nazarene announced plans for a church building in the 1400 block of Abbott Street NW. The church was organized in June and was holding meetings at the home of G. W. Peters on Hanging Rock Road. Rev. Loren Gould was the pastor.

The Russell Johnston family of Salem was selected to kick off National Farm Safety Week in Washington, DC, because of the family's long record of farm safety and community development. The Johnstons were nominated by Virginia Tech and appeared on the *Farm and Home Hour* over NBC the third weekend in July. They also attended a luncheon inaugurating national Farm Safety Week.

Adams Construction Company was awarded the largest contract ever given by the Virginia Department of Highways, the company announced on July 18. The contract was for $1.6 million for work on US 301.

A three-acre tract near Deyerle Road was purchased by the Montgomery Presbytery as a site for a new Presbyterian church. The site was purchased from A. M. Renick.

Roanoke was one of a hundred cities in the United States that participated in an atomic strike Civil Defense preparation exercise on July 20. Members of the city council and top-level staff were evacuated to a high school in Botetourt County, and all National Guard reserve units were activated in the area.

Roanoke Wholesale Furniture Corporation and Roanoke Furniture Mart advertised they were going out of business in mid-July. They were located at 347 W. Campbell Avenue.

Dr. E. G. Gill announced on July 21 the creation of the Elbyrne G. Gill Eye and Ear Foundation through an initial donation by the Gill family. An initial purpose of the foundation was the creation of the first eye bank in Virginia. Headquarters for the foundation would be at Gill Memorial Hospital. Gill was a former president of Lions International.

Showtimers presented *Anastasia* as its third production of their summer season on July 26 at the Lab Theatre at Roanoke College. Lead roles were played by Rosalie Turner, Bob Niemyer, James Gearheart, and Charles Bush. Genevieve Dickenson was the director.

Gene Mason, sixteen, of Vinton died in an auto accident on July 22 at Pollard and Cedar Streets. It was the first traffic fatality in Vinton in seventeen years.

State Senator Earl Fitzpatrick of Roanoke announced on July 23 his support for the governor's plan to stop the integration of public schools. Governor Stanley had called for a special session of the General Assembly to deal with the matter. Fitzpatrick stated, "It is my opinion that those of us charged with the responsibility in this matter should prevent, with all legal means at our command, integration in our public schools."

The annual Roanoke Booster Club trip to White Sulphur Springs occurred on July 25 with some 350 local businessmen making the trip via a special train provided by N&W Railway. Dr. E. G. Gill was the club's president. During the trip, Boosters expressed concern about the failure of the Community Fund and Red Cross campaigns to reach their fundraising goals, defeats of recent bond issues, and the loss of the June school tax referendum. The Boosters adopted a resolution for Mayor Robert Woody to deliver to city council asking for the appointment of a study commission to explore these various setbacks.

The Detroit Stars played the Memphis Red Sox in baseball at Salem Municipal Field on July 25. Both teams were affiliated with the American Negro League.

Williams Blind Shop opened on July 25 at 825 Colorado Street in Salem.

The Roanoke Baptist Ministers' Conference, comprised of all-Black clergy, adopted a resolution at their July 25 meeting censuring Rev. F. E. Alexander for his editorials appearing his newspaper, the *Roanoke Tribune*. Alexander had published an editorial in the *Tribune* that was also reprinted in white newspapers calling for gradual integration of public schools. The conference declared in its resolution, "We request that you (Alexander) will consider whether or not these articles are propaganda to give to the forces of reaction ammunition to use against the aspirations of our people to climb out of the rut of second class citizenship." Alexander was pastor of the First Baptist Church of Buchanan and was in attendance at the meeting.

The congregations of Williamson Road Baptist Church and the Hollins Church of God voted to switch buildings in early August. The Baptists were located at 1907 Williamson Road, while the Church of God was located on Hollins Road. When the church swap occurred, the Baptists planned to rename their congregation Northside Baptist Church.

The leaders of Roanoke's Diamond Jubilee got strong backing from a large crowd that attended a public hearing at the Hotel Roanoke on July 27 to solicit volunteers. Shields Johnson, president of Diamond Jubilee, conducted the meeting that resulted in the appointment of over fifty committees.

The Ortho-Vent Shoe Company of Salem announced on July 27 plans for a new office and warehouse on a four-acre site east of Salem. W. F. Brand was president of the company that was Salem's largest retail business in dollar volume.

The Jefferson Street leg of the Roanoke viaduct opened to traffic on July 21.

Lloyd Price and his band performed for a show and dance at the Star City Auditorium on July 31.

Green Ridge Presbyterian Church was formally organized on July 29 during an afternoon worship service. The church was located west of Roanoke on Route 117.

Roanoke vocalist William Dupree made a guest appearance on the *Ed Sullivan Show* on August 5. Dupree was starring in the New York City Center's production of *Carmen Jones*. Dupree graduated from Addison High School in 1947, then graduated from Howard University, and then toured with the US Air Force Symphony Orchestra.

Showtimers did a production of the comedy *Born Yesterday* the first weekend in August at Roanoke College. Lead roles were performed by Betty Thornton Shaner, Arden Kiser, Bob Lee, and Wilson Price.

Roanoke Radius began publishing with home delivery. It contained feature articles on local events, culture, history, personalities, and sightseeing. Its office was at 317 W. Campbell Avenue.

Appalachian Power Company formally filed on July 31 with the Federal Power Commission in Washington, DC, for a preliminary permit to create a hydroelectric dam on the Roanoke River in the gap of Smith Mountain. The proposed Smith Mountain Dam would be 200-feet high with the storage reservoir extending thirty-eight miles.

WDBJ-TV erected a permanent twelve-bay antenna on top of Poor Mountain as part of the station's plan for a permanent transmission facility there. When completed, it would replace the temporary antenna on Mill Mountain.

Rabbi Morris Graff, who had served Temple Emanuel as rabbi since 1938, accepted a position with the Union of American Hebrew Congregations in Miami, Florida. Graff had served on numerous civic boards during his tenure and authored

The Ayes Have It, a column on parliamentary procedure in the Sunday *Roanoke Times*.

Two warehouses at 101 and 105 Norfolk Avenue SW were razed in early August, having been damaged by fire, to make room for a parking lot.

Harness racing came to the Starkey Racing Grounds on August 4, along with mule and pony races. Music was provided by the Bedford Fireman's Band. Of interest was the appearance of Rowena Grisso of Catawba, who was paralyzed by polio six years prior. Grisso's wish was to see horse racing live, so she was transported by ambulance to the races and given a special view from the infield.

Mobile telephone service was inaugurated in Roanoke on August 2 when Mayor Robert Woody made the first call to Major Frank Webb, superintendent of police. Roanoke was the third locality in the state to have the service that allowed a phone in a car to be operated through a radio transmitter on Mill Mountain that dialed the operator.

A proposed $35 million redevelopment plan involving some 1,500 acres was announced by the Roanoke Redevelopment and Housing Authority on August 3. The area involved extended from Orange Avenue south to the Roanoke River and between Sixth Street SE and Fifteenth Street on the west. If approved, it would be the second-largest urban redevelopment program in the US. The plan called for new roads and bridges and would eliminate what were deemed to be blighted residences. This plan was in addition to the redevelopment already underway at the time in northeast Roanoke by the RRHA.

Roanoke race car driver Curtis Turner won the 150-loop National Championship late model convertible stock car race at Winston-Salem on August 3.

Roanoke Valley Realty Corporation advertised homes in its subdivision Panorama Court off Westside Boulevard NW. A three-bedroom brick home could be had for $250 down and $78 per month.

The New York Black Yankees played the Indianapolis Clowns at Maher Field on August 9. Both baseball teams were affiliated with the Negro National League.

Workers began returning to the American Bridge plant on August 6 due to a new contract with steelworkers that ended a nationwide strike.

Showtimers gave a production of *Life With Father* the second weekend in August. Lead roles were performed by Herbert Harris, Maxine Bulbin, Raymond Doss, Lynn Bond, and Kenneth Hyde. The director was Clara Black.

Roanoke cartoonist James Gibson was profiled in *Parade Magazine* on August 5 for his many cartoons published in a variety of national magazines including the *Saturday Evening Post*.

Milan Brothers held a grand opening at their new location, 106 S. Jefferson Street, on August 7. The business had been operation for forty-six years in Roanoke and advertised as "Roanoke's foremost fountain, tobacco and sundry store."

Roanoke reported its second polio case for the year on August 6 when a two-year-old boy from the city was diagnosed with paralytic polio at Roanoke Memorial Hospital. The child had received two Salk vaccine shots. In addition to the boy, there were three other polio patients at the hospital, including a nineteen-year-old woman from Catawba. The first local case for Roanoke City was an eighteen-year-old who was treated and released for nonparalytic polio in February. A third city case was reported on August 7, an eight-year-old with nonparalytic polio.

The State Highway Commission gave its approval on August 9 for the City of Roanoke to name the $2.6 million viaduct in downtown Roanoke for the late Williams P. Hunter, Roanoke's first city manager and a former mayor. The city planned to place a plaque at the viaduct honoring Hunter.

Claude Settlemire was named as Roanoke's new head librarian, succeeding Harold Sander, who had resigned earlier to assume the position of director of the Indianapolis Public Library. Settlemire was coming from Hutchinson, Kansas.

Ernest Sears was announced as the new football coach at Carver High School on August 11. Sears replaced Irvin Cannaday, who went to Lucy Addison High School to assist head coach Charley Price. Sears, a native of Roanoke, was coaching football, basketball, and baseball at Larkin High School in Mason City, West Virginia.

George Fulton Jr. shot a nine under par 62 at the Cascades golf course at Hot Springs on August 11, setting a new course record for competitive play.

The Kiddie Korner held its grand opening on August 13. The store for infants' and children's clothing was located at the corner of Jefferson Street and Church Avenue.

A billboard for the S&W Cafeteria hangs above Kiddie Korner, Harryettes, Royal Fur Shop, and the Curtain Shop near Jefferson Street intersection in this 1956 photo. *Bob Kinsey*

This undated photo shows Mountain View, the home of J. B. Fishburn, which was gifted by his estate to the City of Roanoke in 1955 for use as a recreation center. *Virginia Room, RPL*

The Williamson Road Church of the Brethren worshipped in their new sanctuary for the first time on August 12. Seating capacity was 550.

Showtimers presented its sixth and final production of the summer season with *The Little Foxes* at Roanoke College the third weekend in August. Kathleen Thornton, David Thornton Rhoda Morgan, and Sam Good had the lead roles. The play was directed by Leroy McFarland.

Nearly forty pioneer Virginia aviators met at Woodrum Field on August 11 to form the Virginia OX-5 Club, named after an early plane engine. The purpose of the group was to foster interest in and advancement of aviation. Two of those from Roanoke who helped organize the club were Clayton Lemon and Marshall Harris.

The Men's Garden Club announced their plans to restore and maintain the two-acre gardens at Mountain View as a public garden. The mansion was the home of the late J. B. Fishburn and had been given to the city for recreational and public use.

Harry Neren, a pioneer in synthetic rayon, died on August 14 in a Roanoke hospital at the age of eighty-eight. A native of Germany, Neren retired as general manager of the American Viscose Corporation's seven plants. He moved to Roanoke in 1917 when the "silk mill" opened in Roanoke and was its first general manager.

A photograph appeared in the August 15 edition of the *Roanoke Times* that showed five Roanoke men who had gathered for lunch, all of whom had held national or international positions. They were E. R. Johnson, past president of Rotary International; Dr. E. G. Gill, past president of Lions International; John Walker, past exalted ruler of the Elks; Clem Johnston, past president of the US Chamber of Commerce; and Francis Cocke, past president of the American Bankers Association.

State officials announced on August 14 that one floor of the new Williams Hospital in Richmond would open on August 28. At that time, twenty Negro tuberculosis patients at the Coyner Springs Municipal Hospital would be transferred there.

The Roanoke County School Board voted on August 14 to name its new high school in the southwest section Cave Spring High School.

Shoppers Mart held a grand opening of their new, enlarged store on August 16. The department store was located across from the Bank of Virginia in downtown Roanoke.

A woman from Baltimore, Maryland, was killed instantly when the car she was in was struck and dragged a half mile by a Virginian Railway coal train on August 16 near Salem. The accident occurred west of the Wabun Crossing. Two others in the car were injured.

The commissioner in chancery of Roanoke County Circuit Court set the debts of Dixie Caverns at $151,557 on August 16. The commissioner recommended the sale of the property, separating the caverns from adjacent land and the restaurant.

Clinton Searle, seventy-six, of Roanoke was killed on August 17 in an auto accident at the intersection of Marshall Avenue and Sixth Street SW.

Gyro Reducing Salon opened at 2509 Melrose Avenue NW on August 20 with steam baths and other strategies for weight loss.

The Salem Rebels won the Virginia Mountain League pennant on August 19 with a regular season record of 16–8. It was the third pennant in three years for the club.

The Roanoke School Board responded to the Roanoke Branch of the NAACP about school integration during its meeting on August 20. The board took three minutes to adopt a response to a letter submitted to them by the branch's president, Reuben Lawson. The board's reaction was in a motion that read, "With regard to your letter of July 14, the board does not contemplate at the present time any change in the operation of the public schools in Roanoke." There was no discussion, and the response was approved by a unanimous vote. The board asserted that desegregation was in the purview of the state, not local boards.

Burrell Memorial Hospital inaugurated Sunday morning worship services for its patients on August 26. Patients could listen to the service over the intercom system. The first service was conducted by Rev. A. L. James, pastor of First Baptist Church, Gainsboro.

Lewis Young Fashions opened on August 23 at 25 W. Church Avenue. The apparel store carried items for infants, toddlers, and young boys and girls.

Aubrey Vaughan, head basketball coach at William Byrd High School, was named as head football coach for the season. Vaughan replaced Vito Ragazzo, who resigned to become a coach at VMI.

E. A. Graybill became the first mayor of Troutville when he was elected in the town's first municipal election held on August 22. The town in Botetourt County was incorporated several weeks prior to the election.

Sissy Graham is on her horse at the Roanoke Valley Horse Show at Maher Field in August 1956. *Sissy Logan*

The seventh annual Roanoke Valley Horse Show was held the third week in August at Maher Field. The three-day event had an entry list exceeding 200 mounts and riders from six states.

One of the most publicized court-martial trials in Germany involved seven Black servicemen who were accused of raping a fifteen-year-old girl at Bamberg. The sensational trial strained US-German relations, and the town council of Bamberg demanded that the US military close their bases and leave the country, much to the support of many Germans. One of the seven accused and on trial was Pfc. Raymond Kasey of Roanoke, who was indicted for restraining the girl's boyfriend while the rape occurred. The two-week trial ended on August 22 when Kasey and his six codefendants were found guilty. Kasey, eighteen, was sentenced to forty years by the US Army.

The Roanoke Fair began its weeklong run on August 27 at Maher Field. The fair included a livestock show, agricultural exhibits, John Mark's Mile Long Pleasure Trail, grandstand acts, a flower show, and displays of agricultural machinery.

Margaret Brown, fifty-three, of Roanoke was killed in auto accident on August 24 at the intersection of Routes 460 and 117.

Jim Reed of Peekskill, New York, won the 200-lap Grand National feature race for late model cars at Starkey Racing Grounds on August 24.

The Roanoke Weaving Plant of Burlington Industries changed its name to the Vinton Weaving Company on August 26. Burlington officials said the name change was in keeping with its policy of decentralization and in recognition of the plant's twenty-year history in the community.

Dr. J. C. Darden of Salem was profiled in the August 26 edition of the *Roanoke Times* in honor of his fifty years of practicing medicine in the town. Darden recalled the early days of his practice when cows huddled on the streets of Salem to keep warm and almost every resident kept a pig in the backyard. He and other physicians lobbied the town council to eventually pass an ordinance that all pigs had to be kept at least 200 feet from a residence. Darden built a house at 103 College Avenue and had his medical office on the main level while he lived upstairs. He said he got tired of walking all over the town to see his patients.

A WDBJ television photographer was seriously injured on August 26 when a two-seat glider he was in crashed near a home in Montvale. Roscoe Perdue suffered a broken nose, broken ankles, and broken ribs. Heinrich Huber, the pilot, suffered only minor injuries.

An estimated crowd of 4,000 attended the second annual model airplane contest at Woodrum Field on August 26 that was sponsored by the Exchange Club.

Charley Turner defeated Doug Craig for the men's singles championship in the annual city-county tennis tournament held at Roanoke Country Club. Lu Merritt and Fred Bromm won the men's doubles title. Catherine Mayhew defeated Marjorie Smithey to claim the women's singles title, and Sugar Ellett and Juanita Stanley won the women's doubles championship.

George Fulton Jr. defeated Landon Buchanan on August 26 to win the Roanoke Country Club golf championship. It was his eighth title at the club in ten years.

Roanoke City Council directed the city manager at its August 27 meeting to explore the possibility of using the planned Smith Mountain Dam as a future water supply source for the city. Council members wondered aloud if the water could be pumped back to the city.

Roanoke area Lions Clubs reported in late August that they had sold $6,700 in bonds to finance the production of the outdoor drama *Thy Kingdom Come* at the Sherwood Amphitheater. The ten clubs were trying to raise $100,000 for the production costs.

Radio station WBLU in Salem went on the air on September 5. M. C. Bowers Jr. was the station manager. The 1,000-watt station had a studio at 212 E. Main Street, and its tower was located on the Grisso farm west of Salem on Route 11. WBLU was at 1480 on the radio dial.

George Fulton Jr. qualified for the National Amateur Golf Tournament during the state amateur qualifying tournament held in Richmond on August 28.

Thom McAn, a shoe store, held a grand opening for its enlarged and remodeled store at 311 S. Jefferson Street on August 30. It had formerly been located at 108 W. Campbell Avenue. Bob Vandergrift was the store manager.

A group of representatives from several counties in Southwestern Virginia met with the Roanoke city manager and other officials on August 31 to support using Roanoke's tuberculosis sanatorium at Coyner Springs as a nursing facility for the chronically ill. The facility had been vacated with the transfer of Black tuberculosis patients to a hospital in Richmond. Roanoke officials were trying to find a new use for the buildings.

Chuck Berry, Willie Mabon, and Bobby Charles performed for a show and dance at the American Legion Auditorium on September 2. The show began at midnight and went on until 4:00 a.m.

Dr. Charles Smith, provost of Roanoke College, endorsed on September 1 Virginia Governor Thomas Stanley's plan that no public funds be provided for integrated schools. Smith's statement read as follows: "If any other legal means of avoiding integration can be found, I would give my warm support. But if no other workable means can be found I can see no alternative to Governor Stanley's proposal for withholding state funds from integrated schools. The time has come when we in the South must act firmly in response to the misinterpretation of the Constitution by the Supreme Court. The rights of the people in the several states to educate their children as they choose must be defended at all costs."

The Rialto Parking Center, former site of the Rialto Theatre, opened in early September. The rate was forty cents per hour.

Roanoke City Council elected Walter Young as mayor in their organizational meeting on September 1. W. B. Carter was selected as vice mayor. Each would serve a two-year term. Benton Dillard, however, voted for himself as mayor even though he had not been formally nominated. All others voted for Young. Carter received five votes for the second spot, and Mary Pickett received two votes. In Salem, the town council elected James Moyer and Leonard Shank as mayor and vice mayor, respectively. In Vinton, the town council elected Shirley Crowder as mayor and J. E. Clifton as vice mayor.

Members of the Roanoke Valley delegation to the Virginia Assembly announced their positions on school integration in early September. State Senator Earl Fitzpatrick stated, "I'm for the governor's plan or any other that will prevent integration." Governor Stanley had advocated a platform of denying state funds to localities that integrated their schools. Delegate Julian Rutherfoord Jr. supported legislation to allow localities to hold referendums on using public funds to support integrated schools. Delegate Nelson Thurman did not commit to Stanley's plan but was exploring other options.

Fullback Don Divers of Roanoke was elected captain of the 1956 Virginia Tech varsity football team on September 2. Divers was a graduate of William Fleming High School.

Cpl. Lynwood Grisso, twenty-four, of Catawba died in an auto accident near Lebanon, Kentucky, on September 1. Grisso was stationed at Fort Knox.

The Children's Zoo on Mill Mountain closed for the season on Labor Day, when 8,911 visitors passed through the gate to the zoo. Total attendance for the season was slightly more than 86,000.

Curtis Turner won the 500-Mile Stock Car Race at Darlington, South Carolina, by two laps on September 3. He also set a new track record of 95.067 miles per hour despite seven caution flags. Attendance at the race was estimated to be 73,000. Turner's winnings totaled $11,520.

This 1950s postcard shows the Willie the Whale exhibit at the Children's Zoo on Mill Mountain. *Nelson Harris*

James Bear, seventy-five, died on September 4. Bear was a former Roanoke mayor and a member of the Virginia legislature. He had practiced law in Roanoke for over fifty years. He was also involved in numerous business and civic organizations.

State Senator Earl Fitzpatrick, Delegate Julian Rutherfoord Jr., and Delegate Kossen Gregory, all of the Roanoke Valley, joined in a state legislative effort to curtail court action by the NAACP relative to integration of public schools. Bills introduced would require the registration of individuals and organizations with the SCC that instigate litigation. The registration would mean filing financial statements, organizational documents, and membership information. Fitzpatrick stated, "It is my belief that if those encouraging litigation and promoting strife among our people are curbed, the problem which confronts Virginia today will much better be solved." Rutherfoord stated that the legislation "will cut down on interferences by outsiders in our state and local affairs." Other former and current Roanoke area legislators supported the "pupil assignment plan" adopted and advocated by the Gray Commission, which left the assignment of pupils to schools to localities. Leonard Muse, member of the state Board of Education and former Roanoke state senator, stated on September 5 the following: "Of course I favor segregation. I know no one who does not. However, a definite commitment was made by the state leadership...that the Gray Commission report would be adopted." The Roanoke Central Council of PTAs gave unanimous approval to a resolution calling on the implementation of the Gray Commission report rather than the Stanley plan.

Byron McKenzie and Ernest Bolling purchased the C. L. Fielder Company, a steel fabricating firm in Roanoke, for $142,500. They renamed the firm, located at Norfolk Avenue and Eighth Street SW, to Structural Steel Inc. The business was started in 1943.

Shenandoah Christian College, a nondenominational institution, opened at 1232 Sylvan Road SE on September 11. Rev. James Comstock was the president.

Star City Realty Company opened at 3014 Christian Avenue NW on September 8. Brokers were W. E. Hale and T. M. Warren.

Williamson Road Church of the Brethren dedicated its new $75,000 sanctuary and fellowship hall on September 9. Dr. Raymond Peters was the guest speaker. The new sanctuary had a seating capacity of 550.

Postal officials announced on September 8 that a new Highway Post Office route had been established between Roanoke and Winston-Salem to become effective September 29. The Railway Post Office between those two points would be discontinued September 28.

The Roanoke Fine Arts Center held its first-ever showing of all-primitive paintings. The two featured artists were Harriet French Turner of Roanoke and Anna Booze of Buchanan.

Salem defeated Blacksburg in the Virginia Amateur League playoffs to claim the championship title. The team also earned the regular season pennant.

Cowboy Bob Cavanaugh, a Hollywood stunt man and movie double, along with his trick horse Dottie, performed in-person for three nights beginning September 12 at the Queen Drive-In Theatre on Route 11, west of Salem.

Nelson Bond, a Roanoke writer, appeared on the NBC TV game show *Tic, Tac, Dough* on September 10 and 11, which was broadcast from New York City.

Fes Saunders pled guilty to charges of making sixty indecent telephone calls to white women and was fined $6,000 in Hustings Court on September 10. Unable to pay, the Black man was given nine years in jail. Saunders had received much the same sentence in Municipal Court.

General Electric officials reported on September 10 that the Salem plant had about 1,600 employees, of which 85 percent were locals.

The League of Women Voters of Roanoke adopted a statement at their September 10 meeting opposing Governor Thomas Stanley's anti-desegregation plan. "In our opinion, the (plan) of an 'efficient' school system as a segregated one will not be upheld in any court tests."

George Fulton Jr. of Roanoke was eliminated in the US Amateur Golf Championship tournament at Lake Forest, Illinois, on September 10. He was eliminated, one up, by a high school golfer from Columbus, Ohio—Jack Nicklaus. The two were even through sixteen holes, but Nicklaus sank a twenty-foot putt on the seventeenth. Fulton shot a 76 and Nicklaus a 75 on the par 71 course.

Clarabelle, the character from the national television show *Howdy Doody Time*, made an appearance at Heironimus on September 13.

John Forbes Nash Sr. of Roanoke died on September 12 in a Roanoke hospital at the age of sixty-four. He had come to Roanoke in 1952 to work for Appalachian Electric Power Company and had lived with his wife in an apartment on Grandin Road SW. Forbes's son, John Nash Jr., had also joined his parents at the apartment for a few years. The son would go on to win the Nobel Memorial Prize in Economic Sciences for his game theory and be the subject of the movie *A Beautiful Mind*. At the time of his father's death, the son was living in Boston.

WDBJ-TV officials announced on September 13 that the station's new 50,000-watt transmitter on Poor Mountain would begin broadcasting on October 1. The new transmitter would allow reception for up to eighty miles and fringe reception to one hundred miles.

The City Rescue Mission began operating a thrift store in early September at 111 E. Salem Avenue to help fund its ministry.

Bill McGaw's Tournament Thrills show came to the Starkey Racing Grounds on September 17. The show featured motorcycle side-car racing, a trapeze artist, and auto jumps.

Several gas stations affiliated with the Phillips 66 service station chain and held grand openings on September 15 as a part of their rebranding. The stations were Town and Country, 3002 Brandon Road; Andrew Lewis Station, Fourth Street and College Avenue; Balthis Service Station, Second Street and Franklin Road; Brook Club, Veteran's Facility Road; Community Cash Grocery in Vinton; Lawrence Grocery, Route 3; Mack's Service Station, 1201 Ninth Street SE; Mount Vernon Service Station, 3234 Mount Vernon Drive SW; and Smith's Market, 3434 Salem Turnpike NW.

Business in Roanoke increased by 7 percent as compared to the previous year, according to a bulletin issued by Rand McNally and Company of Chicago. That jump ranked Roanoke seventh in the nation for business growth according to the company.

Lotz Funeral Home completed its new building at Franklin Road and Highland Avenue SW in mid-September. A public open house was held for three days beginning September 20.

First Church of God began meeting at their temporary quarters at 3031 Preston Avenue NW on September 16. Formerly known as Rugby Church of God, the congregation had sold their building on Rugby Boulevard to another congregation.

The Roanoke chapter of the Sons of the American Revolution was chartered on September 15 at a banquet meeting of the state organization held at the Hotel Roanoke. The Roanoke chapter had twenty-one members, with Everett Repass as organizing president.

The Monroe Junior High School Band took top honors at the "I Am An American" Parade in Baltimore, Maryland, on September 15. They were over one hundred bands in the parade.

Curtis Turner won the 300-mile championship stock car race for convertibles at Lehi, Arkansas, on September 16. Turner had an average speed of 90.498 miles per hour.

M. Sgt. Raymond Riggs, formerly of Roanoke, was killed in the Stratofortress plane crash near Madera, California, on September 17. Riggs, forty-two, was a veteran of WWII and a 1934 graduate of Jefferson High School.

Rev. F. E. Alexander, publisher of the *Roanoke Tribune*, filed suit in Law and Chancery Court on September 17 for $60,000 charging malicious damage in publication of allegedly libelous and defamatory statements and slanderous declarations.

The named defendants were four civic leaders and six Black ministers, including Dr. Harry Penn, Dr. Lawrence Paxton, Reuben Lawson, and Cordelia Williams. The suit stemmed, in part, from a resolution adopted by the Roanoke Baptist Pastors Conference that strongly condemned Alexander for his *Tribune* editorials that seemed to promote anti-desegregation sentiments.

Cave Spring High School opened for classes on September 17, two weeks later than other county schools. The delay was due to completing construction. A total of 694 students attended the first day. The students attended an opening assembly on the importance of character with Rev. Kern Eutsler as the speaker. Con Davis was the principal.

A ground-breaking ceremony was held on September 17 for the new $900,000 YMCA building in Roanoke at Church Avenue and Fifth Street SW. Larry Dow, chairman of the building committee, was the featured speaker. The Roanoke YMCA was started in 1883 with twenty members.

The Roanoke Ministers Conference adopted a resolution at their meeting on September 17 opposing any plan that would remove school authority from local boards, including the withholding of funds from local schools that integrate. The resolution was aimed at the plan of Governor Thomas Stanley.

Randolph Maxwell was acquitted by a Roanoke County Circuit Court jury on September 18 in the April 29 killing of Herman Keaton. Maxwell had argued that the stabbing was in self-defense.

Don Reno, Red Smiley, and the Tennessee Cut Ups, all from the *Old Dominion Barn Dance* radio program, performed at the Queen Drive-In Theatre on September 20.

Kirby Poindexter, forty-one, of Roanoke died on September 21 at Jefferson Hospital from burns he had received a week earlier in an auto accident near Boones Mill.

This June 1959 image shows the new Cave Spring High School along Route 221, which opened in September 1956. *Library of Virginia*

Three squirrel hunters found a balloon on Fort Lewis Mountain that had been launched from Minneapolis, Minnesota. Robert Foutz and his two brothers said attached to the twenty-five-foot long balloon was a letter asking the finder to mail the letter back to Minnesota. The balloon was apparently being tested by Free Press Europe for use in sending pamphlets behind the Iron Curtain.

Fleet Oil Station opened on September 22 at Sunset Village Road (Route 460) near Lakeside Park.

Musicians and entertainers that starred on the national radio program *Midwestern Hayride* performed at the American Legion Auditorium on September 29.

Studio School for K–2 opened for registration at 105 Mountain Avenue SW on September 24.

Mundy Motor Lines announced in late September the acquisition of $1.4 million worth of tractor-trailer equipment. The purchase would increase the company's freight handling capacity by 25 percent, according to the business's president Gardner Mundy. Mundy Motor Lines was founded in Roanoke by Harry Mundy in 1908.

Belmont Baptist Church dedicated its new $183,000 educational building on September 23.

James Taney, sixty-nine, of Salem died on September 24. Taney was a former chairman of the Roanoke County School Board and was a member of Salem's first town planning commission.

WDBJ moved from 124 Kirk Avenue SW to 201 Campbell Avenue SW, which was the Times-World Building, in late September.

This 1956 image shows an expansion to the Times-World Building under construction to accommodate WDBJ television and radio, subsidiaries of the Times-World Corporation at the time. *WDBJ7*

Cave Spring High School played its first football game against Bedford County's B Team on October 2 at the Veterans Administration Hospital field. Billy Edmunds was the coach, and John Creasy was the quarterback. The Cave Spring Knights won, 6–0.

Stuart Saunders, vice president and general counsel of N&W Railway, was appointed executive vice president effective October 1. John Fishwick, general solicitor, became the company's general counsel on the same date.

Crobuck's Drug and Prescription Center opened at 2310 Melrose Avenue NW on September 28.

The nation's first nuclear reactor vessel for commercial electric power stopped in Roanoke on September 28 on its way to Shippingport, Pennsylvania. The 152-ton reactor was the largest single shipment and the widest load ever carried to date by N&W Railway.

Kenneth Mullins, twelve, of Roanoke drowned in the Roanoke River near Piedmont Street SE on September 29.

George Cooke, thirty-three, of Roanoke County was arrested in Tulsa, Oklahoma, on September 29 and charged with the murder and robbery of a service station operator at Shelby, North Carolina, on September 10. According to authorities, Cooke confessed to the crime.

Midas Muffler Shops opened one of its chain stores at 426 Carver Avenue NE in late September.

The Times-World Corporation reported on October 1 that the combined circulation of the *Roanoke Times* and the *Roanoke World-News* was 90,305, an all-time record.

This WDBJ studio shot from the 1950s shows an episode of *Saturday Session* with Dudley Townsend being televised. The pop music show featured local dancers and singers. *WDBJ7*

The congregation of First Presbyterian Church in Roanoke voted on September 30 to call Rev. Albert Edwards as its next pastor. Edwards had been serving a church as pastor in Harrisonburg for nine years.

Officials with Thompson Products announced on October 3 they were building a $10 million center for testing and developing fuel and auxiliary power on a 1,000-acre tract, seventeen miles south of Roanoke in Franklin County. They predicted the center would employ 500 by 1961.

Fats Domino and his orchestra performed for a show and dance at the American Legion Auditorium on October 5. The Friday night event started at 10:00 p.m. and ended at 2:00 a.m.

Roanoke artist Paul Wilke had an exhibition of twenty pieces of his art that opened in the Café Riviera in Greenwich Village, New York, City, in early October. A native of Germany, Wilke had retired to Roanoke to be with relatives and was very involved in the local arts community.

Top Value Enterprises, which controlled the operation of Top Value Stamps, leased a 34,000-square foot warehouse at 105 Bullitt Avenue to use as a zone distribution center.

WDBJ-TV expanded their local program *Saturday Session with Dudley Townsend* to a one-hour format at noon on October 6. The show featured local talent, contests, dancing, and guests.

A new Presbyterian church for southwest Roanoke was launched on October 7. A community Sunday School program was held in a house at 3663 Colonial Avenue SW. Rev. Bernard Bain was leading the effort.

Roanoke firefighters held their annual Fireman's Ball on October 6 at the American Legion Auditorium. Music was provided by Price Hurst and his orchestra.

Roanoke Goodwill Industries marked its twenty-fifth anniversary on October 11 with a luncheon and open house at its Goodwill Building at 3125 Salem Turnpike. Goodwill began in Roanoke in 1931 as an effort to provide the physically handicapped employment. E. H. Ould, president of the First National Exchange Bank, was the keynote speaker.

This October 1959 photo shows the storefront for Goodwill Industries at 3125 Salem Turnpike. Goodwill began in Roanoke in 1931. *Virginia Room, RPL*

This 1950s postcard shows Bradford's Steakhouse on Melrose Avenue NW. *Bob Stauffer*

Rutrough Motors, located at 329 Luck Avenue SW, announced in early October that it would become the new local distributor for the Rambler, Nash, and Metropolitan automobiles in addition to Packards. The new distributorship agreement was through American Motors.

Roanoke City Council voted at its October 8 meeting to purchase the former WDBJ radio property at 124 Kirk Avenue SW for $100,000. The purpose was to relocate the city's water department from East Salem Avenue to the building.

A dirt cave-in near Bradford's Restaurant on Route 460 killed a Roanoke bulldozer operator on October 10. Max Bauman, fifty, was excavating dirt from a cliff when the accident occurred.

Theodore Kauffman, thirty-five, of Salem was killed in a single-vehicle accident on Route 11 on October 10.

Kevin O'Sullivan, a television and Broadway singer, made a personal appearance at Fink's Jewelers on October 12 to promote Ronson Electric Shavers.

Val Balfour played the leading role in the touring production of *Passion Play* at the American Legion Auditorium on October 17 and 18.

Aaron Matthews was shot to death on October 13 at the Horseshoe Café located at 210 First Street NW. The next day, John Poindexter, eighteen, of Roanoke walked into police headquarters and confessed to the slaying.

Jack Andrews of the Roanoke Valley Drama Association reported on October 13 that more than $40,000 on bonds had been sold by area Lions Club for the production of *Thy Kingdom Come*, an outdoor drama. Andrews indicated the funds were sufficient to launch the production next summer at the amphitheater in Sherwood Burial Park.

Hajoca Corporation, wholesale distributors of home equipment supplies, held a formal opening of its new branch office at 1 Boulevard SW on October 15. R. T. Crawford was manager of the Roanoke store.

Burrell Memorial Hospital announced on October 13 a reorganization of its outpatient department and emergency service. Both would be under the direction of Dr. W. R. Brown. The purpose of the outpatient clinic would be to provide medical service for the indigent in the Roanoke region.

A meeting to organize and launch the Roanoke Valley Tennis Association was held in the auditorium of the Times-World Corporation Building on October 17. The effort was led by James Woods Jr.

A private post office subdivision was installed in the new Ortho-Vent Shoe Company building being constructed on Route 460 east of Salem. Cabell Brand, sales manager, stated that postal officials agreed to the arrangement as the company accounted for over half the mail volume of the Salem post office. The company employed over 3,800 salesmen.

The pedestrian underpass beneath the N&W Railway tracks opened on October 18 with little fanfare. The 150-foot long structure in downtown Roanoke was well-lit, had ceramic-tiled walls, and had two entrances from the train sheds. The underpass was part of the viaduct project.

Bluefield State played St. Paul's College in football at Victory Stadium on October 20. Sherley Stuart, former football standout at Addison High School, played for St. Paul's.

A tractor-trailer loaded with diesel fuel crashed into two cars, a bus, and a pickup truck at a construction barricade on Route 460 near Montvale on October 19. Two men were killed, including Wallace Campbell, fifty, of Roanoke, who was a highway construction superintendent.

A Southwest Virginia news bureau was opened in Wytheville to serve the *Roanoke Times*, *Roanoke World-News*, and WDBJ television and radio in late October. Alex Crockett was named the bureau manager.

The *Roanoke Times* endorsed the reelection of President Dwight Eisenhower in its October 21 edition. Among the reasons for the endorsement were that "Mr. Eisenhower has lifted the prestige of the Presidency from the depths to which it had sunk under Harry Truman" and that "he has had a unifying effect on the country which is essential in today's divided world."

The Roanoke Symphony Orchestra performed at the Roanoke Theatre on October 22. The special guest performer was Roanoker Gene Akers, who was the official pianist for the US Marine band. Attendance at the opening concerts of the symphony's fourth season was 3,000.

The Rt. Rev. William Marmion dedicated the parish hall of St. James Episcopal Church on October 21. The hall contained a chapel and Sunday School rooms and was constructed for $60,000. The church was located at 4515 Delray Street NW.

Mayflower Hills Baptist Church dedicated its sanctuary on October 21. The congregation, which was started in 1952, was located on Rutrough Road Extension six miles east of Roanoke. Much of the construction was done by members.

Linda's Beauty Shop opened on October 22 at 715 Thirteenth Street SE. The owner was Mrs. L. D. Setliff.

Dixie Caverns and restaurant were bought by the Trompeter family of Roanoke for $135,100 at a bankruptcy auction on October 22. Herman Trompeter and Albert Trompeter, brothers, purchased the property. The Trompeters owned several business properties in Roanoke, and the family owned H. Trompeter & Son Bakery.

Hollins College held a mock presidential election on October 24. The results were Eisenhower-Nixon, 353; Stevenson-Kefauver, 79; Coleman Andrews, 6; and Senator Harry Byrd, 2.

Luke Barnes, the golf pro at Roanoke Country Club, won the Middle Atlantic Professional Golfers' Association championship at Virginia Beach on October 24. He shot par on the rain-soaked course at the Cavalier Yacht and Country Club.

Piedmont Airlines established a repair facility at Woodrum Field in late October. Two aviation mechanics conducted preflight inspections and minor repairs. Piedmont had twenty-five daily flights out of Roanoke at the time.

The Salem Civitan Club received its charter in ceremonies on November 1 at Bradford's Restaurant. Roy Kinsey was club president.

Dr. Otto Klineberg, psychology professor from Columbia University, stated that there was no scientific proof that any racial or ethnic group is inherently inferior to any other in a lecture at Hollins College on October 25. Klineberg was one of the psychologists whose scientific opinion was used as evidence in the 1954 desegregation decision of the US Supreme Court.

Elvis Presley arrived in Roanoke on October 26 on the *Tennessean*. Presley was on his way from his home in Memphis to New York on the N&W Railway train. The singer did not emerge from his Pullman car during the stopover to grant local media interviews, however.

Hollins College announced plans for a new $500,000 chapel in late October. Almost half the money for construction had already been pledged for the chapel that was designed by the Roanoke architectural firm Frantz and Addkinson.

The former Daleville Academy, which closed in 1933 due to the Depression, was purchased in late October by Carl Ikenberry and Lawrence Garst for $11,000. The academy was located in Botetourt County on Route 220.

The National Swedish Chorus performed at the American Legion Auditorium on October 29, sponsored by the Thursday Morning Music Club. The chorus consisted of seventy-five men.

Virginia Tech defeated the University of Virginia in football 14–7 at Victory Stadium on October 27. Attendance was estimated at 17,000.

A fire scorched the interior of Associate Reformed Church near Williamson Road on October 28 shortly before congregants began arriving for Sunday School. The brick church had been built in 1941 at Lee and Wildhurst Avenues NE. The fire did an estimated $19,000 worth of damage.

WDBJ-TV debuted a local quiz show, *Watch the Birdie*, on October 29. The show was hosted by Irv Sharp and aired weeknights at 6:15 p.m. Viewers were encouraged to submit answers to questions via mail.

This 1950s image shows the control room for WDBJ television. *WDBJ7*

Officials with the Roanoke Community Fund denounced the distribution of what it called "hate pamphlets" being distributed in Roanoke to discredit its annual fundraising campaign. The pamphlets declared, "Community Chest Supports Race Mixing," claiming the Community Fund supported the Urban League. The Community Fund supported thirteen agencies, and the Urban League was not one of them. The pamphlets were published by the National Citizens Protective Association headquartered in St. Louis, Missouri.

Top Ten Review of 1956 came to the American Legion Auditorium on November 1. Performers for the rock 'n' roll show were Little Richard, Bill Doggett, Big Joe Turner, the Moonglows, the Five Keys, Faye Adams, the Five Satins, Etta James, the Robins, Tommy Brown, Johnny Torres, and Big Jay McNeely and his band.

A racial incident occurred in downtown Roanoke on Halloween night. Police reported a clash between over one hundred Blacks and whites on Kirk and Salem Avenues. Police were able to disperse the crowd.

Mrs. E. O. Tinsley was presented a pink dogwood tree by the Women's Missionary Society of Mount Olivet Baptist Church at Bent Mountain. Tinsley had served as the group's president for forty-seven years and was being succeeded by Mrs. Claudia Kefauver.

A woman who called herself Peace Pilgrim walked into Roanoke on October 31 in the last 400 miles of a 10,000 mile pilgrimage to promote world peace. She began her trek in January 1953 and was walking through all forty-eight states.

Crawford Door Sales Company opened at 210 Fourth Street SW in early November. W. L. Sutherland was the company president.

In the mock presidential election held at Roanoke College on October 31, President Dwight Eisenhower received 262 votes to 84 votes for Adlai Stevenson. Coleman Andrews polled 24. Andrews was the candidate for the pro-segregation States Rights Party.

Samples' Amoco Service Station opened at Fourth Street and Alabama Avenue in Salem on November 2. R. F. Sample was the operator.

The Huntsman Motel north of Roanoke on Route 11 was sold for $190,000 to Edwin and Phyllis Bofinger from New York. The couple planned to move to Roanoke to operate the twenty-unit motel.

The Kazim Temple held its sixth annual Shrine Bowl football game at Victory Stadium on November 3 that included a performance by twenty-three bands in the stadium following a parade through downtown Roanoke. An estimated 13,000 fans watched the freshmen team of the University of North Carolina defeat the freshmen of the University of Virginia 52–6.

A hymn composed by Bill Mangus, twelve, of Roanoke was debuted in choir concert at First Baptist Church on November 4. Mangus was assisted in the composition of *Jesus Christ, Our Lord and Savior* by the church's music minister Malcolm Scott.

Fats Domino and his orchestra performed for a show and dance at the American Legion Auditorium on November 8. The show was for white patrons only.

A taxi driver shot a female dispatcher and then himself in an apparent murder-suicide in Salem on November 5. Minnie Cadd, thirty, was shot twice at her residence at 421 E. Main Street by Andrew Rhodes, forty-nine. Police could determine no motive for the incident.

In the US presidential election held on November 6, voters in Roanoke City and County supported Republican incumbent Dwight Eisenhower over his Democratic opponent, Adlai Stevenson. In the city, the vote was 16,708 to 6,750, with States Rights Party candidate Coleman Andrews getting 610. In the county, the vote was 7,509 to 2,899. Andrews received 339 votes. City and county voters also voted for the reelection of Richard Poff, Republican, over his Democratic opponent, John Whitehead, for Congress in the Sixth District. In Roanoke City, voter turn-out was 72 percent—a record. In the county, the turnout was 68 percent.

Two men were captured by the FBI in early November for the attempted robbery of the Melrose Avenue branch of the Mountain Trust Bank on November 2. Stephen Weese, twenty-one, of Georgia was arrested in Phoenix, Arizona, and G. A. Ferrell, twenty-two, of Chicago was taken into custody in Roanoke County.

Roanoke opera singer Jane Stuart Smith performed the role of Brünnhilde in Wagner's *Ride of The Valkyries* at the Belini Opera House in Catania, Sicily, on November 8. The Associated Press reported, "She sang her way right into the hearts of the notoriously critical opera-goers of this Sicilian town."

A twenty-four-page special section was published in the November 10 editions of the *Roanoke Times* and *Roanoke World-News* to commemorate the official opening of the Times-World Corporation's new publishing and broadcasting facilities. A public open house was held the second week in November.

This circa 1956 photo shows the nurses' building on the campus of the Catawba Sanatorium. The sanatorium was established in 1908 to treat patients with tuberculosis. *Virginia Room, RPL*

The number of patients at Catawba Sanatorium fell below estimates for the fiscal year. Administrators had estimated a daily census of 440 patients, but the average was 276. Catawba spent $2,187 per patient during its previous fiscal year.

The first worship service in the new building of Windsor Hills Methodist Church was held on November 11. The church was chartered on November 6, 1955, and had been meeting at Mount Vernon School.

A new Pilgrim Holiness congregation, to be known as the Pleasant View Pilgrim Church, was formed in the Hershberger Road NW section in early November. Rev. C. M. Muse was the organizing pastor.

A group of local artists displayed their paintings at the Bank of Virginia in November, all with an international flavor. The artists, all immigrants, were Andree Messager (France), George Solonevich (Russia), Inga Solonevich (Finland), Paul Wilke (Germany), Beatrice Bell (Canada), and Hercules Sembrakis (Greece). The exhibit was sponsored by the Roanoke City-County Art Club.

American novelist Evelyn Eaton addressed a joint meeting of the American Association of University Women and the Roanoke Writers' Guild at the Hotel Roanoke on November 12.

The Canadian Players of Stafford presented Ibsen's *Peer Gynt* to a capacity audience at Hollins College on November 11.

This 1950s postcard shows the Bank of Virginia, which was located in downtown Roanoke.
Nelson Harris

Foley's, an appliance dealer, moved to its new location at 131 Center Avenue NW on November 12.

Salem Town Council sent a letter of protest to the Chesapeake & Potomac Telephone Company against the company's plan to merge the spring phone directory into one listing—Roanoke. Prior editions had separated listings into Roanoke and Salem. Salem Mayor James Moyer said, "We are two separate communities in every respect."

Captain Julian Wise of the Roanoke Life Saving and First Aid Crew handed over the keys to the John M. Oakey Funeral Home to John Oakey on November 12. The crew had met at Oakey's and used their garage for twenty-six years, but they planned to move into their new quarters on Day Avenue. The crew had met every Monday at Oakey's since 1930.

Woodson Pontiac announced it would move from its location at 425 Marshall Avenue SW to property in the 3500 block of Williamson Road occupied by Hedge Lawn Nurseries. The move would be in a year after the company built its new facilities there.

Kirk's Jewelers, located at 110 S. Jefferson Street, announced on November 15 that it was going out of business. According to its advertising, the owners of Kirk's were building a Holiday Inn motel on Route 11 north of Roanoke and had to devote their time and resources to that endeavor. Kirk's had been in business for almost a decade.

In its editorial of November 15, the *Roanoke Times* took the following position on racial desegregation in general: "Unfortunately, the doctrine enunciated by the Supreme Court when it outlawed separate but equal public education is certain to be declared applicable to a constantly widening field. It seems likely that all public facilities and all services in any way supported by tax revenue will eventually come under the segregation ban…The tragedy is that both races are bound to suffer, for in the South taxpayers simply will not support public facilities permitting racial mixing that is contrary to their traditional social order. Determination to abolish public schools rather than yield to compulsory integration is sufficient proof of the damage wrought by the Supreme Court."

Country Carnival debuted on WDBJ-TV on November 15. The 7:00 p.m. show featured Don Reno and Red Smiley.

A boy came into the restaurant owned by J. T. Oliver and bought a nickel popsicle. Oliver, a coin collector, noted the nickel was a 1913 V nickel. He later had the nickel evaluated and determined its value to be $7,000. There were only six such nickels known to be in private hands.

Dixie Caverns, having been acquired by the Trompeter family, was leased back to Samuel Garrison, the prior owner and operator.

The Police Athletic League boxing team opened their season with an 8–1 win against the PAL club from Charlotte on November 15 at the American Legion Auditorium.

Prominent Roanoke attorney Morris Masinter died on November 16. He began practicing law in Roanoke in 1920 after serving in World War I. He was active in Democratic politics and served as chief district enforcement attorney for the Roanoke Office of Price Administration during World War II. He was one of the founders of the Elks Boys' Camp near Clifton Forge.

Roanoke resident and Virginia's attorney general Lindsay Almond announced on November 17 that he would be a candidate in Virginia's next governor's race in 1957. He planned to seek the Democratic nomination with his main plank being ardent opposition to the desegregation of Virginia's public schools. He stated, "For more than five years I have fought to save our public school system from destruction and to defend Virginia's right to govern in her own internal affairs and in the lawful exercise of her inherent and constitutional sovereignty."

An instructor and a student pilot parachuted to safety after bailing out of a jet training plane on November 16 before it crashed on a hillside near Poages Mill. The wreckage was scattered across five acres and the impact crater was less than 200 yards from the home of Mrs. M. B. Spencer.

Phillips Motor Company, a used car dealership, opened in mid-November at 424 Campbell Avenue SW. The owner was Candus Phillips, and the sales manager was Jack Morris.

Roanoke City Council approved the placing of a bronze plaque set in a concrete marker to honor the late Williams P. Hunter, Roanoke's first city manager, to be set in grass spot on the south side of the Jefferson Street leg of the viaduct. The action was taken at the council's meeting on November 19.

Roanoke City Manager Arthur Owens proposed at a Roanoke City Council budget session on November 20 that the abandoned tuberculosis sanatorium at Coyner Springs be used to house elderly indigent patients and that the almshouse at the City Farm be converted into a new juvenile detention home.

Virginia Tech defeated VMI 45–0 in their traditional Thanksgiving Day football game at Victory Stadium. A crowd of 24,000 watched the game. Tech's Corbin Bailey, a graduate of William Fleming High School, was named MVP of the game by the sportswriters. It was the third straight year a Roanoker had earned that title, as Don Divers had won it the previous two.

Big Jay McNeely and his orchestra, along with the Five Satins, performed at the American Legion Auditorium on November 21. The 8:00 p.m. show and dance was for whites, and the midnight show was for Blacks.

Vinton's Dogwood Festival was granted a state charter on November 23. Ott Goode was listed as the corporate president of Dogwood Festival of Virginia, Inc. H. J. Bolin was secretary.

The Snow Queen selected for the Roanoke Christmas Parade was Mitzi McAlexander. She was a sophomore at Cave Spring High School.

West End Presbyterian Church broke ground on November 25 for its new education building. The structure would adjoin the sanctuary that was built in 1925.

Crystal Spring Laundry and Dry Cleaners opened a branch at Edgewood, opposite Young's Super Market, in late November.

The Addison High School football team, coached by Charles Price, was awarded the Western District Group One trophy on November 25. This was the first season a trophy was awarded. The Bulldogs won three straight games to clinch the title at the end of the season.

The Roanoke Christmas Parade was held on November 27 in downtown. The event featured thirty-five floats, ten bands, thirty clowns, decorated cars, and novelty attractions. The nighttime event was televised live by WSLS and WDBJ using flood lights.

John Poindexter pled guilty in Hustings Court on November 26 to shooting and killing Aaron Matthews on October 3 at the Horseshoe Café. Poindexter, eighteen, was sentenced to twenty-five years.

Mrs. Alma Keyser won the one-hundred-dollar first prize in the Diamond Jubilee emblem contest. Nearly 300 persons submitted entries.

Blue Barron and his orchestra performed for a show and dance at the Dixie Caverns Ballroom on November 29.

The Lee-Hy Swimming Pool was sold on November 27 to the Rayphil Corporation for $65,000. The head of the corporation, Raymond Alouf, stated that efforts would begin to remodel many of the buildings and construct the Candlelight Nightclub. The property, which fronted Lee Highway, was previously owned by Lee-Hy Enterprises.

Garden City Appliance Company opened on November 29 at 3331 Garden City Boulevard SE. It carried Westinghouse appliances.

A sixth National Guard unit was activated at Roanoke on November 30. Company C of the 116th Infantry Regiment was an infantry rifle unit, the first of its kind for Roanoke since World War 1.

Garland's Drug Store opened at 1232 Jamison Avenue SE on November 29. As part of its opening weekend, WBLU radio did live broadcasts from the store every afternoon with Don McGraw, and music was provided by Barney Nash on a Conn organ. It was Roanoke's largest drugstore.

Ideal Laundry and Dry Cleaners opened a new branch at 1226 Jamison Avenue, adjacent to the new Garland's Drug Store.

The first Salem Christmas Parade was on November 30. The evening event was sponsored by the Salem Chamber of Commerce. A crowd estimated at 10,000 greeted Santa Claus as he brought of the rear of the fifty-five-unit parade.

Joseph Clark Jr., fifteen, died on November 30 as the result of being struck by an automobile a half mile west of Stewartsville. The Vinton youth was on his way home from basketball practice at Stewartsville High School when he stopped to help a neighbor alongside Route 24.

N&W Railway announced on November 30 the planned purchase of thirty-five diesel locomotives at a cost of $7 million.

The Norfolk & Western Railway Shops sign was part of Roanoke's skyline for decades, an emblem of the railroad's muscular economic presence in the region. This images dates to the 1950s. *Bob Kinsey*

An old frame structure at 810 Union Street, Salem, burned to the ground on November 30. Arthur Hall, a resident, told officials an oil stove had exploded, igniting the blaze.

Giant Food Properties announced on November 30 that grading would begin within several days on a $4 million shopping center to be built on a thirty-acre tract fronting Melrose Avenue NW, just inside the Roanoke city limits. R. R. Quick was handling the development locally.

The Villa Heights Church of the Nazarene held its first service in its new building at 1422 Abbott Street NW on December 2. The congregation had been worshiping in a nearby residence.

A new Colonial Store, a grocery, opened on December 4 at Twenty-Fourth Street and Loudon Avenue NW.

Percy Keeling was named as the new executive secretary of the Hunton Branch YMCA on December 1. He had been serving in that capacity as an interim.

The department store Shoppers Mart, located at Church Avenue and First Street SW, announced in early December it was going out of business.

Thomas DeLong, twenty, of Roanoke died in a single-vehicle accident on Fourth Street NE in what police determined had been a hot rod race.

The Roanoke Life Saving and First Aid Crew officially moved into its new building at Day Avenue and Fourth Street SW on December 2.

The Shenandoah Club directors awarded a contract for $400,000 to J. M. Turner & Company for its new three-story building to be erected on the club's present site at 24 Franklin Road SW. Frantz and Addkinson of Roanoke were the architects.

Tuba Reid, twenty, was fatally shot on December 1 at a filling station on Franklin Road SW by Charles Gravely. Gravely claimed the shooting was an accident.

This 1956 image shows the Roanoke Life Saving and First Aid Crew's building at 374 Day Avenue SW. *Nelson Harris*

Ray Eliot, football coach at the University of Illinois, addressed the Roanoke Touchdown Club on December 3. Tracy Callis of Jefferson High School received the first annual Clyde Cocke trophy as the outstanding scholastic player for the Roanoke Valley. Hill Ellett received the outstanding sandlotter award.

The Rayphils Candlelite Club opened on December 8 near the Lee-Hy Swimming Pool. Frank Romano provided the dance music.

Carter Burgess, thirty-nine, of Roanoke resigned as assistant secretary of defense to become president of Trans World Airlines. Burgess's appointment as the youngest person to head a major airline was announced in Los Angeles on December 5 by Howard Hughes.

The Roanoke Community Fund exceeded its goal for the first time in six years. The goal was $360,000, and the campaign was headed by Thomas Rutherfoord.

Charles Eastwood of Roanoke was named as the "French Millionaire" following a contest held by the Dr. Pepper Bottling Company. He and his wife received an expense-paid trip to Paris.

Plans for a Presbyterian Church in the Windsor Hills section were discussed in a meeting on December 7 at the home of Joseph Dill. The Presbytery had already purchased a site at the Renick farm.

The bishop of the Episcopal Diocese of Southwestern Virginia dedicated the St. Luke's Episcopal Chapel at 1114 Grayson Avenue NW on December 6.

Rev. William Denson, pastor of Melrose Baptist Church for fifteen years, announced his resignation in early December. He had accepted a position with the Virginia Baptist Mission Board in Richmond. Denson had also served as a member of the Roanoke School Board.

Roanoke's Police Athletic League boxing team defeated a combination team from Washington, DC, and Danville 7–1 before a large crowd at the American Legion Auditorium on December 6. The main bout was one by Roanoke's James Muse over Robert Shifflett of DC.

The Vinton Christmas Parade was held on December 7 and attended by an estimated crowd of 4,000. Of interest was the mid-70s temperature, as the Roanoke Valley was experiencing a heat wave that was breaking records.

Richo the Clown made personal appearances at the Grandin Theatre and Lee Theatre on December 8 as part of each theatre's kiddie show program. Richo was associated with the Ringling Brothers Circus.

Graybar Electric Company announced on December 8 plans for a $225,000 warehouse and office building in the 1200 block of West Salem Avenue. The firm had warehouse and office space at 601 W. Salem Avenue.

W. P. Swartz Jr. and Company announced on December 8 the acquisition of Custom Kitchens at 105 Center Avenue NW.

The Roanoke Symphony Orchestra, along with church choral singers, presented Handel's *Messiah* at the American Legion Auditorium on December 9.

A Roanoke chapter of the Virginia Voting League was organized on December 10 in a meeting at the Virginia Mutual Insurance Building at 407 Gainsboro Road NW. Dr. L. E. Paxton was the temporary chairman of the chapter.

K. C. Rowland of Roanoke had a one-man painting exhibition at the Pietrantonio Galleries on Madison Avenue in New York City that was well received by critics.

Santa Claus, as he had done since 1950, began his tour on the N&W Railway routes the second week in December.

The new Cave Spring High School was officially accepted by the Roanoke County School Board on December 11. The board's action permitted the county to seek additional capital funds from the state.

A suit to seize and sell an eighty-nine-acre farm on Sugar Loaf Mountain was filed by the government on December 11. Law enforcement captured a large still on the property that was hidden in a farmhouse. Theodore Smith was the owner of the property.

The Eagles Nest gift shop in the terminal building at Woodrum Field opened on December 15. Hazel Nelson and Mildred Burnette operated the store.

Downtown Roanoke department stores and women's apparel businesses held their annual Christmas season Stag Night on December 12. The men-only shopping night was patronized by thousands. Many stores provided refreshments and models on runways.

Jack Andrews, assistant professor of drama at Hollins College, was named as the executive director for the upcoming outdoor drama *Thy Kingdom Come* to be performed at the amphitheatre in Sherwood Burial Park.

Roanoker Don Divers, who was captain of the Virginia Tech football team, spoke at the annual Roanoke Sandlot Football Banquet at Monroe Junior High School on December 12. "Sandlot is the backbone of any sport," stated Divers. Some 250 sandlot players attended the banquet.

Hollins College approved a student-proposed plan for sponsoring the education of four Hungarian refugees. The college would provide free tuition, while the student government committed to funds for their living expenses.

The Hotel Roanoke and the City of Roanoke both lit their respective Christmas trees on December 13. The hotel's tree had 1,300 decorations.

Mick-or-Mack announced on December 12 that it would close its downtown Roanoke grocery store at 115 W. Church Avenue on Christmas Eve. The store was being closed due to a lack of space and parking. The store had opened in 1947.

Joshua Stewart, thirty-nine, of Roanoke died in an auto accident on December 14 at Orange Avenue and Ninth Street NE.

Jacob Reid, seventy-two, a prominent Black attorney in Roanoke, and his wife, Mary, were both found dead in their home on Harrison Avenue NW on December 14. The medical examiner attributed their deaths to natural causes. Reid had served on the board of the Roanoke Redevelopment and Housing Authority since 1949, when the authority was created.

The Gen. James Breckenridge Chapter of the Daughters of the American Revolution was organized on December 14 with twenty-six members at the home of the organizing regent, Mrs. Roger Martin.

Roanoke City Manager Arthur Owens included in his draft budget for 1957 a right-of-way engineer position to prepare for a connecting spur at such time as when the state Department of Highways finalizes the route of the interstate highway system passing north of the city.

Appalachian Electric Power Company began work in mid-December on a 145-mile microwave communications system that would connect its Roanoke and Charleston, West Virginia, offices. Once completed, the system would carry voice, teletype, telemetering, and load control data messages.

Henry Johnson, seventy-five, of Roanoke died on December 14 at his home. Johnson was a partner in the real estate firm Reid and Johnson and a prominent member of Roanoke's Black business community. He was one of the founders of the Magic City Building and Loan Association.

The Roanoke Parks and Recreation Department scheduled twice daily organ recitals for the Christmas season on the second floor of the Municipal Building with the music piped over loudspeakers to the outside. The department also sponsored a Christmas pageant for three nights the week prior to Christmas that was held on the steps of the Municipal Building.

The December 16 edition of the *Roanoke Times* profiled Dr. Andrew Groseclose, Roanoke's first doctor practicing obstetrics and gynecology exclusively when he opened his practice in 1926. In the three decades since, Groseclose had delivered over 10,000 babies. Groseclose said that his best lessons in medicine were those he learned early on from a country doctor in Bland County, who advised him, "Ninety percent of your patients will get well if you leave them alone. Be sure you don't do something to keep them from getting well."

A newborn baby, believed to be two hours old, was found dead in a grocery bag on the steps of Lewis-Gale Hospital on December 18. The child was bathed, clothed, and had a clean diaper. In its nightgown were found two ten-dollar bills. Hospital staff stated the child had been delivered in a "professional" manner. The newborn was discovered by nurses entering the hospital. An autopsy the following day determined the male infant had been born alive and may have still been alive at the time of the abandonment.

William Johnson, twenty-one, of Roanoke was fatally stabbed on December 20 by his wife, Sarah, who confessed to the crime.

LaVern Baker, along with Billy Clark and his orchestra, performed for a show and dance at the American Legion Auditorium on December 24. The show began at midnight.

A $750,000 stone and brick structure was announced as the newly planned home for the Allstate Insurance Company Roanoke regional office. The building site was located on Route 11 (Lee Highway) less than a half mile west of Roanoke. The Roanoke office had 339 employees.

B. F. Goodrich Company moved to its new location at 1409 Williamson Road on December 26. Dick Bryan was the store manager. The tire retailer had previously been located at First Street and Luck Avenue SW.

Sixteen girls were presented at the debutante ball sponsored by the Altruist Club on December 28 at the American Legion Auditorium. "A Breath of Spring" was the theme of the event that was attended by over 600 persons. Dr. L. E. Paxton and Queen Williams were honorary cochairs of the ball.

Bob Aveson, a center on the William Fleming High School football team, was named to the All-Southern football team by coaches and sportswriters.

The first refugees from war-torn Hungary that came to Roanoke boarded a bus from Camp Kilmer, New Jersey, on December 26. Twenty-five refugees were resettled in the Roanoke Valley under the sponsorship of the Roanoke Ministers Conference. Most were single men.

Rabbi Tobias Rothenberg of Beth Israel Synagogue was reelected president of the seaboard region of the Rabbinical Assembly of America during the group's meeting in Washington, DC, on December 26.

Burton Levine, president and general manager of WROV radio, announced that he and others had purchased KOMA, a radio station in Oklahoma City, Oklahoma, for $342,000.

Price's Amoco Service Station opened on December 28 at 1535 W. Main Street in Salem. The station operator was Billie Price.

Blake Newton Jr., an attorney, became president of the Shenandoah Life Insurance Company on January 1, 1957. He had been assistant vice president of AT&T in their Washington, DC, office. Newton was forty-one.

Residents of the Mary Louise Home moved into their new quarters at Berkley and Amherst Avenues SW on December 28. The Mary Louise Home was previously located at 1001 Patterson Avenue SW and had been named for the mother of the late J. B. Fishburn. The home was overseen by the local chapter of the King's Daughters, which had been formed in Roanoke in 1892.

Paul Niswander, thirty-eight, of Roanoke was killed on December 30 when he was run over by a Virginian Railway coal hopper on a siding at American Viscose Corporation. Niswander was a conductor for the railway.

Top O' The Mornin', a new local television show, debuted on December 31 on WDBJ-TV. Hosted by Irv Sharp, the show also featured local musicians Don Reno, Red Smiley, and the Tennessee Cut Ups from the *Old Dominion Barn Dance* radio show. Ron McDonald did the news and weather.

Lloyd Price and his band performed for a show and dance on December 31 at the Star City Auditorium.

Governor Thomas Stanley stayed the execution of convicted rapist Frank Snider on December 31 until February 7 to permit time for a possible appeal to the US Supreme Court. Snider had been sentenced to death on June 27 in Roanoke for raping a ten-year-old girl in the city. His execution had been set for January 3.

Jefferson Hospital, founded in 1907 by Dr. Hugh Trout, became a nonprofit charitable corporation on December 31. The hospital was governed by a board of directors and was located in the 1300 block of Franklin Road SW. It had been a stock company since 1914.

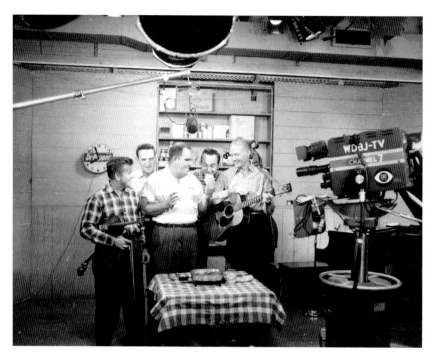

This WDBJ studio shot from the 1950s shows Irv Sharp (center) and Red Smiley (right with guitar) taping a commercial, probably for Sharp's *Top O' The Mornin'* show. *WDBJ7*

1957

Betty Amos of the *Grand Ole Opry* was a guest star on the *Top O' The Mornin'* show on WDBJ during the first week of January.

Leonard Beck became a part owner, manager, and pharmacist at Lipes Pharmacy on January 1. The pharmacy of C. C. Lipes was located at 2201 Crystal Spring Avenue SW.

Ice Vogues of 1957 came to the American Legion Auditorium the first week in January for four days.

What police described as a gunfight broke out in the early morning hours of January 1 during a dance at the Star City Auditorium on January 1 that left two dead. Killed were Robert Boisseau, thirty-five, and David Johnson, eighteen, both of Roanoke. Philip Durham, twenty-one, of Roanoke was charged with murder. Police reported five shots being fired at close range. Durham died on the dance floor, while Boisseau staggered across the street before collapsing near a taxi stand. Hundreds were in the auditorium at the time of the incident. The auditorium was located at Wells Avenue and First Street NW.

Dr. E. G. Gill outlined his plan for the first eye bank in Virginia in an address to the Roanoke Lions Club on January 3. Gill said the eye bank would function with eye donations secured by Lions Clubs across Virginia. Of about 4,100 blind persons in the state, Gill believed 500 could be assisted with corneal transplants.

Dr. Robert Paine Jr., a Salem physician, and Dr. George Tate, a dentist, announced plans to build a one-story duplex for their respective practices on Colorado Street, across from Peacock-Salem Dry Cleaners.

A Greyhound double-decker bus plowed into the rear of a truck loaded with cast iron pipe on January 4 on Route 11 near Lexington killing six and injuring twenty. Killed was the driver Sherer Sutliff of Roanoke, who had been driving for Greyhound since 1942.

The $35 million redevelopment plan proposed by the Roanoke Redevelopment and Housing Authority for southeast Roanoke was so extensive and expansive, covering some 1,500 acres, that the planning commission asked for further study before making any report or recommendations. The commission members also stated in their meeting on January 5 they would like to see the outcomes of the RRHA "slum clearance" program in northeast Roanoke before embarking on another such effort.

Major General Leslie Carter, a native of Salem and alum of Roanoke College, retired from the army in early January after thirty-nine years of service.

A ground-breaking ceremony was held on January 6 for the Franklin Road Chapel at the corner of Twenty-Third Street and Colonial Avenue SW. The original church was located at 2001 Lynn Avenue SW.

The Julliard String Quartet performed at Hollins College on January 9.

Roanoke City Council authorized the acquisition of sixty-six acres of land lying to the west of the northeast-southwest runway at Woodrum Field to create a "clear zone." The city manager indicated the land could be leased for farm use.

Shirlee Hunter, fifteen, known as the "Country Sweetheart" on the *Old Dominion Barn Dance* show, appeared on *Top O' the Mornin'* on January 10. Hunter was a junior at William Byrd High School.

Crystal Hat Cleaners opened at their new location at 514 S. Jefferson Street on January 9, which was the former location of Martha Washington Candies.

George Boyd, sixty-four, of Roanoke County was crushed to death in a screw elevator conveyor at Lone Star Cement plant in Botetourt County on January 9.

William Vest, longtime former Salem police chief, died at age eighty-nine on January 9. Vest began working for the Town of Salem in 1910 as a sergeant and retired as chief in 1942.

The Groundhog Club announced it would no longer hold its customary public meeting in early February that poked fun at local and state politicians. Reasons given were the lack of public participation and the small amount of funds raised for charities as compared to the past. Known as Groundhog Club of America No. 1, the group was organized in 1916 and held meetings through 1934, when it ceased to function. The club was reorganized in 1949.

State Senator Earl Fitzpatrick of Roanoke was elected vice chairman of a General Assembly committee to investigate groups "promoting racial litigation." The group was to be called the Committee on Law Reform and Racial Activities. The committee was expected to focus most of its activities toward the NAACP.

Rev. Merlin Garber, pastor of Central Church of the Brethren, and his foster son, Rev. Bob Richards, appeared on the nationally televised program *Cavalcade of America* on January 15. Garber had taken Richards in when Garber was a pastor in Illinois, and Richards competed in two Olympics in pole vaulting.

The new headquarters of the Roanoke Life Saving and First Aid Crew at 374 Day Avenue SW was dedicated on January 13 with Rev. Harry Gamble, chaplain of the crew, presiding. The main speaker was R. B. Swope, president of Southern Oxygen Company of Washington, DC.

Tena Baxter, four months old, died in a house fire at 812 Gainsboro Road NW on January 11. Her two older sisters were rescued by a passerby, Clarence White, sixteen, who was unaware of the infant inside. The mother of the girls was at a nearby house doing wash.

Over 500 persons attended a Roanoke School Board meeting at Grandin Court School on January 11 to hear an airing by board member Mrs. G. C. Ligon that the school system was spending too much money on "frills" and vocational training. The majority of board members challenged Ligon's assertions and pointed to her faulty math in making inflammatory comments about the school system's budget. After the three hour meeting, Ligon told the press her colleagues' comments "were below the belt."

This is an aerial view of Roanoke Memorial Hospital taken in 1956. *Carilion Clinic*

William Flannagan, administrator of Roanoke Memorial Hospital, announced on January 11 that the hospital would launch a school of practical nursing beginning February 4. The yearlong course would be operated by Roanoke City Public Schools and would be separate from the School of Professional Nursing operated by the hospital.

The Shenandoah Club moved to its temporary quarters in the Patrick Henry Hotel in mid-January after their clubhouse was razed to make way for their new one to be built.

An Evening With Johann Strauss was presented by the Thursday Morning Music Club at the American Theatre on January 16. An ensemble of eight singers presented various Strauss pieces, with most being associated with the New York City Opera. Among the performers was a young lyric soprano, Beverly Sills.

Thomas Hughes Jr. was profiled in the January 13 edition of the *Roanoke Times*, known to many children as the popular "Uncle Looney Toon," the local emcee on WSLS-TV for Saturday morning cartoons. Hughes was the production director for the television station and had had a career in entertainment going back to 1935 when he went to New York City to study acting. His first acting job onstage was in a play in Greenwich Village that also had another actor doing his first stage gig, Van Johnson. Hughes came back to Roanoke in 1946.

Salem Town Council approved a $470,000 bond issue at its January 14 meeting to expand its water system. The plan included funds for the installation of 200,000 gallon water tank in South Salem, improvements to the river pumping station and the filtration plant, and increasing water capacity to five million gallons per day.

This undated studio shot shows Thomas Hughes Jr. in character as "Uncle Looney," a favorite character on the WSLS-TV's local children's programming during the 1950s and '60s. *WSLS-TV*

John Neighbors, seventy-two, of Vinton walked into the Dixie Hardware store on January 14 and purchased a single-barrel, twelve-gauge shotgun. He left the store, loaded it, and committed suicide in public at the corner of Cleveland and Pollard Streets. He had been in ill health for some time.

A bronze portrait of Junius B. Fishburn was unveiled in the lobby of the First National Exchange Bank of Roanoke on January 15 to honor the late banker's many years with FNEB.

The firm of J. M. Harris and Company was sold for $225,000 to E. W. Rose and S. T. Kummer on January 15. The business, a dog food and insecticide manufacturer, was located at 715 Third Street SE.

The Roanoke Merchants Association sponsored its fourth "Greater Roanoke Days" event in early January. The one-week event held in January and June was an effort to promote Roanoke's retailers to shoppers beyond the Roanoke Valley. Over one hundred retailers participated in the promotion.

Dean Goodsell of the Hollins College drama department was selected to direct the Kermit Hunter outdoor drama *Thy Kingdom Come* to be presented in June at the Sherwood Burial Park Amphitheater. The production was planning for a cast of sixty.

James Rhodes, a member of the Roanoke School Board, died suddenly at his home on January 17 at the age of seventy.

Virginia Building Supply Company opened Builders Mart at Eighth Street and Shenandoah Avenue NW on January 18.

An explosion in the furnace room heavily damaged the Bank of Virginia building and an adjoining business on January 18.

Harry Smith, fifty-four, of Roanoke was killed on January 19 when he was struck by a coal car at Lamberts Point Pier at Norfolk. Smith was the superintendent of the eastern general division of N&W Railway.

Architectural plans for twin modernistic homes for Scottish Rite bodies of the Roanoke Valley and Kazim Temple were publicly presented on January 20. The $500,000 project would be connected by a covered walkway and be built on the site of the Shrine Temple facing Campbell Avenue SW. A frame building at 624 Campbell Avenue would be razed to make room for the new construction.

Showtimers presented *Stalag 17* the third week in January that included some local businessmen having minor roles. The cast included Mike Schaffer, Jim Toler, Robert Rogers, Joe Grant, and William Thugut.

A fire destroyed the kitchen and storerooms of Archie's Lobster House on January 20. Archie Parrish, owner of the restaurant, said there were 250 patrons in the restaurant at the time when the fire started but everyone filed out calmly. The restaurant was located at the intersection of Routes 11 and 117.

Mrs. G. C. Ligon resigned her position on the Roanoke School Board on January 21. Ligon cited her disagreements with board colleagues and school administrators for what she deemed "frivolous expenses" as the reason for her stepping down.

Coach Charles Price of the Addison High School bulldogs called his star player, Robert Clark, the best in the state. In the first seven games of the season, Clark had averaged 25.9 points per game.

B. M. Phelps was the high bidder for the site of the former Academy of Music in the 400 block of West Salem Avenue. His offer was $25,007. Roanoke City Council voted to accept the offer.

The Fred Astaire Dance Studios in Roanoke brought in the Fred Astaire Dancers for a three-night show on the stage of the Roanoke Theatre in late January to promote its rock 'n' roll dance classes where students would be taught the Lindy Hop, Bunny Hug, and Charleston.

Bob McLelland (right) receives the Clyde Cocke Memorial Award at the Hotel Roanoke for his many years coaching sandlot football. *Historical Society of Western Virginia*

Dr. Algernon Turner, fifty, operator of the Turner Clinic at Poages Mill, died on January 23. He came to Roanoke in 1940 and established his clinic on Route 221 in 1943.

Bob McLelland, a *Roanoke World-News* sports writer, received the Clyde Cocke Memorial Award by the Roanoke Chamber of Commerce on January 25 in honor of his work with sandlot football.

The new education building at Airlee Court Baptist Church, corner of Hershberger and Williamson Road, was dedicated on January 27.

George O'Hara was named Outstanding Young Man of the Year by the Roanoke Jaycees during their annual banquet on January 26. O'Hara was agency secretary of the Shenandoah Life Insurance Company.

Raleigh Court Presbyterian Church broke ground on its new sanctuary on January 27. Located in the 1800 block of Grandin Road, the congregation's new sanctuary was to be completed at a cost of $340,000. The contractor was Lewis Lionberger, and architects were Smithey and Boynton of Roanoke. The church was organized in 1924.

While doing research for Roanoke's Diamond Jubilee celebration, there arose discussion as to when Big Lick officially became Roanoke. A young lawyer named William Robertson got eighty dollars for drafting the city's charter, and A. S. Asberry turned in expenses of $22.80 for his trip to Richmond to lobby the state legislature to adopt the charter. February 3, 1882, was the date the charter passed the legislature, but the charter did not take effect until July 1. Roanoke historians Raymond Barnes and Griffith Dodson Sr. both suggested the date of July 1 was the more appropriate of the two. Barnes, however, provided evidence that citizens were calling their town Roanoke prior to either of the two dates.

The new Mary Louise Home was formally dedicated on January 27. The home had seventeen residents at the time.

Thomas Crowder opened his home building business in late January at 1227 Patterson Avenue SW. Specializing in contemporary home design, the firm had Stanley Hudson as a designer and Bill Tingle for interior decorating.

The Police Athletic League boxing program moved to new quarters on the third floor of the building at 110 W. Church Avenue in late January. Paul Vest was the director.

Former heavyweight boxing champion Jack Dempsey came to Roanoke on January 29 to referee professional wrestling at the American Legion Auditorium. Dempsey also met with the Police Athletic League boxing team to show them his boxing moves.

Roanoke Vice Mayor W. B. Carter was named managing director of the Diamond Jubilee on January 29. He succeeded Lucian Booth as director. Booth had suffered a heart attack two weeks prior and could not continue.

Officials with the Blue Ridge Parkway and the City of Roanoke held discussions in late January on a temporary connection between the parkway and the city via Mill Mountain. The parkway section between Bent Mountain and Route 220 was to be graded and topped with crushed stone during the year.

The Town of Salem won its battle with the Chesapeake and Potomac Telephone Company to have a separate listing in the phone directory. The phone company had earlier proposed that Salem residents be joined with Roanoke in the directory.

Preliminary work on Smith Mountain Dam began in late January with an access road created to the dam site and core drilling by Grouting Corporation of Salem. The drilling was being done to make certain the rock could bear the weight of the dam.

A group of Presbyterians hoping to start a new church in the Cave Spring section held their first worship service on February 3 at Cave Spring High School. The church would become the Covenant Presbyterian Church.

Evangelist James Vaus conducted a two-week revival at First Baptist Church in Roanoke in early February. Vaus was well-known for his racketeering convictions due to his involvement in the Mickey Cohen-related criminal network in California. During prison, he was converted during a Billy Graham crusade.

The first service of a mission church in the Norwood area, organized by Melrose Presbyterian Church, was held on February 3 at the Draper Construction Company office on Route 117.

The States' Rights Party in the Sixth Congressional District voted on February 1 to affiliate with the Constitution Party in a meeting held at Roanoke's Municipal Building.

Garland's Drug Store No. 2 moved to its new location at 510 Eleventh Street NW in early February. It had been formerly located at 1102 Loudon Avenue NW.

A ground-breaking ceremony was held for the new Greenvale Nursery School on Westwood Boulevard NW on February 4. The school had an enrollment of 130 children.

The Pittsburgh Symphony Orchestra performed at the American Legion Auditorium on February 6. The performance was sponsored by the Thursday Morning Music Club.

The 4-H Clubs of Roanoke County produced their first ever yearbook. The 1956 yearbook became available in early February and included the 800 members of twenty clubs. The publication was dedicated to Lula Crawford.

WSLS-FM radio began broadcasting on the afternoon of February 4. WSLS had had an AM station for many years. The FM station was located at 99.1 on the radio dial.

The Harlem Magicians played the Kentucky Colonels in basketball at the American Legion Auditorium on February 8. The star player for the Magicians was former Harlem Globetrotter Goose Tatum, known as the "Clown Prince of Basketball."

The Roanoke City Council appointed Richard Edwards and Mrs. Gwin Moomaw to the Roanoke School Board at their February 4 meeting. Edwards was a former mayor of Roanoke.

Royce Northcutt was named as manager of US Steel's American Bridge plant in Roanoke on February 4. He succeeded Lester Larison.

Fred Grubb was struck and killed by an auto on February 3 while crossing Route 221 in the Back Creek section. He was struck about 200 yards south of his home.

Robert Hubbard, a retired trial judge for Roanoke County, died at his home in Salem on February 5 at the age of seventy-five. He was a judge for more than twenty years, retiring in 1954.

Felix Brown, fifty-two, of Roanoke was stabbed to death on February 5 at his home on Norfolk Avenue SW. Police charged his wife, Marie, with the fatal attack. The wife confessed to the incident, claiming it was self-defense.

A fire damaged a building at 308 Harrison Avenue NW on February 5. Two businesses occupied the structure, Modernistic Beauty Salon and Southern Aid Life Insurance Company.

The Colonial-American National Bank opened a branch at Twenty-Third Street and Melrose Avenue NW on February 7.

B. F. Goodrich Company opened at an additional location at 1409 Williamson Road on February 7.

Roanoke physicians set aside February 9 in a campaign to get as many Roanokers as possible inoculated for polio with the Salk vaccine. The anti-polio campaign was sponsored by the Roanoke Academy of Medicine. Clinics to receive the shot were set up at local hospitals, doctors' offices, and life saving crew headquarters.

Joe's Grill opened at 1402 Wise Avenue SE on February 8. The restaurant's slogan was "poor man's country club."

This 1957 image shows McKesson & Robbins Wholesale Druggist, which was located at 365 Salem Avenue. *Virginia Room, RPL*

The *Powhatan Arrow*, an N&W Railway passenger train, struck and killed a mother and four children in an auto at a crossing at Fort Gay, West Virginia, on February 8.

Jane Stuart Smith of Roanoke performed to rave reviews for her star soprano performance in Wagner's *Tannhäuser* at the Massime Opera House in Palermo, Sicily, on February 8. It was her first major role in an opera at that venue.

Grandin Washmobile, a car wash business, opened at 1904 Memorial Avenue SW on February 9. According to ads, one car was washed every sixty seconds for $1.50.

Hollins College received $100,000 from the Texas Presbyterian Foundation toward its $500,000 goal for a new chapel on the campus. Hollins was the only non-Presbyterian entity to receive funds from the foundation.

The first corneal transplant eye surgery in Roanoke was performed on Mark Webb by Drs. E. G. Gill and Ronald Harris on January 11. The news was announced by Gill at a meeting of the Roanoke Lions Club on February 9. Gill used the occasion to promote his proposed eye bank for Virginia.

The Roanoke School Board at its meeting on February 11 voted to name the new school in the Lincoln Terrace section Lincoln Terrace Elementary School. The school was being built to replace Gainsboro School that had an enrollment of 375 students. The Gainsboro School at the time still had pot-bellied stoves and no restrooms for the teachers.

Three Black brakemen of N&W Railway filed suit in US District Court in Roanoke on February 11 asserting that they were denied promotions because of their race. The men sued for back pay and $100,000 in punitive damages. The plaintiffs were Sam Clark, Robert Coles, and Robert Hamlar. Coles and Hamlar lived in Roanoke. Judge John Paul heard the case.

Some 500 Boy Scouts paraded through Salem on February 12 to celebrate Boy Scout Week. Other participants included high school bands. The parade was on Main Street.

Mitsuo Fuchida, the Japanese officer who planned and led the air attack on Pearl Harbor and had become a missionary, spoke at Ghent Brethren Church in Roanoke on February 14. Fuchida converted to Christianity following the war and headed the Sky Pilots in Japan.

Fire swept through the One-Hour Valet cleaning service at 26 W. Church Avenue on February 14. Damage was estimated at $60,000. The structure was a complete loss. Thirteen firemen were injured battling the blaze.

Roanoke's City Sargeant Edgar Winstead reported on February 14 that the city jail was so overcrowded inmates had to sleep on the floor of corridors and cells. The jail had a capacity for 158 inmates, but the jail population was regularly over 200.

The Lutheran Synod of Virginia purchased a five-acre tract from Thomas Worrell along Route 221 for the future site of a Lutheran church in the Cave Spring section. Dr. William McCauley was the organizing pastor.

Ortho-Vent Shoe Company held an open house at their new warehouse and retail store off Main Street in Salem on February 15. The store, which stocked some 40,000 pairs of shoes, was believed to be the largest shoe store in the South.

Four persons died in a head-on collision on US 11 four miles west of Salem on February 16. The auto accident took the lives of three members of the same family. Killed were John Griggs, Alma Griggs, Renee Griggs, and Charles Moses. The Griggs family lived on Maiden Lane SW in Roanoke, and Moses was from Elliston. It was one of the worst crashes in Roanoke County's history.

After a series of visits with Jim Vaus, a former criminal turned evangelist, Gail Ferrell entered a guilty plea in US District Court in Roanoke for attempted robbery. Vaus, who was conducting a revival at First Baptist Church, convinced the young man to accept responsibility for his actions. Ferrell repudiated his prior testimony that asserted he was innocent. Judge John Paul sentenced Ferrell to six years.

Roanoke Civic Ballet presented *Coppélia* at Jefferson High School on February 18. Lead dancers were Martha Critzer and Norman Arrington. Miss Floyd Ward was the director.

Ruth Painter Randall, a former resident of Salem, published her work *The Courtship of Mr. Lincoln* by Little, Brown Publishing of Boston in February. It was her third book on Lincoln.

George Solonevich was retained by Simon & Schuster to illustrate their forthcoming book *World Around the Sun.*

Ivory Joe Hunter and his orchestra performed at the Star City Auditorium on February 22.

A Roanoke County couple, Elmer and Jenny Jamison, were killed on February 17 when their car was hit by a westbound N&W Railway train east of Salem. They were killed at a crossing near the Lee-Hi Drive-In Theatre in US 11. The Jamisons were on their way to services at the Peters Creek Old German Baptist Church.

Lt. Gen. Lewis Hershey addressed 300 leaders of the Blue Ridge Boy Scouts Council on the importance of forming young men into leaders a rally at Woodrow Wilson Junior High School on February 18. The rally was to launch plans for the Jubilee Scouting Exposition at Victory Stadium in May.

One-Hour Valet opened at its new location at 415 First Street SW on February 19 following a devastating fire at their prior location.

N&W Railway announced on February 19 that it was ending the use of steam locomotives in its Shenandoah Division. The last steam train in that district came into the Roanoke station on the morning of February 20. N&W had already converted its Lynchburg-to-Durham line to diesel.

James Yates, well-known pharmacist in Vinton, died on February 19. He owned the White Front Drug Store in Vinton for the past eleven years. Prior to that, Yates managed the Preddy-Yates Cigar Store in the Ponce de Leon Hotel.

Johnson-McReynolds Chevrolet celebrated its twenty-fifth anniversary in late February by offering the 1957 Chevrolet 210, a two-door sedan, for $1,995. The auto dealer had two locations, 366 W. Campbell Avenue and 1824 Williamson Road.

Electroplating Inc. opened on February 24 at 3338 Shenandoah Avenue NW.

Carolyn Hale won the Times-World Corporation's Newspaper Cartoon Contest. The contest was for youth, and entries were drawings of their favorite comic page characters. Hale won a Schwinn Hornet bicycle.

Over 450 high school and college singers comprised a chorus that performed with the Roanoke Symphony Orchestra on February 25 at the American Legion Auditorium. The program featured compositions by Copland and Dvorak.

The Paper Rose, a new play by Hollins College drama professor Kermit Hunter, premiered at the college on March 1. Hunter was a well-known playwright, primarily for his outdoor dramas. Those dramas included *Unto These Hills* at Cherokee, North Carolina; *Horn in the West* at Boone, North Carolina; *The Eleventh Hour* at Staunton; and the forthcoming *Thy Kingdom Come* at Sherwood Burial Park.

Novick Transfer Company erected a motor freight terminal on McDowell Avenue at Thirteenth Street NE in late February. The company was headquartered in Winchester.

A new class of hopper cars rolled out of the N&W Railway Shops in late February. The New Class H-10 had eight different improvements, mostly technical, over prior hopper cars. The railway had ordered 5,500 to be built in Roanoke.

Addison High School defeated Dunbar High School, 86–67, on February 23 to win the Group I VIA Western District basketball tournament title. Addison's high scorer both in the game and the regular season was Robert Clark.

The Jose Limon Dance Company performed at Hollins College on February 26. Limon was ranked as one of the best modern ballet dancers in the world at the time.

Roanoke Valley barbers increased their prices on a particular haircut—the flat top. The price went from $1.00 to $1.25. According to one barber, he could give three regular haircuts in the time it took him to do one flat top. The flat top had gained in popularity with young men, such that it was the predominant style for them.

The Roanoke Redevelopment and Housing Authority announced on February 25 plans to apply to the Housing and Home Finance Agency, under a new section of federal law, for funding of its proposed "Greater Roanoke Urban Renewal Project." That $35 million project was to target southeast Roanoke in much the same way the "urban renewal" and "slum clearance" program was progressing in Northeast. The Northeast effort, known as the Commonwealth Project, was being eyed by the planning commission as to results before they intended to vote on the Southeast program.

Plans for a new country club were announced on February 26. The Mountain View Country Club announced it had lease-purchased the Monterey Golf Club and facilities from Martha Read. The purchase included the golf course, clubhouse, and the Col. William Fleming home, all situated on 237 acres. The Monterey golf pro used the Fleming home. Cy Bahakel was president of the new country club, and he stated that plans included the building of a swimming pool, tennis courts, and shuffleboard.

Nelson Hardware closed on February 28. Organized in 1888 by Alexander Nelson, the business had been in the Nelson family since then. The retail hardware was located at 17 E. Campbell Avenue. The family planned to open and operate a wholesale hardware in a new warehouse at Ninth Street and Rhodes Avenue NE. The business was originally located on Second Street SW before moving to Campbell Avenue in 1897. Early in his business, Alexander Nelson had to face down a mob that broke into his store during the riot of 1893 by telling them he would charge the leaders for the stolen merchandise.

The Crystal Spring Beauty Salon opened on February 27 at 2207 Crystal Spring Avenue. It was owned and managed by Frances Hawks.

Moskin's, a clothing store, opened on February 28 at 33 Church Avenue SW.

Grand Ole Opry stars came to the American Legion Auditorium on March 2. Performers were Ernest Tubb, Kitty Wells, Johnnie and Jack, the Wilburn Brothers, the Texas Troubadours, the Tennessee Mountain Boys, Billy Byrd, Shot Jackson, and Rusty Gabbard.

Mill Mountain Garden Club was elected to membership in the Garden Club of America in late February. It was the first garden club in the region to achieve that distinction.

Virginia Prestressed Concrete Corporation purchased nearly seven acres near Starkey for a proposed casting plant.

Robert Conklin, sixty-five, of Kimball, West Virginia, was killed in a head-on collision on March 2 in Salem at the intersection of Union and Calhoun Streets. The driver of the other car, Ralph Agee, was not injured.

United Rent-Alls of Roanoke opened on March 3 at the corner of Tenth Street and Moorman Avenue NW. The owner was Bernie Pruett.

Hollins College convened a "World Affairs Council" panel for a forum on March 4. The panelists were Camille Chautemps, a four-time premier of France; Stefan Osusky, considered one of the founders of the Czechoslovakia; Arthur Webb, a British journalist; and John Metcalfe, an American journalist.

The Roanoke Youth Symphony gave its first public concert on March 3 at Jefferson High School. The forty-four-piece symphony was conducted by Gibson Morrissey. The concert also featured the choirs of Woodrow Wilson Junior High School and William Fleming High School.

Sears Town, the new store of Sears, Roebuck and Company, opened on March 6 on Williamson Road at Wayne Street. George Sellers was the manager. According to Sears officials, it was the largest Sears store in the South with over 55,000 square feet of retail space for fifty departments. The Sears store in downtown Roanoke closed on March 2 after being in that location for twenty-eight years. The new store had 535 employees.

Sears Town opened in March 1957 at 1502 Williamson Road NE. It was the largest such store in the South for the company. *Virginia Room, RPL*

Marc Adams, a 1943 graduate of William Fleming High School, was ranked among the first fifteen in a "King of Hearts" poll conducted by *TV Star Parade* magazine. Adams, whose real name was Kenneth Herman, had appeared on television in *Circle Theatre* and *Fox Theater* as well as the film *Condor's Nest* that starred Cornel Wilde. The No. 1 position in the poll was Elvis Presley.

Archie's Lobster House reopened on March 3 following its recovery from a fire in January. The restaurant was located on US Route 11, five miles north of Roanoke.

Dr. John Jeremiah of Wales took over the Turner Clinic on Route 221 in early March. Jeremiah, twenty-seven, succeeded Dr. A. K. Turner, who had passed away. Jeremiah was selected to run the clinic by Turner's widow. Jeremiah was educated at Queen's University School of Medicine in Belfast, Ireland, and had been with the Central State Hospital in Petersburg, Virginia, since coming to the United States.

The Times-World Corporation exchanged land with Towers Shopping Center in deed transactions recorded on March 5. Towers planned to build on the land it received.

WSLS radio (610 AM) began broadcasting at 5,000 watts on March 8 via a transmitter located at Lakeside. The station had broadcasted at 1,000 watts since 1940.

Roanoke College students voted to affirm the honor system with a vote in the student assembly on March 7. A motion had been made to abolish the system but was defeated 94 to 278.

A group of about sixty persons advocating states' rights met on March 8 in Roanoke and formed a permanent committee of the Constitution Party for the Sixth Congressional District. Herbert Moore Jr. of Roanoke was elected chairman.

The Salem Lions Club held its annual minstrel show the third weekend in March at Andrew Lewis High School. The show was a fundraiser to support its community and sight projects. Interlocutor was Howard Roberts.

Dr. I. M. Levitt, astronomer and director of Fels Planetarium in Philadelphia, gave a lecture to the Roanoke Executives Club on March 18 on the subject of the potential of space travel.

The new and enlarged Police Athletic League gymnasium opened on March 11 at 110 W. Church Avenue.

The Star City Club for the Deaf won the championship in the eleventh annual Southeast Athletic Association of the Deaf basketball tournament held in Roanoke with a 94–77 win over a team from Washington, DC. Top scorers for Roanoke were Owen Bass and Jack Yates.

A milestone for a Christian ministry for the deaf was marked on March 10 when Rev. Steve Mathis III conducted his deaf service at St. John's Episcopal Church in Roanoke on the fifth anniversary of the ministry. Mathis had deaf parishes in Roanoke, Bristol, Lynchburg, and Staunton.

Comic Derwood Kirby portrayed "Jennifer Adams," a member of the Roanoke Garden Club, on the nationally televised *The Garry Moore Show* on March 11. The skit had Kirby dressed in feminine attire and portray a woman from Roanoke.

Robert Spessard and Carroll Rea were named by Roanoke City Council on March 11 as substitute Municipal Court judges. At the same meeting, the council appropriated over $50,000 for improvements to Maher Field which included construction of a concrete pedestrian bridge and concrete floor beneath the west stands of Victory Stadium and the installation of a lighting system under the west stands.

Rusco Window Company opened its new downtown Roanoke showroom at First Street and Church Avenue SW on March 12.

The Roanoke County School Board adopted a $3.8 million building program that called for the construction of four new schools and additions to nine. The new schools included a new high school on the north side of the county and elementary schools at Oak Grove, Vinton, and Glenvar. The school in Vinton was to replace the four-room school on Craig Avenue.

Nelson Hardware officially reopened as a wholesaler on March 13 in its new space at 901 Eleventh Street NE, having moved from its retail space at 17 E. Campbell Avenue.

The Roanoke Chamber of Commerce unveiled plans on March 12 for a half-million-dollar technical institute in the Roanoke Valley. The school would be financed by local industry, Virginia Tech, and the state. The institute would offer a two-year course of study. The effort was being chaired by Roy Herrenkohl.

Homelite, a chain saw manufacturer, opened a branch store in Roanoke on March 12 at 3012 Angell Avenue NW. R. W. Wood was the manager.

Garland's Drug Store formally opened at Eleventh Street and Moorman Avenue NW on March 15.

Actor and future President Ronald Reagan (center) talks with officials at WDBJ television during his March 1957 visit to the Roanoke Valley. *WDBJ7*

This 1957 image shows the General Electric plant located at 1531 Roanoke Boulevard near Salem. The construction of the plant was the largest economic development announcement in the valley in the 1950s. *Virginia Room, RPL*

Actor and future President Ronald Reagan came to Roanoke on March 14 in his role as a spokesman for General Electric. He appeared on two local television programs with WDBJ on March 15, *Panorama* hosted by Ann Howard and the *6 O'Clock Show* with Irv Sharp. On the latter, Roanoke Mayor Walter Young presented Reagan the key to the city. At the time, Reagan was mayor of a city in California. While in Roanoke, Reagan visited the GE plant near Salem and made an appearance at a Soap Box Derby meeting held in the auditorium of the Times-World building. He began his day on March 15 with a press breakfast at the Hotel Roanoke where he recognized local reporter Melville Carico, with whom he had served in the same army unit during World War II. Reagan also made an afternoon visit to the Veterans Administration Hospital. He concluded his daylong visit with an appearance at the National Secretaries Association workshop at the Patrick Henry Hotel. The *Roanoke Times* reported that at the workshop, Reagan "had the apparently pleasant sensation of being engulfed by swarms of women."

Monterey Golf Club officially closed as a public course on March 15 due to its lease-purchase by the Mountain View Country Club. It was the only public course in the Roanoke Valley. The closure prompted area golfers who were not members of country clubs to launch a search for a site for a new public course to be developed. Jubal Angell headed the group.

Leonard Electronics opened at 405 Shenandoah Avenue NW on March 15.

The Roanoke Science Fair was held on March 16, and some 10,000 persons attended the event that had displays by over 250 area high school and junior high school students.

The Student Assignment Plan was developed by Virginia Governor Thomas Stanley and adopted by the Virginia General Assembly as a means to circumvent the US Supreme Court decision regarding integration went into effect in Roanoke city the second week in March. Pupils entering school for the first time, those graduating from one school to another in the same school division, and those transferring into the school division from outside had to go through the SAP process.

Members of Grandin Court Baptist Church posed for this 1955 image during the groundbreaking for their education building, which was completed in March 1956. *Grandin Court Baptist Church*

Allied Sales Company moved into its new building at 2480 Patterson Avenue SW in mid-March.

Grandin Court Baptist Church dedicated its new education building on March 17. The structure had thirty-six classrooms and a sanctuary with seating capacity of 500. It was the second of three buildings planned for the church.

The Junior Achievement Organizational Committee was formed on March 18 to spearhead the effort among local businessmen to form JA throughout the Roanoke Valley. Harry Rosenbaum was elected chairman of the committee.

The Polack Brothers Circus, sponsored by the Kazim Shrine Temple, came to the American Legion Auditorium for three days beginning March 21.

Hundreds gathered in downtown Roanoke to watch a crane lift a five-ton Trane air conditioning compressor on to the top of the new Miller & Rhoads building on March 20.

Clara Black, a longtime director of children's plays in Roanoke, was named as the promotion director for the Roanoke Valley Drama Association. The association was preparing for the debut of its outdoor drama *Thy Kingdom Come*.

Roanoker and Virginia's Attorney General Lindsay Almond officially announced his candidacy to seek the Democratic nomination for governor in the July 9 primary. Almond filed on March 21 and made keeping segregation in public schools a key campaign platform.

The Comas Machine Company in Salem announced on March 21 that it was going out of business in early June. The firm was known for making coin-operated cigarette machines. The company was located at 525 College Avenue. J. W. Burress was company president.

O. Winston Link won the top prize in the national 1957 Graflex photo contest for his image of an N&W Railway mallet locomotive pulling freight through Luray at night. For the image, Link used 36 flashbulbs and one-third of a mile of wire to capture the right effect after two days of test shots. The image was taken on March 23, 1956, with a Graflex View Camera.

Taylor Hardware opened at 410 Twenty-Sixth Street in South Roanoke on March 22.

Evans Evans of Roanoke County, and a student at Yale University, made her national television network debut on March 25 on *Robert Montgomery Presents*. Evans had acted locally with and was a charter member of Showtimers.

The Cardinal Inn restaurant opened on March 24 on Kessler Mill Road.

The Roanoke Academy of Medicine launched a campaign to end polio in the Roanoke Valley by concentrating on the inoculation with the Salk vaccine of all persons under the age of forty. Dr. Louis Ripley headed the effort.

Graham-White Manufacturing announced on March 23 plans for a new $200,000 foundry on Colorado Street in Salem.

Roanoke Diamond Jubilee moved its headquarters from the main library in Elmwood Park to the former site of the S&W Cafeteria at 412 S. Jefferson Street on April 1.

Bush & Hancock, a clothing store, announced on March 24 it was going out of business. The store, located at 106 W. Campbell Avenue, had been in business for almost fifty years.

The Vinton Lions Club held their annual three-night minstrel show the last weekend in March. The interlocutor was Thomas Hill.

Auto Seat Covers Center opened on March 25 at 712 Patterson Avenue SW at the former site of Owens Seat Cover Shop. The owner was Bob Fisher.

Cook's Apparel Shop announced on March 25 it was closing its downtown store at 304 First Street. The clothier also had a shop on Grandin Road that was to remain open.

The US Supreme Court on March 25 refused to review the conviction of Frank Snider for the rape of a nine-year-old Roanoke girl on Mother's Day in 1956. Snider had been sentenced to death in the electric chair.

Moser Furniture Company announced on March 25 that it was closing its showroom at 3326 Williamson Road.

Hollins College opened its new indoor riding rink and stables associated with its equestrian program. Hollins began its equestrian activities in 1929. Countess Judith Gyurky was the riding instructor.

Three Pittsburgh area businessmen returning home from vacation in Havana, Cuba, were killed on March 26 when their private plane crashed at Woodrum Field. The crash was witnessed by many at the airport, who watched in horror as the plane plunged nose-first into the ground at the north end of the airport. Before crashing, the plane barely missed a Piedmont Airlines plane waiting to take off. The pilots of the Piedmont craft rushed to the burning Beechcraft Bonanza with fire extinguishers but could not save the men.

Charcoal Steak House opened on March 27 at 5225 Williamson Road. The restaurant held a formal grand opening on April 12. The owners were James Poulus and George Holevas.

B. F. Goodrich Company held a formal grand opening at 1409 Williamson Road on March 28. The store sold tires, car parts, and appliances. The store had already been in business for a few weeks.

Franklin Moore, sixty-five, died on March 28 at the University of Virginia Hospital. Moore was president of Walker Machine and Foundry Corporation, a post he had held since 1921. He had also served as president of the board of Stone Printing and Manufacturing Company.

The Bulldogs, composed of members of the Addison High School varsity team, won the Negro Division of the Gold Medal basketball tournament in late March. Team members were Arthur Brown, Jimmie Penn, Snake Robinson, Norman Brower, William Barnes, Raymond Perry, Fred Miller, Robert Clark, Wilbur Boyd, and James Prunty.

About 250 golfers who were not members of country clubs met on March 29 at Preston Park School and voted to form the Blue Hills Golf Association with each agreeing to buy stock in the association for twenty-five dollars per share. The association planned to lease the former Blue Hills Golf Club from Clem Johnston. It was estimated that $30,000 would be needed to make the course ready for play.

Gold Seal Window Company opened at its new location at 2308 Melrose Avenue NW on March 30. G. M. Belcher was the manager.

J. C. Penney Company officials announced on March 30 plans for a department store in the thirty-acre Roanoke-Salem Shopping Center being developed on Melrose Avenue NW. It was the first store for the company in the Roanoke market and was the first to publicly announce its plans to locate in the shopping center.

Rose's, a department store chain, opened at Wayne and Wilkins Streets NW near Sears Town on April 4. The 18,000 square-foot store was the first Rose's in the Roanoke area. R. L. Samuel was the manager.

Tryouts for *Thy Kingdom Come* concluded at the end of March with over one hundred persons seeking roles. The cast would number fifty, and some who auditioned came from as far away as New York. Rehearsals were set to begin in early June.

The Starlite Motor Court opened at the end of March on Route 117 midway between Roanoke and Salem.

Carleton Drewry had another book of poetry published. *Cloud Above Clocktime* was published by Dutton, headquartered in New York City. It was Drewry's fifth book of verse. The poet worked for N&W Railway.

Airman First Class Ronald Harris, twenty, was killed instantly when his car was struck by the *Powhatan Arrow* of N&W Railway at a grade crossing near Thaxton on April 1.

Mountain Trust Bank officials announced in early April that a building dating to 1889 at the corner of Church Avenue and First Street SW would be razed to make room for a parking lot. The structure was erected by Tipton Fishburn for the Bridgewater Carriage Company which moved to Norwich in 1891. After that, various businesses occupied the building.

Seen here is Lendy's Big Boy restaurant, which was located on Apperson Drive near the intersection with Electric Road. Note the disc jockey studio on the roof. *Cathy Joyner*

Group Food Plan opened at its new location at 1941 Franklin Road on April 2.

J. D. Altizer and H. C. Altizer purchased the Steak and Shake Drive-In in West Salem for $20,000 in early April. They had been operating the restaurant for four years.

The casting for the lead roles in the outdoor drama *Thy Kingdom Come* were announced by the director Dean Goodsell on April 2 after an extensive tryout period. Bristow Hardin Jr., Leroy McFarland, Dave Lee, James Gearheart, Haddon Dudley, and Larry Cooper, all of Roanoke, were given main parts in the play. The lead character of the Apostle Paul was to be played by Carl Clarke, of Kernersville, North Carolina.

The thirtieth annual spring congress of Gill Memorial Hospital was held the first week in April. Hundreds of physicians and specialists in eye, ear, nose, and throat treatments and surgeries attended. One of the highlights was the closed circuit telecast of Dr. E. G. Gill performing a cataract extraction on an elderly patient. Gill was assisted by Dr. Ronald Harris. It was believed to be the first such telecast in Roanoke.

Rev. William Moore, pastor of Mount Moriah Baptist Church and Morning Star Baptist Church, died on April 3 at his home.

N&W Railway released its annual report for 1956 in early April and reported record highs. Net income was $42,486, 857, while gross income was $254,213,103. N&W also handled the greatest freight volume in its history, $225 million. Coal traffic as well as noncoal traffic also set record amounts. The only decline in any category was in passenger service, down 5 percent.

The Roanoke County School Board announced on April 4 that its offer to purchase the Comas Machine Company building across from Andrew Lewis High School had been accepted. The purchase price was $80,000.

Maple Hardware opened on Route 220 on April 5. It was located adjacent to the Maple Restaurant and Tourist Court a half-mile south of Roanoke.

A group of over thirty British citizens came to Roanoke on April 5 as part of their country's goodwill mission tour of the United States. The delegation was hosted at a dinner at the Hotel Roanoke. The head of the group was Viscount Hailsham and Sir Denys Lawson.

A Multiple Sclerosis Telerama was broadcast live by WDBJ-TV from the American Legion Auditorium on April 7. The sixteen-hour program included live entertainment by nationally known performers George DeWitt, Mr. Green Jeans, Carmel Quinn, Roger Coleman, and Buff Cobb. The broadcast also featured a large number of local entertainers in front of a live audience. The event raised over $40,000.

Shirley and Lee, along with Roland Cook and his orchestra, performed at the Star City Auditorium on April 6.

Italian Spaghetti House, across from Lakeside, celebrated its first anniversary in early April.

A Virginian Railway freight train hit a rockslide about thirty miles east of Roanoke on April 6, derailing forty cars. Two crewmen were injured, and two diesel locomotives were smashed.

Donald Drewery, a teenager, of Vinton was killed in an auto accident near Bonsack on Route 460 on April 6. Two others were seriously injured, Donald Wheeler and Ray Lawhorn.

Kroger opened a new grocery store adjacent to Sears Town on Williamson Road on April 9. It was the third-largest in the Kroger chain of 1,500 stores. Dick Crowder was the manager.

Showtimers presented *Don Juan In Hell* the second week in April. The lead roles were played by Francis Ballard, Robert Niemyer, Bristow Hardin, and Lois Langley. Elizabeth Ross was the director.

Tanya Taylor, age six, of Roanoke was killed on April 9 when she was struck by a truck on Luck Avenue SE. She and her sister darted between two parked cars in front of the oncoming truck.

Kaybee Credit Clothing Store opened on April 12 at 27 W. Church Avenue. The company was headquartered in New York.

Peoples Service Drug Store opened its newest store on April 12 near Sears Town on Williamson Road at 112 Wayne Street NW. T. A. Abbott was the manager. It was the third Peoples in the city, with the other two being at 33 W. Campbell Avenue and 601 S. Jefferson Street.

A group of local talent advertised they would perform every Saturday night on the stage of the American Legion Auditorium beginning April 13. The group consisted of Don Reno, Red Smiley, Irv Sharp, the Tennessee Cut Ups, Joe Vernon, Mac Magaha, John Palmer, Ronnie Reno, and the Webster Brothers. Special guests for the April 13 show were the Stanley Brothers and the Clinch Mountain Boys.

The Roanoke Redevelopment and Housing Authority reported that the Commonwealth Project that was redeveloping much of northeast Roanoke was expected to be completed by December 1958. The project encompassed eighty-three acres. The housing authority report stated 425 of 485 families had been relocated, most of them Black, and that the authority had taken titles to 483 pieces of property out of 524.

A large plank summer cabin, part of the landmark Fort Lewis estate, went up in flames on April 11. A crowd of several hundred gathered to watch the blaze. The cabin, a landmark itself, was set some 200 yards east of the site of the former mansion.

A contract was signed on April 12 with G. A. Traham Company of Cohoes, New York, to decorate business buildings, downtown streets, and highways for Roanoke's Diamond Jubilee scheduled for June 14–23.

The Covenant Presbyterian Church was formally organized on April 14 during a meeting at Cave Spring High School. The congregation had been meeting for about two months.

Diamond Jubilee officials announced on April 13 that a racially mixed chorus composed of church and school choirs would be formed and sing at Jubilee events, notably the religious service at Victory Stadium and the Festival of Music. The chorus was being organized by the Jubilee's Historical Pageant Music Committee chaired by Mrs. R. H. Ligon and Mrs. Helen Robertson.

Television actor John Hart, who played the character Hawkeye in the CBS series *Last of the Mohicans*, came to Roanoke April 16 and 17. He made numerous appearances on local television shows associated with WDBJ and addressed the Optimist Club.

Over 15,000 attended the "Good Neighbor Day" open house at the General Electric plant on April 13. It was the first public open house since the plant opened.

Miller & Rhoads opened a business and credit office at 115 W. Church Avenue in mid-April.

The 1957 racing season opened at the Starkey Racing Grounds on Easter Sunday, April 21, with two features, a 30-lap sportsman race and a twenty-lap amateurs' race.

Curtis Turner won the one-hundred-mile National Championship NASCAR race for late-model convertibles in Greenville, South Carolina, on April 13.

Little Richard performed for an Easter midnight dance and show at the American Legion Auditorium.

Roanoke City Council rejected a proposal that the federal government acquire a parcel of the Shrine Hill property for the location of a branch post office. The government had approached the city in an effort to find a new location for the Grandin Road station.

Hunter Cigar Store opened in its new location at 136 W. Campbell Avenue on April 17, which was directly across the street from its former location. The store also served breakfast and lunch.

A fox terrier was judged Best in Show at the twenty-second annual all-breed dog show of the Roanoke Kennel Club on April 16. The owner was Albert Welty of Short Creek, West Virginia. The event was held at the Merchants Parking Center and had a field of 255 dogs.

David Huddleston, twenty-six, of Vinton was given the role of Barnabas in the upcoming production of *Thy Kingdom Come* to be performed as an outdoor drama at Sherwood Burial Park. Huddleston was one of the last cast members named. At the time he was a student at the American Academy of Dramatic Arts in New York City.

Some 200 Roanokers gathered on April 18 at Addison High School and Lee Junior High School to organize some eighty "Diamond Dandy" chapters throughout the city in connection with the Diamond Jubilee. The chapters' main purpose would be to promote fun and the city's celebration—and growing beards. Mayor Walter Young had issued a proclamation making it "illegal" for men to shave. Women's organizations would also be organized and called "Jubilee Belles."

Roanoke postal officials announced on April 18 that a special cancellation stamp advertising the Diamond Jubilee would be used by the Roanoke post office from April 26 through June 23.

Enon Baptist Church at Hollins occupied its new educational building on April 21. The $84,000 structure contained six assembly rooms and twenty-one classrooms. J. H. Fralin was the contractor.

This 1950s studio photo shows Dudley Townsend (center at podium) with some of the local participants on an episode of *Saturday Session*. *WDBJ7*

More than 37,000 trees containing nearly five million board feet of timber were marked for cutting on the city-owned Beaver Dam and Falling Creek reservoirs to be sold in the summer.

Shopwell Food Stores announced on April 19 that it was opening its Family Stamps redemption store at 401 W. Campbell Avenue. At the same time, the grocery chain advertised that Young's Super Market on Melrose Avenue NW had become a Shopwell Food Store.

The WDBJ-TV local program *Saturday Session* with Dudley Townsend celebrated its first anniversary with a special broadcast on April 20. The show featured local entertainers Nancy King, the Dreamers, Loretta Hundley, and Jo Robertson.

Jimmy's Pitch and Putt Golf Course on Lee Highway opened for the season on April 20.

Sonny Baxter, age three, of Vinton drowned in Tinker Creek on April 20.

Nearly 12,000 Roanoke city schoolchildren and parents were given the Salk polio vaccine as part of the city's participation in the Roanoke Valley Polio Eradication campaign during the third week in April.

The Roanoke Lions Club announced on April 20 it was embarking to raise $10,000 for an eye bank in Western Virginia, the first in the state.

Roanoke's newest radio station, WRKE, went on the air on April 22. It was located at 910 on the radio dial and headquartered in the American Theatre Building. Associated with the station were Johnny Miles, Ron Lindamood, Tom Wade, Sid Tear, Charlie Grant, Ray Mills, and Glen McClellan. The station was owned and operated by Radio Roanoke, of which Elmore Heins was president. It was the sixth station in the Roanoke Valley.

The Thursday Morning Music Club presented its final concert of the 1956–57 Diamond Jubilee series with a performance by pianist Richard Cabb and baritone Miles Nekolny on April 24 at the American Legion Auditorium.

William Dodson, forty-four and a patient at the Veterans Administration Hospital, was struck and killed by an N&W Railway train along the tracks near the rear of the hospital campus. The medical examiner concluded the death was self-inflicted. Dodson was from Blackstone.

The Roanoke Executives Club disclosed on April 21 that it was folding due to a decline in membership. The club had been in Roanoke for seventeen years. At its height, it had 200 members, but only fifty-eight had signed on for the coming year.

Over 18,000 attended the eleventh annual Easter sunrise service at Natural Bridge. The sermon was delivered by Rev. Bob Richards, a former Olympian. The service was broadcast nationally over the CBS radio network.

Curtis Turner won the 150-lap NASCAR convertible race at Hickory, North Carolina, on April 21.

The historical pageant to be presented at Victory Stadium during the Diamond Jubilee was to be known as *The Rising Star*. The name was selected by a committee from among 250 submissions. The winning title was submitted by Miss Una Carter.

Charles Kelly, forty-three, of Vinton died in a doctor's office on April 22. Kelly was the "Santa Claus" on the N&W Railway train that ran each holiday from Norfolk to Cincinnati.

Curtis Turner (inside car) is seen with Bill France in this undated image. Both did much to promote auto racing in the Roanoke Valley and throughout the South. *Pee Wee Ellwanger Collection*

Grand Ole Opry comics Cousin Jody and Odie performed at Reno and Smiley's *Country Music Show* at the American Legion Auditorium on April 27.

The local cast of *Club 88* that aired on Monday evenings on WSLS-TV was profiled in the Roanoke Times on April 27. They were Andy Petersen, emcee, and the members of the Leonard Trio—Thornton Marshall, Gordon Reid, and Roy Lemon.

William Poff, sixty, collapsed with a heart attack in the vestibule of Ninth Street Church of the Brethren on April 27 minutes before he was to escort his daughter down the aisle at her wedding. He died minutes later. The wedding went forward with the bride's uncle stepping for her father, and only after the abbreviated ceremony did family and guests learn the heart attack was fatal.

A&P Super Market opened on April 30 on Melrose Avenue at Peters Creek Road NW.

The Clyde Beatty Circus came to Roanoke on April 29 and gave two performances at Maher Field. The shows were sponsored by the Roanoke Exchange Club. The circus had 600 employees, with 150 being performers and 200 animals.

Talk of the Town, a local radio program sponsored by the Roanoke Chamber of Commerce, first aired on April 28 on WDBJ. The weeknight show combined music with announcements of local events and business updates.

The formation of a fifth country club in the valley was announced on April 27. The new club, Jefferson Hills Golf Club with a nine-hole course, was to be located on the farm of Edgar Jamison just south of Roanoke along Colonial Avenue. Henry Moore was heading the effort. The club's target membership was 250.

Hugh Painter of Andrew Lewis High School was awarded the 1957 B'nai B'rith Athletic Achievement Award on April 27. Painter was on the football and track teams of the high school.

A professional tennis exhibition match between Ken Rosewall and Pancho Gonzales was held on May 1 at the American Legion Auditorium. The exhibition matches had been organized by Jack Kramer and were touring the United States in an effort to promote the sport. Other pro tennis players that participated in the exhibition were Pancho Segura and Dinny Pails.

Anabel Pence of Roanoke had a book of poetry, *This Time Tomorrow*, published by Dietz Press of Richmond. Pence was president of the Roanoke Poetry Society.

A severe thunderstorm passed through Roanoke on April 28, damaging buildings and causing flash floods. Fifth Avenue Presbyterian Church at 301 Patton Avenue NW was struck by lightning, causing the steeple to catch fire. The Ponce de Leon Hotel was also struck and bits of masonry flew into the street.

Cave Spring High School was formally dedicated on April 28 to the "service of mankind and the glory of God" by state superintendent of public instruction Dr. Davis Paschall. More than 450 persons attended the event held in the school's auditorium. The service of dedication was led by Rev. Tom Toler of Haran Baptist Church. The school cost $831,000.

Three bus routes between Roanoke and Salem were leased by the Safety Motor Transit Corporation to Pendleton Bus Lines on May 1 due to low ridership.

Salem voters approved a $470,000 bond issue for water improvements by a 9 to 1 margin in a referendum held on April 30. Only 649 voters cast a ballot.

Roanoke soprano Jane Stuart Smith performed in Roanoke, the first in several years, at the Virginia Federation of Women's Clubs convention at the Hotel Roanoke on April 30. She drew thunderous applause according to reviews.

The Valley Baptist Association voted on April 30 to split into two groups. Montgomery, Giles and Pulaski Counties would become the new western division, while churches in Roanoke, Craig, and Botetourt Counties would remain as the Valley Baptist Association.

The Jubilee Belles held an organizational meeting on April 30 in preparation of celebrating Roanoke's Diamond Jubilee. The Belles decided that no woman should be allowed to wear makeup unless they had a "cosmetic permit," which was a cameo worn around the neck on black ribbon. This was to honor "pioneer great-grandmothers of yore," similar to the men growing beards to honor great-grandfathers.

Academy Award–winning actor and WWII double-amputee Harold Russell addressed the Virginia women's clubs convention at the Hotel Roanoke on April 30. His talk was preceded by the presentation of a $3,000 check from the organization to help fund Camp Easter Seals in Craig County.

This mid-1950s image shows Reid and Cutshall Furniture, which was located at 309 Campbell Avenue SW. *Virginia Room, RPL*

Reid and Cutshall furniture store began their closeout sale at their store at 309 W. Campbell Avenue on May 1 in preparation for their relocation in early June to Campbell Avenue at Third Street SW.

Fink's Jewelers won the Number 1 Certificate of Distinction in the National Brand Names Award Jewelry Division in early May, the first such winner in Virginia. Nathan Fink and his family came to Roanoke from Selma, Alabama, in 1929, in Fink's capacity as a manager and partner of the LeGrand Jewelry Company at 121 S. Jefferson Street. In August 1930, Fink opened his own business at 103 W. Campbell Avenue with three employees. The store was eleven by sixty feet. Later that year, LeGrand moved his business to Atlanta, and Fink moved to the vacated store on Jefferson Street. In 1947, Fink's relocated to 310 S. Jefferson Street.

Roanoke's Community Fund voted on May 1 to back the proposed United Fund and to help establish the broader charity appeal effort.

Kingston Mill Carpet Center opened at 501 Thirteenth Street SWs on May 2. Henry Seay was the manager.

An old steel smokestack, once used at the twine mill in Norwich, was razed on May 1.

Ground-breaking ceremonies were held on May 3 at Camp Easter Seals in Craig County. Monroe Bush, assistant to the president of the Old Dominion Foundation, was the main speaker. The $112,000 camp was on fifty-six acres.

Stars of the *Grand Ole Opry* performed at the American Legion Auditorium on May 5. The show included Hank Snow, Jim Reeves and his Wagon Masters, the Rainbo Ranch Boys, and comedian Sleepy McDaniel.

Vinton held its second annual Dogwood Festival on the first weekend in May. Mitzi McAlexander of Cave Spring High School was crowned Dogwood Queen in ceremonies at William Byrd High School following a parade.

Six women were selected by the Roanoke Merchants Association as Mothers of the Year in various fields. They were Louise Hale (community affairs), Regina Stutts (family life), Betty Bond (business and professions), Mrs. Roy Webber (religious activities), Nancy Rankin (education), and Mrs. Harry Dixon (arts and sciences).

The Virginia Amateur baseball League began its season the first weekend in May. Teams were Pembroke, Glenvar, Salem, Blacksburg, Back Creek, and Catawba.

Curtis Turner set a new 150-mile Grand National convertible stock car record at Langhorne, Pennsylvania, on May 5 with a start-to-finish win time of 1 hour, 45 minutes, and 35 seconds.

The first use of a mobile clinic in the Roanoke Valley Polio Eradication Campaign was used on May 6 at the new Miller & Rhoads building site on Campbell Avenue. The clinic immunized 115 who came to the clinic housed in a tractor trailer provided by Mundy Motor Lines.

Color advertising appeared for the first time in the *Roanoke Times* on May 7. It was a green and black ad for Heironimus.

Government agents who raided a house containing a very large distillery on Sugar Loaf Mountain were justified in doing so without a search warrant was the May 6 ruling in US District Court. The house and ninety acres were seized by the government and scheduled to be auctioned off at the end of May. Three men were charged in connection with operating the illegal still—Theodore Smith, Ulysses Snead, and Howard Easter.

Lakeside Park opened for the season on May 10. Ads from owner H. L. Roberts read, "This is not a public park and is not licensed as such. Drunks and those with jail records are warned not to trespass."

Some 600 young women attended a meeting on May 8 at the Hotel Roanoke to learn details about the Miss Jubilee contest as part of the Diamond Jubilee celebration. They were told that the winner would be chosen on the basis of "beauty, poise, charm, public spirit, and the number of tickets to *The Rising Star* pageant that are sold on her behalf."

A subsidiary of Miller & Rhoads was chartered by the SCC on May 9 to conduct business in Roanoke specializing in men's clothing. The name of the new firm was Stevens-Shepherd of Roanoke.

Alice's Beauty School opened on May 15 at 421 Campbell Avenue.

The Police Athletic League box team opened its season with an 8–0 win over combined teams from Washington, DC, and Chatham. It was the eleventh straight win for the team. The matches were held on May 9 at the American Legion Auditorium before a crowd of 1,600.

Roanoke Vice Mayor W. B. Carter died on May 10 in a Roanoke hospital at the age of seventy. At the time of his death, he was the managing director of Roanoke's Diamond Jubilee program. Carter served as a member of Roanoke City

Council from 1940 to 1948 and was elected to the council again in June 1956. He was involved in numerous civic organizations and was a retiree of N&W Railway.

The Diamond Jubilee Kangaroo Court's Keystone Cops Corps began patrolling downtown Roanoke on May 10 looking for men with clean-shaven faces in violation of the mayoral edict that made shaving "illegal." Howard Hale served as judge, Hassie Hale as prosecuting attorney, and Richard Echols as defense attorney.

The PBX Receptionist School, affiliated with the Switchboard School, opened on May 16 for classes to train adults in switchboards, typing, and reception etiquette. The school was located in the Peoples Federal Building.

Traveltown Amusement Park opened for the season on May 16 with a pool, merry-go-round, miniature golf, and children's rides. The park was located on Route 11 near Cloverdale.

Art Barber Shop opened at its new location, 7 E. Campbell Avenue, on May 16.

Mary Doyle of William Fleming High School placed fourth in the girls' biological science division of the National Science Fair held in Los Angeles, California, on May 11.

This 1950s postcard shows a portion of Traveltown, which was located on Route 11 at Cloverdale. *Bob Stauffer*

Morton Rosenberg and Malcolm Rosenberg announced on May 11 the formation of the Oak Hall Cap and Gown Company. The company was an outgrowth of Oak Hall that rented caps and gowns to schools and colleges. The new company would continue to do rentals but would also do manufacturing of academic regalia and choir robes. The company was located at 116 W. Salem Avenue.

The fifth annual fishing rodeo was held at Lakewood Park on May 11 with over 2,000 youngsters participating. The pond had been stocked with 1,000 trout for the event which was sponsored by the Blue Ridge Game and Fish Club headed by Gerald Cannaday.

Eddie Moylan, the fourth-ranked pro tennis player in the United States, held a tennis clinic at South Roanoke Park on May 13 for free. The program was sponsored by the Roanoke Valley Tennis Association along with the Wilson Sporting Goods Company. Moylan had also been a former member of the US Davis Cup Team.

The Roanoke Bridle Club held its tenth annual horse show at Hidden Valley the second weekend in May. Nearly one hundred horses were entered in twenty-six classes. Sue Provost of Hollins College was the main winner with three first place finishes. Keith Swain served as ringmaster.

The Roanoke Symphony Orchestra presented its final concert of the '56–'57 Season on May 13 at the American Theatre. Judith Justice of Hollins College was featured as a solo violinist. The symphony presented the American debut of Dutch composer Jurrian Andriessen's *Symphonie Concertante*. To honor the occasion, Max Tak, executive secretary of the Committee for Netherlands Music, attended the concert.

Clarence King was appointed the golf pro at Blue Hills Golf Club on May 14.

The Birmingham (AL) Black Barons played the Roanoke Eagles in a semipro baseball game at Salem Municipal Field on May 16.

Richard Hayden, forty-four, of Roanoke died on May 14 in a jail in Hardy County, Florida, following a fight with local police.

Boy Scout Troop 21 of St. Mark's Lutheran Church purchased a thirty-five-acre camp site at Bent Mountain. The land was known as the Craighead farm and was located along the Roanoke-Montgomery County line seven miles northwest of Route 221.

Stedman's, a furniture and interior accents store, announced in mid-May that it was closing its downtown location at 13 W. Church Avenue on May 25.

Romain Lewis, age nine, of Roanoke was struck and killed on May 16 when a car jumped the curb and hit her while she was on the sidewalk near her home. Lewis died at Burrell Memorial Hospital.

Becky Lee was chosen as "Miss Roanoke County" on May 16 in a pageant held at Andrew Lewis High School. She thus qualified for the Miss Virginia pageant. Lee was employed by N&W Railway as a stenographer.

Jettsie Carico, seventeen, was instantly killed and five others injured in a two-car wreck in downtown Roanoke on May 18. The accident occurred at the intersection of Second Street and Salem Avenue SW. The force of the crash hurled both vehicles against the mechanical building of the Times-World Building. In one car were four high school students, and in the other car were Mr. and Mrs. James

Trinkle. All were taken to local hospitals. Carico was a senior at Jefferson High School. The students were returning from a banquet at Dixie Caverns. In addition to Carico, the other teenagers were Sandra Barker, Theodore Weld, and Howard Beamer.

Band leader Paul Whiteman stopped over in Roanoke on May 17 en route to the Martinsville Speedway to help promote stock car racing. While in Roanoke he appeared on local television programs.

Roanoke observed Armed Forces Day on May 18 with the dedication of the new Roanoke army reserve training center opposite the Veterans Administration Hospital. The armory was dedicated in memory of Pfc. Cloyse Hall, who was killed during World War II in Germany in 1945. Virginia Hall, the soldier's daughter, cut the ribbon. The day also included a parade through downtown Roanoke of various military reserve units and veteran organizations.

Queen Swimming Pool opened on May 18 on Route 11 west of Salem. The private pool was owned by J. D. Poff and W. A. Bohon.

A small plane crashed into the Roanoke River near the site of the Smith Mountain Dam construction on May 18. Mary Moss, twenty-one, of Washington, DC, was killed, while a young army officer, Second Lt. Raymond Hemmersmeir, was taken to a Danville hospital with serious injuries. Two men working at the dam site located Hemmersmeir downstream from the crash site and rescued him.

Roanoke Valley gained a new telephone service on May 19. Two letters were added to the digits they usually dialed, and long-distance calls could be made direct without using an operator. The new long-distance service was ceremoniously inaugurated in the valley when the mayors of Roanoke, Salem, and Vinton phoned Congressman Richard Poff at his home in Arlington.

Stevens-Shepherd of Roanoke announced on May 18 that it would take over the operation of Glenn's at 307 First Street SW. Glenn's would continue to operate until May 25. The store would then be remodeled and reopened as Stevens-Shepherd.

Cave Spring Baptist Church formally dedicated its new church on May 19. The church was organized in 1874. The main church building was completed in 1954 and the educational building in February 1957.

Hill Street Baptist Church held a special memorial service for its late pastor Rev. D. R. Powell, who served for the church for thirty-seven years, on May 19. The guest speaker for the occasion was the president of the Virginia State Baptist Convention, Dr. E. C. Smith.

Nearly 500 persons attended a religious liberty rally at Greene Memorial Methodist Church on May 19, sponsored by the local chapter of Protestants and Other Americans United for the Separation of Church and State. The main speaker decried denominations and churches that sought financial support from the government.

The Roanoke Valley Polio Eradication Campaign conducted what it termed "Operation Grand Slam" on May 21 when it set up nineteen clinics in the valley at fire stations. Over 2,500 got shots.

THE CAVE SPRING BAPTIST CHURCH AND PARSONAGE

LOCATED ON U.S. HIGHWAY 221, WEST OF ROANOKE, VIRGINIA

This 1950s postcard shows Cave Spring Baptist Church along Route 221. The house at left was the church's parsonage at the time. *Virginia Room, RPL*

A pedestrian bridge that linked South Roanoke Park with Maher Field at Victory Stadium was completed in mid-May. The bridge cost $25,000 and was done to enhance access and provide more parking for the stadium on the opposite side of the river.

A special song for the Diamond Jubilee was written and composed by G. V. Kromes. *Diamond Melody* was in four-four time, and several thousand copies were printed for distribution.

The Virginia AAU Golden Gloves tournament was held at the American Legion Auditorium on May 22. Roanoke's Police Athletic League boxers earned ten of the following titles: white novice class—Fred McLeod, Charley Masters, Ken Wilson, and George Tebrich; Negro novice class—David Crump; and Negro open class—Robert Carter, Jimmy Muse, and Louis Johnson. The PAL team won the team Golden Gloves title for the second year in a row.

Nu-Way Laundry and Dry Cleaners became Rasnake Laundry and Dry Cleaners on May 23. The business was located at 3756 Mt. Vernon Drive.

Operation of the Colonial Theatre in Salem changed hands on June 1. J. R. McLemore, owner of the Salem Theatre since 1940, took over the Colonial's lease from Harold Depkin. W. R. McCoy would manage both theatres beginning in June.

Enon Baptist Church at Hollins dedicated their new education building on May 26.

Ray-Phil's Swim Club, formerly the Lee-Hy Swim Club, opened for the season on May 25.

This 1957 image is of Oakey's Funeral Home on Church Avenue SW. *Oakey's Funeral Service*

The Pittsburgh Pirates organization named Larry Dorton as the manager of the Salem Rebels in the Class D Appalachian League. Dorton, twenty-eight, had played with other minor league clubs operated by the Pirates.

Windsor Beauty Salon, operated by Ocie Cralle and Dora Pucket, opened on May 26 at 2330 Grandin Road SW.

The owners of Logan's Barn, an antique store located on Route 11, authorized a complete liquidation of their inventory via an auction on June 4 as they were closing to engage in a different business.

At its meeting on May 27, Roanoke City Council voted to fill the vacancy created by the death of Councilman W. B. Carter by selecting Alan Decker. The council also named Councilman Vincent Wheeler as vice mayor, a post Carter held at the time of his death. Both votes were 4 to 2, with council members Benton Dillard and Mary Pickett dissenting. Decker was a retired insurance executive. Dillard and Pickett supported the appointment of Dr. C. M. Cornell to the council vacancy.

John Hart, the actor who played Hawkeye on the CBS network's *The Last of the Mohicans*, returned to Roanoke on June 1. The actor made a special appearance at the Children's Zoo and on local television programs for WDBJ.

The Indianapolis Clowns and the New York Black Yankees played an exhibition baseball game at Salem Municipal Field on May 29. Baseball clown Prince Jo

Henry entertained in the stands. The Clowns won, 14–2, before a crowd of 1,000 spectators.

Lloyd Price and his orchestra performed for a show and dance at the American Legion Auditorium on May 30.

The Cree-Mee Drive-In restaurant opened on May 29 located across from Lakeside at the Minnie Tour Golf Course.

Goodridge Wilson, whose column *The Southwest Corner* appeared regularly in the *Roanoke Times*, wrote about the history of settlements in and around Roanoke City in his column on June 2. "Shortly after the end of the War of 1812 an attempt was made to build locks and make the Roanoke River navigable from Weldon, NC, to Salem, and to make Tinker Creek navigable from its mouth to where it crossed the Lynchburg Road. A city was projected at the head of the navigation on Tinker Creek to be called Prestonville, but it disappeared like the colony of Roanoke Island. Later another town was started near a favorite covered wagon camp ground and stage coach stop, and also near the salt marsh called the 'Big Lick.' It was called Gainesboro after a man named Kemp Gaines who owned the land that was offered as lots. It was also called Big Lick. When the Virginia and Tennessee Railroad came in 1852 the depot was located a half mile or more from the little settlement known as Gainesboro or Big Lick, and the village that started up around the depot and the old Stover home, that stood where the Ponce de Leon Hotel is now, came to be known as Big Lick."

Peters Creek Church of the Brethren broke ground on a new $88,000 sanctuary in early June. The former sanctuary was to be converted to a Fellowship Hall.

Mary Jean Neal, fourteen, of Roanoke was killed in an auto accident on June 1 west of Salem. She was the daughter of John Neal, principal of Fort Lewis Elementary School.

Ray's Garage opened on June 3 at Ray's Auto Sales on Route 24, a mile east of Vinton.

Bracken Lee, the former governor of Utah, spoke at the Hotel Roanoke on June 4 on repealing the federal income tax. Lee's speech was sponsored by the Constitution Party of Virginia's Congressional Sixth District.

WDBJ-TV aired for the first time in Roanoke on June 8 a live broadcast of professional wrestling staged in its studio. The Saturday night match featured Chief Billy Two Rivers, a nationally known wrestling personality. Most of the wrestlers who would appear in future Saturday night matches were normally part of the line up of the Tuesday night professional wrestling at the American Legion Auditorium.

Perry Cunningham opened Perry's Barber Shop at 1503 Williamson Road on June 3.

Daniel Feeney, forty, perished in an apartment house fire at 1510 Franklin Road SW on June 4. A neighbor, William Hopkins, tried unsuccessfully to rescue the man before firefighters could arrive.

Mick-or-Mack opened its newest grocery store on Melrose Avenue at Peters Creek Road on June 6.

A new execution date for convicted rapist Frank Snider Jr. was set for July 9 by Judge Dirk Kuyk on a ruling on June 5. Snider had exhausted all his appeals.

Roanoke Trunk Company, located at 19 W. Church Avenue, advertised on June 6 that it was going out of business. The store sold luggage, briefcases, and travel accessories.

Night Trick, a booklet of night railroad photographs, was published by N&W Railway. It contained eighteen pictures of nighttime steam locomotive operations, all taken by O. Winston Link. Link was a New York industrial photographer.

Millard Townsend was honored as Roanoke's Father of the Year by the Junior Chamber of Commerce. Townsend, fifty-five, was the personnel director at S. H. Heironimus and a resident of Roanoke County. He was commended for his work with disabled children.

Attorney Belford Lawson was the speaker at the graduation ceremony for Addison High School on June 6. Lawson was a graduate of Roanoke schools who went on to attend Harvard and Yale law schools. Lawson denounced segregation and encouraged the 127 graduates to not be content with the ordinary.

Cave Spring High School held its first graduation on June 6 with twenty-one receiving diplomas.

Bill Miller of Lee Junior High School won the city-county marbles tournament on June 6. Coming in second was Gary Conner. Miller earned a trip to the national tournament in Akron, Ohio.

A dozen parents in Roanoke refused to return signed pupil placement application forms that were required by state law, a first for the city. The state forms were largely intended to thwart desegregation, but the parents indicated their refusal had little to do with integration of the schools. Instead, their action was to protest the school board's decision to transfer seventh graders from Oakland School to Lee Junior High School.

Barbara Boitnott of Boones Mill was named "Miss Diamond Jubilee" on June 8. Sharing in court honors was Mrs. Edwina Wertz, who was "Miss Shenandoah Valley." The two were selected from a field of more than 150 contestants and twenty-four finalists. Boitnott was awarded a free trip for two to Hollywood, while Wertz received a free trip to New York City.

The Sunday, June 9, edition of the *Roanoke Times* was the largest in its history. It had 170 pages and weighed over two pounds. Swelling the size was an eighty-four-page Diamond Jubilee supplement.

Stevens-Shepherd, a men's clothing store, held its formal opening on June 10 at 307 First Street. James Foreman was the store manager.

The Roanoke Fine Arts Center held a Jubilee exhibit that showcased the works of the late Allan Ingles Palmer. The show consisted of twenty-four watercolors by Palmer and was held in the Roanoke Public Library Auditorium.

Another meeting aimed at launching a Junior Achievement program in Roanoke was held on June 10 at the Appalachian Auditorium with nearly 200 businessmen in attendance. Harry Rosenbaum was chairing the steering committee, and the main speaker was R. H. Smith, president of N&W Railway.

Kermit Ball of Salem placed second in the Southern Marbles Tournament held in Greensboro, North Carolina, on June 9.

Barbara Boitnott was crowned Miss Diamond Jubilee for Roanoke's celebration in 1957, winning a trip to Hollywood, California. *Nelson Harris*

A brief history of bowling in the Roanoke Valley appeared in the June 9 *Roanoke Times*. According to the article, a primitive version of bowling first came to Roanoke in the late 1890s and was usually found at the back of saloons, typically just four lanes. The Monarch, a saloon, had the first known true bowling alleys. There were early bowling lanes at Mountain Park in South Roanoke which opened in 1904. The Palace opened in June 1914 with seven lanes, adjacent to the old

Rialto Theatre. In 1927, the twenty-five-lane Health Center on West Campbell Avenue opened but closed in 1932, having been operated by Charlie Harris. In 1939, E. W. Shinn opened the fifteen-lane Luckland Alleys on Luck Avenue. The Williamson Road Center with twelve lanes opened in 1948. At Salem, Sherm Sisson opened the only all-tenpin establishment in 1949.

George Fulton Jr. won the city-county golf tournament held the second weekend in June. It was his fourth straight title. He won by eleven strokes over Ralph English and Fred Mueller.

John Lyles of the Roanoke Toastmasters Club won the Zone J speech contest at the Willard Hotel in Washington, DC, on June 9.

Roanoke County voters approved a bond issue in a referendum on June 11. The vote was 10 to 1 in favor. Money from the bond issue would be used to help finance the county's $3.9 million capital plan for the schools. Two previous bond issue votes had failed.

Sales Incorporated advertised in mid-June that it was going out of business. The department store was located at the corner of Church Avenue and Nelson Street.

Roanoke's Diamond Jubilee officially began at noon on Friday, June 14, and ran for nine days. The opening of the $175,000 celebration was marked by sirens, whistles, and the blowing of auto horns. At the Municipal Building, Mayor Walter Young made a brief ceremonial speech and a cut a three-tiered, sixty-pound birthday cake provided by Federal Bake Shop. Merchants had history-themed window displays throughout downtown. That evening, the pageant *The Rising Star* debuted at Victory Stadium with 2,000 cast members. The show was emceed by Ralph Story, quizmaster of television's *$64,000 Challenge*. Prior to the historic drama, performances were held by the Jubilee Chorus, the Jubilee Band, and a drill team from Washington, Pennsylvania. At the stadium was a midway operated by the firm of Caitlin and Wilson that consisted of twenty-three rides and twenty shows. Sally Rand, a burlesque dancer, starred at the midway in performances not open to children.

June 15 was "Governor's Day" at the Diamond Jubilee. Festivities included the dedication of the Williams Hunter Memorial Bridge (viaduct), an industrial exhibition at Victory Stadium known as *Index 57*, a governor's luncheon at the Hotel Roanoke with Governor Thomas Stanley, an afternoon parade from the American Legion Auditorium to Victory Stadium, the nightly performance of *The Rising Star*, and fireworks at the stadium. Governor Stanley formally crowned the queens, "Miss Diamond Jubilee" and "Miss Shenandoah Valley." There was also a Jubilee Ball at the auditorium. Attendance for the parade was estimated at 25,000.

The Williams Hunter Bridge (viaduct) was formally dedicated with the unveiling of a bronze plaque set in stone. Hunter was a former councilman, mayor, and Roanoke's first city manager. The plaque was dedicated by the mayor and unveiled by Hunter's widow. It was positioned on a grassy area at the end of the downtown bridge.

Composer Jack Kilpatrick from Dallas, Texas, flew to Roanoke on June 13 to view rehearsals of *Thy Kingdom Come* for which he wrote the scores. He was a professor at Southern Methodist University. He had also written the music for other outdoor dramas, including *Chucky Jack* in Gatlinburg, Tennessee, and *Horn in the West* in Boone, North Carolina.

Roanoke's Diamond Jubilee kicked off with a grand celebration on the front steps and lawn of the Municipal Building, seen here in this June 1957 image. *Virginia Room, RPL*

A Veterans Administration Hospital patient was killed when struck by an N&W Railway freight train on June 13 on tracks near the hospital. The medical examiner ruled the death of Robert Gutelius a suicide.

Parents of five Black children were the first Black Roanokers to refuse to sign pupil placement forms when they did so in mid-June. The pupil placement act was passed as an anti-segregation effort by the Virginia legislature in 1956 and "froze" all students in their present schools. The placement forms were required if a student was entering a public school system for the first time, was seeking to transfer to a different school, or was moving from a lower school to a high school within the same school division. The parents in Roanoke had children at Loudon School who were to move to the sixth grade at Harrison School.

Day three of the Diamond Jubilee was Sunday, June 16, "Religious Heritage Day." Activities included churches having Jubilee-themed worship services and an interfaith service at Victory Stadium that evening, which included the Roanoke Symphony Orchestra, Diamond Jubilee chorus and band, combined church choirs, and a presentation of *The Three Faiths* written by Kermit Hunter. A rainstorm, however, moved the stadium events to the following day as part of the scheduled music festival.

The long-awaited merger of two large fundraising efforts officially occurred on June 14 when the Roanoke County chapter of the Red Cross and Roanoke's Community Fund became "The United Fund of the Roanoke Valley." John Parrott, a trustee of both organizations, chaired the effort.

Cutting the birthday cake for Roanoke's Diamond Jubilee are (left to right) Miss Diamond Jubilee (Barbara Boitnott), Roanoke Mayor Walter Young, and Miss Shenandoah Valley (Edwina Wertz). *Virginia Room, RPL*

Ground-breaking ceremonies were held on June 17 for the construction of the new Chesapeake and Potomac Telephone Company central office at Cave Spring near the Cave Spring Lions Club.

An agreement was signed on June 14 approving the sale of the Bent Mountain Mutual Telephone Company to the Chesapeake and Potomac Telephone Company. The Bent Mountain company had 160 rural subscribers.

Jane Garman of Catawba was crowned "Miss Washington, DC, Chamber of Commerce" in mid-June. She qualified to compete for "Miss Washington, DC." She was a graduate of Andrew Lewis High School.

Robbie Horak won the first annual city-county junior golf tournament the second weekend in June. Thomas Elkins finished second.

Day four of the Diamond Jubilee was June 17, "Festival of Music Day." In addition to ongoing activities, the day included a time capsule ceremony at the Roanoke Public Library and "Music under the Stars" at Victory Stadium. Following fireworks at the stadium, there was a dance with the Woody Herman Band.

Showtimers presented *Bus Stop* the third week in June. Lead roles were played by George Garretson, Cheryn Coller, Russell Smiley Jr., and Helene Cooper.

Four area high school football players were named by the Virginia Sportscasters and Sportswriters Association to the West All-Star Team. They were Ken McIlhaney (Jefferson), Phil Fracker (Fleming), Warren Gardener (Jefferson), and Bob Aveson (Fleming).

Franklin Publishing Company at 101 Albemarle Avenue SE advertised on June 16 a complete liquidation via auction of its assets, including printing equipment and supplies, on June 26.

Day five of the Diamond Jubilee on June 18 was "Industry and Railroad Day." Events included an industrial parade through downtown, a reenactment of the first train coming to Roanoke, and a third performance of *The Rising Star* at Victory Stadium. It was the first day that the celebration had not been interrupted by rain. The N&W station was the site of the arrival of a replica of the Shenandoah Valley Railroad train that came to Roanoke on June 18, 1882. The train was pulled by a locomotive built by N&W in 1907 and consisted of three cars.

Moss Plunkett, a prominent Roanoke attorney, died on June 18 at the age of sixty-nine. Politically, he was an old-line, antiestablishment figure who mounted several unsuccessful Democratic primary campaigns to topple the Byrd machine in Virginia. He was an ardent opponent of the state poll tax and was a former chairman of the Roanoke County School Board.

Day six of the Diamond Jubilee was "Pioneer and Homecoming Day" which featured a pioneer tea at Buena Vista Recreation Center, a Jubilee Chorus and Band concert at Victory Stadium, a recognition of Roanoke pioneers by Virginia Attorney General Lindsay Almond Jr., *The Rising Star* drama, and a late-evening dance for Diamond Dandies and Jubilee Belles at the Merchants' Parking Garage.

Part of Roanoke's Diamond Jubilee celebration was a parade through downtown Roanoke, seen here in this June 1957 image. *Historical Society of Western Virginia*

In this image, a Diamond Jubilee historical pageant is being held on the field at Victory Stadium. *Historical Society of Western Virginia*

Broaddus Chewning Sr. announced his retirement as executive director of the Community Fund on June 18 to take effect July 15. His successor was Chester Cooley, who would direct the new United Fund of Roanoke Valley Inc. Chewning had served in his post for fifteen years.

Trustees of the Fund of the Protestant Episcopal Diocese of Southwestern Virginia purchased acreage on the north side of Grandin Road, west of Carter Road SW for $23,500 from Mary Neff. It would later serve as the site for St. Elizabeth's Episcopal Church.

Actor Maurice Gosfield, who played Pfc. Doberman on *The Phil Silvers Show*, visited Roanoke on June 19 to help promote the Diamond Jubilee.

Day seven of the Diamond Jubilee, June 20, was "Young America Day" and featured special playground activities at city parks, a fine arts auction, the play *Hansel and Gretel* at Jefferson High School, a fifth performance of *The Rising Star*, and teen dances at South Roanoke Park and Washington Park. The fine arts auction included forty-seven works by local artists, and the top price of $115 was paid for "Southern Cabin" by the late Allen Ingles Palmer.

The *Phillip Morris Country Music Show* came to the American Legion Auditorium on June 22. It featured hillbilly performers which included Carl Smith, Red Sovine, Goldie Hill, Ronnie Self, Mimi Roman, Bun Wilson, the Tune Smiths, Dale Potter, and Biff Collie.

Robert Hall opened his Sunoco Service Station at Twenty-Fourth Street and Melrose Avenue NW on June 20.

Friday, June 21, was "Agriculture, Good Neighbor Day" of the Diamond Jubilee lineup. The day featured a flower show, presentation of agricultural awards by Senator Harry Byrd at Victory Stadium, country music and dancing at the stadium, fireworks, and a sixth performance of *The Rising Star*.

The final day of Roanoke's Diamond Jubilee celebration was Saturday, June 22. It included a parade (the third one of the Jubilee), a final performance of *The Rising Star* at Victory Stadium, a fireworks display, and the singing of *Auld Lang Syne* as the finale. The Diamond Dandies held a beard-shaving ceremony in the afternoon at the stadium and announced the winners of the monthlong beard-growing contest. The winners in five categories were J. R. Noell, Henry Staples, L. E. Saunders, J. B. St. Clair, and Howard Hale.

WSLS-TV did a live broadcast on June 22 from the Sherwood Burial Park Amphitheater of the cast and crew of the outdoor drama *Thy Kingdom Come*. It was the first live broadcast of the station from outside its studios.

The congregation of Green Ridge Presbyterian Church announced on June 22 plans to build a permanent church on a three-acre site along Route 623. The church was meeting in a home on Vivian Avenue.

Thy Kingdom Come opened on Sunday, June 23, to a crowd of 500. The outdoor drama at the Sherwood Burial Park Amphitheater was based on the life of the Apostle Paul, with Carl Clarke in the lead role. The play also featured future Hollywood actor David Huddleston. The three-part play, billed as the nation's first outdoor religious drama, was performed nightly, except Mondays, through Labor Day.

The fifth annual State Junior Golf Tournament opened for a five-day stand at Hidden Valley Country Club on June 25, site of the first tournament in 1953.

This 1957 image shows the 2,000-seat Sherwood Burial Park Amphitheater that was equipped with seats and equipment for *Thy Kingdom Come*. *Sherwood Burial Park*

The steam pump at the Crystal Spring Pumping Station was voted to be retired by Roanoke City Council at their meeting on June 24. The pump would be replaced by electrically driven centrifugal pumps for a cost-savings measure. The steam pump, which had been in operation for more than fifty years, required replacement parts to be made in Roanoke. Interestingly, the end of the steam pump terminated a contract with S. D. Ferguson that dated to 1911. Ferguson, one of the original developers of South Roanoke, had condensate from the pump heat his nearby house.

Reid and Cutshall opened a new furniture store on June 27 on Campbell Avenue SW. It was across the street from their former location. The building was the fourth downtown location for the firm, which was organized in 1924 by C. S. Reid and R. W. Cutshall. It succeeded the firm of H. J. Hartbarger and Son in Roanoke and occupied a building at Salem Avenue and Commerce Street SW. In 1928, the store moved next to the Times-World Building on Campbell Avenue before moving to the 300 block of Campbell Avenue in 1946. It had a branch store on Route 11.

Western Auto opened a new store at 1423 Williamson Road on June 27. It closed its former location at 325 W. Campbell Avenue a few days prior.

First National Exchange Bank opened a branch at 4202 Melrose Avenue NW on June 28. It was their third branch bank.

Emma Lester, seventy-one, of Roanoke was struck by a city bus on June 18 at Kenwood Boulevard and Vernon Street SE. She died from her injuries on June 26 and became the city's seventh traffic fatality of the year.

The Ringling Brothers and Barnum & Bailey Circus was at Victory Stadium on July 2 and 3. The circus performances were held without the traditional big top and sideshows. An estimated 10,000 attended over the two days.

Mack's Sinclair Service Station opened on June 28 on Cove Road at Lafayette Boulevard NW. C. T. McManama was the owner. Andy Anderson and his band performed at the service station for two nights on opening weekend.

Peoples Service Drug Store opened at 112 Wayne Street NE in Sears Town on June 28.

Roanoke attorney Linwood Holton Jr., stated on June 28 that he would not seek the GOP nomination for state attorney general nor would he seek the GOP nomination run for Roanoke's seat in the House of Delegates in the upcoming November election. There had been local speculation that he was considering various candidacies.

The Roanoke Valley Polio Eradication Campaign ended on June 28 with over 35,000 valley residents having received their initial or second vaccine shot. A third campaign was planned for the spring of 1958.

Raymond Willis, forty-four, of Botetourt County was arrested in Philadelphia on June 29 and charged with the murder of Lorraine King on May 31 at her apartment in Roanoke.

Showtimers presented *Angel Street* the first weekend in July. Lead roles were performed by Pat Hooker and Bob Niemyer. Sam Good was the director.

The *Fantabulous Rock 'N' Roll Show of 1957* came to the American Legion Auditorium on July 3. Performers included Ruth Brown, the Coasters, Bo Diddley, the Drifters, the School Boys, Smiley Lewis, the Five Satins, the Spence Twins, and Paul Williams and his orchestra. Ads read, "No white spectators."

Dr. P. T. Goad of Roanoke won the qualifying medal in the senior division of the Virginia State Amateur Golf Tournament at Hot Springs on June 30. He shot a 73, two over par.

Robert Bennington was named to the Roanoke School Board on July 1 for a three-year term. He replaced Barclay Andrews, whose term expired. Dr. L. C. Downing was reelected to the school board by Roanoke City Council.

Construction started on July 1 for a $238,000 building program at Salem Presbyterian Church. A new educational building and remodeling of the sanctuary were the main elements. It was the first major addition to the church since 1914.

Harness racing returned to the Starkey Racing Grounds on July 4, both pacers and trotters. For comic relief, mule races were also held.

Lawrence Vaught, twenty-one, of Roanoke was fatally injured on July 4 when struck by a train in the N&W Railway yards near Sixteenth Street. The brakeman had married just two weeks prior to the accident.

James Carter, a retired building contractor, died at his home in Roanoke on July 4 at the age of eighty-eight. Carter built the first residence in what became Raleigh Court and the second residence in the Williamson Road section. He also helped to organize the Roanoke Booster Club.

Dr. P. T. Goad of Roanoke won the Virginia Seniors Golf Championship at Hot Springs on July 4.

Fairland Lake opened for the season on July 4. The park offered miniature golf, a driving range, swimming, boating, fishing, and picnic areas. It was located off Cove Road in the Villa Heights section.

This 1950s postcard shows the Fairland Lake Club, located in the 2700 block of Cove Road NW. *Nelson Harris*

Kenna Dunn, twenty-one, of Salem died on July 6 from injuries he sustained in an auto accident two days prior on Route 621 near Glenvar. Dunn was a salesman with Roanoke Valley Motors.

WDBJ-TV began broadcasting Sunday School lessons for children on Sunday, July 7, and continued doing so throughout the month as area congregations tuned in for the live broadcasts from Sunday Schools in local churches.

Dixie Cream Donut Drive-In opened on July 7 on Lee Highway in Salem, opposite Shoney's.

Salem Town Council held preliminary discussions on July 8 on an architect's plans for a proposed auditorium, banquet hall, and gymnasium complex for the town. The auditorium would seat 1,500.

The Roanoke Young Democrats Club held a fundraising dinner at Dixie Caverns on July 12. The guest speaker was US Senator Albert Gore of Tennessee. William Hopkins was chairman of the club.

The Ann Howard Show, a local program, celebrated its first anniversary on July 9 on WDBJ-TV.

A school bond issue was defeated in a voter referendum held on July 9 in Botetourt County, 843–1,236. The main element of the bond issue was to create a single consolidated high school for the county.

Roanoke attorney and Virginia's Attorney General Lindsay Almond rolled to an easy Democratic primary win on July 9 to be the party's gubernatorial nominee. His 4-to-1 margin over Howard Carwile was expected. Almond was a staunch segregationist and part of the Byrd machine. In Roanoke City, the vote was 1,742 to 443 for Almond, and in Roanoke County Almond won 877–104.

An all-time attendance record was set on July 9 for professional wrestling at the American Legion Auditorium—2,381. Fans watched a tag-team match between the Gallagher brothers versus George Becker and Dick Steinborn.

Darryl Dellis won Roanoke's fourteenth annual Soap Box Derby on July 10 held at Twenty-Fourth Street and Lafayette Boulevard NW. The event was televised live by WDBJ and WSLS and was the first time a Soap Box Derby had been televised in Virginia. Dellis was a sophomore at Fleming High School. Sixty-three boys participated. Attendance was estimated at 7,500.

The YMCA Completion Fund topped its $300,000 goal in mid-July. The drive was to build a new YMCA, and the effort was chaired by Ben Parrott.

West End Presbyterian Church dedicated its new education building on July 14.

F. C. Amrhein and Sons Jewelers opened at its new location at 32 W. Kirk Avenue in mid-July.

The new fifty-four-unit Holiday Inn motel opened on July 14 on Route 11, a mile north of Roanoke. The half-million-dollar motel was owned by Motel Company of Roanoke of which Joel Krisch was president. Room service for meals was provided by Archie's Lobster House, which also operated the leased gift shop.

The new Goodwill Industries retail store at 11 Salem Avenue NW was dedicated on July 19.

Some 350 businessmen participated in the annual day trip of the Roanoke Booster Club to White Sulphur Springs on July 17. The guest speaker was Bryson Rash, Washington correspondent for NBC.

Evangelist Angel Martinez held a weeklong revival at First Baptist Church, Roanoke, during the last week of July.

Kathy Hill, five, was killed on July 17 when she rode her tricycle from a side road into Route 460 and was struck by an automobile. Her family lived in the Edgewood section of Roanoke County.

Showtimers performed *The Great Sebastians* the third weekend in July. Lead roles were played by Edward Langley, Lois Langley, and Art Glover.

Little Chef Restaurant opened on July 18 at 1907 Williamson Road. It was open 24 hours, except Sundays. A deluxe beef burger, french fries, applesauce and drink were sixty-seven cents.

Auto daredevils gave a show at the Starkey Speedway on July 23.

The City of Roanoke acquired a fourteen-acre tract on July 18 for a new school at the intersection of Westside Boulevard and Hershberger Road NW. The price was $45,000.

Junior Achievement of the Roanoke Valley officially organized on July 19 in a meeting at the First National Exchange Bank. Clem Johnston was elected president.

Rebecca Lee was crowned Miss Virginia in the Hotel Roanoke ballroom on July 20. Lee, a resident of Roanoke, was a stenographer at N&W Railway. The twenty-two-year-old was competing as Miss Roanoke County and was sponsored by the Roanoke County Junior Woman's Club. A bouquet of roses was presented to Lee by Marion McKnight, Miss America 1957, who attended the pageant.

A warehouse for Star Steel was opened in mid-July in the 800 block of Wasena Avenue SW.

WSLS-TV did a live broadcast of the morning worship service from First Baptist Church on July 21. Rev. Angel Martinez, a guest evangelist, was the speaker. It was the first such broadcast from a church in the Roanoke Valley.

Joe Brown, general manager of the Pittsburgh Pirates Major League Baseball team, came to Salem the last week of July to scout the Salem Rebels, a Pirates farm team. He was treated to various dinners and special events by the town's business leaders and baseball enthusiasts.

Clayton Moore, the star of the television series *The Lone Ranger*, along with his horse Silver, gave two performances at Victory Stadium on July 24. The dog that starred in *Lassie* was also there to entertain. All children were given silver bullets.

Vicky Bowers, three, of Roanoke choked to death on an October bean on July 25 while in a garden at home with her parents.

Ground was broken for the new Oak Grove Elementary School the last week of July. The contractor for the $383,000 school was J. M. Turner and Company.

Parents of six Black children refused to sign state pupil placement forms in late July. Their children were to go to Lucy Addison High School, having matriculated through Booker T. Washington Junior High School. The state, as a means of mitigating compliance with court-ordered desegregation, developed the pupil placement forms to regulate where students could attend.

Jackie Wright won the women's City Tennis Tournament at Washington Park on July 26. She defeated Patricia Moore.

A stolen car pursued by police collided with a car of migratory workers on Route 11 at Cloverdale on July 27, killing three people and injuring five. Those killed were Harry Plott of Covington and Julio Santana and Eufracio Lopes, both of Puerto Rico. Two days later, another migratory worker, Nicolas Vesquez, died from his injuries. The three workers were employed by local orchardists.

The National Park Service announced on July 27 that it was taking over the Booker T. Washington Birthplace in Franklin County and planned to make it into a national park. The state cleared the way for the transaction by paying off the $16,000 owed on the property by S. J. Phillips, founder and president of the Booker T. Washington Memorial.

The outdoor drama *Thy Kingdom Come* set records over the final weekend in July. First, it sold out all 2,000 seats at the Sherwood Amphitheatre on July 26 and simultaneously set a record for a first-season crowd at an outdoor drama in the state.

Two Roanoke businessmen, Curtis Turner and Hugh Rakes, purchased over 70,000 acres of timberland in Kentucky in late July. The land was previously owned by the Ford Motor Company.

Showtimers presented their fourth play of the season, *Heaven Can Wait*, during the first weekend in August. Lead actors in the comedy were Chuck Hyman, Fred Bradley, Bob Lee, Thornton Shaner, Wilson Price, Guy Eckman, Joe Grant, Ann Fox, and Betty Thornton Shaner.

Fred Alouf Jr. opened his dental practice at 2610 Williamson Road in late July.

The congregation of First Baptist Church, Gainsboro, held a reception for their pastor Rev. A. L. James on the occasion of his eightieth birthday on August 1. He had been the pastor at the church since 1919.

A new comic strip appeared in the *Roanoke Times* beginning July 29, *The Ryatts*.

In the annual city-county tennis tournament held at the South Roanoke courts in late July, Lu Merritt and Fred Bromm won the men's doubles championships. Stella Popolowski defeated Sugar Ellett for the women's singles title. Charley Turner won his seventeenth men's singles title by defeating Lu Merritt.

The Bargain Center, the third branch store in a chain of Virginia variety stores, opened on August 2 at Luck Avenue and First Street SW. The other stores were in Martinsville and Danville.

Carroll & Lewis, an upscale shoe store, opened on August 5 at 13 W. Church Avenue. It was owned by Carroll Renner and Lewis Miller.

Rutrough Motors in Roanoke was selected to be the local dealership for the new Edsel automobile developed by Ford Motor Company. Henry Rutrough, company president, said the dealership would stop selling Packards, which it had done for thirty-four years. Rutrough Motors also sold Ramblers and Nash autos. It was located at 327 W. Luck Avenue.

The federal investigation led by Robert Kennedy into corrupt labor union leaders revealed in testimony on August 1 in Washington, DC, that racketeer

Johnny Dio was once an organizer for the garment union at a plant in Roanoke. Dio, who had thrown acid into the face of a *New York Times* reporter for his investigative journalism, blinding the journalist, was a well-known criminal. Local labor leaders in Roanoke denied Dio had ever come to Roanoke.

Rev. Troy Weir of Roanoke's Foursquare Gospel Church at 612 Bullitt Avenue SE had his home and church office vandalized. The damage was followed by a letter in early August making a bomb threat. The letter was signed, "An Old Member."

North Cross School, Salem's only private school, was reorganized into a nonprofit school in late July. The school was originally housed in the reception room at the home of Mrs. H. U. Butts in Langhorne Place. First grade began in 1944 and was taught by Margaret Northcross. As enrollment grew, the school moved to what was called the Griffin property on Union Street in 1945. By its second year, the school had an enrollment of seventy-five. Third grade was added in 1946. An addition was built onto the school in 1947. The school was granted a charter by the SCC in 1955.

Dr. Lester Gillespie opened his general medical practice at 2523 Melrose Avenue NW in early August.

Roanoke's PAL boxing team won 10–0 over the team from Whitesville, West Virginia, on August 3. Nine of the ten matches ended in knockouts.

A Patrick County brother and sister, William Atkins and Nancy Atkins, were killed and three other youths injured in a single-car accident at the foot of Bent Mountain on Route 221 on August 4. The car in which all were riding went off the road and down an embankment.

The Roanoke Board of Zoning Appeals denied Fairland Lake Club its request for a nonconforming permit on August 6. The board did grant the swimming club permission for a temporary continuance until January 1, after which the club must have a charter as a nonprofit to continue its operations. The thirty-four-acre club was located at 2611 Ordway Drive NW, which was in a general residence district.

The Blue Eagle Tourist Court at 2302 Williamson Road was sold for $115,000 on August 6 by W. C. Oyler to the Colonial Development Company.

Dixie Cream Donut Drive-In opened at 937 Apperson Drive on August 8, opposite Shoney's. The drive-in was owned and operated by Robert Logan Jr.

Mimi's, a women's clothing store, moved from 7 W. Church Avenue to 19 W. Church Avenue on August 9. A formal opening at the new location was held on August 12. Mr. and Mrs. Daniel Leeds were the owners.

Peters Creek Church of the Brethren held a cornerstone-laying ceremony on August 11 for their new $100,000 church.

Vandals pulled a valve that emptied the five-acre Hideaway Lake in the Bradshaw section of western Roanoke County on August 10. Dr. A. J. Russo of Salem, owner of the lake and 2,000 acres of adjoining land which he was developing for home sites, said it would take through winter for the lake to refill.

Swim Time Pool and Equipment Company opened at 4803 Williamson Road on August 12. The store also sold various sporting goods.

Security personnel with the American Viscose Roanoke plant greet a driver as they approach the new bridge crossing the Roanoke River into the plant's campus. *Avisco News*

Nancy McManaway, eighteen, of Salem was chosen as Miss Virginia Press Photographer in a pageant held at Natural Bridge on August 11. Her crown was made of flashbulbs.

Johnny Cash from the *Grand Ole Opry* performed at the American Legion Auditorium on August 16. Regional musicians also participated in the show, including Don Reno, Red Smiley, the Tennessee Cut Ups, Ronnie Reno, and Bill Price.

Charles McGhee, sixty-six, of Roanoke died in a hospital on August 14 from burns he received on July 11 while repairing a car engine.

Liles Shoe Fashions opened at 106 W. Campbell Avenue on August 15.

An abandoned log cabin in Roanoke County estimated to have been over a century old burned on August 14 in the Cave Spring section. It had once belonged to the Penn family.

Showtimers presented the drama *The Winslow Boy* the second weekend in August. Leading roles were played by Ann deOlazarra, Francis Ballard, and Bill Segall.

Two Roanoke young women appeared in the September issue of *Holiday* magazine. Robin Ould and Jane Ellis were featured in a fashion piece titled "Young Girl Greets the Campus."

General Sales opened at 416 Carver Avenue NE on August 17.

Harold Secord was named the new principal of Jefferson High School, succeeding Gordon Brooks, who resigned to serve as school superintendent in Botetourt County. Secord came to the position with almost twenty years of education experience as a teacher or principal. His prior appointment had been in Petersburg.

Evans Evans of Roanoke County won many accolades for her acting performances in the Williams Summer Theatre in Massachusetts. Evans had also landed acting roles in several television productions, including *Studio One* and *Robert Montgomery Presents*. She was a recent graduate of the Yale School of Drama.

Interiors by Richard announced it was moving from 17 Alabama Street in Salem to a new studio at 506 S. Jefferson Street within the month. Richard Jones was the owner of the firm.

Camp Easter Seals formally opened at its new site in Craig County on August 18 as sixty children from around Virginia attended. The camp had formerly been in Bath County. Sponsors for the camp were the Junior League and Jaycees.

Municipal Court Judge Beverly Fitzpatrick, an organizer and leader of the Roanoke Valley Citizens Traffic Safety Council, lobbied civic groups to become engaged in the work of the council to end "slaughter on the streets and highways" through education, enforcement of safety laws, and better traffic engineering. Fitzpatrick and others had become alarmed at the number of deaths caused by traffic accidents including to pedestrians.

The Coffee Pot, a well-known bar and restaurant at 2902 Brambleton Avenue SW, went up for auction on August 28. Harold LeGrande was the owner.

Over 6,000 fans attended an outdoor professional wrestling event at Victory Stadium on August 20. The Gallagher Brothers wrestled in a tag-team match against Dick Steinborn and George Becker. Fans tossed litter at the villainous Gallaghers. There was also a women's bout featuring Ethel Johnson and Babs Wingo. Walter Buckner was the referee.

Lindsay Almond Jr., candidate for governor and the state's attorney general, held a watermelon feast at Fishburn Park on August 22, sponsored by the Roanoke Young Democrats Club. At the campaign event, Almond declared his fervent support for segregation of public schools. Attendance was estimated at 500. Almond was from Roanoke.

Horace Howell, owner of Howell's Body Shop at 900 Orange Avenue NE, was shot and killed by his brother-in-law on August 22 as he went to visit the home of his ex-wife near Troutville.

A new piece of classroom technology was demonstrated to Roanoke area education officials at Virginia Tech on August 22—the overhead projector.

Junior Achievement formally opened its business center at 15 W. Church Avenue on August 22. It was located on the second floor of the Ewald-Clark Building.

Richard's Sinclair Service Station opened on August 23 at Cove and Hershberger Roads NW. The owner was John Richards.

This September 1957 image shows the Virginian Railway station at Roanoke. *N&W Historical Photographs Collection, VPI&SU Libraries*

Norman Hinchee, owner of Bob's Drive-In on West Main Street in Salem, was arrested on August 22 for shooting one of his employees, Buck Lineberry, on August 21 as Lineberry closed the restaurant. The victim was struck in the neck and partially paralyzed. Lineberry died from his wounds on August 24.

Showtimers presented its final play of the season, *The Man Who Came to Dinner*, at the end of August. Lead roles were played by Herbert Harris, Lynn Eckman, Robert Ayers, and George Garretson.

Burrell Memorial Hospital officials announced on August 24 that the hospital would begin an in-service training program for nurses on September 9. Miriam Smith and Rebecca Stewart would be the directors. The plan was to lay groundwork for a future school or nursing.

The Roanoke Historical Society was organized on August 23 by Dr. D. E. McQuilkin, chairman of the Roanoke Diamond Jubilee Historical Committee. At the meeting were Raymond Barnes, Blair Fishburn, Edmund Goodwin, Shields Johnson, Edward Ould, D. W. Persinger, Claude Settlemire, Tayloe Rogers and Robert Thomas. Goodwin was elected as president, Fishburn as vice president, and Barnes as secretary. The group requested that some of the excess funds leftover from the Diamond Jubilee be appropriated to the group to continue the work of preserving, collecting, and exhibiting items and writings of local historic interest and value.

The Roanoke Fair began a weeklong run at Maher Field and Victory Stadium on August 26. The fair included a livestock show, agricultural exhibits, fireworks, crocheting contest, flower show, commercial exhibits and a beauty pageant. The fair was sponsored by American Legion Post 3. The fair also included a midway operated by Penn Premier Shows that included thirty-five rides and thirty-five sideshows.

The first annual Wild West Rodeo was held at Starkey Speedway for three days that began on August 31. The rodeo featured Brahma bull riding, steer wrestling, bronco riding, calf roping, and clowns.

Bob Payne won the Roanoke Valley Invitational Tennis Tournament held at Roanoke Country Club the last weekend in August. Payne, the top seed, was from Richmond. Bob Bortner and Bob Figg won the doubles title.

Heironimus, Miller & Rhoads and Pugh's Department Store all announced they would remain open evenings until nine beginning September 9 and would include Monday and Friday nights beginning November 15. The stores led the way in trying to bring uniformity for night store openings in downtown Roanoke, an effort encouraged and recommended by the Roanoke Merchants Association.

George Fulton Jr. set a new qualifying record at the Country Club of Virginia in Richmond for the National Amateur Golf Championship. Fulton shot a 143 for a thirty-six-hole total on August 27.

Lindsay Almond Jr. resigned as Virginia's attorney general on August 28 and devoted himself full time to his gubernatorial campaign.

Salem Town Council approved a new town seal on August 28. The new seal, designed by William Paxton Sr. of Salem, had a plain border with a coal tender and a locomotive with an engineer in the cab. The locomotive drawing was based on No. 37, a passenger engine built about 1859 and first used by the A. M. & O. Railroad.

Harry Rosenberg, owner of Oak Hall clothing store, died at the age of sixty-eight on August 29.

Boyle-Swecker Tire Company held a grand opening at its newest store at 104 W. Main Street in Salem on August 30. Bernard Meador was the manager. Its other location was at Church Avenue at Third Street SW in Roanoke.

Shirley & Lee, Roland Cook and his orchestra, and the Solitaires performed for a show and dance at the American Legion Auditorium on September 1. The show began at midnight and ended at 4:00 a.m.

Hollywood actor Don Arrington paid a visit to Roanoke in late August to visit his parents. Arrington of Roanoke was starring in the film *Face in the Crowd* that was playing at the American Theatre. He was a graduate of the Viaud School in Roanoke.

Roger DeBusk of Roanoke, a chemist at the General Electric plant, appeared on the nationally televised quiz show *The Big Payoff* on August 30 that aired over the CBS network.

More than 500 persons from around the nation attended the convention of the National Railway Historical Society at the Hotel Roanoke in late August.

Carolyn Brown was crowned as Miss Roanoke Fair on August 30. Brown of Roanoke competed with thirty-four other contestants. Norma Nunley was runner-up.

J. C. Wheat & Company, a brokerage and investment firm, opened a branch office on September 3 in the Mountain Trust Bank Building at 302 S. Jefferson Street. William Meredith was the manager.

The Jefferson Bowling Alley over the Sportsman on Campbell Avenue reopened on September 9 after being closed for remodeling. It was duck pins only.

Thy Kingdom Come ended its first outdoor summer season on September 2. A total of 22,000 people saw the production.

Miss Mona's School of Dancing opened in early September at 3023 Preston Avenue NW.

Miller & Rhoads opened its new $5 million department store on September 4 with much ceremony. A concert by the Monroe Junior High School band preceded the ribbon-cutting at 9:45 a.m., an event presided over by Webster Rhoads, chairman of the board. Elected officials from Vinton, Salem, Roanoke, and Roanoke County were on hand for the occasion. The night before the opening, the store held a fashion show and dinner at the Hotel Roanoke. The general contractor for the building was B. F. Parrott and Company. Some 4,000 cubic yards of rock were excavated for the structure, necessitating the use of dynamite. John Marchant was appointed as the store's general manager. The fifth floor contained the Tea Room with a full-service kitchen for dining. That floor also contained a beauty salon accented in hues of pink and green. The store, located at the corner of Campbell Avenue and First Street SW, was the fourth for the firm in the state. Over 10,000 went through the store on opening day.

Employees of the Roy C. Kinsey Sign Company of Roanoke install the Miller & Rhoads sign on the front of the store in preparation for its opening in September 1957.
Bob Kinsey

This picture shows the Miller & Rhoads store in 1957, the year it opened in downtown Roanoke. It was the fourth store for the company in Virginia. *Bob Kinsey*

Fines were levied against defendants in Municipal Court on September 4 for operating "girlie" shows in connection with the Roanoke Fair the last week of August. Margarita Allen and Barbara Blake, both of Chattanooga, Tennessee, were fined one hundred dollars each for their starring roles.

Posie Powell of Roanoke won the Old Dominion Checker Association tournament on September 6 in Richmond. The tournament to crown a state champion took place over three days.

O. Winston Link released a high-fidelity recording of *The Sounds of Steam Railroading* in early September. The record also included chimes, freight whistles, and a passenger train. The recordings, all of N&W Railway trains, took over two years to make.

The Roanoke Valley Drama Association proclaimed their production *Thy Kingdom Come* a success based on their metrics. The show drew a total of 22,000 attendees, an average of 350 per night. The association believed about 6,000 of those that attended came from out of town.

Central Baptist Church at Starkey broke ground for a new sanctuary on September 8. The $60,000 structure would adjoin the education building. Rev. Harry Gamble was the guest speaker for the ceremony.

Branecky & White, a real estate development firm, presented a *Better Homes and Gardens* "Idea House" on Cameron Drive that had been constructed as part of their Lindenwood subdivision near Vinton. An open house was held on September 8 with WDBJ-TV personality Ann Howard and music provided by the Frank Romano Orchestra.

A new Lutheran congregation in the Cave Spring section voted to name themselves St. John Lutheran Church. Rev. William McCauley was the organizing pastor. The Lutheran mission board had purchased five acres of land in Cave Spring for a planned building.

Melrose Baptist Church marked its fiftieth anniversary the second weekend in September. As part of their observance, the congregation dedicated a lodge at Eagle Eyrie, a Virginia Baptist retreat. The church was organized on September 15, 1907, with twenty-one charter members. The congregation originally met on Gilmer Avenue near Eleventh Street NW before moving in 1912 to Twelfth Street and Melrose Avenue NW. In 1916, the church erected an education building at the site, followed by a sanctuary in 1925.

Stull's Amoco Service Station opened on September 13 at 671 Brandon Avenue SW. The operator was John Stull Jr.

Roanoke City Councilman Herbert Davies died on September 13 in a local hospital at age sixty-nine. He had been named to council in 1956 to serve the remaining term of Paul Puckett, who had resigned. He was a retired executive with US Steel.

Mr. and Mrs. Edward Atkins of Roanoke appeared as contestants on the CBS network's game show *Beat the Clock* which aired on September 13.

Fred Kenney's *Motor Olympics* came to the Starkey Racing Grounds on September 16 that featured motorcycle side car racing, car stunts, and a '57 Chevrolet shot from a cannon.

The Monroe Junior High School Band won first place for the sixth straight year in a junior high band competition held in Baltimore the second weekend in September. The ninety-piece band competed with eighty-one other bands from a five-state region.

A two-story brick building at 203 E. Main Street in Salem was razed the third week in September. It was once used as a Confederate telegraph office during the Civil War. Walter Oakey of Salem stated he was born in the house in 1873 and believed the structure dated to 1850. It was also used as a post office during the administration of U. S. Grant.

Charles Clark sold his holdings in Ewald-Clark camera and novelty shop to his partner Francis Ewald in mid-September. Clark wanted to devote his full energies to his position as president of Tip and Twinkle, a local manufacturer of novelty items.

The Bank of Salem held an open house on September 20 to showcase its $200,000 expansion and renovations. The bank was located at 100 E. Main Street. The open house included exhibits of counterfeit money used to train personnel and the currency and coin collection of George Walton.

An organizational meeting for Windsor Hills Baptist Church was held on September 19 at the home of Mrs. T. L. Crowder on Grandin Road Extension SW. The meeting was conducted by Rev. Charles Watkins of Grandin Court Baptist Church.

The Bank of Salem is seen here in this 1957 image by George Davis. It was located at 100 E. Main Street in Salem. *Virginia Room, RPL*

Old Dominion Candies did a $25,000 expansion on their plant on E. Main Street in Salem. The expansion would allow the company to increase its production capacity to one million pounds of candy per year.

The Mountain View Country Club Invitational Pro Am Tournament was held the third weekend in September and drew a field of 150 golfers. Those competing included Arnold Palmer of Latrobe, Pennsylvania, who was the fourth leading money winner on the professional circuit. The top prize for the professional was $350. Palmer won the event with a 135 in the thirty-six-hole tournament. He was four strokes ahead of John Musser of Baltimore. George Fulton Jr. of Roanoke ended tied for third at 143.

Pro golfer Arnold Palmer (left) holds his trophy after winning the Mountain View Invitational Golf Tournament. Roanoke's George Fulton Jr. is at right, as he was the low-scoring amateur. *WSLS-TV News Film Collection, UVA Libraries*

The Roanoke Star on Mill Mountain would begin burning red during the evening following each traffic fatality occurring in Roanoke City starting in mid-October. The Roanoke Merchants Association, owner of the star, agreed to the plan based upon the urging of the Roanoke Valley Citizens Traffic Safety Council headed by Beverly Fitzpatrick. The announcement of the plan was made on September 21 by Fitzpatrick. The plan would be for a fifteen-month trial basis.

Valley Steel Corporation began operating in its new fabricating plant on Kessler Mill Road in late August. The business was a subsidiary of Roanoke Iron and Bridge Works.

Construction of a new parish building for College Lutheran Church in Salem began in late September, along with alterations to the existing building. The total cost of the work was estimated to be $190,000. Martin Brothers was the general contractor. A formal ground-breaking ceremony was held on October 6.

The second annual Star City Classic football game was held at Victory Stadium on September 28 between Hampton Institute and Bluefield State.

Roanoke Valley Home Week was held the third week in September. To honor the occasion, the *Roanoke Times* forecasted what Roanoke would be like in 1975. The population would be 225,000. Old landmarks would completely disappear. The Roanoke City Market would be eliminated in favor of a modern downtown, and Woodrum Field would have separate terminals for jets.

Christopher Stevens, two, died at his family's home in Roanoke County on September 23 when he fell from a small stool and struck his head on a bathroom fixture.

Miss Harriet Simpson, the retired principal of West End School, was named as Woman of the Year for 1957 by the Roanoke Business and Professional Women's Club on September 24.

Kraft Foods announced in late September that its distribution plant in Salem would close in November and its building at 1338 W. Main Street would be vacated. The structure was built by Kraft in 1947 and opened in 1948.

St. John's A. M. E. Church purchased the Melrose Presbyterian Church building at Fifteenth Street and Moorman Avenue NW for $20,100 in late September. The St. John's congregation planned to occupy the Melrose building once that congregation completed their new building in the Norwood section.

Johnson-McReynolds Chevrolet closed their Campbell Avenue location to consolidate all their operations at 1824 Williamson Road effective October 1. They also began operating their service department until midnight on weekdays.

Louis Huffman, forty, of Troutville was killed instantly on September 30 when he was struck by a car on US Route 11 near the entrance to Hollins College. The victim was crossing the highway when the accident occurred.

Dr. Benjamin Beckham, founder of Ferrum College, died in a Roanoke hospital on September 30 at the age of eighty-nine. A retired Methodist minister, Beckham was president of Ferrum College from its founding in 1913 until 1934.

Roanoke City Council at its September 30 meeting authorized the purchase of sixty-six acres to be used for the creation of a safety zone at the west end of the northeast-southwest runway at Woodrum Field. The cost of the land was $101,730.

Virginia House of Delegates member Kossen Gregory of Roanoke, in a campaign speech for reelection on October 1, stated his commitment to opposing desegregation of public schools. "Schools should be maintained on a segregated basis" was a major part of his reelection platform.

Gauges on the No. 4 pump engine are explained to the C Shift of the Viscose Fire Brigade in this September 1957 image. The volunteer fire brigade at the American Viscose Roanoke plant was organized in November 1941. *Avisco News*

Wilbert Pruett, twenty-eight, of Salem died on October 1 from injuries he sustained two days prior in an auto accident on Route 11 in Salem.

Chester Brooks, first superintendent of the Booker T. Washington National Monument in Franklin County, set up a temporary office in the Blue Ridge Parkway Headquarters at 625 First Street SW.

The Coffee Pot restaurant at 2902 Brambleton Avenue SW was sold to Joseph Grayeb in early October.

Woodson Pontiac held a grand opening at its new location at 3926 Williamson Road on October 3. They offered shuttle service from downtown using station wagons for the event. Over 1,000 attended the opening.

Sylvan Lincoln-Mercury moved all sales and service operations to 425 Marshall Avenue SW in early October.

William Henritze, of Roanoke and a prominent real estate holder, died on October 3 at the age of seventy-eight. Henritze lived on Mill Mountain and once owned the mountain before it was acquired by Junius Fishburn. A native of Marion, Henritze came to Roanoke in 1907 and entered the real estate business. He constructed a road up Mill Mountain in 1923 and planned for a 300-room resort hotel at the summit, a plan that was later abandoned.

The first worship service for the newly organized North Roanoke Baptist Church was held on October 6 in a renovated house across from Burlington School on Route 117. The organizing pastor was Rev. H. W. Connelly.

Over 18,000 spectators watched the football game between Jefferson High School and Fleming High School on October 4 at Victory Stadium. Jefferson won, 32–7. Jay Blackwood was the Jefferson quarterback.

The biggest fundraising drive in the history of Roanoke was announced on October 5. It was the campaign for the United Fund of Roanoke Valley with a goal of $590,230. Bolling Izard was the campaign chairman.

Jerome Hines of the Metropolitan Opera performed at the American Legion Auditorium on October 7. His concert was sponsored by the Thursday Morning Music Club.

Frank Maddox, fifty-seven, of Roanoke died at Grayson, Kentucky, on October 5. He was an assistant to the president of the Richardson-Wayland Electrical Corporation and was a pioneer in the field of radio. Maddox built for his employer the first radio station in the area, WDBJ. The station was operated by Richardson-Wayland from June 20, 1924, until it was purchased by the Times-World Corporation in May 1931.

The Fabulous Rock 'N' Roll Show of 1957 came to the American Legion Auditorium on October 9. The performers were Ray Charles, Mickey and Sylvia, Larry Williams and his orchestra, Joe Turner, Bo Diddley, Roy Brown, Mary Ann Fisher, Annie Laurie, the Moon Glows, Tiny Topsy, Vicki Nelson, Nappy Brown, and the Velours. A concert was given for Black and white audiences from 8:00 p.m. until 10:00 p.m., with a "colored dance" from 11:00 p.m. until 3:00 a.m.

Kohen's Lingerie at 3 W. Campbell Avenue advertised on October 6 it was going out of business.

Goodyear Shoe Shop opened on October 8 at 34 W. Kirk Avenue. The owner and manager was Jimmy Hagan.

Gospel singers Hovie Lister, the Statesmen, the Blackwood Brothers, Jackie Marshall, and the Eastland Harmony Quartet performed on October 10 at the American Legion Auditorium.

Hustings Court had its first female juror on October 7, Mrs. Duvall Adams. Judge Dirk Kuyk was responsible for her appointment to the jury.

Westinghouse Electric Supply Company purchased the home of Blue Ridge Post 484 of the VFW on October 8. The building in the 1900 block of Salem Avenue SW was to be razed according to Westinghouse officials for a warehouse and office building.

The Benson Brothers Wild Animal Circus came to the American Legion Auditorium on October 12.

Over 350 antique automobiles were brought to Roanoke the second weekend in October for the start of the National Glidden Tour on October 14. The cars were temporarily stored at the Downtown Parking Garage. The local Antique Automobile Club was the host for the tour which went from Roanoke to Hershey, Pennsylvania.

Twenty residents of the Windsor Hills section gathered on October 10 and organized Windsor Hills Baptist Church. Rev. Charles Watkins led the effort.

First Church of the Brethren at Carroll Avenue and Twentieth Street NW, dedicated their new education building on October 12. Dr. Warren Bowman, president of Bridgewater College, was the guest speaker.

Edwin West Jr. was elected by Roanoke City Council on October 10 to fill the unexpired term of Herbert Davies. The vote was unanimous. West was a retired banker who had been appointed to council once before in 1945 to serve the remaining term of Robert Cutshall.

General Sales opened its newest department store on Williamson Road at Carver Avenue NE on October 12.

The oldest bank in southwestern Virginia, Farmers National Bank in Salem, held an open house on October 18 to showcase its $200,000 expansion and renovation. Located at College Avenue and Main Street, the bank held an exhibit of artifacts used by the bank and its presidents during its eighty-six-year history. The bank was organized in 1871. Over 4,000 attended the open house.

Graybar Electric Company opened its new office and warehouse at 1125 Salem Avenue SW on October 14. The branch store had formerly been located at 601 Salem Avenue SW since 1928.

Dr. Pepper Bottling Company of Roanoke was named in mid-October as the top company among Dr. Pepper bottlers all over the world. J. W. Davis started the local bottling company in 1936 and was notified by corporate headquarters in Dallas that the Roanoke plant was the top seller per capita in the world. The plant was located at 421 McClanahan Street SW and could produce 144,000 bottles per day. The Roanoke plant's first location was at 214 Fifth Street.

This late 1950s image shows the Dr. Pepper Bottling Company, located at 451 McClanahan Street SW. *Virginia Room, RPL*

The Roanoke Symphony Orchestra opened their fifth winter season with three concerts in one day on October 14 at the American Theatre. Two daytime concerts were provided for local schools. The cumulative attendance was around 4,000.

Cosa Reynolds of Roanoke had a book of religious poetry published by Poetry Library of New York in October. The title was *As Sure as the Dawn*. She was employed by the Baptist Children's Home in Salem.

Voters in Botetourt County approved a $2.4 million bond issue in a referendum on October 15 by a 2-to-1 margin. The vote essentially gave approval to consolidating the county's high schools into two schools.

The Chesapeake and Potomac Telephone Company erected a permanent microwave tower atop offices on Second Street SW in mid-October. The new tower would permit line-of-sight transmission to the relay station on Green Knob near Vinton that would carry long-distance telephone calls in addition to programs of local television stations.

Several Roanokers attended a dinner in Williamsburg on October 16 honoring Her Majesty, Queen Elizabeth, and His Royal Highness, Prince Philip. The dinner was hosted by the governor of Virginia. Locals who attended were Mrs. Lee Trinkle, Mr. and Mrs. C. B. Houck, Dr. and Mrs. Z. V. Roberson, and Mr. and Mrs. Julian Rutherfoord.

Jefferson Hills Golf Course opened on October 15. The nine-hole, par 33 course had a membership of 500. The first foursome off the tee was K. L. Perkins, David Vaught Sr. and Jr., and Dick Morgan. Henry Moore was the manager.

Rosa Carney, eighty-one, of Roanoke County died on October 16 in a local hospital after she suffered a stroke in her backyard and laid there overnight before being found. The medical examiner ruled that her death was due to exposure.

Linwood Holton Jr., Republican candidate for the House of Delegates, showed up unannounced at a Democratic meeting in South Roanoke on October 17 to ask the two incumbents, Delegates Kossen Gregory and Julian Rutherfoord, questions regarding segregation, poll taxes, and school board appointments. Holton openly challenged the incumbents to defend their support of "Massive Resistance" in light of Holton's opposition to the same.

The Roanoke Astronomy Club held a night watch on October 18 from a hill near Bonsack to view the passing of the Russian Sputnik satellite as it passed over the Roanoke Valley.

Charles Williams, seventy-eight, of De Land, Florida, died on October 18. Williams had served on Roanoke City Council under the early ward system beginning in 1910 and was a former publisher of the *Radford Advance*.

First Christian Church of Salem held a note burning ceremony on October 20. Rev. Virgil Lilly was the pastor.

The US Supreme Court's ruling against Virginia's Massive Resistance strategies to school desegregation loomed large at the Roanoke School Board meeting on October 21. Dr. L. C. Downing, the sole Black member of the board, questioned Superintendent E. W. Rushton on teacher qualifications and overall education quality, inferring that Black students were not getting the same level of teaching and education as white students. The Supreme Court had struck down Virginia's pupil placement law, a cornerstone of Virginia's Massive Resistance program. Representatives of the Southwest Progressive Citizens League, a Black civic organization, addressed the board and pointedly asked why Black children in southwest city were not being sent to West End School, a white school, but being sent to overcrowded schools in northwest. Further, the delegation asserted that schools in northeast were inferior to schools elsewhere in the city.

Construction began on October 21 on a new women's dormitory at Roanoke College. The dorm was projected to cost $310,000. Fifty-six female students were being housed at the remodeled Methodist church educational building that the college had acquired.

Nine hundred prospective voters turned out on October 22 for a gubernatorial campaign debate between Democrat Lindsay Almond Jr. and Republican Ted Dalton. Both candidates argued that their opponent's plan would lead to wholesale race mixing in schools. Almond championed Massive Resistance, a multipronged approach to keeping schools segregated that had been developed by Democrats under the leadership of the Byrd machine. Dalton favored the pupil placement plan administered by local school boards. Almond supported the "right" of the state to cease funding schools that integrated, while Dalton opposed cutting off funds.

Mary Curtis-Verna, a graduate of Hollins College, gave a concert at the college on October 22. Since her graduation, Curtis-Verna had been singing as a lead soprano with the Metropolitan Opera in New York.

Irvin Graybill, twenty-eight, was sentenced to five years, suspended, on October 23 in the fatal shooting of his brother-in-law Horace Howell, a Roanoke businessman, on August 22. The shooting occurred a few miles north of Troutville. Graybill's defense was that he was defending his sister and other family members from domestic violence at the time of the shooting.

Leonard Muse of Roanoke and a member of the state board of education endorsed Lindsay Almond Jr. for governor in a televised speech on October 23. The Roanoke attorney stated that Almond was the state's best hope for keeping schools segregated. Muse stated that segregation was "as much a part of our way of thinking and living as the freedom of speech and the freedom of the press."

Lucky's Radio & TV Service opened at its new location at 3520 Williamson Road on October 24. It had formerly been located at 1132 Ninth Street SE.

Nicholas Pugh Sr. of Roanoke died at his home on October 24 at the age of sixty-eight. Pugh was the founder and chairman of the N. W. Pugh Company, a department store. He came to Roanoke in 1921 and founded the department store at 24 W. Campbell Avenue. In 1928, he acquired the Hancock Dry Goods Company and moved the store to 35 W. Campbell Avenue. He was president of the Roanoke Chamber of Commerce in 1930.

Roanoke's PAL boxing team defeated the Quantico Marines 5–3 before an estimated 1,500 at the American Legion Auditorium on October 24. Local winners were Lewis Johnson, Robert Carter, Fred McLeod, Bruce Durham, and Nick Nichols. The Roanoke team was undefeated after thirteen competitions.

Stuart Six, forty-two, of Roanoke died on October 25 from a gunshot wound. John Slaydon, seventy-three, of Boones Mill was arrested for the killing.

The Jane Morgan Harris cottage at Mercy House, a Roanoke County nursing home, was dedicated on October 25. The $35,000 cottage was to house twenty men. Harris was the general manager of Mercy House.

Sidney Weinstein announced in late October plans to double the size of his women's apparel store, Sidney's. Located at 501 S. Jefferson Street, the renovation would incorporate an adjacent building occupied by Advance Stores Company. Advance planned to move to the 100 block of Church Avenue SE. The total cost of the project was to be $175,000. Sidney's had been in business for about twenty-five years and was first located directly across the street at 502 S. Jefferson Street.

Virginia Military Institute defeated George Washington University 26–20 in football at Victory Stadium on October 26. Attendance was 3,500.

Katherine Tyler Ellett of Roanoke had a children's book published by Dietz Publishing in Richmond. *Young John Tyler*, about the tenth US president, had originally been written for Ellett's children. Ellett was a collateral descendant of President Tyler.

Greenvale Nursery formally dedicated its new building on Westwood Boulevard on October 27. About 300 persons attended the event and open house for the nursery that served about 150 children.

Mick-or-Mack opened its newest grocery store at 5301 Williamson Road on October 29.

Advance Stores opened at its new location at 19 E. Church Avenue on October 28. The store was formerly at 503 S. Jefferson Street. Arthur Taubman purchased the company in 1932, when Advance consisted of three stores, two in Roanoke and one in Lynchburg. Taubman soon thereafter closed one of the Roanoke stores and opened another in Winston-Salem. By 1957, Advance had forty-one stores across four states.

Magic City Laundry at 902 Thirteenth Street SW was sold and became Sunshine Laundry & Cleaners.

Richardson-Wayland Electrical Corporation discontinued their wholesale and retail Merchandising Division on October 31 in order to concentrate on their expanding contracting and construction division. Those employed in the Merchandising Division organized the Progressive Products Corporation and became the General Electric and Iron Fireman dealer in Roanoke.

Allstate Insurance Company held an open house on October 29 at their new regional office building west of Roanoke at 3517 Brandon Avenue SW.

The Fairland Country Club in the Villa Heights section was granted a charter as a nonprofit club by the SCC on October 28. The owners of the club were Roy Giles Sr. and his son.

The Roanoke City Parks and Recreation Department sponsored Halloween teen dances at parks throughout the city on October 31. Each park had its own local disc jockey, and they were as follows: Lansdowne, Ken Tanner (WROV); South Roanoke, "Jackson" (WROV), Preston Park, Lou Farraye (WDBJ); Raleigh Court, Dudley Townsend (WDBJ); Washington Park, Moses Lipscomb; Fishburn Park, Art Glover (WDBJ); and West End School, Bill Spahr (WDBJ).

Joseph Spigel, a women's apparel store, celebrated its fiftieth anniversary in early November. The store was located on Campbell Avenue at First Street SW.

Woody's Appliance Supermarket opened on November 1 at 3237 Woodlawn Avenue SW, next to Grandin Court Elementary School.

Draper Construction Company razed the former water department office building at 20 E. Salem Avenue in early November. Draper did the demolition for Roanoke City.

A proposed three-stage community center for Longwood Park in Salem was presented to the Salem Town Council in late October. The conceptual drawings had been drafted by the Roanoke architectural firm Wells and Meagher. The proposed center called for an assembly hall that could seat 500 for dining, a 1,500-seat auditorium, and a 1,200-seat gymnasium. The estimated cost was $803,000. Many in Salem felt a civic auditorium of some kind was needed as the carriage house at Longwood had burned several years prior, a place often used for plays, concerts, and other events.

First Church of God at Curtis ad Hildebrand Avenues NW dedicated its new $60,000 building on November 3. The building included a 275-seat sanctuary. First Church was the former Rugby Church of God that had sold its building to Pilgrim Baptist Church two years prior.

Firefighters do their best to extinguish the fire that engulfed the American Legion Auditorium in November 1957. *Historical Society of Western Virginia*

Hollywood University of Beauty Culture opened in early November in the Carlton Terrace Building. The owners and instructors were Melvin and Mary Ann Martin.

Evans Evans of Roanoke, and formerly with Showtimers, landed a role in the Broadway play *Dark at the Top of the Stairs*. The production would tour New England cities before its Broadway debut on December 5 at the Music Box Theatre. The William Inge play was directed by Ella Kazan.

A spectacular fire on November 3 destroyed the American Legion Auditorium, Roanoke's main venue for events and entertainment. Located at Wells Avenue and Williamson Road, the auditorium was a total loss despite the efforts of over one hundred firefighters. Many guests at the nearby Hotel Roanoke were awakened by the early-morning fire. The auditorium was built by the Roanoke Auditorium Company in 1916 and sold in September 1939 to the Virginia Holding Company, a subsidiary of N&W Railway. The auditorium was closed for about a year in 1946–47 when it was used for storage during a major expansion and renovation of the Hotel Roanoke. American Legion Post 3 purchased the building in August 1947 and reopened it the following month.

Kappa Alpha at Roanoke College moved into their newly acquired fraternity house at 316 High Street in early November. Their former house had been at 415 High Street.

The Roanoke County School Board moved into its new offices the first week in November, which were located in the Andrew Lewis High School annex. The board offices had formerly been in the courthouse.

Roanoker Lindsay Almond Jr. was elected Virginia's governor in the election held on November 5. A staunch segregationist, Almond won over Republican nominee Sen. Ted Dalton by a 2-to-1 margin statewide. In local elections, incumbent House of Delegate members were reelected. Julian Rutherfoord Jr. and Kossen Gregory were returned to the General Assembly, defeating the Republican opponents Hazel Barger and Linwood Holton Jr. The vote totals were as follows: Rutherfoord, 10,228; Gregory, 9,847; Barger, 6,515; and Holton, 6,394. Roanoke's Commonwealth's Attorney C. E. Cuddy was reelected over Republican challenger Ben Richardson. Roanoke City voters favored Almond over Dalton by a vote of 9,860 to 7, 866, while in Roanoke County, Almond's margin was 4,219 to 3,706. In Roanoke County incumbent House of Delegates members Nelson Thurman defeated his Republican opponent Frank Angell by a margin of 4,775 to 2,919.

Roanoke's J. Lindsay Almond Jr. was elected Virginia's governor in 1957 after having served as the state's attorney general. *Nelson Harris*

Roanoke Moose Lodge 284 acquired the former Cardinal Inn on Kessler Mill Road as its new meeting hall. The lodge was formerly located at 10 W. Kirk Avenue. The local lodge was one of the charter members when the National Moose was organized in 1913.

The *Roanoke Times* added another news service to its coverage beginning October 10, the Women's New Service. Stories acquired from that source had the byline of WNS.

Declining passenger service forced N&W Railway to drop three more local trains. The SCC gave the railroad permission to cease operating train No. 7 from Petersburg to Roanoke, train No. 8 from Roanoke to Norfolk, and train No. 27 from Norfolk to Petersburg, all effective January 1. N&W had also petitioned the SCC to discontinue trains No. 9 and 10 that operated between Bristol and Roanoke.

The seventh annual Shrine Bowl Classic was held between the freshmen of Virginia Tech and Virginia Military Institute at Victory Stadium on November 9. The football game was a benefit for the Shriners' Hospitals for Crippled Children. The game was preceded by a parade. An estimated 11,000 viewed the game, including Governor-elect Lindsay Almond. VMI won, 14–13.

A Presbyterian minister, two deacons, and an elder reported seeing a strange light over the Peaks of Otter as they were leaving a church meeting on the evening of November 7. The flying saucer moved left to right, made rapid movements, was still, disappeared, and then reappeared. All viewed the phenomenon from the Laurel Grove Presbyterian Church at Kelso in Bedford County.

Lucinda Terry, eighty-three, of Roanoke died on November 8. She was prominent in women's civic work and a member of one of Roanoke's founding families. She was the daughter of Peyton Terry, one of the founders of Big Lick. Terry helped organize the Roanoke YWCA in 1913 and was a delegate in 1937 to a convention of the Women's International League for Peace and Freedom in Czechoslovakia.

Green Ridge Presbyterian Church held a ground-breaking ceremony on November 10 for its first building. The church was organized in 1956.

Former President Harry Truman passed through Roanoke in the early morning hours of November 12 while sleeping on Train No. 16 from Welch, West Virginia, en route to Washington, DC. His sleeping car was transferred to Train No. 42 in Roanoke, but Truman never awoke.

Jefferson High School won the Group I football championship on November 11 when it defeated Covington 27–0. Rudy Rohrdanz was the coach.

Lowe's held a grand opening of its store at 3324 Melrose Avenue NW on November 14. The hardware store specialized in Hotpoint appliances. Edward Greene was the manager. It was the ninth store in the corporation's chain of stores in Virginia and North Carolina.

A fire heavily damaged the Crystal Spring Pumping Station on November 15. The fire destroyed the roof of the boiler room before being brought under control.

Julian Wise announced on November 16 that he was retiring as head of the Roanoke Life Saving and First Aid Crew after nearly thirty years as captain. His retirement was to take effect January 6, 1958. Wise said his reason was to devote more personal time to the field of research in rescue work. Wise organized the crew in October 1928 and was the first independent all-volunteer rescue squad in the United States.

Virginia Tech played North Carolina State in football at Victory Stadium on November 16. State won 12–0 before a crowd of 7,500.

Formal Wear Shop opened on November 18 in the Ponce de Leon Hotel Building.

Mrs. Augusta Bailey organized the Junior Women's Auxiliary of Burrell Memorial Hospital in early November. The teenage girls made dolls for children, prepared Thanksgiving baskets, and performed skits for patients among other activities.

Richard Beck, executive director of the Roanoke Redevelopment and Housing Authority, revealed plans for a major redevelopment project on a twenty-eight-acre tract south of Orange Avenue and east of Peach Road NW during comments to the Roanoke School Board on November 18. He called the proposal the Gainsboro Project, but he noted it had not yet been formally presented to city council. It was the fourth major redevelopment project planned, proposed or underway by the RRHA in the city. Dr. L. C. Downing, the only Black member of the school board, stated, "This is good news," and added that substandard housing was "too close to the heart of the city."

Graybar Electric Company held a public open house on November 21 at its new building at 1125 Salem Avenue SW. Graybar was a wholesaler and distributor of electrical equipment. Graybar opened its first office in Roanoke in 1928 at 601 W. Salem Avenue.

Mrs. June Goodloe Ferguson, formerly of Roanoke, was selected as the fashion model for the television game show *The Price Is Right* being broadcast from New York.

Cavalcade of Song was presented by the Thursday Morning Music Club at Jefferson High School auditorium on November 22. The show featured mezzo-soprano Carol Jones and an eighteen-voice male choir directed by Ralph Hunter.

The old Roanoke City Water Department building at 20 E. Salem Avenue was razed the third week of November.

Carver High School shared the state Group II V.I.A. state football championship title with Robert Moton High School in Farmville. The two teams played to a 13–13 tie in a title game at Farmville on November 22.

Anton Brees, a world-famous carillon virtuoso, inaugurated the electronic carillon at Greene Memorial Methodist Church on Thanksgiving morning. The carillon was dedicated during a Thanksgiving morning worship service that was followed by a carillon concert from Brees, a native of Belgium. The carillon at Greene Memorial cost about $20,000 and was installed by Schulmerich Carillons of Sellersville, Pennsylvania.

Roanoke Volvo opened in early December at 622 Eleventh Street NW. The owner was B. D. Peters, and the sales manager was Paul Key.

Ground was broken in late November for construction of the new 10,000 square-foot office building for Lindsey-Robinson at Seventh Street and Shenandoah Avenue NW. The company manufactured feed and flour.

Two Roanoke boys were named to All-American Sandlot Team for 1957, which consisted of twenty-two select players. The boys were Eddie Scruggs and Jerry Cecil. Both played for the one-hundred-pound Salvation Army Boys Club team.

The former home of Veterans of Foreign Wars Post 484 at the corner of Nineteenth Street and Salem Avenue SW was razed the last week of November. The old residence was considered a local landmark, but it had been acquired by Westinghouse Electric Supply Company as the site for its new warehouse and offices.

Reuben Clay, race relations officer for the Federal Housing Administration, addressed the Forum Hour at High Street Baptist Church on November 24. "In the problem of decent housing, enough decent housing, for Roanoke's minority families, we have a challenge that must be met." He also provided details about how families displaced by a redevelopment project could secure other housing.

Four Roanoke residents reported seeing unidentified flying objects in the early evening sky over the city on November 24.

The site of the American Legion Auditorium was sold back to the Virginia Holding Corporation, a subsidiary of N&W Railway, on November 26. The transaction essentially canceled the remaining debt that American Legion Post 3 still owed on the burned-out property. The sale dispelled any notion that the auditorium would be rebuilt.

Virginia Military Institute defeated Virginia Tech 14–6 in the annual Thanksgiving Day football game at Victory Stadium. With the win, VMI completed an undefeated season, their first in thirty-seven years. The 25,000-seat stadium was sold out for the game, which was preceded by a parade of the military cadets from both colleges along with school bands and veteran organizations.

The Salem Die-Casting Company was incorporated in late November. It was formerly the Keller Machine Company, which was founded in Roanoke in 1945 by George Keller but moved to Salem in 1952. The company was located at 1022 Tennessee Street.

A fourteen-foot-long hole appeared for the second time in the exact same location in as many weeks in the median strip of College Avenue at Eighth Street in Salem in late November. The cave-in was the farthest away from the river of any that the town had experienced. The prior cave-in had been filled in the fourteen truckloads of loam and broken concrete. A VPI geologist, who had studied prior cave-ins in Salem, indicated there were caverns under the town.

Liza Venable, fourteen and a student at Lee Junior High School, was selected as Snow Queen and would lead the mile-long Santa Claus Parade in Roanoke on December 3. Venable was selected among other contestants by the Roanoke Merchants Association, sponsor of the parade.

Kohen's Lingerie at 3 W. Campbell Avenue announced in early December it was going out of business.

Internationally known cellist Antonio Janigro performed at Hollins College on December 4.

Roanoke's teenagers were given copies of *Here's How*, a book produced and published by the Central Council PTA in collaboration with student representatives.

The free books, given to every junior and senior high school student in the city, dispensed advice on parties, dating, rules of conduct, curfews, and manners and suggested that church and home were the better places to go on dates.

Employees and volunteers with the Juvenile and Domestic Relations Courts and the Juvenile Detention Home delivered unexpected remarks at the meeting of Roanoke City Council on December 2. Some half-dozen employees had already resigned their positions prior to the council meeting, but statements made asserted that there was misappropriation of food, clothing, and other items at the home. Council decided to ask Judge K. A. Pate to address the wide-ranging concerns and report to the council any recommended actions.

The body of a premature baby was found on December 2 near the old Hollins Quarry. The body was discovered by Billy Orange and was contained in two paper bags stuffed inside a trash can. The child was a white male born about four months premature, according to the medical examiner.

Ten bands and forty-five floats were among the over one hundred units in Roanoke's annual Santa Claus Parade that was held on December 3. It was the biggest parade to date in Roanoke's history. The mile-long parade took about forty-five minutes to complete.

Salem's Christmas Parade was held on December 6, its second. The parade proceeded down Main Street from Shank Avenue to College Avenue, then along College Avenue to the Boulevard. The reviewing stand was located in Younger Park. WSLS televised the parade that was attended by an estimated 20,000 persons.

Mountain View Country Club announced on December 4 that it would become a public golf course again. The stockholders voted to give up their lease to Cy Bahakel, who would become the owner of the course formerly known as Monterey Golf Club. Johnny Johnston, the club pro, agreed to stay.

Local players named to the 1957 Group I All-Western District scholastic football team of the Associated Press were Clarence Tarpley, Andrew Lewis; Mike Rapp, Jefferson; Lee Fracker, Fleming; Arthur Price, Jefferson; Carlton Waskey, Jefferson; Tracy Callis, Jefferson; and Jerry Smith, Fleming.

A contract post office opened at Taylor Hardware Store, 410 Twenty-Sixth Street SW, on December 4. It was the second contract post office in the city. The other had operated for several years at Garland's Drug Store at 1232 Jamison Avenue SE.

A contract to raze the charred remains of the American Legion Auditorium was awarded to J. C. Hoelle, a Roanoke general contractor. Work was slated to begin December 16 and expected to take two months.

The Roanoke Central United Labor Council, formed by the merger of the Roanoke Central Labor Union (AFL) and the Roanoke Industrial Council (CIO), received its charter and installed officers at its first meeting on December 4. Frank Mundy was elected president.

Vinton held its annual Christmas Parade on December 5, which featured thirty units. Some 1,500 spectators lined Pollard Street for what was believed to be the largest Christmas Parade in the town's history.

Sunnybrook Shell Service Station held a grand opening on December 5. The station, owned by D. N. Thompson, was located at 7443 Williamson Road.

Huntington Court Methodist Church dedicated its new children's wing on December 8. The new wing adjoined the south side of the church.

Ground was broken for a new dance hall in the Bennett Springs section of Roanoke County in early December. The cinderblock building would contain a dance floor and snack bar and was owned by W. V. Arrington and Johnnie Moore. The building was off Bradshaw Road a mile north of Bain's store.

Roanoke's PAL boxing team defeated the team from Charlotte 4–2 in a meet at the City Market Auditorium on December 7. Attendance was 550, and it was the team's fourteenth consecutive victory.

James Comer, eighty-two, died at his home in Roanoke on December 8. He was the last surviving member of the first Roanoke City Council under the city manager form of governance. He was first appointed to the council in 1922 and was reelected eighteen times before retiring in 1942. He helped organize the Hicks-Palmer Company, from which he retired in 1949.

Peyton Jamison, seventy-three, of Salem died on December 8. He was the grandson of one of Roanoke's pioneer developers, Peyton Terry, and was president of the Exchange Lumber Company. He was also a charter member of the Roanoke Rotary Club.

Rev. A. L. James announced on December 8 his retirement as pastor of the First Baptist Church, Gainsboro. He had served the church for thirty-eight years. He was a past member of the Roanoke School Board and was active in numerous civic and charitable organizations.

Joe's Coffee Pot at 2902 Brambleton Avenue SW had a reopening on December 12 following an extensive remodeling. The owner held a renaming contest for the restaurant.

A patient missing from the Veterans Administration Hospital for two weeks was found dead in woods near the 2500 block of Maiden Lane SW on December 10 by four boys. The medical examiner determined the cause of death was exposure. The deceased was Ernest Wright, thirty-six, of Maryland.

A ground-breaking ceremony for Lincoln Terrace Elementary School was held on December 12. Dr. L. C. Downing, a member of the Roanoke School Board, turned the first spade of dirt. The contract for construction of the fourteen-room school at Liberty Road and Burrell Street NE had been awarded to Days Construction Company of Salem.

John Slaydon was sentenced to five years in prison after being found guilty of voluntary manslaughter in the death of Luther Six, a Roanoke taxi driver. The fatal shooting occurred at the Slaydon home on October 25. Attorneys argued that Slaydon had acted in self-defense.

Officials with Piedmont Airlines announced on December 13 they planned to establish fixed base operations at Woodrum Field in 1958. At the time of the announcement, Piedmont Airlines had thirty-three daily departures from the airport.

Santa Claus boarded the westbound *Tennessean* at Bristol on December 14 to begin his annual trip to spread cheer along the lines of N&W Railway. Santa passed out candy to children, corsages to women, and cigars to men on passenger trains and at station platforms. It was the seventh year for the Santa train.

This shows the groundbreaking ceremony for Lincoln Terrace Elementary School in Roanoke in December 1957. *Harrison Museum*

The Cosmopolitan Club of Roanoke was organized in mid-December with ten charter members. John Hart was elected president. The club planned to hold weekly luncheon meetings. The club was affiliated with Cosmopolitan International, one of the oldest service clubs in the nation.

Roanoke's Christmas tree on the lawn of the Municipal Building was lit on December 15. Philip Young, the mayor's son, flipped the ceremonial switch to light the tree. Grand Piano Company donated the life-size Nativity scene placed next to the tree.

The Roanoke Symphony Orchestra, four soloists, and hundreds of church and school choir members gave a performance of Handel's *The Messiah* on December 15 at Jefferson High School. The soloists were Hartwell Philips, Helen Wood, Charlean Eanes, and Oscar McCullough.

Larry Dorton was reappointed to manage the Salem Rebels in the all-rookie Appalachian League for the 1958 baseball season. The announcement was made by the Pittsburgh Pirates, the major league affiliate of the Rebels. A book of season tickets cost ten dollars.

E. N. Mustard of Charlottesville qualified at Luckland Alleys on December 15 for the fourth annual BPPA National Duckpin All-Star Match Game Championship held in Washington, DC. Otis Shepherd qualified as the alternate with a second-place finish in the qualifying tournament held at Luckland.

Seventeen boys at Jefferson High School were suspended in mid-December for initiation activities related to two groups, the Revelers and Delta Chi. The suspensions consumed a significant amount of time at the Roanoke School Board meeting on December 16 as the suspensions were due to the boys' haircuts.

A new volume of poems by Leigh Hanes of Roanoke was published by Golden Quill Press. *Wide the Gate* was a selection of Hanes's best work from over three decades. Hanes edited *The Lyric* for over twenty years and had been published in several national magazines.

The Roanoke County School Board renewed its efforts to acquire land across from the Veterans Administration Hospital for a stadium that would be shared by Andrew Lewis High School and the planned Northside High School. The board had already purchased fifteen acres from the federal government and made a request to add about twenty acres to the tract.

Becky Blevins of Roanoke was the state winner in the Voice of Democracy contest sponsored by the state Junior Chamber of Commerce. Blevins, a student at William Fleming High School, was presented her award by Virginia Governor Thomas Stanley on December 19 in Richmond.

Ruth Lynch, eighteen months old, of Salem died from burns on December 18 that she sustained when she turned on a hot water faucet in the home's bathtub.

Halfback Tracy Callis of Jefferson High School was named Virginia's outstanding high school football player of the year by members of the Virginia Sports Writers and Sportscasters Association in their annual poll that was released on December 20. Callis led all Group I scorers during the year with 97 points and gained 759 yards in 88 carries.

Gordon Watson of Roanoke announced on December 21 his plan to open a new funeral home at 1701 Melrose Avenue NW on January 1. An open house was set beginning December 29 for Watson Funeral Home.

The first in-service training for nursing program at Burrell Memorial Hospital held its inaugural graduation on December 22 at the YWCA on Orange Avenue. The guest speaker for the first graduating class was Mrs. Sylvia Hines, RN, a nurse educator from Richmond.

Tracy Callis and Carlton Waskey, both on the Jefferson High School football team, were named on December 21 to the All-South Scholastic Team, which was composed of sixty players from twelve states.

John Wheeler, believed to have been Roanoke's oldest resident, died on December 23 at his home. He was 101.

Salem Town Council voted against a National Guard armory for the town at its December 23 meeting. The effort for an armory failed to gain traction with the council due to vagueness in the proposed contract as to public use of the facility if built.

Rev. Edward Thompson died on December 23 at his home in Vinton. He was the pastor of Back Creek Baptist Church in Roanoke County and Promised Land and Olive Branch Baptist Churches in Bedford County.

Buttress Goria, a pioneer Roanoke businessman, died on December 26 at the age of seventy-three. A native of Lebanon, Goria came to America with his mother and siblings at the age of seven and settled in Roanoke in 1892. His family helped to establish the first Catholic school in Roanoke, and he and his brothers later started a wholesale grocery business in the city, Goria Brothers, which was the first such business in Roanoke.

The Jefferson High School band left Roanoke on December 26 for Jacksonville, Florida, to perform at the Gator Bowl during halftime on December 28.

Roanoke native Carter Burgess resigned as president of Trans World Airlines on December 27 to take effect January 1. Burgess made the joint announcement with TWA's major stockholder Howard Hughes in New York City.

David Huddleston, who appeared in the production of *Thy Kingdom Come* at the Sherwood Burial Park Amphitheater, had appeared in three off-Broadway plays since the summer. He had performed at the Actor's Playhouse, Chanlon Theatre, and the Carnegie Playhouse. He was a student at the American Academy of Dramatic Arts in New York.

The sixth annual debutante ball, sponsored by the Roanoke Altruist Club, was held on December 30 at the Star City Auditorium.

Curtis Hardware opened in late December at 5301 Williamson Road. It was owned and operated by Mr. and Mrs. Curtis Simmons.

An N&W Railway freight train hit an N&W passenger train on December 30 near Cloverdale. A fireman, W. R. Harris of Roanoke, was severely injured, while others managed to emerge from the wreck with minor injuries.

An 800-pound bull elk escaped from the Children's Zoo on Mill Mountain in late December. The elk was found by Henry Turner on his farm near Cave Spring. Unable to subdue the elk, the animal was shot by the game warden, and the meat was given to a local charity.

Roy Giles died on December 31 at his home in Roanoke at the age of forty-nine. He was secretary-treasurer of Giles Realty Company and part owner and operator of the Fairland Lake Club.

1958

N&W Railway continued its dieselization of the railroad on January 1, when three through trains operated in conjunction with the Southern were pulled by Southern diesels from the start of their runs to their destinations in Washington, DC. The end of the use of steam passenger trains prompted photographer O. Winston Link to photograph the last runs from Radford to Bristol. Included in the conversion was the Bristol-Roanoke run.

Dorothy Stuart, sixteen, of Roanoke died on January 1 from injuries she sustained in an auto accident on December 19. She was a student at Addison High School. Her death was the first time the Roanoke Star on Mill Mountain was turned red in keeping with an effort to promote traffic safety. The star was turned all-red on January 2.

The Safety Motor Transit Corporation announced the purchase of ten new thirty-seven-passenger buses on January 2. It was the first purchase of new buses since 1947. The exterior color scheme was cream over red.

Wiley Burton, thirty-eight, of Salem was killed in an auto accident near Dixie Caverns on Route 11 on January 3.

Fire heavily damaged the residence and grocery store of Joe Monsour at 902 Peach Road NW on January 3.

Hook-Fast, a wholesaler of transportation uniforms, opened in its new building at 2121 Salem Avenue SW in early January. Paul Dodson was the firm's president and treasurer. Dodson began selling bus driver uniforms as a sideline while working for Greyhound and laid the groundwork for Hook-Fast.

The new $1 million First Federal Savings and Loan Building opened on January 3 at Church Avenue and First Street SW. In addition to the bank, the building housed numerous other businesses.

A fire cause significant damage to the Dean and Catron Coal Company at 402 Shenandoah Avenue NW on January 5. A gasoline tank truck was the cause of the fire.

N&W Railway announced on January 6 that its experimental steam engine "Jawn Henry" would be scrapped. Built in 1954 and known as locomotive No. 2300, the engine was designed to travel over the most mountainous terrain on N&W's lines.

Over 350 persons attended a public hearing at Jefferson High School on January 7 to share support for a new civic auditorium as the American Legion

Auditorium, a main venue, had burned. Some thirty persons spoke, all in favor, representing various civic and business organizations.

Eight leaders of Roanoke's Black community ran a paid advertisement in the *Roanoke Times* on January 8 apologizing to Rev. F. E. Alexander, a minister and editor of the *Roanoke Tribune*. The signatories apologized for a prior ad they had issued in the newspaper on July 31, 1956, that questioned Alexander's commitment to school integration and their personal criticism of his thinking and theology. The signatories were Harry Penn, Lawrence Paxton, Reuben Lawson, C. S. Williams, Samuel Stone, William Henter, and Winslow Medley. Alexander had filed a $60,000 libel suit against the men, which was settled out of court.

A new Baptist Mission Center opened in early January at 1619 Wise Avenue SE. The new center replaced the Baptist Goodwill Center on Tazewell Avenue SE and was sponsored by the Roanoke Valley Baptist Association. Programming was set to begin on February 1 under the direction of Mr. and Mrs. Allen Seward.

Outgoing Virginia Governor Thomas Stanley proposed on January 8 that the Catawba Sanatorium near Salem be closed as a tuberculosis sanatorium. The response from Roanoke area legislators was mixed. Stanley's reason was the decreasing number of TB patients statewide. The state health commissioner indicated plans were being drafted to use the hospital for the treatment of other diseases.

Chesapeake and Potomac Telephone Company announced on January 8 that it was taking over the Bent Mountain Telephone Exchange. The exchange had about 160 customers. C&P's decision meant an end to Wilbert King serving as the Bent Mountain switchboard operator once more modern C&P equipment was installed, a process that would take two years.

J. Lindsay Almond Jr. of Roanoke took the oath of office to become governor of Virginia during ceremonies in Richmond on January 11. In his inauguration speech, Almond, fifty-nine, pledged a no-integration school policy and a shutdown of public schools if the Eisenhower Administration chose to use federal troops to desegregate as had been done in Arkansas. Almond stated, "To sanction any plan which would legalize the mixing of the races in our schools would violate the clear and unmistakable mandate of the people."

Unidentified flying objects were reported in the skies over the Roanoke region on January 11. State police indicated that they received calls from persons in Salem, Floyd County, and Pulaski County.

Hi Mac Hardware opened at 20 E. Church Avenue on January 13. The firm also had another location at 1102 Brandon Avenue SW.

Roanoke Times reporter Melville Carico was assigned to cover the General Assembly in Richmond, an assignment he would continue to for most of his career spanning four decades. His coverage began with his inaugural *Capitol Columns* that ran in the January 12 edition of the newspaper.

Rev. W. M. Gilbert, pastor of Sweet Union Baptist Church, announced on January 12 his plans to retire from the pastorate effective April 7. Gilbert had served as Sweet Union's minister for forty-three years.

Roanoke Building Supplies opened its new warehouse and office at Cleveland Avenue and Seventeenth Street SW on January 13.

Grace Creswell, a folk singer from Nashville, performed at Hollins College on January 13.

Local financial institutions published their balance sheets in mid-January for their fiscal year that ended on December 31, 1957. Assets and liabilities were reported as follows: First National Exchange Bank, $101.6 million; Mountain Trust Bank, $32.7 million; Colonial-American National Bank, $42.2 million; Bank of Virginia, $124.2 million; and Roanoke Industrial Loan Corporation, $723,400.

Roanoke City Council voted at its January 13 meeting to allow professional wrestling promoter Pete Apostolou use of the National Guard armory for his weekly pro wrestling events that had formerly been held at the American Legion Auditorium.

The new and enlarged Baptist Bookstore at 36 Kirk Avenue SW was formally dedicated by Baptist leaders in ceremonies on January 16. Kittie Sullivan was the store manager.

Episcopalian leaders announced on January 14 a meeting to be held on January 22 at the Virginia Heights Masonic Temple on Grandin Road SW for the purpose of organizing a new church in Roanoke. The new church would be called the Raleigh Court Mission. The diocese had acquired land on Grandin Road at Guilford Avenue SW for the new church, which would become St. Elizabeth's Episcopal Church.

L. O. Brown announced that his Brown Motor Sales at 306 Seventh Street SW would begin selling and servicing the new British sports car, the Standard-Triumph, in January.

Lowell Heaton, twenty-five, of Salem died on January 15 from injuries he received in an auto accident on Big Hill on Route 11 in Roanoke County the day prior.

Norman Hinchee pled guilty to involuntary manslaughter on January 15 and was sentenced to four years in prison for the fatal shooting of Theodore Lineberry. The three-day trial drew capacity crowds at the Roanoke County Courthouse.

Roanoke Postmaster Robert Via announced on January 15 that the Grandin Road postal station would move to a new building at the corner of Grandin and Sherwood Avenue SW. The new structure was to be built by Lillian Fowlkes and then leased to the postal service for twenty years. The postal station had been at 1418 Grandin Road and would remain there until the new building was ready.

Vinton Town Council voted on January 15 to seek a change in its charter from the Virginia General Assembly to allow the town's mayor to be elected directly by the voters rather than by the town council.

Eighty-one retail stores participated in "Greater Roanoke Days" in mid-January. The twice-annual event of the Roanoke Merchants Association asked participating businesses to discount selected items up to half off.

Clifford Hollandsworth, twenty-three, of Roanoke County died on January 17 when the car he was driving was struck by an N&W Railway train on a crossing near Glenvar.

Carter Burgess addressed the annual dinner meeting of the Roanoke Chamber of Commerce on January 17 and warned, "Communism is on a fresh march. It is a more devastating march than the one made by Sherman to the sea."

The *Salem Times-Register* was sold to Mr. and Mrs. Kermit Salyer of Rocky Mount in mid-January. The couple also published the *Franklin News Post*.

Jerry Lee Lewis was scheduled to perform at Andrew Lewis High School in the afternoon on January 18 and then that night at the marine armory, but the entertainer failed to show for the afternoon performance. Some 600 teenagers who showed up at Andrew Lewis were refunded their ticket prices. Lewis claimed bad road conditions delayed his Roanoke arrival.

Dr. Pierre Hill, the first pastor of West End Presbyterian Church, died at San Antonio, Texas, at the age of eighty-one on January 17. He served the church from 1909 until 1912, when it was originally located on Thirteenth Street off Patterson Avenue SW. He left West End to serve as a missionary in Korea.

This 1958 image shows some of the warehouses located along Norfolk Avenue SW. *Virginia Room, RPL*

First Federal Savings and Loan Association held a formal grand opening at their new headquarter building on Church Avenue at First Street SW on January 20. The main lobby contained a large mural depicting a family watching the construction of a new home in the Roanoke Valley that was painted by Marion Junkin of the art department at Washington and Lee University.

Showtimers presented *Solid Gold Cadillac* in late January. The lead romantic roles were played by Maurita Wiggins and Curtis Kirby.

Dutch paintings from the Metropolitan Museum of Art were the January exhibit by the Roanoke Fine Arts Center. The paintings were displayed in the Roanoke Main Library auditorium, and most were 300 years old.

The Canary Cottage Restaurant at 2117 Williamson Road was liquidated at an auction on January 20. Mrs. Allen Reedy was the owner.

This 1958 postcard shows the First Federal Savings & Loan Association on the corner of First Street and Church Avenue SW. *Nelson Harris*

Scruggs Garage opened at its new location at 2902 Williamson Road on January 20.

Kroger permanently closed its store at 1205 Patterson Avenue SW on January 25.

James Sigmon, fifty-one, of Roanoke died on January 27 at work when he was crushed under the bed of a dump truck at the City Garage. Sigmon's death was the first for a municipal employee on the job since the death of city fireman C. L. Ferguson on September 2, 1955.

The Virginia Council on Higher Education lent its support to efforts by Roanoke leaders to secure funds from the Virginia General Assembly to launch a technical institute in the city during its meeting on January 27. Roanoke Mayor Walter Young along with Roy Herrenkohl presented the proposal to the Virginia Council. The Roanoke legislative delegation had introduced legislation seeking funds for the project. Dr. Walter Newman, president of Virginia Tech, had indicated his willingness to have VPI operate the institute.

The Cave Spring Rescue Squad was organized in late January with Capt. Robert Monahan of the Cave Spring Fire Department serving as captain of the squad. Other officers were J. D. Hinchee, Ralph Bailey, and Norman Martin. Other founding members were Fred Tanner, Jesse Hambrick, G. E. Hinchee Jr., and G. C. Winstead.

W. J. Jenks resigned as president and chairman of the board of N&W Railway on January 28. The board, meeting in Philadelphia, named Stuart Saunders, executive vice president of the railway, to fill the vacancy.

Stuart Saunders was elected president of the 1958 Roanoke Valley United Fund on January 30, succeeding Thomas Rutherfoord.

A class for "mentally disabled children" was opened in early February at Academy Street School in Salem. The class had been long-planned for by the Salem Junior Woman's Club. It was the first such class for students in Roanoke County, as the county had been sending its students to a similar class at Roanoke's West End School. Mrs. Leland Jamison was the teacher of the class.

A ten-man committee to study the feasibility of a new municipal auditorium was announced on January 30 by John Fishwick, president of the Roanoke Chamber of Commerce. W. P. Booker was committee chairman.

Catherine Penn, two, of Roanoke County drowned in Spring Valley Lake off Deyerle Road near her home on January 31.

The newly organized Episcopal mission in Raleigh Court decided to call their church St. Elizabeth's Episcopal Church at a meeting on January 31. The first service of the mission was held on February 2 at the Virginia Heights Masonic Lodge, 110 Grandin Road SW. Andrew Thompson was chairman of the organizing committee.

King Funkhouser died at his home in Roanoke on February 1. Funkhouser was a president of the Roanoke Bar Association and a former director of Mountain Trust Bank. He established his law practice in Roanoke in 1919.

Plans for the Spring Run Swim Club in the Cave Spring section were announced on February 1. The club had about 200 members and had purchased a seven-acre plot for a planned swimming pool and picnic area. Long-term plans also called for a clubhouse. The club was located on Route 745, just off Route 221.

The Roanoke Valley SPCA announced a campaign on February 1 for an animal shelter. The $30,000 building was to be located on the corner of Tinker Road and Eastern Boulevard NE. James Hart Jr. was the SPCA president.

Goose Tatum and his Harlem All Stars came to the Roanoke College Gym on February 3 for a basketball exhibition game.

Clarence White, an eighth grader at Booker T. Washington Junior High School, was given a humanitarian award in early February for rescuing a child from a burning building a year prior while he walking home from school. The award ceremony was televised live on WSLS. A sister of the rescued child died in the blaze that happened on January 11, 1957. The rescued child was one-year-old Marilyn Baxter.

Newman's Pharmacy opened on February 3 in the Carlton Terrace Building, 920 S. Jefferson Street. The owner was David Newman.

A talent show for children up to age sixteen was held each Saturday at the Lee Theatre preceding the regular kiddie show of movies. Auditions were held on Wednesday afternoons, and the theatre's manager Jim Hawkins was the emcee.

The newly organized Roanoke Oratorio Society gave its first performance on February 9 at the Huntington Court Methodist Church. The ninety-voice society performed Mendelssohn's *Elijah*. Mildred Helmlich was the society's head.

Second Lt. Louis Caplan of Roanoke was killed on February 1 when two military planes collided over Norwalk, California. He was among forty-eight victims. A graduate of Jefferson High School, Caplan was twenty-six.

The Roanoke Ministers Conference adopted resolutions denouncing parimutuel betting and racial segregation as "contrary to Holy Scripture" during their meeting on February 3. The ministers also reaffirmed their opposition to funerals on Sundays.

Carter Burgess of Roanoke was named president of American Machine and Foundry Company of New York on February 5.

Roanoke Mayor Walter Young and a delegation from the Roanoke Chamber of Commerce spoke at a hearing on February 6 in Richmond before the House Appropriations Committee seeking $905,000 in state aid to launch the Roanoke Technical Institute. The money was to be used for construction and vocational training equipment. Dr. Dabney Lancaster, chairman of the Virginia Council on Higher Education, also spoke in favor of the request.

The Roanoke Ministers Conference reported the results of a religion door-to-door-survey that was conducted in early February. Some 28,000 homes were visited. The survey found that 93 percent indicated they were Protestants, 4 percent were Catholics, and not quite 1 percent was Jewish. About 750 families indicated no religious affiliation.

A new puzzle feature began running in the *Roanoke Times* on February 10, *Make-A-Word*.

Station At Dawn, an oil painting by Iva Moore, was judged as Best in Show in the eighth annual AAUW Art Exhibit of Roanoke area artists in mid-February. The exhibit was held on the first and second floors of Heironimus Department Store.

LiCona Dance Studio opened on February 9 at 507 Second Street SW. The studio offered lessons in ballroom dancing.

Grand Ole Opry star Grandpa Jones appeared on the local television program *Top O' the Morning* on WDBJ for two weeks in mid-February. Jones played his signature banjo and sang the show's theme song to begin each broadcast.

Roanoke Goodwill Industries opened a branch store in Danville on February 8.

The aurora borealis put on a display in the night skies over Roanoke on February 10. The northern lights were described as having a blood-red glow. The lights appeared to the north of Fort Lewis Mountain.

Clarence Dunnaville Jr. of Roanoke attained the distinction of becoming the first Black person to be employed as a special attorney for the IRS in the New York region. Dunnaville graduated from Addison High School in 1950 and obtained his law degree from St. John's University in Brooklyn.

Roanokers spotted for the first time on February 11 the US satellite Explorer in the night sky. The satellite was launched from Cape Canaveral on January 31.

Carter's Fruit Market at 1916 Williamson Road was liquidated at an auction on February 14.

Peyton Tabernacle, an interdenominational church on Eighteenth Street at Orange Avenue NW, dedicated its new building on February 16. Rev. Harry Peyton was the founding pastor.

This 1958 image shows the Southern States Cooperative Mills, which was located at 1003 Walnut Avenue. *Virginia Room, RPL*

Vance's Hardware Company opened at 2319 Melrose Avenue NW on February 14.

Temple Emanuel consecrated the site and broke ground for its new sanctuary on Brambleton Avenue SW on March 2. The new building was estimated to cost $250,000. Participants in the ceremony were Isadore Forman, Rabbi Samuel Shillman, Samuel Spigel, Frederick Bulbin, and Harry Rosenbaum and his wife.

A corporation was formed in Roanoke in mid-February to operate the former Fairland Lake Club as a country club. Roy Giles Jr. was chairman of the board of directors.

A formal dinner was held on February 14 to open the new Shenandoah Club at 24 Franklin Road, and women were allowed to enter the male-only areas of the club for the first time in the club's history. About 370 guests attended the dinner at the three-story, $400,000 building. The first floor was rented to two local businesses, and the second floor with an entrance off Bullitt Avenue contained a buffet dining room. The third floor was a men-only gathering area and den. Thomas Parsley was president of the club.

On February 17, the weather station at Woodrum Field recorded the lowest temperature on record for Roanoke, three above zero. At Apple Orchard Mountain in Bedford County, the temperature reading was twenty-three degrees below zero with wind gusts at ninety miles per hour.

Representatives of the Southwest Progressive Citizens League, a Black civic organization, made an appeal for a Black elementary school in southwest Roanoke before the Roanoke School Board at the board's meeting on February 17.

Ginnee Beauty Shop opened on February 19 at 125 Lee Street in Vinton.

The Virginia House of Delegates passed an appropriations bill on February 19 for $50,000 for planning work on the proposed Roanoke Technical Institute. The bill was forwarded to the Virginia senate.

A late-night fire swept through the three-story building of L. Cohn and Son clothing store at 208 S. Jefferson Street on February 20. There was smoke damage to the adjacent Smartwear-Irving Saks store. I. J. Cohn, owner of the store, indicated the store had $60,000 of new merchandise that was a total loss.

Sherwin-Williams Paints opened at 3653 Williamson Road on February 21.

The Virginia Senate passed the appropriations bill for the Roanoke Technical Institute on February 21 and forwarded the measure to Governor Lindsay Almond for his signature. The senate made one amendment to the House bill and that was to change the name from Virginia Technical Institute to Roanoke Technical Institute. The proposed institute would be a division of Virginia Tech.

The Roanoke District Conference of the Methodist Church decided on February 21 to purchase the former Crockett Springs resort property in Montgomery County for $23,000. The resort contained 350 acres and several buildings.

A new Lutheran Church in the Burlington area of Roanoke County held Charter Sunday on February 23 for those who wished to be founding members. The church was meeting in a house-chapel at the corner of Peters Creek Road and Deer Branch Road. The church had been meeting at Burlington School. Rev. Willis Buchanan was the organizing pastor.

Norman Lavinder opened Lavinder's Appliance and Furniture Store on Route 221 at Cave Spring on February 24.

Curtis Turner won the 160-mile NASCAR national championship race for convertibles in Daytona Beach, Florida, on February 22. Turner took home $4,100 for first place.

The *Roanoke Times* began running a new comic strip *Dilly* on February 24. The main character was a blonde model named Dilly Divine.

Charles Hancock, a retired Missionary Baptist pastor formerly of Salem, fired eight bullets into his estranged wife as she was working in a department store in Coeburn on February 22. Edla Hancock died almost immediately from the wounds.

Roanoke City Council appointed James Flippin, thirty-eight, as a municipal court judge during its meeting on February 24.

N&W Railway announced on February 25 that John Fishwick would become a vice president. Fishwick, forty-one, was the railroad's general counsel and a native of Roanoke. The following day, the N&W board of directors announced that Stuart Saunders would succeed R. H. Smith as president of the railway on April 1. Smith had been with the railroad for almost half a century. Saunders had been with N&W since 1939.

Lee Hartman & Sons, a sound equipment firm, opened at 3236 Cove Road NW on March 1.

Virginia's first state women's ten-pin bowling tournament was held the first two weekends in February at the Salem Bowling Center. Doris Layne won the singles tournament, and Evelyn Shelton and June Buchanan won the doubles tournament.

The Roanoke Symphony Orchestra presented a concert at the American Theatre on February 3. Internationally known Mischa Elman was the featured violinist. The symphony gave two concerts with a combined attendance of 4,000.

Professional wrestling which went on a hiatus following the American Legion Auditorium fire returned to Roanoke for a twelve-week run on Friday nights at the National Guard armory that began on March 7. The Roanoke Sports Club promoted the matches.

City Auto Wrecking Company at 1001 Orange Avenue was sold in early March and became Howell's Auto Parts.

The Roanoke Cosmopolitan Club formally received its charter on March 1. John Hart was president of the club.

Curtis Turner won the first Grand National late-model stock car race of the year at Concord, North Carolina, on March 2 before a crowd of 12,000.

A fire damaged the Assaid Grocery at Gainsboro Road and Patton Avenue NW on March 3.

A building at 305–07 West Campbell Avenue was razed the first week of March to make room for a parking lot. The office building had been used as a doctor's office.

Frank Mitchell was shot and killed by Leroy Hale on March 4. Hale walked into police headquarters and confessed to the crime. Hale stated the two had been arguing.

This circa 1958 image shows Mountain Trust Bank, which was located at 302 S. Jefferson Street. *Virginia Room, RPL*

Hodges Lumber Company opened its new showroom at 528 Shenandoah Avenue NW on March 5.

The possibility of using Coyner Springs as the site for a regional juvenile detention home was to be studied by a committee headed by Mrs. A. B. Camper. Coyner Springs was not being used and had been the former site of a tuberculosis sanatorium. In addition to several buildings, the site also contained 130 acres.

The Dublin Players, on their fifth American tour, presented *Shadow and Substance* at Hollins College on March 6.

Salem Furniture Company began advertising in early March that it was going out of business. The business was located at 113 E. Main Street in Salem.

Darling Shoe Store opened at 2308 Melrose Avenue NW on March 6.

Richard Pence, forty-four, of Roanoke announced on March 7 that he would seek the Democratic nomination to oppose Sixth District incumbent Congressman Richard Poff in the general election. Pence, an attorney, had the support of Governor Lindsay Almond Jr.

The Roanoke Historical Society elected Edmund Goodwin as its first president in a meeting of the board of directors at the Roanoke Public Library on March 7. The society reported 120 charter members. The society also reported that it had received $3,820 in Diamond Jubilee funds.

Ground was broken in early March to add a banquet hall to Bob's Drive-In at 3801 Williamson Road. The restaurant also changed its name to Bob Preddy's Drive-In Restaurant.

The cornerstone for the new Green Ridge Presbyterian Church was laid on March 9. The first section of the building was an $85,000 educational unit.

The *Roanoke Times* began publishing a daily word puzzle on March 10. *Add One* was developed by a Roanoke School teacher Mrs. Eugene Hale.

The ninety-member Pittsburgh Symphony gave a concert at the Jefferson High School auditorium on March 12, sponsored by the Thursday Morning Music Club. William Steinberg was the conductor.

Bethel Baptist Church in Salem dedicated its new education building on March 9. Rev. Landon Maddox, pastor of Villa Heights Baptist Church, was the guest speaker. The building cost $75,000 and could hold up to 350 persons.

The congregation of Westminster Presbyterian Church on Peters Creek Road worshipped for the first time in their new sanctuary on March 9.

Fink's Jewelers received the Brand Name Retailer of the Year Award for 1957 in the jewelry store category. It was the nation's highest retail award in the jewelry business. The national competition was sponsored by the Brand Names Foundation in New York. Nathan Fink was head of the firm.

Roanoke freeholders voted for an $8 million school building program in a referendum held on March 11. The vote was 6,412 to 5,259. Business and civic leaders rallied behind the bond issue in a campaign to improve overcrowded classrooms and aging school buildings.

Loft's Candy, part of a national chain headquartered in Long Island, New York, opened at 9 W. Campbell Avenue on March 13.

Three high school basketball players were named to the Group 1 All-Western Team. They were Ron Henry, Andrew Lewis; Jack Taylor, Jefferson; and Garland Berry, William Fleming.

Rev. R. R. Wilkinson began serving as pastor of Hill Street Baptist Church in early March. He was formerly the pastor of First Baptist Church in Rocky Mount.

The body of Frances Lorden, thirty-four, of Roanoke was pulled from Carvins Cove reservoir on March 12. Lorden's five-month-old daughter had died two days prior. The medical examiner believed the cause of death was suicide.

B. R. Hall Plumbing and Heating opened at their new location at 2727 Shenandoah Avenue NW on March 12. The company had been in business for eleven years.

Two navy guided missiles were exhibited at the Robert E. Lee Plaza across from the post office in downtown Roanoke in mid-March.

Ground was broken for the St. James Episcopal Church parish hall addition on March 16. The church was located at 4515 Delray Street NW. Rev. Manly Cobb was the rector.

Ramon's Club 460 opened west of Lakeside on Route 460 on March 15. The Saturn Trio performed at the dance club on opening night.

Club Oasis opened on March 15 at 323 W. Campbell Avenue. Woody Mashburn and his Wanderers of the Wasteland performed for both round and square dances on opening night.

A fire on March 14 caused significant damage to the Hannabass Food Market at 109 Lee Avenue in Vinton. The store was owned by A. V. Hannabass.

The Town of Vinton launched "Plant A Dogwood Week" on March 17 with the goal of planting 500 dogwood trees in advance of its annual Dogwood Festival scheduled for early May.

Colonial-American National Bank opened a new branch at 1941 Franklin Road SW on March 17.

Virginia Home Improvement Company at 2518 Center Avenue NW became Miller Improvement Corporation in early March.

Well-known historian and philosopher Dr. Arnold Toynbee spoke at Hollins College on March 18.

Richard Beck announced his resignation as executive director of the Roanoke Redevelopment and Housing Authority on March 12 to take effect April 1. Beck planned to return to being a realtor. Beck had led the RRHA program of redeveloping northeast Roanoke through its "slum clearance" project. He had been the RRHA executive director since January 1950.

Burrell Memorial Hospital opened a recovery room for postoperative patients on March 19. The room was located in the second floor solarium of the hospital and offered special-duty nursing and team physician care.

Smartwear-Irving Saks reopened on March 21 after suffering smoke damage from a fire at an adjacent store. Customers found a new interior in soft shades of pink and green throughout the four-story store.

Ronnie Reid, a senior at William Fleming High School, was the first-place winner in the state American Legion oratorical contest for the second straight year.

Arthur Early, sixty, of Roanoke was killed while working in the N&W Railway yards near Fifteenth Street SW on March 20. The car inspector apparently became caught between two cars when his leg was run over, causing him to bleed to death.

The trustees of Roanoke Memorial Hospital announced on March 20 plans to begin construction of a $600,000 nursing school building in the summer. William Flannagan, hospital administrator, said the residence and school would accommodate 124 students.

A wrecking ball demolishes some of the last remaining walls of the American Legion Auditorium in this March 1958 news clip. The auditorium had suffered a devastating fire some weeks prior to the demolition. *WSLS-TV News Film Collection, UVA Libraries*

The Roanoke Chamber of Commerce asked Roanoke City Council on March 24 to amend the city code to permit the use of firearms in an all-out war on pigeons and starlings in downtown Roanoke. The city had already begun using a spray said to deter pigeons, and Appalachian Power Company suggested electrocution of certain areas where the birds gathered.

J. W. Davis of Roanoke was honored on March 21 as the world's top bottler of Dr. Pepper soft drinks by company officials from Dallas, Texas, during a dinner at the Hotel Roanoke.

Two Roanoke City Council incumbents announced they would not seek reelection. Roy Webber, a former mayor, and Edwin West, who was serving an unexpired term, declined to run in the June 10 general election. Incumbent Mayor Walter Young announced that he would seek reelection but to the two-year, unexpired term of the late Councilman W. B. Carter.

Woodson Pontiac opened in mid-March at its new location at 3926 Williamson Road. The dealership had been formerly located on Marshall Avenue SW.

The University Club at 9 Elm Avenue SW went out of business on March 22.

The Roanoke Children's Theatre, sponsored by the Junior League of Roanoke, presented *Nutcracker Prince* the third week in March under the direction of Clara Black. The Roanoke Youth Symphony accompanied the production.

This late 1950s image is looking east on Campbell Avenue. The Ponce de Leon Hotel is on the left. *Historical Society of Western Virginia*

Wilma Lee, Stoney Cooper, and their band, all of the *Grand Ole Opry*, performed each weekday morning on the *Top O' The Mornin'* show on WDBJ the third week in March. "Cousin" Irv Sharp was the emcee.

The Addison High School Bulldogs captured the Gold Medal Championship in basketball in the Negro Division. The coaches were Irvin Cannaday and Charles Price. Players James Prunty and Arthur Brown were named to the all-tournament team.

After seven hearings and weeks of investigation, a special committee chaired by Roanoke City Manager Arthur Owens delivered a thirteen-page report on the Juvenile Detention Home to Roanoke City Council. The council had received numerous complaints about the operation and finances of the home, which culminated in an investigation. Among the main recommendations were creating a new home, discovering a new location for the juvenile court, relieving the judge of administrative work, and limiting the authority of outside assistance.

Claude Settlemire, director of Roanoke's public library, announced on March 25 that he was resigning effective May 1 to take a similar position in Boulder, Colorado.

Plans for a proposed interstate highway spur into Roanoke were reviewed by Roanoke officials and executives of N&W Railway on March 25. The spur had been planned to run from the proposed interstate near Kingstown, north of

Roanoke, through the Williamson Road section and connect with Second Street at Orange Avenue NW. City engineers planned to ask federal officials to extend the spur to the Hunter Memorial Bridge.

A landmark home in Roanoke was razed on March 25. The home stood at Orchard Hill and Mountain Avenue SE and was the former home of C. S. Churchill, an executive of N&W Railway.

Brown Derby Drive-In Restaurant opened on March 27 at the intersection of Route 460 and Peters Creek Road. Their opening special was a barbeque sandwich with coleslaw and a jumbo milkshake for fifty cents.

The third and final round of the Roanoke Valley Polio Eradication Campaign, sponsored by the Roanoke Academy of Medicine, began on March 27 with inoculation clinics at five schools in Roanoke County. Dr. Louis Ripley was chairman of the campaign for the final round. The goal was to administer 22,000 shots.

Officials with International Telephone and Telegraph (ITT) announced on March 27 plans for a new plant in the Roanoke Valley that would have a $1 million payroll. Construction on the $2.5 million facility was to begin in April and would manufacture electronic vacuum tubes for the military.

City Hall Barber Shop opened on March 28 at 304 Second Street SW.

The City Rescue Mission opened a branch thrift store at 10 First Street SE on April 1. The Rescue Mission was located at 111 E. Salem Avenue.

Calvary Tabernacle was formally dedicated on March 30. The church was located at 1802 Orange Avenue NW.

The Salem Recreation Center at 620 Florida Street, which opened in January, proved to be popular after a few months of use. Charley Turner was the recreation director and had scheduled numerous meetings, after-school clubs, and teen dances.

Henry Giles, seventy-five, of Roanoke died on March 28 at his home. Giles came to Roanoke in 1922 and went into the real estate business. He developed the Fairland and Southern Hills subdivisions.

Hollins College officials announced that the school would begin its first-ever graduate degree program beginning with the 1958–59 academic year. Hollins would offer the MA degree in psychology, and the program would also be open to males.

Actor-producer Douglas Fairbanks Jr. and his family spent the last weekend in March on holiday in Roanoke. His daughter was the reigning queen of the Apple Blossom Festival in Winchester. The Fairbanks spent the weekend at the home of Mr. and Mrs. Charles Burress, as Mrs. Fairbanks and Mrs. Burress were sisters.

The Gold Medal basketball tournament concluded the last weekend in March after beginning some weeks prior with 110 teams in various divisions and numerous sponsors. All-tourney players named by division were as follows: A Division—Dom Flora, Dick Kepley, Herb Weaver, Lefty Driesell, and Bill Matthews; B Division—Bob Stone, Carlos Chase, Dave Blondine, Charles Saul, and Paul Hall; and C Division—Dick Flinchum, Paul Richlin, Denny Weddle, Dick Calvert, and Bobby Fetter.

R. H. Smith officially left N&W Railway on March 31, retiring as president. Smith started with the railroad as an axman in the engineering department. He was appointed general manager in 1936 and became vice president and general manager in 1939. In 1942, he was promoted to vice president in charge of operations and then president in June 1946. Smith would remain on the board of directors.

In Roanoke City's campaign to rid downtown of pigeons, city officials agreed to pay any citizens ten cents per live bird trapped in downtown, effectively placing a bounty on pigeons. The limited trapping program adopted by the city had failed to yield desired results. A worker at N&W Railway found an estimated one hundred pigeons feeding on grain in a boxcar. The worker slammed the door shut to give the birds free passenger service out of town.

Shoney's Big Boy opened its "downtown walk-in" restaurant at 115 W. Church Avenue on April 1. It offered its Big Boy sandwich and a ten-ounce Royal Crown Cola for fifty cents. Disc jockey Jerry Jones of WROV was on hand to greet patrons and record them for his broadcast *Moonlight Serenade* that was heard nightly from 9:00 until midnight. Leonard Goldstein was the owner and manager of both Shoney's.

A. R. Minton Sr., who had operated a meat market in Roanoke for forty-five years, closed his store at 24 E. Campbell Avenue on April 1 due to declining business. Minton was also a former mayor of Roanoke.

Northside Fish Market opened on April 2 on Eleventh Street at Moorman Road NW.

Roanoke Lookout, a motor lodge and gift shop, opened on Route 221 at the top of Bent Mountain in early April. The gift shop offered handmade Appalachian crafts.

This 1950s postcard shows the Look Out Lodge and Gift Shop along Route 221 at Bent Mountain. *Virginia Room, RPL*

Members of the Peters Creek Church of the Brethren worshipped in their new $110,000 sanctuary for the first time on April 6. The sanctuary was designed by the Roanoke firm of Eubank and Caldwell.

Rev. J. E. Stockman of Roanoke's St. Mark's Lutheran Church delivered the sermon for the Easter sunrise service at Natural Bridge on April 6. Music was provided by the choir of Calvary Baptist Church under the direction of Helen Robertson. The service was broadcast nationwide over the CBS radio network. A heavy rain diminished attendance to about 7,000, and the choir had to sing the last hymn a cappella.

David Spencer, a twenty-six-year-old student at Virginia Tech, of Arlington plunged more than one hundred feet to his death during a cave exploring expedition on April 5 near the Botetourt-Roanoke County line in the Catawba section. He was one of fourteen Cave Club members from Virginia Tech on the expedition. The cave being explored was known locally as the "Murder Hole."

A 550-pound cake was cut at the Kroger Grocery at Sears Town on April 5 to mark the observance of the store's first anniversary.

Roanoke's PAL boxing team remained undefeated after over two years of matches as they sparred to a 4–4 deadlock against boxing teams from Eunice and Whitesville, West Virginia, on April 5.

Roanoke City school leaders in a meeting with architects on April 8 agreed to move forward with campus-style school buildings for future schools and additions to existing ones. The campus plan of one-story structures was advocated by James Tyson, city supervisor of secondary education, and architect William Caudill. Some fifty educators and architects participated in the meeting at the Hotel Roanoke.

Starkey Racing Grounds opened for the season on April 13 with eight races totaling 130 laps.

Thomas Beasley announced on April 8 plans to build a drag strip along Route 679 near Starkey. The $20,000 strip would consist of a 3,000-foot, dual-lane straightaway and a parking area for 2,500 cars. Beasley planned to lease the strip to Roanoke Dragsters, a local club affiliated with the National Hot Rod Association.

Roy Webber reversed a previous decision and announced on April 8 that he would seek reelection to Roanoke City Council. At the time of his announcements, seven other candidates had also announced for seats on the council in the general election.

The state highway department announced on April 9 plans to make Peters Creek Road a four-lane highway. Some $300,000 had been allocated for the project.

William Green of Roanoke deeded a three-acre tract on Catawba Mountain to the Fraternal Order of Police, Old Dominion Lodge No. 1, as a site for a boys' camp. The tract was located just off Route 311.

Covenant Presbyterian Church held a ground-breaking ceremony on April 13 for its new building on Deyerle Road SW.

High's Ice Cream opened at 1701 Williamson Road on April 11. "Cactus Joe" of WDBJ television entertained families on opening day.

Rocca Drive-In restaurant opened on April 11 on Lee Highway.

St. Phillip Evangelical Lutheran Church was formally organized on April 13. Services were held in a house near the entrance to Tinker Knoll subdivision in Roanoke County.

Showtimers presented the play *Major Barbara* the third weekend in April. Husband-wife team George and Elizabeth Garretson performed the leading roles.

Rev. A. L. James concluded his ministry at First Baptist Church, Gainsboro, on April 15. The church gave the minister a reception in honoring his thirty-eight-year pastorate there.

The thirty-first annual spring congress of the Gill Memorial Eye, Ear, Nose and Throat Hospital opened on April 14. Lectures were presented at the hospital and the Patrick Henry Hotel. The congress had been occurring since 1927 and attracted noted doctors from around the world. The congress had registered over 300 doctors from forty-two states and Canada for the 1958 gathering.

Night dances for teenagers at the marine reserve armory were banned beginning in mid-April due to what US Marine officers called "rowdyism" at the events. An estimated 600 youth regularly attended the dances.

The US Navy announced on April 14 that the *USS Roanoke*, a light cruiser, would be mothballed effective July 1. The ship, which cost $30 million, was commissioned in April 1949.

Buddy Morrow, trombonist, brought his nationally known dance band to play for the Roanoke Symphony Ball on April 18 at the Colonial Hills Club.

First National Exchange Bank opened its South Roanoke Branch on April 18 at 301 McClanahan Street.

Biff-Burger Drive-In restaurant opened on April 17 at 4317 Williamson Road.

Roanoke began planning for the arrival of NBC television personality Dave Garroway. Garroway planned to broadcast his *Today* show live from Roanoke in mid-May. Wanting to broadcast from Mill Mountain, the city erected a wooden overlook platform at the base of the Roanoke Star and trimmed treetops to create an unobstructed view of the city for Garroway's backdrop.

Wheelers' Amoco Service Station opened on April 18 at 3733 Williamson Road. Operators were Alvin Wheeler and Calvin Wheeler.

Larry Poff, seventeen, of Salem drowned in Bottom Creek while fishing on April 18. Poff was a senior at Andrew Lewis High School. Speculation was that he fell and knocked himself unconscious when he entered the creek.

The Traveltown Auction House opened on April 12 on Route 11 behind the Traveltown Amusement Park.

South Roanoke Dry Cleaners opened on April 21 at 1850 S. Jefferson Street.

Mrs. R. B. Jennings, eighty-five, of Roanoke died on April 19. A well-known civic leader, Jennings helped start the Roanoke YWCA and the Red Cross Chapter.

Over a hundred persons showed up on April 19 for initial tryouts for *Thy Kingdom Come*. The tryouts were held at the Sherwood Amphitheater, which was the stage for the outdoor drama, set to begin its second season. Dean Goodsell was the director.

Tracy Callis, a senior at Jefferson High School, received the 1958 B'nai B'rith Athletic and Achievement Award on April 19.

Former professional boxing champion Rocky Marciano (center) gestures to local media and visitors to enter his newly purchased warehouse in Salem in this April 1958 news clip. *WSLS-TV News Film Collection, UVA Libraries*

Howard Woody, a Roanoke artist, had a one-man show of fifteen oil paintings at Panoras Gallery in New York City in April.

Roanoke poet Carleton Drewry was named a regional vice president of the Poetry Society of America. Robert Frost was honorary president of the national organization.

The State Highway Commission began finalizing its recommendations for the routes of the new interstate highway system through Virginia in mid-April. Key supporters in Roanoke and Lynchburg advocated for the Roanoke to be the main crossroads for two such highways, one routed north-south and the other east-west via Lynchburg. Two other options were also under consideration, one with Lexington being the crossroads and the other being Staunton.

Former boxing heavyweight champion Rocky Marciano flew into Roanoke on April 24 to join his business associates in closing a purchase on a warehouse in Salem. Marciano Enterprises acquired a warehouse at 1338 W. Main Street, formerly occupied by Kraft Foods, and planned to convert it into a plant for packaging fruits and vegetables.

The State Corporation Commission (SCC) granted a charter on April 24 to organizers of the Citizens Bank of Vinton. Charter signers included W. P. Vinyard, E. B. Lassiter, and W. B. Huddleston, all of Vinton. The group planned to sell $500,000 in stock to capitalize the bank.

Marshall McClung, a prominent Salem attorney and businessman, died by his own hand on April 25. McClung was president of McClung Lumber Company and was involved in numerous civic organizations. He had been in declining health for several months.

Estill Auto Sales opened in mid-April on Route 460 between Lakeside and Salem.

Hazel Barger of Roanoke won a seat on the Republican National Committee during a meeting of the state central committee in Lynchburg on April 26. Barger was chairman of the Roanoke Republican Committee.

Rutrough Motors at 329 Luck Avenue SW became the authorized dealer for Renault in late April. The French auto manufacturer produced the Renault Dauphine and the Peugeot.

The third annual Vinton Dogwood Festival was held the first weekend in May. It began with a Dogwood Festival Ball in the William Byrd High School gymnasium on Friday night. A parade was held on Saturday afternoon through Vinton with Tod Andrews, star of the television western *The Gray Ghost*, as the grand marshal. Andrews rode in a full Confederate uniform while mounted on a horse during the parade and later crowned the Dogwood Festival queen, who was Pat Poindexter. The festival's theme was the history of the town. According to local history, the Town of Vinton got its name by combining "Vin" from Vinyard and "Ton" from Preston. Prior to this, the town had been called Gish, Gish's Mill, Vinyard, or Preston at various periods. The town was chartered in 1884.

Before a crowd of 1,000, Roanoke's PAL boxing team went down to defeat in three matches against boxers from West Virginia. It was the team's first defeat in two seasons.

One of the most horrific crimes in Roanoke's history happened on the night of April 28. Grover Lucas, forty-nine, bludgeoned to death his wife, Connie Maxey Lucas, forty-eight, and their two children, Mildred, age eleven, and Dennis, age nine. Seriously wounded was a daughter of Mrs. Lucas from a prior marriage, Dorothy Smith, fifteen. The brutal slayings occurred in the couple's home, a second-story apartment at 1126 Center Avenue NW. The medical examiner determined that all three deaths were due to each having multiple skull fractures caused by a pick. All victims were apparently attacked in their sleep. The slain children were students at Melrose Elementary School. Suspicion that something was wrong was raised by Mrs. Lucas's sister, Rosa Williams, of Roanoke County. Unable to get her sister on the phone, she went to the home and did not get a response when she knocked. Patrolmen W. A. Kelley and G. K. Ford were summoned and discovered the scene. According to Mrs. Williams, Grover Lucas had a day or two prior gone to the Crystal Spring Laundry where his wife was employed to collect her paycheck and told the supervisor that his wife and children had died in an auto accident in West Virginia. A laundry official alerted Mrs. Williams to Lucas's story. Neighbors were able to locate Grover Lucas a block away after police arrived and escorted him back to the scene where he was arrested. After two hours of questioning by Det. Captain Kermit Allman and others, Lucas confessed to the slayings. The slain were buried in the Huff Cemetery at Bent Mountain a few days later following a triple funeral service at Lotz in Roanoke officiated by Rev. Wade Bryant.

Fisher Optical Company opened at a new location, 507 Second Street SW, in early May.

Grover Lucas (right) is being escorted in jail in 1958. Roanoke police arrested Lucas for what they called "the most heinous crime in the city's history." *WSLS-TV News Film Collection, UVA Libraries*

Russell Henley was appointed executive director of the Roanoke Redevelopment and Housing Authority in late April. Henley, the director of Danville's housing authority, was to assume his post on June 1.

The Roanoke Valley Polio Eradication Campaign closed out its third-round effort on April 30 with a total of 30,445 injections reported. This brought the grand total of all three rounds to 94,449 shots of the Salk vaccine given, with the majority dispensed through school clinics.

Mary Cheatham, thirty-eight, of Roanoke was shot and killed by her husband, Luther Cheatham, as she entered their home on May 3 returning from work. An ambulance was summoned, and the husband handed the gun over to Harry Curtis of Hamlar-Curtis Funeral Home and confessed to the crime when Curtis arrived.

About 2,000 children participated in a fishing rodeo on May 3 at Lakewood Park that was sponsored by the Blue Ridge Game and Fish Association. About 1,200 children participated in a similar event at Salem's Lake Springs Park.

The Roanoke Fine Arts Center sponsored an exhibition of original paintings by Roanoke residents Peter Wreden and William Owen in May. The exhibit was held at the Roanoke Main Library.

The Cristiani Brothers Circus came to the Starkey Speedway on May 6 and 7. The circus was held under a big top that seated 5,000. Featured performers were animal trainer Capt. Eddie Kuhn and Zachinni "The Human Missile."

The Roanoke Symphony Orchestra and Roanoke Youth Symphony combined for three performances on May 4. Featured performer was Alfred Myers, a graduate of William Fleming High School, who was a member of the Cincinnati Symphony.

The Virginia Mountain League opened its baseball season on May 10 with six teams—Buchanan, Clifton Forge, Glasgow, New Castle, Hot Springs, and Salem-Glenvar. The Salem-Glenvar home field was the Veterans Administration Hospital stadium.

Harry Sherman and John Harris of Addison High School won the doubles tennis championship in the State Negro High School tournament held at Portsmouth on May 4.

Wells Gas and Oil Company Service Station at 227 Eleventh Street NW was liquidated at an auction on May 6. The business closed due to the death of one of the partners.

The Roanoke Ministers Conference adopted resolutions at their meeting on May 5 that chastised local newspapers for accepting advertising for alcoholic beverages. Local editors either declined to respond or claimed the resolutions were misleading in their facts.

The Virginia Amateur League opened its baseball season on May 11 with six teams—Ellett, Blacksburg, Pembroke, Newport, Back Creek, and Christiansburg. It was the twelfth season for the league.

General Electric announced in early May it was closing its Milwaukee, Wisconsin, plant and shifting that work to its Roanoke facility in July.

Dr. Corbett Thigpen, the well-known psychiatrist who worked on the multiple-personality case which was the basis for the film *The Three Faces of Eve*, spoke at Hollins College on May 10.

The Roanoke Board of Zoning Appeals approved construction of the Grandin Road Postal Station by a 3–2 vote at their meeting on May 6. Some 120 nearby residents had appealed to the board in opposition to the station's construction at 1733 Grandin Road SW.

A Civil Defense alert exercise was held on May 6 in which public buildings and schools were evacuated in a simulated hydrogen bomb attack on the Roanoke Valley. An estimated 18,500 schoolchildren participated in "Operation Alert 1958."

A fire swept through Bert's Slipper Salon at 9 W. Campbell Avenue on May 7 and caused damage to two adjacent buildings, Loft's Candies and the Young Men's Shop. Fire Chief John Brown estimated damage to the three structures at $60,000.

The Roanoke Merchants Association named their honorees for Mothers of the Year. Those named were as follows: Mrs. Curtis Scott (business and professions), Mrs. Edward Moomaw (education), Mrs. Edward Ould Sr. (religious affairs), Mrs. Charles Young Jr. (arts and sciences), Mrs. Hubert Leonard (family life), and Mrs. Emmett Albergotti (community affairs). Each woman was presented a silver bowl during ceremonies televised live on WDBJ and WSLS on May 8.

William Barton, former manager of the American Viscose plant in Roanoke, died on May 7 while on his way back from vacationing in Florida. Barton, a native of England, came to Roanoke in 1916 to help establish the Roanoke plant. He became plant manager in 1954 and retired the same year.

Johnson-McReynolds Chevrolet became Diamond Chevrolet on May 8. The dealership was formed in 1941 when Harry McReynolds established a partnership with the late L. C. Johnson, president of Johnson Chevrolet, which had been founded in 1932. Charles Freeman was president of the new Diamond Chevrolet Corporation.

Mary Doyle, a senior at William Fleming High School, placed second in the ninth annual National Science Fair that was held in Flint, Michigan, on May 8. Doyle's project focused on earthworms.

The Monroe Junior High School and Woodrow Wilson Junior High School marching bands placed first and second, respectively, in the school safety patrol band national competition held the second weekend in May in Washington, DC. It was the third consecutive first-place win for Monroe. Over 150 junior high bands from across the nation competed.

Some 2,500 Roanoke homes and offices received new phone numbers on May 11. The Chesapeake and Potomac Telephone Company switched them to the Williamson Road office. The change moved the customers from the Diamond prefix to Empire prefix.

Frank Snider, convicted of raping a ten-year-old Roanoke girl on Mother's Day in 1956 and sentenced to death, was moved from death row in Richmond to a state pen in Norfolk due to a last-minute appeal.

The Clearbrook Community Center was the site of a reunion on May 10 for a retired teacher and her pupils, whom she taught four decades earlier. Mrs. Sue Ferguson taught at the one-room Dry Hollow School, which was near the location of the community center, from 1917 until 1920. She had all seven grades with a total enrollment of seventy-two students. According to the newspaper report, she "saw that they were vaccinated, taught them Sunday School lessons, and mothered them generally." She also sent students to the woods to fetch switches she used on misbehaving students.

Heironimus opened its own book shop and lending library on the mezzanine of its store on May 12. Mrs. Mabel Porterfield was the manager. You could rent a book for two cents per day.

Curtis Turner of Roanoke won the Rebel 300 late-model auto race at Darlington, South Carolina, on May 10. He also set a new speed record for the annual race, with an average speed of 109.062 miles per hour. A crowd of 22,000 was in attendance. Turner took home $5,600 for his win in the NASCAR event.

Evangelist Morris Cerullo brought his ten-day Pentecostal healing crusade to Victory Stadium on May 19. The services were held under a "giant tent cathedral" that seated thousands.

The Park Drive-In restaurant opened on May 12 on Jefferson Street across from Elmwood Park.

Dorothy Smith, fifteen, who was injured when her mother and step-siblings were killed in late April, regained consciousness in mid-May following a lengthy surgery at Lewis-Gale Hospital. Doctors indicated she was still unable to speak.

Dave Garroway, host of the NBC network's *Today* show, arrived in Roanoke on May 14. Other personalities on the show also joined Garroway, including

Kokomo Jr. (a chimp), Bonnie Pruden, Jack Lescoulie, Joe McMichaels, and Dick McClutcheon. Upon arriving at Woodrum Field, Garroway and his cast were paraded along Jefferson Street, where they were received by Mayor Walter Young and John Fishwick, representing the Chamber of Commerce, and James Moore of WSLS. On May 15, Garroway broadcast his three-hour-long *Today* show live from a platform erected at the base of the Roanoke Star on Mill Mountain. Victory Stadium served as a secondary camera position with the west stands available for spectators. Highlights of the morning's program included performances by Virginia Tech's Hightie-Tighties Band and Pershing Rifle Drill Team, the Radford College Highlander All-Female Kiltie Band and Bagpipes, and Troop 76, Girl Scout Mounted Patrol. McMichaels interviewed officials with N&W Railway for a segment titled "The Plight of American Railroads." A film showing the Shenandoah Valley through the eyes of Garry Baker, a fourth grader at Wasena Elementary School, highlighted the scenic beauty of the region. Local personalities featured on the broadcast were Sgt. William Dupree and Jim Walsh. On May 16, the *Today* show was telecast from the campus of Hollins College and Dixie Caverns. Featured on the broadcast were performances by the Roanoke Symphony Orchestra from the front steps of the Hollins library, modern dance students from Hollins, and the VMI Glee Club, along with a taped interview with John Salling—a 112-year-old Civil War veteran living in Slant, Virginia. The show also did a spelunking segment from Dixie Caverns, the first time the show broadcast from underground.

Dave Garroway, host of NBC's *Today* show, waves to a crowd from his motorcade in downtown Roanoke in May 1958. *WSLS-TV News Film Collection, UVA Libraries*

WSLS-TV broadcasts the Glee Club of Virginia Military Institute performing on the campus at Hollins University for NBC's *Today* **show that aired on May 16, 1958.** *Virginia Military Institute*

One humorous incident from Garroway's visit was the *Today* show's chimp pulling a muscle while swinging through trees on Mill Mountain. Kokomo Jr. was taken to Roanoke Memorial Hospital for an X-ray. As the hospital, administrator William Flannagan approached the chimp, Kokomo moved toward him as if to give Flannagan a hug. Instead, the administrator was bitten on the chin. Kokomo later that day entertained patients on the children's ward with his trainer.

Salem Furniture Company, located at 201 College Avenue, held a formal opening on May 15.

Goodwill Industries held a ground-breaking ceremony for its Training Center for Adult Mentally Retarded on May 15 at 3125 Salem Turnpike NW. Dave Garroway was the guest speaker.

June Ferris was crowned Miss Roanoke County on May 15 in a pageant sponsored by the Roanoke County Junior Woman's Club. Ferris was a sophomore at Radford College and resident of Roanoke.

A crowd of 4,200 attended races at the Starkey Speedway on May 15 that featured thirty drivers from around the nation affiliated with NASCAR. The event was promoted by NASCAR and local driver Curtis Turner. Jim Reed won the 150-lap late model stock car feature race.

Five Black children, all from the same family, were withdrawn from Roanoke Catholic High School and St. Andrew's School on May 16 by their parents. The Black students had learned they would not be allowed to attend the high school's prom, only the banquet. When their parent, Mrs. Harvey Dudley Jr., protested to school officials, the school canceled both the prom and the banquet slated for the Hotel Roanoke, prompting retaliatory action by other students toward them. The Dudley children had attended Roanoke Catholic Schools since 1954. Sister Miriam, principal of the high school, confirmed to local media that Blacks were permitted to attend the prom. A few days later, the Dudleys sent their children back to Catholic schools after assurances that there would be no further harassment by other students.

Roanoke Lodge, No. 133, Knights of Pythias held an open house at their new Castle Hall located at 310 W. Campbell Avenue on May 18. The lodge hall was located on the top floor.

An Armed Forces Day Parade was held in downtown Roanoke on May 17. Over 1,000 marched in the parade, representing a variety of military and veterans' organizations. Mayor Walter Young was the grand marshal.

Raphael Ostrov opened Ostrov Furs at 815 Franklin Road in mid-May as a wholesale business for servicing stores within a hundred-mile radius.

Brambleton Auto Service opened in mid-May at 3205 Brambleton Avenue SW.

Brenda Dyer, sixteen, of Roanoke County died on May 18 in a Buchanan doctor's office after being taken there from an auto accident. She and four other young people hit a bridge abutment on Route 11. She was a junior at William Byrd High School.

This May 1958 photo shows a Girls in Action coronation service at Virginia Heights Baptist Church. The GA program was popular among Southern Baptist churches. *Heights Community Church*

Two Roanoke County men drowned in a pond at Crumpacker Orchards near Bonsack on May 18. James Hall, twenty-four, and Elwood St. Clair, thirty, were in a rowboat on the pond when it overturned and capsized.

Linwood Holton Jr. was elected chairman of the Roanoke City Republican Committee on May 19. Holton had been elected to the same position in 1952 after his faction ousted the "old guard" from committee leadership.

The Roanoke Ministers Conference adopted a resolution at their meeting on May 19 petitioning Roanoke City Council to create a biracial commission to "promote communications and understanding between the races."

Dorothy Smith was discharged from Lewis-Gale Hospital on May 19, having been severely beaten by her step-father, Grover Lucas, who attacked and killed her mother and step-siblings on April 28. Smith was released to the care of her older sister in Roanoke County.

Joint cornerstone-laying ceremonies were held for the new Scottish Rite and Kazim Temple of Roanoke on May 23. Over 500 attended the event, including Virginia Governor Lindsay Almond Jr. The new temples were 624 Campbell Avenue SW.

Shopwell Food Store No. 7, a grocery, opened on May 23 at 1205 Patterson Avenue SW.

Nearly 1,000 Boy Scouts and their leaders assembled south of Roanoke, just off Colonial Avenue, the third weekend in May for the annual Roanoke-Botetourt District camporee.

Goodyear Service Store opened on Melrose Avenue at Peters Creek Road on May 26.

Winton Churchill opened their storm windows and doors store at 131 Center Avenue NW on May 26. Erwin Katz was the store manager.

The Children's Zoo on Mill Mountain announced the arrival of some new animals in late May. The zoo opened for its seventh season on Memorial Day with a chicken from Brazil, four golden spider monkeys from Florida, and an eagle from Chatham named "Chang."

Chitwood's Auto Daredevils show came to Victory Stadium on May 28.

The new YMCA building at 425 Church Avenue SW was officially dedicated and opened to the public on May 26. William Grede, former national YMCA president, was the guest speaker at the occasion. Nearly forty Hi-Y members gave guided tour of the $1 million facility following the ribbon cutting. Over 1,000 attended the opening.

Denny Huff of Highland Park Elementary School won the city-county marbles championship on May 26 and a trip to the national tournament in Asbury Park, New Jersey. The last stage of the tournament was held at Elmwood Park. The second- and third-place winners, Kermis Ball and Elbert Caldwell, respectively, qualified for the southern championship in Greensboro, North Carolina. Hundreds of boys entered the multiphased tournament.

Final routing of the interstate spur into Roanoke would be complicated due to schools, school sites, a park, a cemetery, and homes, according to planners with the state's highway department. Highway officials met on May 28 to discuss a variety of options. In the vicinity of the proposed interchange at Orange Avenue and Second Street was Old Lick Cemetery, which contained approximately 2,700 graves. The route would also take a portion of the Booker T. Washington Elementary School site, as well as a site designated for a new school at Oakland Boulevard and Rockland Avenue NW.

The Junior League of Roanoke, Virginia Tech, and UVA officials announced on May 29 plans for a Harvest Festival to be built around the Tech-UVA football game in Roanoke slated for October 11. The Junior League would sponsor the event that all three organizations believed would lead to an annual Harvest Bowl football game between the two schools at Victory Stadium. Mrs. John Locke, co-chair of the Festival Committee, outlined plans for a queen to be selected each year along with a parade to precede the games.

Johnnie's Steak House opened on May 31 at 510 S. Jefferson Street, formerly the location of the Metropolitan Café. John Tsahakis was the proprietor.

The Park Drive-In restaurant that had already opened held a formal grand opening on June 1. The drive-in was located on Jefferson Street across from Elmwood Park, adjacent to the Angus House restaurant. Marvin Babb was the manager of both restaurants.

Fairland Country Club, formerly Fairland Lake Club, held a formal opening with a public open house on June 1. Advertisements announced swimming, miniature golf, picnic facilities, and refreshments. The club was located off Cove Road in the Villa Heights section.

The *Roanoke Times* changed its home delivery subscription rates effective June 1 to forty-five cents per week.

R. D. Hunt aced the 115-yard seventh hole at the Jefferson Hills Golf Course on June 1. It was the first hole-in-one ever recorded at the all-par 3 course.

A Hustings Court grand jury indicted Grover Lucas on June 2 for the murders of his wife and two small children in late April. It was anticipated that the unemployed auto mechanic would be committed to Southwestern State Hospital at Marion for psychiatric examinations prior to the June 26 start of his trial. G. W. Reed was Lucas's court-appointed defense attorney. The grand jury also returned a murder indictment against Luther Cheatham for the killing of his wife on May 3. Cheatham asserted his gun went off accidentally while cleaning it.

Rehearsals began on June 9 for the second season of *Thy Kingdom Come* at the Sherwood Burial Park Amphitheater. Most of the leading actors returned to play their former roles. The religious outdoor drama would run June 21 through August 31. The role of the Apostle Paul would again be played by Carl Clarke.

Oakey Cleaners in Salem was sold in early May to Vincent Wheeler and C. J. Mays of Fast Service Laundry and Cleaners in Roanoke. The plant, located at Colorado Street and Boulevard, would be known as Salem Fast Service Shirts and Cleaning. The cleaning business had originally been established by Frank Oakey.

Nearly 6,000 persons visited the Children's Zoo on Mill Mountain during its opening Memorial Day weekend. The zoo was under the management of the Roanoke Parks and Recreation Department.

Virginia Governor Lindsay Almond Jr. of Roanoke held a press conference on June 3 in light of court rulings against his program of Massive Resistance. At his media event in Richmond, Almond stated the tuition grants would be made available to parents to send their children to private schools should their local public schools integrate. "I am more convinced than ever before that we cannot have mixing of the races in the schools."

Fair-Acre Farm Store and Garden Center opened its new store at 2601 Franklin Road SW on June 5. The retail store was owned by Lindsey-Robinson and Company.

The forty-five-foot, 2.5-ton steeple was placed atop the Hollins College chapel on June 3. The $500,000 chapel was still under construction at the time.

The new $250,000 distribution station at Kumis in Roanoke County was put into operation on June 4 by Appalachian Electric Power Company. The station provided additional electric power to customers between Salem and Shawsville along Route 11.

Officials with the Soap Box Derby announced in early June a change of venue for the annual event. The new location would be at the Parkway Center on Route 679, midway between Starkey and Route 220. The race had formerly been held at the Salem Turnpike and prior to that on Crystal Spring Avenue SW. The new location was also being developed for drag races.

The Roanoke Merchants Association named its Fathers of the Year honorees, and they were as follows: Alan Wilson (family life), Roy Herrenkohl (religious activities), William Griggs Sr. (youth leadership), and Warren Stansbury (civic affairs).

The B and F Skating Rink opened at 1312 Riverland Road SE, near the American Viscose plant, on June 13. The rink had 6,000 square feet of floor space and a concession stand. It was owned by Logan Brown and H. R. Farmer.

Dunn Brothers Miniature Circus was displayed at Heironimus for a three-week period that began June 6. The circus, which consisted of thousands of wood-carved pieces, had been used as props in Paramount Studios movies including *The Greatest Show on Earth.*

Lee Hy Beauty Bar opened on Lee Highway on June 8 and was operated by Mildred Johnson and Marie Hopkins.

Roanoke Department of Parks and Recreation began their evening teen dances on tennis courts during the summer on June 2. Dances were held every Monday at Preston Park, Wednesday at Raleigh Court Park, and Friday at South Roanoke Park. Area radio disc jockeys provided the music. Jim Gearhart and Ken Tanner of WROV were at Preston Park, Bill Spahr of WDBJ was at Raleigh Court, and Doug Newton of WSLS was at South Roanoke. The dances went through August 27 and were sponsored by Roanoke Coca-Cola Bottling Works.

The cornerstone for a new parish building at College Lutheran Church in Salem was laid on June 8. The $200,000 structure would house classrooms and an assembly hall.

The Salem Avenue Parking Garage in Roanoke underwent a new management contract in early June with Allright Virginia Company.

This June 1958 photo shows the N&W Railway passenger station in Roanoke. *N&W Historical Photographs Collection, VPI&SU Libraries*

Professional wrestling, typically held at the National Guard armory, moved to Victory Stadium for some nights during the summer. The first such night was June 10, which featured Red Bastein against "Cry Baby" Corby. There was also advertised "midget wrestling" that featured Ivan the Terrible and Tom Thumb in a tag-team match versus Cowboy Bradley and Lord Little Brook. Advance tickets could be purchased at the Sportsman. Pro wrestling was sponsored by the Roanoke Sports Club.

Elbert Caldwell of Roanoke shot his way to win the championship in the 1958 Southern Marbles Tournament at Greensboro, North Carolina, on June 7. He was a fifth grader at Jamison School.

Richard Guerrant and William Mounfield announced the formation of a new architectural firm on June 7 with plans to locate in their own building on Lee Highway.

Walter Henry launched an egg factory in the Poages Mill section in early June. Henry expected an output of about 1,800 eggs per day. He had nearly 2,200 DeKalb pullets. Eggs were collected four times per day.

Roanoke golfer George Fulton Jr. squandered a final-round lead to earn a third-place finish in the Virginia State Open golf championship held at Staunton the first weekend in June. His four-round score was 284.

The Birmingham Black Barons and the Kansas City Monarchs, both of the Negro American League, played at Salem Municipal Field on June 9.

In the general election for Roanoke City Council on June 10, voters returned incumbents Walter Young and Roy Webber to office and elected newcomers Willis Anderson and Dr. C. M. Cornell. Cornell edged out Caldwell Butler by a mere fourteen votes. Young, Webber and Anderson were viewed as more establishment candidates, while Cornell was viewed as an outsider who had criticized the council and city administration during his campaign. Two ballots were held, as eight candidates vied for three four-year terms and two candidates vied for a two-year term. Young defeated Robert Wagner for the special election, 4,601 to 3,014. Those on the main ballot finished as follows: Webber, 4,351; Anderson, 3,763; Cornell, 3,231; Butler, 3,217; James Brice, 2,810; Alan Decker, 2,572; Carl Woodson, 1,953; and I. V. Jessee, 1,064. Anderson, twenty-nine, was one of the youngest council members in the city's history.

In Salem's general election for town council, James Peters, Jeff Hart, and Jack Dame were elected. An incumbent, Howard Roberts, placed fourth. In Vinton, voters directly elected their mayor for the first time since 1934, and Shirley Crowder was elected to the post. He defeated J. W. Leggett and Letcher Adkins. Elected to the Vinton Town Council were O. L. Horn and Leonard Hale. They defeated Marvin Craig, Norman Dowdy, and Walter Wainwright.

William Bier, eleven, of Roanoke died on June 11 as a result of being run over by the Roanoke Water Department truck when his bike skidded underneath the moving vehicle. The accident happened just off Hollins Road.

A group of Roanoke residents petitioned Roanoke City Council to lease them land adjacent to Woodrum Field as a golf course for Blacks. The land had been earmarked for park purposes. Those petitioning were Justin Plummer, Lawrence Hamlar, Carroll Holland, William Thomas, and Ira Womack.

Joe Stern Clothiers advertised in mid-June that it was going out business. The store was located at 124 W. Campbell Avenue, and the reason for the closing was due to the illness of the owner.

Two new self-service Save Stations opened in mid-June at Nineteenth Street and Melrose Avenue NW and on Route 11 between Roanoke and Salem. There were a total of five such gas stations in the valley.

The Roanoke Booster Club made its annual trip to White Sulphur Springs on June 18. "Roanoke in 1980" was the theme of the dinner, with John Fishwick being the keynote speaker. Dr. E. G. Gill was president of the club. A special train was provided by N&W Railway for the trip. Attendance was 350. For the first time in the club's history, females were permitted to take part, albeit briefly. Five women with the Junior League rode the train from Roanoke to Buchanan and passed out literature promoting the new Harvest Festival football game in the fall. At Buchanan, they disembarked. In Fishwick's remarks about Roanoke's future, he predicted that by 1980, the city would have a population of 250,000, a consolidated city-county government, and a new downtown. The boosters also adopted two resolutions calling for a new civic auditorium to be built and for the expansion of Woodrum Field.

Raleigh Court Presbyterian Church consecrated its new $340,000 sanctuary on June 15. Lewis Smithey was the local architect, and Lewis Lionberger was the general contractor. Work on the sanctuary was begun in January 1957.

This 1958 image shows Raleigh Court Presbyterian Church at 1837 Grandin Road SW. The sanctuary (right) was consecrated in June 1958. *Virginia Room, RPL*

Green Ridge Presbyterian Church worshipped in its new sanctuary for the first time on June 15. The church was located at Alpine Road and Starmount Avenue.

Roanoker E. C. Ninde Jr. was cast as Peter Felham in the outdoor drama *Common Glory* at Williamsburg for its summer season.

Ralph English won the annual city-county golf tournament the second weekend in June. George Fulton Jr. finished second. Their respective scores were 287 and 289. The tournament was held at Mountain View Country Club.

Cave Spring Methodist Church voted on June 15 to sell its old sanctuary for $17,500. The property, located at the junction of McVitty Road and Mt. Vernon Drive, was to be vacated once the congregation moved into its new sanctuary off Colonial Avenue SW. The old sanctuary was believed to be over one hundred years old.

A cornerstone-laying ceremony was held on June 17 for the new Central YMCA. Ben Parrott, board vice president, presided at the event.

Beamer Motors, a Lincoln-Mercury dealer, opened at 425 Marshall Avenue SW on June 18. The dealership was the successor to Sylvan Lincoln-Mercury Sales that had gone into receivership.

Showtimers presented the comedy *Teahouse of the August Moon* the third weekend in June. Lead roles were played by Wilson Price, John Willett, Bob Ayers, Francine League, Beverly Scott, George Brown, Dennis Pendleton, and Ken Cook. Betty Garretson was the director.

This image shows a performance of *Thy Kingdom Come* in the Sherwood Burial Park Amphitheater during the summer of 1958. *Salem Historical Society*

The first golf league in Roanoke started playing at Mountain View Country Club on June 17. The scratch league consisted of eight teams—Viscose, Vinton Weaving, N&W Railway, C&P Telephone, General Electric No. 1 and No. 2, Moore Appliance, and Stone Printing. Johnny Johnston headed the league.

A new section of Williamson Road was opened on June 20 "through the slum clearance project" in northeast Roanoke. The new section opened at Orange Avenue and was four lanes south to Second Street. The new section was part of the overall Commonwealth Project that involved the redevelopment of some eighty-four acres.

The Kazim Shrine Circus was at Victory Stadium on June 20 and 21.

Bonnie Richardson, eighteen and a student at William Fleming High School, was killed in an auto crash in Roanoke County on June 19. The accident occurred on Route 676 between the Salem Turnpike and the Veterans Administration Hospital. Four other teenagers in the car received minor injuries.

The outdoor religious drama *Thy Kingdom Come* opened on the night of June 21 for its second summer season in the amphitheatre of Sherwood Burial Park. The second season's production was shortened to two hours.

Fulton Motor Company became the local dealership authorized to sell the economy-sized import Simca Aronde automobile. The motor company was a dealership for Chrysler-Plymouth.

Paul Anderson, billed as the world's strongest man, was the main attraction at the professional wrestling event held at Victory Stadium on June 24. Anderson was the reigning Olympic and world weight lifting champion. He squared off against Gypsy Joe. The other main mat event was between the Great Bolo and Red Bastein.

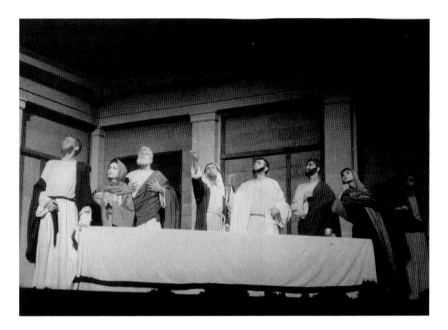

The outdoor drama *Thy Kingdom Come* ran for three summers during the late 1950s and was the only outdoor religious drama in the United States at that time. *Salem Historical Society*

The Appalachian League opened its minor league baseball season on June 25. The five-team circuit consisted of teams from Bluefield, Johnson City, Pulaski, Salem, and Wytheville. The Salem Rebels team was affiliated with the Pittsburgh Pirates and was managed by Larry Dorton.

Annie Kennett of Roanoke died on June 23 of injuries she sustained in an auto accident on June 7 at the intersection of Fleming Avenue and Winslow Street NW.

A former resident of Salem had a butterfly named after him. Dr. Carl Gottschalk, an assistant in the medical department at UNC in Chapel Hill, discovered the species of butterfly on his family's farm when he was a student at Andrew Lewis High School. The Strymon cecrops gottschalki has a yellow band, while the ordinary Strymon cecrops had a red band.

Officials with N&W Railway announced on June 25 plans to purchase 268 new diesel locomotives at an estimated cost of $50 million. Railway president Stuart Saunders also stated that 1960 was the year for retirement of the last of the N&W's steam engines. N&W was the last major railroad company in the United States to use steam locomotives. The last locomotives made by N&W in Roanoke were made in 1953.

The Roanoke County School Board announced on June 25 the purchase of thirty-four acres of land as the site for the planned Northside High School. The purchase price was $35,000 and involved two tracts owned by Mary Firebaugh and Hugh Womack, respectively. The tracts adjoined the Southview School campus on Route 117.

The Miss Virginia pageant began on June 27 with a reception at the Patrick Henry Hotel. The event was sponsored by the Valley Junior Woman's Club with the competition held at the Hotel Roanoke. Featured guest was Marilyn Van Derbur, Miss America. The winner was Barbara Guthrie, nineteen, of Martinsville.

Colonial Avenue Sinclair Service Station opened on June 27 on Colonial Avenue at Broadway SW. Opening day featured pony rides for children and a variety of drawings for prizes. Clarence Etue and Earl Etue were the owners.

The Roanoke Drag Strip opened on June 29 near Starkey. The half-mile asphalt strip was owned by Thomas Beasley and leased by the Roanoke Dragsters Auto Club. Bob Bateman was president of the club. It was one of only two sanctioned drag strips in the state recognized by the National Hot Rod Association, with the other being in Petersburg. Roanoke police fully supported the strip in the hope that it would curb drag racing on city streets. Nearly 2,000 attended the opening day.

Rutrough Motors announced in late June it was canceling its contract to sell Edsels. Henry Rutrough said sales had been insufficient to warrant the overhead.

Officials with US Steel announced on June 27 that more employees from its American Bridge Division in Roanoke would be transferred to Birmingham, Alabama, effective July 1. All employees affected worked in the design and estimating department.

The proposed leasing of land adjacent to Woodrum Field for a Black golf course was opposed by Roanoke City Council's Airport Committee at their meeting on June 27. The committee indicated the land was needed for the airport's planned expansion.

This undated image shows the Roanoke Drag Strip at Starkey. The strip opened in June 1958. *Pete Wheeler*

Sinclair Brown, T. J. Andrews, and E. K. Mattern were reappointed to new terms on the Roanoke County School Board by the Roanoke County School Trustee Electoral Board on June 27. The appointments were formally made by Circuit Court Judge Fred Hoback.

Nehi Bottling Corporation at 302 Fifth Street SW advertised on June 28 a new product, Nehi Lemonade.

Roanoke lost its long-held third-place ranking in the list of Virginia's most populous cities on July 1. Roanoke fell to fourth place, with Newport News moving into third. Norfolk was first, with Richmond second. Roanoke's population was estimated at 104,400.

Showtimers presented the Irish comedy *The Loud, Red Patrick* the first weekend in July at Roanoke College. Lead roles were performed by Carol Cundiff, Pam Divers, Alden Willis, Joan Turner, George Garretson, and Tommy O'Neill.

Kroger Company announced in late June plans for new distribution center located on a thirty-acre tract west of Salem near Glenvar. The center would serve Kroger stores in four states. The projected cost for the new facility was $7 million. Paxton Judge was head of Kroger's Roanoke division.

Loebl Cleaners and Dyers opened a drive-in at 2923 Brambleton Avenue SW on June 30.

Roanoke City Council on June 30 endorsed the proposed east-west interstate highway, known as I-64, along a route that generally followed US 460 and 220. That link would serve Lynchburg, Bedford, and Clifton Forge. The route favored by the council was in contrast to an already-approved route that took I-64 through Charlottesville and Waynesboro.

Dr. L. C. Downing was appointed to the seven-member Virginia Advisory Committee of President Dwight Eisenhower's Civil Rights Commission. It was Downing's second three-year term on the committee.

David Burrows, a Roanoke contractor, was named by Roanoke City Council to the school board along with two incumbents, Richard Edwards and Clarence Hawkins.

Roanoke City Council denied a request made by the Roanoke Ministers Conference to appoint a biracial committee to promote communication and understanding. The council expressed support for the sentiment but decided that with no racial legislation coming before it, such a committee was unnecessary.

Norman Moore was appointed as a full-time judge on Roanoke County Court and the Juvenile and Domestic Relations Court. The appointment was made by Judge Fred Hoback.

The Chesapeake and Potomac Telephone Company announced on June 30 plans to spend $41,000 on improvements to the Bent Mountain Exchange that would include 465 new poles and twenty-two miles of new lines for the section.

Colonial-American National Bank bought the former L. Cohn and Son building on South Jefferson Street for $90,000 on July 1. The bank planned to use the former clothing store for its expansion.

The Spring Run Swim Club opened its private pool, just off Route 221, near Poages Mill, on July 6.

The Sun Valley Swim Club, shown here in 1958, was located on Route 116 in the Mount Pleasant section. *Vinton Historical Society*

Rev. Gustaf Johnson and his wife marked ten years of service at the Roanoke Rescue Mission in early July. Johnson, a native of Sweden, came to the United States in 1914 and was converted to the Christian faith in 1942. He and his wife came to Roanoke from Chicago's United Mission, which had been directed by his father-in-law for thirty years.

High's Ice Cream opened its newest dairy products store at 3302 Brambleton Avenue SW on July 4.

WDBJ-TV began a new local program on July 5, *Russian – So To Speak*. The thirty-minute Saturday program was taught by Russian native George Solonevich, a local artist.

Hollywood Beauty Salon opened on July 7 in the Carlton Terrace Building at 920 S. Jefferson Street. Owners were Melvin Martin and Dick Allen.

An all-star lineup of professional wrestlers was on the card for the matches at Victory Stadium on July 8. The roster included Irish Mike Clancey, Hans Schnabel, the Great Bolo, Red Bastein, Angelo Martinelli, and Gory Buerrero.

Luther Cheatham pled guilty in Hustings Court on July 7 to second-degree murder in the May 3 death of his wife, Mary Cheatham. Cheatham was sentenced to nine years.

The Roanoke School Board met on July 7 and adopted a slightly revised master plan for the Shrine Hill site, which was to contain a new high school, elementary school, football stadium, auditorium, baseball diamond, fire station, and nature area atop Shrine Hill. The master plan was endorsed by the city's planning commission on July 9.

The first Black woman to serve on a jury in Roanoke Hustings Court served in that capacity on July 7. She was Bessie Hall.

The Everly Brothers perform at Lakeside in this July 11, 1958, photo. Doug Talbert of Roanoke is at right playing the piano. *John Ewald*

Elbert Coulter, president emeritus of National Business College, died on July 7 at the age of eighty-seven. Coulter came to Roanoke in 1896 from St. Joseph's Business University in Missouri. He began as an instructor at the college, then located in the Bear Building at Salem Avenue and Jefferson Street. He purchased a half-interest in the school in 1898 and acquired the remaining interest in 1901.

The Everly Brothers, accompanied by Doug Talbert and his orchestra, performed at the Lakeside on July 11.

Charles Poole purchased the Whitehall Motor Lodge at 3016 Williamson Road NW on July 8 from William McPhilamy for $200,000.

The Roanoke Development Association was founded in early July by Dr. Harry Penn, who stated that the association's purpose was to influence area politics and to support economic development projects for the benefit of Blacks. Others holding leadership in the group included Walter Wheaton, Virginia Belcher, Annabell Keeling, and Annabelle Adkins.

Over thirty residents petitioned the Roanoke County Circuit Court on July 9 for the creation of the Town of Lakeside between Roanoke City and the Town of Salem. The residents claimed they were county residents with city problems and treated as "orphans." The proposed town included most of the area between the Salem Turnpike and Cove Road. The head of the citizens' group was Albert Lurie. The group also indicated in its petition that the City of Roanoke had shown little interest in annexing the section.

Virginia Lee received a thirty-year service pin on July 9 in recognition of being the librarian at the Gainsboro Branch Library. She became a librarian with the city on July 1, 1928.

Lutheran Church House, the first permanent headquarters of the Lutheran Synod of Virginia, opened in early July at 317 Washington Avenue SW. The house was the former home of N. W. Pugh.

The PAL boxing team squared off against opponents from various localities before 1,000 spectators at Victory Stadium on July 10. The PAL team prevailed in six of the eight bouts. PAL boxer Jimmy Muse, twenty, had announced prior to the event that he planned to turn pro.

The 1958 Soap Box Derby trials were held on July 11 with a record number of entrants. The qualifying trials were held at the Parkway Center, a local drag strip near Starkey.

Toppie the Elephant, mascot of Top Value trading stamps, made his first appearance in Roanoke on July 11 at George Hartman's Texaco Station on the corner of Maple Avenue and Jefferson Street SW.

State and federal highway officials gave tentative approval to a multimillion-dollar interstate highway spur into Roanoke extending to from Orange Avenue and terminating at Elm Avenue.

The south corner of the Shrine Hill property was recommended as the site for the Roanoke Technical Institute on July 11. The recommendation came from the advisory committee to the Virginia Tech Board of Visitors. The committee passed a resolution to ask Roanoke City Council to provide the land. The committee also believed the site was far enough removed from the other planned developments at Shrine Hill.

Irv Sharp (seated at piano) and a bluegrass band on the set in the WDBJ-TV studios in the 1950s. *WDBJ7*

On July 17, 1958, the last steam engine, the J-Class 610, used by train No. 25,comes into Roanoke in this image. *N&W Historical Photographs Collection, VPI&SU Libraries*

Carl Montgomery and C. G. Peters, Roanoke real estate developers, announced on July 11 plans for a shopping center and subdivision that would straddle Peters Creek at the city-county line and run along the north side of Shenandoah Avenue to the Salem Turnpike. The project would encompass a total of 161 acres. The developers were seeking a rezoning on some of the acreage.

The Roanoke Junior Chamber of Commerce launched a study of erecting a sports coliseum in Roanoke that could also be used for trade shows and conventions. The Jaycees believed such a venue would not compete with a proposed civic center. The Jaycees suggested a 2,500-seat coliseum could host indoor tennis, ice skating, basketball, boxing, and wrestling events.

Showtimers presented *Kind Lady* the third weekend in July. The title role was played by Dorothy Turner.

American Legion Post 3 voted to purchase the former Harvey Apperson home in Salem as its new post home. The legion had been without a permanent place to meet since a fire had destroyed the American Legion Auditorium.

WDBJ-TV announced a new weekday morning lineup beginning July 14. *Happy Valley Hymn Time* would begin at 6:45 a.m., followed by an hour-long *Top O' the Morning* at 7:00. The same personalities were featured on both programs— Don Reno, Ronnie Reno, Red Smiley, John Palmer, the Tennessee Cut Ups, and Irv Sharp.

Oak Grove Church of the Brethren observed its fiftieth anniversary on July 13. The church began as a mission of the Peters Creek Church of the Brethren.

W. B. Coles, an egg farmer at Bent Mountain, opened an additional egg factory at Airpoint that housed 15,000 chickens. Coles had been in the egg business since 1925.

Salem Town Council voted on July 14 to annex 1.7 square miles of Roanoke County, including the site of the General Electric plant. The area also included the land for the proposed town of Lakeside. The boundaries of the area were Salem corporate limits on the west, Roanoke River on the south, Masons Creek on the east, and Route 631 and the old Valley Railroad right-of-way on the north.

On July 14 Roanoke City Council agreed to pay $3,500 to relieve the outstanding debt of the defunct Roanoke Red Sox baseball club. The action settled a long-standing controversy involving liens and unpaid taxes.

Frank Woods was sentenced to four years on July 15 for the March 23 slaying of his wife, Gracie Woods. He pled guilty to voluntary manslaughter.

Roy Rinehart won the fifteenth annual Soap Box Derby on July 16 at the Parkway Center drag strip. His brother Jim won the derby in 1956. Rinehart prevailed over a field of seventy-seven boys. The derby attracted a crowd estimated at 5,000. The derby sponsors were the *Roanoke Times*, the Optimist Club, and Diamond Chevrolet.

Herman Garrison was killed on July 16 from injuries he sustained in a fight in Bedford County. The city medical examiner ruled that death was caused by acute alcoholism in addition to internal injuries.

Sterling White was shot and wounded by Vinton police on July 17 after threatening his neighbors near the W. D. Vinyard farm and assaulting the town's police chief with the butt of a rifle.

Darden Phlegar of Salem saved a drowning boy when he drove by Lake Spring on July 17. Hearing the boy's yells, Phlegar stopped his car, jumped in the lake, and got the choking boy to the pond's rim.

N&W Railway announced on July 17 that it would begin using leased diesel locomotives to replace the remaining steam locomotives for passenger trains. The diesels replaced fourteen J-Class locomotives.

This photograph, taken on July 18, 1958, shows the first leased diesel on train No. 25 coming into Roanoke. *N&W Historical Photographs Collection, VPI&SU Libraries*

This June 1959 image shows Lincoln Terrace Elementary School with the addition that was approved and funded in 1958. *Library of Virginia*

Rev. C. A. Ivory, pastor of Hermon Presbyterian Church at Rock Hill, South Carolina, addressed a meeting of the Roanoke Development Association on July 22 at First Baptist Church, Gainsboro. Ivory was president of the Committee for Human Rights and leader of the year-old bus boycott in Rock Hill. In Ivory's address to the Black civic organization, he said, "We must learn to get what we want and not wait for it to be handed down to us." Dr. Harry Penn, organizer of the group, was elected president.

Members of Rosalind Hills Baptist Church broke ground on July 20 for an education-fellowship hall addition. The $90,000 three-story building was being constructed by H. A. Lucas and Son. Rev. Alan Neely was the pastor. The church's first building had been erected in 1954.

Lu Merritt defeated Fred Bromm to win the city-county men's singles tennis championship on July 20. Merritt and Bromm won over Bob Bolling and Jack Miller to gain the doubles title. Suzanne Glass won the women's singles title over Stella Peplowski. The tournament was held at South Roanoke Park.

At its July 21 meeting, the Roanoke School Board agreed both to plans for a $132,000 addition to Lincoln Terrace Elementary School and to "Monterey" as the name for new elementary school planned near Hollins Road.

The Roanoke City Planning Commission and the Roanoke Redevelopment and Housing Authority met on July 21 to discuss the proposed interstate spur into Roanoke (later known as I-581). The spur would split in half the Commonwealth Project, a redevelopment project in northeast Roanoke. The spur would consume 50 percent of the land, meaning that many of the 350 families displaced by the RRHA's program would not be able to move back into the section. The RRHA objected to the route of the spur on that basis.

Carnis Poindexter retained his men's singles title in the Washington Park tennis championship played on July 23. He defeated John Penn. Doris Ballou won the women's title over Doris Mason.

Lester Flatt, Earl Scruggs, and their Foggy Mountain Boys of the *Grand Ole Opry* performed on WDBJ's *Top O' The Mornin'* show on July 25.

The Riverside Drive-In Theatre was sold in late July for $25,000 to the owners of the Lee Drive-In in Lexington. The prior owners were Mr. and Mrs. J. R. Pence. The theatre was located at 1942 Bennington Street SE.

Jonah Penn of Roanoke County died on July 25 at Burrell Memorial Hospital from injuries he sustained in a single-car accident a week prior. The accident occurred on Route 221, one mile west of Roanoke.

Mrs. W. J. McCorkindale Jr. of Roanoke won the first Virginia Seniors golf tournament for women on July 25 at Hot Springs.

Chuck Berry, the Clovers, Lloyd Price, and Diane Dove performed at the Star City Auditorium on July 27. Doors opened at 10:00 p.m. for the concert and dance. Tickets at the door were two dollars.

Larry LeGrande, a graduate of Carver High School, was selected to play in the 1958 East-West All Star Game of the Negro Leagues. The baseball game was held at Comiskey Park in Chicago. LeGrande played originally for the Memphis Red Sox and then the Detroit Stars. Following the 1958 season, LeGrande went to the Kansas City Monarchs, where he played as catcher for Satchel Paige. In 1959, LeGrande was recruited by the St. Petersburg Saints, played a half season, and returned to the Monarchs.

Benno Forman announced on July 27 that B. Forman Sons, a women's clothing store, had obtained a long-term lease on the former S&W Cafeteria building at 412 S. Jefferson Street. Forman planned to remodel the structure and relocate there from 418 S. Jefferson Street, where Forman had been for thirty-five years.

Officials with Roanoke Memorial Hospital reported they had treated twenty-four polio patients in the first six months of the year. At the time of the late July report, there were ten polio patients in an isolation ward due to an early summer outbreak of the disease in southwestern Virginia. The hospital also was treating six paralytics of polio that were not in isolation. The number of polio patients treated by the hospital peaked in 1950 at 450 cases. The cases in 1958 were mostly due to parents' failures to get their children vaccinated.

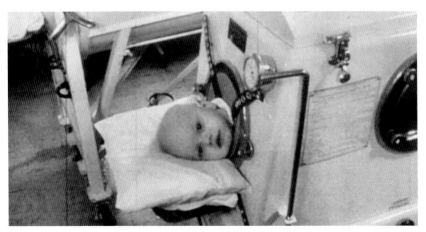

This news clip shows a child in an iron lung due to polio being treated at Roanoke Memorial Hospital in August 1958. *WSLS-TV News Film Collection, UVA Libraries*

The Roanoke Historical Society announced in late July that it had acquired temporary quarters in the Peoples Federal Building.

Mr. and Mrs. Mitchell Saba of Roanoke were subpoenaed and appeared before the Congressional House Committee on Un-American Activities on July 29 when the committee met in Atlanta. The couple refused to tell the committee whether they were members of the Communist party. Mrs. Saba indicated that she had been fired from a Roanoke medical office because the doctor feared publicity stemming from her appearance before the committee. Mrs. Saba was questioned extensively about her employment background and asked if she had been trained "on party penetration methods in the South." She refused to answer. When her husband testified, he received the same line of questioning. According to the committee's lead investigator, Armand Penha, the Communist party had recruited Southerners to "raise political and economic issues of Negroes, spreading propaganda to cultivate workers, and promoting strikes and slowdowns." The Sabas refused to comply with the committee's inquiries.

Major Kirk Myers, formerly of Roanoke, died on July 29 when the B52 jet bomber he commanded crashed near Loring Air Force Base at Limestone, Maine. The crash killed seven others. Meyers attended Jefferson High School and went into the air force in 1942. He was the son of Mr. and Mrs. William Myers. He was also survived by his wife and two young children.

Showtimers presented the comedy *Three Men on a Horse* the first weekend in August. Lead parts were played by Betty Parrish, Jim Kelly, Ed Langley, Joe Grant, Robert Ayers, and Clarence Dobbins. George Garretson was the director.

Some 7,000 spectators attended the open-air professional wrestling match at Victory Stadium on July 29. The main attraction was the long-awaited grudge match between Red Bastein and the masked Great Bolo. The referee eventually stopped the fight, declaring it no decision. Other match events included strongman Paul Anderson against Hans Schnabel.

Owen-Weaver, a sporting goods store at 4221 Melrose Avenue NW, petitioned in Law and Chancery Court for the liquidation of assets and the appointment of a receiver. A. C. Owen was president of the company.

The *Roanoke Times* launched its Sunday Book Page on August 3, which used local critics, mostly college professors, to review books. Prior to this, the newspaper used syndicated book reviews.

The Roanoke Valley Regional Planning and Economic Development Commission released a study on July 31 that reported more than 2,000 dilapidated houses in the Roanoke Valley. Running water was not available in half of the houses that received that designation.

Norwich Fuel Company opened on August 1 at 607 Warwick Avenue SW.

Hidden Valley Country Club broke ground on a $276,000 clubhouse the first week in August. The clubhouse would be connected to the locker room, pro shop, and grill built in 1954.

George Thompson was appointed principal of William Byrd High School in early August, succeeding E. E. Barnett.

N&W Railway completed construction on its new freight car shop in early August. The shop was located just east of the main entrance at Eight-and-a-Half

Street and Campbell Avenue SE. The shop employed about 500 and could produce twenty cars a day. Construction of the shop began in the summer of 1955.

American Viscose Corporation, the third-largest industry in the Roanoke region, announced on August 4 that it was closing its Roanoke plant. At the time of the announcement, the plant employed 1,750 workers. No set date was given, but company officials indicated the plant would close in a matter of months. The plant covered 226 acres between Riverland Road SE and the Virginian Railway. It began operations in Roanoke in 1917. Company officials also indicated other plants were being closed, and there was little opportunity for Roanoke employees to find jobs elsewhere within the company. At its peak in 1929, the Roanoke plant employed close to 5,500. It annual payroll was estimated at $7 million, making it the third-largest employer behind N&W Railway and General Electric. Employees were given little notice of the company's decision that was announced from headquarters in Philadelphia. The plant occupied a prominent place in Roanoke's history. W. A. Barton and James Breakell, both from England, came to Roanoke to set up the plant. H. C. Neren became the plant manager in 1917 and was succeeded by LeRoy Smith in 1938. The facility closed only once for six weeks in 1932 due to the Depression. Technological changes and lack of business caused a gradual decline in production during the 1950s, forcing its closure.

This October 1958 photograph provides an aerial view of the American Viscose Roanoke plant in southeast Roanoke. The announcement that Viscose was closing the plant was a severe economic blow to the Roanoke Valley. *N&W Historical Photographs Collection, VPI&SU Libraries*

This late 1950s postcard shows Woodrum Field. The airport went through several runway and other expansions during the decade. *Bob Stauffer*

Westinghouse Electric Supply Company moved to a new warehouse and office at Nineteenth Street and Salem Avenue SW on August 4.

Work to improve Woodrum Field began on August 5, including an expansion of the apron and the partial relocation of Route 118 for runway extensions.

The University of Virginia's Division of Extension and General Studies leased a former residence at 1713 Grandin Road SW for offices and classroom space. The division planned to use the home for its operations within a month.

Antrim Motors, located at 510 McClanahan Street SW, was appointed as the local dealer for Fiat cars imported from Italy. They were the first dealership in southwest Virginia to offer the car.

Seventy-four sets of twins attended the first annual "Twin Day" at Mill Mountain Children's Zoo on August 6. They ranged in age from toddlers to seventy-one.

Toot's Drive-in No. 2 opened on August 7 at 2406 Franklin Road SW. The location was formerly the Snack Shop.

Roanoke Mayor Walter Young led a delegation from Roanoke that flew to American Viscose headquarters in Philadelphia to meet with company officials on August 7 about the closing of the Roanoke plant. Members of the delegation included John Fishwick and E. H. Ould. All three indicated the plant would be offered for sale, but there was no success in avoiding the plant's closure.

Piedmont Airlines took delivery on the first of eight F-27 Fairchild Pacemaker prop-jet transport planes on August 8. Their pilots began training on the thirty-six-passenger planes with regular use of them by Piedmont slated for September.

The remaining portion of the McClanahan property at McClanahan and South Jefferson Streets was acquired by Roanoke Memorial Hospital for future expansion. The hospital trustees signed a contract for the purchase of the two-acre tract on August 7.

R&S Building Company announced in early August that it would build over thirty residences in the Ridgewood Park subdivision, with each home having an approximate value of $7,500.

Westward Lake Estates Club offered nonresident memberships for one hundred dollars per year. The club had a five-acre lake on 3,000 wooded acres with beaches, piers, and picnic areas. The club's site was on Route 3 near Salem.

Tommy Huddleston, twenty-one, of Vinton was killed when a car in which he was a passenger struck a bridge on Route 24 between Vinton and Stewartsville on August 8. Three others were injured, and they were Roy Kirk, Kenneth Campbell, and Glenn Campbell.

The Social Security Administration opened its new offices at 306 W. Campbell Avenue on August 8.

Lewis Young Fashions held a grand reopening on August 11 following an extensive remodeling and expansion of its store at 25 W. Church Avenue.

Paul Thompson, manager of employee and community relations at the valley's General Electric plant, was selected to chair the 1958 United Fund campaign with a goal of $619,000.

Showtimers presented *The Heiress* the second weekend in August. The lead role was played by Yvonne Slonaker, a teacher at Oakland Elementary School.

Red Hill Baptist Church held a ground-breaking ceremony on August 10 for its education building. The church was located along Route 220 near Clearbrook.

Chuck Berry, the Clovers, and Lloyd Price and his orchestra performed at Lakeside on August 10.

Dixie Bar-B-Que at 900 Colorado Street in Salem closed on August 11.

City Home operations were transferred from the home's site on Colonial Avenue to the former tuberculosis sanatorium at Coyner Springs by Roanoke City Council at their August 11 meeting. At the time of the council's action, forty persons were residents at the City Home, which served as a convalescent facility for the poor.

The Bean Pot, a restaurant, opened at 3719 Williamson Road the second weekend in August. Jack Boettcher was the owner.

The Roanoke County School Board adopted a new policy on August 12 that any students who married while still in high school must make a written application to the board and appear before a special committee that would determine if they could continue their high school education. The action was part of a broader policy that enforced the same requirements for unwed mothers.

Grover Lucas, who killed his wife and children on April 27, was judged mentally competent to stand trial on August 12. The report and assessment were made by doctors at the Southwestern State Hospital in Marion.

An abstract painting by Roanoke artist Peter Wreden was chosen by Virginia Tech as the first item for its permanent art collection. The selection was made by a committee that reviewed works by more than thirty artists.

The Montgomery Presbytery purchased a 400-acre conference campsite in Botetourt County in mid-August for $25,000 from A. A. Woodson. The location included a cabin and a five-acre lake and was about four miles north of Fincastle off Route 666.

Singer Chuck Berry was convicted in absentia in Roanoke County Court on August 15 on a Peeping Tom charge. Judge Norman Moore ordered that Berry's cash bond of $156 be forfeited, and he sentenced the singer to sixty days in jail. Berry had posted bond when he was arrested Saturday night after his concert for allegedly peeping into the women's restroom at Lakeside Amusement Park. If he returned to the area, the judge indicated Berry could be forced to serve time in jail.

Waverly Market opened on August 16 at 1344 Jamison Avenue SE.

Boxley Hill Clinic opened at 5501 Williamson Road on August 16 by Dr. Herman Brubaker.

Lester Hairston of Roanoke County was fatally wounded on August 16 when he was shot near Dixie Caverns. He died at Burrell Memorial Hospital within a few hours of the incident. Sylvester Campbell was charged with murder.

Bill Monroe performed on the *Top O' The Mornin'* show on WDBJ-TV on August 18.

Roanoke County Sheriff H. W. Clark announced that he and his officers seized one of the largest stills in the county's history when they raided a moonshine operation in the Clearbook area on August 17. No arrests were made because no one was at the 800-gallon still when it was raided.

Rev. Harry Peyton of Roanoke's Calvary Tabernacle announced plans for a transcontinental trip that he, his family, and several others would start in early September. The group planned to travel in three specially built Conestoga wagons from Hinton, West Virginia, to Los Angeles for the purpose of "bringing people back to the faith of the Founding Fathers." Calvary Tabernacle was located at Eighteenth Street and Orange Avenue.

Major Frank Webb of the Roanoke Police Department announced on August 19 plans to establish a special juvenile section within the department to investigate cases involving juvenile offenders.

Sidney's held a formal reopening of its clothing store on August 22 following an extensive remodeling. The store was at 503 South Jefferson Street.

Lewis Lionberger, speaking on behalf of neighbors near Shrine Hill, spoke in opposition to the Roanoke Technical Institute being located on the southern corner of the Shrine Hill tract. About forty families were in attendance to support Lionberger at a hearing before the Roanoke Planning Commission on August 20. The objections were due to what Lionberger termed "the integration problem" and "the mixing of age groups" on the tract which was to include a high school and elementary school. The planning commission tabled discussion due to the absence of three of its members.

The US Coast Guard closed its recruiting station at 211 W. Campbell Avenue on August 29. The Roanoke station opened in January 1957.

Hake Manufacturing Company announced on August 22 plans to erect a new plant on a ten-acre tract along the east side of Hollins Road NE. The new plant would allow the company to consolidate its plastics production operations. It would then vacate its two other locations at 1215 Midvale Avenue SW under Memorial Bridge and the plant at Bullitt Avenue and Second Street SE.

Due to a breakdown in their air-conditioning unit in mid-August 1958, the Roanoke office of Allstate Insurance did what no other business in the Roanoke Valley had ever done before—allowed their female employees to wear shorts. *WSLS-TV News Film Collection, UVA Libraries*

Local members of the Virginia General Assembly expressed strong support for Governor Lindsay Almond's stance on school integration. In a press conference on August 22, Almond stated "there will be no enforced integration in Virginia." Those concurring were Senator Earl Fitzpatrick and Delegates Kossen Gregory and Nelson Thurman.

Maude Fischer, eighty-four, of Roanoke County died on August 23 after being struck by an auto the day before on Peters Creek Road.

Julian Wise presented resuscitators on behalf of the Roanoke Valley Heart Association to three life saving crews—Cave Spring, Clearbrook, and Mount Pleasant—on August 23.

Professional women's tennis player Maureen Connolly came to Roanoke on August 28 to conduct a tennis clinic at Roanoke Country Club. She was ranked first in 1952, 1953, and 1954.

Bob Bortner of Richmond won the Roanoke Valley Invitational Tennis Tournament, which concluded at Roanoke Country Club on August 24. He defeated Bobby Schwartzman of Washington, DC.

Kroger opened a new grocery store at the corner of Brambleton Avenue and Kenmore Street SW, opposite Mount Vernon School, on August 26.

Mrs. M. F. Hubbard did something she had wanted to do for years. She flew over Roanoke on August 25 in a small plane piloted by Clayton Lemon. The ride was a gift from her children on her ninety-eighth birthday. As she stepped from the plane after the fifteen-minute ride, she said, "I wasn't any more afraid than if I'd been in a car. If you had seen as many things as I have during ninety-eight years, you wouldn't think about being afraid either."

Showtimers concluded its performance season with *Arsenic and Old Lace* the last weekend in August at Roanoke College. The cast included Elizabeth Pettrey, Betty Jean Michie, Jim Kelly, and John Marstellar.

The Veterans Administration Hospital held a two-day carnival on its campus the last weekend in August for its patients and the community. Some 1,600 patients attended the carnival, which included clowns, games, and exhibition booths. The most popular prizes were cigars.

Over 3,000 teenagers attended the final summer dance of the season held on Roanoke's tennis courts. "Record Romp" was at South Roanoke Park on August 27 and was the thirty-eighth dance of the summer sponsored by the city's parks and recreation department.

Joseph Jackson, a thirty-seven-year-old migrant worker from Florida, was killed on August 27 in a single-car accident on Route 864 five miles north of Salem.

Grover Lucas returned to Roanoke on August 28 from the state hospital in Marion to await trial for the murder of his family.

Windshield Glass Distributors moved to 1003 Orange Avenue NE on September 1, which was the former location of City Auto Supply.

Florence Thames, a former model of Roanoke, began reporting the weather on the 11:00 p.m. news broadcasts of WDBJ-TV on September 1. She was the first on-camera female for a local television news show.

The Roanoke Fair opened for a weeklong run on September 1 at Maher Field and Victory Stadium. Sponsored by American Legion Post No. 3, the fair included a livestock show, agricultural exhibits, nightly fireworks, grandstand acts, the Marks-Manning Midway, boxing matches, a flower show, a beauty pageant, and wrestling contests.

WSLS-TV began broadcasting its popular *Top Ten Dance Party* on weeknights on September 1. The show had previously been seen only on Saturdays since its debut six months prior. The cohosts were Bob Fenderson and Doug Newton. Dance contests, games, and novelty dances were featured with local teens.

The 5 O'Clock Supper Club opened on Route 220 a half-mile south of Roanoke on September 2. The restaurant was owned by Hunter Dews.

US Air Force Master Sergeant William Dupree of Roanoke sang "They Call It Ireland" on the *Ed Sullivan Show* on August 31. His father was C. C. Dupree of Loudon Avenue NW.

Vincent Wheeler was selected as Roanoke's mayor by his colleagues on Roanoke City Council during their reorganizational meeting on September 1. He was chosen by a vote of 4–3, with other nominees being Benton Dillard and Mary Pickett. Wheeler had served as vice mayor for the past two years. Roy Webber was chosen as vice mayor.

The Salem Town Council reelected James Moyer to his sixth consecutive two-year term as mayor during their reorganizational meeting on September 1. Leonard Shank was selected as vice mayor.

This 1950s aerial shows the Children's Zoo on the top of Mill Mountain. *Virginia Room, RPL*

Roanoke's PAL Boxing Team won five of six matches against opponents from North Carolina, West Virginia, and Virginia on September 1. Some 600 spectators watched the bouts at Maher Field.

The Children's Zoo on Mill Mountain set a new attendance record with the 1958 season having 93,403 visitors to the zoo. N. J. Dalton was the "Zooperintendent."

Thy Kingdom Come had a total attendance of 20,298 for its 1958 season. The figure was about 1,100 less than attendance at the outdoor drama the previous year. Attendance was held down by significant rains during the first month of the summer season. Clara Black, president of the Roanoke Valley Drama Association, indicated the production was planned for 1959 at the Sherwood Amphitheatre.

A new daily cartoon titled *Gil Thorp* began running in the *Roanoke Times* on September 8. The comic strip was described as "showing today's high school students as they see themselves."

The Olen Dollar Department Store opened at 17 E. Campbell Avenue on September 4.

Mrs. Peggy Looney of Roanoke appeared on the nationally televised game show *The Price Is Right* the last week in August and won $2,500 in prizes.

John Falwell, Roanoke's first director of public welfare who retired in 1957, died on September 3 from a self-inflicted gunshot wound. Falwell had been diagnosed with a terminal illness according to his relatives. He had been appointed as director of the city's welfare department in 1936.

The assets of Owen-Weaver, a sporting goods store, were purchased by Northwest Hardware for $13,500 in early September. The former store was opened as the Melrose branch of Northwest Hardware on September 3. Northwest's main store was at 611 Eleventh Street NW. F. W. Overstreet was the president of Northwest Hardware.

Shrine Hill Sinclair Service Station opened on September 5 at 2402 Grandin Road SW. Those associated with the service center were Julian King, Herman Whitenak, B. E. Whitenak, and Ollie Witcher.

Roanoke County schools reported a record enrollment of 12,253 students on September 4 for the start of the school year. The figure represented an increase of almost 500 students over the previous year.

Roanoke's oldest hook-and-ladder fire truck was officially retired on September 4 after being in service for forty years. "Old Kate," as the engine was called by the department, had logged over 35,000 miles since the engine was first used on August 1, 1918. The truck had been at Fire Station No. 1.

Pat Poindexter of Salem was crowned "Miss Roanoke" at the Roanoke Fair on September 6. The eighteen-year-old would represent Roanoke at the Miss Universe state elimination pageant in Richmond on September 19.

Hollywood actor and Roanoke native John Payne returned to his hometown the first weekend in September to visit with friends. The actor had appeared in ninety-five films since he left Roanoke in the 1930s.

Eliot Clark spoke at the formal opening of his one-man show at the Roanoke Main Library on September 8. The exhibition of his paintings was sponsored by the Roanoke Fine Arts Center.

Colonial-American National Bank opened a branch bank on Franklin Road at Brandon Avenue SW on September 10.

John Norman held a formal reopening of its store at 505 S. Jefferson Street on September 10 following an extensive remodeling. The store included the new Cambridge Shop, a department store exclusively for high school and college men's fashions. The store had been at its South Jefferson location for fourteen years, having originally opened in a room over Kingoff's Jewelers in 1932 and then relocated over the Park Theatre for nine years.

Eighteen feet of a smokestack at the water department's Crystal Spring Pumping Station were removed on September 8 due to its deteriorated condition.

Frank Thomas Jr., forty-seven, of Salem was killed on September 9 when his bulldozer tilted and crushed him on a carport beam. The well-known contractor was working on a new home in the Boxley Hill subdivision. He was part owner of Thomas Brothers Construction Company.

Over 400 business and government officials attended a barbeque and rally at Lakeside on September 10 to lobby the state highway department for the Interstate 64 route that would go from Richmond to Roanoke via Lynchburg. Several speakers supported the "southern route" as opposed to the one proposed to go through Charlottesville to Staunton. The outcome of the rally was the selection of a sixty-one-member board of directors for the newly organized Water Level Route Association.

Gainsboro Elementary School was permanently closed in early September, and its students were transferred to Lincoln Terrace Elementary School. The Gainsboro School was built in 1898 for $11,500 for Black students. The school board closed the school, deeming it a fire trap.

The *Roanoke Times* added a new comic strip to its daily editions with *Pogo*, which began running in the newspaper on September 15.

The Helen Spahr School of Dance and Voice opened on September 15 in Salem.

Roanoke City Public School reported their enrollment for the school year at 18,824, an increase of more than 500 pupils from the previous year.

W. T. Smith opened the Shenandoah Avenue Esso Station in mid-September at Shenandoah Avenue and Twenty-Fifth Street NW.

John Easter, eighty-eight, of Roanoke died on September 12. Easter owned and operated Easter Produce Company before retiring from the business in 1920. In 1923, he founded Easter Supply Company and remained active with the company until 1957. He was also a leader in numerous civic and church-related organizations.

West End Methodist Church observed its fiftieth anniversary with special services the third week in September. The church was organized in 1908 with sixty-six charter members. The site of the church on Thirteenth Street SW was acquired in 1910.

Mrs. Bernice Mitchell, thirty-seven, blacked out while driving her car in downtown Roanoke on September 13. The car went into the front of Pugh's Department Store, struck three pedestrians, and careened back onto Campbell Avenue, where she hit three parked cars. A thousand people rushed to the scene following the crash.

Leonidas Ziompolas of Roanoke was instantly killed when he was struck by a pickup truck as he crossed Route 220 six miles south of Roanoke.

The Colonial Theatre in Salem closed on September 13 due to dwindling audiences.

The Times-World Corporation announced on September 13 that its two broadcast entities, WDBJ radio and WDBJ-TV, would split effective October 1 due to the growth of each department. John Harkrader was named as manager of WDBJ-TV, while Frank Koehler was named as manager of the radio station.

Preston Oaks Baptist Church held a ground-breaking ceremony on September 14 for its first building. The church, which was organized in October 1957, was located at Preston Avenue and Oakland Boulevard NE. The building would have educational space and serve as a temporary sanctuary.

The Eastern States Championship Drag Races held qualifying races at the Roanoke Drag Strip near Starkey the third weekend in September. The championship was sponsored and sanctioned by the National Hotrod Association.

The City of Roanoke purchased a large residence off Lafayette Boulevard NW for use as a recreation center. An advisory committee recommended that it be called the Villa Heights Community Center. It was the seventh community center in the city.

Poole's Appliance and Refrigeration Service opened at 3202 Williamson Road NW on September 15. C. E. Poole was the owner.

A new syndicated comic strip titled *Johnny Reb* began running in the Sunday editions of the *Roanoke Times* on September 21.

Teresa Barger, an infant, and Flossie Smith, sixty-seven, of Salem were killed when their station wagon collided head-on with a truck on Shenandoah Avenue NW on September 17.

Roanoke officials deemed their downtown pigeon eradication program a success in a report submitted in mid-September. Some 4,000 pigeons were caught, with about one-third being sold to a processing plant on Long Island.

The second annual Mountain View Invitational golf tournament began on September 19 with a field of forty-six in the Pro Am event. Top prize was $350.

Carter and Jones Dry Cleaning and Dyeing opened a branch at 3211 Brambleton Avenue SW on September 22.

Hollins College had something it had not had in over a century—male students. Three men were admitted to the college's new graduate program in psychology beginning with its fall semester. The school used to have male students before it became an all-female institution in 1852, when it became the Female Seminary at Botetourt Springs.

About 320 Boy Scouts participated in the Scouts' camporee at Longwood Park in Salem on September 20.

Aubrey Kendrick, fifty-seven, of Roanoke died on September 21 from injuries he received when a car struck him as he crossed Maple Avenue SW that same day.

The Rt. Rev. Karl Block, the seventy-one-year-old bishop of the Episcopal Church Diocese of California, died in San Francisco on September 21. Brock had been the rector of St. John's Episcopal Church in Roanoke from 1920 to 1926.

North Roanoke Baptist Church held a ground-breaking ceremony on September 21 for its first building. The church was organized eleven months prior and was located along Peters Creek Road opposite Burlington School. Rev. Burrel Lucas was the pastor.

Salem Presbyterian Church completed a $250,000 building program that included remodeling the sanctuary and creating a new educational wing. The congregation worshipped in its renovated sanctuary for the first time on September 21.

Second Presbyterian Church completed a large stained glass Gothic window in its narthex in mid-September, which concluded the installation of memorial windows at the church, a process that began in 1941. The stained glass windows were designed and erected by the Henry Keck Studio of Syracuse, New York.

Pat Poindexter was named Miss Virginia at the Virginia State Fair on September 21. The Salem resident would represent Virginia in the Miss Universe contest to be held in July 1959 at Long Beach, California.

Hollins College opened its new $650,000 chapel with a worship service on September 21.

Chuck Alexander of High Point, North Carolina, won the second annual Mountain View Invitational golf tournament on September 21 with a thirty-six-hole total of 136. Jim Ferree came in second. Both men were touring professionals. The low amateur was Connie Sellers, who shot a 144.

The Hollins College chapel was dedicated in 1958 and cost $650,000. *Historical Society of Western Virginia*

Some sixty persons of Italian descent attended a dinner at Ciotti's Spaghetti House near Lakeside on September 22 to launch the formation of a "Sons of Italy" social and civic group.

Patients at the City Home were moved from the Colonial Avenue property to the former tuberculosis sanatorium at Coyner Springs on September 23.

American Viscose announced the closing of three departments at its Roanoke plant effective in October. The departments were spinning, engineering, and maintenance. The three areas employed about 325 persons.

Ground was broken on September 22 for a $100,000 addition the Holiday Inn on Williamson Road. The new building would hold thirty rooms and a breakfast bar.

Roanoke and state engineers began surveying Old Lick Cemetery on September 24 in preparation for the proposed route of the interstate spur into the city. Crews had also begun clearing the site that had been neglected for years. The cemetery contained an estimated 2,700 graves. Ownership of the cemetery was unclear, with the exception of about 300 gravesites on the eastern side that were maintained by the trustees of First Baptist Church in Gainsboro. The study of the cemetery had been suggested to city officials by the state highway department. Roanoke City Manager Arthur Owens indicated that he would like for the spur route to avoid the cemetery.

A small plane crashed on the M. E. Petty farm in Roanoke County on September 26. Lawrence Peverall and his flight instructor, Don Brown, were both injured. The plane was at 2,500 feet when the engine failed.

Betty Graybill, twenty, was shot and killed by her estranged husband in the kitchen of her home on Montrose Avenue SE on September 26. Emory Graybill, twenty-nine, of Troutville was arrested and charged two hours later. The couple married in 1957 and had been separated for about three months.

The Park Street Gulf Service Station at 4426 Melrose Avenue NW became the Melrose Phillips 66 Service Station in late September under the management of Herbert Glovier.

Oak Grove Development Corporation began advertising house lots in its Sugar Loaf Estates in late September. Lot prices ranged from $3,000 to $4,000 and homes from $18,000 to $30,000.

Virginia Plastics and Chemical Company on Starkey Road reported the Hula-Hoop craze was a boon to their business. The small company had been producing about 4,320 hoops per day and shipping them all over the East Coast. One key ingredient in the production was molasses. The company made several kinds of these hoops.

Nelson Bond, a noted Roanoke author, opened Nelson Bond Associates in late September. The award-winning writer's business was for public relations and advertising.

Dr. Louise Wensel, an independent candidate for the US Senate in Virginia, and Judge Hubert Delany of New York City addressed the quarterly meeting of the Roanoke Development Association on September 28 at Addison High School. Attendance was estimated at 600.

The Junior Workshop of Creative Drama for children in grades one through eight opened for enrollment in late September. The school was run by Heather Barton, a former professional actress.

Star City Furniture Company, located at 131 E. Campbell Avenue, advertised in late September that it was going out of business.

Vester Campbell was sentenced to five years in prison by Roanoke County Circuit Court on September 29 for the fatal shooting of Lester Hairston on August 16. Campbell claimed self-defense.

Dot's Salon of Beauty opened in the First Federal Building on October 1. The owner was Dot Stanley.

Grover Lucas was sentenced to death in the electric chair on October 1 for the April 27 garden-pick slaying of his family. The Hustings Court jury deliberated for less than an hour before returning its verdict in the three-day trial. Lucas's attorney had used a defense of insanity, but physicians, neighbors, and coworkers testified that Lucas was an alcoholic who suffered epileptic seizures but was not mentally incapacitated.

G. C. Armistead, eighty-five, died on October 1. Active in business and civic affairs, Armistead had served on the Roanoke City Council prior to the adoption of the city manager form of government in 1918.

This late 1950s aerial shows Victory Stadium. The stadium was built in 1942 and razed in 2006. *Virginia Room, RPL*

Rev. Maurice Ivie, an interdenominational evangelist, leased the former Johnson-McReynolds Chevrolet building at 366 W. Campbell Avenue beginning October 1 for the purpose of holding continuous revival services there. He erected a sign on the building that read "Roanoke Gospel Center."

Dr. Arnett Macklin, fifty-two, of Petersburg died on October 2. He was on the faculty of Virginia State College. A native of Roanoke, Macklin was a former principal of Addison High School.

A crowd of 16,000 attended the football game at Victory Stadium on October 3 between Jefferson High School and William Fleming High School. Ticket sales were used to raise funds for the city's sandlot football program. Fleming won, 27–20, breaking a sixteen-year loss record to Jefferson. Jackie Null, a student at Lee Junior High School, was crowned Roanoke's Sandlot Football Queen at halftime by Barbara Guthrie, Miss Virginia of 1958.

Roland Clark, seventy, of Roanoke County died on October 4. He had represented the Salem District on the Roanoke County Board of Supervisors since 1955.

The new chapel at Hollins College was named for Jessie Ball du Pont, a member of the college's board of trustees. The October 5 decision was made to honor du Pont for her many years of service to the college.

Lucy Carter King, eighty-seven, was identified as the last surviving widow of a Confederate veteran in the Roanoke Valley. She had been a widow for forty years. At the age of nineteen, she married Thomas King, who was forty-eight at the time, at Newbern. Her husband died in 1918 of the Spanish flu, and Mrs. King moved to Roanoke a month later. She had been receiving a small pension from the City of Roanoke since 1932, as localities were authorized to provide pensions to Confederate widows by the Virginia General Assembly. The city had imposed a levy in 1909 to underwrite the pensions from its general fund.

A half-mile-long parade through downtown Roanoke kicked off the United Fund campaign on October 4. Twenty-seven organizations participated in the fund.

The Roanoke Valley Chapter of the Order of DeMolay was organized in early October with thirty-seven charter members. The order was a division of the Masons and was open to young men ages fourteen to twenty. John Eades was master councilor. On October 6, a local television program was aired live from the Hotel Roanoke ballroom featuring local talent to also hype the start of the fund drive.

Grand Ole Opry stars Johnny and Jack with Kitty Wells appeared on the local television program *Top O' The Morning* on October 7 on WDBJ.

The Roanoke Business and Professional Women's Club named Clara Black as its Woman of the Year during a dinner at the Hotel Roanoke on October 6. Black was known as a drama coach and director in the Roanoke Valley and was president of the Roanoke Valley Drama Association.

A three-person committee of Roanoke City Council was named to study the feasibility of providing the Roanoke Valley with a civic auditorium due to the loss of the American Legion Auditorium. The idea of such a regional effort had been forwarded by Councilman Willis Anderson. Joining him on the committee were Mayor Vincent Wheeler and Councilman Walter Young. They planned to meet with other governing bodies to discuss the need.

Roanoke launched its first annual Harvest Festival on October 8. The four-day event was cosponsored by the Junior League of Roanoke and the Virginia Tech Athletic Association. The event began with an "International Fashion Tour" sponsored by Miller & Rhoads that featured Nancy Cooke, a recognized fashion authority. On the second day, the Roanoke Council of Garden Clubs opened its Color and Fashion for Living Exposition at the armories on Reserve Avenue. More than 140 businesses and organizations had displays. There were also lectures, presentations, and parties at the Hotel Roanoke. Live models wearing the latest fashions were used by downtown businesses to attract shoppers on Friday evening followed by a Harvest Ball at the Patrick Henry Hotel. On Saturday, the Harvest Parade kicked off midmorning with special guest Mary Ann Mobley, Miss America. In the early afternoon, the Harvest Bowl football game between Virginia Tech and UVA kicked off in Victory Stadium, where Governor Lindsay Almond Jr. was in attendance, along with 26,000 others. Tech won, 22–13. That evening, the Roanoke Country Club hosted a dance and honored Miss America as being the first Harvest Queen.

Amo's Restaurant at 1436 W. Main Street in Salem went up for auction.

John Fishwick, N&W Railway vice president, identified four major problems facing the Roanoke area in an address to the Roanoke Better Service Club at the Hotel Roanoke on October 7. The main issues were recruitment of new business and industry, annexation, regional planning, and a new civic auditorium. He also stated to the 500 in attendance, "It is essential that in 1960 we pass the 100,000 mark…because industries and businesses frequently exclude from consideration cities with populations of less than that."

A Congressional Sixth District political council was organized by the region's Black leaders to help determine the outcome of the pending Congressional House race between Richard Poff and Richard Pence. M. U. Thornhill of Lynchburg was elected the council's chairman, and Dr. Harry Penn of Roanoke was elected vice chairman. Both Poff and Pence were strong segregationists.

Mill End Fabric Center opened the second week in October at 309 First Street SE.

Roanoke city engineer H. C. Broyles provided a report that he, along with traffic engineers from the state highway department, believed would spare Old Lick Cemetery from being moved with the planned interstate spur into Roanoke. He redesigned the Orange Avenue cloverleaf interchange with the northeast segment moved further to the east and west such that all graves, estimated at 2,700, would be able to remain. Final approval rested with state and federal authorities, however.

Edgar Crockett, a lineman with the Town of Salem's electrical department for four years, was electrocuted on October 9 while changing a transformer on a utility pole at the intersection of Craig Avenue and Hawthorne Road. The location was just two blocks from his home. Crockett was thirty-six.

Roanoke City Councilman Willis Anderson in a speech to the Fraternal Order of Police on October 9 urged valley consolidation. Anderson cited the interdependence of the various governments upon one another for the valley's future and stated it was time "to start talking out loud" about consolidating the four political subdivisions in the valley. The idea was panned the next day by Mayor James Moyer of Salem, who stated it sounded good in theory, "but I don't know if it would prove out in practice."

The Grandin Road Post Office opened on October 11 at 1731 Grandin Road SW. The new post office replaced a smaller one that was located at 1418 Grandin Road, which had been in use for almost eleven years. The postal station was officially dedicated on October 18 in a ceremony emceed by Roger Hodnett of the Lions Club. To make room for the post office on the corner lot at Sherwood Avenue, a large home, formerly owned by Louise Fowlkes, was moved from the lot to the adjacent lot.

First Church of the Nazarene, located on Highland Avenue at Eighth Street SE, celebrated its fiftieth anniversary on October 12.

John Logan, a Salem businessman, was appointed to the Roanoke County Board of Supervisors by Circuit Court Judge Fred Hoback on October 11. Logan was named to fill the unexpired term of Roland Clark, who died while in office.

Eileen Farrell, a nationally known soprano, gave a concert at the Jefferson High School auditorium on October 13, sponsored by the Thursday Morning Music Club.

Witten-Martin Furniture Company advertised on October 14 that it was going out of business and began liquidating its stock due to the retirement of J. E. Zeigler. The company was located at 115 E. Campbell Avenue. The company was established in 1904 as Reams, Jones and Blankenship, which later became Witten-Blankenship and then Witten-Martin in 1926. The store's first slogan was, "You marry the girl; we furnish the home."

The Roanoke Symphony Orchestra opened its sixth season on October 15 with a concert at the American Theatre. The featured performer was Jeryl Powell, an organist at St. John's Episcopal Church.

Pendleton Thomas Jr., a teacher at Andrew Lewis High School, was dismissed from his position after being arrested on a morals charge on October 10.

Harvest Motors opened on October 17 at 1337 W. Main Street in Salem as a Ford dealership. Harold Ferguson was the general manager. The dealership had formerly been Roanoke Valley Motors. To celebrate its grand opening, Harvest gave away a free pony.

The Virginia Department of Highways opened its new district offices in Salem on October 17. The new offices were located on Harrison Avenue. The department's district headquarters had formerly been on Water Street.

Carl Andrews, editorial page editor of the *Roanoke Times*, was elected chairman of the National Conference of Editorial Writers during the group's annual meeting in Philadelphia on October 18. Andrews had been the editorial page editor at the newspaper since 1945.

Central Methodist Church in Salem celebrated its fiftieth anniversary on October 19.

Green Hill Church of the Brethren near Salem dedicated its new education building on October 19. The $80,000 facility contained classrooms and a 200-seat meeting hall.

Nineteen original paintings by French masters went on display in mid-March as an exhibit sponsored by the Roanoke Fine Arts Center. The exhibit included two Picassos, two paintings by Henri Matisse, and works by Raoul Dufy, Paul Klee, Jean Lucrat, and George Braque. The works were on loan from the Virginia Museum of Fine Arts in Richmond.

Marian Duckwiler, thirty-four, of Vinton was stabbed to death on October 18. Police reported nearly one hundred stab wounds on her body. LeRoy Wynn of Roanoke was arrested for the killing. Duckwiler's body had been found in an alley behind a house on Loudon Avenue NW.

Johnson-Carper Furniture Company broke ground in mid-October on a new three-story warehouse addition to its plant on Hollins Road. Donald Jordan was president of the company, which was organized in 1926.

Kroger opened its newest grocery store at 2711 Franklin Road SW on October 21. Virgil Porter was the store manager.

This 1957 image shows the Kroger grocery located on Franklin Road near the present-day I-581 on-ramp. It closed when the new Kroger opened a short distance away at 2711 Franklin Road SW. *Virginia Room, RPL*

Pulitzer Prize–winner Mark Van Doren of Columbia University came to Hollins College for two days of lectures the week of October 19. Van Doren won a Pulitzer in 1940 for poetry. His visit came on the heels of his son, Charles Van Doren, being involved in the *Twenty-One* game show scandal. His son was given answers in advance to win out over other contestants on one of the nation's most popular TV quiz shows.

The Vinton Town Council decided against trying to annex any new territory from Roanoke County during its meeting on October 21. The council believed annexation would not make sense financially.

Raymond Carter of Henry was named as the Sportsman division champion at Starkey Speedway for the season. He won the most points in the class. Charlie Williamson of Roanoke placed second. Jesse Hambrick of Roanoke won the Class A Jalopy championship.

William Dowdy Jr. of Roanoke was killed in a single-car accident on Brandon Avenue SW on October 21.

Playwright Kermit Hunter wrote a play about the Protestant Reformation titled *The Mistress of the Inn.* The play was sponsored by the Roanoke Ministers Conference, and a performance was given for the first time at First Baptist Church on October 26. Attendance was 2,000.

All-Star Lanes bowling alley opened at 3439 Melrose Avenue NW on October 24.

Dr. E. G. Gill announced on October 25 that the Eye Bank and Sight Conservation Society of Virginia housed at Gill Memorial Hospital became one of eleven eye banks around the country to be affiliated with the Eye Bank for Sight Conservation, New York City.

The *USS Roanoke*, the third ship in US naval history to bear the name Roanoke, was retired in late October. Its final decommissioning was on October 31. The ship served for eleven years and had a regular crew of sixty officers and 980 men. The keel of the ship was launched on May 15, 1945, in Camden, New Jersey. Miss Julia Ann Henebry, daughter of Roanoke's mayor at the time, officially launched the ship on June 15, 1947. Its home port was Norfolk before it was transferred in 1955 to the Pacific fleet.

A Florida man who had hopped in an N&W Railway gondola car for a free ride was found crushed to death at the railway's repair shop at Shaffer's Crossing on October 27. Local police believed the man, Pierce Todd, thirty-eight, had hopped on the train near Richmond. He had forty-five cents in his pocket.

Two Roanoke sisters died in an auto accident on October 28 at Boones Mill. Rebecca Bell, sixty-seven, and Retta Thornburg, seventy-seven, lived together on Westover Avenue SW. Bell drove into the path of a southbound car on Route 220.

Watson Funeral Home opened at 305 E. Washington Avenue in Vinton on October 29. The company also had a funeral home at 1701 Melrose Avenue NW. Gordon Watson was the owner.

Broadway actress Evans Evans visited family in Roanoke in late October. The actress had gotten her start with Showtimers and was appearing in the William Inge play *The Dark at the Top of the Stairs* in New York City. Evans, originally from Salem, had a reunion with her former Showtimers colleagues at the home of Mrs. David Thornton.

Wash & Dry Laundry opened at 3008 Williamson Road in late October.

Hollywood actress Esther Williams came to Roanoke on October 29 to boost sales of her Esther Williams Swimming Pools. Williams had been scheduled to participate in the Harvest Festival, but illness had postponed her visit. A brunch was hosted in her honor at the Hotel Roanoke, which was followed by her offering comments at the United Fund's final report meeting at the hotel. Williams also spoke to the Roanoke Kiwanis Club at the Patrick Henry Hotel and appeared on WSLS-TV midafternoon at the Fair-Acre Farm and Garden Center.

James and Estelle Leonard, both forty-four, of Roanoke were sentenced to a year in prison and fined $1,500 by Federal District Judge A. D. Barksdale on October 28 for sending obscene materials through the mail. The couple was involved in a "friendship club" where they sought to "swap partners for sexual purposes." The couple was the former owner of Leonard Electronics. Barksdale called the offense "a vile and loathsome thing." The Leonards' defense attorney, Linwood Holton Jr., asked the judge for leniency in that the couple had already "paid a severe price" due to the local publicity.

Hollywood actress Lynn Bari, formerly of Roanoke, sought to gain custody of her son, John, in a high-profile court case in Los Angeles. The son was living with Bari's ex-husband, Sid Luft, and Luft's new wife, Judy Garland.

The eighth annual Shrine Bowl football game was held at Victory Stadium on November 1 between the freshmen squads of VMI and Virginia Tech. Tech won 43–0. The game was a benefit for the Shriners Hospitals for Crippled Children. Prior to the game was a parade with twenty-five high school and college bands. Attendance at the game was estimated at 9,000.

All-Star Lanes held a bowling clinic the first weekend in November with three top professional bowlers—Frank Clause, Anita Cantalina, and Henry Nosakowski.

Thomas Franklin, twenty-seven, of Roanoke was killed on October 31 in a single-car accident on Yellow Mountain Road. His parents were Mr. and Mrs. Stuart Franklin Sr.

A ground-breaking service was held on November 2 for the first building of Colonial Presbyterian Church just off the 3500 block of Colonial Avenue SW. Rev. Robert Field was the pastor. The church was chartered on May 5, 1957, and had been meeting at Cave Spring High School. The first building was to cost $65,000, and Walker Caldwell was the contractor.

Folk artist Harriet French Turner had a one-woman exhibition of her work at Hollins College that opened on November 2. The works were for sale and ranged in price from $75 to $125. She began painting in 1952.

All-Star Lanes held a formal ribbon-cutting ceremony on November 2. Participants included Mayor Vincent Wheeler and business leader Carter Burgess. The bowling alley—which had already been open a week—had twenty-four lanes, a restaurant called the 300 Room, and a billiard parlor. George Kissak was the owner.

Travelmasters, a travel agency, opened on November 3 at 305 First Street SW. Mrs. Odessa Bailey and Gwen Moomaw were co-owners.

Incumbent Sixth District Congressman Richard Poff, a Republican, defeated Democrat Richard Pence in a spirited general election on November 4. The district vote was 37,937 to 28,530. Poff was one of the few Republicans in the South to retain his seat. In Roanoke, the vote was 11,952 to 7,758 in favor of Poff. In Roanoke County, Poff won by a vote of 5,676 to 3,390.

Clover Creamery Company advertised its newest ice cream flavor in early November—coffee candy.

A second Top Value Stamps redemption store opened in Roanoke on November 6 at 2817 Williamson Road.

The Sable Room, a dinner club with dancing, opened on November 8 at Dixie Caverns.

The location of a proposed sports and trade coliseum on the thirty-acre tract of Roanoke-Salem shopping plaza along Melrose Avenue NW was studied by the shopping center's developers, Giant Food Stores. The Jaycees supplied details for the project. The Jaycees had proposed a three-unit coliseum with 8,200 permanent seats.

Yoda's Big Boy Drive-In restaurant opened on November 7 on Route 460 at Lakeside. Local disc jockeys broadcasted from the parking lot.

A group of twelve Explorer Scouts and two leaders were trapped for eight hours on November 8 in a remote mountain cave nine miles west of the Catawba Sanatorium in a section called Millers Cove. No one was seriously injured. The scout troop was from Richmond.

John Reid, eighty-six, of Roanoke died on November 9. He was the last surviving charter member of Roanoke Country Club and was a former director of First Federal Savings and Loan Association.

The Roanoke County School Board decided on the name of its newly proposed elementary school at their November 11 meeting. The name originally given was Monte Vista Elementary School, but board members did not like it. After much discussion and several suggestions, the board's clerk, Hazel Ballentine, offered Mountain View Elementary School as a name. The suggestion passed unanimously.

A truck was sliced in two while crossing the N&W Railway tracks on November 12 at the Kroger warehouse. The driver, Claude Larch of Roanoke, was injured by the westbound *Tennessean* passenger train's collision with his delivery truck.

Andrew Lewis High School and Cave Spring High School had to be evacuated due to prank bomb threats in mid-November.

Howard Johnson's Motor Lodge opened in mid-November on Routes 11 and 220, north, adjoining the Howard Johnson's restaurant. The sixty-unit $350,000 motel had two swimming pools and was managed by Frank Meadows.

Herman Weaver of Roanoke was elected president of the International Rescue and First Aid Association at the group's annual meeting in Jacksonville, Florida, on November 15. Two other Roanoke men had also served previously in that capacity, Julian Wise and Marcellus Johnson.

The Brice Trio performed at Addison High School on November 20, sponsored by the Hunton Branch YMCA.

The first worship service of Ridgewood Baptist Church was held on November 16 in a home on the corner of Ridgewood Road and Deaner Drive NW. Rev. Wallace Altice was the pastor.

Wills Grocery at 2415 Hollins Road NE was liquidated in an auction on November 19 due to the death of its owner, W. L. Wills. The grocery had been in operation since 1914.

A fire heavily damaged a large shed at the United Cooperage Company in the 1800 block of Shenandoah Avenue NW on November 16. That same day, fire destroyed a large barn on the Huff Farm, which attracted 1,000 spectators.

The Villa Heights Recreation Center was officially opened and dedicated on November 16. About 700 persons attended the opening in the former Bateman home. The center was owned and operated by the Roanoke Parks and Recreation Department. Clara Dodson was the leader of the center.

The Roanoke Ministers Conference elected a Black clergyman to an office within the organization for the first time during its meeting on November 17. Rev. C. H. Pierson, a chaplain at the Veterans Administration Hospital, was elected as secretary.

Stephenson & Aldridge, a furniture store, opened a second location on November 20 on Lee Highway between Roanoke and Salem. Its other store was at 111 E. Campbell Avenue.

The City of Roanoke began work the third week in November for a six-inch water main from the Crystal Spring Pumping Station to the top of Mill Mountain. The main would replace a two-inch line.

Officials with both N&W Railway and the Virginian Railway announced on November 19 plans to study a merger of the two historic railroads. Both railroads connected the coal fields of West Virginia to ports on Virginia's eastern shore.

Piedmont Airlines landed its first turbojet, an F-27, at Woodrum Field on November 19. The plane was one of eight that Piedmont was putting into service. The F-27 could carry up to thirty-six passengers and reach a speed of 280 miles an hour.

Two Virginian Railway trains sideswiped each other on November 20 at the Kumis siding west of Salem. The freight-train accident derailed thirty-seven coal cars and injured two men. The accident was blamed on a mix-up in communications. Coal was scattered for several hundred yards on both sides of the track. J. W. Kesling of Roanoke, engineer of the westbound train, said, "Ninety seconds earlier and we'd all be dead. We would have met head-on on the bridge."

The Roanoke City 115-pound sandlot football championship game between South Roanoke and the Salvation Army Boys' Club was held at Victory Stadium on November 22. It was the first time the sandlot championship was televised live via WSLS.

Glidden Paint Company opened a store at 4915 Williamson Road on November 20.

The Roanoke Redevelopment and Housing Authority asked Roanoke City Council for permission to study additional blighted areas in northwest and northeast Roanoke for possible "slum clearance" and urban renewal. The RRHA sought to apply for federal funding. The RRHA was already engaged in the Commonwealth Project for northeast Roanoke. The additional sections being eyed by the RRHA were Gainsboro and an industrial area.

Scotchwash Laundromat opened on November 22 on Jamison Avenue at Ninth Street SE.

St. John Lutheran Church was formally organized during a service on November 23 at the Cave Spring Lions Club building. Rev. Luther Mauney conducted the Act of Organization.

A fire swept through and destroyed the H. H. Carter Lumber Company at 619 Brandon Avenue SW on November 22. Damage was estimated at $150,000. The Franklin Road Chapel, across from the lumber firm, was threatened as firemen poured water on it to prevent it from catching fire. Thousands watched the blaze from a nearby hillside.

Shell Homes, a housing contractor, held a grand opening on November 23 at 1617 W. Main Street in Salem.

Three members of Roanoke City Council walked out of a meeting on November 24 in protest of the council's decision to receive a report on annexation in closed session. Benton Dillard, Charles Cornell, and Roy Webber refused to attend the closed-door session, which had been adopted on a 4–3 vote.

A forest fire consumed nearly one hundred acres on Coyner's Mountain in Botetourt County on November 24. It took sixty-three firefighters to bring the blaze under control.

WDBJ radio placed its new mobile unit into service on November 24. The unit, housed in a Volkswagen van, contained two audio consoles, two turntables, a tape recorder, a two-way radio, and a public address system. The mobile unit allowed the radio station to host live remote broadcasts with better quality and frequency.

Vinton Furniture Company in Vinton advertised in late November that it was going out of business.

The first three of 268 new passenger diesels were put into service by N&W Railway in late November. Nos. 506, 507, and 508 were operating on the Shenandoah Division.

M. W. Armistead III president of the Times-World Corporation, stated, "We've got three more governments than we need," in an address to the Rotary Club about the status of the Roanoke Valley on November 25. He called it "a reflection of our own stupidity as evidenced by a narrow provincialism that would be really ludicrous if it weren't so expensive."

Santa arrived at Sears Town on November 28, the day after Thanksgiving. He arrived by helicopter, landing on the Sears roof. Santa was at Heironimus the following day, where children could ride a miniature *Powhatan Arrow* on the fourth floor.

John Kingery was acquitted in the October 19 death of George Furrow by a Roanoke County Circuit Court jury on November 26. The jury believed Kingery acted in self-defense.

An estimated crowd of 27,500 attended the annual Thanksgiving Day football game between Virginia Tech and VMI at Victory Stadium. For the first time in the tradition's history, VMI brought female cheerleaders…from Lexington High School. Tech won the game 21–16. The City of Roanoke flew twenty-four Confederate flags on the top of the stadium's east and west sides in keeping with the game's tradition. Half were taken as souvenirs, though police recovered most of them.

A log cabin that was dismantled in Roanoke and rebuilt in Rockbridge County was profiled in the November 30 edition of the *Roanoke Times*. According to the article, the cabin was believed to have been the home of Roanoke's first postmaster when the city was known as Big Lick. The weather-boarded cabin was put up for sale by a contractor when widening Williamson Road and purchased by a couple who had it disassembled and moved fifty-two miles to southeastern Rockbridge County. When the building was being dismantled, a penny dated 1802 was discovered.

Addison High School opened its varsity basketball season on December 3 with a game against Waid High School at Rocky Mount. It was the Bulldogs' first game under their new head coach, Irvin Cannaday Jr. Cannaday had been the assistant coach for two years at Addison and prior to that was the head coach at Carver High School in Salem.

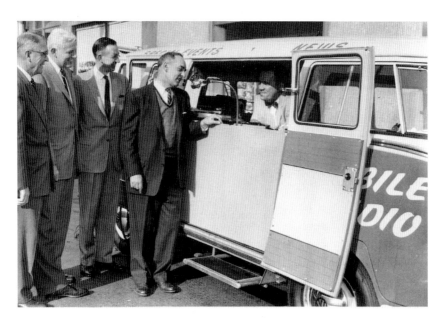

WDBJ radio created a mobile studio in 1958 using a Volkswagen van. Shown here are Roanoke Mayor Vincent Wheeler (hand on the door) and Irv Sharp (inside the van), along with others. *WDBJ7*

The Fading Giant, a recording of steam locomotives on N&W Railway in Southwest Virginia, was made by O. Winston Link, a New York photographer. It was his second such record.

Over 200 persons attended a public hearing on December 1 regarding the Roanoke Redevelopment and Housing Authority proposal to do "slum clearance" in large areas of northeast and northwest Roanoke, adjacent to their ongoing redevelopment project in northeast Roanoke. The crowd, which was biracial, stated that the areas in question were not "slums." Those in opposition included Dr. L. E. Paxton, Robert Burrows, Reuben Lawson, Rev. Frederick Sampson, and Rev. W. N. Hunter. Most based their opposition on the city's experience with the Commonwealth Project and urged the city to not continue such projects in the future.

The Lemarco Manufacturing Corporation, a stock corporation, came into existence on December 1. About 150 members of the Roanoke Development Association, an organization of Black businessmen and citizens, voted to create company to be a Black-owned manufacturer of dresses. Dr. Harry Penn, president of the association, was a primary financial backer of the new business. According to Penn, the name "Lemarco" was Italian for "move forward."

An estimated 35,000 attended the eighth annual Roanoke Christmas Parade in downtown on December 2. City officials believed it was the largest in the city's history. The Roanoke Merchants Association was the sponsor of the 130-unit parade. Carolyn Epperson, a senior at Jefferson High School, was the parade's Snow Queen.

Miller & Rhoads sponsored a Santa Claus Train on December 6, the second one of the season for the department store. The train departed in the early afternoon, picked up Santa along the route, and returned in late afternoon. The train had local television personalities, the Snow Queen, fairy princesses, and Santa's helpers. Tickets were fifty cents. Over 4,000 bought round-trip tickets to ride the *Santa Claus Special* that went from Roanoke to Elliston.

The Town of Salem filed a formal petition in Roanoke County Circuit Court on December 4 to annex part of Roanoke County. The town sought to annex the area east of the town limit to Mason's Creek and south to the Roanoke River.

The Roanoke Planning Commission recommended on December 5 that the proposed Roanoke Technical Institute be built on a ten-acre site adjacent to Forest Park School in the 2400 block of Melrose Avenue NW. The tract, known as the Horton property, was offered as a donation by Mrs. W. H. Horton in memory of her husband. The second choice of the planning commission was in Shrine Hill Park on Grandin Road SW.

Salem held its Christmas parade on December 5. A crowd of 15,000 viewed the seventy-five-unit parade, which went down Main Street and College Avenue.

The new Garden City Church of the Brethren on Bandy Road SE was dedicated on December 7.

The Roanoke Symphony Orchestra gave a concert of Handel's *Messiah* on December 7 at Jefferson High School. Twenty-three church choirs also participated. Jane Stuart Smith was a guest soloist.

A new Torah scroll was presented to Beth Israel Synagogue on December 7. It was a gift from Hyman Katz of Baltimore in honor of the bar mitzvah of his grandson, Dennis Brumberg.

The Golden Crucible, an outdoor drama by Hollins College professor Kermit Hunter, was chosen to be performed in Pittsburgh, Pennsylvania, on the occasion of the city's bicentennial. It would run for six weeks during the summer of 1959.

Bud Skeens was selected as host of a new local television program titled *Spotlight* that aired on WSLS on Saturday mornings beginning December 13. The show dramatized scientific problem-solving using local guests and high school students. It was sponsored by the Junior League.

The proposed extension of the interstate highway spur from Orange Avenue, near Second Street, to Elm Avenue SE was approved by Roanoke City Council on December 8. The proposed extension of 1.1 miles was estimated to cost $13.4 million. It was a reaffirmation of a decision made by a prior council.

Due to opposition from residents to the proposed site for the Roanoke Technical Institute along Melrose Avenue NW, Roanoke City Council decided to ask a subcommittee of the Board of Visitors at Virginia Tech to revisit the issue of location. There was also opposition to the Shrine Hill Park site.

The workforce at the American Viscose plant in Roanoke had dwindled to 250 as of the first of December due to the phased closure of the plant. Only the Filatex department remained in full operation.

This circa 1958 photo shows the W. T. Grant Company, a chain department store, which was located at 17 Campbell Avenue. *Virginia Room, RPL*

Leroy Wynn was ordered to undergo a psychiatric exam prior to his murder trial slated to begin December 30. Wynn had been arrested for the killing of Marian Duckwiler of Vinton on October 18. Her mutilated body had been discovered by police in an alley behind 133 Loudon Avenue NW.

The annual pre-Christmas Stag Night was held by numerous stores in downtown Roanoke on December 10 to provide male customers an opportunity to shop for their wives and girlfriends. Some stores offered dinner, live models, and live music.

The Roanoke Fair, after losing $4,000 in 1958, was canceled for 1959 by its sponsor, American Legion Post No. 3. It had been an annual event in Roanoke since 1937. The 1958 fair had attracted 22,000 to Victory Stadium but still was not profitable.

Representatives of the valley's four governing bodies met on December 11 at the invitation of Roanoke Mayor Vincent Wheeler to discuss the need for a new civic auditorium. The group named an eight-person committee to continue meeting about a sports coliseum and auditorium. The consensus of the group was to approach officials of N&W Railway and ask that they consider expanding the Hotel Roanoke to accommodate conventions and large cultural events. The group also believed that a large auditorium would most likely have to be located outside downtown Roanoke to accommodate parking.

Henry Rolley, a graduate of Roanoke's National Business College who once served as vice president of the Virgin Islands, died at age fifty-nine at Williamsburg on December 12. Rolley held the post in the Virgin Islands from 1948 to 1953.

A double shooting occurred in the predawn hours of December 13 at Norman's Restaurant at 201 E. Main Street in Salem. Police determined Norman Potts of Roanoke was killed due to a self-inflicted gunshot. Ruth Waddell of Salem was also shot. Investigators believed Potts accidentally shot Waddell and then shot himself.

Grace Baptist Church (also known as Judy Memorial Baptist Church) at 727 Jamison Avenue SE reopened on December 14 after being closed for three months. It reopened under the name of Central Baptist Church.

Covenant Presbyterian Church on Deyerle Road SW dedicated the first of a planned three-unit building on December 14. The newly completed building was estimated to have cost $140,000.

Pendleton Thomas Jr. was sentenced to six years on December 13 by Judge Fred Hoback in Roanoke County Circuit Court. Thomas had been convicted of "aiding and abetting sodomy." Two teenagers testified against Pendleton, who had been fired from his teaching position at Andrew Lewis High School.

Louise Weeks, fifteen, of Roanoke County died on December 15 from wounds she received that day from being shot in the abdomen. Bobby Clark, twenty-two, was detained by police for the shooting. Police believed the shooting was accidental.

Annie Fisher, thirty-seven, of New Castle died in a Roanoke hospital on December from burns she sustained on December 5 when her husband poured gasoline on her and lit her on fire. Howard Fisher had been arrested for the attack. Mrs. Fisher was survived by the couple's nine children.

The Roanoke School Board adopted new plans for two new high schools at their meeting on December 15. The first of the schools would be a high school located in Shrine Hill Park. The architectural firm of Smithey and Boynton had been retained to develop the schools.

The pouring of Roanoke's first community Christmas candle, made from thousands of used candles, was on December 18. The candle was displayed on the lawn of the Municipal Building and was ten feet high. The project was sponsored by the Roanoke Ministers Conference and WDBJ-TV.

Officials with American Viscose announced on December 18 that the 1,900 hourly employees would get an average separation wage of $800, and some would receive up to $2,500 as the company began closing down the Roanoke plant.

East Coast Service Station opened on December 19 on Patterson Avenue SW at Shaffers Crossing.

Roanoke City Council released a map showing 3.6 square miles for possible annexation lying to the west of Roanoke. The report was the culmination of weeks of study behind closed doors. The area generally was between Peters Creek, the western boundary, and Masons Creek, and was bounded roughly by US 460 to the north and US 11 to the south. It encompassed the N&W and Virginian Railway yards, the Hancock substation of Appalachian Power Company, and the

Veterans Administration Hospital. The chairman of the Roanoke County Board of Supervisors, W. E. Cundiff, responded to the plan by stating that the board would oppose it "with all legal means necessary."

H. K. Howell became the new owner and operator of the Auto Trading Post at 713 Thirteenth Street SW in mid-December.

The community Christmas candle was officially lit on December 23. Located on the lawn of the Municipal Building, the ceremony included the eighty-five-voice choir of Jefferson High School and city officials. The project was undertaken by the Roanoke Ministers Conference to symbolize "the oneness of all Christian people in Christ." Molding of the gigantic candle was done by Chuck Verna of WDBJ.

Stevens-Shepperd men's store announced on December 24 that it would merge with its parent organization, Miller & Rhoads, on January 2. The men's store was located at 307 First Street SW.

A combination store and gas station owned by George Powell on Bent Mountain was destroyed in a Christmas Day fire. The store, formerly owned by C. G. Bohon, was on Route 221.

A soft-drink truck ran off the road along Route 220 on December 26 and crashed through the front of the Virginia Grocery Store. E. L. Craighead, owner of the store, heard the truck approaching and jumped on a table to avoid being hit. The truck had blown a tire, causing the driver to lose control.

A late-night fire on December 27 damaged the Angus House restaurant at the corner of Jefferson Street and Elm Avenue SW. A. A. Jamison, owner, had opened the restaurant in 1954.

Bailey's Gifts, located at 1025 S. Jefferson Street, advertised that it was going out of business effective December 31.

A public auction was held on December 30 to liquidate the assets of H. Fox and Brothers, a retail store, due to bankruptcy. The store was located at 117 W. Campbell Avenue.

The Star City Furniture Company closed its doors for the last time on December 29.

A committee of the Virginia Tech Board of Visitors reiterated its preference for Shrine Hill Park as the location for the planned Roanoke Technical Institute in a report to Roanoke City Council on December 29. The council remained split on that location.

"White Christmas" was the theme of the annual debutante ball sponsored by the Altruist Club at the Star City Auditorium on December 29. Twenty-four girls were presented at the event, which was the culmination of a weeklong set of social activities for the participants. John Reeves was the grand marshal of the pageant, and music was provided by the Aristocrats Orchestra.

Roanoke's George Preas, offensive tackle for the Baltimore Colts, returned home to his real estate business following the Colts' 23–17 sudden-death victory over the New York Giants in the National Football League championship game. It was the Colts' first championship title. The 245-pound Preas told reporters, "We out-gutted them. Everybody was mighty happy. It was hard to believe for awhile."

Preas got his start in football at Jefferson High School and was a standout player at Virginia Tech.

A number of New Year's Eve dance events were held at various locations with local bands, including the City Market Auditorium with Andy Anderson's Band, Club 323 with the Country Cousins, Hillbilly Barn on Route 311 with Carl Decker and the Happy Valley Boys, Colonial Hills Club with Rusty Nichols and his orchestra, Candlelite Club with the Stylists, the Sable Room with Dave Burgess and his orchestra, Sammy's with the Flames, and the Preston Club with the Tempos.

1959

WDBJ radio hosted a "Record Romp and Dance" at the National Guard armory on January 2 with their disc jockey, Bill Spahr, broadcasting live. The dress code was skirts and sweaters for women and coats and ties for men.

Patterson Drug Company opened on January 2 at 101 McClanahan Street SW. It held a formal grand opening on January 9. Roy Moon and Homer Stokes were the pharmacists.

Blue Ridge Motors opened in their new building at 625 W. Campbell Avenue on January 3.

Woodrum Field began receiving more than $2 million worth of electronics installations to improve traffic safety and reduce the number of flyovers in weather. The infusion of new equipment in early January was paid for by the Federal Aviation Agency, successor to the Civil Aeronautics Association (CAA) that went out of existence on January 1. The new equipment allowed the airport to better handle jet aircraft. Marshall Harris, the airport manager, also reported that 1958 was a "banner year," with a total of 84,038 outbound passengers despite two national airline strikes. Woodrum Field was served by Eastern, American, and Piedmont Airlines.

Goliath Imports, a German automaker, appointed Huffman Motor Company at 424 W. Campbell Avenue as its dealer.

Associated Advertising was formed in early January by Fred Corstaphney and John Will Creasy. Corstaphney had been with WDBJ, and Creasy was formerly employed as the director of publicity for S. H. Heironimus Company. The firm was located in the First Federal Building.

Economy's Restaurant at 110 Campbell Avenue SW was liquidated in an auction on January 6.

Alvin Hickson, twenty-five, of Salem died in an auto wreck at the intersection of Electric Road and Salem Turnpike on January 4.

The N&W Café building at 114 E. Salem Avenue was ravaged by fire on January 6. The former restaurant had been purchased by the Roanoke Rescue Mission a few weeks prior.

Alexander Terrell resigned as captain of the Hunton Life Saving and First Aid Crew on January 5, a position he had held since he helped organized the crew more than seventeen years ago. Terrell remained with the crew as captain emeritus.

A couple engaged to be married was killed when their car was struck by an N&W Railway diesel train on January 7. Robert Smelser, thirty-six, and Ruth Crook, thirty-five, were in a car that stalled on the rail crossing at Bonsack.

Roanoke and Roanoke County were one of five areas in the nation to participate in a pilot study of home preparedness for Civil Defense in the event of an atomic attack. The study was being conducted by the Office of Civil and Defense Mobilization and was overseen locally by a thirteen-member steering committee. Some 10,000 kits were distributed to homes for the purposes of the study.

Dr. Harry Penn announced on January 8 that the Lemarco Manufacturing Corporation hoped to begin production on March 1. The dressmaking company was owned by local Black businessmen. Phil Jacobs was named as the plant manager. The new business was to be located at 204 Fifth Street NW, which was formerly occupied by Binswanger & Company.

Former Roanoker Herbert Moseley was named president and chief executive officer of the Bank of Virginia on January 9, which was headquartered in Richmond. Moseley had been head of the bank's Roanoke branch from 1948 to 1953.

Roanoke City Council rejected on January 12 the request of the Roanoke Redevelopment and Housing Authority for permission to apply for federal funds to study two more areas for potential redevelopment. The council voted 5–2 to prevent the RRHA from moving forward primarily due to the opposition from the Black community and to ongoing problems with the Commonwealth Project. At the same meeting, the council favored the Shrine Hill Park site for the planned Roanoke Technical Institute. By a vote of 4–3, the council favored a 7.5-acre tract of the park and conveyed that via resolution to the Virginia Tech Board of Visitors.

Judge Beverly Fitzpatrick was honored on January 13 for his work as president of the Roanoke Valley Safety Council. Fitzpatrick was instrumental in forming the organization as a means of promoting better traffic laws and safety to reduce the number of accidents and fatalities caused with vehicles.

The Roanoke Broadway Theater League was formed on January 15 and began planning a four-play season by bringing Broadway touring shows to Roanoke. Don Leslie, representative of the Broadway Theater Alliance, was the organizer.

A committee appointed by the Episcopal Diocese of Southwestern Virginia held a listening session at St. John's Episcopal Church and St. James Episcopal Church on January 16 and 17 to hear comments regarding the use of Hemlock Haven, an Episcopal camp, by Blacks. There had been spirited discussion surrounding the issue of desegregating the camp's summer youth programs. Dr. Dabney Lancaster chaired the committee.

A fire heavily damaged the Hamlar-Curtis Funeral Home on January 16. The funeral service was located at Tenth Street and Moorman Avenue NW.

The Wilmont Realty Company announced plans for a 600-home subdivision to be built that would stretch from Thirty-Sixth Street NW into Roanoke County. The tract encompassed 182 acres and was known as the Stevens farm property. Carl Montgomery was president of the company.

The Zoo Choo at the Children's Zoo on Mill Mountain became debt free in early January. The miniature train was a project initiated by the Roanoke Jaycees.

In the 1958 season, there were 34,172 children's tickets sold to ride the train and 21,471 for adults.

The Plantation Grille restaurant at 829 W. Main Street in Salem was liquidated in an auction on January 21 due to the retirement of the owner.

The new building of Preston Oaks Baptist Church was dedicated on January 19 with a crowd of 250 in attendance. Rev. Lewis Bates was the guest speaker.

The Virginia Supreme Court struck down Virginia's various Massive Resistance strategies in a 5–2 ruling on January 19. The court gutted Governor Lindsay Almond's plan to maintain segregated schools despite the US Supreme Court's *Brown* decision. The decision was also followed by a decision by a three-judge federal court striking down Norfolk's segregation plan. In the wake of the court decisions, two Roanoke legislators advocated switching to "locally owned and operated schools" as a means to continue noncompliance. Delegates Julian Rutherfoord Jr. and Kossen Gregory provided little details as to their plan.

The building that once housed the N&W Café at 114 E. Salem Avenue was razed on January 19 due to fire damage.

Roanoke City Council delayed finalizing a decision on the site of the Roanoke Technical Institute when significant opposition from surrounding residents was demonstrated at the council's January 19 meeting. A petition with 900 signatures was presented to the council. Edwin Young, an attorney representing some of the residents, stated that the recent court ruling striking down segregation and the fact that Virginia Tech was integrated made the Shrine Hill site "not the proper place for the school."

Cynthia Isaebelle, four, of the Big Hill section in Roanoke County was killed on January 21 when four sticks of dynamite exploded accidentally in a woodshed in which she was playing at her home.

The Roanoke Regional Blood Program changed its name to Appalachian Regional Blood Program on January 21. The blood bank was operated by the Roanoke Red Cross.

This January 1959 clip shows skaters on Lakewood Park's pond. The park was along Brandon Avenue SW. *WSLS-TV News Film Collection, UVA Libraries*

Showtimers presented Gore Vidal's comedy *Visit to a Small Planet* the third weekend in January. Lead roles were played by Bristow Hardin, George Garretson, Jim Shipp, Betty Lou Hunter, Harold Hall, and Cindy Weeks. The play was directed by Betty Thornton Shaner.

Hamlar-Curtis Funeral Home opened temporary offices at 512 Gainsboro Road NW on January 22 due to remodeling of its funeral home following a fire. The temporary location had formerly been the site of Hughes Funeral Home.

A mental examination for convicted rapist Frank Snider Jr. was ordered on January 23 by the Fourth Circuit Court of Appeals. Snider had been convicted of the Mother's Day 1956 attack on a young Roanoke girl. He had been given the death sentence.

Richard Fowlkes, partner in the Roanoke real estate firm Fowlkes and Kefauver, died on January 23 aboard a cruise ship he was taking from Nassau to Florida on vacation. He became a partner in the firm in 1933.

The first-ever garden club for Black men in Virginia was formed in Roanoke in mid-January. The Men's Garden and Improvement Club, which had twelve charter members, was sponsored by the Golden Harvest Garden Club. Alexander White was president.

The firm of Agnew and Connelly, a seed firm, dissolved in early January, but the two partners continued to operate in the same business individually. Frank Agnew took over the stores at 301 Nelson Street SE, the Vinton branch at 201 Maple Avenue, and the warehouse at 919 Third Street SE. Willard Connelly took over the Christiansburg branch and leased the former Virginian Railway passenger station on South Jefferson Street, which he planned to convert to a garden store and warehouse. The firm of Agnew and Connelly had been in operation for twelve years, having taken over the seed and garden supply business of J. M. Harris and Company. The Virginian Railway station had been vacant since the run of the last passenger train, old No. 3, from Norfolk to Roanoke on January 30, 1956. The train arrived forty-five minutes late and had 115 paying passengers.

Holiday Homes opened its offices and plant at 2011 Salem Avenue SW in late January. The home design and manufacturing firm offered three mainly ranch-styled models ranging in price from $2,325 to $3,475.

The Angus House restaurant was liquidated by auction on February 3 due to fire damage as the owners decided to not reopen. It was located at 723 S. Jefferson Street.

The Roanoke District Methodist Conference voted to call for an end "to the tragic program of massive resistance to racial integration" during a meeting on January 27. On the same day, the Montgomery Presbytery also called for an end to segregation in public education, passing a resolution to that effect by a vote of 63–28.

Bobby Clark of Roanoke pled guilty to involuntary manslaughter in Hustings Court on January 27 in the death of his girlfriend, Louise Weeks, fifteen, of Roanoke County on December 14, 1958. He was sentenced to one year in jail.

Governor Lindsay Almond Jr. gave a fiery thirty-nine-minute speech to the General Assembly specially convened in Richmond on January 28 in response to court rulings gutting his Massive Resistance program. Almond proposed that compulsory attendance be revoked and that the state provide tuition grants for parents who wished to send their children to nonintegrated schools. His proposals were met with full support by the Roanoke Valley's delegation, including Senator Earl Fitzpatrick, who escorted the governor into the assembly's chamber.

Rudy Rohrdanz, the football and track coach at Jefferson High School, announced on January 30 that he had accepted the head football coach position at Chattanooga High School in Tennessee.

The subcommittee of the Board of Visitors at Virginia Tech studying the site for the Roanoke Technical Institute changed their recommendation from Shrine Hill Park to the former City Farm property located along Colonial Avenue SW on January 30. The group had visited the site the previous day. The committee's recommendation to Roanoke City Council was to convey the twenty-acre tract and remove a cemetery that was also on the property.

James Trinkle of Roanoke was elected president of the Young Democrats of Virginia and became the first person from western Virginia to head the organization. He was elected during the group's convention at Virginia Beach on January 31.

The Cosmopolitan Club founded the Roanoke Valley Speech Clinic in late January. The clinic was temporarily housed at Gill Memorial Hospital. The director of the clinic was Mrs. Bobbie Lubker.

The Roanoke Valley Drama Association named James Heizer to the newly created position of promotion director on January 31 for its production of *Thy Kingdom Come* for the 1959 season. The group also adopted an operating budget of $112,500 for the season.

Professional Business Service opened on February 2 in the Shenandoah Building.

Geraldine Williams, thirty-five, and her son Thomas, eighteen months, perished in a house fire at 11 Gilmer Avenue NE on February 1. The husband, Thomas Williams Sr., was rescued by firefighters.

J. C. Wheat & Company, a securities firm, opened its new offices on the ground floor of the Shenandoah Building on February 2.

A Vortac station went into service atop Fort Lewis Mountain on February 3. The station aided air navigation for planes flying to Woodrum Field. The electronics aid station was one of two planned for airport traffic. The other was to be near Vinton.

Hair Fashions Beauty Salon opened on February 3 at 1107 Main Street SW. Mrs. Lois Roatenberry was the owner.

Travis-Kelley Fish Market at 205 First Street SE was liquidated by public auction on February 5.

Mountain View Golf Club became the Colonial Country Club on February 4. The 250-acre layout had also been known as Monterey Golf Club in the past. Officials with the Colonial Country Club planned to continue work on a new 3,200-square-foot swimming pool, bath house, and pro shop.

Plans for a subdivision known as Cherry Hill were filed on February 4. Some eighty-eight acres had been purchased for the development, just east of the Veterans

Administration Hospital, from Fairview Cemetery Company for $57,750 by B. L. Radford and others.

Roanoke city leaders began assessing the task to moving some 500 graves at the old City Home site due to city council's plans to convey the land for the Roanoke Technical Institute. Burials were started at the City Home tract in 1929 and averaged fifteen or more per year, with many being residents of the home.

A February 7 fire heavily damaged a structure in Salem that was one block west of the post office on Main Street. The building housed Richardson's Supermarket, H. R. Johnson Furniture Company, and the offices of dentist W. S. Mayo Jr.

By the end of the first week of February, only 150 workers remained actively employed at the American Viscose plant in Roanoke. The skeletal crew was helping to close down the various departments and buildings. The 208-acre site with 1.6 million square feet of buildings was officially for sale.

June Reed of Salem had a novel published by Vantage Press titled *Jest Olga*. The novel was about the WAVES in World War II.

An appreciation dinner was held in honor of Rudy Rohrdanz, the departing football coach of Jefferson High School, on February 11. Speakers included George Preas, Jay Blackwood, and Rev. Harry Gamble.

Frank Bowler Jr., forty-six, of Salem died from suffocation due to a house fire at 1031 Homestead Drive on February 8. His body was found about two feet from his front door.

This February 1959 photo shows the Top Value Stamps Gifts Store at 318 Second Street SW. *Virginia Room, RPL*

This is the Top Value Stamps Gifts Store at 2613 Franklin Road SW in March 1959.
Virginia Room, RPL

The Roanoke Commission on Interracial Cooperation held its annual Race Relations Sunday observance on February 8 at First Baptist Church in Gainsboro. Rev. Edward Ziegler of Williamson Road Church of the Brethren delivered the sermon underscoring the need for racial integration in all aspects of society. The racially mixed crowd numbered about 200.

At a meeting of the Roanoke Development Association, it was decided to have a committee meet with the Retail Merchants Association, managers of four large grocery stores, the Roanoke city manager, and the Roanoke police chief about more employment for Blacks. The group also endorsed renewed attempts to have Roanoke hire Black firemen. About 300 members of the association met on February 8 at High Street Baptist Church.

WRIS Radio announced on February 9 that it had banned "rock and roll" music from being played on its station. The 5,000-watt station was located at the corner of Mountain Avenue and Jefferson Street SW.

Roanoke City Council formally adopted an ordinance at its February 9 meeting to convey a sixteen-acre tract of the City Farm property, which also used to have the City Home, for the Roanoke Technical Institute. The vote was unanimous and ended a protracted debate on the site for school. The ordinance called for the removal of an estimated 509 graves before the deed could be executed. City Manager Arthur Owens suggested the graves be removed to Coyner Springs, where the City Home had also been relocated.

Roanoke's PAL boxing team had a 5–2 triumph over the Quantico Marines team on February 12. The bouts were held at the Marine Corps armory before a crowd of 1,100. PAL victors were Jimmy Muse, Jimmy Tucker, Louis Johnson, Mike Thompson, and Billy Sahnow.

Carper's Barber Shop opened on February 16 at 1910 Memorial Avenue SW. Lloyd Carper was the owner.

This clip shows Alexander Terrell (left) receiving an award from Julian Stanley Wise in February 1959 for his years of service to the volunteer rescue squad movement. Terrell founded the Hunton Life Saving and First Aid Crew in 1942. *WSLS-TV News Film Collection, UVA Libraries*

Roanoke's Negro PTA Alliance announced on February 13 that they were reviewing the city schools' curricula and comparing those used in Black schools versus those in white ones. The study was being conducted because Black parents did not want their children set back a grade should their children be made to attend formerly all-white schools when integration was adopted in Roanoke City. School administrators indicated there were only slight differences at the high school levels, with the white schools offering advanced foreign languages while Addison High School did not.

Rosalind Hills Baptist Church dedicated its new multipurpose building on February 15. The $90,000 building was the first one erected by the church, which was located at 2711 Laburnum Avenue SW. H. A. Lucas and Sons was the general contractor. The guest speakers were Rev. W. H. Connelly and Rev. Harry Gamble.

Richard West, twenty-three, of Roanoke was killed in a single-vehicle accident on February 14 on Route 24 west of Stewartsville.

Congressman James Van Zandt of Pennsylvania addressed Sixth District Republicans at their annual Washington-Lincoln Day dinner at the Patrick Henry Hotel on February 20.

Playwright and Hollins College professor Kermit Hunter debuted his newest drama, *Homecoming in Magdala*, on February 20 at the college in connection with the dedication of the Jessie Bal Dupont Chapel. The production was directed by Dean Goodsell.

John Crowe Ransom, well-known poet and former editor of the *Kenyon Review*, lectured at Hollins College on February 19.

B. Forman Sons opened their new store at 412 S. Jefferson Street on February 16. The women's clothier had been in business for seventy-one years.

A Roanoke harness shop closed in mid-February after being in business for six decades. Andrew Hansbrough started a leather harness shop in 1898 on Henry Street and moved the business to Campbell Avenue and Second Street SE in 1918. When the Hunter Viaduct was constructed, the shop building was razed and Joseph Hansbrough (son of Andrew) moved the business to the basement of his home off Williamson Road. Business was good during World War II due to farmers having to often use horses because repair parts for tractors could not be found. By the early 1950s, the business was a sideline.

St. Elizabeth's Episcopal Church began using the chapel of Raleigh Court Presbyterian Church on Sunday afternoons in early February for its worship services. St. Elizabeth's had been using the Masonic Hall on Grandin Road.

About 250 people attended a meeting of the Citizens Protective Association at First Baptist Church in Gainsboro on February 15. The group's aim was to lobby local officials for equal treatment of white and Black sections in regard to the city's toughened housing ordinance that sought to improve substandard residential properties. The city council had enacted tougher regulations in light of rejecting any further expansions of the urban renewal program beyond the Commonwealth Project. Dr. L. E. Paxton was president of the newly organized association.

The Roanoke PTA asked Roanoke City Council at its February 16 meeting to mitigate the fires and danger of disease at the Washington Park dump. The PTA also advocated for a plan to close the dump which was a former rock quarry.

Dr. Curtis Woodford of Vinton was appointed on February 17 to the Roanoke County School Board to serve the unexpired term of Wilson Adkins, who had moved out of Vinton.

The old Big Lick Post Office, one of the few remaining landmarks from that era, was moved on February 18. The little white cottage long stood on the east side of Williamson Road, just south of Orange Avenue NE. It was relocated to the west side of Williamson Road, not far from its former site. The relocation was necessitated by the Roanoke Redevelopment and Housing Authority work relative to the Commonwealth Project. While the former site was not the original site of the old post office, it was undisputed that the building itself was the original post office. It was believed there was an additional post office in Big Lick, however, likely located near Shenandoah Avenue and Second Street NW.

Officials with N&W Railway and the Virginian Railway announced on February 19 that an agreement had been worked out for exchange of stock leading to the merger of the two railroads. An evaluation of the exchange basis had been conducted by the First Boston Corporation. The agreement was to be presented for ratification by the shareholders of both railways. Company officials reported that the merger would save the two systems a combined $1 million per month in operating expenses.

Vinton officials complained to the City of Roanoke that debris from the "slum clearance" project of the Roanoke Redevelopment and Housing Authority was creating problems for some of the town's residents as razed buildings were piled on vacant lots in Vinton. The piles were drawing rats and creating other health hazards.

Everett Freazell, seventy-eight, of Roanoke County was struck and killed by a car on February 21 on Hershberger Road. The man was walking to his mailbox when hit.

Roanoke Times columnist Ben Beagle penned a piece on the paper's February 22 edition about the lack of passengers on N&W Railway's *Powhatan Arrow*. "The relative emptiness of the *Arrow* as it leaves Roanoke is a poignant reminder that railroad travel isn't what it used to be."

The Jessie Ball du Pont Chapel at Hollins College was formally dedicated on February 22. The main speaker was Rev. John Baille, dean of the divinity faculty at the University of Edinburgh, Scotland. His sermon was titled "The Christian's Attitude to College Education." Over 800 attended the service.

The Canadian Players presented George Bernard Shaw's *The Devil's Disciple* at Hollins College on February 26. The drama troupe from Ontario was on a US tour.

Roanoke County's night jailer was reunited with his mother the third weekend in February after being separated from her for forty-five years. Howard Kropff of Salem had been placed in a Richmond orphanage in 1914 with two siblings following the separation of his parents. The mother returned to claim the children, taking two with her but being told the third child, Howard, had died. In reality, Howard had been adopted by Mr. and Mrs. W. J. Kropff of Copper Hill. When they died in 1924, he was sent to an orphanage in Illinois. Kropff had been searching for his mother since 1931. He was able to locate her in Philadelphia through a network of police officials.

Holiday Homes held an open house of its model home on February 21. The prefabricated residence was located at 3044 Melrose Avenue NW. Thomas Crowder was the company president.

Oren Roanoke Corporation began advertising on February 23 that it was open to the general public to work on trucks—built, rebuilt, or repaired. Oren had been exclusively a manufacturer for fire trucks. It was located at 1201 W. Salem Avenue.

Local hospital officials reported that the average daily cost of hospital care per person in Roanoke was $19 for 1958.

Operation of the Crystal Spring Pumping Station switched from steam to electricity on February 24. Earl Mitchell, chief engineer, shot down the old steam pump that morning and switched to electricity seven hours later. The switchover marked the passing of an era as steam had been used at the pumping station since 1905.

R. H. Smith, retired president of N&W Railway, was named Boss of the Year for 1958 by the Roanoke Jaycees during their annual dinner meeting on February 25. Warren Stansbury of Chesapeake & Potomac Telephone Company received their Distinguished Service Award.

Pitney-Bowes, maker of business machines, opened a sales and service office at 3741 Williamson Road NW on February 25.

Woods Brothers Coffee Company announced in late February it had a new blend, Seven Star Coffee.

This clip shows a city employee at the Crystal Springs pump station tending to the fire in the boiler of the steam-powered water pump a few days prior to the station's conversion to electrified water pumps. *WSLS-TV News Film Collection, UVA Libraries*

Roanoke City Manager Arthur Owens announced on February 25 that he and his staff had selected a site at Coyner Springs as the site for a new municipal cemetery. It would replace the cemetery at the former City Home on Colonial Avenue. The new site would also be used for the relocation of more than 500 graves at the old City Home cemetery.

Cindy Saul, nine, of Salem recorded her newest song, *Shabby*, in February. Her other recordings included *Happy Birthday Jesus* and *It Must Have Been the Easter Bunny*. Her lyricist and agent was Donald McGraw.

A commission studying the racial policies of Hemlock Haven, an Episcopal camp near Marion, for the Episcopal Diocese of Southwestern Virginia was divided 11–8 on whether to maintain segregation or not in its activities. The diocesan executive board referred the matter back to the committee for further study during its meeting in Roanoke on February 26. The commission had conducted several input sessions at churches throughout the diocese on the matter, including three in Roanoke. No summer youth conferences were held at the camp in 1958 due to a lack of agreement on the issue.

David Sirry, forty-six, of Catawba confessed to police in St. Louis, Missouri, in late February that he had killed his wife, Betty Jo, at their Catawba home on August 7, 1958. Sirry was charged with murder and was returned to Roanoke County for trial. Sirry had originally told local authorities that he found his wife dead when he returned home that day from work. Evidence indicated the woman had been smothered.

This February 1959 photo shows Mullens Place located at 307 Ninth Street SE. *Virginia Room, RPL*

The Salem District headquarters of the Virginia Division of Forestry opened on February 27 at 210 Riverland Drive in Salem. The office had been formerly located in the Farmers National Bank of Salem.

The former library building in Elmwood Park, the 129-year-old Elmwood home, was found to be in deteriorating condition in late February such that city officials restricted its use to the first floor. The building commissioner had recommended that it be razed. The building served as the city's library from 1921 until 1952 and then was turned over the Roanoke Council of Garden Clubs.

A five-year-old girl was found starved, beaten, and locked in a dirt-floor basement of a home on February 27 in the Back Creek section of Roanoke County. Her stepfather and mother, Everett Ray and Ann Ray, were jailed for child neglect. The child weighed twenty-nine pounds. Her three siblings seemed well and were attending school. A suspicious neighbor reported the situation to officials.

North Roanoke Baptist Church dedicated its new building on Peters Creek Road on March 1. The sanctuary was contemporary in its design. It began in August 1957 as a mission of Calvary Baptist Church.

The Roanoke Symphony Orchestra performed at the American Theatre on March 2. Gibson Morrissey conducted the symphony performance in the US premier of Stevan Hristic's *Legend of Orchid*. In 1950, Morrissey had conducted the Wiesbaden Symphony in the German premier of the same piece. Sara Rhodes of New York was the guest soloist. The performance was attended by the Yugoslavian ambassador to the United States and his wife.

Pfc. Howard Perry, twenty-two, of Vinton appeared on the nationally televised CBS show *Ted Mack's Amateur Hour* on March 1. The Irish tenor sang *Dear Old Donagal.*

The *Roanoke Times* named its All City-County basketball team in early March. The First Team consisted of the following players: Al Johnson, Jefferson; Butch Cox, Jefferson; Nelson Powell, Lewis; Buddy Firebaugh, Fleming; and Doug Meador, Byrd. Coach of the Year was Jimmy Moore of Fleming, and Player of the Year was Al Johnson.

Opera soprano Camilla Williams performed at the Addison High School auditorium on March 4, sponsored by the Alpha Kappa Alpha sorority. Williams had been touring in Africa and Germany. A native of Danville, Williams was accompanied by her pianist, George Malloy.

A spirited battle for Roanoke's seat in the state senate was launched on March 4 when William Hopkins, a young attorney, chose to oppose incumbent State Senator Earl Fitzpatrick for the Democratic nomination for the seat. Fitzpatrick had held the seat since 1948 and was widely viewed as aligned closely with the Byrd-Almond wing of the party. Hopkins represented a challenge to the status quo and was more accommodating to civil rights and integration.

The Bargain Center, a department store on First Street at Luck Avenue SW, began advertising in early March that it was going out of business.

The colors of the 314th Field Artillery Battalion were retired on March 6. The battalion had been in Roanoke since 1947, having originated in 1917 at Fort Lee. Its 114 men would combine with the 318th Infantry to form the 319th Basic Combat Training Regiment under the command of Lt. Col. William Reynolds.

The filling of the dump in Washington Park "should be continued until the ultimate plan of the city is completed," as the report of the State Department of Health stated in early March. The dump received a state inspection due to complaints from nearby residents. Roanoke officials had estimated it would take two more years to fill the dump and then close it.

Everett Ray and his wife were sentenced to twelve months of suspended jail terms on March 6 when they pled guilty to charges of child neglect. The couple claimed they kept their five-year-old daughter in the basement because she "wet and messed herself." The child was turned over to the Roanoke County welfare department for adoption.

Southwest Kwik-Wash, a laundromat, opened at the corner of Patterson Avenue and Thirteenth Street SW on March 7.

Jim Walter Corporation, a modular homes business, opened at 1166 E. Main Street in Salem in early March.

A well-preserved Windsor writing chair used by Roanoke County's first delegate to the General Assembly of Virginia was bequeathed to the Roanoke Public Library. The chair was willed by the heirs of Capt. Henry Snyder, who represented the county in the legislature in 1840 and 1841. The chair was believed to be 125 years old.

The Paganini Quartet performed at Hollins College on March 9. The members played instruments made by Stradivarius.

This March 1959 image shows the exterior of the Lemarco Manufacturing Company.
WSLS-TV News Film Collection, UVA Libraries

The Minneapolis Symphony Orchestra performed at Jefferson High School on March 13 under the sponsorship of the Thursday Morning Music Club.

The twenty-fourth consecutive performance of the Salem Lions Club minstrel show was held the second weekend in March at Andrew Lewis High School. The club had been in existence since 1936 and had been doing its annual minstrel show since 1937 as a fundraiser for its sight conservation projects.

Rev. D. Z. Roberson, pastor of Raleigh Court Presbyterian Church, announced his retirement to his congregation on March 8 to take effect September 29. Roberson had been the church's pastor since 1925, when the church started.

The Roanoke Redevelopment and Housing Authority announced in mid-March that vacant land within the Commonwealth Project was for sale to private developers. Russell Henley, RRHA executive director, stated that the authority was looking for developers "who will build blocks of houses and sell them to Negroes" in a presentation he made to the Roanoke Home Builders Association.

The US House of Representatives approved statehood for Hawaii on March 12. The US Senate had done the same a few days prior. Sixth District Congressman Richard Poff was one of eighty-nine who voted against statehood, and he had done the same in regard to Alaska the previous year. Poff explained his negative vote in a radio address on March 17 as being based on his impression that Hawaii was under the social and political influence of Communists.

A 1.1 mile extension of the planned interstate spur into Roanoke from Orange Avenue NE to Elm Avenue SE was given approval by the US Bureau of Public Roads on March 13. The road would link to an already-approved spur from Interstate

81 near Kingstown through the Williamson Road section to Orange Avenue near Second Street. The cost of the extension was estimated at $13.4 million.

The new Lemarco Manufacturing Company, a Black-owned dress factory, was dedicated on March 15. The factory, located at 206 Fifth Street NW, was a project of the Roanoke Development Association, an association dedicated to providing economic opportunity for Blacks. The guest speaker was Rev. A. L. James. Dr. Harry Penn, president of the company, stated that Lemarco planned to employ fifty-five people. About 350 attended the dedication ceremony.

Sarah Kingery, one hundred, of Boones Mill died on March 15. She was survived by three sons, four daughters, forty-four grandchildren, ninety-one great-grandchildren, and fifty-eight great-great-grandchildren.

Grover Lucas, convicted of killing his wife on April 27, 1958, and also charged with killing two of his children and injuring a third, was sentenced to die by the electric chair on June 5 by Judge Dirk Kuyk. When asked if he wanted to say anything by the judge, the passive Lucas shook his head in the negative.

Roanoke's annual two-week-long Gold Medal basketball tournament began March 17. Nearly one hundred teams had entered the contest.

The Roanoke County International Telephone and Telegraph Corporation plant was dedicated on March 17. The main speaker was Governor Lindsay Almond Jr., who addressed a gathering of 250 businessmen. The plant was located just north of Hollins College. Fred Farwell, ITT vice president, also spoke.

This October 1959 clip is of the interior of Lemarco Manufacturing Company, a dressmaking business launched to employ Black women. *WSLS-TV News Film Collection, UVA Libraries*

This October 1959 photo shows the ITT building under construction at 7635 Plantation Road. *Virginia Room, RPL*

Frank Snider Jr., who was convicted of raping a nine-year-old Roanoke girl on May 13, 1956, was sent back to Southwestern State Hospital in Marion for another mental evaluation. Snider had been sentenced to death but had been given several reprieves due to his many appeals. His defense attorneys were Warren Messick and Harvey Lutins.

A committee formed to create a transportation museum in Wasena Park announced on March 18 that its request to get a jet plane for the museum met with success. A formal request had been sent by the city manager, Arthur Owens, to a federal disposal depot in Arizona, and the city would be able to select from a F84, F86, or F94. The nucleus of the museum would consist of a locomotive and tender donated by N&W Railway and one of the first motorized fire engines purchased by the city.

Planters opened a new Peanut Store at 7778 Williamson Road on March 19. It was the second store in Roanoke for the company. The first Peanut Store was at 14 W. Campbell Avenue, where it had been since opening in 1939.

The new Cave Spring Central Office of the Chesapeake and Potomac Telephone Company opened on March 20. The million-dollar facility was located near Route 221. W. E. Cundiff placed the first call on the Spruce Exchange to Arthur Ellett, president of the Roanoke Chamber of Commerce.

Double Envelope Company announced on March 18 plans to build a 75,000-square foot building in Roanoke County across from the new ITT plant near Hollins.

Roanoke Memorial Hospital announced on March 19 the purchase of an artificial kidney machine, one of only 135 in the nation. The Travenol Coil Kidney removed poisons from the blood stream of a patient whose own kidney failed to do so. The unit cost about $2,000.

Roanoke played host to Virginia's annual Gold Gloves boxing tournament the third weekend in March. Bouts were held at the Marine Corps armory. Roanoke's PAL boxing team won ten titles. The winning boxers included Ray Robrecht, Fred McLeod, Robert Carter, Jimmy Muse, Carl Thompson, Phil Webb, Bruce Durham, Robert While, Allen Camper, and Garland Bush. The PAL won the team Gold Gloves title for the third straight year. The event had a tragic note when Laymon Gravely of Martinsville in the Middleweight Novice Negro Division was fatally injured in the ring during the title bout against George Ford of Richmond. Gravely was knocked unconscious and died at Burrell Memorial Hospital having never regained consciousness. Efforts to revive the boxer in the ring by trainers were unsuccessful. A few days later, a coroner reported the death was caused by a cerebral hemorrhage.

A steering committee chaired by Franklin Hough Jr. was organized in mid-March to help organize and plan for a Roanoke Valley Community Council. Several organizations were represented in an effort to consolidate fundraising and other efforts by groups involved in recreation, juvenile problems, unemployment, and services for the elderly.

Red Hill Baptist Church dedicated its new education building on March 22. The $65,000 addition was three stories with thirty-six rooms and a fellowship hall. The church was located on Route 220 South.

Riverland Road Baptist Church was formed in southeast Roanoke. It was chartered in early March with thirty-three charter members. A frame building at Riverland Road and Laurel Street SE served as a temporary meeting space. Rev. Walter Lubinsky was the pastor.

An Easter sunrise pageant sponsored by the women's auxiliary of Burrell Memorial Hospital was held at Victory Stadium on March 29. The "Star City Sunrise Service" was directed by Pearl Fears and featured an hour-long drama that was televised by WSLS. Principal speaker was Rev. A. L. James. Some 400 school students participated.

Sixteen famous paintings of Christ were portrayed by students on the stage of Andrew Lewis High School. It was the tenth year of the high school's annual Easter pageant. The high school choir sang for the production. Mrs. Arnie Cook and Harry Simmers were the directors.

Roanoke Linen Service officially opened its new $750,000 plant at 3401 Shenandoah Avenue NW on March 26. Robert Evans Jr. was the plant manager. The plant was a division of National Linen Service, headquartered in Atlanta. It was the third plant in Roanoke since National Linen came to the city. The first was built in 1934 on Salem Avenue, and the second was at 1111 Shenandoah Avenue NW.

Breeden Motor Company opened at its new location at 2724 Williamson Road on March 22.

The Filatex operation at the shuttered American Viscose Roanoke plant shut down on March 27. The process, purchased from Viscose, was being transferred to Waxhaw, North Carolina.

Former House of Delegates member Raye Lawson of Roanoke was convicted on two counts of forgery on March 24. Lawson faced his second time in prison, having been sentenced to prison the first time in 1937. Lawson was elected to the General Assembly in 1935 from Roanoke and was convicted on October 27, 1936, of grand larceny and embezzlement. He served a year sentence at that time.

James Long, forty-two, of Roanoke was killed on March 25 when a coal train struck his car at the Sites Crossing just east of Salem. The car was dragged about 150 feet along the tracks after being hit by Virginian Railway engine No. 127. It was the third such death in two years at that crossing.

An Easter sunrise pageant was held at the Sherwood Burial Park Amphitheater on March 29. The service featured an outdoor drama written by Kermit Hunter titled *Dawn of Promise*. The play involved a 200-voice Roanoke County school choir and a brass choir from Cave Spring High School. The pageant was televised live by WDBJ and was directed by Del Shook.

Chuck Cabot and his orchestra, along with The Ink Spots, performed at the Colonial Hills Club on March 27.

The Roanoke Association of Retired Railway Employees was organized on March 26 in a meeting at the Pythian Hall, 310 W. Campbell Avenue. Charles Kelly was elected president.

Leroy Wynn was deemed mentally competent and ordered to be returned to Roanoke from Central State Hospital to stand trial for the October 18, 1958, murder of Marian Duckwiler.

The largest prestressed concrete beams ever used in Virginia were placed on a Blue Ridge Parkway bridge just southeast of Starkey in late March. The fifty-two-ton beams were six feet high and one hundred feet long. The bridge spanned Back Creek and Route 613. Charlottesville Hauling Company did the placement.

The thirteenth annual Easter sunrise service was held at Natural Bridge on March 29. Rev. Paul Lottich of Christ Lutheran Church in Roanoke delivered the sermon. The choir of Calvary Baptist Church provided a choral anthem. The service was broadcast over the radio by WDBJ and to other stations in Virginia. Attendance was estimated at 8,000.

Dorcas St. Clair, twenty-three, of Roanoke County died on March 27 in the home of Mr. and Mrs. S. F. Taylor. Upon investigation, Roanoke County Sheriff Henry Clark charged Lewis Reed, thirty-three, of Floyd County and Mrs. S. F. Taylor of Roanoke County with murder. According to investigators, St. Clair had died after an attempted abortion.

Dr. Farris Logan opened his dental practice on April 1 in the Garlands Drug Store Building at the corner of Eleventh Street and Moorman Avenue NW.

Mrs. Margurite Belafonte, an actress, came to Roanoke on April 7 to appear in a fashion show at Addison High School sponsored by the Roanoke Branch NAACP. Belafonte was cochair of the National NAACP's Freedom Fund campaign.

Three boxers from Roanoke represented Virginia and competed in the A. A. U. National Senior Boxing Championships in Toledo, Ohio, the first weekend in April. They were Carl Thompson, Fred McLeod, and Jimmy Muse. Paul Vest, president of the Roanoke PAL, accompanied the boxers.

George T. Hitch Jeweler opened at its new location at 34 W. Church Avenue on April 1.

The Vinton Lions Club held their annual minstrel show the first weekend in April at William Byrd Junior High School as a fundraiser for their various sight-related projects.

Gene Tingler became the new owner and operator of Oakland Esso Service Center on April 1, formerly Bower's Esso. The station was located at Tenth Street and Williamson Road.

The Roanoke Valley delegation in the General Assembly endorsed the Perrow Commission on Education's report giving "freedom of choice" to local school boards and parents on how to operate their schools. The Perrow report was largely viewed as another means of skirting court-ordered integration, though ardent segregation-ists viewed it as too accommodating to the US Supreme Court's *Brown* decision. State Senator Earl Fitzpatrick called the report "the best we could do to preserve our schools." Delegate Kossen Gregory summarized the report as follows: "The plan contemplates the continuance of public schools but at the same time if the problem becomes intolerable for any locality, it recognizes the right of that locality to close its schools by the simple method of refusing to appropriate funds." The *Roanoke Times* lead editorial on April 2 opined, "In its broad outline, we believe it embraces general principles…to provide schooling for the maximum number of children and to erect legal safeguards against indiscriminate integration."

The first burial took place on April 1 in the new municipal cemetery at Coyner Springs. The unnamed deceased was a Roanoke native who had died out of the area.

Officials with the Chesapeake and Ohio Railway announced on April 2 that they would not oppose the merger of N&W Railway and Virginian Railway.

Structural steel for the world's largest radio telescope to be built at Sugar Grove, West Virginia, would be fabricated at US Steel's American Bridge Division plant in Roanoke. Company officials made the announcement on April 2 and mentioned that two other US Steel plants would also be involved.

Roanoke Drag Strip opened with its first races of the season on April 5.

More than 1,200 persons rode the last N&W Railway passenger train between Bluefield, West Virginia, and Norton on April 4. The final runs ended seventy years of passenger service in the railway's Clinch Valley District.

The thirty-second annual spring congress in diseases of the ear, eye, nose and throat opened on April 6, sponsored by Gill Memorial Hospital. The lectures were held at the Patrick Henry Hotel. Four hundred persons attended from forty states and five foreign countries.

WBLU radio station in Salem increased its power from 1,000 to 5,000 watts the second week in April. The station was at 1480 on the radio dial.

The Starkey Speedway opened its racing season on April 12.

Daniel Saunders, a seventy-five-year-old farmer in the Dundee section of Roanoke County, was found shot to death on April 5. The sheriff believed robbery was the motive, but he had no suspects. The coroner indicated Saunders had probably been dead three to four days prior to being found.

Joseph Spigel declared itself insolvent in a court filing on April 6. The women's apparel shop at 101 Campbell Avenue SW was granted thirty days to develop a reorganization plan. Charles Spigel was president of the firm.

Mrs. Frank Long of Roanoke was named as Virginia's Mother of the Year for 1959. Her husband had been named as Roanoke's Father of the Year in 1951.

Mrs. Donnie Gordon, seventy-nine, of Roanoke was struck and killed by a car on April 7 as she walked to her mailbox along Hollins Road NE.

Preliminary plans for the new William Fleming High School were approved by the Roanoke School Board on April 8. The main topic of discussion was the use of electric heat for the school.

Blanche Binns, formerly of Roanoke, was named Missouri's Mother of the Year for 1959. Binns was the wife of Rev. Walter Binns, pastor of Roanoke's First Baptist Church from 1931 to 1943.

Emory Graybill Jr. was sentenced to thirty years in the state penitentiary by Judge Dirk Kuyk on April 8. Graybill had been found guilty of first-degree murder in the slaying of his wife in 1958.

Del Webb, co-owner of the New York Yankees, was the main speaker at the annual banquet of the Gill Memorial Hospital Spring Congress at the Hotel Roanoke on April 8. His topic was "creating a winning team."

A Doberman pinscher, owned by Mrs. G. F. Barron, was awarded Best in Show at the Roanoke Kennel Club's twenty-fourth annual all-breed dog show held at Victory Stadium on April 9. A total of 371 dogs competed in the show.

The new Roanoke County library was dedicated on April 11 and was viewed as the culmination of almost three decades of effort by numerous individuals. The library, at 526 College Street in Salem, was the first stand-alone library in the county's history. About 150 persons attended the ceremony. The library had occupied space at Conehurst, the Roanoke Junior Woman's Club headquarters, since its inception in 1931. It was financed through private donations until 1941, when it became a county library. Delegate Nelson Thurman was the main speaker. The library had about 27,000 books and was headed by Mrs. Blanche Pedneau.

Southern Credit Store, a department store of both new and used items, advertised in mid-April that it was closing. The store was located at 10 E. Campbell Avenue and had been at that location since its opening in 1906. The store's owner, M. J. Schlossberg, was retiring.

Showtimers presented Shakespeare's *The Taming of the Shrew* the second weekend in April. The cast included Edward Langley, Lois Langley, Ralph Hatchell, Charlie Bell, and Ken Cook. The play set an all-time attendance mark for the drama group with 1,150 paid admissions over four performances.

Save Station, part of a chain of auto gas and service stations, opened in the 1300 block of Dale and Jamison Avenues SE on April 17. It was the eighth Save Station in the Roanoke area.

Lightweight Block Company opened its new plant at 3002 Shenandoah Avenue NW on April 20.

Nino's Restaurant opened on April 20 at the corner of First Street and Day Avenue SW.

The new Kazim Temple and the new Scottish Rite Temple near Jefferson High School were dedicated jointly on April 17. George Stringfellow, imperial potentate of more than 800,000 Shriners in North America, was the main speaker. More than 1,500 attended the evening ceremony. The dedication was a four-day event for the Shriners that included a ceremonial ball and a parade through downtown Roanoke.

A one-engine plane made an emergency landing at Woodrum Field on April 17, injuring two marines, one of whom was the pilot. Two other marine passengers were uninjured. The plane was en route to Wheeling, West Virginia, when the plane ran out of gas.

The Council of the Episcopal Diocese of Southwestern Virginia voted on April 17 to postpone resuming youth conferences at its Hemlock Haven campground due to a strident division among its ranks over integrating summer youth conferences. The result was that no youth conferences would be held during the summer, as was the case in 1958. The decision was widely viewed as a victory for pro-segregation elements within the denomination.

Phyllis Barnard was crowned Miss Roanoke County on April 18. She was a senior at William Byrd High School. The pageant was sponsored by the Roanoke County Junior Woman's Club and qualified Barnard to compete in the Miss Virginia pageant.

The Williamson Road Recreation Club was formed in mid-April.

Jimmy's Golf Driving Range opened in mid-April on Route 11 between Roanoke and Salem and near the Lee-Hi Drive-In Theatre.

National Cash Register Company opened at 902 S. Jefferson Street on April 21. Charles Mayhew Jr. was the branch's manager.

Salem Furniture Company began advertising in mid-April that it was going out of business. The store was located at 201 S. College Avenue in Salem.

The Roanoke Children's Theatre, under the direction of Clara Black, performed *The Sleeping Beauty* using eighty-three children as part of the cast the last week in April. The performance was staged in the Scottish Rites Temple on Campbell Avenue and was the first event held in the Temple since its dedication.

Roanoke Lookout Gift Shop at Bent Mountain was auctioned off on April 25 as the owners had moved to Florida.

John Freeman, eighty, of Roanoke died on April 21 from burns he received at his home in the Catt Hill section when he fell while carrying a kerosene lamp.

Reuben Lawson, a Roanoke attorney, announced on April 22 that he planned to file a lawsuit to integrate the public schools of a nearby county. Most reporters identified the county as Pulaski. Lawson planned to attend a May 10 meeting with the Negro PTA of the county. A petition had been filed in September 1956 in Pulaski County by parents of six Black students to desegregate the school system, and Lawson was the attorney for the parents. While Lawson hoped to not have to take legal action, if a suit were to be filed, it would be the first such suit in southwest Virginia. Several counties did not have high schools for Blacks, including Pulaski, Floyd, Carroll, Giles, Grayson, Craig, and Lee. Most of those counties sent their high school students to the Christiansburg Institute. In its April 24 edition, the

Roanoke Times editorial board wrote the following in light of Lawson's comments: "Hints have been made that Roanoke may also soon become a target of the integrationists…It is important that the people of Roanoke be prepared for such a development. Perhaps the excellent provisions made for separate Negro education here – Addison High is far superior to any high school Roanoke has been able to provide for its white students – has contributed to a feeling that our Negro citizens would be content with separate but equal facilities."

St. Paul's Lutheran Church on Peters Creek Road at Melrose Avenue NW purchased a six-acre site about a mile north of the intersection on Peters Creek Road for the purpose of erecting a new church.

The counties of Roanoke, Botetourt, and Franklin were the footprint of a new organization, the Gateway Tuberculosis Association, which was formed in mid-April. Mrs. Arthur Deyerle was president. According to Gateway leaders, the combination into a larger association was for efficiency and more effective outcomes.

Double Envelope Company broke ground on April 23 for its new plant opposite of the ITT plant north of Roanoke.

Ernest Ellington, thirty-five, of Roanoke was stabbed to death on April 22 in his home. Police arrested his wife, Edith, for the murder.

Ethel Viaud, ninety-five, of Roanoke died on April 25. Viaud, along with her husband Gustave Viaud, founded the Viaud School in 1924. A native of England, she taught public school in Roanoke for many years prior to starting her own, from which she retired in 1946. Originally at 105 Mountain Avenue SW, the school relocated in 1954 to 1101 First Street SW.

The fourth annual Vinton Dogwood Festival got underway on April 30 for four days. The festival began with a band concert at the Vinton War Memorial on Thursday evening, with the Dogwood Pageant and fireworks at the memorial the next evening. On Saturday, there was an afternoon one-hundred-unit parade through the town and a coronation ball and crowning of the Dogwood Queen that night. The grand marshal for the parade was television star Steve McQueen, who played Josh Randall in the western *Wanted: Dead or Alive*. While in Roanoke, McQueen appeared on the local WDBJ television program the *Ann Howard Show* and the *Betty Bond Show* on WSLS. McQueen attended the Friday night pageant and was swarmed by young women and autograph seekers immediately afterward such that he left the war memorial by exiting through an open window and running to his car. Attendance at the parade was estimated at 12,000, a record for the festival. Nancy Garland, a senior at William Fleming High School, was crowned queen of the festival.

The Roanoke Symphony Orchestra performed three concerts on April 27, with two being primarily for the benefit of children and youth. The concerts featured pianist Carolyn Finfgeld, the Roanoke Youth Symphony, and a 125-voice combined choir from Fleming High School and Jefferson High School. All three concerts were held at the American Theatre with a combined attendance of almost 5,000.

Earl Camper Jr., twenty-three, of Vinton died on April 27 from drowning while fishing on Bottom Creek near Bent Mountain. It was the same spot where another drowning had occurred a year previous, that of Larry Poff.

The actor Steve McQueen participates in the Vinton Dogwood Festival Parade as he rides a horse and waves to the crowd in this May 1, 1959, clip. *WSLS-TV News Film Collection, UVA Libraries*

Sidney Robertson of Roanoke was selected to receive the first annual Good Samaritan Award presented by the Roanoke Civitan Club on April 27. Robertson was cited for his many volunteer activities.

The Roanoke School Board voted at its April 27 meeting to make chest X-rays for tuberculosis mandatory every two years for all school employees.

Charles Tucker from Prince George High School was named as the new head football coach for Jefferson High School on April 27.

Roanoke City Council voted on April 27 to remove some 500 graves from the old municipal cemetery on Colonial Avenue at the former City Home to Coyner Springs. The process was to begin in the fall. The city manager suggested the cost might run as high as $15,000. The council resolution stipulated that each grave be identified by a suitable marker.

For the second straight year, the Dr. Pepper Company in Dallas, Texas, reported that Roanokers drank more of the soft drink per capita than anywhere else in the world. As a thank-you, coupons were made available in local newspapers for free cartons of Dr. Pepper.

Hennis Freight Lines, a trucking company, opened its new Roanoke terminal in the 3300 block of Salem Turnpike in late April.

The Roanoke Valley Golf Association was organized on April 28 in a meeting at Blue Hills Golf Club. Membership was restricted to men. Connie Sellers was president. The group planned to publish a monthly magazine, *Roanoke Golfer*, for its membership beginning in June.

Virginian Railway stockholders approved the merger of its railway with N&W Railway on April 30 by an overwhelming margin with 92 percent in favor.

Kane Furniture Company closed its doors for the last time at 22 E. Campbell Avenue on May 1.

An expert in annexation from St. Louis shared with Roanoke City Council on April 30 that Roanoke should seek to annex almost twenty square miles from Roanoke County for economic development reasons. Based on the city's population trends, the expert estimated that Roanoke's population by 1980 would be 153,000.

Harold Ross became Roanoke's new postmaster on April 30, succeeding Robert Via who had retired.

Joyce Bryant, a former professional singer at nightclubs and on television, gave a concert at Addison High School on May 2 as a benefit for the Macedonia Seventh-Day Adventist Church, a denomination to which she belonged.

Nearly 3,000 attended the sixth annual Children's Fishing Rodeo at Lakewood Park. Some 1,000 rainbow trout had been stocked in the pond for the event.

Colonial Presbyterian Church dedicated its new $60,000 sanctuary and education building on May 3. The church was located at 3550 Poplar Drive SW. Rev. Robert Field was the pastor.

Billy Talbert, a professional tennis player, came to Roanoke for a May 5 fashion show to promote the McGregor brand's European wear at Miller & Rhoads. Talbert was a seven-time member of the US Davis Cup team. While in Roanoke, he also appeared on the *Ann Howard Show* on WDBJ.

The Lucy Addison High School majorettes strike a pose in front of the Gainsboro Branch Library in May 1959. *Virginia Room, RPL*

A profile on Dewey Marshall appeared in the *Roanoke Times* on April 26. Marshall, who went by "Rube," was a former professional baseball pitcher in the major leagues. A resident of Roanoke, he was signed by the Cincinnati Reds and the Boston Red Sox in the 1920s. Marshall signed with the Reds on June 9, 1921, for $500 per month along with a $1,000 signing bonus. In 1923, he went to Boston, but an arm injury forced his early retirement from the pro sport and subsequent return to Virginia, where he became a Prohibition agent in Roanoke.

Lloyd Price and his orchestra performed at Lakeside Amusement Park on May 8. Admission was twelve Pepsi-Cola bottle tops, as Pepsi-Cola Bottling Company at Hollins was the sponsor. A crowd of 10,000 attended.

Pope Johnson set a new record for the Roanoke Drag Strip near Starkey on May 3 by being clocked at 126.58 miles per hour.

The John Puhl Products plant in Salem was sold to the Purex Corporation in early May for $564,000. The Salem plant made Little Bo Peep household ammonia and Fleecy White detergent. The Salem plant was built in 1953.

Floating metal docks for Carvins Cove were put into use on May 8. The docks could accommodate about thirty boats. This was part of a larger effort to make the lake more accessible for recreation.

Red Barn Antique Loft opened on May 6 at Cloverdale. It was part of the Traveltown business section.

The Roanoke Merchants Association named its Roanoke Mothers of the Year on May 6, and they were as follows: Mrs. McHenry Stiff Jr. (business and professions), Mrs. Richard Edwards (family life), Mrs. Robert Pickett Jr. (community affairs), Mrs. English Showalter (arts and sciences), Mrs. Millard Townsend (education), and Mrs. Clara Carter (religious activities).

The Roanoke German Club marked its seventy-fifth anniversary on May 9 with a formal dinner-dance at the Hotel Roanoke. Formed in 1884 by men who had come to Roanoke to work but found there to be a scarcity of young women, the men created a formal dance club that invited young ladies from outside the Roanoke Valley to attend. Dance cards were used, and N&W Railway provided reduced fares for the females. The name was derived from a popular nineteenth-century form of dance.

The Virginia Mountain League opened its baseball season on May 9. The six-team league included Buena Vista, Virginia Foundry, New Castle, Clifton Forge, Hot Springs, and Glasgow. Virginia Foundry's home field was Veterans Field at the Veterans Administration Hospital.

Larry Mills, ten, of Roanoke died on May 9 from injuries he sustained on that same day when he fell off the roof of his home while retrieving a baseball.

Woodrum Field celebrated thirty years of air service in May. The notion of having air service apparently got attention when a barnstormer landed a plane on the Horton farm near the intersection of Twenty-Fourth Street and Melrose Avenue NW in the fall of 1919. By May 1929, the city of Roanoke leased seventy acres of the old Cannaday farm for an airstrip that ultimately developed into Woodrum Field. The airport held its official anniversary celebration on May 16.

The Monroe Junior High School Band won its fourth straight first place title on May 9 in the annual National Schoolboy Patrol Parade in Washington, DC. Andrew Hull was the band director.

Huffman's Organ Shop opened at its new location at 424 W. Campbell Avenue on May 10.

Robert Hunt of Andrew Lewis High School was the recipient of the ninth annual B'nai B'rith Athletic and Achievement Award, which was presented in a televised ceremony on May 9.

The New York burlesque production of *A Night on Lenox Avenue* came to the Club Morocco on May 9.

Rev. Frederick Sampson of High Street Baptist Church advocated for the hiring of Black firemen in Roanoke City in remarks to the Roanoke Development Association on May 10. "We feel we have enough taxpayers in Roanoke that we ought to have Negro firemen. And the number of Negro policemen ought to be increased."

A landmark building at the southeast corner of Jefferson Street and Salem Avenue was razed on May 11, having been condemned by the building commissioner when it became clear the building was literally crumbling. The structure was erected in 1886 and was known as the Bear Building. Originally the City Hotel, it became the home of the National Exchange Bank in 1889. National Business College occupied the structure beginning in 1898. Being condemned in 1926, the top two stories of the four-story building were removed to bring the structure back into compliance. Since that time, occupants had included a restaurant, cigar store, pool hall, saloon, newsstand, and a palm reader. Its lone tenant at the time of its second condemnation was United Pawn Shop, operated by brothers Adolph and Joel Krisch.

Roanoke attorney Reuben Lawson announced on May 11 that he planned to file a petition with the Floyd County School Board on behalf of the parents of fourteen Black high school students in the county to seek admission to Floyd County's two white high schools. The Black high school students were forced to attend the Christiansburg Institute, a seventy mile-round trip from their homes. If the Floyd County School Board denied the petition, then Lawson said he would file suit in US District Court in Roanoke. Lawson was part of Virginia NAACP's legal staff.

A third Goodwill Industries store opened in Roanoke on May 14 at 3125 Salem Turnpike NW. The other stores were at 13 W. Salem Avenue and 122 E. Campbell Avenue.

A new office building for the Salem bureau of the *Roanoke Times* and *Roanoke World-News* was opened on May 11 at Colorado and Clay Streets.

The study of a merger between Jefferson Hospital and Lewis-Gale Hospital became public on May 12. The two Roanoke hospitals had formed a six-person study committee to examine such a proposal. Both hospitals were overcrowded and in outdated buildings, and both had been operating for fifty years.

Kane Furniture Company closed its store at 22 E. Campbell Avenue and opened at its new location at 131 E. Campbell Avenue on May 13.

This postcard from the 1950s shows Lewis-Gale Hospital, which was located in downtown Roanoke. *Nelson Harris*

The Maracibo, a dining and dance club, opened at 1209 Center Avenue NW, on May 15.

Salem opened its new water filtration plant at Fourth and Main Streets on May 13. The plant cost $516,000 and would provide water treatment until 1980 according to town manager Frank Chapman.

Dan's, a men's clothier at 104 W. Salem Avenue, began advertising on May 14 that it was going out of business.

Stockholders of N&W Railway approved the merger with the Virginian Railway in a vote on May 14 with 99.6 percent of the stock being voted in favor.

Nineteen former professional baseball players met in Salem on May 14 to discuss a plan to promote baseball in the region. Guy Spruhan was head of the group.

High Street Baptist Church marked its seventy-fifth anniversary in special services on May 17. Dr. E. C. Smith, pastor of the Metropolitan Baptist Church in Washington, DC, was the guest speaker. The church was established in 1884, with the first building being on Salem Avenue near Jefferson Street. The congregation purchased a second site on December 30, 1886, and relocated shortly thereafter. A brick sanctuary replaced a wooden A-frame structure in 1907 but was destroyed by fire in 1914. The church rebuilt a new sanctuary in 1915.

Roanoke Coca-Cola Bottling Works and the Roanoke Department of Parks and Recreation held an Airport Hop dance on the north ramp at Woodrum Field on May 16 in the morning. Music was provided by Bill Spahr of WDBJ radio. The event was part of the airport's anniversary celebration. Other events to mark the occasion at Woodrum Field were plane exhibits, a military parade, and an air display by local pilots.

The Colony House Motor Lodge on Franklin Road SW is shown in this November 1959 image. A man appears to be practicing his putts on a putting green at the lodge. *Julia Elliott*

Ground was broken for a new motel in mid-May. The Colony House, a forty-three-unit motel, was on Route 220 between Avenham Avenue SW and the entrance to Edgehill. The owners were Glover Trent and Richard Trent, and the motel was expected to cost around $250,000. The Trents stated that a public stenographer and babysitting would be available for guests.

The Roanoke Valley Training Center for Retarded Children at 726 Thirty-First Street NW was dedicated on May 16. The center was a joint project by numerous civic organizations.

Cave Spring Methodist Church broke ground for its new church off Colonial Avenue on May 16. The church building was anticipated to cost $110,000. It would replace the congregation's frame sanctuary at McVitty and Bent Mountain Roads SW.

Earl McDonald, billed as the world's champion high-shallow water diver, performed at Lakeside Amusement Park for six nights the third week of May. He leapt from a high-dive platform into a five-foot water tank covered with flaming gasoline.

United Pawn Shop set up temporary quarters at 9 E. Salem Avenue after their former location had been razed.

Eddie Moylan, former member of the US Davis Cup team, gave a tennis exhibition at the Roanoke Country Club on May 19. The event was sponsored by the Roanoke Valley Tennis Association.

A public hearing conducted by the state highway department drew a large crowd at the Roanoke Public Library on May 21. Two members of Roanoke City Council—Benton Dillard and Charles Cornell—spoke in opposition to the proposed extension of the interstate spur from Orange Avenue to Elm Avenue SE, even though the majority of the council had endorsed the extension through a resolution. Dillard and Cornell argued that the extension would disrupt businesses, create traffic congestion at Elmwood Park, and break the trust of displaced home-owners affected by the Commonwealth Project who would not be able to relocate back to their former residential area due to the spur.

The Blue Ridge Council Scout-O-Rama brought some 3,000 Boy Scouts to South Roanoke Park to camp for two days the third weekend in May. Arrangements were made for water, electricity, cooking, and sanitation for the temporary tent city.

Residents impacted by the Commonwealth Project, the redevelopment of northeast Roanoke by the Roanoke Redevelopment and Housing Authority, com-plained that families had paid for their residential lots but were never given deeds to the property even after two years. Eugene Brown, representing the Citizens Protective Association, demanded on May 21 that housing officials provide deeds immediately. The RRHA indicated that deeds had been withheld pending the out-come of the planned interstate highway spur.

The Virginia Amateur League opened its baseball season in early May. Teams in the league were Pembroke, Newport, Back Creek, and Floyd.

Shank Furniture Company in Salem filed for bankruptcy on May 22. Henry Shank was the owner.

Ground was broken for the new $55,000 education building at Grace Methodist Church at 4404 Williamson Road on May 24.

Professional wrestling opened its season in Roanoke at Victory Stadium on May 26. Argentino Rocca squared off against Larry "Bruiser" Hamilton, and a second main attraction was a match between the Great Bolo and Cyclone Anaya. Attendance was 1,500.

Kennedy's Restaurant opened on May 25 at 411 Fifth Street SW.

An early-morning fire on May 25 destroyed Greenfield, a historic Botetourt County landmark visited by George Washington when he surveyed that section of Virginia. Only the chimney remained on the 200-year-old home near Amsterdam. Valuable antiques and documents were also consumed. The home had been in the Preston family since 1759.

Ground was broken on May 25 for a new $350,000 warehouse and office building for Roanoke Grocers on Kessler Mill Road near Lakeside.

Major James Sink of Roanoke was one of four members of the famed 116th Infantry Regiment of the Twenty-Ninth Division that returned to Normandy, France, in late May to participate in the dedication of a special memorial to the 116th. The regiment was officially disbanded on June 1 when the Virginia Army National Guard reorganization took effect.

Julian Fulcher, fifty-four, of Roanoke was found shot to death in his car that was on Route 117 near Woodrum Field.

Mrs. Betty Ikenberry, twenty-one, of Roanoke was named as Mrs. Virginia of 1959 in a contest held on May 27 at Virginia Beach. The contest was largely based on appearance and cooking skills. She qualified to compete in the Mrs. America contest to be held on June 11 at Fort Lauderdale, Florida.

This 1950s postcard shows many of the attractions at Lakeside Amusement Park. *Bob Stauffer*

Lakeside Amusement Park launched a new ride on Memorial Day—Track Rabbit. The ride consisted of "gas-powered midget automobiles operated on a concrete track," according to ads.

Charles Cook, forty, and his wife, Lucille Cook, of Salem were both found dead in their home on Lake Street on May 29. The coroner believed that the husband shot his wife and then turned the gun on himself based on the position of the bodies. The couple's four children were found unharmed in the home when police arrived.

On May 30, Gene Beeme, the "human bomb," performed between races at the Starkey Speedway. Beeme got in a casket loaded with dynamite and ignited it.

The Children's Zoo on Mill Mountain opened for the season on May 29 with clowns, free balloons, and Cactus Joe on hand. WSLS-TV broadcast live from the zoo that morning.

Elbert Caldwell won the city-county marbles tournament in a final round playoff on May 29, the first playoff in the tournament's twenty-seven-year history. Caldwell was a student at Jamison School. Coming in second was Frank Carter of Garden City School.

The semipro Roanoke Dodgers played the Clifton Forge Giants in baseball at Salem's Municipal Field on May 31.

Three stained glass windows were dedicated at Christ Evangelical Lutheran Church on May 31. The windows depicted miracles and parables, and the donors were Governor and Mrs. Lindsay Almond Jr., Mrs. M. R. Shull, and Mr. and Mrs. A. S. Craft. The windows were made by the Henry Lee Willet Studio in Philadelphia.

The Bent Mountain Volunteer Fire Department purchased land near Poff's Garage and launched a fund drive to erect a fire department building. Roanoke County had agreed to provide a fire truck by July.

Joey Maxim, former lightweight boxing champion, was the guest referee for the professional wrestling matches held at Victory Stadium on June 2.

The U. D. Smith Lumber Company, located five miles west of Salem on Route 796, was liquidated at an auction on June 6 due to the retirement of the owners.

Raymond Cruey, sixteen, of Vinton died on May 31 at Vinton's municipal swimming pool. His death was due to natural causes. Before he collapsed, he had complained of chest pains.

US Senator Willis Robertson spoke at a Memorial Day service at Sherwood Amphitheatre on May 31. His address praised Confederate General Robert E. Lee as an example of duty and valor. Other participants included veterans' organizations, the Andrew Lewis High School band and choir, and clergy.

John Cruickshank and Mrs. Edward Moomaw were reappointed to the Roanoke School Board on June 1.

Brammer's Automatic Laundry opened on June 2 at 914 Orange Avenue NE.

Interiors by Richard, located at 504 S. Jefferson Street, was liquidated in an auction on June 8 due to bankruptcy.

Minnie Pearl from the *Grand Ole Opry* performed at an outdoor show and square dance held at the Roanoke Drag Strip on June 5. Andy Anderson called the figures.

Rev. H. W. Connelly of Roanoke received an honorary doctoral degree from the University of Richmond for his work in planting Baptist churches, most of which had been done in the Roanoke area. Connelly was directly involved in the founding of Connelly Memorial, Rosalind Hills, North Roanoke, Emmanuel, and Grandin Court Baptist Churches.

An independent political party was formed on June 4 in Roanoke County headed by Ernest Robertson of Salem, a former member of the Virginia House of

Delegates. The group was called the Independent Citizens Committee of Roanoke County.

Charles Beasley of Ferguson, Kentucky, was named as the new head coach for the William Byrd High School basketball team. He succeeded Aubrey Vaughan, who had been named as principal of Byrd Junior High School.

Marathon Calloway, seven, died on June 5 from wounds he accidentally inflicted upon himself while playing with a revolver in his home. The parents were not at home at the time of the accident.

Howard Fisher was convicted of second-degree murder on June 5 in the burn death of his wife at their Craig County home. Fisher was sentenced to ten years. The accused set fire to his wife by pouring gasoline on her.

Bobby Phoenix captured the Salem marbles championship title on June 5 for the second straight year. His victory qualified him to compete in the national tournament.

Warner Hughes, a pioneer Roanoke mortician for the Black community, died on June 5 at age ninety-three. He came to Roanoke from South Carolina in 1899 and had operated the W. F. Hughes Funeral Home since 1909.

Over 1,000 graduated from area high schools in early June. The number of graduates was as follows: Jefferson High School, 450; Andrew Lewis High School, 180; William Fleming High School, 160; Lucy Addison High School, 128; William Byrd High School, 76; and Cave Spring High School, 76. Valedictorians were Tommy Edwards (Jefferson), Betty McDonald (Lewis), James Baird (Fleming), Kathleen Hackley (Addison), Wendell Kelly and Judy Overstreet (Byrd), and Thomas Fralin (Cave Spring). No information was published in regard to Carver High School.

Brothers Donald Sisk, twenty, and Albert Sisk, twenty-three, of Roanoke County drowned in the James River at Rocky Point on June 7. Both were swimming, and one drowned trying to save the other, according to witnesses.

The Floyd County Board of Supervisors met on June 8 and decided to adopt a budget plan that would allow for the closing of their schools within thirty days. The budget allocated funds to the school system on a month-by-month basis. The action was taken a day prior to the school board's meeting to discuss a petition filed with the board by Roanoke attorney Reuben Lawson seeking to admit Black students to the county's high schools. The next day, the Floyd County School Board denied Lawson's school integration petition on the grounds that it did not comply with state law. Instead, the board asked the petitioners to make applications via the pupil transfer forms, which the board would forward to the State Pupil Placement Board for processing to determine their admission to the county's high schools.

Showtimers began their ninth season with a production of *Witness for the Prosecution* the second weekend in June. The cast included Betty Shaner, Harold Hall, and George Garretson.

A new S&H Green Stamps redemption store opened on June 11 at 5319 Williamson Road.

Robert Bennington, a member of the Roanoke School Board, died on June 10 of an apparent heart attack. Bennington, seventy-six, was appointed to the board in 1957.

This 1957 image shows the façade of one of Roanoke's S&H Green Stamps stores. *Virginia Room, RPL*

The Roanoke Junior Chamber of Commerce announced its annual Fathers of the Year honorees on June 11. They were as follows: Henry Kiser (youth leadership), Richard Edwards (family life), Robert Hutcheson Jr. (religious affairs), and John Eure (civic affairs).

Larry Ruhl and Sandy Winters, aerial trapeze artists, performed at Lakeside Amusement Park the first week in June. Their act was performed while being suspended 500 feet in the air from a helicopter.

The State Highway Commission voted 5–3 on June 11 for the southern route of I-64, which would take the east-west path from Richmond via Farmville, Lynchburg, and Roanoke to Clifton Forge. Those advocating for the northern route vowed to protest the decision to federal officials. The commission also approved the 1.1 mile extension of the I-81 spur in Roanoke from Orange Avenue to Elm Avenue NE.

Dr. L. E. Paxton, president of the Citizens Protective Association, stated on June 12 that the organization was considering legal action against the Roanoke Redevelopment and Housing Authority if Blacks were forced to give up their homes in the Commonwealth Project. Families who had been displaced had not received deeds to lots as promised, according to Paxton.

State Civil Defense officials classified Roanoke as one of five areas in Virginia classed as a "target area" in the event of an enemy attack on the United States. The state recommended a plan of evacuation be developed by local Civil Defense officials as a key to survival in case of a nuclear attack.

The Fabulous Brunos, billed as the world's greatest high-pole sway act, performed at Lakeside Amusement Park the second week of June.

The Blue Ridge Parkway was under construction through Roanoke County during the 1950s. This June 1959 image shows bridge construction at Milepost 114.7. *National Park Service*

Lu Merritt defeated Frank Snow to win the men's single title in the Roanoke Valley Spring Tennis Tournament on June 13. Merritt and Fred Bromm won the men's doubles title. The matches were held at the Roanoke Country Club. Buddy Saunders and David Burrows won the Junior and Boys Division titles, respectively, in the same tournament in their matches at South Roanoke Park.

Connie Sellers won the eleventh annual city-county golf championship the second weekend in June with a seventy-two-hole total of 288. George Fulton Jr. placed second at seven strokes behind, and Ralph English was third.

The Wilson Six-Horse Hitch Wagon made an appearance at each Mick-or-Mack grocery store on June 17.

Four members of Roanoke City Council met with representatives of the Roanoke Redevelopment and Housing Authority about some Black families within the Commonwealth Project not getting deeds. Mayor Vincent Wheeler and the other council members asserted that all families who had purchased lots should have deeds. The matter continued to be complicated by the State Highway Commission's decision to locate an interstate spur through a corner of the area.

Over 300 local businessmen took the annual day trip to the Greenbrier Hotel sponsored by the Roanoke Booster Club. The trip was designed "to sell Roanoke to Roanokers," according to Dr. E. G. Gill, club president.

Bill Veeck, president of the Chicago White Sox, came to Roanoke and Salem on June 17, holding a press conference at the Patrick Henry Hotel and then addressing the Roanoke Kiwanis Club. Later in the day, he spoke at Salem just prior to an intra-squad scrimmage by the Salem Rebels and then at Joe's Grill on Wise Avenue SE, all in an effort to promote professional baseball.

The Rocky Marciano Enterprises produce packing plant in Salem was sold to Tom Black Inc. of Knoxville, Tennessee. The Knoxville firm planned to move its "Tom's" potato chip, peanut, and popcorn processing plant on Williamson Road to the Salem site.

Charles Mundy of Catawba and Maggie Hoffman of Roanoke, both in their fifties, were struck and killed by an auto on June 18 as they crossed Route 220 about one mile south of Roanoke.

Rev. Edward Zeigler, pastor of the Williamson Road Church of the Brethren, was elected moderator of the 215,000-member Church of the Brethren denomination during its annual convention at Ocean Grove, New Jersey, on June 18.

Rocky Marciano Enterprises announced plans to construct a new building near Cloverdale on Route 11 for the packing of apples. The plan was for the plant to be operational by mid-August.

Bob Sommardahl won the annual Roanoke Valley Junior Golf Tournament on June 18 with a thirty-six-hole total of 155 at Blue Hills Golf Club. His younger brother, Don, won the Midget Division with a score of 95.

Lt. Col. Harold Mosley, a former Roanoke resident, was killed in the crash of a US Air Force T-33 jet in February, but the crash with Moseley's body was not discovered until June 19 in California. Mosley was a flight surgeon.

The Fair-Acre Farm Store and Garden Center at 2601 Franklin Road SW announced it was going out of business on June 20. Its assets were scheduled to be liquidated at an auction on June 25.

Plans for a palatial three-story, one-hundred-room hotel to cost over $1 million were announced on June 20 for South Jefferson Street opposite the Patrick Henry Hotel. The hotel was to be called the Roanoke Downtowner, and construction was slated to begin in early 1960. A hotel firm headquartered in Memphis, Tennessee, was the developer. The structure would necessitate the razing of the remnants of the former Gale home that had been converted into a Gulf service station, the Elmwood Minit Car Wash, and the Elmwood Diner. All were owned by Paul Hunter.

Showtimers presented *The Fourposter* the last weekend in June. The two-person comedy was performed by Betty Jean Michie and John Jennings.

Water Follies of 1959 opened at Victory Stadium on June 23 for a six-day run. The show featured diving, water stunts, and music, all revolving in and around a 150-foot portable pool.

Tennis-court dances were held the last week in June at Preston Park, South Roanoke Park, Fishburn Park, and Washington Park, sponsored by the Roanoke Parks and Recreation Department. Local disc jockeys provided the music. The Salem Recreation Department did the same at the Salem tennis courts.

Buddy Saunders won the Roanoke Valley Junior Tennis Tournament held at South Roanoke Park the third weekend in June.

The construction of the Roanoke River Bridge at Milepost 114.7 for the Blue Ridge Parkway was a major undertaking. The bridge was located just south of Roanoke and was one of the highest parkway bridges in Virginia. *National Park Service*

The all-rookie Appalachian League began its baseball season on June 25. The teams were Lynchburg, Salem, Bluefield, Wytheville, Johnson City, and Morristown, Tennessee. The teams played a seventy-game schedule. Larry Dorton was the manager for the Salem Rebels, which was affiliated with the Pittsburgh Pirates.

Ten Black parents and eleven Black students, represented by Roanoke attorney Reuben Lawson, filed applications for the assignment of the students to two Floyd County high schools with the county's superintendent's office on June 23. The action was pursuant to the procedures outlined by the state's Pupil Placement program. The superintendent, J. H. Combs, stated that the school board would review the applications and, if found properly completed, would forward them to Richmond for assignment.

Buford's Airstrip along Route 460 at Montvale was sold at auction on June 27.

Rev. Arthur Camper, the former minister of Ebenezer AME Church in Roanoke, was named president of Kittrell College in North Carolina in mid-June. He was a pastor in Roanoke from 1951 to 1958.

Thy Kingdom Come opened for its third season at the Sherwood Amphitheatre on June 26. The outdoor religious drama had a cast of sixty with Louis Catching in the lead role as the Apostle Paul.

Dr. James Barringer spoke at High Street Baptist Church on June 28. Barringer, a native of Roanoke and graduate of Addison High School, had completed his doctoral degree at the University of Amsterdam, Holland, having been awarded a Fulbright Scholarship in 1955.

A $1.1 million contract for construction of the new Northside High School was awarded to J. H. Fralin and Son contractors of Roanoke on June 25. The school was slated to open for the 1960–1961 school year.

Babb's, a new restaurant, opened on Route 220, three miles south of Roanoke, at the Parkway Motel.

Western film comic Smiley Burnette entertained fans between races at the Starkey Speedway on June 27.

The death of Julian Fulcher in May was determined to be self-inflicted by the Roanoke County medical examiner in his June 25 report. Police had originally arrested Fulcher's wife for the death.

Sue Williams, nineteen, won the Miss Virginia pageant on June 27. She was competing as Miss Williamsburg. The pageant was sponsored by the Roanoke Junior Woman's Club and was held before a capacity crowd in the Hotel Roanoke ballroom.

Jarrett-Chewning Company opened at its new location at 1854 S. Jefferson Street on June 29. They sold Studebakers and Mercedes-Benz automobiles and had been in business for thirty-eight years. The dealership opened in 1921 and was the first new car dealership in Roanoke at the time. Broaddus Chewning was president of the company.

Plans for a $5 million shopping center on Lee Highway between Roanoke and Salem were announced on June 27. The developer was Morris Skilken of Columbus, Ohio, who had acquired twenty-two acres of what was formerly the Cook farm. The farm had been the site of one of the valley's earliest airfields. Construction was slated to begin in the fall.

Miss Liberty Belle, Eleanor Englehart, came to Roanoke the last week in June as part of her East Coast tour promoting Freedom Week in Philadelphia that was to begin on July 1.

This June 1959 image shows the Jarrett-Chewning Company at 1854 S. Jefferson Street.
Virginia Room, RPL

The State Jaycee Tennis Tournament was held at Roanoke Country Club in late June. C. W. Shackelford of Danville captured the state junior division championship.

John Eure, an executive of the Times-World Corporation, was appointed to the Roanoke School Board on June 29 by Roanoke City Council to fill the unexpired term of Robert Bennington, who had died.

The Roanoke Chamber of Commerce proposed a campaign for a multimillion dollar civic center for the Roanoke Valley on June 29. They had a petition to present to Roanoke City Council asking the council to take the initial step of acquiring land. The COC request asked for a civic center that could seat 2,500 in an auditorium and 10,000 in a coliseum and that it be located outside of downtown due to parking. The COC planned to appoint a committee that would solicit other municipalities to join in the effort. Five potential sites were identified by the COC—land opposite the Veterans Administration Hospital, the "Horton tract" along Melrose Avenue, the Huff Farm on the south side of Hershberger Road, a tract along Shenandoah Avenue, and the Andrews Farm near the airport.

George Barger, forty, of Roanoke County shot and killed his wife, Irene Barger, twenty-nine, in the front yard of their home on June 30 as their twelve-year-old daughter watched. Barger then turned the gun on himself, committing suicide. The Bargers lived in the Bradshaw section of the county.

Frank Cook, a high-wire comedian, performed at Lakeside Amusement Park the first week in July.

Vinton Laundry Center opened at 123 Lee Avenue in Vinton on July 2.

A single-engine plane with three men from Marion aboard was forced to make an emergency landing in a field at Mount Regis Farm south of Salem on July 1. No one was injured.

Crane Company, a plumbing firm, closed its Roanoke branch at 404 Center Avenue NW, on July 1.

The former Loch Haven Drive-In Theatre, which had been closed for a year, reopened in late June as the Kingston Drive-In and was for Black patrons. The drive-in was located on Route 118 near Woodrum Field. Ernest Grimes was a co-owner.

Lakeside Amusement Park opened a zoo as park attraction in early July. The zoo featured monkeys, an ocelot, and an ant bear from South America. The park also advertised its newest ride, a fifty-foot high Ferris wheel.

This image from the summer of 1959 shows Lakeside Amusement Park. *Jeff Goldstein*

Lakeside, seen here in 1959, added a small zoo that year to provide an added attraction. It had also become a major concert venue for the Roanoke Valley. *Jeff Goldstein*

Showtimers performed *The Reluctant Debutante* the second weekend in July. The cast included Mary League, Lorri Gregory, and Shelby O'Bryan.

Joseph Spigel's, a clothing store, began advertising on July 8 that it was going out of business after fifty-one years. The store was located at 101 W. Campbell Avenue.

The Silver Line of Virginia, a manufacturer of storm windows and doors, was liquidated at an auction on July 8. The business was located at 3346 Shenandoah Avenue NW.

The Roanoke County Citizens League voted on July 7 to oppose a proposed regional civic center to be built in Roanoke with the cooperation of neighboring localities. The league believed that if Roanoke County wanted an auditorium, it should build one on its own. Ernest Robertson was chairman of the 535-member group.

Boxley Hill Garden and Farm Center opened on July 13 on Route 11 just north of Roanoke city. C. F. Kefauver was the owner.

Mill End Fabric Center opened on July 1 at 829 W. Main Street in Salem.

John Saxon's Hell Drivers car stunt show came to the Starkey Speedway on July 9.

A sixty-year-old landmark at the intersection of Routes 601 and 11 was razed on July 9. Known as Wilson's Store, the structure formerly housed the Hollins Post Office and had also been used as a canning factory.

A plan for a five-story municipal office building to cost $2.5 million was presented to Roanoke City Council at their meeting on July 13. The structure was designed to be built on the site of the school administration building fronting Church Avenue. The plan was the result of a study by city officials for more space to house municipal offices.

N. W. Kelley, a longtime Roanoke business leader and civic official, died on July 10 at the age of sixty-six. Kelley led efforts to develop Woodrum Field and was a member of Roanoke City Council from 1940 to 1945. He served as president of the Virginia Chamber of Commerce in 1948.

A special annexation court ruled on July 11 that the Town of Salem could annex more than three square miles lying east of the town from Roanoke County to take effect on December 31. The annexed territory would add about 2,700 residents to Salem.

Roanoke Memorial Hospital observed its sixtieth anniversary on July 12 and dedicated its new $500,000 addition to its school of nursing and dormitory. The hospital began on May 11, 1899, when ten women and two men met to discuss the needs of caring for the sick. This resulted in the creation of the Roanoke Hospital Association, a nonprofit corporation with a capital stock of $1.00. It is believed that a "Home for the Sick" had existed in Roanoke prior to that, having started around 1888 and located on Fifth Street at Campbell Avenue. About that same time, Dr. Charles Cannaday established the Rebekah Sanatorium on Elm Avenue at Commerce Street, believed to have been the first medical and surgical hospital in southwest Virginia.

The former YMCA building at the corner of Second Street and Church Avenue SW was sold at auction on July 15. It had 126 furnished bedrooms. Walter Green and Frank Calcara, both of Washington, DC, were the high bid at $109,500. The men owned various hotels in Virginia.

Willie McGuire, sixty-three, was struck and killed by a car as he crossed Williamson Road on July 12. McGuire lived in the Hardy area.

Union Carbide Corporation signed an option for purchase of the American Viscose plant in Roanoke on July 14. The option on the plant was good until August 31. Union Carbide planned a number of feasibility studies in connection with the plant.

William Hopkins defeated incumbent State Senator Earl Fitzpatrick in the July 14 primary for the Democratic nomination for the general election. After a very spirited campaign, Hopkins garnered 4,171 votes to Fitzpatrick's 3,373. Fitzpatrick was closely aligned with the Byrd Machine in state Democratic politics. The Republicans nominated Leigh Hanes Jr. as their candidate for the November general election for Roanoke's seat in the Virginia senate.

In Roanoke County, the Democratic primary resulted in the defeat of the county treasurer Janie McNeal to James Peters, a member of the Salem Town Council. Also nominated for the general election were incumbent Sheriff Henry Clark, who defeated Emmett Waldron and R. R. Goodwin; Luck Richardson for commissioner of revenue, who defeated Murphy Scott; and Commonwealth's Attorney Edward Richardson, who defeated Derwood Rusher. Hampton Moulse was nominated to run for the Salem District for the Board of Supervisors, defeating incumbent Tyler Nash by sixty-eight votes.

This July 1959 image shows storefronts in the 10 block of Campbell Avenue SW. *Virginia Room, RPL*

Two N&W Railway trains collided near Roanoke on July 14 when a passenger train crashed the rear of a northbound freight train. Five persons were taken to the hospital but with no serious injuries.

The Roanoke Valley Drama Association announced on July 14 that their outdoor drama *Thy Kingdom Come* would close on August 2 due to lack of attendance. The play had been slated to run through September 6. Total attendance in 1957 had been 21,707, and in 1958 it was 20,296. During the first fifteen showings of the 1959 season, total attendance was 2,447.

Richard Scott, fourteen, of Radford won the 1959 Roanoke Soap Box Derby on July 15. A crowd of 4,000 watched the event that was held at the Roanoke Drag Strip near Starkey. Richard Jennings placed second.

The north-south runway at Woodrum Field was officially designated as an instrument landing strip in mid-July, a major step forward for the airport in attracting and retaining airlines.

John Fishwick, vice president of N&W Railway, was named chairman of the United Fund campaign for the fall. The Fund had twenty-nine participating groups and agencies.

La Norma, billed as the nation's foremost trapeze artist, performed at Lakeside Amusement Park the third week in July.

Showtimers presented the comedy *The Seven Year Itch* the fourth weekend in July. The cast included Bill Segall, Betty Shaner, Frances Ebeling, Cindy Wees, Ann Fox, and John Jennings.

Johnson's Pie Shop opened on July 22 at 4209 Williamson Road.

The first annual Mill Mountain Music Festival was held on July 29 at the Children's Zoo. The event was sponsored by the Roanoke Parks and Recreation Department.

Catherine Bryan Smith, niece of three-time presidential candidate William Jennings Bryan, died in Roanoke on July 22 at the age of eighty-seven. She was the widow of John Smith, a Roanoke attorney.

Lewis-Gale Hospital began a three-day observance of its fiftieth anniversary on July 24 with a dance at the Hotel Roanoke. The hospital was founded in 1909 by Drs. James Lewis and Sparrell Gale as a private, twenty-six-bed hospital to serve their patients and industrial cases from N&W Railway. In 1910, the hospital opened in a new building at Luck Avenue and Third Street. The X-ray department was started in 1914, while the school of nursing had begun in 1912. Additions were made to the original hospital facility in 1916 and 1938. Over the course of a half-century, the hospital had served 169,922 patients.

N&W Railway donated Locomotive No. 2156, a Y-6a steam engine, to the National Museum of Transport in St. Louis on July 22. The locomotive had been built in the Roanoke Shops.

The congregation of Emmanuel Baptist Church announced a capital campaign to build a church on Thirty-Seventh Street at Troutland Drive NW in mid-July. A ground-breaking service was held on July 26.

Members of the cast of *Thy Kingdom Come* went on a tour of towns in southwestern Virginia as a means of promoting the final performances of the outdoor drama. Area Lions Clubs provided autos for the touring caravan. Promoters of the play indicated poor attendance in the third season was due to a lack of locals attending, as most who had purchased tickets were tourists.

Modern Dress Shop at 212 E. Main Street in Salem announced in mid-July it was going out of business.

Shenandoah Company, a printing and mailing services company, opened at 702 Shenandoah Avenue NW in late July. The company was owned by William Mahone and Alex Williams Jr.

The Catawba Sanatorium observed its fiftieth anniversary on July 30. The sanatorium received its first patient on July 30, 1909. In a half-century, the sanatorium had cared for over 17,000 patients. It was Virginia's first state-supported facility for the treatment of tuberculosis.

Betty Bond, hostess of the *Betty Bond Show* on WSLS-TV, announced in late July that she planned to give up television to help her husband, Nelson Bond, with his advertising agency. The show first aired in 1955 and was a pioneer local television program.

Lu Merritt won the annual city-county tennis tournament, capturing the men's singles title by defeating Jack Miller. Merritt and Fred Bromm won the men's doubles title. Suzanne Glass defeated Gingie Higgins to win the women's title, and then Glass and Higgins won the women's doubles title in a victory over Sugar Ellett and Juanita Stanley. The matches were played at South Roanoke Park the last weekend in July.

This 1959 clip shows the Tenth Street Bridge in Roanoke that crossed the tracks of N&W Railway. The bridge would eventually be replaced years later. *WSLS-TV News Film Collection, UVA Libraries*

Parents who had filed pupil placement forms with the Floyd County School system were asked to testify before the Boatwright Commission on July 27 in a hearing held at the Floyd County Courthouse. The commission had been established by the Virginia General Assembly as a means of challenging lawyers of the NAACP from practicing law on behalf of clients by being paid through the NAACP. Bearing the brunt of the criticism and investigation by the commission members was Roanoke attorney Reuben Lawson. The commission concluded that Lawson did not follow the wishes of his clients but acted instead to advance the agenda of the NAACP, a charge Lawson denied.

US Secretary of Agriculture Ezra Taft Benson came to Roanoke and addressed the Virginia Association of Electrical Cooperatives at the Hotel Roanoke on July 28.

Shenandoah Hospital at 712 Campbell Avenue SW completed an $8,000 improvement to its lab at the end of July.

Showtimers presented the *Diary of Anne Frank* the first weekend in August. The cast included Kathy Thornton, David Thornton, Suzanne Kraige, Bettie Matthews, Larry Cooper, and Richard Heninger.

Thy Kingdom Come, which had been scheduled to close on August 2, was given an extension of two weeks by the board of the Roanoke Valley Drama Association due to increased attendance.

Hidden Valley Country Club held a formal opening of their clubhouse on August 1.

The first annual city-county women's golf tournament began on August 3 at Blue Hills Golf Club with sixty-three entrants. The winner of the tournament, which was three rounds over three days, was Connie Gorsuch with a score of 240. She won by thirty-two strokes. Finishing second was Barbara Ann Pope.

Mortgage Investment Corporation opened a branch office in Roanoke in the Shenandoah Building on August 3. S. S. Edmunds was the branch manager.

Union Carbide Corporation announced on August 5 it was dropping its option to buy to the American Viscose plant in Roanoke. The company did not provide details on its decision.

Boxley Hills Texaco Service Station opened on August 6 at 5220 Williamson Road.

Ralph Via Hardware Company opened on August 15 at 3239 Brandon Avenue SW.

Al and Ruth's, a restaurant and dance club in the Starkey section, became Freddie's in early August.

United Pawn Shop moved to a new location on August 7 at 22 E. Campbell Avenue. The site was formerly Kane Furniture.

The Burrell Memorial Hospital's school of practical nursing, established a year prior in cooperation with Addison High School, received full approval from the State Board of Nurse Examiners in mid-August. The first class had nearly thirty students.

Norman's Restaurant at 201 E. Main Street in Salem was liquidated in an auction on August 19.

Drivers stand next to their Sears delivery trucks in Roanoke in this August 1959 image.
Virginia Room, RPL

A coliseum report presented to Roanoke City Council by the Roanoke Junior Chamber of Commerce on August 10 was filed by the council for future study.

James Combs, school superintendent of Floyd County, announced on August 10 that applications for admission to white high schools by the parents of thirteen Black students had been denied. The State Pupil Placement Board had denied all the applications. Reuben Lawson of Roanoke was the attorney for the Black families.

Kayletta, a gymnast who did tricks using a 125-foot high ladder, performed at Lakeside Amusement Park the second week in August.

Phelps & Armistead, a furniture store, opened at 2 W. Main Street in Salem on August 14 in what was formerly Shank Furniture Company. Its flagship Roanoke location was at 20 E. Church Avenue.

A "miracle" happened at Lewis-Gale Hospital on August 13 when Larry Wade, twelve, of Troutville woke up. He had remained in a coma in the hospital since July 13, when he was struck by a car on Route 11 near his home in Troutville while riding his bicycle. His mother had never left his bedside.

Diamonds worth $3,000 were stolen from Henebry's Jewelers at 209 S. Jefferson Street on August 14 during a Dollar Days noon rush. The unidentified thief simply reached over the counter and swiped the diamonds from their display tray, according to store manager Joe Burkholder.

The Roanoke Fair opened at Victory Stadium for six days beginning August 17. The fair included exhibition boxing matches, a midway, agricultural exhibits, a flower show, and grandstand entertainment nightly. The entertainers included Roy Acuff, the Wilburn Brothers, and June Webb.

Captain Cresso and his rocket car performed at Lakeside Amusement Park the second week in August. The performance included a midair summersault by Cresso in the car.

The final public performance of *Thy Kingdom Come* was on August 15 at the Sherwood Amphitheatre. The total paid attendance for the third and final season was 12,000. Total attendance over its three seasons was 54,095, but it was not enough to financially sustain the outdoor religious drama. The following night, Mick-or-Mack grocery stores gave tickets away to customers for a final, private showing of the play, and attendance was 3,200.

Showtimers presented its final play of the season the third weekend in August, a production of *State of Mind*, which was written by Nelson Bond of Roanoke. Leading the cast were Bob Marvin, Doreen Heard, Charlie Bell, and Ariene Bell.

Saleth Wilds, fourteen, of Salem drowned on August 18 at Ray-Phil's Swimming Pool on Lee Highway west of Roanoke.

Two Philadelphia consulting firms provided a study of the Commonwealth Redevelopment Project to the Roanoke Redevelopment and Housing Authority on August 20 and concluded that the eighty-three-acre area should be used only for business development and not for residences. The report put in jeopardy Black families who were waiting on deeds to residential lots they had purchased on the promise they would be able to relocate back to their former neighborhood. Some deed-holders had already constructed new homes. The report also asserted that families still residing in the project boundaries should be relocated. A review of the report by local media found several inaccuracies about Roanoke in general.

Carl Fayen Jr., of Christiansburg who played the role of Saint Peter in *Thy Kingdom Come* filed litigation against the Roanoke Valley Drama Association on August 20 seeking compensation for his full contract through early September. His weekly pay was forty-five dollars. The total persons employed for the drama was fifty-two.

Don McGraw's Drag Hop and Square Dance was held every Friday night at the Roanoke Drag Strip beginning August 21.

Sunnyside Awning and Tent Company was delighted that Hawaii became the fiftieth state on August 21. The company had been producing forty-nine-star flags and was set begin production of fifty-star flags. Roscoe Robertson, vice president of the business, believed the short-lived forty-nine-star flags would become collector items.

Alfred Goodwin was selected by members of the Salem Town Council to complete the unexpired term of James Peters, who had resigned from the council.

Carnis Poindexter of Roanoke won the National Intercollegiate men's singles championship of the American Tennis Association on August 21 in Wilberforce, Ohio. Poindexter, a 1956 graduate of Addison High School, had previously won the Southwestern Conference championship. He was a student at Arkansas State.

Eddie Phillips of Richmond won the Roanoke Valley Invitational Tennis Tournament singles championship on August 23. The tournament was held at Roanoke Country Club.

Grace Whitefield of Roanoke signed a contract with Naylor Company of San Antonio, Texas, to publish her book of poetry, *The Bloom of Time*. Whitefield was president of the Roanoke Poetry Society.

Excavation began in late August for a $225,000 addition to be built behind Garland's Drug Store No. 6 at 1327 Grandin Road SW. The addition would include a rooftop parking area for forty cars with an entrance on Westover Avenue.

Delong's, a clothing store, opened at its new location at 212 E. Main Street in Salem on August 28. The store had been in business for five years.

Salem Office Supply opened on September 1 at 9 S. College Avenue in Salem.

Officials with the Roanoke Redevelopment and Housing Authority met with residents impacted by the Commonwealth Redevelopment Project on August 27 and asked for sixty-day options to purchase all the privately owned properties remaining in the eighty-three-acre redevelopment area. The proposal was primarily directed toward Black families who had been living in the section without deeds to their properties. Residents were presented with an eight-page document that stated, in part, that purchases would be made "based on the present-day, fair market value…it should be pointed out that if the project is approved for commercial use, the authority – as originally - has the right to condemnation to acquire such properties." The meeting was held at the Lincoln Terrace Center and was attended by about one hundred persons. Reuben Lawson, an attorney, served as legal counsel for many in attendance.

Joseph Spigel's closed its doors for the final time on August 31. The clothing store was located at the corner of First Street and Campbell Avenue. Brady's Discount Shoe Mart opened in the building on September 4.

A new two-story church and education building was used for the first time by Windsor Hills Methodist Church on August 30.

Webber's Pharmacy, operated for thirty-five years by Ted Webber, in Salem was purchased by Ervin Brooks and Ray Byrd in late August. The name was changed to Brooks-Byrd Pharmacy. The store was located at 2 E. Main Street.

The Fiestas, the Roulettes, and the Rockteens performed at Lakeside Amusement Park on September 7. The show was sponsored by radio station WBLU.

Rufus Ellett Sr., sixty-nine, died on September 1 in a Roanoke hospital. Ellett had been a longtime business and civic leader in the Roanoke Valley and was an N&W Railway retiree.

Polio made a comeback in southwest Virginia such that throughout the spring and summer, there were numerous admissions to the polio ward at Roanoke Memorial Hospital. On September 1, a three-year-old died at the hospital from the disease, having never been vaccinated. There were twenty-seven victims from Henry County alone.

George Fulton Jr. of Roanoke qualified for the National Amateur Golf Tournament in early September during a sectional qualifying tournament at the Country Club of Virginia in Richmond.

The potential condemnation of homes in the Commonwealth Redevelopment Project would be "the most flagrant disregard for the welfare and well-being of a minority people," as Dr. L. E. Paxton of the Citizens Protective Association asserted. Paxton delivered his comments during a meeting of the association on September 3. The CPA agreed to stand with eleven families who had purchased residential plots in the project area but had not been given deeds to them by the Roanoke Redevelopment and Housing Authority.

The Roanoke County Board of Supervisors passed a local compulsory school attendance law during their meeting on September 4. The Virginia General Assembly had abolished the statewide law the previous year as part of massive resistance to court-ordered desegregation.

Ophelia Barrett, forty-six, died at Burrell Memorial Hospital on September 7 after being shot by her husband, Herbert Barrett, the same day. The husband confessed to the murder, which occurred in the couples' home on Loudon Avenue NW.

The Children's Zoo on Mill Mountain set a new attendance record with its paid admissions of 92,612 for the 1959 season.

A three-pronged school integration filing was heard in the US District Court in Roanoke on September 8. Roanoke attorney Reuben Lawson filed injunction suits against Galax, Grayson County, and Floyd County to seek admission of Black students to all-white high schools in those localities. Floyd County warned it may close its high schools. None of the three localities provided high school educations for Black students but instead sent students to other counties. Lawson was joined by Oliver Hill from Richmond, chief counsel of the Virginia NAACP. On September 10, Judge Roby Thompson issued his ruling that forced an end to segregated schools in Galax and Floyd County. Thompson instructed the localities to begin integrating their school systems in January 1960. He held off on a similar ruling for Grayson County, as the Black litigants had petitioned to enter Galax schools. He asked them to first apply to schools in Grayson County.

Roanoke attorney Reuben Lawson (left) speaks with a reporter as he leaves Roanoke's federal court after filing the first school desegregation lawsuit in southwest Virginia. *WSLS-TV News Film Collection, UVA Libraries*

The former Sears Building at 12 E. Church Avenue was razed the second week in September. Sears had vacated the building, which they had occupied for twenty years, when Sears Town opened in 1957. Prior to Sears, the structure had been known as the Bear Building after John Bear, who was an early owner. A cornerstone indicated the structure had been erected in 1905.

Roanoke Valley orchardists began harvesting their apples in early September. There were about 160 orchards in Botetourt, Roanoke, Franklin, and Bedford counties. It was estimated that one million bushels would be harvested.

Groff Awnings held a grand opening at 3346 Shenandoah Avenue NW on September 11.

Kroger opened its new five-acre distribution center at Glenvar on September 15.

William Flannagan, administrator of Roanoke Memorial Hospital, reported on September 10 that Western Virginia had more polio cases through early September than in all of 1958. Of the sixty-seven polio cases treated through August at the hospital, forty-three had been diagnosed as paralytic.

The congregation of Locust Grove Methodist Church broke ground for its new church on a six-acre site in the Beverly Heights section of Roanoke County on September 13. The church was founded in 1915 and the first sanctuary was built in a locust grove about one mile north of the Fort Lewis area on a site gifted by George Butts.

Roanoke's first sidewalk art show was held on September 12 in Elmwood Park and was jointly sponsored by the Roanoke Fine Arts Center and Miller & Rhoads. Attendance was 8,000. J. M. Yeatts won top honors for his *Country Road* painting and was named Best in Show.

Sandra Kay Jones, seventeen, of Salem was named as "Miss Index II" meaning she would reign over the state industrial exposition at Victory Stadium in late September.

The Roanoke Jaycettes were granted the franchise for selecting Virginia's contestants in the national Junior Miss Pageant. Virginia had never fielded a contestant.

Arrington and Bussey Funeral Home of Rocky Mount was the sole bidder on September 14 to move 112 graves from the old City Farm cemetery to Coyner Springs. The graves were being moved to make way for the Roanoke Technical Institute.

The board of the Roanoke Valley Drama Association, producer of *Thy Kingdom Come*, voted on September 14 to go into bankruptcy or receivership. Liabilities of the organization were listed at $95,525; cash on hand at $1,703; and fixed assets such as chairs and building and stage equipment at $46,050. Those assets had little value, however, except for salvage.

Hollywood actor and director Orson Welles filed a $425,000 suit against CBS on September 14, alleging that his 1938 *Men From Mars* radio program was used without permission in a television drama written by Nelson Bond of Roanoke. Welles's suit referred to *The Night America Trembled* that aired over the CBS television network on September 9, 1957. Bond, who was not named in the suit, called Welles's suit "ridiculous."

George Preas of Roanoke was honored by the Baltimore Colts on September 14 in Baltimore as the team's "unsung hero" for the 1958 season. Preas, an offensive tackle, had been a starter with the team for five seasons, including the pending 1959 season. Preas was the fifth draft choice of the Colts after playing in forty consecutive games for Virginia Tech.

H&S Stores, a discount department store, opened at 1705 Franklin Road SW on September 17.

The former City Home was dedicated on September 15 as a day care center for preschool children with intellectual disabilities. The school was named in memory of Dr. Jerome Natt, a Roanoke physician and former president of the Roanoke Council for Retarded Children. The council had been formed in 1951.

The Pelican Club was opened by Fred Joseph on September 17 on Route 221, five miles south of Roanoke.

Roanoke City's public schools experienced a mass exodus for the start of the 1959 school year as compared to one year prior. Enrollment was down by 790 students. School officials indicated most of the drop was due to families moving out of the city.

Coach House Restaurant on Route 11 west of Salem opened on September 18. The owners were Mr. and Mrs. J. A. Whitley.

The Green Shed, a restaurant, opened on September 19 at the intersection of Colonial Avenue and Cave Spring Road. Charles Hite was the manager.

Green Ridge Presbyterian Church dedicated its new education building on September 20.

Pratt's Store, formerly Bain's Place, on Old Catawba Mountain Road was sold at auction on September 26. The building contained a country store, barbershop, beer parlor, service station, and living quarters.

George Fulton won the Roanoke Valley Invitational Open golf tournament on September 20. Fulton had a thirty-six-hole total of 140. The Pro Am tournament was held at the Colonial Country Club in Roanoke.

Minnie Snyder, eighty-seven, of Salem died on September 20. She was the owner of Snyder Nursing Home and other business properties in Salem. She had owned and operated a millinery shop in Salem for fifty years.

Billy Rumberg, his wife, and five children became stranded in Phoenix, Arizona, in early September but made it back to their home in Roanoke two weeks later by hitchhiking.

A new Top Value stamp premium redemption store opened at 1519 Williamson Road on September 24. The store had relocated from 318 Second Street SW. A second store was located on Franklin Road SW.

Lester's Toy and Gift Shop opened on September 25 at 113 E. Main Street in Salem.

Several in the Roanoke Valley reported seeing an unidentified flying object in the sky on September 24. All described the object as having a bluish-green color with a tail flame. The control tower at Woodrum Field reported seeing the object, as did an Eastern Airline pilot flying into the airport. In Southside Virginia, witnesses reported seeing a cigar-shaped object in the sky.

Webster Brick, located on Webster Road, is the subject of this September 1959 photograph. *Virginia Room, RPL*

More than 400 persons attended a reception at the Patrick Henry Hotel on September 25 that honored Rev. Z. V. Roberson of Raleigh Court Presbyterian Church. He was retiring after serving the church for thirty-four years as their pastor. At the time, no other Roanoke clergyman had served the same church longer than he had.

Hal March and Sheila Copelan performed in the touring production of *Two for the Seesaw* at the American Theatre on October 1. The play was sponsored by the Roanoke Broadway Theater League.

Willie Hopkins Jr., thirty-six, of Roanoke died on September 26 from injuries he sustained that day in a car wreck on Loudon Avenue NW.

A plane carrying four Californians collided with a car driven by Charles Stump Jr. of Roanoke when the plane made an emergency landing on Route 11 west of Salem on September 27. No one was seriously injured.

The odor of Roanoke County's dump was the subject of a petition presented to the Salem Town Council on September 28 by residents of the Stonewall Forest section.

Roanoke's Harvest Festival began September 30 for a four-day weekend. The festival included an industrial exposition of 116 booths at Victory Stadium known as "Index '59," a fashion and interior design show, military exhibits, and a football game between Virginia Tech and William and Mary. The halftime show at the football game included an appearance by television actor John Bromfield, star of the western *Sheriff of Cochise*. Julie Payne was crowned Queen of the Harvest Bowl.

She was the daughter of actor John Payne. Bromfield was also the grand marshal for the mile-long parade through downtown that preceded the football game. Unfortunately, the remnants of Hurricane Gracie caused havoc with some of the events due to flooding. A crowd of 19,000 attended the football game.

A fire caused significant damage to the Skyline Motel on September 29. The motel was located on Route 220, three miles south of Roanoke. H. R. Brugh was the motel's owner.

Spigel's of Roanoke, a women's clothing store, held a grand opening at 506 Jefferson Street. The owners were Leo and Lorraine Peyser, formerly with Joseph Spigel's. The formal evening opening featured live models.

Valleydale Packers of Salem purchased Lindsey-Robinson and Company of Roanoke in late September. The latter produced Fair-Acre Test-Fed Feeds. Valleydale officials said the Lindsey-Robinson name would remain. Lindsey-Robinson had been operating in the Roanoke area since the 1860s. Valleydale was founded in Lynchburg in 1933.

Northminster Presbyterian Church held a ground-breaking ceremony on October 4 for their $215,000 education building at the church's new site at Greenland and Avalon Avenues NW. The church was meeting at 3406 Williamson Road NW. The church was organized on March 1, 1942, and originally met at Oakland School.

The Citizens Protective Association urged Roanoke City Council on October 5 to appoint more Black policemen and to also hire Black firemen, which the city had never done. The city had four Black policemen.

Attendance was 18,000 at the Jefferson High School football game against Fleming High School held at Victory Stadium on October 2. The game also served as a fundraiser for city's sandlot football program. Jefferson won, 19–0.

The new Crawford-Maury Building at Mercy House, located west of Salem, was held on October 4. The annex was named for Mrs. Aline Crawford and Sally Maury. Both had been nurses.

Ground was broken on October 5 for the new Towers Shopping Center at the intersection of Colonial Avenue and Brandon Avenue SW. Pioneer Construction Company of Roanoke was the general contractor. The shopping center was located on a thirty-acre site and estimated to cost $2.5 million. The land was being leased for fifty-five years from the Times-World Corporation by developers from Norfolk. Many retailers had already signed leases to be in the center.

Greene Memorial Methodist Church began a monthlong celebration of its centennial on October 4. The church began in 1859 as the Methodist Society of Old Lick and held services in a Presbyterian church located on the Old Lynchburg Road. In 1866, the congregation became Roanoke Methodist Church on the Roanoke circuit. From 1868 to 1872, the congregation worshipped in a frame school on the west side of Commerce Street (Second Street) which was across the street from the site of Greene Memorial. Then it met in a Lutheran church on High Street (later Loudon Avenue) before occupying its first sanctuary in 1875 on Henry Street at High Street. That building was sold to a black Methodist congregation in 1883, which they razed in 1920. In 1875, Roanoke Methodist Church moved to a building on Church Avenue and then worshipped in the Opera House on Market

Square in 1887. The congregation eventually erected a new brick church in 1890 at Third Street and Campbell Avenue SW. That building campaign was begun while Rev. Leonidas Greene was pastor, but he died before the building was completed. The church voted to name the building in his memory. In 1902, Greene Memorial made its last move when it acquired the unfinished St. Mark's Lutheran Church at the corner of Church Avenue and Second Street in an exchange of the two buildings by the two congregations. The Lutherans had been unable to complete their building due to the stock market crash of 1890.

Foster Gallery opened at 2404 Williamson Road in early October. Edwin Foster, a painter and sculptor, was the owner.

Miller & Rhoads held a seminar in its Tea Room on "Effective Living" for professional women. A main speaker for the October 6 event was Ivy Baker Priest, treasurer of the United States.

Dr. Allen Barker of Roanoke was elected president of the Medical Society of Virginia on October 5 during the organization's annual meeting at the Hotel Roanoke.

Ruth Cuddington, principal of Belmont School, was named Roanoke's Woman of the Year by the Roanoke Business and Professional Women's Club on October 6. Cuddington was presented a silver tray by Mayor Vincent Wheeler.

Vinton First Aid Crew celebrated its twentieth anniversary on October 6 with a dinner at Yearly Haven. The crew was founded on October 5, 1939.

This October 1959 image shows the grading for Towers Shopping Center along Brandon Avenue SW. Wheeler's Fast Service Laundry and Brandon Amoco are in the background. *Virginia Room, RPL*

Mountain View Elementary School in Roanoke County opened on October 7. The opening had been delayed due to construction.

Auctioneer Joe Stewart conducted an all-night livestock auction on October 7 at the Roanoke Livestock Market at Shaffers Crossing. A glut in livestock resulted in 1,850 head being sold.

Bradford's Seafood and Steakhouse on Melrose Avenue at Peters Creek Road was sold to the Lewis Restaurant Corporation of Lynchburg on October 7. The seller was Bradford Lipscomb.

The streets in downtown Roanoke were washed with a detergent on October 9 that caused the streets to smell like "the pine odor of Virginia," according to City Manager Arthur Owens. The experiment was well received.

L. E. Ward Jr., manager of N&W Railway's industrial and agricultural department, presented to Roanoke City Council on October 8 the idea of creating an industrial park in the Roanoke Valley. Officials with the railroad had been advocating the idea for several months within the business community.

The congregation of Windsor Hills Baptist Church held a ground-breaking service on October 11 for their new education building at 4436 Grandin Road Extension. A sanctuary was planned for later. Rev. Lawrence Dodson was the pastor.

A rodeo came to the Starkey Speedway the second weekend in October that featured bull riding, wild steer roping, and trick riding.

The Virginia All-State Championships in drag racing were held at the Roanoke Drag Strip the second weekend in October with a record 127 entrants.

Westside Elementary School in Roanoke opened on October 9 after two construction-related delays. Enrollment at the school was 227. Anna Barker was the principal.

Lynn Deyerle of Salem joined the Fred Waring Orchestra as a percussionist and tympanist. A graduate of Andrew Lewis High School, Deyerle had been playing in New York City for four years. Waring's orchestra was known as the Pennsylvanians.

The United Fund officially launched its 1959 campaign on October 12. John Fishwick was the general campaign chairman. The goal was $672,951.

Roanoke and Vinton funeral homes discontinued providing ambulance service on October 14, and the service was taken over by the Roanoke Ambulance Service operated by Lowell Voorhees of Staunton. John M. Oakey Funeral Service, Lotz Funeral Home, and Watson Funeral Home made a joint announcement of the change. John M. Oakey & Son of Salem planned to continue their ambulance service.

Raleigh Court Presbyterian Church extended a call on October 11 to Rev. James Allison Jr. of Fort Defiance, Virginia, to serve as pastor.

Lemarco Manufacturing Company, a dressmaking firm owned and operated by local Black businessmen, was labeled a financial failure in mid-October with losses at $50,000. Dr. Harry Penn, one of the founders and president of the company, promised to pay back those that had purchased stock.

The Star City Wrecking Company began demolishing the former Gale home at the northeast corner of Jefferson Street and Bullitt Avenue on October 12 to make way for a planned motel. The Gale home was considered a local landmark. The home was once part of early Roanoke's most upscale neighborhood, Orchard Hill.

This January 1959 image is of a John M. Oakey Funeral Home hearse. For years, funeral homes also provided ambulance services, which many discontinued doing in the late 1950s. *Virginia Room, RPL*

The Interstate Commerce Commission formally approved the merger of N&W Railway and Virginian Railway on October 13. N&W President Stuart Saunders stated it was "a great day in the history of the railroad industry." It was expected that the merger would take legal effect on December 1.

A one-acre plot of ground at Coyner Springs was consecrated as a new city cemetery on October 14. Graves from the former City Home on Colonial Avenue SW were to be moved to Coyner Springs.

Robert Shropshire, sixteen, of Roanoke was diagnosed on October 15 with paralytic polio. A patient at Roanoke Memorial Hospital, Shropshire became the first polio victim in Roanoke for 1959. The number of polio cases in Virginia was double that of the same period for 1958.

Oak Hall celebrated its seventieth anniversary in October. The store first opened on Railroad Avenue in October 1889 and had been owned and operated by members of the Rosenberg family for seventy years.

Sports Car Center opened at 117 Williamson Road NE on October 17. The dealership primarily sold German-made Goliath cars and trucks in addition to Porsche, Fiat, and Alfa Romeo.

His New Creation, an original drama by Nelson Bond, was presented the third week in October as a climax to the centennial celebration of Greene Memorial Methodist Church.

The Roanoke Symphony Orchestra launched its seventh season the third weekend in October with concerts at the American Theatre. Solo performances were given by Harold Thompson, John Loban, and Margaret Conrad.

Lord Botetourt High School was formally dedicated at Daleville on October 18. The $1 million school was the result of the consolidation of three high schools—Blue Ridge, Fincastle, and Troutville.

Officials with Roanoke Memorial Hospital announced on October 20 that permission had been granted to them by the state for construction of $2 million, 124-bed rehab center, the only one of its kind in the United States. The Roanoke Memorial Rehabilitation Center would be erected on a two-acre site at the corner of Jefferson Street and McClanahan Avenue SW. It was estimated that one fourth of the patients in the hospital could be moved to the rehab center in the future.

The Lemarco Manufacturing Company in Roanoke was sold to a New York City firm for an undisclosed price on October 20. Dr. Harry Penn, president of the company, said the firm would continue to operate with its forty-five employees.

Roanoke City Young Republicans announced on October 20 a write-in campaign for Linwood Holton to the House of Delegates. Both Democratic incumbents were unopposed for Roanoke's seat in the general election.

Southern Building Products Distributors opened on October 27 at 2580 Broadway SW.

A cornerstone-laying ceremony was held on October 21 for the new animal shelter of the Roanoke Valley SPCA. The shelter was located off Orange Avenue at Easter Avenue and Thirteenth Street NE.

Roanoke attorney Reuben Lawson filed applications on October 22 with the Pulaski County School Board requesting the transfer of eighteen Black students to the all-white Pulaski County High School. The students were attending the Christiansburg Institute, which served grades eight through twelve. The students were requesting admission for the start of the January 1960 term.

Gene Kay Health Studios, a gym, opened at 2601 Franklin Road SW in late October. The facility offered a handball court, steam baths, massages, personal trainers, a weight room, and weight loss programs.

The Roanoke Fraternal Order of Police began putting the finishing touches on a camp they created for boys in an effort to thwart juvenile delinquency. The J. L. C. Medley Camp was located on four acres in Catawba and included a bunk house, camping sites, and a swimming pool. The camp would open for the summer in 1960. Murray Cochran was chairman of the building committee.

NAACP civil rights attorney Oliver Hill spoke at Fifth Avenue Presbyterian Church in Roanoke on October 25 as part of Laymen's Day. His topic was the "The Responsibilities of Christians."

The Roanoke branch of the National Council of Negro Women gave the new Lincoln Terrace Elementary School a portrait of its first principal, Mrs. Fannie Watson, on October 26. The portrait was painted by Mrs. Audrey Whitlock.

Harris & Huddleston Super Market opened their new store at 119 S. Pollard Street in Vinton on October 29.

Eleven Roanoke city employees had moved 254 of 550 graves from the former City Farm site on Colonial Avenue SW to Coyner Springs as of October 27. The city manager estimated the effort would take about a month. Some of the bodies were studied by Virginia's chief medical examiner as a means of learning more about identifying the deceased. The first burial at the City Farm occurred in November 1932.

This 1959 photo shows the Harris & Huddleston Super Market on S. Pollard Street in Vinton during its grand reopening following an expansion. *Judy Cunningham*

Belle-Aire Lawn and Garden Center opened on October 31 on Lee Highway (Route 11) near the intersection of Keagy Road. The store was managed by Roland Cook and T. F. Franklin.

A report recommending an $8 million hospital be built in the southwest section of Roanoke was submitted on October 27 to a merger study committee of officials from Lewis-Gale Hospital and Jefferson Hospital. The 253-page study envisioned a 400-bed hospital and was prepared by John Stacey, director of the UVA Hospital.

Hake Manufacturing Company of Roanoke was sold to Eli Lilly & Company of Indianapolis on October 28 for $2.5 million. Hake manufactured plastic containers and would be managed and operated by Paper Package Company, a subsidiary of Eli Lilly. George Kissak was the sole owner of Hake. A few days later, Hake was renamed Diamond Plastic Industries.

Family Service Association moved to a residential building at 442 King George Avenue SW in late October to expanded staff and an increase in its caseload. It had been formerly located at 14 Albemarle Avenue SW since 1954.

A Piedmont Airlines plane with twenty-seven passengers aboard bound for Roanoke went missing on October 30. Air traffic officials announced that day their belief the plane had crashed in an area north of Charlottesville. The DC-3 was three hours overdue for its landing at Woodrum Field and was last heard from as it approached the Charlottesville airport. Persons in the Ruckersville area reported seeing a midair explosion that the Civil Air Patrol was investigating. The plane had departed from Washington. The following day, the search, involving over 300 personnel, shifted to the Buena Vista area in Rockbridge County. Two of the passengers were identified as being from Roanoke—David Findlay, an executive with WDBJ-TV, and William Peake, a salesman. On November 1, the crashed plane was finally located on the side of Calf Mountain near Waynesboro. Searchers found the bodies of the three crew members and twenty-three passengers. There was one survivor—Phil Bradley of Clifton Forge—who was taken to UVA Hospital. Most of the bodies were found in front of the ripped-open fuselage, indicating they were thrown through the plane and onto the slope. Rescuers believed almost all had died on impact. Bradley, however, was conscious and even raised his hand for a photographer. It was the first fatal crash for Piedmont Airlines, which had been operating since February 1948.

The new Temple Emanuel at Brambleton Avenue and Persinger Road SW was dedicated on October 30. The main speaker was Dr. Sidney Regner of the Central Conference of American Rabbis. The illumination of the sanctuary was led by Mrs. Morris Harrison, the oldest member of the congregation. The religious school was dedicated the next morning. Temple Emanuel began in Roanoke in the 1890s with meetings of Reform Jews. The congregation purchased its first building in 1904. In 1937, Temple Emanuel moved to McClanahan Street SW.

Dr. Hubbard Padgett, seventy-one, of Roanoke died on October 31 from injuries he sustained in a hit-and-run a week prior while crossing Jefferson Street near the Carlton Terrace Building. He had been a physician for forty years. Charged with manslaughter was Jackie Price, twenty-three, also of Roanoke.

Workers disinter graves at the cemetery on the City Farm at Colonial Avenue SW for reburial at Coyners Springs in this October 1959 clip. *WSLS-TV News Film Collection, UVA Libraries*

This 1950s postcard shows a DC-3 used by Piedmont Airlines during that decade. *Nelson Harris*

Lorin Hollander, fourteen and a virtuoso pianist, performed at the Jefferson High School auditorium on November 5, sponsored by the Thursday Morning Music Club.

Roanoke City Council voted 5–2 at its November 2 meeting to authorize an annexation ordinance that would take in 31.2 square miles of Roanoke County. Councilmen Benton Dillard and Charles Cornell voted against the motion. The intent was to file an annexation suit in early December.

Three teenagers were killed in an automobile accident near Troutville on November 2. Roy Strickler, Bill Strickler, and Shirley Mullins were all from Botetourt County. The Stricklers were brothers.

The Roanoke City School Board awarded contracts to J. M. Turner & Company for the construction of two new elementary schools during the meeting on November 2. Raleigh Court Elementary School and Fishburn Park Elementary School were expected to be completed for the next school year. Smithy and Boynton was the architectural firm.

William Hopkins was elected to represent Roanoke City in the Virginia senate as a result of the general election on November 3. The Democrat defeated his Republican opponent Leigh Hanes Jr. by a vote of 7,490 to 4,414. In the Twenty-First Senatorial District that included Roanoke County, James Turk, a Republican, defeated Democrat John Spiers, 9,028 to 7,872. Turk was elected to a seat that had previously been held by Ted Dalton, who had been appointed to a federal judgeship. In the House of Delegates, the only contested race in the Roanoke Valley was between incumbent Democrat Nelson Thurman and Republican Edward Garner. Thurman won, 4,958–2,397. In local elections, Roanoke County returned all their constitutional officials back to their offices. Sheriff Henry Clark defeated Thayer

Morris by a margin of 660 votes; Commissioner of the Revenue Luck Richardson defeated Burman Bowman; and Commonwealth's Attorney Edward Richardson won over Charles Shelor. In the county Board of Supervisors races, A. C. Harris won the Big Lick District seat, defeating C. C. Crockett, the former mayor of Vinton; and Minor Keffer defeated Oval Gillespie for the Catawba District seat. In the Salem District, Hampton Moulse won over C. R. Brown, and Edwin Terrell defeated Harry Wiseman for the Cave Spring District seat. The county treasurer, James Peters, and county clerk, Roy Brown, were unopposed.

A special three-judge annexation court awarded the town of Salem 3.68 square miles of Roanoke County in a ruling on November 4 to take effect January 1. Salem would gain about 2,700 new residents.

The Floyd County school superintendent announced on November 5 that the thirteen Black students who had sought admission to the county's all-white high schools would be admitted to those schools on January 25 in compliance with a court order. The students and their families had been represented by Reuben Lawson, a Roanoke attorney.

High Street Baptist Church in Roanoke held a weeklong celebration of its Diamond Jubilee the second week in November. The church was established in 1884.

The congregation of Woodlawn Methodist Church approved plans for a $124,000 church sanctuary in early November. The congregation hoped to raise the funds and begin construction by the summer of 1960. An education unit had been constructed in 1955. The church was located at 3301 Ashby Street SW.

The new sanctuary of First Christian Church of Salem was used for the first time on November 8. Rev. Virgil Lilly was the pastor.

The annual Shrine Bowl football game was held at Victory Stadium on November 7. The freshmen squad of Virginia Tech defeated those of VMI by a score of 24–6 before a crowd of 12,000. A parade preceded the game, which was a fundraiser for the Shriner's programs benefiting crippled children.

Charles Cornell, a member of Roanoke City Council, reported at the body's meeting on November 9 that he had received reports of children being "horribly abused" at the Juvenile Detention Home. The council responded by asking for an investigation, the second in two years. Cornell indicated that children had been struck, sexually abused, and choked—and that there had even been a death. The home was located at 622 Rorer Avenue SW. The one death referenced by Cornell was a teenage boy who died from an epileptic seizure.

The superintendent of schools in Galax announced on November 9 that Rita Brooks, sixteen, would be admitted to the all-white Galax High School effective January 19, making Galax the first locality in southwestern Virginia to integrate in compliance with a court ruling. Roanoke attorney Reuben Lawson was the attorney for the Brooks family in the matter. The parents, however, turned down the admission as their daughter had been sent to attend schools in Plainfield, New Jersey, while living there with relatives.

Henebry's Jewelers in both Roanoke and Salem were sold to Reliable Stores Corporation, a Baltimore chain, on November 16 by Leo Henebry. The names of the stores would not change. The Roanoke store was located at 209 S. Jefferson Street and the Salem store at 215 E. Main Street.

Barr's Variety Department Store held its grand opening on November 12 at 1318 Grandin Road SW.

The Roanoke School Board purchased a sixteen-acre site for an elementary school at the foot of Round Hill on November 10. The purchase price was $46,000.

Clay Ferguson Sr., former head of the Roanoke police, died at his home of an apparent heart attack on November 11 at the age of seventy. Ferguson was police superintendent from 1946 to 1949, when he retired after more than twenty-five years with the department.

Hennis Freight Lines opened its new terminal in the 3300 block of Salem Turnpike on November 14.

In its mid-November issue, *Billboard* magazine ranked Don Reno and Red Smiley as tenth among "favorite small country and western vocal groups." Reno and Smiley appeared regularly on WDBJ's *Top O' the Mornin'* show hosted by Irv Sharp. The two performed on the national broadcast of the *Grand Ole Opry* on November 14, along with Mac Magaha and John Palmer, also known as the Tennessee Cut Ups.

Gospel singer Mahalia Jackson performed at the Addison High School auditorium on November 14 before a sold-out crowd of 850. Her final number was her signature song, *His Eye is on the Sparrow*, which was followed by three encores. She was accompanied by pianist Mildred Falls. She gave a second performance at Addison the following day. Jackson was presented a key to the city by Mayor Vincent Wheeler. Her concerts were sponsored by St. Paul's Methodist Church.

Whitehall Motor Lodge opened their new dining room and coffee shop on November 16 at 3016 Williamson Road NW.

This November 1959 image shows Barr's Variety Department Store at 1318 Grandin Road SW. McVey's Hardware is to the right. *Virginia Room, RPL*

The Carver High School football team was awarded the Group II, District 4 VIA championship on November 16 by VIA officials based on the team's record and opponents.

Three persons were killed in a plane crash in Botetourt County on November 17. Among the dead was the pilot, Jack Miller, of Vinton who flew for Virginia Airmotive based at Woodrum Field. The plane crashed within sight of the Covington airstrip, where it was scheduled to land as the two passengers were going to the Homestead at Hot Springs. The plane went down in rugged mountains, known to locals as Rich Patch. It was the first accident for the charter aviation service, which was owned by Clayton Lemon. Eyewitness accounts from hunters led officials to believe the plane experienced engine failure.

The Little Chef Restaurant at 1307 Williamson Road opened its new Walnut Dining Room on November 19.

The Roanoke Broadway Theater League presented *The Dark at the Top of the Stairs* on November 19 at the American Theatre. The touring production's cast included film actress Joan Blondell in the lead role.

Directors of Jefferson Hospital voted on November 19 to consolidate with Lewis-Gale Hospital, whose directors had approved the merger on November 9. The plan called for a new 400-bed hospital to be erected.

The Pittsburgh Pirates announced on November 19 that they would not operate a farm team in Salem for the 1960 baseball season. The Salem Rebels were in the Class D rookie Appalachian League. The Pirates had operated a farm team in Salem for three years.

Cashiers and shoppers are shown in this November 1959 interior image of Barr's Variety Department Store on Grandin Road SW. *Virginia Room, RPL*

Concord, a men's and boy's clothing store, began advertising in late November that it was going out of business. The store was located at 509 Second Street SW.

Hunter Roberts, a real estate broker, announced on behalf of the Valley Development Corporation on November 20 that the group planned to raise funds to erect at $1 million coliseum with a seating capacity of 6,500 on a twenty-three-acre tract at Salem Turnpike and Thirtieth Street NW. The site was opposite Fairview Cemetery. Roberts stated that many investors from outside the valley were interested. The new facility would be called the Starland Coliseum with grading expected to begin in early January. Roberts was hopeful that the coliseum would eventually attract a minor league hockey team to Roanoke.

Mrs. Edward King was shot and killed in the kitchen of her home on Madison Avenue NW on November 20. King's sister-in-law, Beatrice King, was arrested for the slaying.

Peter Faries, fifty-one, of Roanoke was fatally injured on November 20 when he was struck by a moving motor car at the 16th Street Yard. He was a foreman with N&W Railway. Witnesses stated that Faries stepped into the path of the car while he was supervising two work crews.

Roanoke NAACP attorney Reuben Lawson filed a letter with the Grayson County School Board on November 20 seeking admission of two Black students to Independence High School. The students' families had applied via forms from the State Pupil Placement Board. The superintendent had returned the forms to the students stating they were incomplete.

English Village Restaurant opened on November 21 at 7206 Williamson Road.

Roanoke city officials expressed doubt that the city would achieve a population of 100,000 or more by the 1960 census due to residents moving to new subdivisions in Roanoke County coupled with the closing of the American Viscose plant.

Richard Tucker, tenor with the Metropolitan Opera, performed at the American Theatre on November 23 under the sponsorship of the Thursday Morning Music Club.

The Roanoke Male Chorus was organized in late November with forty-one men. Rehearsals were held at Greene Memorial Methodist Church with Eula Ligon as the conductor. James Evans was president of the group.

Tazewell Lancaster, seventy-two, of Roanoke died on November 23 from injuries he sustained on November 20 when he was struck by a pickup as he crossed Melrose Avenue NW. It was the city's sixth traffic fatality of the year.

Holiday Ice Arena, a skating rink, opened the third week in November. It was located at the rear of Archie's Restaurant on Route 11. It was a portable ice rink opened for the winter season.

A navy pilot was killed when his plane crashed just short of the runway at Woodrum Field on November 24. Richard Leach, twenty-four, of Virginia Beach was asphyxiated, according to officials, when he inhaled carbon dioxide in the closed cockpit. He was piloting a Douglas AD-6 Skyraider. Leach was alive at the time of the crash and tried to free himself, but rescuers said they were unable to help due to the flames. The pilot was en route to Little Rock, Arkansas.

The Rainbow Room opened for dining and dancing at the Normandie Inn, corner of Thirteenth Street and Patterson Avenue, on November 25.

C. J. Wray and his wife, driving past 401 Walnut Avenue SE on the evening of November 25, noticed the two-story frame house was on fire. They pulled the nearest fire box, raced into the house, and found W. F. Brown and his five children asleep. Waking them, all were able to exit the home before flames engulfed the residence.

Santa arrived at Sears Town by helicopter on November 27. It was his first appearance in Roanoke for the Christmas season.

The Bloom of Time, a collection of poetry, was authored by Grace Whitefield of Roanoke County and published by Naylor Company of San Antonio, Texas. Whitefield was president of the Roanoke Poetry Society.

VMI defeated Virginia Tech 37–12 in the annual Thanksgiving Day football game between the two at Victory Stadium on November 26. With the win, VMI won the Southern Conference title, the first time in the history of the Thanksgiving Day games that the match was for the conference championship. A crowd of 27,500 attended the game, which was preceded by a parade through downtown Roanoke.

George T. Hitch Jeweler opened at its new location at 34 W. Church Avenue on November 27.

The merger of the Virginian Railway and N&W Railway became a physical and legal reality on at 12:01 a.m. on December 1. It was the first merger of two wholly independent American railroads in modern history.

The Roanoke Valley Unitarians leased the former Cave Spring Methodist Church and began meeting there on December 6. The congregation had about forty adults and had been meeting at the Central YWCA and in members' homes.

Alice Plunkett, a senior at William Byrd High School, was named as Snow Queen for the annual Santa Clause Parade in downtown Roanoke which was held on December 1. The selection was made by the Roanoke Merchants Association, sponsor of the event.

In the first annual Sand Bowl at Victory Stadium on November 29, Roanoke's sandlot football all-stars defeated Lynchburg's sandlot all-stars, 30–7. The games was attended by 350 and televised live on WSLS.

A fire on November 29 heavily damaged the Fifth Avenue Presbyterian Church at 301 Patton Avenue NW. The church was burned such that it could not be restored, according to Rev. Andre Kearns. The fire broke out on Sunday morning just minutes before congregants began arriving for Sunday School. The frame church had been built sixty-five years prior by its members. The 335-member congregation was offered temporary meeting space by other churches. The following Sunday, the congregation began meeting at the Macedonia Seventh-Day Adventist Church, located at Eighth Street and Madison Avenue NW.

An estimated crowd of 35,000 to 40,000 lined the streets of downtown Roanoke on December 1 for the Santa Claus Parade, sponsored by the Roanoke Merchants Association. Salem's annual Christmas parade was held on December 4.

The Roanoke Broadway Theater League presented the touring production of *Odd Man In* at the American Theatre on December 2. The lead actress was Ann Sheridan.

Roy Stump, fifty-two, of Roanoke County died on December 2 from injuries he sustained in an auto accident in Salem on December 1. It was the first fatal traffic accident to happen in Salem in three years.

Clayton Lemon announced plans for a $10,000 nine-hole golf course near Woodrum Field. Lemon, president of Airport Golf Club, said the organization had acquired a twenty-eight-acre site for the course that he hoped would open in the spring.

The home of James Tinnell and his wife in the Dixie Caverns area was destroyed by fire on December 3. Frustrating to the Tinnells and fire officials was the couples' inability to phone the fire department due to a neighbor refusing to give up his call on the party line telephone. Tinnell was forced to walk two miles to the nearest alternate phone, delaying the fire department's arrival.

Frank's Restaurant opened on December 6 on Williamson Road, across from Archie's Lobster House, in what was formerly Howard's Restaurant.

The Roanoke Symphony Orchestra presented its fifth annual performance of Handel's *Messiah* on December 6 at the American Theatre. Guest soloists were Oscar McCullough, Jane Stuart Smith, Walter Carringer, and Phyllis Rochow. The concert also featured a 150-voice choir from nearly twenty local churches.

Cave Spring Methodist Church met in its new sanctuary for the first time on December 6. The first service of the day in the $10,000 380-seat sanctuary was Holy Communion. The church was organized in 1853.

Miller & Rhoads department store sponsored its second annual Santa Train on December 5. The special N&W Railway train carried children and parents on a round trip from Roanoke to Elliston with Santa Claus and Roanoke's Snow Queen on board. Some 3,400 passengers made the trip.

The Moose Home of Roanoke Lodge 284 was dedicated on December 6. The home was located on Kessler Mill Road.

Tom Nugent, football coach at the University of Maryland, spoke at the annual awards banquet of the Roanoke Touchdown Club on December 7. His main thought was, "Take the positive approach to life. You can't sell anyone else on you unless you believe in yourself."

Capt. Cecil Crockett Jr., formerly of Roanoke County, was announced as "presumed dead" by military officials on December 7 after being missing on a jet training flight from Chicago to Waco, Texas. The US Air Force had abandoned further search of the aircraft. His parents still resided in Roanoke County at the time of the news.

Cundiff's Drug Store held a grand opening on December 11 at 116 Pollard Street in Vinton.

Lewis Reed was convicted in Roanoke County Circuit Court on December 10 for voluntary manslaughter in the death of Dorcas St. Clair, whose body had been found in the home of Mary Taylor earlier in the year. St. Clair died due to a botched abortion performed by Reed, who had no medical training. Judge Fred Hoback sentenced Reed to five years of probation.

Mamie Gordon, sixty-five, of Roanoke died on December 10 from injuries she received a few days prior when she was struck by a car on Williamson Road. It was the fifth such pedestrian fatality in the city for the year.

A faulty automatic direction finder on the ill-fated Piedmont Airlines flight destined for Roanoke that crashed near Waynesboro in late October was to blame for the airliner careening into a mountainside. That was the conclusion of an investigation by the Civil Aeronautics Board announced on December 11 following a three-day hearing. The crash claimed twenty-six lives.

The new sanctuary of First Christian Church of Salem was dedicated on December 13.

The Town of Salem completed a census on December 15 of the population within the 3.58 square miles it had annexed. The count showed 4,914 people in 931 living units.

Mayor Vincent Wheeler, with the assistance of his seven-month-old granddaughter, Nina Dooley, lit the municipal Christmas tree on the lawn of the Municipal Building on December 16. Carols were provided by the Roanoke Catholic High School choir.

St. Elizabeth's Episcopal Church voted to construct a chapel and Sunday School building at its annual business meeting on December 17. Construction on a four-acre site at Guilford Avenue and Grandin Road SW was expected to bring in the spring of 1960. The congregation was meeting in the chapel of Raleigh Court Presbyterian Church.

Krispy Kreme advertised in mid-December that both of their locations at 4141 Melrose Avenue NW and 1923 Williamson Road had been remodeled into doughnut and coffee bars, open 24-7.

Elm's Barber Shop opened at 3613 Shenandoah Avenue NW on December 19. Elmer Morton was the barber.

The Virginia General Assembly's Boatwright Committee formally asked the Virginia Bar Association to examine the activity of lawyers that had represented Black clients in desegregation suits. The pro-segregation committee believed it was unlawful for the NAACP to pay attorney fees rather than the plaintiffs being represented. One of those targeted by the committee's concern was Reuben Lawson of Roanoke.

Star City Junior Lodge No. 8 of the IOOF was formed on December 19 with sixteen charter members, all in their teens. Chief ruler of the junior lodge was Donald Pittman of Salem.

The Roanoke School Board approved names for three new schools at their December 21 meeting. The names chosen were Fishburn Park Elementary School, Round Hill Elementary School, and Hurt Park Elementary School. All three schools were still under construction at the time.

William Cundiff and John Logan were recognized for their service as members of the Roanoke County Board of Supervisors on December 21. Neither had sought reelection.

Roanoke's giant community Christmas candle was lit in a ceremony on December 22. The candle, a symbol of Christian unity, was sponsored by the Roanoke Ministers Conference and WDBJ-TV. The candle was made from the wax of used candles donated by area congregations and was located on the lawn of the Municipal Building. The ten-foot-tall candle was lit by Mayor Vincent Wheeler.

Forty women employed by Lemarco Manufacturing showed up at the commonwealth's attorney office of C. E. Cuddy on December 21 claiming that their paychecks had bounced. A preliminary investigation into the matter by Cuddy showed that the sale of Lemarco by Dr. Harry Penn to Seymour Kaplan of New

York had not actually occurred in October as announced. Other investors also indicated that Kaplan had not purchased their shares in the company either, leaving the finances of the dress-making company in doubt. Dr. Penn stated to the *Roanoke Times*, "From all indications it is in my lap again. But, I don't want all those liabilities and they are numerous."

A fire destroyed the trailer home of Randy Simmons and his family in the Starkey area on December 22. Only a skeleton of the trailer was left, as the fire consumed all the contents, including his children's Christmas presents. Officials believed a faulty oil heater was the cause.

A recording of N&W Railway's last steam engine operations at Blue Ridge was released the third week in December by O. Winston Link Railway Productions in New York. It was Link's third such recording.

Clifton Woodrum Jr. died Christmas night from a single gunshot wound to the chest while alone at his home. Woodrum was the son of the late Congressman Clifton Woodrum, for whom Woodrum Field was named. He was an attorney and prominent in Roanoke's civic affairs. Police indicated there was no foul play involved.

A religious drama by Kermit Hunter, titled *Mistress of the Inn*, was staged at First Presbyterian Church on December 27. The play was produced by a newly organized religious drama group called Faith in Dramatic Presentation. The play was first produced in Roanoke in 1957.

Lester Banks, the executive secretary of the Virginia NAACP, addressed the Roanoke Branch of the NAACP in a meeting at Sweet Union Baptist Church on December 27. Lester appealed for civil rights, stating, "Colored people are sick and tired of being treated like underlings. All the people of Virginia…want is to be treated like human beings." Lester also took aim at Roanoke's leadership in the early 1950s. "Don't fool yourselves. Addison High School was built because your city fathers discriminated against Negroes and feared some parents would have guts enough to file a suit." Lester was on hand for the charter presentation to a new junior department of the Roanoke branch.

Dr. Harry Penn indicated on December 29 that he had asked his attorney to place Lemarco Manufacturing Company into receivership. Penn was the former owner and chief creditor of the dressmaking firm. The company formally filed for Chapter 11 in Western District Federal Court on December 31.

Wright Furniture Company, located at 118 E. Campbell Avenue, sponsored a personal appearance in their store of Jim Lemon of the Washington Senators professional baseball team on December 31. Lemon signed autographs on baseballs and photos.

Various Roanoke Valley financial institutions filed their statements of condition effective December 31. They were as follows: First National Exchange Bank, $107.8 million; Colonial-American National Bank, $45.1 million; Southwest Virginia Savings and Loan Association, $10.1 million; and Mountain Trust Bank, $37.2 million.

Appendix:
Roanoke Valley Korean War Casualties

The information was compiled from three sources—the printed records of the Roanoke Valley War Memorial Committee, online archives of the Department of Defense, and death notices from the *Roanoke Times*.

Akers, James F., killed in action on December 2, 1950; age twenty; son of Mr. and Mrs. Peter Akers of 1801 Warrington Road SW; member of the Roanoke Marine Corps Reserves; joined the First Marine Division in September 1950; rank was corporal

Atkins, Irvin L., killed in action on September 22, 1950; joined the Army in 1946; rank was corporal

Barns, Jim Bob, killed in action on April 23, 1951; age eighteen; son of Mr. and Mrs. Robert Barnes of Orange Avenue NW; member of the Roanoke Marine Corps Reserves; rank was private

Boitnott, Charlie, died from a fall while climbing a mountain in Korea on April 13, 1951; rank was private

Boyden, Stewart Stanley, killed in action on October 4, 1951; age twenty-four; husband of Lillian Paxton Boyden of 327 Patton Avenue NE; attached to the Third Infantry Division; rank was lieutenant

Broughman, Woodrow H., died on September 2, 1950; rank was private first class, US Army

Brown, G. Ernest Jr.

Brown, Ralph G., killed in action on January 3, 1953; age thirty; son of Mrs. Zenella Brown of Roanoke County; US Air Force; rank was captain

Bruner, Herbert S., killed in Korea on July 5, 1951; age twenty; son of Mrs. Edna Bruner of 525 Eighth Street NE; rank was corporal

Cauley, George C., killed in Korea in 1951; son of Mr. and Mrs. George Cauley of RFD 6, Roanoke; rank was sergeant

Coggin, Carl L., died on July 31, 1952; army rank was corporal

Coggin, George W.

Cole, Thomas Edward, declared presumed dead by the Defense Department in January 1954, having been missing in action since December 12, 1950; son of Mr. and Mrs. E. H. Cole of 3107 Shenandoah Valley Avenue NE; rank was corporal

Cox, Robert C., died on January 8, 1951; army rank was sergeant

Craig, Gordon W.

Craighead, Rufus Pleasant, died on December 1, 1950; remains were never recovered; army rank was private first class

Crowder, Paul E., died in Korea from drowning on June 20, 1951; age twenty-one; son of Mr. and Mrs. Charles Crowder of 1216 Tazewell Avenue SE; rank was corporal

Custer, Vernon C., died on July 20, 1950; army rank was private first class

Dent, Dan Webb, killed in action on November 6, 1950; age nineteen; son of Mr. and Mrs. T. S. Dent of 1325 Rugby Boulevard NW; joined the army in May 1950; rank was private

Dickerson, Paul, killed in action in December 1950 at the Chosin Reservoir; son of Mr. and Mrs. Willie Dickerson of Brownlee Avenue SE

Dickerson, W. E., declared presumed dead by the Defense Department in January 1954, having been missing in action since December 1, 1950; son of Mr. and Mrs. W. E. Dickerson of 1517 Brownlee Avenue SE; rank was private

Dille, John A. Jr., killed in a plane crash on April 13, 1952, en route to Japan; age twenty-five; son of Mr. and Mrs. John Dille of 362 Walnut Avenue SW; had flown twenty-four combat missions over Korea; survived by a wife and son; rank was first lieutenant

Dressler, William E., died on July 14, 1950; army rank was major

Duncan, Raymond E., killed in action on June 16, 1951; son of Mr. and Mrs. C. A. Duncan of 2633 Oregon Avenue SW; member of marine reserve unit; rank was private

Earles, James S., killed in action on December 6, 1950; age twenty-four; husband of Mrs. J. S. Earles of 3730 Melcher Street SE; served with the marines in World War II and Korea; rank was private first class

Edwards, Elzia M., killed in action on September 22, 1951; age nineteen; son of Mr. and Mrs. C. R. Edwards of 1211 Jamison Avenue SE; had enlisted in the army on August 29, 1950; rank was private first class

Edwards, James S., killed in action in 1951; son of Mrs. Alice Edwards of 270 Cotton Avenue NW; rank was private

Edwards, James Sterling, killed in action on October 22, 1951; age eighteen; son of Mr. and Mrs. W. W. Edwards of 416 Wells Avenue NW; entered the army on October 25, 1950; rank was private first class, paratrooper

Ellis, Henry Edward, killed in action on November 29, 1950, near Koto-ri; age twenty-two; son of Martin Ellis of 410 Harrison Avenue NE; joined the marines in 1948; rank was private first class; Ellis's remains were not identified until 2020 as a result of Operation GLORY, an effort to repatriate and identify some 850 remains of soldiers returned to the United States by North Korea. He was interred in Salisbury, North Carolina, in 2021.

Ferris, Vernon G., killed in action on August 14, 1950; age eighteen; son of Mr. and Mrs. J. W. Ferris of Shenandoah Avenue NW; joined the army on September 3, 1949; rank was private

Fitzgerald, Lawrence E., killed in action on September 1, 1950; son of Mr. and Mrs. Fred Fitzgerald of Route 1, Roanoke County; rank was private

Francis, Joe M. Jr.

Goad, Homer J., killed in action on June 1, 1951; age twenty-five; son of Mr. and Mrs. W. F. Goad of Roanoke County and husband of Ruth Goad of Salem; was serving with the army's 82nd Airborne Division; rank was private first class

Gravely, James C. Jr., killed in action on November 4, 1952; son of Mrs. Ida Gravely of 420 Gregory Avenue NE; entered the army in November 1951; rank was private

Hairston, Wilbur C., killed in action, had previously been reported as missing, in 1951; son of Mr. and Mrs. Roy Hairston of Center Avenue NW; rank was private

Hassell, John T., killed in action on September 21, 1950; son of Mr. and Mrs. John Hassell of Cove Road NW; joined the service in October 1949 and went to Korea on July 5, 1950; rank was private

Hazelgrove, W. Perkins Jr.

Hill, Herman E., killed in action; son of Flora Hill of Route 3, Salem; rank was private

Hopkins, Frank Sherrill, killed in action on March 31, 1951; age twenty-two; son of Mr. and Mrs. Frank H. Hopkins of Mount Pleasant section; had entered the service on August 13, 1950; rank was private

Johnson, Walter M., killed in action on September 30, 1950; age twenty-three; son of Cora Johnson of 612 Elm Avenue SW; had served in World War II; marine reserves; rank was sergeant

Kelly, Eugene T.

King, Andrew W. IV, died on July 6, 1953; army rank was sergeant; remains were not recovered

Lowe, James Alfred Jr., reported as dead by the US Air Force on March 5, 1954, having been shot down over Korea in September 1952; rank was captain

Martin, Paul Edward, killed in action on November 28, 1950; age twenty-two; son of Mr. and Mrs. M. R. Martin of 822 Day Avenue SW; husband of Freda Morgan and father of four-month-old Mark Martin; member of the Roanoke Marine Corps Reserves; rank was corporal

McGuire, Clyde A., declared presumed dead by the Defense Department in January 1954, having been missing in action for over a year; stepson of Mrs. Ruth McGuire of 1139 Murray Avenue SE; rank was corporal

Moore, William Lee, died of wounds on October 13, 1950, at a navy hospital in Yokosuka, Japan, that he received in Korea; age twenty-two; husband of Elizabeth Moore of Sweetbrier Avenue SW; member of Roanoke's Marine Corps Reserve Unit; rank was private first class.

Parker, James R.

Payne, Eugene, died from wounds on July 28, 1950; age nineteen; son of Mr. and Mrs. Ralph Payne of Wise Avenue SE; enlisted in the army in 1949 and went overseas in March of that year; served with the Field Artillery; rank at death was corporal

Perry, Willie E., killed in action in 1951; son of Mr. and Mrs. Lewis Perry of 22 Fourteenth Street SW; rank was corporal

Powell, John H.

Rogers, Carl R., killed in action; was reported missing in action on July 26, 1950; age seventeen; son of Dillard Rogers, of Route 3, Salem; enlisted in the army on August 23, 1949; rank was private

Rule, Lawrence G., declared presumed dead by the Defense Department in January 1954, having been missing in action for over a year; son of Mrs. Mary Rule of 2913 Williamson Road; rank was sergeant

Short, Marvin E., killed in action on September 3, 1950; son of Mrs. Doshie Short of Dunkirk Avenue NE; joined the army in October 1949 and went to Korea on August 15, 1950; rank was private

St. Clair, Willie A. Jr., killed in action on June 3, 1953; husband of Mrs. Ida Spradlin St. Clair of Vinton; entered the army in March 1952 and went to Korea that August; rank was corporal

Turner, Elmore Carlton, Jr., killed in action in 1951; age nineteen; son of Mr. and Mrs. E. C. Turner of Eureka Circle NW; member of Roanoke Marine Corps Reserve Unit; ranks was private

Underwood, Guy L. Jr., killed in action in September 1950; son of Guy Underwood of Route 1, Salem; rank was private first class

Ware, Cecil O., killed in an accident in Japan on February 7, 1951, while preparing for operations in Korea; age thirty-one; husband of Doris Vest of Larchwood Avenue NE, Roanoke; rank was captain in the US Air Force

Whitt, John T., reported as missing in action in Korea on October 27, 1951; reported as killed in action in January 1952; husband of Katherine Bowling Whitt of Roanoke; rank was private

Witt, Wallace D., killed in action on September 2, 1950, at Haman; age twenty-one; son of Mrs. Ruby Bernard of Eleventh Street NW; enlisted in the army in 1947 and had served during the occupation of Japan; rank was private first class

Index

719

Cundiff, William 711
Curtain Shop 461
Curtis Hardware 570
Curtis, Harry 159, 592
Curtis, Mary 3, 559
Custer, Carl 255
Custer, Everett 47
Cutts, Louise 238, 256

D
Dairy Bar 103
Dairy Fountain 197, 216, 323
Dairy Queen 123
Dalton, Ted 122, 141, 278, 419, 424, 558, 562, 704
Dame, Jack 187, 370, 602
Damewood, Lawrence 193
Daniels, Johnny 213
Dan's, clothing store 671
Darden, J. C. 472
Darling Shoe Store 582
Darnell, G. B. 195
Darnell, Larry 12, 287
Daughters of the American Revolution 29, 493
Davidow Paint and Wallpaper Company 108, 112, 127
Davidsons 270
Davidson's Restaurant 173
Davies, Herbert 355, 367, 377, 382, 551, 556
Davis, Con 56, 445, 477
Davis, Floyd 214
Davis, J. G. 222
Davis, J. W. 406, 556, 584
Davis, Othia 140
Davis, William 374
D&D Auto Upholstery Shop 445
Dean and Catron Coal Company 571
Deb Fashions 404
DeBusk, Roger 548
Decker, Alan 529, 602
Decker, Clarence 15, 25
Decker, Nettie 15, 25
Dellis, Darryl 541
Delong's, clothing store 692
DeLong, Thomas 491
Deluxe Laundry and Dry Cleaners 111, 258
Dempsey, Jack 69, 126, 270, 503

Dennis, John 14
Densmore, Arthur 419
Densmore Poultry Farm 419, 434
Denson, William 492
Dent, Dan 76
Denton, Sonny 221
desegregation 116, 334, 388, 389, 394, 395, 402, 413, 421, 423, 425, 440, 459, 470, 475, 477, 483, 487, 488, 531, 542, 554, 558, 693, 711
Detroit Stars 461, 465, 614
DeVault, Robert 363
DeVries, Lourens 154
Deyerle, Dorothy 313
Deyerle, Lynn 699
Diamond Chevrolet 594, 612
Diamond, Eduoard 56
Diamond Jubilee 399, 441, 463, 466, 489, 502, 503, 514, 518, 519, 520, 522, 524, 525, 528, 531, 533, 534, 535, 536, 537, 538, 547, 582, 705
Dickens, Jimmy 30, 125, 221, 291, 298, 323, 369, 456
Dickerson, Warren 169
Dickinson, Genevieve 217, 257, 263, 327, 395, 399
Dickinson, Jeanne 103, 376
Dickson, Ruth 400
Diddley, Bo 397, 411, 539, 555
Dillard, Benton 8, 12, 24, 35, 59, 458, 473, 529, 621, 637, 672, 704
Dillard Paper Company 375, 410
Dille, John 172, 714
Dillon, Shirley 198
Diplomat Civic Committee 140
Dirksen, Everett 88
Divers, Don 352, 422, 473, 489, 493
Division of Motor Vehicles 97
Dixie Bar-B-Que 618
Dixie Caverns 101, 322, 329, 342, 353, 402, 408, 411, 426, 432, 451, 470, 483, 488, 489, 527, 541, 571, 595, 619, 634, 710
Dixie Cream Donut Drive-In 541, 544
Dixie Drive-In 131, 144, 395
Dixie Hardware 262, 500
Dixie Playboys 38
Dixon's Hardware 197
Doctors Ambulance Service 224
Dogwood Festival 103, 436, 450, 489,

344
Schilling, Otey 28
Schley, Daisy 381, 416
Schlossberg, Arnold 20
Schlossberg, Arthur 122
Schlossberg, M. J. 43, 664
Schneider, Leroy 197
Schneider Oil Company 112, 267
Schnore, Edward 213
Scholz, Arthur 290
Schuler, Charlie 89
Schulte-United 193
Scotchwash Laundromat 636
Scott, Clinton 44
Scott, Horner & Mason 448
Scott, Lee 6
Scott's Cash Grocery 156
Scott, Walter 146, 154, 341
Scruggs, Earl 130, 143, 167, 613
Scruggs, Eddie 565
Scruggs Garage 576
Seal, Bobby 74
Searle, Clinton 470
Sears 139, 392, 432, 445, 446, 461, 509,
    515, 517, 539, 588, 637, 694, 709
Second Methodist Church 315, 340, 345
Second Presbyterian Church 3, 309, 625
Secord, Harold 546
See, Earl 273, 285, 327
See, Elvin 273, 285, 327
Segall, Bill 19, 115, 208, 545, 687
segregation 104, 292, 315, 322, 346, 361,
    387, 422, 425, 427, 428, 438, 445,
    447, 451, 453, 474, 485, 487, 513,
    531, 534, 546, 558, 559, 577, 647,
    648, 665, 711
Self-Service Station 57, 253
Sellers, Connie 114, 115, 126, 183, 195,
    251, 318, 323, 333, 625, 667, 678
Semones, Alton 188, 196, 207
Semones, Mrs. Harry 161
Senter, Eugene 337
Serkin, Rudolph 157
Seventh-Day Adventist Church 92
sewage treatment plant 71, 187, 212, 263,
    275
Shank Furniture Company 316, 330, 331,
    352, 673, 690
Shank, Henry 113, 673
Shank, Leonard 182, 458, 473, 621

Shanks, David 101
Shapiro, Andrew 369
Sharp, Irv 63, 77, 201, 268, 412, 483,
    495, 512, 517, 585, 611, 706
Shaw, George 56, 117
Shay Produce Company 12
Sheena 452
Sheets, Foster 47
Sheets, J. G. 366
Shell Homes 636
Shelor, Charles 204, 705
Shelton, Ruby 376
Shenandoah Avenue Esso Station 624
Shenandoah Christian College 360, 372,
    475
Shenandoah Club 43, 128, 342, 491, 499,
    579
Shenandoah Company 688
Shenandoah Drive-In 131, 143, 152, 239,
    444, 459, 461
Shenandoah Hospital 309, 689
Shenandoah Hotel 188, 242
Shenandoah Life Insurance Company 132,
    257, 283, 299, 309, 313, 406, 495
Sherman, Harry 593
Sherrill's Antiques 159, 268
Sherwin-Williams 167, 579
Sherwood Burial Park 9, 263, 319, 343,
    377, 444, 464, 481, 493, 501, 507,
    519, 538, 570, 599, 604, 662
S&H Green Stamps 195, 396, 410, 676
S&H Green Stamp Store 77, 432
Shirley's Drive-In 17
Shirley's Restaurant 295, 414
Shoaf, Ralph 24
Shober, Wayne 24
Shoney's 458
Shoney's Big Boy 587
Shoppers Mart 418, 470, 491
shopping centers 404, 419, 421, 422, 429,
    430, 432, 491, 515, 611, 634, 681,
    697
Shopwell Food Store 88, 223, 270, 520,
    598
Shorter, M. B. 425
Short, Marvin 62
Showtimers 98, 115, 116, 120, 122, 124,
    186, 187, 188, 189, 192, 253, 255,
    256, 257, 258, 260, 263, 293, 322,
    323, 325, 327, 328, 361, 362, 376,

About the Author

Local historian Nelson Harris is a native and former mayor of Roanoke, Virginia. He has been the pastor of Heights Community Church (formerly Virginia Heights Baptist Church) since 1999 and is an adjunct faculty member at Virginia Western Community College. He holds degrees from Radford University (BA, cum laude) and Southeastern Baptist Theological Seminary (MDiv) and has done postgraduate work at Princeton Theological Seminary and through Harvard University. A past president of the Historical Society of Western Virginia, he is a history columnist for the *Roanoker* magazine and producer, writer and host of the award-winning *Eye on the Past with Nelson Harris* on Blue Ridge PBS. He has been instrumental in obtaining numerous Virginia state historical markers for the Roanoke Valley for which he received a Kegley Award from the Roanoke Valley Preservation Foundation. He is the author of the following books:

The 17th Virginia Cavalry

Roanoke in Vintage Postcards

Images of Rail: Norfolk & Western Railway

Virginia Tech

Stations and Depots of the Norfolk & Western Railway

Downtown Roanoke

Salem and Roanoke County in Vintage Postcards

Roanoke Valley: Then and Now (co-author)

Greater Raleigh Court: A History of Wasena, Virginia Heights, Norwich & Raleigh Court

Hidden History of Roanoke

Aviation in Roanoke (co-author)

A History of Back Creek: Bent Mountain, Poages Mill, Cave Spring and Starkey

The Grand Old Lady on the Hill: An Informal History of the Hotel Roanoke (co-author)

The Roanoke Valley in the 1940s